The Last Dance

THIRD EDITION

Encountering Death and Dying

LYNNE ANN DeSPELDER
Cabrillo College

ALBERT LEE STRICKLAND

Mayfield Publishing Company
Mountain View, California
London • Toronto

Library of Congress Cataloging-in-Publication Data

DeSpelder, Lynne Ann
     The last dance : encountering death and dying / Lynne Ann
DeSpelder & Albert Lee Strickland. — 3rd ed.
        p.   cm.
     Includes bibliographical references and indexes.
     ISBN 0-87484-995-0
     1. Death — Social aspects — United States.   2. Death — United States —
Psychological aspects.   I. Strickland, Albert Lee.   II. Title.
HQ1078.3.USD48   1991
155.9′37 — dc20   91-33988
                                                                                                                 CIP

Manufactured in the United States of America

10 9 8 7 6 5 4

Mayfield Publishing Company
1240 Villa Street
Mountain View, California 94041

Sponsoring editor, Franklin C. Graham; *managing editor*, Linda Toy; *manuscript editor*, Carol
Dondrea; *text designer*, Albert Burkhardt; *cover designer*, Donna Davis; *manufacturing manager*,
Martha Branch. The text was set in 10/12 Monticello by TypeLink, Inc. and printed on 50#
Mead Pub Matte by R. R. Donnelley & Sons.

Credits and sources are listed on a continuation of the copyright page, p. 642.

Contents

CHAPTER 4

Health Care Systems: Patients, Staff, and Institutions   125

CHAPTER 5

Facing Death: Living with Life-Threatening Illness   163

C H A P T E R   6

Last Rites: Funerals and Body Disposition   *197*

CHAPTER   9

Death in the Lives of Adults   297

C H A P T E R   10

C H A P T E R   11

CHAPTER 12

Environmental Encounters with Death 423

CHAPTER 13

Suicide 477

C H A P T E R   *14*

Beyond Death/After Life   *527*

CHAPTER 15

The Path Ahead: Personal and Social Choices   567

Preface

*T*he study of death is concerned with questions that are rooted at the center of human experience. Thus, the person who sets out to increase his or her knowledge of death and dying is embarking on an exploration that must be in part a journey of personal and experiential discovery. This text evolved out of the practical experience of teaching college and university courses in death and dying. It provides the reader with a solid theoretical grounding as well as methods for applying what is learned about death and dying to real-life situations. In writing *The Last Dance: Encountering Death and Dying*, our aim has been to offer a comprehensive and readable introduction to the study of death and dying that highlights the major issues and questions.

Each chapter conveys the depth of research and range of applications pertinent to its particular topic area. For those wishing to pursue further study, each chapter includes a list of recommended readings, and the chapter notes also suggest source materials for consultation. Thus the reader is introduced to a wide range of topics in thanatological studies and is also guided toward more detailed presentations on topics of particular interest. When citing such source materials, we have tried to achieve an appropriate balance between classic works in the field and publications of more recent vintage. Throughout the text, concepts and principles are made more meaningful by the use of examples, anecdotes, boxed material, and other illustrative materials. Contributions from anthropology, art, ethics, health science, history, literature, philosophy, psychology, public policy, religion, and sociology can all be found here in their relevant contexts.

Following an introductory chapter in which American attitudes toward death form the major focus, the perspective is broadened by examining, in the second chapter, cross-cultural and historical attitudes and practices relative to dying and death. Chapter 3 deals with the question of how we learn about death during childhood, taking up issues concerning the processes of socialization. Chapters 4 and 5 deal, first, with the health-medical care system, including alternatives for providing care at the terminal phase of life and, then, with the personal experience of life-threatening illness and patterns of coping with it. Chapters 6 and 7 focus, respectively, on the topics of funerals and grief.

The middle chapters of the book, Chapters 8 and 9, use a developmental approach in examining encounters with death throughout the lifespan. Together, these chapters elucidate logically the types of bereavement and experiences with death that commonly occur at various ages. In Chapters 10 and 11, the ethical and legal issues surrounding death are discussed, including such topics as informed consent, organ donation and transplantation, euthanasia, definitions of death, living wills and natural death directives, and the processes involved in making a will and probating an estate.

The next three chapters are devoted to a number of specific topics that are crucial to a comprehensive view of death and dying. In Chapter 12, important issues are addressed relating to risk taking, accidents, disasters, violence and homicide, war and the nuclear threat, and stress. Chapter 13 covers the subject of suicide, including a discussion of various theoretical models that have been developed for better understanding the dynamics of suicide and a section describing methods of suicide prevention, intervention, and postvention. Chapter 14 provides a wide-ranging survey of concepts of immortality and beliefs about what might follow death, drawing from religious and secular traditions as well as modern research into near-death experiences.

The final chapter summarizes some of the personal values and societal applications that can be gained from a study of dying and death, concluding with a discussion of how one might define a "good death."

Although topics are organized in a way that we believe serves the needs of most readers, some may wish to rearrange the sequence in which chapters are read. Accordingly, the book has been written to allow for such flexibility. We urge readers to use the extensive boxed quotations and other illustrative material which is designed to expand upon or provide counterpoint to the textual presentation.

In short, *The Last Dance: Encountering Death and Dying* embodies an approach to the study of death and dying that combines the intellectual and the emotional, the social and the individual, the experiential and the scholarly. Thus, intensity is balanced with relief. The book emphasizes the positive and necessary values of compassion, listening, and tolerance for the views of others, and it encourages the reader to engage in a constructive process of self-discovery about death and dying.

This book is a comprehensive survey of a field of study that is still in the process of formation. It is not an indoctrination to any one point of view, but an introduction to diverse points of view. The reader is invited to join in the process of discovering the assumptions, orientations, and predispositions that have, for much of this century, inhibited discussion of death and dying in this country. Readers may well form their own opinions, but we hope that, when they do, they will choose them only after considering other possibilities in a spirit of tolerance and open-mindedness. A major theme of this book is that such an unbiased investigation makes choices available that might otherwise be neglected because of prejudice or ignorance.

With the publication of the third edition of *The Last Dance*, we again express our appreciation to the many individuals who contributed to the success of the first and second editions and whose contributions are evident in this edition as well, including Thomas Attig, Bowling Green State University; Linda C. Kinrade, California State University, Hayward; Anthony Lenzer, University of Hawaii at Manoa; Wendy Martyna, University of California, Santa Cruz; Marsha McGee, Northeast Louisiana University; Walter L. Moore, Florida State University — Tallahassee; Judith M. Stillion, Western Carolina University; Jeffrey S. Turner, Mitchell College; and Joseph M. Yonder, Villa Maria College of Buffalo. For their suggestions as reviewers for the third edition we thank John B. Bond, The University of Manitoba; Tom Bruce, Sacramento City College; John Harvey, Western Illinois University; Judith M. Stillion, Western Carolina University; and John B. Williamson, Boston University.

Special thanks to Linda Toy, whose good humor and keen management skills eased the production process, and to Frank Graham, whose editorial guidance and warm friendship are deeply valued. To all whose help was instrumental in bringing this edition of *The Last Dance* to print, our sincere thanks.

L. A. D.
A. L. S.

P R O L O G U E

I don't know how much time I have left. I've spent my life dispensing salves and purgatives, potions and incantations — miracles of nature (though I admit that some were pure medicine-show snake oil). Actually, half the time all I offered was just plain common sense. Over the years, every kind of suffering person has made his or her way here. Some had broken limbs or broken bodies . . . or hearts. Often their sorrow was an ailing son or daughter. It was always so hard when they'd lose a child. I never did get used to that. And then there were the young lovers. Obtaining their heart's desire was so important to them. I had to smile. I always made them sweat and beg for their handful of bark, and for those willful tortures I'll probably go to hell . . . if there is one. My God, how long has it been since I had those feelings myself? The fever, the lump in the throat, the yearning. I can't remember. A long time . . . maybe never. Well, there have been other passions for me. There's my dusty legion of jars. Each one holds its little secret. Barks, roots, soils, leaves, flowers, mushrooms, bugs — magic dust, every bit of it. There's my book — my "rudder," a ship's pilot would call it. That's a good name for it. Every salve, every purgative . . . they're all in there. (Everything, that is, except my stained beard, scraggly hair, and flowing robes — they'll have to figure those out on their own.) And then there's my walking stick (always faithful) . . . and the ballerina. And ten thousand mornings, ten thousand afternoons, ten thousand nights. And the stars. Oh, I have had my loves.

It hurts to move. My shelf and jars seem so far away, though I know that if I tried I could reach them. But no. It's enough and it's time . . . almost. I hope he makes it back in time. He burst through my door only two days ago. A young man, well spoken. Tears were streaming down his face. He looked so bent and beaten that I could not refuse him. He told me that his wife had died over a month ago and that he had been inconsolable since.

"Please help me," he pleaded, "or kill me." He covered his face with his hands. "Perhaps they're the same thing. I don't know anymore."

I

I let him cry awhile so I could watch him, gauge him. When at last he looked up, with my good hand I motioned him to take a seat. Then, between coughing fits, I went to work. "Do you see that toy there?" I said. "The little ballerina . . . Yes, that's it. Pick it up."

"Pick it up?"

"It won't bite. Pick it up." (He probably thought it was a trick—that's what they expect.) He grasped it carefully, with one hand, then wiped his eyes with the other. "That's better," I continued. "That's just a toy to you. You don't know what meaning to put to it, yet. So I want you to look at that ballerina."

He was hesitant, but I waited, stubbornly, until he looked down and fixed his attention on the little toy dancer. I went on: "I knew a young man once who was very handsome—always had been. He not only turned every head, he was strong and smart, and his family was wealthy. His main concern each day was which girl he should court that evening. He had planned that after several seasons of playing at love he would marry a beautiful girl, have beautiful children, and settle down to spend the money his father had promised him. And he had plans for that money. He had already purchased the land he wanted to live on and was having built there the biggest house in the area. He was going to raise and race horses, I think. One morning he got on his favorite horse and went for a ride. He whipped that horse into a gallop; it stepped in a hole and threw him. The young man broke his neck, and died." I stared at my guest and waited.

"That's a tragedy," he finally croaked.

"For whom? For those he left behind, perhaps. But was it for him? When he opened his eyes that morning, he didn't know he would die that day. He had no intention of dying for another sixty years—if then. None of us does." The young man looked confused. "His mistake was that he forgot that he could die that day."

"That's a morbid thought," he replied, and he looked as though he had just smelled something putrid.

"Is it? A moment ago you asked me to end your grieving by ending your own life. Suppose I oblige?" I stared at him for a few moments with my most practiced penetrating glare. "Suppose I did agree to kill you. How would you spend your last few minutes?"

He was still a little wary of me, but relieved that I seemed to be suggesting a hypothetical situation, rather than a serious course of action. He considered the possibilities for a while, then straightened in his chair. "Well, I guess I would step outside and take a last, best look at the sky, the clouds, the trees."

"Suppose you lived that way all the time?" He stared at me, then looked down at his hands, searching them. "That young man I told you about . . . perhaps the tragedy for him was not that he died, but that he failed to use the eventual certainty of his death to make him live! Did he woo each of those ladies as though it might be his last romance? Did he build that house as though it might be his last creation? Did he ride that horse as though it would be his last ride? I don't know; I hope so." My young guest nodded, but he was still sad. I pointed to the toy ballerina he was holding. "That was given to me by a young lady who understood these things."

He looked at the figure closely. "Is she a dancer?"

"Yes, she is, and she is dead." The young man looked up, once again off balance. "She has been dead for, oh, a very long time." After all these years, a tear fell onto my cheek. I let it go. "She was many things. A child, a woman, a cook and a gardener, a friend, lover, daughter . . . But what she really was—who she was—was a dancer. When she was dying, she gave that doll to me, smiled, and whispered, 'At the moment of my death, I will take all of my dancing and put it in there, so my dancing can live on.'"

Tears welled in my guest's eyes.

"I can help you," I said, "but first there is something that you must do." He became very attentive. "Go to town and knock on the door of the first house you come to. Ask the people inside if their family has ever been touched by death. If so, go to the next house. When you find a family that has not *been touched by death, bring them to me. Do you understand?" He nodded, and I sighed. "I'm tired now."*

He got up, set the ballerina back on the table, and started for the door. I stopped him. "Young man!" He faced me from the doorway. "Come back as soon as you can."

David Gordon

*In a Spanish village, neighbors and relatives peer through the doorway
upon the deathbed scene of a villager.*

Attitudes Toward Death:
A Climate of Change

O f all human experiences, none is more overwhelming in its implications than death. Yet, for most of us, death remains a shadowy figure whose presence is only vaguely acknowledged. Although American attitudes toward death have changed greatly during the recent past, the predominant outlook and social customs of our society still reflect a queasy uncertainty that some observers have characterized as a denial of death. Life styles influence death styles. Attitudes, which develop out of the interplay between an individual and his or her environment, include components of belief, emotion, and behavior. Anxiety in the face of death is not new, of course. Death has always been the central question of human experience, although it is one that, for the greater part of the twentieth century, most Americans have tried in various ways to avoid.

Formal education about death is a relatively recent phenomenon. To provide a context for the journey that follows, we begin by looking at several factors that have stimulated the recent interest in death studies and by reviewing the pioneering contributions that have shaped this new field of study. Following this introduction, and with the aim of gaining a better understanding of our own attitudes toward death, we then cast a glance backward in time. Look-ing to the past can provide clues about how and why present attitudes evolved. By acquiring a sense of the way that people believed, behaved, and felt about death in the late nineteenth century, we can appreciate more fully how modern attitudes are influenced by a variety of factors that tend to lessen our familiarity with dying and death. In subsequent sections of this chapter, we examine how attitudes toward death are revealed through language, literature, music, and the visual arts, as well as by the mass media in the form of news and entertainment.

The Present Milieu: Awareness of Death

The experience of world war, the atomic bomb, and the aftermath of Hiroshima and Nagasaki have been followed in the recent past by assassinations of political leaders, wars in Vietnam and the Middle East, international terrorism, and nuclear brinkmanship, not to mention the prospect of global pollution. We have been forced to contemplate our mortality. Robert Lifton and others have described children of the present era as *hibakusha*, a Japanese word meaning "explosion-affected" that was initially applied to the survivors of Hiroshima. Anxiety about these threats of possible annihilation is surely sufficient reason for searching out the meaning of life and death.

Most of us, however, want to learn about death and dying for the more obvious reason that we have been largely ignorant of the experience. Our understanding of death has been blurred by euphemistic language, by the isolation of the dying, by technologies that alter our understanding of life and death, and by the various institutions that have assumed the tasks of dealing with the dying and the dead, as well as by our vicarious acquaintance with death through presentations in the media.

The ambivalent attitudes toward death in our society are reflected when one educator applauds the study of death as the "last of the old taboos to fall" while another contends that it is "not a fit subject for the curriculum." During the latter part of the 1980s, this ambivalence was also reflected by a brief flurry of media interest in death education, largely in response to a campaign initiated by a small group of people determined to expose the "evils" of death education. In at least one instance, students who had agreed to be interviewed by a network film crew felt angry and violated when they saw their positive comments twisted and misrepresented by the way the resulting "film bites" were pieced together, apparently in an effort to create a more interesting or sensational story for the evening news.[1] The question remains: What price do we pay for the lack of firsthand experience with death?

David Stannard tells us that in societies in which each individual is unique, important, and irreplaceable, death is not ignored but is marked by a "community-wide outpouring of grief for what is a genuine social loss." But in societies in which one individual is not considered to be very different from any other, "little damage is done to the social fabric by the loss of an individual," and outside one's immediate circle there is little or no acknowledgment of the death.[2]

The first step in gaining new choices among behaviors and attitudes toward death is to become aware of how a climate of denial or avoidance prevents us from honestly confronting death, thus estranging us from an integral aspect of human

The obituary pages tell us of the news that we are dying away, while the birth announcements in finer print, off at the side of the page, inform us of our replacements, but we get no grasp from this of the enormity of scale. There are 3 billion of us on the earth, and all 3 billion must be dead, on a schedule, within this lifetime. The vast mortality, involving something over 50 million of us each year, takes place in relative secrecy. We can only really know of the deaths in our households, or among our friends. These, detached in our minds from all the rest, we take to be unnatural events, anomalies, outrages. We speak of our own dead in low voices; struck down, we say, as though visible death can only occur for cause, by disease or violence, avoidably. We send off for flowers, grieve, make ceremonies, scatter bones, unaware of the rest of the 3 billion on the same schedule. All of that immense mass of flesh and bone and consciousness will disappear by absorption into the earth, without recognition by the transient survivors.

Less than a half century from now, our replacements will have more than doubled the numbers. It is hard to see how we can continue to keep the secret, with such multitudes doing the dying. We will have to give up the notion that death is catastrophe, or detestable, or avoidable, or even strange. We will need to learn more about the cycling of life in the rest of the system, and about our connection to the process. Everything that comes alive seems to be in trade for something that dies, call for call. There might be some comfort in the recognition of synchrony, in the information that we all go down together, in the best of company.

Lewis Thomas, *The Lives of a Cell: Notes of a Biology Watcher*

life. In the final analysis, sufficient motive for studying death and dying and for encountering the reality behind the image is framed by Octavio Paz: "A civilization that denies death ends by denying life."[3]

Precursors of Current Interest in Death and Dying

A few books serve as signal examples of the modern impulse to systematically study death and dying. A convenient watershed from which to date the beginnings of this effort is Herman Feifel's book, *The Meaning of Death*. Based on a symposium held in 1956 at the annual meeting of the American Psychological Association and published in 1959, Feifel's compilation brought together authorities from various disciplines whose essays encompassed theoretical approaches, developmental and attitudinal studies, cultural and religious concepts, and clinical aspects of death. Death was shown to be an important topic for public as well as scholarly consideration. Despite initial signs of recognition for the validity of investigating the emerging "thanatological domain," there was nevertheless considerable resistance from professional personnel. Feifel says:

The realization soon began to sink in that what I was up against were not idiosyncratic personal quirks, the usual administrative vicissitudes, pique, or nonacceptance of an inadequate research design. Rather, it was personal position, bolstered by cultural structuring, that death is a dark symbol not to be stirred—not even touched—an obscenity to be avoided.[4]

Looking back on those pioneering efforts, Feifel recently recalled that he was emphatically told that "the one thing you never do is to discuss death with a patient."

Essentially the same message was communicated to Elisabeth Kübler-Ross, whose publication of *On Death and Dying* ten years later encouraged public demand for a more realistic assessment of how dying and death was being dealt with in this country. The book's major contribution was its focus on the needs and feelings of the dying patient. The notion that dying patients could provide important lessons for health care professionals and for their own families was regarded by many people as a radical innovation.

In the meantime, two books published in 1965 contributed significantly to the development of studies dealing with death and dying. *Awareness of Dying*, by Barney G. Glaser and Anselm L. Strauss, used sociological field work to study how a dying patient's awareness of his or her impending death affected hospital staff and family members. Glaser and Strauss found that medical professionals and the general public were reluctant to discuss the process of dying and tried to avoid telling a patient that he or she was dying. Robert Fulton's *Death and Identity* brought together contributions from various fields bearing on death and dying from both theoretical and practical points of view. During this period, other writers focused attention not on the processes of dying or the meaning of death, but rather on the social practices and customs for dealing with death.

Geoffrey Gorer's essay, "The Pornography of Death," published in 1955, was an early instance of this kind of inquiry. It marked the beginning of what would become an energetic and often critical appraisal of how we deal with death. Jessica Mitford's *The American Way of Death* and Ruth Harmer's *The High Cost of Dying*, both published in 1963, criticized American funeral practices. Evelyn Waugh had earlier employed satire in *The Loved One*, published in 1948, to cast light on hypocritical and death-avoiding attitudes. Books like these directed public attention to practices and customs relating to death. Indeed, such publications helped to stimulate subsequent efforts by consumer advocates to regulate American funeral practices.

Much has happened in the last several decades to increase our awareness about how people try to ignore the inevitability of death or construct elaborate deceptions to avoid its reality. Not long ago, a person seeking information about death would find precious little on the subject, and even that only after considerable effort. Today many bookstores devote a special section to death-related books, some of which are bestsellers. Among these are biographical accounts of coping with terminal illness and bereavement, as well as essays and anthologies written by professional thanatologists. Many of these books are in the self-help category, offering advice to the bereaved and to the dying. Such books, as one survey reports, have "become a ubiquitous part of American health care and culture."[5] Indeed, Kübler-Ross's *On Death and Dying* was found to be the self-help book most read, as well as most prescribed, by psychologists who responded to the survey. Children, too, can find a wide selection of books, both nonfiction and fictional stories, with themes relating to death.

At the same time, there has been a burgeoning professional and scholarly literature, with two journals devoted exclusively to scholarly articles in thanatology: *Omega: Journal of Death and Dying* and *Death Studies*. Care of the dying is the precinct of such scholarly periodicals as *The Journal of Palliative Care* and *Hospice Journal*, and ethical issues related to dying and death are addressed in such journals as *The Hastings Center Report* and *Second Opinion*. There now seems to be no shortage of interest in death and dying nor of publications intended to satisfy this interest.

The Rise of Death Education

As we have noted, public discussion of death and dying is a fairly recent phenomenon in modern American society. Among the factors cited as responsible for the emergence of death studies and the so-called death awareness movement are: (1) the increasing number of aged persons in American society; (2) the prolongation of the dying process; (3) the destruction of Hiroshima by the atomic bomb, which ushered in the nuclear age and its attendant anxieties; (4) the "psychology of entitlement," which became prominent in the 1960s and which asserted the rights of the dying as well as entitlements for other groups previously ignored in varying degrees by society; (5) a reaction against what has been characterized as a dehumanizing technology and advocacy of humane and natural approaches to such biological phenomena as birth and death; and (6) a sociocultural need to confront death meaningfully in a secularized society.[6]

People are now examining the subconscious cultural message that death is "bad." The western and the detective story are modern versions of the morality play in which the villain dies and the hero lives. We are just beginning to acknowledge that death and failure are not necessarily synonymous, that the true meaning of death lies beyond such categories. Still, there are frequent reminders that death remains a taboo and fearful topic for many people. Take a death-and-dying course or read a book such as this one and quite likely someone will ask, "Why would you want to take a class about death?" or "Why in heaven's name would you be reading about death?"

Clearly, we are witnessing a period of transition. In 1964, a bibliography of death-related publications comprised about 400 references; by 1975, it had increased tenfold, and its compiler, Robert Fulton, estimated that more books and articles about death and dying had been published in the previous decade than had been written during the whole of the previous hundred and fifty years.[7] This trend has continued unabated since the time of Fulton's remarks.

Considered broadly, death education includes both formal instruction dealing with dying, death, and grief, as well as informal exploration of these topics. Informal death education may occur in the context of "teachable moments" arising out of death-related events occurring in daily life. The event precipitating this instruction may be the death or bereavement of a child in a given classroom, or it may be an event experienced more widely, as was the case when an explosion killed the *Challenger* astronauts. This event, watched as it happened by millions of schoolchildren in their classrooms, stimulated immediate discussion of issues related to death in schools throughout the country. Teachers had little choice but to help students deal with their concerns, questions, and anxieties.

More formally, education about death is offered as part of the curriculum in a small percentage of elementary and secondary schools, most often in conjunction with courses on health or family living.[8] More widespread are courses in death education at the college and university level. The first regular course in death education at an American university was offered by Robert Fulton at the University of Minnesota in the spring of 1963.[9]

The decades of the 1960s and 1970s, says Herman Feifel, "were characterized by the introduction of workshops and courses on dying, death, and mourning in various universities and professional schools."[10] When the first conference on death education was held at Hamline University in Minnesota in 1970, there were only about twenty death education courses above the high school level. Within the next four years, that number increased more than fiftyfold.[11] Today, it is estimated that several thousand such courses are offered on college campuses. In 1982, Brooklyn College began offering a master's degree in thanatology within its program in community health, and other graduate schools now offer similar programs.

The Interdisciplinary Nature of Death Education

Courses in the field of death education are taught in a wide variety of departments and academic disciplines. Most courses can be found in sociology (including social work) and psychology departments, followed by religious studies, philosophy, health education, nursing, gerontology, English, law, and education departments.[12] Death education benefits not only from this broad base of academic support but also from the contributions of physicians, nurses, counselors, ethicists, hospice workers, and other professionals and lay people involved in various aspects of death education, counseling, and care. The recurring themes in thanatology, as Mary Ann Morgan points out, include its interdisciplinary nature and its conjoining of both cognitive and affective content.[13] In other words, to be complete, death education must address both objective facts and subjective concerns.

Curricula focused on dying and death have also been proposed for students preparing to become healthcare professionals. Care of the dying has been a major responsibility of professional nurses throughout the history of nursing. Even before specialized training in nursing was instituted, as Leslie Degner and Christina Gow point out, "lay nurses both in Europe and the New World provided comfort to soldiers dying on the battlefields and to civilians dying as a result of large-scale epidemics."[14] During the modern period, however, changing patterns of disease and treatment have altered the role of the nurse vis-à-vis the dying process. Degner and Gow cite two implications of this change in the nature of nursing care: "First, prior to entering nursing, young people are relatively protected from both seeing and talking with the dying. However, as soon as they begin their education they are expected to adapt to death as a visible phenomenon and to respond sensitively and effectively in providing care." Second, "nurses are exposed primarily to curative-oriented care and are less likely to encounter effective nursing models of comfort-oriented care." In light of the variability in the type of education currently available to nursing students, Degner and Gow reaffirm the conclusion of a landmark study by Jeanne Quint Benoliel more than two decades ago in which she called attention to the need for "systematic death education for nurses."[15]

Specialized training programs for other professionals whose duties bring them into frequent contact with dying and bereaved persons are also part of the larger picture of death education.[16] Professionals such as police officers, fire fighters, and emergency medical technicians are witnesses to human tragedy in the line of duty. Being present in crises involving death, they are called upon to comfort victims and survivors. Thus, besides the skills needed to carry out their primary role, they are also expected to exhibit sensitivity and expertise in human relations. The stress that results from being on the scene when tragedy occurs may take an emotional toll on their own lives, however. The image of the police officer, emergency medical technician, or fire fighter who "keeps it all in" and never shows his or her emotions is being challenged by the recognition that such a strategy is, ultimately, physically and psychologically harmful. Death education, "in advance of experiencing the deaths of others," can identify the range of emotional responses that are likely to be encountered, and, through previous contemplation and analysis of their own mortality, these professionals can become better prepared to deal not only with their own feelings but with the feelings of others as well.[17]

As death education has achieved greater prominence, a number of organizations have become catalysts for multidisciplinary communication about death and dying. Groups like the Association for Death Education and Counseling (ADEC) and the Foundation of Thanatology have achieved a national or even international scope; others, such as the Minnesota Coalition for Terminal Care, are focused primarily on regional or local concerns.[18] The International Work Group on Death, Dying, and Bereavement (IWG), an organization that is comparatively small in numbers but one that includes many of the leaders in the field, has provided a forum for consensus on important issues in the field and for disseminating policy statements on various aspects of death, dying, and bereavement to the larger community. In addition, institutions like the Center for Death Education and Research at the University of Minnesota and the National Center for Death Education in Boston serve to focus interest and gather resources pertaining to death education, counseling, and care.

Where death is concerned, the adage, "What you don't know won't hurt you," is a fallacy. Avoiding the thought of death doesn't remove us from its power. Such ostrichlike behavior only limits our choices for coping effectively with the experience of death. When we bring death out of the closet, we give ourselves the opportunity to clear away the accumulated rubbish and preserve what we find valuable. As Robert Kavanaugh said, "The unexamined death is not worth dying."

The churchyard cemetery is a reminder of human mortality as well as a focal point for memories of deceased members of the community. Here, the tombstones face the doorway of the church, so that the names of the memorialized dead can be seen as parishioners exit this Canadian church.

Patterns of Death and Dying: Then and Now

In contrast to the death-related experiences of most Americans today, consider those that were commonplace to someone living before the turn of the century. Death usually took place in the home, with all family members present, down to the youngest child. After death, the family washed and prepared the body for burial. The local carpenter, or perhaps the family members themselves, built a coffin that was then set up in the parlor of the home.

Friends and acquaintances from the community, along with other relatives, came to the family's home to view the body of the deceased in an open coffin and to share in the ritual of mourning. Children kept vigil along with adults, sometimes sleeping in the same room as the corpse. Later, the body was carried to the gravesite, perhaps a family plot on the property or at a nearby cemetery. There, a local parson would read a few appropriate verses from the Bible as the coffin was lowered and the grave filled in by relatives. Each person learned about death firsthand. From caring for the dying family member through disposition of the corpse, death was within the realm of the family.

If you were a person of the nineteenth century suddenly transported through time to the present, you would find a rich source of information about current attitudes toward death by observing modern funeral practices. Walking into the "slumber room" of a typical mortuary, you would experience culture shock. The familiar coffin has been replaced by a more elaborate "casket," and the corpse shows the mortician's skill in cosmetic "restoration"—the stark appearance of death diminished.

At the funeral, you would observe the ritual as family and friends eulogize the deceased. Ah, that's familiar, you say—but where is the dear departed? Off to the side a bit, the casket remains closed, death tastefully concealed.

When the service at the gravesite concludes, you look on with amazement as the mourners begin to leave although the casket lies yet unburied. The cemetery crew will complete the actual burial. As a nineteenth-century onlooker at a twentieth-century funeral, you are perhaps most struck by a sense that the family and friends of the deceased are observers rather than participants: The tasks of preparing the dead for burial are handled by hired professionals who are paid to perform these services. Compared to a time when skills for dealing with a dead body were an ordinary aspect of domestic life, our present participation in the rituals surrounding the dead is minimal.

Factors Lessening Familiarity with Dying and Death

Both social and technological factors have altered how people in modern societies deal with death and dying. The size, shape, and distribution of the population—that is, its demographics—have changed greatly since the turn of the century. Increases in average life expectancy, coupled with lower mortality rates, have had a tremendous influence on our attitudes and implicit expectations about life and death. The extended family has been replaced by a smaller family unit, the nuclear family; this is a significant demographic change whose effects have been accentuated by increased geographical mobility. At the same time, advances in medical science and in applied health care technologies have not only contributed to demographic change, they have altered the usual causes of death as well as the setting where dying ordinarily occurs.

Life Expectancy and Mortality Rates

Since the turn of the century, average life expectancy at birth in the United States has increased from forty-seven years to about seventy-five years.[19] Figure 1-1 gives changes in life expectancy by sex and race over a period of more than eighty years. In 1900, over half of reported deaths involved persons fourteen years of age and younger. Today, less than 3 percent of total reported deaths occur among this age group.[20]

Imagine a time when death at an early age was not uncommon. Today we might characterize such persons as "struck down in their prime." Most of us take it for granted that a newborn child will live on into his or her seventh or eighth decade, perhaps beyond.

Of course, the expectation that a baby will survive and mature into old age is not shared equally by all Americans, nor by those elsewhere who live where

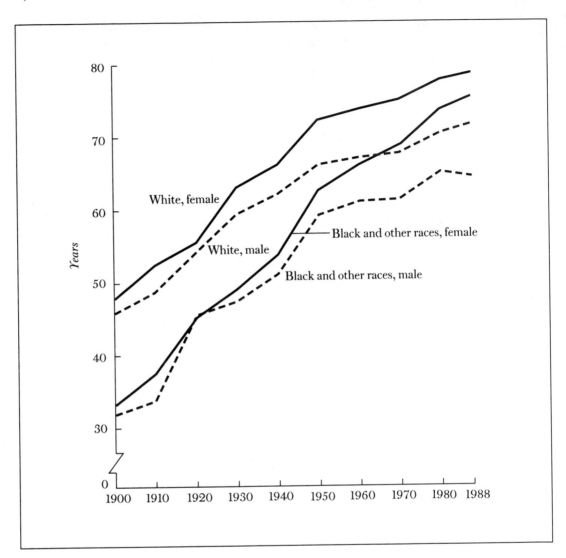

Figure *1-1*.   *Life Expectancy at Birth, by Race and Sex, 1900–1988*
Source: U.S. Department of Commerce, Bureau of the Census, *Social Indicators III*, p. 71;
U.S. National Center for Health Statistics, *Statistical Abstract of the United States 1990*,
p. 71, and *Health, United States 1989*, p. 106.

poverty and poor living conditions contribute to high rates of mortality during
infancy and childhood. The death rates among people living in conditions of bare
subsistence have been altered only minimally by the advances in modern medicine and health care that we enjoy as a given. Despite these obvious inequities, for
most North Americans and Europeans the expectation of a long life seems almost
a birthright.

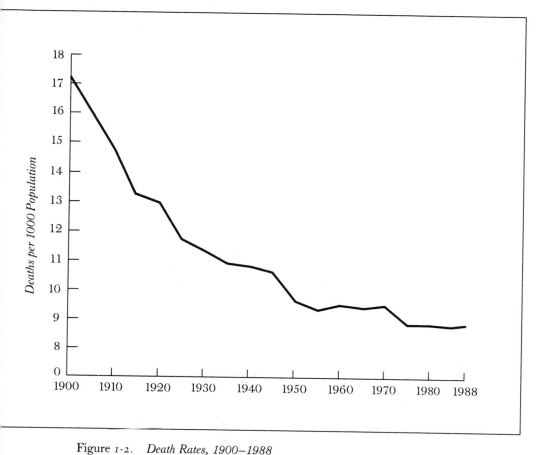

Figure *1-2*.   *Death Rates, 1900–1988*
Source: U.S. National Center for Health Statistics, *Statistical Abstract of the United States 1990*, p. 75; *Health, United States, 1989*, p. 119; and U.S. Bureau of the Census, *Historical Statistics of the United States, Colonial Times to 1970* (Washington: Government Printing Office, 1975), p. 59.

How unlike times past, when one or both parents might die before their children had grown to adolescence. Mothers died during childbirth; babies were stillborn. People commonly experienced the deaths of brothers and sisters during the early years of childhood from such diseases as whooping cough, diphtheria, and polio.

At the turn of the century, the death rate in America was about 17 per 1000. Today, the death rate has declined to about 8.8 per 1000 (see Figure 1-2).[21] A high mortality rate, of which infant deaths were a considerable percentage, made it difficult for people of earlier times to deny the fact of death.

Young and old experienced death as a natural and inevitable part of the human condition. The typical household of the nineteenth century contained an

Death brought the community into play for the last time: the food discreetly left in the kitchen; the condolence calls; the preparation of the corpse in the bed in which [the person] had died — and perhaps slept in for many years — without benefit of the mortician's cosmetics; the laying out in the parlor; a stream of people filing softly by throughout the day paying respects to the family; the old friends who sat up with the body through the long lonely night; and then the funeral the next day, with family, friends, numerous townspeople, members of the husband's lodge, ladies of the burial society who had decorated the grave site. Funerals were long and doleful; the minister droned on interminably about the virtues of the deceased and hymns were sung; then the black hearse with white-gloved pallbearers in attendance and a black-plumed horse drawing it made its slow progress to the cemetery. It was not unusual for town businesses to close down completely for a funeral, and nearly everyone joined the procession to the burying-place, where at graveside a few last words were said, before the finality of the earth raining down on the coffin. Back at home neighbors had cleaned and dusted, leaving a neat — and empty — home for the grieving family to return to. There they sank down wearily and talked in numbed voices and at last went to bed, to try to get some rest in preparation for the new day.

Richard R. Lingeman,
Small Town America

extended family: aged parents, uncles, aunts, and grandparents, as well as children of varying ages. In this setting, the chances of experiencing death firsthand were much greater than in today's much smaller family. The typical American family may now expect statistically to live twenty years without experiencing the death of one of its members.[22]

Changing Causes of Death

Changes in the major causes of death are another reason why the experience of death today differs from what it was at the turn of the century. Then, the typical death was rapid and sudden, often caused by acute infectious diseases such as tuberculosis, typhoid fever, syphilis, diphtheria, streptococcal septicemia, and pneumonia. In 1900, these microbial diseases accounted for about 40 percent of all deaths in the United States; today they account for only about 4 percent. Now the typical death is a slow, progressive process related to such maladies as heart disease and cancer (see Table 1-1). The result is a tendency to assume that death is something that happens only in old age.

This shift in disease patterns has been referred to as an *epidemiologic transition* and is characterized in modern societies by a redistribution of deaths from the young to the old.[23] As the risk of dying from infectious diseases is reduced, more people survive into older ages, where they face the likelihood of dying from degenerative diseases. Although many demographers believe that the maximum

T A B L E *1-1*   *Leading Causes of Death, 1988*

Cause of Death[a]	Estimated Death Rate Per 100,000	% of Total
All causes	883.0	100.0
Diseases of the heart	312.2	35.4
Malignancies (cancer)	198.6	22.5
Cerebrovascular diseases	61.1	6.9
Accidents	39.7	4.5
Pulmonary diseases	33.3	3.8
Pneumonia and influenza	31.5	3.6
Diabetes mellitus	16.1	1.8
Suicide	12.3	1.4
Chronic liver disease	10.6	1.2
Atherosclerosis	9.6	1.0
Infective diseases (including AIDS)	9.4	1.0
Homicide	9.0	1.0

Source: U.S. National Center for Health Statistics, *Statistical Abstract of the United States 1990*, p. 79.
[a]The top three causes of death currently account for nearly two-thirds of all deaths in the U.S. population.

possible human life span has held steady at about eighty-five years, in earlier times few individuals actually survived to such a ripe old age. In modern societies, a diminishing mortality rate among younger members of the population results in a larger, and steadily increasing, proportion of aged persons.

In 1900, persons sixty-five or older made up 4 percent of the American population; today, they make up about 12 percent, or 30 million persons. In 1900, this segment of the population accounted for only about 17 percent of all deaths; today, of the slightly more than 2 million deaths each year in the United States, more than two-thirds occur among persons sixty-five and older.[24] Reflecting on this dramatic change, one can appreciate Robert Fulton's statement that "the elderly in America have a monopoly on death."[25]

Geographical Mobility

Our geographical mobility is another factor influencing the lessened incidence of firsthand experience with death. Every year, about one-fifth of the American population pulls up stakes, says goodbye to relatives, friends, and neighbors, and moves elsewhere.[26]

Whereas in previous times relationships were closely tied to place and to kinship, relationships now are characterized more by present function than by a lifetime of shared experiences. How many college friendships continue through marriage and the childrearing years on into retirement? Children, once grown, rarely live in the same house with their parents or, even less likely, with brothers and sisters in an extended family.

Five generations of the Machado family form an extended family network rarely seen today. Firsthand experiences of death in such a family come through the closeness of multigenerational living.

Distance separates family and friends as changes in life style and changes of employment necessitate moving on. In such circumstances, death is less likely to occur among family and friends. This highly mobile pattern of living is, of course, experienced in varying degrees. Among certain racial, ethnic, or socioeconomic groups who place exceptional value on family ties, several generations may maintain a high degree of intimacy and closeness. But, for most people, a highly mobile life style contributes to making death less immediate, less intimate.

Reduced Contact Among Generations

Geographical mobility, an increasing proportion of elderly people in the population, a declining percentage of deaths among the young, and the rise of the nuclear family combine to create a situation wherein few people are present when close family members die. Grandparents and grandchildren do not typically reside in the same home (or perhaps even in the same city) and thus, unlike times past, have intermittent rather than daily contact. Senior citizen subdivisions and trailer parks tend to discourage close intermingling of the generations.

Consider, for instance, the experience of two small children on a Halloween trek, going door to door in their neighborhood. After knocking to no avail on several well-lighted doors in a large mobile-home park, their cries of "Trick or treat!" were finally answered by a woman who said, "You'll not get any Halloween treats in this place. Only old people live here, and they leave their lights on for security and safety, not to welcome children on Halloween!"

In addition, illness or failing health may lead to confinement in hospitals or in nursing or convalescent facilities. Death, when it comes, is not likely to occur amid familiar surroundings with family and friends present. Even for those elderly who are able to live more or less independently in their own homes, the onset of the final illness usually brings admittance to a hospital followed by death in an institutional setting.

The Displacement of Death from the Home

Not only is death less prevalent than it once was, it is less visible, as is dying. In 1900, two-thirds of the Americans who died were less than fifty years old. Most died in their own beds. This was true even in the cities, where perhaps 75 to 80 percent of deaths occurred at home.

The present pattern of death in our society is such that, regardless of age, about 80 percent of all persons die in an institutional setting — hospital, nursing or convalescent facility, or retirement home providing care for the aged — often surrounded by an astonishing array of machinery that is designed to sustain life until the last electrical impulse fades from the monitor. Institutionalized and given over to professional caretakers, death is kept apart from the rest of us. A long-distance phone call announcing the passing of grandpa or grandma takes the place of the intimate, firsthand experience of a loved one's death.

Life-Extending Technologies

Striking advances in modern medicine have created immense changes in how we relate to death. With its invention in 1954, the kidney machine became the first in a steadily lengthening line of sophisticated biomedical technologies intended to help prolong life. These life-sustaining technologies have also affected our attitudes about dying and death.

Biological malfunctions that once were lethal may now be restored by highly skilled techniques. The replacement or repair of dysfunctional organs is an accepted, even expected, part of current medical practice. The surgeon's skill is

Grandmother, When Your Child Died

Grandmother, when your child died
hot beside you
in your narrow bed,
his labored breathing kept
you restless
and woke you when
it sighed,
and stopped.

You held him through the bitter dawn
and in the morning
dressed him, combed his hair,
your tears welled, but you didn't weep
until at last he lay
among the wild iris in the sod,
his soul gone inexplicably to God. Amen.

But grandmother, when my child died
sweet Jesus, he died hard.
A motor beside
his sterile cot
groaned, and hissed, and whirred
while he sang his pain —
low notes and high notes
in slow measures
slipping through the drug-cloud.
My tears, redundant,
dropped slow
like glucose or blood
from a bottle.
And when he died
my eyes were dry
and gods wearing white coats
turned away.

Joan Neet George

extended by companion technologies. Sophisticated machinery monitors biological functions, including brain wave activity, heart rate, body temperature, respiration, blood pressure, pulse, blood chemistry, and a host of others. Signaling changes in body function by light, sound, and computer printout, such apparatus often make the crucial difference in situations of life or death.

Modern medicine is the beneficiary of advances in many scientific disciplines and technologies, including electronics, materials science, engineering, nuclear physics, molecular and cellular biology, immunology, and biochemistry. Recombinant DNA technologies, for example, now yield clues that may aid in treating some of our most troubling diseases. The computer, too, has become an important tool in medicine, where it is used in sophisticated physiological monitoring as well as in diagnostic and therapeutic procedures. The familiar X-ray machine has been joined by new and innovative imaging systems such as the CAT scanner, which by "computerized axial tomographic" scanning provides images of plane sections through the patient's body.

Despite the advantages, however, this marriage of medicine and technology also has confusing consequences. The technological device that seems to one person a godsend, extending life, may to another person seem only to prolong dying. Thus, these modern medical miracles raise questions: In what situations should life-saving technologies be used to sustain biological life? Does the preservation of human dignity imply limits to their use? What are the social and economic costs? Can we construct workable ethical guidelines for their use, and who will decide? The highly publicized case of Karen Ann Quinlan, whose death in 1985 came nearly a decade after she was removed from a respirator as a result of a

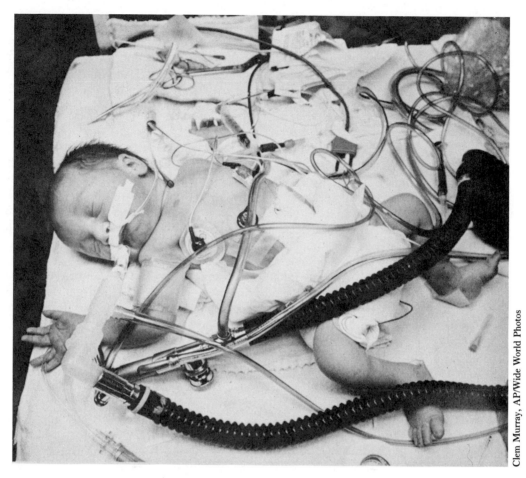

Lifelines — tubes and wires monitoring heartbeat, breathing, and blood pressure — increase this premature baby's chances of survival in the intensive care unit of Philadelphia's Children's Hospital. The special-care nursery often becomes an arena for many of the most difficult ethical decisions in medicine.

Clem Murray, AP/Wide World Photos

New Jersey Supreme Court decision, is a familiar example of the complex questions associated with decisions about the use of such life-sustaining technologies.

With the advent of modern biomedical technologies, the definition of death has itself come under question. The traditional understanding that death is the "cessation of life, the total and permanent cessation of all vital functions" must be superseded in some instances by a complex medicolegal definition, one that recognizes the modern reality that biological life can be artificially sustained. The definition of death has evolved considerably from the child's simple statement, "When you're dead, you're dead."

Expressions of Attitudes Toward Death

Prevailing cultural attitudes toward death can be seen in the language people use to describe the fact of death, as well as in the portrayal of death by the mass media and in literature, the visual arts, and music. Although direct contact with death is uncommon for most of us, it is worth noting that death nevertheless occupies a significant place in our cultural environment.

Language

Many people have difficulty talking about death at all. The language used to discuss the process of dying or the fact of death is rarely direct. More often, we take refuge in euphemisms, substituting mild, indirect, or vague expressions for ones considered harsh or blunt (see Table 1-2). We rarely speak of someone dying; instead they "pass away" or "were called home." The dead person is "laid to rest," and burial becomes "interment"; the undertaker is replaced by the "funeral director" — all terms that suggest a well-choreographed production for disposing of the dead in a tasteful manner.

In our etiquette for acknowledging a person's bereavement, death is seldom mentioned without the adornment of euphemistic language. Sympathy cards allow the sender to express condolences without violating the cultural taboo against explicitly mentioning the event of death. In a study of over one hundred sympathy cards, none mentioned the word "death" or "died." The person who had died was referred to only indirectly, usually within the context of memories or the healing process of time. Contemporary cards often include images of sunsets or fields with grain or flowers, apparently intending to convey an impression of "peace, quiet, and perhaps a return to nature."[27]

Death is a metaphor in such sentiments as "What is death but a long sleep?" and is denied in verses like James Whitcomb Riley's "He is not dead, he is just away." Greeting card companies, perceiving American attitudes toward death, apparently agree with the advice given by arbiters of etiquette that words like "death" and "died" should be avoided when writing letters of condolence. Such advice reflects the view that euphemisms can be a way of talking about death without offending another person's sensibilities, a way of avoiding disrespect of the bereaved's feelings of loss. However, euphemisms may also be employed to mask the reality of death and, thus, to distance oneself from the experience.

The military adds to our lexicon of substitutions for plain talk about death by citing "body counts" or "KIAs" (killed in action) and by describing soldiers as "being wasted" by an adversary or civilian deaths as "collateral damage." Defense briefings include elaborate charts depicting the capability of new weapons systems to inflict "megadeath" on the enemy. Euphemisms replace words that would more directly describe the harsh and horrible reality of death in battle. Death is depersonalized, devalued.

Whereas euphemism represents an attempt to blunt the reality of death, the intensity and immediacy of a person's encounter with death may also be revealed through the way language is used. For example, in a study of "danger of death" narratives — stories about close calls with death — a tense shift was found to occur

T A B L E *1-2*   *Euphemisms*

Passed on	Made the change
Croaked	Got mertelized
Kicked the bucket	On the other side
Gone to heaven	God took him/her
Gone home	Asleep in Christ
Expired	Departed
Breathed the last	Transcended
Succumbed	Bought the farm
Left us	With the angels
Went to his/her eternal reward	Feeling no pain
Lost	Lost the race
Met his/her Maker	His/her time was up
Wasted	Cashed in
Checked out	Crossed over Jordan
Eternal rest	Perished
Laid to rest	Lost it
Pushing up daisies	Was done in
Called home	Translated into glory
Was a goner	Returned to dust
Came to an end	Withered away
Bit the dust	In the arms of the Father
Annihilated	Gave it up
Liquidated	It was curtains
Terminated	A long sleep
Gave up the ghost	On the heavenly shores
Left this world	Out of his/her misery
Rubbed out	Ended it all
Snuffed	Angels carried him/her away
Six feet under	Resting in peace
Consumed	Changed his/her form
Found everlasting peace	Dropped the body
Went to a new life	Rode into the sunset
In the great beyond	That was all she wrote
No longer with us	

when the narrator came to the crucial point in his or her story when death seemed imminent. In one instance, a man who had experienced a frightening near-accident some years earlier while driving in a snowstorm began his story in the past tense, describing the circumstances surrounding the incident. As he reached the point in the story when his car went out of control on an icy curve and slid into the opposing lane of traffic, he switched to the present tense. As he spoke, it was as if he were *reliving* the experience of watching an oncoming car heading straight for him and believing in that moment that he was about to die.[28]

In summary, then, language usage can reveal much about our personal as well as cultural attitudes toward death. By becoming aware of the metaphors, euphemisms, and other linguistic patterns that people use when talking about dying and death, we come to more fully appreciate the range of such attitudes.

© Albert Lee Strickland

In place of the conventional sentiment usually engraved on tombstones, a touch of whimsy adorns this memorial to B.P. Roberts at a cemetery in Key West, Florida.

Humor

Serious and somber matters may be easier to deal with when there is comedic relief. Clowns poke holes in our pretensions, thereby shedding a glimmering light on ourselves and the situations that we deem so crucial to our secure self-identity. Laughter can defuse some of the anxiety we feel toward death. Occasionally, however, we find a bravado toward death that some may find startling.

It is possible, for example, to obtain a build-it-yourself coffin that doubles (before it's needed for its ultimate purpose) as a stereo cabinet, wine rack, or coffee table. "Rent-a-caskets" have been used at birthday parties and mock wakes, and as cocktail bars. One hostess asked to be placed in the casket and rolled into her yule party so that, at the appropriate moment, she could leap up dressed as Santa Claus — thus laying to rest, no doubt, the rumors of Santa's untimely demise. Another woman chose to be buried in a luxury convertible (with the top down?) while she was adorned in furs and jewelry, apparently in an effort to prove that it *is* possible to take it with you. And, in California, passing motorists are taken aback by a gleaming white hearse with the cryptic license plates, "Not Yett."

Poking fun at death or casting it in an unconventional light may or may not be genuinely confronting death. Still, finding humorous aspects to death, or considering it in a less than somber fashion, may make it possible to reduce the anxiety that comes with awareness of one's own mortality.

"The Far Side," drawing by Gary Larson, Chronicle Features

"Wouldn't you know it! Now the Hendersons have the bomb."

Humor comes in many different forms, from humorous epitaphs to so-called black or gallows humor, which often reflects a thumbing of one's nose at death, as if attempting to minimize its power and gain a sense of mastery over it. Since the advent of the atomic bomb, the threat of horrendous death has given rise to humor that seeks to put such an incomprehensible possibility into a more manageable perspective.

There are constraints, however, on the kind of humor that a particular person or group finds acceptable, especially when it concerns dying or death. A joke that is shared gleefully among the members of one group might be shockingly unacceptable to others with a different set of assumptions about what is funny. When a syndicated newspaper columnist wrote a parody of "USA for Africa" and its efforts to alleviate the Ethiopian famine, even loyal readers reacted with disgust. Apparently, the heartrending facts of the famine and the positive image of USA for Africa outweighed what seemed by comparison a feeble and unfeeling attempt at humor.[29]

Mary Hall observes that "what is humorous to each of us depends on our particular cultural set, our own experience, and our personal inclination."[30] She notes that humor can function in several ways relative to death. First, it can raise our consciousness about a taboo subject, allowing us to talk about the indescribable. Humor can also give us an opportunity to rise above the immediate sadness of death, thus giving us momentary release from the pain and helping us feel more in control of the situation, even if we cannot change it. Third, humor is a great leveler in that it treats us all alike and confronts us with the fact that there are no exemptions from the human predicament. Thus, humor binds us together and promotes the closeness we need as we confront the fearful unknown. Finally, after a death has occurred, humor can comfort the survivors as they recall the funny as well as the painful events of a loved one's life.

Humor also provides relief and release for caregivers whose jobs bring them into frequent contact with dying or death. A firm that distributes instructional

---

The Undertakers

Old Pops had been stone cold dead for two days. He was rigid, gruesome and had turned slightly green and now he lay on a slab at the undertakers, about to be embalmed by two lovable old morticians.

"At least he lived to a ripe age," said one.

"Yep," said the other. "Well, let's get to 'er."

Suddenly, Old Pops bolted upright and without opening his eyes, began to utter this story:

"In 1743, Captain Rice set sail from England with an unreliable and mutinous crew. After three days at sea, the mast of the mainsail splintered, and then broke completely in half. The ship tossed about at sea for two days; the men mutinied, and the ship tossed about for another two days. At the end of the third day, a ship appeared on the horizon and rescued them and good Captain Rice failed to mention to the admiral the incident of mutiny, and his crew became faithful and hard-working and devoted themselves to their captain."

Old Pops laid back down on the marble.

"Well," said one mortician, "there goes the old saying, 'dead men tell no tales'!"

Steve Martin, *Cruel Shoes*

materials for emergency medical technicians includes in its catalog a musical recording entitled "You Respond to Everyone But Me." At a teaching hospital, doctors avoided using the word "death" when a patient died because of their concern that other patients might be alarmed. One day, as a medical team was examining a patient, an intern came to the door with information about another patient's death. Knowing that the word "death" was taboo and finding no ready substitute, she stood in the doorway and announced, "Guess who's not going to shop at Woolworth's any more?" Soon, this phrase became the standard way for staff members to convey the news that a patient had died.

For individuals with a life-threatening illness, humor can be an important means of coping with the debilitating effect of a shattering diagnosis as well as with the attendant pain and anxiety of illness. Death may be humorously treated as a way to achieve a comforting perspective on a painful situation, as in the offhand remark, "Halitosis is better than no breath at all." Humor can help us confront our fears and thereby gain a sense of mastery over the unknown.

Mass Media

Death touches our lives not only when close friends or family members are affected. Death is almost constantly before us through dramatic portrayals and news reports in the mass media. Technology now has the potential to make us all instantaneous survivors. When Egyptian president Anwar el-Sadat was assassinated in October 1981, news of the event was flashed around the world almost immediately. Stunned television viewers watched in disbelief as news footage was repeatedly broadcast showing the terrorist attack that came as the Egyptian political leader sat reviewing a military parade in Cairo.[31] Similar reactions occurred in the wake of the space shuttle *Challenger* disaster in 1986. Because most of us no longer experience death firsthand, the way we think about death is shaped largely through vicarious experiences provided by the media. Newspapers, magazines, books, movies, and television have become the secondhand sources from which we learn about death and dying.

In the News

As you read the daily newspaper, what kinds of encounters with death vie for your attention? Perhaps, scanning the day's news, you find an assortment of accidents, murders, suicides, and disasters involving violent deaths. A jetliner crashes, and the newspaper announces the fact with banner headlines. Here you see a story about a family perishing when trapped inside their burning home; in another, a family's vacation comes to an untimely end when they become the victims of a spectacular fatal automobile collision on the interstate.

And there are the deaths of the famous. Whereas most deaths are reported in *death notices* — brief, standardized statements, usually printed in small type and listed alphabetically in a column of vital statistics "as uniform as a row of tiny grave plots"[32] — the deaths of the famous are announced by means of more extensive *obituaries*. Obituaries vary in length as well as in content and style. Prefaced by individual headlines and set in the same size of type used in other newspaper stories, obituaries indicate the newsworthiness that editors attribute to the deaths of famous persons. Most media organizations — wire services, metropolitan newspapers, and network news bureaus — maintain files of pending obituaries on persons whose deaths would be considered newsworthy. These obituaries are updated periodically so they can be printed or aired when the occasion demands.

The death of a neighbor or of the person working alongside you on the job is not likely to be reported with such emphasis. Indeed, efforts by family members to obtain an obituary rather than the smaller death notice may meet with resistance from the press. To illustrate, the family of a young woman who died of Hodgkin's disease sent her photo and a brief account of her life to the local newspaper. Despite their efforts and the efforts of a local funeral director, a newspaper spokesperson maintained that it was against policy to run obituaries instead of death notices in such cases; neither the photograph nor the biographical sketch was printed. This refusal frustrated the family as well as many people in the community who had become acquainted with the young woman's accomplishments. Ordinary deaths — the kind most of us can expect to experience — tend to be neglected or else mentioned only in the most routine fashion. The spectacular obscures the ordinary.

Whether routine or extraordinary, these encounters with death in the news influence the way we think about and respond to death. According to communication scholar Wilbur Schramm, the nature of news has changed from simply providing information to sharing experience. News, he says, has less to do with an *event* than with how that event is *perceived*, by reporters as well as their audience.[33] When the space shuttle *Challenger* exploded shortly after lift-off, killing the seven crew members aboard, it evoked shared grief as people read newspapers and watched television. Reaction to the tragedy was intense, heightened by public interest in a mission involving the first private citizen slated for space flight, Christa McAuliffe, a schoolteacher.

In describing the role of television during this crisis, some likened it to a "national hearth" around which Americans were symbolically gathered as they witnessed the disaster and contemplated its meaning, while others said television fulfilled its function no better and no worse than one would expect of any household appliance. The repeated broadcasts of the shuttle exploding were criticized by some as exhibiting a macabre fascination by the media for the "pornography of grief."

Whether television is perceived as a national hearth or simply as an appliance, most people have come to expect the media not only to provide information about events, but also convey some sense of their meaning. When the news involves death, a question arises about the propriety of focusing upon those most closely affected. For example, during the memorial service for the *Challenger* crew, which was viewed on television by millions of Americans, the astronauts' grieving families were shown in close-up. Was such coverage of the bereaved an intrusion on their private sorrow, or was it legitimate news that helped to focus a nation's shared experience of loss? The distinction between *public* event and *private* loss is not always easily drawn.

When a Canadian newspaper ran a photograph of a distraught mother as she learned of her daughter's fatal injuries from an accident, many readers were outraged, calling the picture "a blatant example of morbid ludicrousness" and "the highest order of poor taste and insensitivity."[34] Interestingly, the mother did not share these feeling. On the contrary, she said that seeing the photo had helped her to comprehend what had happened. Indeed, many survivors of sudden, unexpected deaths want to reconstruct the events surrounding the death in as much detail as possible, as a means of coping with the reality of the loss. What, then, are we to make of the outrage expressed by some members of the community at what they considered to be the newspaper's insensitivity? John Huffman, commenting on this incident, suggested that, because most people are unfamiliar with death and the emotions it elicits, they are likely to "ascribe emotions to the grief-stricken that are not really present."[35] Were the outraged readers defending what they imagined to be the prerogatives of the grief-stricken mother who was seen as the victim of a too-intrusive press? Or were volatile emotions related to readers' own uncomfortable feelings about death unwittingly triggered by publication of the photo?

Such questions are not amenable to simple answers. The media's proclivity to focus on the dramatic does at times raise issues regarding its ethical integrity. As Huffman points out, "Photographs mirroring and evoking intense emotions can sometimes cause pain and suffering to those pictured and those close to them." In addition, the rapid reporting made possible by the current technology of news transmission can even alter the conventional death notification process. This occurred, for example, when the parents of a boy killed by the Mount St. Helens volcanic eruption learned of their son's death when they saw a photograph of his body in the newspaper.

Television, with its visual power and intimacy, has heightened the privacy question. When Pan Am Flight 103 crashed at Lockerbie, Scotland, enroute from London to New York, television crews rushed to Kennedy Airport to cover the reaction of grief-stricken relatives and friends who learned the devastating news only after arriving at the airport. Writing about how this event was reported on television, Sydney Schanberg noted that the image of one mother's grief "became the symbol of that grief-torn passenger lounge."[36] While acknowledging that coverage of this kind is intrusive and that reporters ought to be sensitive to issues of privacy, Schanberg also argued that there was "community value in running it — briefly, not at length, not ghoulishly."

For victims of disaster, the media's actions may stimulate a "second trauma," following upon the initial trauma of the horrible event itself. Reporting on the survivors of Aloha Airlines Flight 243, Barbara Hastings notes that opportunistic journalists may attempt to "capture the experience" of a tragedy at the expense of the victim.[37]

Recall from your experience both the types of death reported on television and the commentator's manner of presenting this information. The "detached and captionlike quality" of network news coverage, observes Michael Arlen, results in "snippets of information" about the deaths that are reported.[38] News of the bus crash or the mine disaster is interposed between reports about stock market prices and factory layoffs. Fulton and Owen comment that such news reports "characteristically submerge the human meaning of death while depersonalizing the event further by sandwiching actual reports of loss of life between commercials or other mundane items."[39] Television, they add, "portrays grief and the ruptured lives that death can leave in its wake only superficially." Michael Arlen contrasts these media messages about death with the experience of death in our own lives, where death evokes "myriad expressions of grief, incomprehension, and deep human response." Only rarely does television suspend its detachment somewhat to present the communal dimensions of death, the public as well as private loss that accompanies bereavement.

Entertaining Death

The pervasive influence of television is well known. Ninety-eight percent of American homes have at least one television set, and television programs are viewed an average of seven hours per day per household.[40] Far from being ignored, death is a central theme of much television programming. Although estimates vary, it is said that the average American child has seen between 13,000 and 18,000 deaths on television by the age of twenty-one. In a typical week of program listings in *TV Guide*, about one-third describe programs in which death or dying is a featured theme. Out of a possible total of 168 hours of weekly viewing time, an avid television viewer could spend more than two-thirds of those hours watching programs that feature death in some way.

These figures are even more striking in that they take into account only such programs as talk shows, crime and adventure series, and movies. Not included are newscasts (which typically feature several stories about death in each broadcast); nature programs (which often depict death in the animal kingdom); children's cartoons (which often present caricatures of death); soap operas (which seem always to have some character dying or recently deceased); sports programs (which give us descriptions such as "the ball is dead" and "the other team is killing them today"), or religious programming (which includes theological and anecdotal discussions of death). Concerning this last, a recent study found that the social topic most referred to in religious programming was death and dying, including the physical process of dying as well as the emotional process of preparing for death.[41]

Despite this massive volume of programming in which death is prominent, the televised image of death seldom adds to our knowledge of its reality. Few programs deal with such real-life topics as how people actually cope with a loved one's death or confront their own dying. Instead, television presents a depersonalized image of death, an image characterized most often by violence.

Consider, for example, the western or detective story, which glazes over the reality of death by describing the bad guy as "kicking the bucket" or as having "croaked" — relegated, no doubt, to Boot Hill at the edge of town, where the deceased now "pushes up daisies." Think about the last death you saw portrayed in a television entertainment or movie. Perhaps the camera panned from the dying person's face and torso to a close-up of hands twitching — then all movement ceases as the person's breathing fades away in perfect harmony with the musical score. Or, more likely, the death was violent: the cowboy gunfight at the OK Corral; high noon. The gent with the slower draw is hit, reels, falls, his body convulsing into cold silence.

Recall the Saturday morning cartoon depiction of death. Daffy Duck is pressed to a thin sheet by a steamroller, only to pop up again a moment later. Elmer Fudd aims his shotgun at Bugs Bunny, pulls the trigger, bang! Bugs, unmarked by the rifle blast, clutches his throat, spins around several times, and mutters, "It's all getting dark now, Elmer. . . . I'm going. . . ." Bugs falls to the ground, both feet still in the air. As his eyes close, his feet finally hit the dirt. But wait! Now Bugs pops up, good as new. Reversible death!

Realistic portrayals of death are not the media's standard bill of fare. When told of his grandfather's death, one modern seven-year-old asked, "Who did it to him?" The understanding of death offered by the media is that it comes from outside, often violently. It has been found, for example, that adolescents typically vastly overestimate the number of murders that actually occur in a society.[42]

Such notions of death reinforce the belief that dying is something that *happens* to us, rather than something we *do*. Death becomes an accidental rather than a natural process.

Persons who have been present at a death describe a very different picture. Many recall the gurgling, gasping sounds as the last breath rattles through the lungs; the changes in body color as flesh tones tinge blue; the feeling of a once warm and flexible body growing cold and flaccid. They often say, "Death is not at all what I thought it would be like; it doesn't look or sound or feel like anything I see on television or in movies!"

According to George Gerbner, television portrayals of death are embedded in a structure of violence that is essentially a "ritualistic demonstration of power" from which viewers derive "a heightened sense of danger, insecurity, and mistrust." Such televised portrayals reflect what Gerbner and his colleagues have termed the "mean world" syndrome. This symbolic use of death contributes, Gerbner says, "not only to a structure of power but also to the irrational dread of dying and thus to diminished vitality and self-direction in life."[43]

Gerbner's conclusions are based on a study that has been ongoing at the Annenberg School of Communications since 1967.[44] The results of this study indicate that Americans are entertained by about sixteen violent acts, including two murders, in each evening's prime-time programming. Children are exposed to more than twenty acts of violence during each *hour* of television on Saturday and Sunday mornings. Based on these findings, the researchers concluded that "our children are born into a home in which—for the first time in human history—not the parents, church, or school, but a centralized commercial institution tells most of the stories most of the time."

And what is the content of this story? "For most viewers," Gerbner says, "television's mean and dangerous world tends to cultivate a sense of relative danger, mistrust, dependence, and—despite its supposedly 'entertaining' nature—alienation and gloom." This "mean world" of television, Gerbner adds, "invites not only aggression but also exploitation and repression. Fearful people are more dependent, more easily manipulated and controlled, more susceptible to deceptively simple, strong, tough measures and hard-line postures—both political and religious. They may accept and even welcome repression if it promises to relieve their insecurities and other anxieties."

Turning our attention to the cinema, we find that here, too, death is a major theme, although it is the rare film that deals realistically with dying and death. Fantasy often replaces reality to enhance the story line. Many films exhibit what critic Roger Ebert calls "Ali McGraw Disease," in which characters with terminal illness are depicted as becoming more and more beautiful until ultimately "they're so great that they die."[45] In the aftermath of the Vietnam conflict, a number of films have portrayed the combat experience and its devastating and lasting effects on the warriors, as did the 1989 film, *Born on the Fourth of July*, which was based on an account written by Ron Kovic.

Fascination with death can sometimes turn bizarre, as in the "blood and gore" movies, often released at Halloween, as well as in pseudo-documentaries

AP/Wide World Photos

Facing the possibility of death heroically, lawman Will Kane (played by Gary Cooper) strides courageously toward a showdown with his adversary at "High Noon." Attitudes toward death portrayed in the movies help shape how we relate to risk and to death in our own lives.

like *Faces of Death*, which depicts graphic scenes of animal and human death, including suicide and autopsies. Robert Fulton has suggested that the lack of firsthand experience with death, combined with the pervasive threat of nuclear annihilation, may cause people to exhibit a fascination with *anything* related to death. This fascination is frequently manifested more as a kind of necrophilia or obsession with death—as displayed in some contemporary novels and films—than as a healthy capacity to cope with mortality.

One researcher notes that what we are experiencing today may not be so much "a lack of death symbolism, but a lack of symbols that represent rebirth, continuation, and the positive aspects of death and dying. We have become sated with violent deaths resulting from war and terrorism that are perpetually presented in the media, if not in art."[46]

The comparatively few exceptions to the usual media presentation of death demonstrate that television, movies, and other media can provide more realistic coverage of issues related to dying and death. Over the past few years, a number of documentaries as well as fictional dramas have shown individuals and families coping with the experience of terminal illness. Unfortunately, the positive contributions of the media to our awareness of death are nearly buried under an avalanche of messages about death that bear little resemblance to its reality.

Literature

Death is one of the enduring themes in literature. From Sophocles' *Oedipus the King*, to Shakespeare's *King Lear*, to Leo Tolstoy's "The Death of Ivan Ilych" and James Agee's *Death in the Family*, death has been treated by writers as significant and meaningful to human experience. Recall for a moment a literary work you have read recently. Was death an element of the plot? How did the author portray dying or death in the story? In many works of poetry, prose, and drama, the meaning of death is explored as it relates to society as well as the individual. Thus, literature is a rich source of information about attitudes toward death. By expressing the human dimension and portraying the range and subtlety of death-related experiences, literature can balance a strict diet of facts and technical information.

Literature has been applied in just this way as a teaching tool within the medical profession. Medical school curricula now routinely include courses in literature and medicine.[47] At Johns Hopkins, the Mayo Clinic, and other such institutions, plays such as Marsha Norman's *'night, Mother*, which dramatizes the factors behind suicide, and Laurence Housman's *Victoria Regina*, which focuses on issues of aging, have been presented to audiences made up of physicians and other medical personnel. The aim of these programs is to foster insight into human behaviors and problems that generally receive little discussion during formal medical training.

Michael Cristofer's play *The Shadow Box* was inspired by the deaths from cancer of two close friends. While writing the play, Cristofer became familiar with the work of Elisabeth Kübler-Ross, and a description of her well-known outline of the "stages of loss" was printed in the program distributed to playgoers. *All the Way Home*, another play featuring death as a theme, was adapted by Tad Mosel from James Agee's well-known novel, *A Death in the Family*. The

From way back, our major development as a race of frightened beings has been towards how to avoid facing the discomfort of our existence, primarily the possibility of an accident, immediate death, ugliness, and the ultimate departure. In terms of all this, television is a very pleasing medium: one is always the observer. The life of discomfort is always accorded to others, and even *this* is disqualified, since one program immediately disqualifies the preceding one. Literature does not have this ability to soothe. You have to evoke, and by evoking, you yourself have to provide your own inner setting. When you read about a man who dies, part of you dies with him because you have to recreate his dying inside your head.

Jerzy Kosinski, quoted in *The Paris Review*

threat of nuclear annihilation is dramatically confronted in Lee Blessing's *A Walk in the Woods*, a play centering on issues of disarmament as viewed through the relationship between two negotiators — one Soviet, the other American — during their informal talks in Geneva. The AIDS Memorial Quilt, created to memorialize persons who died as a result of acquired immunodeficiency syndrome, inspired the writing of *Remember My Name*, a play by David Lemos.

Literary accounts of the Vietnam war have created a distinct genre depicting the trauma of combat as well as the quest to restore meaning to a shattering experience of loss. The best of these accounts are more than mere war stories. The authors' personal experiences form a basis for dealing with the overwhelming magnitude of the losses resulting from the war, individually and as a society.[48]

Another literary category of special interest to the student of death and dying is that which seeks to express and understand the Holocaust. The experiences of Nazi incarceration and extermination, as well as life and death in Soviet labor camps, have been reported and analyzed through a rich literature. Holocaust literature has found expression through victims' diaries as well as persecutors' memoirs, in novels as well as psychological studies. Examples include Anne Frank's *Diary of a Young Girl*, Chaim Kaplan's *Warsaw Diary*, Charlotte Delbo's *None of Us Will Return*, and Elie Wiesel's *Night*. Yet this literature is not merely topical. Rather, it forces the reader to contemplate fundamental aspects of human nature. As one writer says, "The human imagination after Auschwitz is simply not the same as it was before."[49] Some of these writings explore the syndrome of the observer-victim whose familiar self, by means of radical detachment bordering on schizophrenia, deteriorates to the point that it finally allows "business as usual" amid unspeakable horror. The victim becomes indistinguishable from the violence, a situation the cartoon character Pogo once described by the phrase, "We have met the enemy and he is us."

Increasingly, literature has focused on what Frederick Hoffman calls the "landscape of violence" that pervades life in the twentieth century.[50] Reflecting human experience in a century that has seen the mass deaths of two world wars and innumerable smaller conflicts, the modern fictional hero tries to come to terms with sudden and violent death in situations that allow no time for survivors to express their grief fully or to mourn the dead ceremonially.[51] It seems that whatever meaning death may have is no longer clear.

Modern warfare as well as the common street violence that receives so much attention in the media has the effect of reducing individuals to the status of *things*. This phenomenon is seen, too, in the popular detective novel, which has been described as "vigilante literature."[52] The hero in these stories sets out to avenge evil but is often corrupted by a self-justifying morality that perpetuates violence.

Frederick Hoffman points out that modern literature includes many attempts to delineate and explore the meaning of death in situations that are apparently absurd and ultimately incomprehensible. The modern writer, says Hoffman, tries to deal with death in a variety of ways: by creating a mythology or metaphor significant enough to account for the evil; by portraying the violence within an ideological melodrama or showing it as a farce, alternating between the

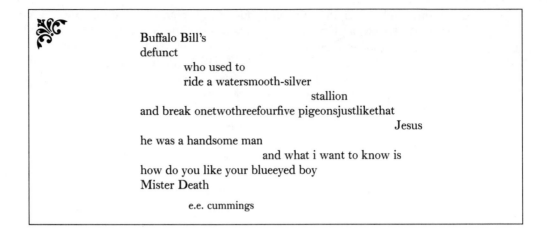

Buffalo Bill's
defunct
           who used to
           ride a watersmooth-silver
                                    stallion
and break onetwothreefourfive pigeonsjustlikethat
                                              Jesus
he was a handsome man
                          and what i want to know is
how do you like your blueeyed boy
Mister Death

        e.e. cummings

trivial and the grotesque; or by simply presenting experiences in a manner that is as impersonal as the events themselves seem to be, to let the bare violence speak for itself. "The history of violence," Hoffman says, "is dominated by examples of ambiguous dying."[53]

As you review the messages conveyed by the literature with which you are familiar, you may find that much of it reflects the belief that death in the twentieth century is so horrendous in its violence and impersonality that it is impossible to truly comprehend. For modern writers, death often elicits less a contemplation of judgment or concern for immortality than a deep anxiety about annihilation and loss of identity.

Visual Arts

As with literature, the visual arts present a range of attitudes toward death. Death themes in art are revealed through the symbols, signs, images, and concepts used by the artists. Richard Pacholski has remarked that "to declare an interest in death themes as expressed in the visual arts is to declare an interest in iconography," which can be defined as "that branch of the history of art which concerns itself with the subject matter or meaning of works of art."[54] In Western art, one often finds themes and images related to classical mythology or to the Judeo-Christian tradition. Comparable sources inspire artists of other cultures with respect to death themes in art. (Interestingly, when death is personified in the visual arts, the figure is usually portrayed as having masculine attributes — a perception that was echoed in a recent study of college students' concepts, which found death to be significantly perceived more in masculine than in feminine terms, especially by females.)[55] Themes that draw upon the processes observed in nature with respect to life, growth, decay, and death transcend cultural boundaries.

Tomb art is a rich source of information about the predominant beliefs of a culture. Scenes inscribed in relief on the limestone sarcophagi of ancient Egypt, for example, often depicting the life of the deceased, attest to that culture's beliefs about what follows upon death, beliefs that are also portrayed in the illustrations accompanying Egyptian religious texts. Graphically portrayed is the common expectation that, after death, a person will be judged according to his or her deeds during earthly life.

By contrast, the sarcophagi constructed by Greek and Roman artisans express the somewhat different views common to these Mediterranean societies. A first-century Roman urn, whose text is addressed to the "Manes" or spirits of the dead, shows the deceased reclining on a couch before a table lavishly set with dishes while three servants offer him food and drink. Birds, commonly used in art as a representation of the soul, are perched on laurel trees, and the urn's cover depicts a bird's nest with four young being fed by their parents. The use of such symbols as the banquet scene and the family of birds communicates visually the deceased's hopes for a peaceful afterlife.

In ancient China, tomb figures, hundreds of which were sometimes buried in a single tomb, were created to represent persons of various status and occupation. These artworks indicate the presence of a belief in the desirability of preserving and perhaps even recreating after death the social interrelationships known to the deceased.

The artistic history of Western civilization is full of images of death. When we view a work such as the thirteenth-century French sepulchral effigy of Jean d'Alluye, which shows the recumbent knight in chain mail, sword girded and shield at his side, feet resting on the image of a lion, it expresses something of the intellectual and social milieu of medieval Christendom and the age of chivalry, the tension between faith and heroism that influenced the way people of that time related to death.

In the fifteenth and sixteenth centuries, there arose in Western Europe one of the most arresting expressions of death ever to emerge in the graphic arts: portrayals of the Dance of Death. Growing out of widespread fears related to the spread of bubonic plague, known as the Black Death, these images of the Dance of Death reflect a preoccupation with mortality and the possibility of sudden, unexpected death regardless of one's station in life. As an artistic theme, the Dance of Death continues to fascinate contemporary artists. Fritz Eichenberg's twentieth-century woodcuts reveal the frightening possibilities inherent in our own time's Dance of Death: humankind facing the prospect of universal annihilation resulting from total war.[56]

The encounter with dying and death is also expressed through art that depicts scenes of the deathbed and persons *in extremis*. One such painting is Franco José de Goya's *Self-Portrait with Dr. Arieta*. This work, which Goya painted for the doctor who aided his recovery from life-threatening illness, shows the doctor holding medicine to Goya's lips and includes the figure of Death alongside persons who may be Goya's priest and his housekeeper.

Suicide, too, has been given artistic expression. In *The Death of Lucretia*, painted in 1666, Rembrandt portrays Lucretia with a tear in her eye, moments after she has stabbed herself with a dagger. Painted shortly after the death of his wife and one of his sons, this work expresses the artist's saddened mental state.

Early American attitudes toward death can be seen in Charles Wilson Peale's painting, *Rachel Weeping* (1772 and 1776), which shows a mother mourning her dead child. Lying on her deathbed, the child has her jaw wrapped with a fabric strap to keep it closed and her arms bound with a cord to keep them straight at her sides. Various medicines, all of which have proven ineffective, sit on a bedside table. The child's mother gazes heavenward and holds a handkerchief as tears roll down her face, a contrast to the dead child's peaceful countenance.

In the early nineteenth century, Americans combined both classical and Christian symbols of death to memorialize public figures and family members. Influenced by earlier practices in England and continental Europe, the images associated with American mourning reflected the Romantic views of the time toward death. Found on jewelry and pottery as well as textiles and prints, common motifs included the urn, trees, gardens, and the mourner—symbols that expressed qualities associated with the deceased as well as religious and secular meanings associated with death. Young women embroidered and painted mourning memorials on silk that were "shared with family and friends by being hung in the most important room of the house, the parlor."[57] The making of a memorial quilt provided not only a focus for physically working through grief, but also a means of perpetuating the memory of the loved one. Much the same motivation lies behind the actions of those who have recently come together in the making of a massive quilt commemorating the lives of loved ones who died from AIDS (acquired immunodeficiency syndrome)[58].

Death themes in art can be found in our own time in the works of artists such as Edvard Munch, Ernst Barlach, Käthe Kollwitz, and American sculptor Richard Shaw. For artists like Kollwitz, art becomes an expression of the painful impact of personal loss. In contrast, Shaw's 1980 work, *Walking Skeleton*, expresses a whimsical attitude toward death: The skeleton is composed of twigs, bottles, player cards, and similar found objects. Some modern artists have taken it as their mission to communicate the impact of the Holocaust, to ensure that the slaughter of more than six million people will not be forgotten. Others address the tragedy of AIDS. Before his death from AIDS in 1989, Robert Mapplethorpe had begun making portraits "filled with gaunt men and hollow-eyed skulls."[59] In Joseph Beuy's "The End of the 20th Century," a scattering of toppled stone pillars suggests a fragile civilization giving way to decay.

It has been suggested that actually few images of death appear in modern art compared with the art, for example, of medieval Europe. Whereas people of medieval times sought relief by materializing their horrors, modern people seem to prefer to deal with oppressive thoughts by burying them. One commentator has observed that, when modern artists depict death, the focus often becomes the moment "after"—that these artists portray death as an accomplished fact.[60] It may be, however, that a greater willingness to discuss death openly, coupled with the unavoidable impact of AIDS and the ever-present threat of nuclear or environmental destruction, is affecting how dying and death are expressed in the works of modern artists.

Of the modern artists who have expressed death themes in art, few have done so more frequently or more powerfully than German artist Käthe Kollwitz—as in this 1925 woodcut, Proletariat—Child's Coffin.

Music

Themes of death and loss can be frequently heard in both serious and popular music. Indeed, such themes form the *raison d'être* for some music. A modern composition, Leonard Bernstein's *Symphony No. 3* (Kaddish), is based on the Jewish prayer for the dead. The Requiem Mass, or Mass for the Dead, has attracted numerous composers, including Mozart, Berlioz, and Verdi. One section of the Requiem Mass, the *Dies Irae* ("Day of Wrath"), which dates from the early thirteenth century, has become a kind of musical symbol for death that can be heard in the works of many composers. In Berlioz's *Symphonie Fantastique* (1830), this theme is heard, first following the ominous tolling of bells and then, as the music reaches its climax, in counterpoint to the frenzied dancing of witches at a *sabbat*. The *Symphonie* tells the story of a young musician who, spurned by his beloved, attempts suicide with an overdose of opium. In a narcotic coma, he experiences fantastic dreams, including a nightmarish "march to the gallows." The *Dies Irae* is also heard in Saint-Saëns' *Danse Macabre* (1874) and Liszt's *Totentanz* (1849), two of the best known musical renditions of the Dance of Death. Opera, too, often includes themes having to do with violence, suicide, and death.[61]

Church music is a rich source of death-related themes. Passion music, for example, centers on the suffering and death of Christ. Death-related themes can also be heard in psalms and psalmody, as well as in hymns and other popular church music. Traditional American gospel music, with its roots in various strains of ethnic folk music, is replete with images of death, loss, grief, and mourning. Examples include songs such as "Oh, Mary Don't You Weep" (mourning), "Will the Circle Be Unbroken" (death of family members), "Blood Done Signed My Name" (sacrifice and redemption), "This May Be the Last Time" (impermanence of life), "Pilgrim of Sorrow" (relationship losses), "When the Saints Go Marching In" (vision of afterlife), "Known Only to Him" (fatalism in the face of death), "If I Could Hear My Mother Pray Again" (grieving the death of a mother), and "Precious Memories" (integration of loss).

In the world of jazz and blues, the so-called jazz funeral is perhaps the best example of a popular version of the *dirge*, a musical form associated with the funeral procession and burial.

Related to the dirge are *elegies* and *laments*, musical settings for poems marking the loss of a person. Beethoven, Schubert, Schumann, Strauss, Brahms, Mahler, and Stravinsky are among composers in the Western musical tradition who have written elegies. As a means of ritual leave-taking, the lament is a musical form found in many societies — as in the music for bagpipes played at Scottish clan funerals. Typically, laments are characterized by a vocal expression of mourning called "keening," which conveys feelings of longing that are also heard in chants composed to mark the event of death.

In pre-Christian Hawaii, the *chant* was the basic form of musical expression and served to commemorate both happy and sad occasions. One type of chant, known as *mele kanikau*, was the traditional Hawaiian lament to commemorate someone who has died.[62] *Kanikau* might be chanted at the funeral or sent to the surviving relatives. In more recent times, *kanikau* have been published in newspapers as a tribute. The lament would be chanted only once at the appropriate occasion, and then it remained in the family as part of its chant repertoire. The *kanikau* could be either carefully composed ahead of time or a spontaneous chant used during the funeral procession. Imagery of the natural world was used to portray the writer's experience of loss.[63] Subtlety and levels of meaning were important. *Kanikau* might compare the deceased person to the wind or to the rain. Things that were experienced together were mentioned: "My companion in the chill of Manoa" or "My companion in the forest of Makiki." The things that bound people together were recalled. Not "I am bereft without you," but "These are the things I cherish about you."

American folk songs and country music are also replete with death themes. Examples include "Where Have All the Flowers Gone?" (war), "Long Black Veil" (mourning), "The Wreck of the Old 97" (accidental death), "The School House Fire" (disaster), "The TB is Whipping Me" (terminal disease), and "John Henry" (occupational hazards). Indeed, murder, mayhem, and misery have long been staples of American music.

Death themes have been a standard genre in rock music since its earliest performances. In fact, some believe that the presence of such imagery in rock

One Tree Hill

We turn away to face the cold, enduring chill
As the day begs the night for mercy
Your sun so bright it leaves no shadows, only scars
Carved into stone on the face of earth
The moon is up and over One Tree Hill
We see the sun go down in your eyes
You ran like river to the sea
Like a river to the sea
And in our world a heart of darkness, a firezone
Where poets speak their hearts, then bleed for it
Jara sang, his song a weapon, in the hands of love
You know his blood still cries from the ground
It runs like a river to the sea
Like a river to the sea
I don't believe in painted roses or bleeding hearts
While bullets rape the night of the merciful
I'll see you again when the stars fall from the sky
And the moon has turned red over One Tree Hill
We run like a river to the sea
Like a river to the sea

Bono, U2. For the funeral of Greg Carroll
(1960–1986), Wanganui, New Zealand,
July 10, 1986.

music may have played a role in breaking the taboo against public mention of death. Rock lyricists have written songs expressing a variety of death-related themes, ranging from the humorous to the poetic and deeply moving. Examples include Elton John's "Candle in the Wind" (the death of Marilyn Monroe); "Abraham, Martin, and John," by Dion (assassination); "Fire and Rain" by James Taylor (suicide); "The Living Years" by Mike and the Mechanics (unfinished business); and Jackson Browne's "For a Dancer" (a eulogy). Regular listeners to rock music could easily cite additional examples. Indeed, criticism and concern have been expressed at the proliferation of so-called heavy metal rock lyrics that convey stark images of homicide, suicide, and various bizarre manifestations of dying and death.[64] At issue is the apparent glorification of death that is suggested in titles like "Skeleton on Your Shoulder," a song performed by a Swiss group that goes by the name Coroner. Whether such lyrics are truly "destructive," as some have characterized them, or merely provide an outlet for adolescents to deal with death-as-boogeyman, it is clear that death themes, albeit less explicit and perhaps more sentimental in the past, continue to be well represented in the lyrics of rock music.

As you listen to music, note the references to death and ask yourself what themes or images are being conveyed and what attitudes are being expressed. Whether your taste runs to rock, folk, country, gospel, or classical, you will discover a rich source of information about attitudes to death.

Examining Assumptions

Robert Fulton and Greg Owen have noted that the changes that have taken place in American society since the beginning of this century can be observed in the lives of two age groups whose encounters with death have been distinctively different.[65] The first group was born prior to the advent of the atomic bomb, whereas the second group was born subsequent to the nuclear age. Between these two groups, there has been a dramatic shift in human experience. For the first group, "death was visible, immediate, and real." Families generally "lived in terms of the simple round of life that humankind had known and accepted since the beginning: birth, copulation, and death. . . . Illness, dying, and death took place at home, and was observed by child and adult alike." The second group, by contrast, "has, for the most part, experienced death at a distance." In this chapter, we have reviewed the impact of social forces, technological innovations, and demographic changes on our lives and on our relationship with dying and death.

Many people are rethinking their assumptions about death. In a society as pluralistic as ours, however, the quest for a more personally meaningful attitude toward death leads to diverse and even conflicting outcomes. For example, the consumer debate about funerals has caused many people to take another look at their own preferences for last rites. The trend away from traditional funeral rituals and the increasing popularity of memorial societies, with their emphasis on swift and inexpensive disposition of the body, is considered by many death researchers to be a significant indicator of changing attitudes toward death.

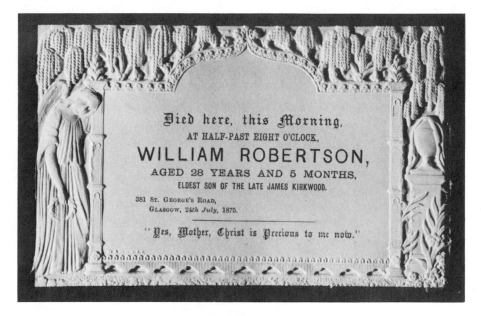

Figure *1-3*   *Embossed Linen Death Notification Card, 1875*
This card exemplifies the formality of nineteenth-century mourning customs. The etiquette books of the period often devoted considerable space to the procedural details associated with the wearing of mourning clothes, the issuance of funeral invitations, and other behaviors appropriate to the survivors of a death.

While some people criticize funerals as perpetuating death-denying behaviors and would as soon eliminate them altogether, others find the trend away from conventional funeral practices disturbing. Traditionally, ceremonies marking a person's death have provided a framework for meeting the social and psychological needs of survivors, and for acknowledging the place and meaning of death in human life. Something important may be lost when survivors are not given the opportunity to participate in a social ritual designed to commemorate the death of a significant other and to facilitate the mourning of his or her passing from the community (see Figure 1-3).

Underlying these contrasting attitudes, a common intention can be discerned; namely, the desire to find a personally meaningful response to the fact of death. That various options exist is itself a positive sign. As people examine their own attitudes and investigate the choices that are available to them, new ways of dealing with death and dying become evident.

There is a growing freedom for individuals and families to make choices that are personally satisfying, rather than simply conforming to some preconceived social norm. For example, just as there is now greater personal creativity in the design of wedding ceremonies, we are beginning to see similar creativity with regard to matters of death and dying.

Luke Stanoš

Luke Stanoš, you took me by surprise:
how unexpected to find the year of my birth
chiseled on your tombstone in this shady graveyard
in Yugoslavia, so far away from home.

Luke Stanoš
OBITELJ
1936–1976

On the marble headstone, your black-and-white photograph,
inside a glass bubble, stares without irony at my surprise,
head and shoulders posed at a slant like a movie star's:
wavy black hair, square face, pain-smudged eyes,
and lips, below a well-trimmed mustache, that reveal
neither a grimace nor a smile.

Luke Stanoš, who were you?
Born the same year as I, you grew as I grew
through summers and winters of Hitler and Mussolini,
although your childhood was not spent
knowing that cloudbanks out at sea
hid a distant war. Your war was as close
as the foreign men who slept in your bed,
forcing you to sleep on the floor —
their growling language at the table,
their black boots and gray wool uniforms,
their glinting rifle breeches smooth with sour oil.
For five years the grapes swelled, the valley bloomed,
then withered, then bloomed again,
and in every season the wind licked a long tongue
under your bedroom door. While you and your friends
played tag and the German soldiers watched,
helmets off, smiling and cheering your every move,
I listened to the radio underneath my pillow
and knew Jack Armstrong and General Eisenhower
would win the war. Did you pray the Partisans
would come and kill the Nazi *svinja*?
Did you cheer for them?

Truman, Stalin, Tito;
sixth grade, seventh: I could barely read,
didn't know my times tables past the 6s.
Did you excel in history and grammar?

Did you listen to Roy Orbison sing
about his pretty woman in the '60s
and smile at a woman of your own?
Did the Beatles make you imagine all the people
you would never know? And did you suspect, even once,
that through all those years each of us, on opposite sides
of the planet, was growing separately yet the same
toward our different deaths?

How did you die?
An auto accident? A fall, head first, against a stone?
The old woman who we've come to visit,
my wife's great aunt, says you had been ill for years —
cancer, she thought, and that your death
was a blessing in the end to both family and friends.
Luke Stanoš, you were trudging inevitably to 1976,
to forty years packed in the crate of your body
that in the end was packed in the earth,
leaving this marble gravestone and your photograph.

I turn to walk away and then turn back,
conscious of each step that will take me from you,
aware that once again our lives must separate
and I shamble toward a date I do not know,
already thirteen years beyond your caring.

Luke, give me a sign: make a branch fall,
a pebble drop, a swallow screech and wing away,
something to let me know where all of us are headed,
something to tell me that all this suffering,
all this uncertainty, are for a reason.
No, of course not. Silence, even in the trees.
What answers I receive will come from the living,
not the dead; I know that. Nor does this meeting
obligate me to do those things you never did
for the rest of every hour, month and year
that I continue to breathe the planet's souring air.

It's time to go. This has been a stopping place
on a sunny afternoon where for a moment things are clear —
a place worth marking on any map. Luke Stanoš,
I take my leave, but do not leave you here.

                                        Morton Marcus

The hospice movement, which focuses on giving emotional support for the dying person and for his or her family, is an example of how some people are acknowledging the reality of death by restoring, in ways appropriate for the present, some of the attitudes and practices that were prevalent in the past. Among the Amish, who have maintained traditional practices, death is considered part of the natural rhythm of life. Death initiates a time for reinforcement and support, for the bereaved family as well as the larger society. Kathleen Bryer summarizes the social patterns that the Amish find helpful in coping with death as including: the continued presence of the family, open communication about the process of dying and its impact upon the family, maintaining a normal life style as much as possible during the course of illness, commitment to the independence of the dying person, opportunities to plan for one's own death, and continued support of the bereaved.[66]

Many of our attitudes toward death are closely connected with our notions about what medical technologies can and cannot accomplish. Coupled with the ethical maxim that whatever *can* be done *should* be done to keep an individual alive, such technologies have reduced the intimate contact with death experienced by our forebears. As a society, the care of our dying and of our dead is no longer part of our common experience. Instead, there are now professionals—ranging from the cardiologist to the coroner to the cremator—to whom we turn.

When the death of a loved one or life-threatening illness touches our own lives, the experience transcends the merely academic or theoretical. Our inquiry must therefore be practical. Death is universal, intrinsic, to human experience. Yet many of us try to cram it into a dark closet and shut the door. There death stays until, bursting its hinges, the door flies open and death is once again forced upon our awareness.

Like a mysterious stranger at a costume ball, whose mask conceals the face beneath, death waits. Perhaps the disguise is more terrifying than the reality, yet how can we know unless we risk the experience of uncovering the face that lies hidden behind the mask? Learning about death and dying can help us identify the attitudes and behaviors that keep us from lifting the mask so that we may each confront our mortality in a way that is meaningful for our own lives.

Further Readings

D.J. Enright, ed. *The Oxford Book of Death*. New York: Oxford University Press, 1983.

James J. Farrell. *Inventing the American Way of Death, 1830–1920*. Philadelphia: Temple University Press, 1980.

Kathi Meyer-Baer. *Music of the Spheres and the Dance of Death: Studies in Musical Iconology*. Princeton, N.J.: Princeton University Press, 1970.

Mary Jane Moffat, ed. *In the Midst of Winter: Selections from the Literature of Mourning*. New York: Random House, 1982.

Dan Nimmo and James E. Combs. *Nightly Horrors: Crisis Coverage by Television Network News*. Knoxville: University of Tennessee Press, 1985.

Martha V. Pike and Janice Gray Armstrong. *A Time to Mourn: Expressions of Grief in Nineteenth Century America*. Stony Brook, N.Y.: The Museums at Stony Brook, 1980.

Charles Shively. *A History of the Conception of Death in America, 1650–1860*. New York: Garland, 1988.

Vivian Alpert Thompson. *A Mission in Art: Recent Holocaust Works in America*. Macon, Ga.: Mercer University Press, 1988.

Robert F. Weir, ed. *Death in Literature*. New York: Columbia University Press, 1980.

In January 1879 frontier photographer L. A. Huffman recorded this scene showing the burial platform of a Sioux warrior who had died and been placed on the scaffold only a few days before. Surrounding the gravesite is a vast plain, crisscrossed with the trails of wild herds of buffalo.

CHAPTER 2

Perspectives on Death: Cross-Cultural and Historical

*D*eath is a universal human experience, yet the response it elicits is shaped by attitudes and beliefs that are prevalent in a particular culture. This shared consciousness among its members makes a culture distinct; it gives a particular cast to experiences and the meanings ascribed to them. In the previous chapter, we saw how social and cultural changes during the past century have affected the characteristic American mode of dealing with death and dying. To gain a broader perspective, we expand our study by surveying attitudes and behaviors relative to death in cultures that, in many respects, are quite different from our own. In doing so, we may find that customs which seem unfamiliar or even exotic in fact share a common ground with our own practices. Indeed, understanding the perception of death in other cultures sheds light on our own beliefs and behaviors.

It has been suggested that cultures can be ranged on a continuum from "death-welcoming" to "death-denying." As you read about the societies discussed in this chapter, note where each of these societies might be placed on such a continuum. You may also find it interesting, as you reflect on your study of these cultures, to decide where your own "cultures"—the national, ethnic, and family groups of which you are a part—might fit on such an attitudinal continuum. Notice that, whatever the particulars of a culture's belief system, death attitudes represent efforts to rationalize—that is, make sense of—the world as it is known at a particular time and in a particular place. In this sense, it is important to recognize that there are no absolute right or wrong ways to view the end of life.

Death in Early and Preliterate Cultures

As archaeological evidence demonstrates, human concern for the dead predates the advent of written history. In the Neanderthal burials of more than 50,000 years ago, food, ornamental shells, and stone implements were buried with the dead, implying a belief that the deceased would find these items useful during the passage from the land of the living to the land of the dead. In many of these ancient burials, the corpse was stained with red ochre and positioned in a fetal posture, suggesting beliefs about the revitalization of the body after death and subsequent rebirth (see Figure 2-1.)[1] This evidence from the earliest known burials demonstrates a characteristically human concern with beliefs about the meaning of death and with rituals that serve to formalize the relationship between the living and the dead.

Death seems to have been viewed not as an end or as extinction but as a radical change of status: a transition from the land of the living to the world of the dead. Thus, the living took precautions to aid the deceased on the journey to the spirit world and — among some societies — to offset fears about the potential malevolence of the dead toward the living.

Beliefs like these are characteristic of societies in which mythological themes about life and death provide the foundation for human attitudes, values, and behavior. Joseph Campbell observed that traditional mythologies normally serve four functions: (1) to reconcile human consciousness with the conditions of its own existence; (2) to render an image of the cosmos that is consistent with the science of the time; (3) to validate and maintain some specific social order; and (4) to shape individuals to the aims and ideals of their various social groups, "bearing them on from birth to death through the course of a human life."[2]

It is clear from evidence such as the Neanderthal burials that speculations about death and its meaning date from the earliest human societies. Although the cultural environment of a people who lack written language or advanced technology may appear rudimentary by modern standards, it is a mistake to think that the terms *preliterate, primitive*, or *traditional* imply ignorance or dullness. The so-called primitive, whose learning simply takes place in a different schoolhouse, is no less capable of intelligent consideration of the fundamental areas of human experience. The essential lessons for living well — and for dying well — would seem to have a common basis throughout all human experience.

The Power of the Dead

In many preliterate or traditional societies, the dead are considered to be potentially harmful, especially during the period of transition immediately following death. In one society, grief may be expressed with loud wails, in another with silent tears; but almost always there is deep respect for the still-powerful soul of the deceased. Often there is a concern that the soul or spirit of the de-

after the Smithsonian exhibit
—eric mathes—

Figure 2-1   *Neanderthal Burial*

ceased, if not treated properly, could inflict harm upon the living. Thus, elaborate funeral rituals are conducted to ensure not only the successful journey of the soul into the realm of the dead, but also the well-being of the living community. Often, of special concern are malevolent, or evil-intentioned, spirits — perhaps of those who suffered catastrophic deaths or deaths in childbirth — which are believed to wander about aimlessly, seeking to harm or disrupt the living.

To understand how such beliefs about the dead might have a very real effect on the living, think about the eerie feelings that people associate with "haunted houses" or the strange sense of foreboding experienced when passing through a cemetery at night. Experiences that include an element of mystery commonly provoke awe and uncertainty. In preliterate societies, the context may be different, but the impulse is strikingly similar: One simply has no wish to disturb the dead.

Yet this is not to say that people in preliterate or traditional societies always shun their dead. Often the contrary is true. Ceremonies may be held periodically to celebrate and honor the dead, who are thought to be still present in some way as members of the community. In its totality, the community is composed of both the living and the dead; in the rhythm and flow of communal life, the individual — in death as in life — is part of the whole. As unseen members of a continuing social order, the dead may be valuable allies and may even perform services for the living — as interpreters, intermediaries, and ambassadors in the realm beyond the reach of sensory perceptions. In some traditional societies, communication with the dead is facilitated by the *shaman*, a kind of visionary who, by projecting his or her consciousness to other realms, functions as intermediary between the worlds of living and dead.[3]

For the ancient Hawaiians living within the intimate relationships of the *'ohana*, or family clan, a close bond existed between the living members of a family and their ancestors.[4] Besides serving as role models upholding standards of conduct, ancestors provided a crucial spiritual link between human beings and powerful, but distant and impersonal, gods. Keeping alive the memory of one's ancestors and calling upon them to intercede with the gods sustained family loyalties beyond the boundaries of death. Furthermore, memorizing the names and characteristics of one's ancestors enhanced an individual's sense of identity and self-worth.

Individuals are born, procreate, and die. Yet, just as those who are now deceased gave life to the community while they were living, the community sustains the dead's participation by celebrating their shared identity in the whole. This communal consciousness embraces both living and dead who, together, comprise the clan, the tribe, the people. This intimate relationship is also celebrated as a sign that the community endures — even beyond the limits imposed by death.

Thus, in societies that retain a strong sense of community between the living and the dead, it seems as if "the land echoes with the voices of the ancestors."[5] In Japan, where a deeply rooted reverence for ancestors continues to influence present practices, many Japanese consider the tomb to be the dwelling place of the deceased's spirit.[6]

We find a semblance of this communal sense in mentions of the "founding fathers" of a nation or of a college. These deceased figures are spoken of metaphorically as "being with us in spirit" on those occasions when the members of the living group — be it nation or college convocation — meet to celebrate their common aims with those who preceded them in the life of the community.

Death-Song

If they ask for me
　Say: He had some
　Business
In another world.

　　　Sokan

The Names of the Dead

The proximity and deep relationship between the worlds of living and dead may, as we have just noted, result in fear of what the dead can do to affect the living. If calling a person's name is a way of summoning the person, then refraining from using a name will presumably leave its bearer undisturbed. Hence, one of the most prevalent of all quasi-magical practices related to the dead is name avoidance: The deceased is never again mentioned or else is referred to only obliquely, never by name.

Among some of the aboriginal tribes of Australia, for example, a dead person is never mentioned by name after burial, but is referred to instead only as "that one." In other traditional societies, an allusion may be made to particular traits or to some special fame that the person was known for during his or her lifetime or the deceased may be referred to by his or her relationship to the speaker — but again, never by name. Thus, "Uncle Joe," who gained great renown as an expert fisherman, might be referred to after his death as "that relative who caught many fish." Or a woman who had demonstrated extraordinary bravery might be called "that one who showed courage." In some societies, there is a demand that living members bearing the same name as the deceased must adopt new names, or even that words describing ordinary objects be erased from the society's vocabulary when they are the same as the name of the deceased.

In other societies, the name of the deceased, rather than being avoided, may receive special emphasis, such as being conferred on a newborn in the deceased's family. This practice may simply reflect the desire to honor the memory of a loved one, or it may be a means of ensuring that the soul of the dead person is reincarnated. When a Lapp woman is near the time of giving birth, a deceased ancestor appears to her in a dream and informs her which of her ancestors is to be reborn in her infant. This is the name her new baby receives.[7] Among the Hawaiians, children sometimes were named for ancestors or were named by the gods. Names bestowed by the gods, which came in a family member's dream, were most important, followed by names linking a child with his or her forebears, given for the sake of identification as well as commemoration. Sometimes the name of a child who died would be given to a child born later. It was felt that "to name a child for a deceased relative was to make the name live again."[8]

The desire to spare oneself or others grief may at least partly account for the effort to avoid mentioning the name of someone recently dead; this desire motivates the behavior of many in our own society. The deceased person may be referred to in terms of family relationship or by other substitutions. If the member of a traditional society avoids a name from fear of evoking the deceased's ghost, is this "ghost" much different from the mental images conjured up by mention of the deceased's name to a bereaved relative in a more developed society? While one society manages grief by postulating the existence of ghosts, another does so by relying on custom and etiquette. Likewise, when we name a child after a beloved parent or some person that we respect, aren't we hoping that some of the qualities we value in the namesake will be "reborn" in the child?

The Causes of Death

Why do humans die? One might respond that death occurs because human beings are biologically programmed to die. In the scientific view, death is an intrinsic part of human development: a natural event. In many primitive societies, however, there are no "natural" causes of death. Instead, death is always viewed as an unnatural event, an accident. Death may result from a wound sustained in battle or from a mishap that strikes a person unexpectedly in the course of daily life. In such cases, the proximate cause of death is clear. When the cause of death is not obvious, it is attributed to some unseen, malign influence, possibly induced by magical means. Although a magical explanation does not lend itself to either proof or disproof, it can provide comfort by making sense of what otherwise seems inexplicable.

Something of this attitude can be seen occasionally even among modern people. Sometimes diseases that are not well understood become the objects of magical thinking, attempts to provide a rationale that satisfies despite the lack of clear and logical information. When the causes of such diseases as tuberculosis in the nineteenth century and cancer today are not scientifically clear, some people fall prey to magical explanations that seem to provide the missing link. Among the Senufo of Africa's Ivory Coast, for example, the unexpected death of a child or young person is considered abnormal and brings an obligation to discover the supernatural cause of such misfortune. Likewise, when death occurs suddenly, perhaps resulting from an accident or from violence outside the village, it threatens the welfare of the entire village and sets into motion "an elaborate series of precautions, sacrifices, and medicines that will purify the land and protect the villagers from further calamity."[9]

This is not to say that traditional societies attribute the causes of disease and death solely to the supernatural. On the contrary, such societies typically reflect an "ecological orientation" that takes into account not only the supernatural, but also the following domains:[10]

1. The *natural* domain, which includes such phenomena as the wind and the moon, as well as bodily conditions and processes, the life cycle (e.g., aging), heredity, food or hunger, behavioral excesses (e.g., not getting enough sleep), and the adverse effects of proposed remedies
2. The *socioeconomic* domain, which consists of income, sanitation and general living conditions, type of work, health resources, and the like
3. The *psychosocial* domain, which consists of emotions related to social interactions, such as anger, anxiety, fright, and envy

Although traditional societies do tend to express the cause and cure of disease in terms of a "personalistic idiom"—that is, as due to "the purposeful intervention of an agent and to the personal characteristics of the healer and the patient"—Paul Katz and Faris Kirkland note that this attribution is not really so different from what can be found in the context of modern medicine.[11] Perhaps the major distinction is that traditional societies usually view illness as a "public, not a private, event," an event that can ultimately involve the whole community, the dead as well as the living. This holistic view of health is seen in traditional Navajo culture, which regards health as "the correct relationship between man and his environment."[12] Illness, therefore, is a sign that "one has fallen from balance." For the traditional Navajo, religion and medicine are not separated; rather, they are perceived as aspects of a unified whole. Thus, we find a common human desire for suitable explanations when death occurs, explanations intended to satisfy those who seek the cause of an individual's illness or death.

The Origin of Death

How did death become part of human experience in the first place? Traditional societies provide responses to this fundamental enigma in the form of myths. Although easily as useful and as pertinent to their believers as any provided by the modern, scientific frame of reference, the insights couched in myth can be coaxed out only by patient study and reflection. The outlines given here only suggest the riches to be found in much primitive myth.[13]

Some myths portray death as originating because the ancestral parents or an archetypal figure transgressed against divine or natural law through poor judgment or disobedience (see Figure 2-2). Sometimes a person or a group is put to a test. When the test is failed, death becomes a reality. Among the Luba of Africa, one such myth describes how god created a paradise for the first human beings and endowed it with everything needed for their sustenance. However, they were forbidden to eat of the bananas in the middle of the field. When the humans ate the bananas, it was decreed that humankind would die and be buried in the earth after a lifetime of toil. This motif is akin to the biblical story of Adam and Eve's transgression and subsequent expulsion from the Garden of Eden, an account of the origin of death that continues to have relevance in three major religious traditions: Judaism, Christianity, and Islam.

In other myths, a crucial act that would have ensured immortality was not properly carried out. A common theme is that of a messenger whose task it is to

When the first man, the father of the human race, was being buried, a god passed by the grave and inquired what it meant, for he had never seen a grave before. Upon receiving the information from those about the place of interment that they had just buried their father, he said: "Do not bury him, dig up the body again." "No," they replied, "we cannot do that. He has been dead for four days and smells." "Not so," entreated the god, "dig him up and I promise you that he will live again." But they refused to carry out the divine injunction. Then the god declared, "By disobeying me, you have sealed your own fate. Had you dug up your ancestor, you would have found him alive, and you yourselves when you passed from this world should have been buried as bananas are for four days, after which you shall have been dug up, not rotten, but ripe. But now, as a punishment for your disobedience, you shall die and rot." And whenever they hear this sad tale the Fijians say: "Oh, that those children had dug up that body!"

Figure 2.2 *Fijian story (traditional): The origin of death*

When Hare heard of Death, he started for his lodge & arrived there crying, shrieking, *My uncles & my aunts must not die!* And then the thought assailed him: *To all things death will come!* He cast his thoughts upon the precipices & they began to fall & crumble. Upon the rocks he cast his thoughts & they became shattered. Under the earth he cast his thoughts & all the things living there stopped moving & their limbs stiffened in death. Up above, toward the skies, he cast his thoughts & the birds flying there suddenly fell to the earth & were dead.

After he entered his lodge he took his blanket and, wrapping it around him, lay down crying. *Not the whole earth will suffice for all those who will die. Oh, there will not be enough earth for them in many places!* There he lay in his corner wrapped up in his blanket, silent.

Figure 2-3   *Winnebago myth: When Hare Heard of Death*

deliver the message of eternal life, but who either garbles the message out of forgetfulness or malice, or does not arrive on time to save the day. The Winnebago Indian story involving the trickster figure, Hare, is an example of this motif (see Figure 2-3). Momentarily forgetting his purpose, Hare fails to deliver the life-saving message. A variant of this motif is seen in myths that tell how two messengers are sent — one bringing immortality, the other bringing death — and the messenger bringing death arrived first.

In the "death in a bundle" motif, death is introduced into human experience when a bundle containing the fate of mortality for all humankind is opened, either inadvertently or because of poor choice. A story told by Aesop based on Greek mythology gives a variation on this theme (see Figure 2-4). Another motif, involving sleep and death, describes how a message of immortality was addressed to human beings, but people were not awake to receive it. Still other myths describe death as resulting from a sexual transgression.

Although most myths portray death as something unwelcome, a few portray it as welcomed, even actively pursued. In some such myths, death is welcomed because of weariness with life or disgust with its misery; in other myths, death is sought in order to prevent overpopulation. Many such myths describe human beings bartering for or buying death from the gods so that life will not continue interminably.

Despite their variety, these myths echo a theme that is surprisingly familiar: Death comes from outside; it cuts short what otherwise would be an immortal existence. The notion that death does not originate within ourselves but comes from outside continues to influence our attitudes toward death. Death seems somehow foreign, not really part of ourselves. Even when we understand the biological processes of disease or deterioration, there is often a sense that, if only this defect could be repaired or the deterioration reversed, we would live forever. Although eons separate us from the preliterate myth makers, death still seems an anomaly.

It was a hot, sultry summer afternoon, and Eros, tired with play and faint from the heat, took shelter in a cool, dark cave. It happened to be the cave of Death himself.

Eros, wanting only to rest, threw himself down carelessly — so carelessly that all his arrows fell out of his quiver.

When he woke he found they had mingled with the arrows of Death, which lay scattered about the floor of the cave. They were so alike Eros could not tell the difference. He knew, however, how many had been in his quiver, and eventually he gathered up the right amount.

Of course, Eros took some that belonged to Death and left some of his own behind.

And so it is today that we often see the hearts of the old and the dying struck by bolts of Love; and sometimes we see the hearts of the young captured by Death.

Figure 2.4. Aesop: *Eros and Death*

Yet when a loved one dies, it is difficult to avoid the recognition of our own mortality. An early story on the theme of death, the epic of Gilgamesh, describes this awakening. The epic relates the odyssey of Gilgamesh, a king whose journey is precipitated by the death of his friend, Enkidu. After undergoing great peril in his search for the power to renew his youth, Gilgamesh returns from his quest empty-handed. There, grieving the death of his beloved friend Enkidu, Gilgamesh realizes that he too will die.

Cultural Case Studies

The foregoing has provided a broad outline of beliefs and customs about death that can be observed more or less universally in human culture, although perhaps most strikingly among traditional societies. To fill in this picture, we now focus on particular aspects of these customs by taking up, in turn, the attitudes toward dying exemplified by the heterogeneous cultures of the Indians of North America, the traditional death ceremonies practiced by the LoDagaa in Africa, and the celebration of community between living and dead known as *El Día de los Muertos*, or the Day of the Dead, in Mexico.

From the broad spectrum of the anthropology of death, we have chosen to highlight these three cultures because they are distinctive enough to provide the necessary perspective and yet similar enough to shed light on our own customs and beliefs — customs and beliefs with which we may have grown all too familiar.[14]

At first glance, the highly formalized mourning rituals among the LoDagaa appear quite different from the death ceremonies that most Americans have encountered. Likewise, the boisterous flaunting of death that occurs during the Mexican fiesta El Día de los Muertos may appear the opposite of the reverential attitude that most Americans associate with death. Yet, closer examination reveals significant correspondences between the "foreign" and the "familiar," correspondences that may elicit insights about behaviors and attitudes that, because they are familiar and our own, we have never really observed. Appreciating something of another culture's relationship to death may help us to more truly recognize that of our own culture and may suggest opportunities for enlivening practices and beliefs that have become for us merely a matter of rote rather than a considered response to human needs.

Native American Culture

In the traditional Native American culture, with its intimate knowledge of the natural environment, death is accepted as part of a cyclical process that can be observed wherever one chooses to look. Generally speaking, the attitude toward death of the tribal societies of North America can be summarized as follows: Death is not something to be ignored, but neither should it become an obsession, something to be feared. Death demands attention only when it impinges on one's present situation, here and now. At such times, it is good to make room for death. The traditional view of the North American Indian societies emphasizes "the significance of living one day at a time, with purpose, grateful for life's blessings, in the knowledge that it could all end abruptly."[15]

This characteristic way of relating to death is typified in the Sioux battle cry: "It's a good day to die!" Many accounts can be found of individuals who faced death stoically, even indifferently. Some individuals composed "death songs" as expressions of their confrontation with death. Sometimes a death song would be "composed spontaneously at the very moment of death" and "chanted with the last breath of the dying person."[16]

These death songs express a resolve to meet death fully, to accept it with one's whole being, not in defeat and desperation, but with equanimity and composure. As part of the natural cycle, dying is not something to be feared or struggled against; a place can be made for death when the time comes. As an expression of this attitude, the death song represents a summary of a person's life and an acknowledgment of death as the completion of being, the final act in the drama of earthly existence.

Although there is a tendency, both for social scientists and the public as a whole, to view Native American societies in a generic, collective manner, there is, in fact, extraordinary diversity among the Indian populations of North America.[17] Furthermore, traditional practices that had held sway for hundreds of years were in many instances altered dramatically by the cultural upheaval caused by the "westward expansionism" of white society.[18] Thus, even within a particular tribal group or culture area, the beliefs and practices of the past typically have not persisted unchanged down to the present time. With this in mind, our examination of Native American beliefs and practices relative to death includes discussion both of commonalities that are shared among the various tribal groupings and of distinctive beliefs and practices that are specific to particular tribes.

For most traditional Native American societies, dying was less feared than were the ghosts of the dead. Although these societies share a view of time as a recurring cycle, as Åke Hultkrantz points out, "they are mainly interested in how

Two Death Songs

In the great night my heart will go out	The odor of death,
Toward me the darkness comes rattling	I smell the odor of death
In the great night my heart will go out	In front of my body.
Papago song by Juana Manwell	A song of the Dakota tribe
(Owl Woman)	

this cycle affects people in this life and have only a vague notion of another existence after death."[19] Often, he says, "One individual might hold several ideas about the dead at the same time" because "different situations call for different interpretations of the fate of humans after death."

Among the Wind River Shoshoni, for example, the state of the dead can be thought about in various ways. The dead may travel to another world or may remain on earth as ghosts; they may be born again as people or may transmigrate into "insects, birds, or even inanimate objects like wood and rocks." Hultkrantz remarks that "most Shoshoni express only a slight interest in the next life and often declare that they know nothing about it."

Among many tribes, the soul or spirit of the deceased is thought to linger for several days near the site of death before passing on to the afterworld. Typically, this is seen as a time that requires great care, both to ensure the progress of the deceased toward the supernatural realm and to safeguard the living.

The Ohlone (Costano) of the California coast, for example, adorned the corpse with feathers, flowers, and beads and then wrapped it in blankets and skins. Dance regalia, weapons, medicine bundle, and other items owned by the deceased were gathered together and, along with the corpse, were placed on the funeral pyre. The mourners sometimes threw some of their own valued possessions onto the pyre as gifts for the deceased. The destruction of the deceased's possessions was intended to facilitate the soul's journey to the "Island of the Dead" and also to remove any reminders of the deceased that might cause his ghost to remain near the living. A Yokut funeral chant says: "You are going where you are going; don't look back for your family."

For the Ohlone, the dangerous period lasted from six months to a year; afterward, a ceremony was held to acknowledge that the widow was free of taboos and that her life could return to normal. However, it was still considered disrespectful to utter the deceased's name. In *The Ohlone Way*, Malcolm Margolin writes: "While the mere thought of a dead person brought sorrow, the mention of a dead person's name brought absolute dread."[20] By destroying the deceased's belongings and avoiding his or her name, the tribal members confirmed the separation of the dead from the living.

Other tribes exhibit less fear of the dead. Indeed, in some tribes, the dead are thought of as guardian spirits or as special envoys of the shamans or medicine

Burial Oration

You are dead.
You will go above there to the trail.
That is the spirit trail.
Go there to the beautiful trail.
May it please you not to walk about where I am.
You are dead.
Go there to the beautiful trail above.
That is your way.
Look at the place where you used to wander.
The north trail, the mountains where you used to wander, you
  are leaving.
Listen to me: go there!

Wintu tribe

men. The memory of deceased members of a tribe might be sustained through rituals exhibiting reverence or even worship of the ancestors, whose burial places are considered sacred. This attitude toward the dead was stated eloquently by Chief Seattle: "To us the ashes of our ancestors are sacred and their resting place is hallowed ground. . . . Be just and deal kindly with my people, for the dead are not powerless. Dead, did I say? There is no death, only a change of worlds."[21]

Burial customs also reflect a society's attitude toward its dead. For many of the Plains tribes, it was customary to expose the corpse on a platform above ground or to place the corpse in the limbs of a tree. This not only hastened the decomposition of the body, but also was thought to speed the soul's journey to the spirit world. Later, the sun-bleached skeleton would be retrieved for burial in sacred grounds. As Old Chief Joseph of the Nez Percé lay dying, he told his son, "Never forget my dying words. This country holds your father's body. Never sell the bones of your father and mother." These words would be remembered later by the Younger Chief Joseph as he led his warriors into battle to preserve the sanctity of the tribal lands that held the bones of the ancestral dead. (This respect for ancestral burial places has led to disputes in recent years concerning artifacts and bones retrieved by archaeologists; public display of such items in museums is at odds with maintenance of the sanctity of ancestral remains.)[22]

Attitudes toward death and the dead in a society arise from the general cultural life of the group and its members. Death rituals symbolize the separation of the dead from the living, the transition of the deceased to some afterlife state, and the reincorporation of the community after its loss of the deceased. Even when the dead are feared and the corpse is disposed of quickly, the deceased may nevertheless become the object of ritual attention. This is illustrated by David Mandelbaum's instructive comparison of death customs among the Hopi and the Cocopa.[23]

Warrior Song

I shall vanish and be no more
But the land over which I now roam
Shall remain
And change not.

Hethúshka Society, Omaha tribe.

Traditionally, when a Cocopa dies, surviving family members wail and scream in an "ecstasy of violent grief behavior" that generally lasts twenty-four hours or more, continuing until the body is cremated. Clothes, food, and other articles are burned with the body. It is thought that the deceased will make use of these items in the afterlife, but the Cocopa also intend that they will help persuade the spirit of the deceased to pass on from the earth.

Later, the bereaved family gives a ceremony to mourn and commemorate the deceased. Speeches and lamentations are heard on this occasion. Although the names of the dead cannot be spoken at other times, at this special time relatives who have passed into the spirit world are publicly summoned, and their presence may be impersonated by living members of the tribe. Occasionally, a ceremonial house constructed especially for the spirits is burned as a gift. The mourning ceremony is conducted both to honor the dead and to try to persuade lurking spirits to come out in the open and depart from the earthly realm. Whereas the cremation ritual focuses on the grief and emotional needs of the bereaved family, the subsequent ceremony is designed to affirm the integrity of the family and the community.

The Hopi, on the other hand, prefer to keep death at a distance. Death is unwelcome; a person's death causes fear. Death threatens the "middle way" of order, control, and measured deliberation that the Hopi cherish. As we would expect, this attitude toward death is reflected in Hopi funeral rituals, which are attended by very few and are held privately. The death is mourned, but without public ceremony. Mourners tend to be reticent in expressing their grief. The Hopi desire that the whole matter be "quickly over and best forgotten."

Among the Hopi, burial follows soon after death. Unlike the Cocopa, the Hopi have no wish to invite departed ancestors to a communal gathering. Once a person's spirit leaves the body, it becomes a different class of being, no longer Hopi. The Hopi want to make sure that the "dichotomy of quick and dead is sharp and clear."

Mandelbaum's description of the death customs of these two Native American societies shows how, even within a similar cultural setting, different social groups may develop quite distinctive responses to death. The Hopi and the Cocopa both fear the dead, but the Hopi avoid the dead, whereas the Cocopa choose to invite the ghosts of deceased ancestors to come out in the open.

Probably each of us feels drawn more strongly to one than the other of these styles of mourning. Reflecting on the different emphases within the Hopi and Cocopa societies can help us evaluate our own attitudes and determine our own values relative to death. In thus pondering cross-cultural examples, we can ask, What is valuable about each of these ways of coming to terms with death? The common elements of the rites of passage surrounding death — the themes of separation, transition, and reincorporation — are present whether the ritual is elaborate or simple. But the manner in which these essential elements are realized through ceremony and other ritual practices is a reflection of a society's attitudes toward death and its particular way of finding resolution when death takes a member of the group.

The LoDagaa of Africa

The term *ancestor worship* has frequently been used to label customs in Africa that could be more accurately described as reverence for and continuing communication with the deceased members of a community who are still remembered by name. As time passes, generations come and go, and memory fades, these ancestral members of the community are replaced by the more recently deceased.[24] The ongoing community of the living dead consists, then, of deceased ancestors who are still recalled in the minds of the living.

Communion with the "living dead" in traditional African societies can be compared with our own relationships to deceased loved ones. At those times when some event or stimulus evokes the memory of a person who was dear to us, we may pause a moment, reflecting on the qualities that made that person beloved, experiencing again our feelings of affection. Our momentary reverie may include a sense of "communion" with the deceased. Perhaps we even feel that the experience has given us some insight or some direction that is helpful in our lives. Although modern societies tend not to provide formal rituals for acknowledging or encouraging this kind of experience, the essential elements seem much the same as those described in the context of traditional African culture.

The relationship between the living and the dead in African societies is indicated quite clearly by the system of age grouping practiced by the Nandi in Kenya. Once past childhood, a male member of the tribe moves through the junior and senior warrior levels and eventually enters the age group of senior elders; he next becomes an old man and ultimately, at death, an ancestor, one of the living dead whose personality is remembered by survivors. After a while, when he is no longer remembered by persons now alive, he merges with the anonymous dead. By this time, however, the Nandi believe, the dead man's "soul stuff" may have already reappeared in a newborn child of the tribe, thus continuing the recurrent pattern of a person's passage through the levels of the age-group system.[25]

According to Kofi Asare Opoku, the traditional African attitude toward death is positive "because it is comprehensively integrated into the totality of life."[26] In the modern Western world, we generally conceive of life and death as

> If we knew the home of Death, we would set it on fire.
>
> Funeral song, Acholi (Africa)

opposites; for the traditional African, however, "the opposite of death is birth, and birth is the one event that links every human being, on the one hand, with all those who have gone before and, on the other, with all those who will come after." The death of a person elicits a response from the entire community, and the rituals connected with death function as "symbolic preparations for the deceased to enter the abode of the ancestors." Messages may be given to the deceased to take to the other side, just as one might give a message to a person going on a trip to convey to those he meets at his destination. There is, indeed, a "this-worldly orientation" to the traditional African conception of the afterlife. "The land of the dead is geographically similar to our own," says Kwasi Wiredu, and "its population is rather like us."[27]

This reverence toward deceased members of the community is of the greatest importance to those who follow the way of traditional African religions. When the body of a Nigerian villager of the Ibo people was recently shipped by air from the United States to her home village, the coffin arrived in a damaged condition and, somewhere along the line, her body had been wrapped in burlap and turned upside down—violating strict tribal taboos concerning abuse of a corpse. Despite the family's offerings of yams, money, and wine to appease the insult, members of the tribe reported seeing the woman's spirit roaming about, and relatives began to experience various reversals of fortune, which they characterized as a "curse" brought about because of the mistreatment of their dead relative. According to the woman's son: "My mother was treated as if she were nothing." As a result, her spirit was angry and not at peace. In bringing suit against the airline to which the body had been entrusted, the son said, "If this had been done to us by an individual, my whole tribe would have gone to war. If I win the case, it would be like bringing back someone's head. It would prove I'm a warrior . . . it will show the gods I have done something against someone who shamed my mother."[28]

The study of the LoDagaa of Northern Ghana by Jack Goody provides an excellent description of the death customs practiced within a traditional African tribal society.[29] Among the LoDagaa, funeral ceremonies span at least a six-month period and sometimes continue over several years. They occur in four distinct, successive phases, each focusing on specific aspects of death and bereavement. Altogether, the LoDagaa funeral ceremonies last about twelve to fifteen days.

The first stage begins at the moment of death and lasts for six or seven days. During the first half of this initial stage, the body is prepared for burial; the deceased is mourned by bereaved relatives and other members of the community;

rites are performed to acknowledge the separation of the deceased from the living; the solidarity of kinship ties are affirmed; and some minor social and family roles that had been occupied by the deceased are redistributed. These public ceremonies, which last about three days, end with the burial of the corpse. During the remaining three or four days of this first stage, in private ceremonies, preparations are made for redistributing the dead man's rights over his widow, children, and property.

About three weeks later, in a second funeral ceremony, the cause of death is established. Whereas modern people would typically consider, say, a snakebite to be the cause of death, the LoDagaa would view the snakebite as an intermediate agent but not the final cause of death. Among the LoDagaa, the real cause of death "is seen as a function of the network of spiritual and human relationships." So inquiries are made to uncover any tension that may have existed between the deceased and others. The LoDagaa also frequently rely on divination as a mode of inquiry into the causes of a person's death.

At the beginning of the rainy season a third stage of the funeral ceremonies is held. Many of these rites, although resembling those of the first stage, mark a transitional stage in the deceased's "passage from the role of living father to that of ancestral father." A provisional ancestral shrine is placed on the dead person's grave.

The final stage follows the harvest, provided that sufficient time has elapsed since the death. The final ancestral shrine is constructed and placed in the grave, and the close relatives of the deceased are formally released from mourning. The care of offspring is also formally transferred to the deceased's tribal "brothers," and final rites are conducted to conclude the redistribution of the deceased's property.

Virtually no one in our society is likely to experience such prolonged or extensive funeral rites as those of the LoDagaa. What is the function of the LoDagaa death ceremonies? Throughout the long period of mourning, the ceremonies serve two purposes. First, some rituals *separate* the dead person from the bereaved family and from the larger community of the living; by these rites, certain social roles formerly occupied by the deceased are gradually assigned to living persons. Second, some rites gather together, or *aggregate*; the dead person is joined with the ancestors, and the bereaved are reincorporated into the community of the living in a way that reflects their changed status.

This rhythm of separation and gathering together is, of course, common to all funeral ceremonies, even when only minimally acknowledged. The rites of the LoDagaa are noteworthy because of the formality with which these basic functions of funeral ritual are accomplished. They provide a model of explicitness in mourning against which our own customs for coping with death and bereavement can be compared and contrasted.

The explicitness of LoDagaa mourning is evident in the use of "mourning restraints," made of leather, fabric, and string. These restraints, which are generally tied around a person's wrist, indicate the relationship of the bereaved to the dead person. For example, at a man's funeral, his father, mother, and widow wear restraints made of hide; his brothers and sisters wear fiber restraints; and his

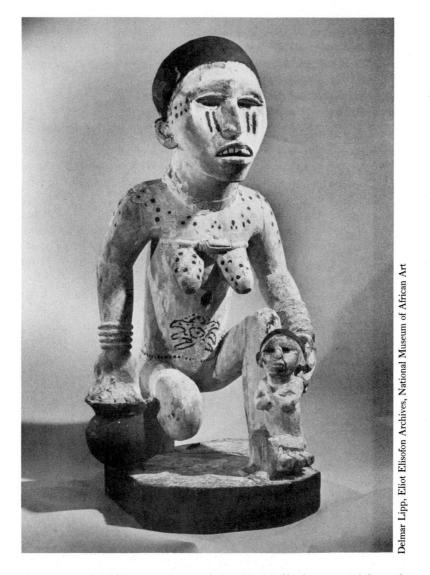

Delmar Lipp, Eliot Elisofon Archives, National Museum of African Art

A woman and child in mourning are depicted in this Yombe memorial figure from Zaire. Installed in a shed constructed on the grave, such adornments are thought to provide the deceased with companionship or protection in the afterlife.

children wear restraints made of string, tied around the ankle. Thus, the strongest restraints are provided to the mourners who had the closest relationship with the deceased—usually through kinship and marriage, but sometimes through extraordinarily strong friendship bonds. Weaker mourning restraints are given to persons who had been correspondingly less intimate with the deceased. One end of the mourning restraint is attached to the bereaved person while the other end is held by a "mourning companion," who assumes responsibility for the bereaved's behavior during the period of intense grief.

Mourning restraints thus serve two related purposes: Being something that can be seen and felt, they validate that the bereaved's expression of grief at the loss of someone close is commensurate with the intensity of relationship with the deceased. Second, they discourage expressions of grief that would exceed the norms of LoDagaa society.

Immediately following the death, LoDagaa expressions of grief are likely to be fervent. Gradually, during the three-day period of the initial funeral ceremonies, expressions of grief become more routine and systematized as the mourners begin adjusting to and accepting their loss.

The LoDagaa way of mourning invites considerable public participation by members of the community, but the grave is dug and made ready for the burial by men specially designated and trained for this function. In their training they learn not only how to prepare a grave properly but also how to protect themselves against the mystical dangers that surround care of the dead. The LoDagaa pay for these funeral services by giving offerings of food and other goods to the gravediggers at the conclusion of the ceremonies.

Even though gravedigging is performed by specialists, the LoDagaa occasionally make therapeutic use of this task to counteract excessive fear of the dead. For example, if a LoDagaa boy displays debilitating fear at the sight of a dead person or during a funeral, he may be forced by his father to join in the work of digging the grave. The LoDagaa believe that a repulsive act performed under controlled circumstances can have curative as well as preventive effects. This kind of direct confrontation with the reality of death is considered to be a way of working through fears about death.

In LoDagaa society, people come to terms with death by confronting it directly. The prolonged and elaborate funeral ceremonies, the use of mourning restraints to show degrees of relationship to the deceased, and the therapeutic use of digging the grave as a means of confronting fears about death all demonstrate the LoDagaa choice to deal with death explicitly.

Traditional African customs surrounding death have, in some instances, helped to maintain cultures threatened by change in the modern world. Writing about the Sakalava of Madagascar, Gillian Feeley-Harnik notes that members of this society continue to organize their lives around the royal ancestors who once governed them, while participating only marginally in the national political economy.[30] The Sakalava have resisted the destruction of their indigenous institutions and have "protected their values by 'hiding' them in the now-illicit realm of the dead." Despite the changes wrought by colonization and independence, ancestral tradition remains the ideal guide to action.

Similarly, obituary publications among the Yoruba of southwestern Nigeria provide a modern form for the ancient customs. The status and prestige of the deceased is denoted in various ways, most obviously in the size of the obituary publication, which may be a costly, full-page advertisement. It is common, writes Olatunde Bayo Lawuyi, to "mark the return of the dead every ten years," although this practice decreases over time. Obituary publication "demonstrates the possibility of continuity in ancestral beliefs" and "is a symbolic manifestation of a tradition that has taken a new cultural form."[31]

Mexican Culture

From ancient times, Mexican culture has echoed the interrelated themes of life, death, and resurrection. Life and death are seen not as opposites, but as different phases of an underlying process of regeneration. The Aztecs of pre-conquest Mexico believed that the very creation of the world was made possible by sacrificial rites enacted by the gods. The warrior killed in battle and the sacrificial victim in Aztec religious rites were confident that they were participating in a destiny that had been determined in the origins of the world.

The Spanish conquerors brought to Mexico a cult of death (or, "cult of immortality," to use the term preferred by Miguel de Unamuno, the great Spanish writer and philosopher) that in many respects resembled indigenous beliefs. The willingness to die for ideals espoused by the larger society is exemplified in Spanish history by the mass suicide at Sagunto in 219 B.C., when the city's leading citizens demonstrated that death was preferable to capture by the Carthaginians. Such an acceptance of fate was familiar to the Aztecs.

For the Mexican, death is intimately related to identity. Octavio Paz says, "Death defines life. . . . Each of us dies the death he is looking for, the death he has made for himself. . . . Death, like life, is not transferable."[32] Common folk sayings reiterate this deep connection between death and identity, as in "Tell me how you die and I will tell you who you are." In the Mexican consciousness, death mirrors a person's life.

Symbols of death are visible everywhere. In churches, the suffering Savior is portrayed with a bloody vividness. Glass-topped coffins display the remains of martyrs, saints, and notables of the Church. Death is manifested in graffiti and in the ornaments that decorate cars and buses. Newspapers seem to revel in accounts of violent deaths, and obituaries are conspicuously framed with black borders that call the readers' attention to the fact of death. Art and literature are replete with images of death, and in Mexican poetry one finds similes comparing life's fragility to a dream, a flower, a river, or a passing breeze.[33]

Whereas Anglo artists and writers seem in awe or even fearful of death, their Mexican counterparts seem to confront death with an attitude of humorous sarcasm. But it is not really death that is parodied, but life. In Mexican art and literature, death is portrayed not so much as an end, but as an equalizer that not even the wealthiest can escape; the emotional response it generates is often one of apparent impatience, disdain, or irony. Although the engravings of Antonio Guadalupe Posada, for example, may superficially resemble the woodcuts of the medieval *danse macabre*, in which people of all walks of life danced with their own skeletons, Posada's skeletons do not have the "anxious premonition of death" one associates with similar works by artists in other cultures.[34] Surrounded by references to death, Paz says, the Mexican "jokes about it, caresses it, sleeps with it, celebrates it," and makes it "one of his favorite toys and his steadfast love."

Once a year, death is celebrated in a national fiesta, *El Día de los Muertos*, the Day of the Dead. Occurring annually in November, the Day of the Dead generally lasts one or two days and coincides with All Souls' Day, the Catholic Church's feast of commemoration for the dead. Blending both indigenous pre-Spanish Indian ritual and the imposed ritual and dogma of the Church into a unique celebration, the fiesta is an occasion for communion between the living and the dead. This amalgamation is especially evident in the traditional observances found on the Island of Janitzio in Michoacán and in the Zapotec villages in the Valley of Oaxaca.[35]

The fiesta's purpose and spirit are described by Glenn Whitney, a reporter who observed the celebration in Mixquic:[36]

> Bearing food and singing songs, millions of Mexicans head for the cemetery to welcome their relatives back — at least symbolically — from the grave. The holiday centers on the belief that dead relatives, who return once a year to visit the living, would not want a somber and silent welcome. Instead, they are greeted with tamales, enchiladas, and even their preferred brands of tequila and cigarettes.

Although the sequence and shape of events varies from village to village, the pattern followed in Mixquic — and described to Glenn Whitney by Marie Nunez, a caretaker of the village — can be taken as representative. The fiesta begins on October 31, "with the tolling of twelve bells at midday to mark the return of all dead children." In each house, the family "sets a table adorned with white flowers, glasses of water, plates with salt (for good luck), and a candle for each dead child." The next day — following a special breakfast of chocolate, bread, fruit, and atole (a thick, sweet drink made of corn starch) in honor of the children — families gather at the church, where bells are rung at noon to signify the departure of the "small defunct ones" and the return of the "big defunct ones." Then, "before nightfall, some 3000 graves near San Andres Church will be cleaned and covered with ribbons, foil, and the marigold-like cempasuchil flower." Nunez says:

> The celebration kicks into high gear on the evening of November 1 and into the next morning, when thousands file into the small candle-illuminated graveyard carrying tamales, pumpkin marmalade, chicken with "mole" — a spicy sauce of some 50 ingredients including chili peppers, peanuts, and chocolate — and "pan de muerto," or bread of the dead — sweet rolls decorated with "bones" made of sugar.
>
> People sit on the graves and eat the food along with the dead ones. They bring guitars and violins and sing songs. There are stands for selling food for the visitors. It goes on all night. It's a happy occasion — a fiesta, not a time of mourning.

Throughout Mexico, bread in the shape of human bones is eaten. Sugar-candy skulls and tissue-paper skeletons poke fun at death and flaunt it. The fiesta is a time for excess, for revolting against ordinary modes of thought and action. It is, says Paz, "an experiment in disorder, reuniting contradictory elements and principles in order to bring about a renascence of life." During the Day of the

An ironic attitude toward death characterizes the Day of the Dead fiesta in Mexico.
Death is satirized while memories of deceased loved ones are cherished by the living.
Family members often place the names of deceased relatives on ornaments such as
this candy skull and these candy coffins. This practice assures the spirits of the dead
that they have not been forgotten by the living and provides solace to the living in the
form of tangible symbols of the presence of deceased loved ones.

Dead, celebrants seek to break through the ordinary bonds that separate the dead
from the living. Families clean and decorate the graves of deceased family members, placing food offerings and lighted candles before the souls of the ancestors.
The dead are said to partake of the spirit of the foods and gifts brought to them.
The entire night is often devoted to meditative communion with dead loved ones,
as the ancestors are urged to come forth this one special night of the year to aid
and comfort the living. The failure to pay respect to the dead can bring scorn to
the family that neglects its responsibilities.

Fiesta night, as Paz observes, is also a night of mourning. However, mourners are cautioned against shedding too many tears. Excessive grief may make the
pathway traveled by the dead slippery and thus burden them with a tortuous
journey as they try to return to the world of the living on this special night of fiesta
and communal celebration.

Day of the Dead

It was several mornings after the celebratory fiesta of El Dia de Muerte, the Day of the Dead, and ribbons and ravels of tissue and sparkle-tape still clung like insane hair to the raised stones, to the hand-carved, love-polished crucifixes, and to the above-ground tombs which resembled marble jewel-cases. There were statues frozen in angelic postures over gravel mounds, and intricately carved stones tall as men with angels spilling all down their rims, and tombs as big and ridiculous as beds put out to dry in the sun after some nocturnal accident. And within the four walls of the yard, inserted into square mouths and slots, were coffins, walled in, plated in by marble plates and plaster, upon which names were struck and upon which hung tin pictures, cheap peso portraits of the inserted dead. Thumb-tacked to the different pictures were trinkets they'd loved in life, silver charms, silver arms, legs, bodies, silver cups, silver dogs, silver church medallions, bits of red crape and blue ribbon. On some places were painted slats of tin showing the dead rising to heaven in oil-tinted angels' arms.

Looking at the graves again, they saw the remnants of the death fiesta. The little tablets of tallow splashed over the stones by the lighted festive candles, the wilted orchid blossoms lying like crushed red-purple tarantulas against the milky stones, some of them looking horridly sexual, limp and withered. There were loop-frames of cactus leaves, bamboo, reeds, and wild, dead morning-glories. There were circles of gardenias and sprigs of bougainvillea, desiccated. The entire floor of the yard seemed a ballroom after a wild dancing, from which the participants have fled; the tables askew, confetti, candles, ribbons and deep dreams left behind.

Ray Bradbury, "The Next in Line," in
The October Country

Much of the traditional attitude toward death has persisted to the present, both in Mexico and among Mexican-Americans. Surveying Mexican-American customs, Joan Moore notes that "uniformly, one meets the flat assertion that the funeral is the single most important family ceremony. . . . It far outstrips marriage, baptism, or any other family or church-related rite of passage." Indeed, she adds, "to the Mexican, a visit to the graveyard is potentially a visit to his personal antiquity and his connection with the land."[37]

Familiarity with death, however, may breed contempt, not understanding. Paz argues that both the American and Mexican deny the reality of death, albeit in different ways. In the one culture, death is brought to the forefront of consciousness; in the other, it is pushed aside. It is possible to deny or avoid death even though surrounded by images that constantly suggest it. When death is devalued — is made to seem less than the radical event it truly is — then we are not looking squarely at death, and life loses meaning.

Death and Dying in Western Civilization

We might expect cultures like those just discussed to reveal attitudes and behaviors different from our own. However, we might be surprised to discover the contrasts that exist in the more familiar setting of Western civilization if we go back in time. To better understand our modern response to death, let us trace some responses that were characteristic of Western culture during the last fifteen hundred years or so.

For well over a thousand years (if we count from A.D. 500, roughly when the Middle Ages began), those living in the Western world accepted death as an integral part of human existence. Despite gradual changes, as Figure 2-5 shows, the attitude toward death remained generally consistent with a view of the universe as bound together by natural and divine law. Death was part of this natural design, and, for most people, the teachings of the Church were a source of hope for the afterlife. This outlook, which prevailed from about the sixth to the nineteenth centuries, has been characterized by Philippe Ariès as one of "tamed death."[38]

Using Ariès' analysis, we can discern relatively distinct periods during this epoch of Western cultural history as regards death and dying. In the first period, during the early Middle Ages, a sense of collective destiny was prevalent. Death was understood in this context as the common fate of all people: "All people die." In the religious mentality of the time, the dead were "asleep in Christ," and their bodies entrusted to the Church until the Last Day, when they would be resurrected at the time of Christ's Apocalyptic return. Salvation was achieved less through individual merit or freedom from sin than through the good graces of the Church.

By the twelfth century, this mentality had gradually been transformed into a more particular awareness of one's own death as having a personal meaning: "Everyone dies" had become "I will die my own death." This transformation came about as a result of a general enrichment in medieval culture and the greater complexity of social structure. Innovations had been made in commerce, agriculture, education, and political life. The works of ancient writers having been preserved by Byzantine and Moslem scholars, Greek thought and Roman law became influential, opening the way for new intellectual pursuits. Above all, people in the West gained a new sense of individual identity and self-awareness. As a result, the act of dying became an event of supreme importance for the individual.

This increased emphasis on individual identity brought dramatic changes in the religious sphere as well. Whereas in times past, residing in the bosom of the Church was enough to ensure resurrection on the Last Day and acceptance into heaven, now people developed personal anxieties regarding the Judgment that would separate the just from the damned. The *liber vitae*, or Book of Life, which previously had been conceived as a sort of vast cosmic census, now became the biography of an individual life, a balance sheet by which each person's soul would be weighed.

The third great transformation of the meaning of death occurred toward the end of the seventeenth century, when the death of the other, "thy death," began to receive emphasis. Death was romanticized, and the loss felt by the bereaved gave rise to impassioned expressions of grief and to desires to memorialize the dead. The romantic ideal of the beautiful death was part of a more general fascination

Ritual of dying; the recumbent figure of the dying person, presiding amidst protocol and custom, over an essentially public ceremony. Everything done with simplicity, no great show of emotion. Custom and social observances dictate the style of dying and the deathbed scene. Death is familiar; there is an awareness of dying: "I see and I know that my death is near."

As the initiative passes from the dying person to the family and then to the medical arena, there arises a desire to spare the dying person, often by means of pretence, from the "ugliness" of death. Death becomes taboo.

Place of burial is the charnel house, the outer part or courtyard of the church. With the rise of the cult of martyrs there is a desire to be buried near the great saints of the church; burials take place near or in churches instead of outside cities as during pagan times.

Gradually, a greater sense of individuality is reflected in death customs. A new self-awareness becomes evident first in the use of inscriptions and plaques to mark a person's biography and death; later, effigies and death masks herald the individuality of the dead. Eventually, the tombs of the notable dead are embellished with sculptures portraying both the appearance of the body when alive and its ultimate putrefaction after death, a stark reminder of mortality and individual responsibility.

The "cult of memory" demonstrated by ornate memorials to the dead was often accompanied by hysterical mourning on the part of the bereaved survivors. More recently, however, these once-customary signs of mourning have been largely replaced by the avoidance of emotional display and by discreet and brief funeral ceremonies. Uncertainty and anxiety become the characteristic emotions elicited by "forbidden death" in the twentieth century.

500 600 700 800 900 1000 1100 1200 1300 1400 1500 1600 1700 1800 1900 2000

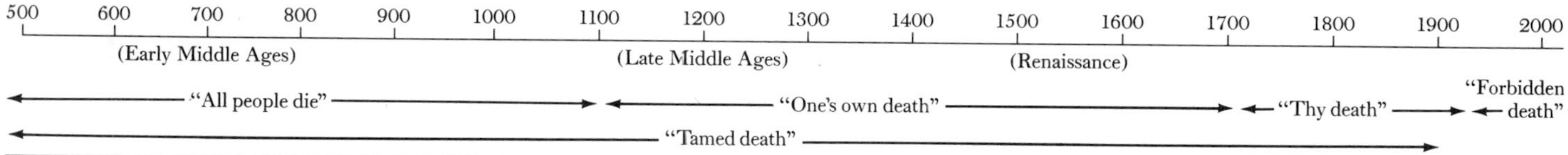

	(Early Middle Ages)	(Late Middle Ages)	(Renaissance)	
Timeline	500 — 600 — 700 — 800 — 900 — 1000 — 1100	1200 — 1300 — 1400 — 1500	1600 — 1700 — 1800	1900 — 2000

Arrows: "All people die" — "Tamed death" — "One's own death" — "Thy death" — "Forbidden death"

Universe bound together by natural and divine law. Death a familar and accepted part of this order. Individuals experienced themselves as participants in a collective destiny of humankind, presided over by the Church.	Belief in the Apocalypse (Christ's return at the end of time). Resurrection of the dead on the Last Day. The dead "asleep in Christ," to awake in Paradise. Salvation based on participation in the communal Body of Christ, not on individual moral actions.
General enrichment throughout culture; intellectual advances, influenced by Greek thought and Roman law.	Concept of the Resurrection incorporates belief in the Last Judgment, when the soul will be judged on its record in the "Book of Life," an individual account that is closed on the Last Day.
Age of exploration and conquest; old geographic and intellectual boundaries giving way.	Emphasis on Judgment predominates; the "Second Coming" fades into background. The time of Judgment shifts to the deathbed scene, which becomes the final test in the cosmic struggle. Between death and "the Last Day" there is an extension of being into purgatory.
Increasing secularization of social and intellectual life.	Challenges to religious belief lead to a reexamination and reinterpretation of scripture and sacred traditions. The interplay between reason and faith creates a diverse and pluralistic religious and social environment.

Figure 2-5   *Death and Dying from the Middle Ages to the Present*

Death Knells

During many centuries one item of expense for survivors was the fee that must be paid for the ringing of the soul bell. Every cathedral and church of medieval Christendom had such a bell, almost always the largest one in the bell tower.

By the time John Donne wrote the immortal line "for whom the bell tolls," ringing of the soul bell—in a distinctive pattern, or knell—was popularly taken to be merely a public notice that a death had occurred. This use of the soul bell came into importance relatively late, however.

Not simply in Christian Europe but also among primitive tribes and highly developed non-Christian cultures of the Orient, bells have been linked with death. Notes from bells (rung in special fashion) served to help convince a spirit that there was no need to remain close to a useless dead body. At the same time, noise made by bells was considered to be especially effective in driving away the evil spirits who prowled about hoping to seize a newly released soul or to put obstacles in its path.

Ringing of the soul (or passing) bell was long considered so vital that bell ringers demanded, and got, big fees for using it. Still in general use by the British as late as the era of King Charles II in the seventeenth century, bell ringers then regulated the number of strokes of the passing bell so that the general public could determine the age, sex, and social status of the deceased.

Webb Garrison,
Strange Facts About Death

with the imaginative and emotional appeal of the heroic, the mysterious. The sad beauty of death elicited feelings of melancholy, tinged with optimism that there would be an eventual reunion of the family in a Heavenly home.

Survivors began more and more to visit the graves of beloved relatives and friends. Expressions of mourning became highly visible. The arts were pressed into service to memorialize the dead: Memorial brooches contained pictures of the deceased, and watercolors depicted such scenes as ladies weeping at receiving the news of a death. By the nineteenth century, the deaths of others tended to overshadow one's own sense of mortality.

Then, with great rapidity, all this changed. By the early decades of the twentieth century, the deathbed had been displaced from the home to the hospital. What had been a response to the death of another became a desire to spare the dying person the pain of knowing about the imminence of his or her death. Funerals became shorter, more discreet. Grief was suppressed. The customary signs of mourning disappeared. These changes were particularly dramatic in the United States. Attitudes and behaviors that had been common since the early Middle Ages, and that remained essentially unchanged through most of the nineteenth century, were quickly superseded as death became taboo. No longer familiar, death was ugly and forbidden. This modern mentality has been characterized as "invisible death."

Although it is possible to discern a chronology in the occurrence of these changes in the Western attitude toward death, one may also, as Ian Gentles suggests, regard the various stages as "different mentalities, each of which has been dominant at different times."[39] This suggestion has merit, first of all, because widespread social change does not affect all elements of a culture equally or at precisely the same time. For example, the attitude characterized by the term "tamed death" was found up until the end of the nineteenth century among Russian peasants and, indeed, could be identified among some social groups even today. Furthermore, conceiving of these different attitudes as "mentalities" rather than as distinct chronological periods can help us understand how our own attitudes toward death may change depending on various circumstances.

Nevertheless, tracing the changes that have occurred during the past fifteen hundred years of Western culture reveals that the predominant attitude toward death today is dramatically different from what it was even as recently as a hundred years ago. What is the significance of this break in the continuity of Western humanity's relationship with death? To answer this question, we must examine how patterns of dying and of death evolved from the Middle Ages to the present.

Anticipated Death

Dying was a grim business in the Middle Ages. In the absence of surgery or adequate means of alleviating pain, the pangs of death were real indeed. On pious deathbeds, the dying person offered up his or her suffering to God, expecting nothing more than to meet death in the customary manner.

Sudden death was rare. Even wounds received in battle or injuries resulting from accidents seldom brought instantaneous death. "I see and know that my death is near": Thus did the dying person acknowledge his or her impending demise. (The possibility of sudden, unexpected death was greatly feared because it caught the victim unawares and unable to properly close earthly accounts and turn toward the divine.)

Those who stood near the deathbed, too, could say with confidence that the dying person "feels her time has come" or "knows that he will soon be dead." Only rarely did death come without warning. Usually it was anticipated either by natural signs or by a conscious inner certainty. Death seemed manageable.

A good teacher both of the body and the soul is perfect remembrance of death, when a man, looking beyond everything that is between (that is, between the present moment and the hour of death), is always seeing forward to that bed upon which we shall one day lie, breathing out our life; and at that which comes after.

Hesychius of Jerusalem, circa A.D. 400

The Deathbed Scene

A person realizing that death was near began to prepare for it. The dying person customarily enacted certain ritual gestures to make sure that dying was done properly. Philippe Ariès describes the main features of a dignified death during the early Middle Ages: Lying down, with the head facing east toward Jerusalem, perhaps with arms crossed over the chest, the dying person first expressed sadness at his or her impending end, "a sad but very discreet recollection of beloved beings and things." Then, the many companions—family and friends—surrounding the deathbed received the dying person's pardon for any wrongs that they might have done, and all were commended to God.

Next, the dying person turned his or her attention away from the earthly and toward the divine. A confession of sins to a priest was followed by a short prayer requesting divine grace. The priest then granted absolution. With the customary rites completed, nothing more was said. The dying person was ready for death. If death came more slowly than expected, the dying person simply waited in silence.

The recumbent figure in the deathbed, surrounded by parents, friends, family, children, and even mere passersby, remained the predominant death scene until modern times. Dying was considered a more or less public ceremony, with the person who was dying clearly in charge. Emotion was neither suppressed nor given especially vivid expression. Everything was directed toward simplicity and ceremony.

As a new individualism evolved, beginning about the twelfth century, the scene around the deathbed began to change imperceptibly. *How* you died was profoundly important. Over the entourage of public participants now hovered a great and invisible army of celestial figures, angels and demons, battling for possession of the dying person's soul. As the awareness of selfhood grew, death became the *speculum mortis*, the mirror in which each person could discover his or her nature and destiny as an individual. Because free will implied moral responsibility for one's acts, each person facing death tallied the moral balance sheet of his or her life. As a unique occasion for reviewing one's actions and making a final decision for good or ill, the moment of death became the supreme challenge and the ultimate test of an entire lifetime. An indicator of this evolution toward greater emphasis on the individual can be seen in the fact that the drafting of written wills became increasingly prevalent. Unlike the wills drafted today, however, which are generally concerned only with the disposition of a person's wealth and property, the wills of this period became "a personal testament" to a person's whole view of life.

From the seventeenth century on, the religious understandings of death began to gradually give way to secular understandings that emphasized reason and the natural order rather than the divine. Although still an important force in Western culture, religion now shared the stage with the more materialistic orientation of scientific rationalism. Thus, the world view of the Middle Ages, embodied in the iconography of the Church, with its attendant comforts and fears, gave

W. Eugene Smith. Center for Creative Photography, University of Arizona, © Heirs of W. Eugene Smith

This deathbed vigil in a Spanish village is characteristic of the way in which human beings have responded to death for thousands of years. Only recently have such scenes been superseded in modern societies by the specter of dying alone, perhaps unconscious, amid the impersonal technological gadgetry of an unfamiliar institutional environment.

way to a mentality that viewed nature as chaotic and sometimes frightening, but also fascinating in its beauty. Still, for the dying person, there remained a familiarity with death that seems quite foreign today. It was not uncommon for people to have possessed what seems an uncanny knowledge of when they were going to die, even waiting until death drew near before drafting their wills.

The scene around the deathbed remained little changed outwardly; family and friends still gathered as participants in the public ritual of a person's dying. But the religious images and understandings that had characterized the earlier world view no longer served to channel the spontaneous grief of the survivors. The idea of death as untamed yet beautiful, like nature, gave survivors a means to express their emotions. The old notions of Heaven and Hell that had so motivated people in an earlier time were replaced by a hoped-for immortality of the soul and an eventual reunion of loved ones in the afterlife. Whereas the Puritan child in seventeenth-century New England was counseled to contemplate the terrors of death and the torment of a fiery Hell as prods to good behavior, the Romantic child of the eighteenth and early nineteenth centuries was instructed to think of death as beautiful, graceful, and serene. Dying was likened to the emergence of a butterfly from its cocoon.

Along with this changed outlook, the initiative in the ceremonies surrounding death was transferred from the dying person to the grief-stricken survivors. But not until the twentieth century, with the displacement of the scene of death from the home to the hospital, would a major change in the manner of dying occur.

Burial Customs

Until the sixth or seventh century, burial customs remained much the same as they had been during Roman times. These customs reflected the pagan belief that the dead might come back to haunt the living. To prevent such unhappy events, gravesites were usually located away from towns and cities. Despite the differences in their beliefs about the state of the dead, Christians followed these customary practices. Early Christians were buried in the pagan cemeteries; later, Christians were buried in their own cemeteries, but still outside of populated areas.

With the development of monasticism (a practice whereby individuals chose to live in seclusion or ascetic simplicity in order to more faithfully pursue their religious vows), a cult of martyrs arose that gradually introduced a new element into Christian burial practices. It came to be believed that the martyrs' saintliness remained powerful even in death, and could help others avoid the pitfalls of sin and the horrors of hell. The early martyrs had been buried alongside the pagan dead, as was the custom. But, over time, many Christians began to want to be buried near the graves of the martyrs in hopes of gaining merit by such proximity. (A rough, modern analogy might be that of a person wishing to be buried near a famous person at Forest Lawn or a veteran requesting burial near a Medal of Honor winner, although those living in the early Middle Ages were concerned with eternal welfare rather than earthly prestige.)

At the same time, pilgrims began journeying to the gravesites to venerate the martyrs, creating a need to establish a focal point for their worship, and altars, chapels, and eventually churches were built on or near the graves. At first these developments took place in the old pagan burial grounds because burials were still prohibited within the cities. However, as the cemeteries adjoining rural churches became increasingly used for Christian burials, the great urban cathedrals also began allowing burials to take place within their precincts. Initially this practice was limited to the notables and saints of the Church, but by the ninth century or so the burials of the faithful were taking place in the churchyards and surrounds of the urban cathedrals as well as the rural churches. Thus, the state of the dead had become intimately linked with the Church.

The Charnel House

The custom of burial within the churchyards of the urban cathedrals eventually led to the development of *charnel houses*, arcades and galleries that ran the length of the churchyard, where the bones of the dead were entrusted to the Church. Limbs and skulls were arranged artistically along various parts of the churchyard, as well as within and near the church. Many of these bones came from the great common graves of the poor, which were periodically reopened to remove the bones, which were then given over to the church for safekeeping until the Resurrection. The final destination of the bones was unimportant, so long as they were associated with the church or with some saint or holy relic. "As yet unborn," Ariès says, "was the modern idea that the dead person should be installed in a sort of house unto himself, a house of which he was the perpetual owner or at least the long-term tenant, a house in which he would be at home and from which he could not be evicted." Most burials were anonymous; except for those of a few notables of the Church or royalty, gravesites had nothing to identify who was buried in them.

With the coming of the new individualism in the twelfth and thirteenth centuries, however, there was a growing tendency to preserve the identity of the person buried in a particular place. Simple grave markers, usually of the "Here lies John Doe" variety, began to appear on the graves of even common folk, although not until the seventeenth century or so would this practice become prevalent. In the abbey church of Saint-Denis, this evolution in burial practices is reflected by the beautifully sculpted figures that adorn the tombs of the kings and queens interred there. The earliest figures are shown sleeping the long, placid sleep of the pious who are awaiting resurrection; during the Renaissance, the figures have become more worldly monuments to family and dynastic greatness.[40]

Throughout the Middle Ages, burial practices for most people remained little changed; the characteristic resting place of the dead was an unmarked grave in the charnel house, a place where the dead awaited eventual resurrection in the care of the Church. The charnel house itself was a public place, which reflected the medieval familiarity with death. Much as the Romans had congregated in the Forum, their medieval counterparts met in the charnel houses. There they would find shops and merchants, conduct business, dance, gamble, or simply enjoy being together.

In Paris, one can still visit catacombs where, as one wide-eyed visitor exclaimed, "piles of femurs and skulls" are "stacked eight feet high and ten yards deep, as neatly as lumber in an Oregon mill yard." The bones are "painstakingly arranged in elaborate geometric patterns" and "above them, inscribed in French and Latin, phrases like 'Death is all around us' or 'Stop! This is the Empire of the Dead' are strategically posted on the walls lest you forget where you are."[41]

Yet another indication of this familiarity with the dead is the public anatomy demonstrations that were attended by surgeons and students as well as by curious townspeople. During the sixteenth century, the University of Leiden chose

This ossuary located at a European monastery is a survival of the medieval charnel house, a gallery of skeletons and skulls and bones.

the apse of a church as the setting for such public dissections of the human body. In this "Anatomical Theater," as it was called, specimens were collected and even displayed artistically or posed in dramatic gestures. Gonzalez-Crussi cites an example from the eighteenth century: a child's arm "clad in an infant's lace sleeve," as the hand holds, "between thumb and index finger — as gracefully as an artist's model might hold a flower by the stem — a human eye by the optical nerve."[42] Such a display would seem shocking today; dissection is performed strictly for scientific purposes. "We have," says Gonzalez-Crussi, "banished the dead from our midst."

The Dance of Death

As funeral inscriptions and tombs — at least of the notable — became more personalized, macabre themes also developed. Effigies of the dead appeared, and as time passed became increasingly realistic. By the early seventeenth century, the striving for realism had become so great that sometimes the deceased was portrayed twice; first as he or she looked while alive and a second time as a severely decomposed corpse. In death as in life, the focus was on the individual. Although these effigies portrayed only the most notable personages, they nevertheless represent an important development in how the dead were perceived by the living. Survivors had found a means for continuing their relationship with the dead in the custom of perpetuating the *memory* of the deceased.

To understand some of the influences leading to this change, we can trace the evolution of the Dance of Death, or *danse macabre*, which found expression in a variety of art forms including drama, poetry, music, and the visual arts. The Dance of Death is thought to have its origin in ecstatic mass dances that date from the eleventh and twelfth centuries. But it is not until the late thirteenth and early fourteenth centuries that the Dance of Death begins to become formalized, combining ideas of the inevitability of death with its impartiality.

The Dance of Death was sometimes performed as a masque, a short dramatic entertainment in which actors costumed as skeletons danced with other figures representing persons of all levels of society. The rich as well as the poor were invited to join in the Dance of Death, which conveyed the notion that death comes to *all* people, and to *each* person. A series of paintings, dating from the early fifteenth century, depicted the living being escorted to their destination by skeletons and corpses, a grim reminder of the imminence of death and a call to repentance.[43]

A major influence on the Dance of Death was the mass deaths caused by the plague, called the Black Death, of the mid-fourteenth century. The plague arrived in Europe via a Black Sea port in 1347, and by the time the first wave of the pestilence ended in 1351, a third of the population, twenty-five million people, had died.[44] The plague wiped out three-quarters of the population during the next eighty years, and its ravages continued at irregular intervals until the eighteenth century, with the last large outbreak striking Moscow in 1771. The devastation of the Hundred Years' War (1337–1453) between France and England also contributed to the sense that death was omnipresent.

In the oldest versions of the Dance of Death, death seemed scarcely to touch the living, to warn or single out the person. Even as death took on a more personal meaning with the rise of individualism, it was still an accepted part of the

Hans Holbein the Younger, British Museum

Antonio Guadalupe Posada, Swann Collection Library of Congress

MIGUEL Y LA CRIADA.

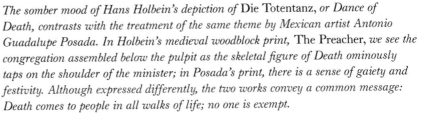

The somber mood of Hans Holbein's depiction of Die Totentanz, *or Dance of Death, contrasts with the treatment of the same theme by Mexican artist Antonio Guadalupe Posada. In Holbein's medieval woodblock print,* The Preacher, *we see the congregation assembled below the pulpit as the skeletal figure of Death ominously taps on the shoulder of the minister; in Posada's print, there is a sense of gaiety and festivity. Although expressed differently, the two works convey a common message: Death comes to people in all walks of life; no one is exempt.*

natural order of things. But, about the end of the fifteenth century and the beginning of the sixteenth, a great shift in attitudes was reflected in the Dance of Death: The person was now portrayed as being forcibly taken by death. Death was seen as a rupture, a radical and complete break between the living and the dead.

With this change, the Dance of Death took on certain erotic connotations. Death was seen as a radical break with ordinary modes of consciousness, and thus was likened to the "small death" that occurs during the sexual act when, for a moment, there is a break with ordinary consciousness.[45] These blatantly erotic ideas about death were sublimated by the larger society, so that death was transformed into the obsession with beauty that became the hallmark of the Romantic ideal of death. The relationship between love and death that previously was seen in martyrdom now extended to include romantic love as well. Romances like those of Tristan and Isolde or Romeo and Juliet demonstrated the notion that where there is love, death can be beautiful—and even desirable.

> Death is a subject to me which you can see and think of but cannot talk of. Indeed however ill he be I could never think of the death of one I love. It may be reconed [*sic*] as a want of faith! I know it is not. I do not mean by that, that I shall not be prepared to die when the time comes.
>
> From the *Diary* (1858) of Annie de Rothschild,
> age thirteen

By the Romantic period of the late eighteenth and nineteenth centuries, these concepts, which bear a historical relationship to the code of chivalry and the notion of courtly love, found currency in the popular imagination. Thus, we have followed the progression from the communal mentality that "we all die," to the personal awareness that "I will die," to finally arrive at the death of the other, "thy death." As Ian Gentles says: "The center of attention now shifted to the bereaved. *Mourning* became profoundly important, and people again became apprehensive, not about their own death, but about the death of their loved ones."[46] Exalted and dramatized, death became important because it affected the loved one, the other person, whose memory was perpetuated in the ornate cemeteries of the eighteenth and nineteenth centuries.

Memorializing the Dead

We have already noted how, as individualism took hold, practices evolved to preserve the identity of the deceased. These practices came into broad use in the seventeenth century or so, when all the various social and cultural changes combined to produce a fascination with the death of loved ones and a desire to perpetuate their memory. In the eighteenth and early nineteenth centuries this memorialization of the dead was evidenced by elaborate mourning rituals, ornate tombstones, and a variety of mourning paraphernalia. The acceptance of death as universal and inevitable, an attitude that reflected religious and social concepts of order that had endured for more than a thousand years in Western culture, began to give way to a desire to mute the harsh reality of death, to blunt its finality. The finality of death was made less severe by perpetuating the memory of the deceased and by imagining his or her continued existence in heaven, where survivors hoped to be eventually reunited with loved ones (see Figure 2-6).

The untended graveyards of the seventeenth-century Puritans, who disdained the body whether living or dead, were replaced by lush, well-kept cemeteries like Mount Auburn in Cambridge, Massachusetts, and Woodlawn in New York City. By the 1830s, the rural cemetery movement had begun in America, and resplendent monuments were erected to honor the dead in perpetuity. In these parklike settings, the bereaved could come to commune in memory with the deceased.[47]

DIED,

On the 23d instant, Mrs. HARRIET R. DAI-
LEY, aged 44 years
    The friends of the family are respectfully invited
to attend her funeral, to-morrow, at 3 o'clock, from
the residence of her husband, corner Seventh and
F sts., south.

On the morning of the 24th instant, WILLIAM,
aged 4 years and 10 days, youngest child of M. H.
and Susan B. Stevens
    His funeral will take place from No. 48 Missouri
avenue, to-morrow (Friday) at 2 o'clock. The
relatives and friends of the family are respectfully
invited to attend, without further notice.

On the morning of the 24th instant, at 4½ o'clock,
after a brief but painful illness of pneumonia,
which she patiently bore as only an humble believer in Him of Calvary can bear. and in the peaceful hope of an eternal life to come, surrounded by
the family circle, ELIZABETH LARCOMBE,
wife of John Larcombe, Sr., aged 61 years and 7
months.
    The relatives and friends of the deceased are cor-
dially invited to attend her funeral, from her late
residence, on Virginia avenue, below 6th st., to-
morrow (Friday) afternoon, at 3 o'clock, without
further notice.

On the 23d instant, at 5 o'clock, of chronic croup,
JOSEPH WM ARTHUR, aged 2 years and 5
months, eldest child of Richard and Rachel Gorm-
ley.
    The friends of the family are invited to attend
the funeral, from the residence of the parents, on
Third st. east, between D and E sts. south, at 2
o'clock to-morrow evening.

Figure 2-6
*Newspaper Death Notice
from the 1860s*

Invisible Death

Beginning around the turn of the twentieth century, the Romantic attitude
toward death waned. It was replaced by what Ariès and others have characterized
as "invisible death," an attitude corresponding to the lack of firsthand familiarity
with death that characterizes people living in modern societies. Care of the dying
and the dead gradually was delegated to professionals, and death was no longer a
familiar element of life. Care of the dying came to be dominated by efforts to delay
death by all means available.

In recent times, the *meaning* of death is hardly considered at all. Especially
in technological societies, death is generally thought to be synonymous with
extinction. Some despair about the meaning and value of life itself. Herman Feifel
writes: "In the Middle Ages man had his eschatology and the sacred time of
eternity. More recently, temporal man lived with the prospect of personal immortality transformed into concern for historical immortality and for the welfare of
posterity. Today we are vouchsafed neither."[48]

It might be argued that the foregoing portrait of a time when people died
more serenely than people do today is drawn too much in black and white. Were
there not as many reasons to fear death in the past, especially during the recurring
epidemics of plague, as we have today with the threats of nuclear catastrophe and
environmental pollution? Was religion necessarily a comfort for the dying, given
that the terrors of hell as well as the joys of heaven were likely to be among the

images envisioned by a dying person? And what about the physical agony of dying? Today we have access to modern medical techniques for alleviating pain.

Although the foregoing historical portrait may indeed be drawn in broad strokes, it is nevertheless generally agreed that dying persons of earlier times had access to a source of comfort that is comparatively lacking in modern health care institutions: the familiar presence of other people. Fulfillment, as Norbert Elias wrote, is closely tied to "the meaning one has attained in the course of one's life for other people."[49]

Even when a person has reached his or her goals in life and feels a sense of completion, the act of dying may be painful and difficult if it is felt to be a meaningless end. Caregivers may alleviate pain and attend to physical comfort, but this effort may be perceived as mechanical and impersonal. Family members, in an unaccustomed situation and unfamiliar setting, may be at a loss as to what to say or do.

Thus, in tracing the evolution of attitudes toward death in Western culture, the most significant change may involve the dying person's sense of his or her meaning for others. Today, feeling that he or she has scarcely any significance for other people, the dying person may feel truly alone.

The advent of the hospice movement and other forms of palliative, or comfort-oriented, care has undoubtedly mitigated some of the harsher aspects of the "invisible death" scenario, at least for those with access to such care. Even though the taboo against discussing death has been somewhat lessened in the recent past, the effect may be only to replace "invisible death" with "objectified or alienated death." Despite a veritable flood of conferences, studies, books, courses, and other forums dedicated to humanizing care of the dying and instituting greater openness regarding death, observers like Ian Gentles question whether this "habit of talking incessantly about death" has not led to "the suppression of authentic emotion about the subject?"[50] According to Gentles, the problem lies partly in the fact that "death, which was once a public and corporate experience, has become increasingly private." This change is due partly to such factors as demographic change and population mobility, as well as to the increasingly secular nature of modern technological societies. Charles O. Jackson says: "Because the dead world is largely understood as irrelevant to our lives, death tends to become without significance and absurd," and, "because we have this perspective on the end of life, it becomes difficult to avoid the same view on all of life."[51]

In every age, dying and death have been confronted with the aid of various cultural support systems. Now, however, the ritual dimensions of dying have largely been replaced by a technological process in which death occurs, as Ariès says, "by a series of little steps," making it difficult to discern the moment of "real death." He adds: "All these little silent deaths have replaced and erased the great dramatic act of death, and no one any longer has the strength or patience to wait over a period of weeks for a moment which has lost a part of its meaning."

The cultures surveyed in this chapter exemplify the sense of community and shared experience that have traditionally shaped people's beliefs and behaviors relative to dying and death. Some would argue, as Gentles does, that "the ability to deal with one's own death, and to find consolation following the death of a loved one, flows most naturally out of a living faith." Absent such faith, or living in a secular environment, what can be done to infuse modern-day customs with a sense of community, a sense of shared values, that allows room for death?

"Man," says Gentles, "is a ceremonial animal, and it has been the experience of all cultures that ceremony has the power to ennoble and glorify." He suggests that the following customs may help to restore a greater sense of community relative to death:

1. *Feasting*. English accounts of the seventeenth century show that food was the most costly single item in a funeral budget, and, Gentles says, "The sharing of food and drink between people has always had great psychological significance."

2. *Exchanging of gifts*. In earlier times, such items as ribbons, lace, gloves, clothing, and mourning rings were commonly distributed among mourners— to the young especially. Gentles notes that, besides serving as a concrete and visible affirmation of the community of mourners, this custom "also performed the function of reducing children's fear of dying by linking funerals in their minds with the happy experience of receiving gifts."

3. *Presence of children at funerals*. Of this custom, Gentles says that it demonstrated that "the community was united in observing the passing of one of its members, and it showed that the species would continue despite the loss of a valued person. Life was reaffirmed in the face of death."

This emphasis on the central role of children seems quite a contrast to what commonly occurs today. Perhaps the question most frequently heard in connection with modern-day funerals is: "Should the children be allowed to attend?" Most people seem to be more prone to exclude children from situations involving death than to make a special place for them. Yet, as Gentles points out, children are indeed members of the total community and represent its future.

As is true of any culture, it is through the various processes of socialization— including the customs associated with funerals—that children learn about the concepts and conventions that have currency in a particular society. Thus, the customs that are followed in connection with a community's dead or dying communicate the attitudes, values, and behaviors that are associated with death. We explore these processes of socialization in the next chapter.

Further Readings

Maurice Bloch and Jonathan Perry, eds. *Death and the Regeneration of Life*. New York: Cambridge University Press, 1982.

Peter Brown. *The Cult of the Saints: Its Rise and Function in Latin Christianity*. Chicago: University of Chicago Press, 1981.

Joseph Campbell. *Historical Atlas of World Mythology*. 5 vols. New York: Harper and Row, 1988, 1989.

James Stevens Curl. *A Celebration of Death*. New York: Charles Scribner's Sons, 1980.

Loring M. Danforth. *The Death Rituals of Rural Greece*. Princeton, N.J.: Princeton University Press, 1982.

Elisabeth Darby and Nicola Smith. *The Cult of the Prince Consort*. New Haven, Conn.: Yale University Press, 1983.

Richard A. Etlin. *The Architecture of Death: The Transformation of the Cemetery in Eighteenth-Century Paris*. Cambridge, Mass.: MIT Press, 1984.

Robert S. Gottfried. *The Black Death: Natural and Human Disaster in Medieval Europe*. New York: The Free Press, 1983.

Richard Huntington and Peter Metcalf. *Celebrations of Death: The Anthropology of Mortuary Ritual*. New York: Cambridge University Press, 1979.

John S. Mbiti. *African Religions and Philosophy*. Garden City, N.Y.: Anchor Press/ Doubleday, 1970.

Paul Radin. *The Road of Life and Death: A Ritual Drama of the American Indians*. Princeton, N.J.: Princeton University Press, 1973.

The "Endings" exhibit at the Boston Children's Museum, with its range of activities for learning about various aspects of death, offers an innovative means of sharing attitudes about death in our culture.

Socialization:
How We Learn About
Death as Children

*I*magine yourself as a child. Someone says, "Everybody's going to zittze one of these days. It happens to all of us. You, too, will zittze." Or, one day as you're playing, you are told, "Don't touch that, it's zittzed!" Being an observant child, you might notice that when a person zittzes, other people cry and appear to be sad. Over time, as you put together all your experiences of "zittzing," you begin to develop some personal feelings and thoughts about what it means to zittze.

The understanding of death evolves in much this way. As a child grows older, incorporating a variety of experiences related to death, his or her concepts and emotional responses to death begin to resemble those of adults in the child's culture. Like other aspects of children's development, the understanding of death gradually evolves during the years of childhood. Just as a child's understanding of "money" changes over time—at first it is a matter of little or no concern; later it seems to come into the child's experience almost magically; and finally, it engages the child's attention and participation in many different ways—so, too, does the child develop new understandings about the meaning of death.

The child's responses change over time through the interplay between experiences and the level of maturity that he or she brings to understanding them. Or, put another way, the child's understanding of death usually fits with his or her model of the world at each stage of development. Thus, an adult could give a young child a lengthy, detailed explanation of the concept of

Death has a different emotional meaning to young children. In the game of Cowboys and Indians death is not final; the game must continue. The common threat when angered may be, "I'll kill you." One can readily see that the concept of killing is not viewed as final and that there is no association of pain with killing. Perhaps the following example will best prove the point. Upon arriving home from a business trip, a young child's father brought her a gun and holster set. After buckling on her new present she took out the gun, pointed it at her father and said, "Bang, bang, you're dead! I killed you." Her father replied, "Don't hurt me." His daughter's innocent answer was, "Oh, Daddy, I won't hurt you, I just killed you." To many children death is seen only as something in the distant future; "only old people die."

Dan Leviton and Eileen C. Forman,
"Death Education for Children and Youth"

death as adults understand it, yet the child will grasp its components only when he or she is developmentally ready to understand. However, a child's cognitive and emotional readiness to understand is not simply a matter of age: Experience plays an important role. A child who has had firsthand encounters with death may arrive at an understanding of death beyond that which is characteristic of children in the same age group.

What a child understands about death reflects a process of continuous adjustment and refinement as new experiences cause a reexamination of his or her values and responses. This process is often quite rapid; a child's understanding of death can change dramatically in a very brief time. The progression of a child's understanding about death can be placed in a framework that gives the adult observer an orderly picture of the relevant processes. By observing and questioning to gather information, and then analyzing the data, researchers can discern certain characteristic patterns of childhood development. (You have probably done this yourself by observing the changes that occur in children with whom you have frequent contact. For example, the kinds of play activities that engross a child change over time; the toys that elicited great excitement at one age become uninteresting at a later time.) By such observations of children's behaviors, developmental psychologists and theorists devise models to describe the characteristic concerns and interests of children at various ages. These models are like maps that describe the major features of the territory of childhood at different stages of development. These models can be very useful for describing the characteristics of a typical child at, say, age two or age seven. They give a general picture of each particular stage of development. But the map should not be mistaken for the territory.

Like maps, models of childhood development are abstractions, representations, interpretations of the actual territory (see Figure 3-1). Such maps can be useful for guiding one's way, for locating certain landmarks, and for sharing knowledge with others. But the particular features of the landscape will always

Freud: The Psychosexual Model

Oral   Anal   Phallic   Latency   Genital

Erikson: The Psychosocial Model

Trust Autonomy Initiative   Industry   Identity

Piaget: The Cognitive Development Model

Sensori- Preoperational   Concrete   Formal operational
motor   operational

B 1 2 3 4 5 6 7 8 9 10 11 12 13 14 15 16 17 18 19 20

Infant-toddler-preschool   School age   Adolescence

Figure *3-1*   *Comparison of Major Developmental Models, or Theories, Concerning Childhood Phases of Development*

possess a uniqueness that cannot be fully described by a map. Children vary widely in individual rates of development—not only physically but also emotionally and cognitively, or intellectually. Thus, with respect to a child's understanding of death, as with other human traits, developmental levels do not correspond neatly to chronological age.

Components of a Mature Concept of Death

Whatever our beliefs about death or what it is like to die or what happens afterward, the known facts can be easily summarized: Death is inevitable and happens to one and all. Death is final; physical death spells the end of our known existence. A formal statement of these empirical, or observable, facts includes five components. These are the understanding that:

1. Death involves the *cessation* of all physiological functioning, or signs of life.
2. Death is biologically *inevitable*.
3. Death is *irreversible*; organisms are unable to return to life after death.
4. Death involves *causality*; there are biological reasons for the occurrence of death.
5. Death is *universal*; it eventually comes to every living organism.

Recognition of these facts constitutes possession of a complete or mature concept of death, although other, nonempirical ideas about death may be associated with an understanding of these observable facts.

I was astonished to hear a highly intelligent boy of ten remark after the sudden death of his father: 'I know father's dead, but what I can't understand is why he doesn't come home to supper.'

Sigmund Freud, *The Interpretation of Dreams*

Such nonempirical issues, for adults as well as for children, are: What happens after someone dies? Does the self or soul continue to exist after the death of the body? What is the meaning of death? Such questions impinge on our understanding of death. Children also deal with these questions in various ways as they develop their own concepts and feelings about death.

In addition, what a person "knows" about death may differ from time to time, according to circumstances. Even as adults, we may discover that we harbor conflicting notions about death, especially our own. Under certain conditions, a hard-nosed acceptance of the facts may give way to a more childlike attitude that presumes an ability to bargain where death is concerned. For example, a patient told by a doctor that he or she has only six months to live may imagine that by some kind of "magical" act, some bargain with the universe, the death sentence can be staved off. A child's understanding of death may also fluctuate among different ways of "knowing" as he or she develops a personal framework in which to place it.

Early Childhood Encounters with Death

When does a child first become aware of death? By the time children are four or five, death-related thoughts and experiences are usually evident in their songs, their play, and their questions. Although the awareness of death among younger children is not so readily observed (and, of course, is manifested differently from that of older children), researchers like Adah Maurer suggest that such experiences begin quite early.[1] The infant's experience of the difference between sleep and wakefulness may involve a perception of the distinction between being and nonbeing, and Maurer believes that children begin to experiment with this difference at a very early age. The "peekaboo" game, for instance, may represent the polarities of being and nonbeing. The infant's experience of having a cloth thrown over her face, shutting out sensory awareness of the environment, is analogous to death. The "boo," when the cloth is removed, is like being alive again. Thus, death may be experienced in games of this kind as separation, disappearance, and return.

The child's earliest encounter with death usually comes with the ability to distinguish between the animate and the inanimate. The child perceives whether or not something has life. The following story illustrates how this may occur in quite ordinary circumstances. An eighteen-month-old boy was out for a walk

Summaries of Early Studies of Children's Concepts of Death

Paul Schilder and David Wechsler (1934): Schilder and Wechsler listed general statements about children's attitudes toward death:

1. Children deal with death in an utterly matter-of-fact and realistic way.
2. Children exhibit skepticism concerning the unobservables.
3. Children often accept conventional definitions.
4. Children often remain insensitive to contradictions between convention and observation.
5. Children exhibit naivete in solving problems.
6. Children regard death as deprivation.
7. Children believe the devil punishes orally by withdrawing food or by devouring the dead.
8. Children do not believe in their own death.
9. To very young children, death seems reversible.
10. Children believe death may result from disease.
11. Children have a tendency toward undue generalization of limited knowledge.
12. Children believe in death from overeating, violence, and acts of God.
13. Fear of death is rare.
14. Children often fail to understand the meaning of death, but base their attitudes on the actions of adults.
15. Children may exhibit suicidal ideas.
16. Children are always ready to believe in the deaths of others.
17. Children are ready to kill.
18. The tendency to kill may come only in play.
19. The degree of preoccupation of children with violence and death can be seen by the way in which they react to ghost pictures.
20. God appears as a stage magician, controlling ghosts and death, etc.
21. Appearance and reality are not sharply differentiated.
22. Children exhibit the urge to pass moral judgments on every person and picture.
23. Children's professed morality is utilitarian, since children fear punishment.
24. Religious morality enters relatively rarely into children's attitudes toward death.

Sylvia Anthony (1940): Before the age of two years, the child has no understanding of death. After age two, most children think often of death. The idea of death seems to take much of its emotional component from its links with birth anxiety and aggressive impulses. Magical thinking pervades much of the child's thoughts about death (i.e., belief that events happen in a certain way because he or she thinks about them happening in a certain way; for example, angry thoughts directed toward someone who subsequently dies makes the child feel himself or herself to be a murderer). As a result, guilt is one of the child's reactions to death.

Maria H. Nagy (1948): Nagy identified three major developmental stages among children three to ten years of age.

Stage 1 (3–5 years): Death is understood as separation, a state of being less alive, a departure or disappearance (i.e., the dead go away and continue to "live" on under

continued

continued from previous page

changed circumstances). The child does not yet recognize that death involves complete cessation of life; nor is the finality (irreversibility) of death comprehended.

Stage 2 (5–9 years): Death now understood as final. However, still present is the notion that one might be able to elude death; the inevitability (all die) and personal reference (I die) components are not yet established. Belief that one might be able to outwit or outluck the "Death Man."

Stage 3 (9 or 10 years and older): Death recognized as final and inevitable.

Irving E. Alexander and Arthur M. Alderstein (1958): Death has a greater emotional significance for children with less stable ego self-concepts than for children with adequate self-concepts. The ages five to eight and the period of adolescence are times of great emotional upheaval and changing demands of growth, which are likely to put existing self-images to a severe test. As a result, the concept of nonbeing (death) may be more threatening during these periods of development.

Sources: Paul Schilder and David Wechsler, "The Attitudes of Children Toward Death," *Journal of Genetic Psychology* 45 (1934): 406–451; Sylvia Anthony, *The Discovery of Death in Childhood and After* (New York: Basic Books, 1940, 1972); Maria H. Nagy, "The Child's View of Death," *Journal of Genetic Psychology* 73 (1948): 3–27; Irving E. Alexander and Arthur M. Alderstein, "Affective Responses to the Concept of Death in a Population of Children and Early Adolescents," *Journal of Genetic Psychology* 93 (1958): 167–177.

with his father when the father inadvertently stepped on a caterpillar. The child kneeled down, looked at the dead caterpillar lying on the sidewalk, and said, "No more!" That is the typical genesis of a child's awareness of death: *No more*.

It should be recognized that similar experiences may produce quite different responses in different children. Encountering a dead caterpillar or dead bird may set off a reaction in one child that lasts for several days, during which time the child is eager to find some answers. Another child may seem to pay such an encounter little heed, apparently without a moment's reflection about an event that the first child found provocative and mysterious.

Some theorists believe that much of the behavior shown by infants and very young children is *protothanatic* — that is, preparation for concepts about life and death that will eventually emerge in the child's later interactions with the environment. To what degree such early experiences influence the child's later concepts about death is not clear. However, there is greater certainty that children do exhibit some awareness of death quite early.

Psychoanalytic theory suggests that our earliest experiences of separation and loss mark the beginning of death-related anxieties that continue throughout life.[2] According to this view, the infant's lack of physical and psychological resources of self-care leads to anxiety, which is mitigated by the parent's nurture and care.

A central feature of an infant's existence is helplessness. From the infant's perspective, care takes place because of his or her own control over the environment. The infant's cries result in some action on the parent's part to relieve the child's discomfort. Diapers are changed; the child is fed. It's as if imagining or thinking about the breast causes it to appear. The symbiotic union with the parent is so complete that there seems to be no separation between the child's subjective and objective realities.

Inevitably, however, there will be times when the infant's attempt to satisfy needs meets with frustration. Over time, the infant gradually perceives that the parent is a separate entity; the child is alone, a separate self. This perception is the beginning of a kind of love-hate relationship with the parent — who both satisfies and frustrates the striving to have needs met. If mother arrives at the crib for feeding because she has been wished there, then angry thoughts may lead to her disappearance as well. This kind of magical thinking, which operates on the premise that wishing something can make it a reality, equates separation or disappearance with nonbeing or "death."

The process of individuation, of arriving at a separate self-identity, occurs most notably within the context of the intimate bonding between an infant and parent, and anxiety is likely to be especially acute at the major turning points in a child's development — such as weaning, toilet training, beginning school, or the birth of siblings.

The fears associated with the separation-individuation process during infancy and early childhood may appear in an altered context during adolescence. Just as the infant comes to perceive separation from parents, so too the adolescent strives to come to terms with that separateness on a much broader scale. Since the adolescent's developmental tasks with regard to forging an individual identity are conceptually quite different from the younger child's, the anxieties aroused by death also differ.

Death-Experienced Children, Ages One to Three

It used to be assumed that children between the ages of one and three are simply too young to know anything about death. Because of this assumption, and because obtaining data for research on very young children requires greater effort, most research has been conducted with children older than four years. However, a study conducted by Mark Speece to investigate the impact of death experiences on children ages one to three suggests that very young children do indeed try to come to terms with death-related experiences.[3] Speece says, "It seems safe to conclude that death experiences occur in the lives of a sizable proportion of children of this age and that those children who do have such experiences attempt to deal with and integrate their specific death experiences into their understanding of the world in general."

Speece found that slightly over half of the children he studied had some experience with death: in some cases, a human death (for example, a grandmother, a cousin, a neighbor); in others, a nonhuman death, such as that of a pet (most often birds, dogs, and fish). Speece found that these young children responded to death in observable ways. For example, some actively looked for the deceased pet or person. That these children were trying to come to terms with the experience of death was indicated by their questions about the immobility of the deceased and what happens after death, and by their expression of concerns for the welfare of the living. Children may also display emotions in response to death, including anger. One child became angry when a pet bird that had died would not come back to life. Thus, the idea that very young children do not experience a meaningful response to the deaths occurring in their environment is falling away as new evidence reveals this notion to be a fallacy.

The Very Young Child and Death: An Example

So, how does one answer the question, "When does the understanding of death begin, and what governs its development?" The dialogue between a twenty-seven-month-old child and his psychologist father provides an illuminating and suggestive case study.[4] (Note how the father's professional skills in listening and his sensitivity to his child's behavior helped him engage in this kind of conversation.)

For two months the child had been waking several times each night and screaming hysterically for a bottle of sugar water. The father describes getting up one night, for the second or third time, and deciding with his wife to use firmness in refusing to meet the child's demand. He went into his son's room and told him that he was too old to have a bottle and would have to go back to sleep without it. The father, his mind made up that enough was enough, started to leave the room.

But then he heard a frightened cry, one of desperation that sounded like the fear of death. Wondering what could be causing the child such alarm, the father turned back into the room, took his son out of the crib, and asked, "What will happen if you don't get your bottle?" The child, no longer hysterical, but very tearful and sniffling, said, "I can't make contact!" The father asked, "What does that mean, 'you can't make contact'?" His son replied, "If I run out of gas, I can't make contact — my engine won't go. You know!"

The father then remembered several family excursions during the previous summer, when vehicles had run out of gas. "What are you afraid will happen if you run out of gas?" Still crying, the child replied, "My motor won't run and then I'll die." At that point, the father recalled another incident his son had witnessed. Some time earlier, when they were selling an old car, the prospective buyer had tried to start the engine, but the battery was dead and the engine wouldn't turn over. The child had heard remarks like, "It's probably *not making contact*," "the *motor died*," and "I guess *the battery's dead*."

With this incident in mind, the father asked, "Are you afraid that your bottle is like gasoline and, just like when the car runs out of gas, the car dies, so, if you run out of food, you'll die?" The child nodded his head, "Yes." The father explained, "Well, that's not the same thing at all. You see, when you eat food, your body stores up energy so that you have enough to last you all night. You eat three times a day; we only fill up the car with gas once a week. When the car runs out of gas, it doesn't have any saved up for an emergency. But with people it isn't anything like that at all. You can go maybe two or three days without eating. And, even if you got hungry, you still wouldn't die. People aren't anything like cars."

Edward C. Clark, UPI/Bettman Newsphotos

Children who experience the death of someone close may look to adults for models of appropriate behavior. Amidst the regalia of high military and political office that characterized the funeral of President John F. Kennedy, young John F. Kennedy, Jr., salutes the flag-draped coffin containing his father's body as it is transported from St. Matthew's Cathedral to Arlington National Cemetery. The day also marked John-John's third birthday.

This explanation seemed to do little toward alleviating the child's anxiety, so the father tried a different tack. "You're worried that you have a motor, just like a car, right?" The child nodded, "Yes." "So," continued the father, "you're worried that if you run out of gas or run out of food you'll die, just like the motor of a car, right?" Again, the child nodded yes. "Ah, but the car has a key right? We can turn it on and off anytime we want, right?"

Now the child's body began to relax. "But where is your key?" The father poked around the boy's belly button: "Is this your key?" The child laughed. "Can I turn your motor off and on? See, you're really nothing like a car at all. Nobody can turn you on and off. Once your motor is on, you don't have to worry about it dying. You can sleep through the whole night and your motor will keep running without you ever having to fill it up with gas. Do you know what I mean?" The child said, "Yes."

"Okay. Now you can sleep without worrying. When you wake in the morning, your motor will still be running. Okay?" Never again did the child wake up in the middle of the night asking for a bottle of warm sugar water.

Think of the impressive reasoning that goes on in a child's mind—the way he or she strings together concepts. In this case, the father speculates that two experiences contributed to his child's understanding: First, the child had decided that sugar water would give him gas because he had overheard his parents saying that a younger sibling had "gas" from drinking sugar water; second, when the child's parakeet died, his question "What happened to it?" was answered by his father: "Every animal has a motor inside that keeps it going. When a thing dies, it is like when a motor stops running. Its motor just won't run anymore."

Thus, a child strings together concepts about death until eventually a coherent understanding of it develops. Although there is still some uncertainty about when infants begin to develop concepts about death, the description of this twenty-seven-month-old's complex associations of language and death demonstrates that children are capable of formulating some kind of understanding about death very early in life.

Developmental Studies of the Child's Understanding of Death

Children first conceive of death as partial, reversible, and avoidable. As their understanding matures, they eventually arrive at a concept of death as final and inevitable. Until recently, although important studies had been done on the general parameters of child development, few focused on how children learn about death. As some of the blanks are being filled in by current research, the picture provided by earlier researchers is being refined.[5]

From early studies, undertaken in the 1930s and 1940s, it was generally concluded that children had little or no awareness of death before the age of three or four. Early theoretical models proposed a series of stages with fixed corresponding ages within which particular kinds of behaviors and conceptual developments occurred. Current research, however, demonstrates that *sequence* is more reliable in describing how children learn about death than correlating stages of

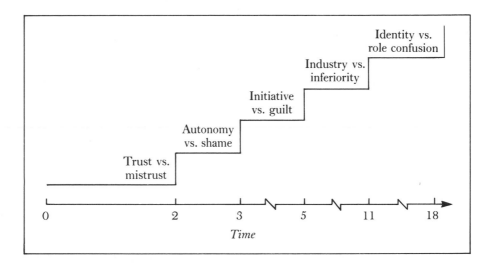

Figure 3-2   *Five Stages of Preadult Psychosocial Development Proposed by Erikson*
Source: Based on Erik H. Erikson, *Childhood and Society* (New York: Norton, 1964), pp.
247–274.

understanding to age. In addition, until recently it was generally thought that the
cognitive resources to conceive of death as final and inevitable were acquired at
around the age of nine. Despite deemphasizing a correlation between age and
stage, current research nevertheless places this occurrence between the ages of
five and seven for most children.[6]

In tracing the development of the death concept in children, it is useful to
have a theoretical framework within which to place the distinctive attitudes and
behaviors that pertain to various phases of childhood. We will use two theories of
development — namely, those devised by Erik Erikson and Jean Piaget — in the
discussion that follows.

The model of human development devised by the psychologist Erik Erikson
focuses on the *stages of psychosocial development*, or psychosocial milestones, that
occur successively throughout a person's life (see Figure 3-2).[7] In this chapter,
only the stages of childhood will be discussed. In Erikson's model, psychosocial
development depends significantly on the environment and is linked to the individual's *relationships* with others. Each stage of development involves a turning
point, or crisis, that requires a response from the individual.

Applying Erikson's model, we find that, depending on an individual's psychosocial stage, certain aspects of death are likely to be more important than
others. For instance, to an infant, the sudden loss of a parent may be a major blow
to the child's development of *trust* in the environment. The preschooler's fantasies
of a parent's death may be accompanied by feelings of *guilt*. The adolescent's
experience of a close friend's death may trigger *anxieties* concerning whether
death could thwart the realization of his or her own goals and dreams as well.

TABLE 3-1   *Piaget's Model of Cognitive Development*

Age (approximate)	Developmental Period	Characteristics
Birth-2 years	Sensorimotor	Focused on senses and motor abilities; learns object exists even when not observable (object permanence) and begins to remember and imagine ideas and experiences (mental representation).
2-7 years	Preoperational	Development of symbolic thinking and language to understand the world. (2-4 years) *Preconceptual subperiod:* sense of magical omnipotence; self as center of world; ego-centric thought; all natural objects have feelings and intention (will). (4-6 years) *Prelogical subperiod:* beginning problem solving; seeing is believing; trial and error; understanding of other points of view; more socialized speech; gradual decentering of self and discovery of correct relationships.
7-12 years	Concrete operational	Applies logical abilities to understanding concrete ideas; organizes and classifies information; manipulates ideas and experiences symbolically; able to think backwards and forwards; notion of reversibility; can think logically about things experienced.
12 + years	Formal operational	Reasons logically about abstract ideas and experiences; can think hypothetically about things never experienced; deductive and inductive reasoning; complexity of knowledge; many answers to questions; interest in ethics, politics, social sciences.

Thus, as we consider the various periods of childhood development, Erikson's model can help to supply insight into what kinds of issues children may pay particular attention to at different times in their lives.

Jean Piaget is generally considered to have been the world's foremost child psychologist, a profound theorist as well as an astute observer of children's behavior. Piaget's focus was on the *cognitive transformations* that occur during childhood (see Table 3-1).[8] In his view, an individual's mode of understanding the world changes significantly, in sequential stages, from infancy into adulthood. According to Piaget, four different periods of cognitive, or intellectual, development can be distinguished, based on the characteristic ways in which children organize their experience of the world: *sensorimotor, preoperational, concrete operational*, and *formal operational*.

The rate of cognitive development for each child is unique, but all children move through these periods in the same order. Thus, Piaget's theory also emphasizes *sequence*, not a direct age-stage correlation. Although particular cognitive abilities tend to fall within a specific age range, these abilities develop earlier in some children and later in others. When statements about age are made in discussing children's development, therefore, they should be understood as approximations, not as norms.

Infancy and Toddlerhood

According to the psychosocial model devised by Erikson, infancy is characterized by the individual's development of an adequate sense of *trust* concerning the environment. If the infant's needs are not adequately met, the result may be distrust. Thus, other persons in the infant's environment — typically, his or her parents — play an important part in the child's psychosocial development.

During Erikson's second stage, toddlerhood (roughly between one to three years of age), the child begins to grapple with the issues of *autonomy* versus shame and doubt. As the toddler explores the environment, developing greater independence, there is sometimes a clash between what the child wants to do and what others want the child to do. Toilet training typically occurs during this time, and it may become a focal point of conflicts involving greater autonomy. In both physical and psychosocial development, this is a period of "letting go" and "holding on."

Turning our attention to Piaget's cognitive model, we find that the first two years of life are characterized as the *sensorimotor* period. During this period, the child begins to develop and strengthen sensory and motor abilities, becoming acquainted with the body and learning about the environment. Since the child has not yet acquired the ability to name objects by using language, this is not considered to be a period of conceptual development. A parent who leaves the room has simply vanished from the scene; there is no thought "My parent is in the other room." Piaget says, "As long as there is no subject, that is, as long as the child does not recognize itself as the origin of its own actions, it also does not recognize the permanency of objects other than itself."[9]

As the child experiences the changing flow of events in the environment, he or she gradually begins to perceive certain patterns that become generalized into what Piaget terms *schemes*. These schemes tie together the common features of actions that occur at different times. During this stage of development, Piaget says, "a Copernican revolution takes place," with the result that "at the end of this sensory-motor evolution, there are permanent objects, constituting a universe within which the child's own body exists also."

Early Childhood

During the years of preschool and kindergarten, roughly between the ages of three to five years, Erikson's model postulates that the child's psychosocial development involves issues of *initiative* versus guilt. The child increasingly desires to find his or her own purpose and direction, yet is also concerned about how parents (or other adults) may perceive these tentative efforts to express initiative and individuality. Thus, the overwhelmingly egocentric orientation of the infant gives way to the more socially integrated self of the older child, which assumes its

I saw death. At the age of five: it was watching me; in the evenings, it prowled on the balcony: it pressed its nose to the window; I used to see it but I did not dare to say anything. Once, on the Quai Voltaire, we met it: it was a tall, mad old woman, dressed in black, who mumbled as she went by: "I shall put that child in my pocket." Another time, it took the form of a hole: this was at Arcachon; [we] were visiting Madame Dupont and her son Gabriel, the composer. I was playing in the garden of the villa, scared because I had been told that Gabriel was ill and was going to die. I was playing at horses, half-heartedly, and galloping round the house. Suddenly, I noticed a gloomy hole: the cellar, which had been opened; an indescribable impression of loneliness and horror blinded me: I turned round and, singing at the top of my voice, I fled. At that time, I had an assignation with it every night in my bed. It was a ritual: I had to sleep on my left side, my face to the wall; I would wait, trembling all over, and it would appear, a very conventional skeleton, with a scythe; I then had permission to turn on my right side, it would go away and I could sleep in peace.

Jean-Paul Sartre, *Words*

place as one among many. Making this transition, however, may involve situations that induce feelings of guilt. For instance, a child who has fantasies of doing away with a parent—expressed perhaps by the frustrated scream, "I wish you were dead!"—may feel guilt about having such thoughts. Again, how others respond to this conflict plays an important part in determining whether the crisis is resolved positively for the child's development. This period marks the beginning of the child's moral sense, the ability to function effectively within socially sanctioned modes of behavior.

One of the fears that may surface during this period is that of bodily mutilation. Children at this age are racing around on tricycles or big wheels, learning to cut small pieces of paper very precisely, making their muscles work for them, gaining greater control over their bodies. The body becomes very important to the child's self-image.

This preoccupation with the body can be illustrated: A five-year-old witnessed the death of his younger brother, who was killed when the wheel of a truck rolled over his head. The parents, who were considering having a wake in their home, asked their surviving son how he might feel if his younger brother's body was brought into the house for a wake. This five-year-old's question was, "Does he look hurt?" This child's concern about bodily disfigurement, which in this instance was directed toward the appearance of another's body, is characteristic of this stage of psychosocial development (see Figure 3-3).

In the developmental model proposed by Piaget, these years of early childhood are characterized as the *preoperational* period. The child's mental development centers on learning to use language and symbols to represent objects. Vocabulary develops at an astounding rate as the child becomes interested in naming everything is sight. During the preoperational period, the child's pri-

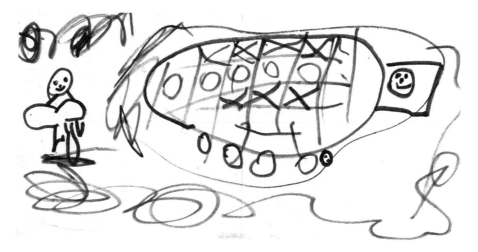

Figure 3-3   *Accident Drawing by a Five-Year-Old*
In this drawing by a five-year-old who witnessed his younger brother's accidental
death, the surviving child is depicted as riding a "big wheel" on the left side of
the truck that ran over his brother. The four wheels of the truck are shown, and
the younger brother's head is drawn next to the wheel farthest to the right. This
drawing is similar to one drawn by the child on the night of the fatal accident
when he told his parents, "I can't sleep because I can't get the pictures out of my
head." The act of externalizing these disturbing images by making a drawing had
therapeutic value for this child in coming to terms with the traumatic experience
of his sibling's death.

mary developmental task is to explore and appraise his or her situation in the
world. Frequently, this entails an intense questioning about nearly everything in
the child's environment. Whereas during the earlier sensorimotor period the
child perceives the subjective and objective worlds as more or less fused into a
single reality, now the child seeks causes and explanations.

How does Piaget's model of cognitive development apply to children's concepts of death? A partial answer is supplied by a study conducted by Gerald
Koocher.[10] After the children were tested to determine which of Piaget's periods
each fitted into, each child was asked four questions about death. You might want
to answer each of these questions for yourself.

The first question asked was, "What makes things die?" Children in the
preoperational stage made use of fantasy reasoning, magical thinking, and realistic causes of death, expressed in some cases in egocentric terms. Here are some
sample responses:

- *Nancy:* "When they eat bad things, like if you went with a stranger and they
  gave you a candy bar with poison on it. [*The researcher asks, "Anything
  else?"*] Yes, you can die if you swallow a dirty bug."

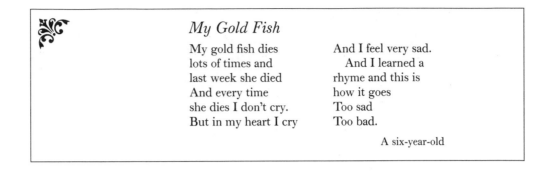

My Gold Fish

My gold fish dies   And I feel very sad.
lots of times and   And I learned a
last week she died   rhyme and this is
And every time   how it goes
she dies I don't cry.   Too sad
But in my heart I cry   Too bad.

A six-year-old

- *Carol:* "They eat poison and stuff, pills. You'd better wait until your Mom gives them to you." [*Anything else?*] "Drinking poison water and stuff like going swimming alone."
- *David:* "A bird might get real sick and die if you catch it. [*Anything else?*] They could eat the wrong foods like aluminum foil. That's all I can think of."

Koocher's findings were corroborated in a study done by Helen Swain that described some general traits of the preoperational child.[11] When the concept of finality was investigated, most of the children in Swain's study expressed the notion that death was reversible. They attributed the return of life to the good effects of ambulances, hospitals, or doctors, whose participation is often summoned magically, as if a dead person could ring up the hospital and say, "Will you send me an ambulance over here? I'm dead and I need you to fix me up."

About two-thirds of Swain's study group said that death is unlikely or avoidable, or is brought on only by unusual events such as an accident or catastrophe. About one-third expressed disbelief that death could happen to them or to their families. Nearly half were uncertain whether they would ever die or else thought they would die only in the remote future.

The Middle Years of Childhood

In Erikson's model, the years from about six to eleven generally correspond to the stage of *industry* versus inferiority. This is typically a time when the child is busy in school, interacting with peers in a variety of ways. As the child's efforts begin to gain recognition and bring satisfaction, the child may develop anxieties about those areas in which he or she senses a failure to measure up. Overcoming these feelings of inadequacy or inferiority becomes the major task of this psychosocial stage. As in all of the psychosocial stages, encouragement from others is crucial to the child's well-being.

In Piaget's framework, this period is denoted by the term *concrete operations*. At this stage, the child begins to use logic to solve problems and to think logically about things without having to have their relationships demonstrated directly. The ability to do arithmetic, for instance, requires the recognition that numbers are symbols for quantities. The child is able to manipulate such concepts in a

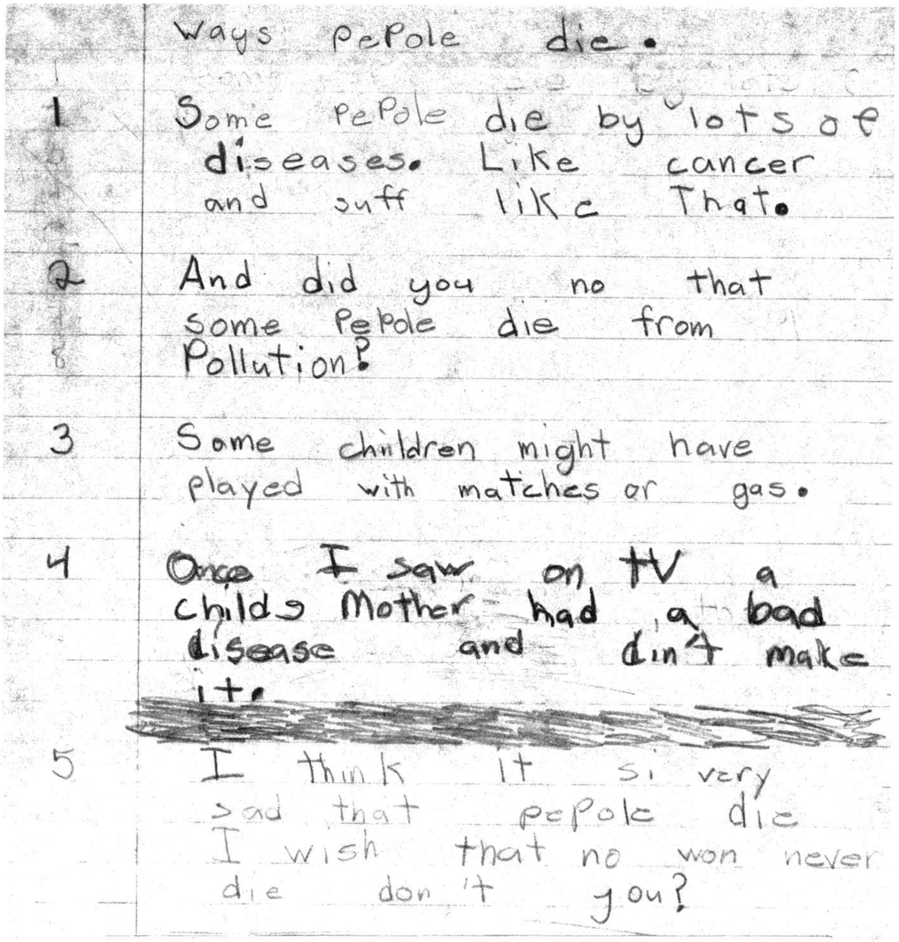

Ways pepole die.

1 Some pepole die by lots of diseases. Like cancer and suff like That.

2 And did you no that some pepole die from Pollution?

3 Some children might have played with matches or gas.

4 Once I saw on TV a childs Mother had a bad disease and din't make it.

5 I think It si very sad that pepole die I wish that no won never die don't you?

Figure 3-4   *Ways People Die: A Child's Explanation*

logical fashion, although still unable to engage in abstract thinking. That is, the ability to think logically can be applied to objects, but not yet to hypotheses, which require the ability to carry out operations on operations. Thus, the characteristic mode of thought in this period emphasizes simultaneously the concreteness and the logic of *things*. During this period, children can think forward and backward in time, and they demonstrate an appreciation of time as "passing" although their comprehension of such measurements as time and space does not yet allow them to manipulate these concepts with the flexibility or abstraction that comes with the ability to engage in formal operations of thought.

During this period of cognitive development, children tend to name intentional as well as unintentional means by which a person may die (see Figure 3-4).

The child has become familiar with, and can name, a wider range of causes of death. Here are some responses from the children in Koocher's study when they were asked about causes of death:

- *Todd:* "Knife, arrow, guns, and lots of stuff. You want me to tell you all of them? [*As many as you want.*] Hatchets and animals, and fires and explosions, too."
- *Kenny:* "Cancer, heart attacks, poison, guns, bullets, or if someone drops a boulder on you."
- *Deborah:* "Accidents, cars, guns, or a knife. Old age, sickness, taking dope, or drowning."

Adolescence

According to Erikson's model of psychosocial development, the years of adolescence are marked by the milestone of establishing an individual *identity*. This period is considered to be a particularly important time of personality development. A bridge must be established between the past — the years of childhood and dependency — and the future — the years of adulthood and independence. Thus, this is a time of integration as well as separation.

Remember what it's like being a teenager? Becoming more your own person? Striving to express your own ideas and beliefs? Sorting out the unbelievable tangle of all that's happening to you? Deciding what you want for your life?

These years can be confusing as well as challenging. With the desire for a greater sense of one's own identity — an answer to the question "Who am I?" — there may also come anxieties about framing an adequate answer. Adolescents are just on the edge of beginning to achieve what they want for themselves. The achievement of their goals and dreams seems nearly within their grasp. The possibility of death is a serious threat to that achievement.

When a major publishing company ran a "young adult" novel competition, the editors were initially surprised to find that the submissions from adolescents predominantly revealed what they called negative themes: illness, death of a loved one, suicide, loss. One editor commented that this result indicated "that kids are writing about what they want to know about."

In Piaget's theory, the years of adolescence are characterized by the term *formal operations*. Marking the fourth and final phase of cognitive development, this period begins at about the age of eleven or twelve and extends into adulthood — although a person's fundamental way of seeing the world is thought to be fairly well established by about the age of fifteen. With the arrival of formal operational thinking, the child is able to "think about thinking" — that is, to formulate or master concepts that are purely abstract or symbolic. As the end point of a complex process of cognitive development, this period is characterized by highly sophisticated operations of thought.

Relations of correspondence or implication between complex sets of statements can be perceived, analogies recognized, and assumptions or deductions made. Such operations make it possible to predict outcomes without having to try them out in the real world. In a chess game, for example, formal operations of thought allow the player to consider a number of complicated strategies, and to predict the likely result of each move, without having to touch a single piece on the board. Likewise, by mentally manipulating related ideas and possibilities, the child can hypothesize the implications of an ethical or political issue. The child is capable of using analysis and reflection to make sense of his or her experience and to formulate a coherent model of the world.

By this point, children typically demonstrate possession of a mature concept of death: They understand that death is irreversible and permanent, that it is universal and inevitable, and that it involves the cessation of physiological functioning. Although in Koocher's study most of the children who used formal operations of thought were twelve or older, some were as young as nine or ten. The mature understanding of death is reflected in their responses to the question "What makes things die?"

- *Ed:* "You mean death in a physical sense? [*Yes.*] Destruction of a vital organ or life force within us."
- *George:* "They get old and their body gets all worn out, and their organs don't work as well as they used to."
- *Paula:* "When the heart stops, blood stops circulating. You stop breathing, and that's it. [*Anything else?*] Well, there's lots of ways it can get started, but that's what really happens."

A Mature Concept of Death

Through three successive periods of cognitive development — preoperational, concrete operational, and formal operational — children's responses to the question "What makes things die?" reflect progress toward a mature understanding of death.

Answers to the other three questions asked by Koocher also elicited recognizable differences among the three stages. Asked "How do you make dead things come back to life?" children who conceived of death as reversible gave answers like: "You can help them; give them hot food and keep them healthy so it won't happen again." Another child said, "No one ever taught me about that, but maybe you could give them some kind of medicine and take them to the hospital to get better." Children in the later stages, however, were able to recognize death as permanent: "If it was a tree, you could water it. If it's a person, you could rush them to the emergency room, but it would do no good if they were dead already." Another child said, "Maybe some day we'll be able to do it, but not now. Scientists are working on that problem."

Asked "When will you die?" children in the preoperational period provided answers ranging from "When I'm seven" (from a six-year-old) to "Three hundred years." At this age, children understood too little about time and death to be able to relate the two to make sense of them realistically. In contrast, older children

© Carol A. Foote

Childhood activities such as "playing dead" can be a means of experimenting with various concepts, trying them on for size, and thus arriving at a more comprehensive and manageable sense of reality.

typically expected to live out a statistically correct lifespan, or a bit more; the usual age at which death was expected was about eighty.

In answer to the researchers' fourth question, "What will happen when you die?" one nine-and-a-half-year-old said, "They'll help me come back alive." The researcher asked, "Who?" "My father, my mother, and my grandfather," the child responded. "They'll keep me in bed and feed me and keep me away from rat poison and stuff."

According to some early developmental models of how children learn about death, a child of nine would understand that none of those measures would work. Thus, this example illustrates the point that age-and-stage correlations provide, at best, a rule of thumb concerning how children develop. As with any *model* of human behavior, the age-stage developmental framework is indicative, not rigorously descriptive.

In answer to the same question, an eight-and-a-half-year-old replied, "You go to heaven and all that will be left of you will be a skeleton. My friend has some fossils of people. A fossil is just a skeleton." Notice how the child uses comparison to help interpret what happens when death occurs. An eleven-year-old said, "I'll feel dizzy and tired and pass out, and then they'll bury me and I'll rot away. You just disintegrate and only your bones will be left."

A twelve-year-old said, "I'll have a nice funeral and be buried and leave all my money to my son." One ten-year-old said, "If I tell you, you'll laugh." The researcher assured the child, "No, I won't, I want to know what you really think." Thus encouraged, the child continued, "I think I'm going to be reincarnated as a plant or animal, whatever they need at that particular time." The ability to imagine what things might be like in the future is seen in these responses.

Play activities can help the child deal with his or her concerns about death. Play can be a means of exorcising fears, trying out roles, making decisions, investigating consequences of actions, experimenting with value judgments, and finding a comfortable self-image.[12] Games like cowboys and Indians and cops and robbers reflect, in part, the child's attempt to reach some understanding about the place of death in his or her world.

Sources of Attitudes Toward Death

Just as the ability to grasp a mature concept of death develops gradually throughout childhood, so too do attitudes toward death. These attitudes derive from a complex array of interrelated sources, including the cultural environment, personal experiences with death, and messages from parents and peers.

It is often difficult, if not impossible, to pinpoint the genesis of ideas about death that a child may acquire in the natural course of social interactions. Take, for example, the following incident: Two children, ages eight and ten, were asked to draw a picture of a funeral (see Figure 3-5). They got out their colored pencils and immersed themselves in the task. After a while, Heather (who is ten) said to Matt (eight), "Hey, you've got smiles on those faces! This is supposed to be a funeral. What are they doing with smiles on their faces?" In her model of appropriate death-related behavior, people don't smile at funerals; to her younger brother, smiles are perfectly acceptable. One can only surmise the influences that led to such a strong statement about the kind of behavior appropriate at funerals; in interactions such as this one between siblings, however, attitudes about death that are expressed by others become incorporated into a child's understanding of death.

Early Parental Messages

To consider parental messages about death, think back to your childhood. What messages did you receive about death that remain to this day in the back of your mind? Possibly some messages were conveyed directly: "This is what death is" or "This is how we behave in relation to death." Or perhaps the messages were indirect: "Let's not talk about it. . . ." How would the rest of that sentence go? Let's not talk about it—because it's not something that people talk about? One woman, for example, was told, "You shouldn't look at it." When there was a dead animal on the highway, her mother admonished, "Put your head down; children

A

B

Figure 3-5   *Children's Drawings of a Funeral*

Instructed to draw a picture of a funeral, a sister (age ten) and brother (eight) did so. The ten-year-old, whose drawing is A, emphasizes the emotional responses of the survivors. We see the picture as if we are looking in (and down) upon their grief. The figures in the first two pews have tears streaming down their faces and one woman shouts "No!" At ten, this child reflects on the sorrowful and unwelcome nature of death. When questioned about the empty pews, she said they were for anyone who came late.

The eight-year-old's drawing (B) is viewed from a similar perspective (looking in and down at the scene). Here we see the survivors group around a flag-draped and flower-bedecked coffin. The figures are portrayed with smiles on their faces. The focus in this drawing is on the symbols of death (e.g., the casket) and the ceremony rather than emotions. During the drawing session, the older sister commented that her brother's picture was "too happy" for a funeral scene.

The Shroud

A mother once had a little seven-year-old boy with such a sweet, beautiful face that no one could look at him without loving him, and she loved him more than anything in the world. Suddenly, the child fell sick, and God took him. The mother was inconsolable and wept day and night. Soon after he was buried, the child began to appear in places where he had sat playing in his lifetime. When his mother wept, he too wept, and when morning came he vanished. Then when the mother could not stop crying, he appeared one night wrapped in the little white shroud he had been buried in and wearing a wreath of flowers on his head. He sat down at her feet and said: "Oh, mother, if you don't stop crying I won't be able to sleep in my coffin, for my shroud is wet with all the tears that fall on it." When she heard that, the mother was horrified, and from then on she shed no tears. The next night the child came again. He held a candle in his hand and said: "You see, my shroud is almost dry. Now I can rest in my grave." After that, the mother gave her grief into God's keeping and bore it silently and patiently. The child never came again, but slept in his little bed under the ground.

Grimm's Tales for Young and Old

---

shouldn't see that." That is a very clear message about what constitutes appropriate behavior toward death.

Other messages about death may be communicated unconsciously. Consider the notion of replaceability. A child's pet dies, and the parent says, "It's okay, dear, we'll get another one." When one woman was talking about the shock of her husband's recent death, her young child broke in and said, "Don't worry, Mommy, we'll get you another one."

Parental attitudes shape the behavior not only of the child but also of the adult that the child will become and how that adult conveys attitudes toward death to his or her own children. A woman now in her thirties tells the following story: "I can remember a time when my mother ran over a cat. I wasn't with her in the car, but I recall my mother coming home and just totally falling apart. She ran into the bedroom and cried for hours. Since that time, I've never killed anything. I'm extremely conscientious about that—if there's an insect on me or in my house, I'll pick it up and carry it outside."

Cultural Influences

The cultural factors described in Chapter 1 as influencing attitudes toward death affect children as well as adults. Television programs, cartoons, movies, and jokes frequently refer to death. Even when not directed specifically toward children, these cultural influences are pervasive. Some children's television programs—one of the most notable being "Mister Rogers' Neighborhood"—have produced segments dealing specifically and creatively with the topic of death.[13]

News reports of disasters or death, and the reactions of adults to such reports, also convey to the child information about cultural attitudes toward dying and death. A child's response to such messages is related to his or her level of cognitive development, as Martha Wolfenstein and her colleagues found when they conducted a study of children's reactions to the death of President John F. Kennedy.[14] From the mass of details about the president's assassination, children tended to select those particular aspects related to their own developmental concerns: Children of elementary school age tended to express concerns about the appearance of the president's body and the effect of the death on members of his immediate family; older children voiced concerns about the impact of the president's death on American politics and society.

Similar developmentally related concerns appear in reports of children's reactions to the deaths of the *Challenger* astronauts. For example, when a group of first graders was asked to draw pictures of the shuttle accident, the astronauts were often depicted returning safely to earth where they could be saved by rescue teams.[15] One child's picture showed the astronauts coming down in parachutes while debris falls around them. Another picture showed all seven astronauts in the water, apparently waiting to be rescued.

In some of the drawings, the astronauts' bodies were shown as intact; in others, although the bodies were in pieces, the children said they could be made whole again by rescue crews or hospital workers. One boy drew a picture of an astronaut in the grass and told his teacher that rescue crews would find the astronaut and take him to a hospital, where he would be made well again. As we have seen, this interest in the condition of the astronauts' bodies and in the possibility of rescue is appropriate and usual for children of this age group.

Children's literature also communicates messages about life and death related to cultural attitudes. Of about two hundred nursery rhymes examined in one study, about half described the wonder and beauty of life and the other half dealt with "the many ways in which humans and animals die or are mistreated."[16] These included accounts of murder, choking to death, torment and cruelty, maiming, misery and sorrow, stories of lost or abandoned children, and themes depicting poverty and want. A number of the classic stories for children also depict deaths, near-deaths, or the threat of death. In addition, themes of death and violence have been found in the lullabies of various countries.[17] Some of the lullabies were "mourning songs" that described the death or funeral of a child; others were "threat" songs that warned of violence if a child did not go to sleep. Researchers noted that the content of many lullabies changed as higher standards of living, better nutrition, and a more secure future evolved.

Traditional children's stories, rhymes, and fairy tales have been joined in the recent past by a genre of children's books designed especially to help children find answers to their questions about dying and death. (A selected listing of these books can be found in Chapter 8.) In many of these books, particularly those for very young children, death is presented as an event occurring within the natural cycle. Often these stories include the suggestion that, like the transition from one season to the next, after each ending in nature there is renewal. One writer has remarked that "it is consistent that a society which produced children's books

---

The Three Little Pigs

. . . This made the wolf so angry that he vowed he would eat the pig, and that nothing should stop him. So he climbed up on the roof and jumped down the chimney.

But the wise little pig was ready for him, for he had built a big fire and hung a great kettle of water over it, right under the chimney. When the pig heard the wolf coming he took the cover off the kettle, and down fell the wolf right into it. Before he could crawl out, the little pig popped the lid back on again, and in a trice he had the wolf boiling.

That night the little pig had boiled wolf for supper. So he lived in his brick and mortar house till he grew too big for it, and never was he troubled by a wolf again.

Journeys Through Bookland, Volume One

---

explaining the mysteries of molecules and atoms, of evolution and birth, should also produce works of facts and fiction which attempt to define and explain death."[18]

Cultural attitudes toward dying and death also can be communicated through educational programs and presentations designed specifically to provide children with opportunities to discuss these topics with parents and other adults. One of the most innovative examples of this phenomenon occurred when the Boston Children's Museum held a participatory show entitled "Endings: An Exhibit About Death and Loss." Included were songs, stories, games, videotapes, and other exhibits designed to stimulate the sharing of thoughts and feelings about death between parents and children. Although many parents, educators, and other professionals praised the exhibit, it was criticized by some for impinging upon children's "innocence" and "sense of joy" by forcing them to think about dying and death.

Cultural influences on children's socialization are also found in distinctions that appear to be correlated with gender roles. For example, a study of junior high students found that attitudes toward death differed between males and females, and these differences were normally "in the direction expected based on traditional sex roles."[19]

In comparison with males, for example, females were generally more in favor of abortion, valued funerals, and expressed greater concern about what might happen to their bodies after death. On the issue of capital punishment, boys were about equally divided, pro and con, whereas girls expressed uncertainty or disagreement. With respect to the students' beliefs about life after death, males were described by researchers as "more decisive" and females as "more variable" in their beliefs.

Developmental models and surveys of cultural factors are useful in gaining a perspective on ways in which children generally formulate understandings about death. For any given child, however, we must fill in this general framework with

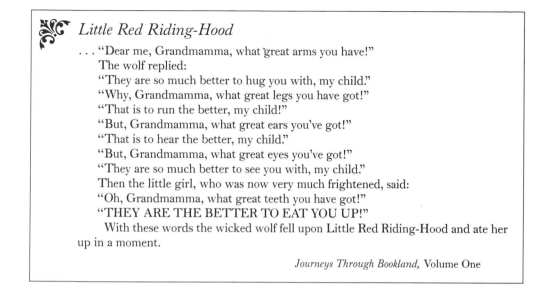

Little Red Riding-Hood

... "Dear me, Grandmamma, what great arms you have!"
The wolf replied:
"They are so much better to hug you with, my child."
"Why, Grandmamma, what great legs you have got!"
"That is to run the better, my child!"
"But, Grandmamma, what great ears you've got!"
"That is to hear the better, my child."
"But, Grandmamma, what great eyes you've got!"
"They are so much better to see you with, my child."
Then the little girl, who was now very much frightened, said:
"Oh, Grandmamma, what great teeth you have got!"
"THEY ARE THE BETTER TO EAT YOU UP!"
   With these words the wicked wolf fell upon Little Red Riding-Hood and ate her up in a moment.

Journeys Through Bookland, Volume One

specific information: the child's personality, unique life experiences, and the kind of family and social resources available for learning about death. All these factors are influential.

Life Experiences

As Ernest Becker pointed out in his landmark study, *The Denial of Death*, there are two schools of thought regarding the presence of a "fear of death" in human beings.[20] The "healthy-minded" argument maintains that individuals are not *born* with a fear of death; rather, this fear is engendered by experiences of parental deprivation, or "hostile denial" of a child's life impulses by his or her parents (or by society more generally). The "morbidly minded" argument, on the other hand, maintains that the fear of death is natural and affects everyone. Indeed, in this view, fear of death is the "basic fear that influences all others." Although evidence can be arrayed in support of either of these views, as a practical matter it can be said that most people do exhibit, if not fear, at least anxiety toward death; and these feelings surface during childhood.

Self-concept seems to influence a child's ability to cope with death. Research indicates that a child with a good self-concept is generally less fearful about death. This correlation also applies to adults. People who feel good about themselves and are comfortable with themselves, who see themselves as active, vital, and interesting, and who have caring relationships with others tend to be less fearful about dying and death.

Consider adult responses to death that you may have observed. How did different persons demonstrate their particular understanding of and attitudes

I recall with utter clarity the first great shock of my life. A scream came from the cottage next door. I rushed into the room, as familiar as my own home. The Larkin kids, Conor, Liam and Brigid, all hovered about the alcove in which a mattress of bog fir bedded old Kilty. They stood in gape-mouthed awe.

I stole up next to Conor. "Grandfar is dead," he said.

Their ma, Finola, who was eight months pregnant, knelt with her head pressed against the old man's heart. It was my very first sight of a dead person. He was a waxy, bony specimen lying there with his mouth open showing no teeth at all and his glazed eyes staring up at me and me staring back until I felt my own ready to pop out of their sockets.

Oh, it was a terrible moment of revelation for me. All of us kids thought old Kilty had the magic of the fairies and would live forever, a tale fortified by the fact that he was the oldest survivor of the great famine, to say nothing of being a hero of the Fenian Rising of '67 who had been jailed and fearfully tortured for his efforts.

I was eleven years old at that moment. Kilty had been daft as long as I could recall, always huddled near the fire mumbling incoherently. He was an ancient old dear, ancient beyond age, but nobody ever gave serious consideration to the fact he might die.

Leon Uris, *Trinity*

about death? What kind of personal and social resources were mobilized to cope with death? Whereas one person might be curious about all the details surrounding a death, someone else might prefer to know as little as possible. The ten-year-old's phrase, "It's sickening, don't talk about it!" can survive into adulthood.

Significant experiences, such as the death of someone close, are likely to influence both the child's attitude and understanding of death. The attitude of a child who is allowed to ask questions about such an experience is likely to be quite different from that of the child who is told that death is not an appropriate topic for children's questions. The experience of a young child who observes the dramatic changes occurring among family members as a result of death, but who is not permitted to participate in any of the funeral rituals or to ask questions, may long afterward carry the notion that death is unmentionable.

At the same time, the child who experiences the death of a close family member or a friend may arrive at an understanding of death that generally would be associated with a later stage of development. One study showed that when children younger than six years had experienced a concrete encounter with death, they gained an understanding of it that was precocious for their stage of development.[21] One six-year-old who witnessed the accidental death of her sibling expressed what seemed to be a very clear understanding that death is final, that people die, and that she herself could die. She was concerned about how she could protect herself and her friends from the dangerous circumstances that led to her brother's death. This attitude toward death was reflected in her admoni-

Cpl. Edward Belfer, U.S. Army Photo

Children's early encounters with death may come in ways that are extraordinary. The child seen here was one of many German citizens who, at the end of World War II, were ordered by the provisional military government of the U.S. Third Army to view the exhumed bodies of some 800 Russians, Poles, and Czechs who had been killed while imprisoned in the concentration camp at Flossenberg.

tions to schoolmates to be especially aware of preventing accidents. Along with her understanding of the reality of death, she possessed an attitude toward death that reflected the particulars of her experience.

Another kind of experience is reflected in drawings made by Cambodian children in refugee camps.[22] Death is the predominant theme in those drawings. These children had experienced starvation, and they represented that fact in their drawings. One child's picture depicted a woman in the midst of about six smaller bodies; the caption read, "Mother's Dead Children." When they have such catastrophic experiences with death, children seem to develop understandings of death earlier than they would in more ordinary circumstances. Children who

"Calvin and Hobbes," drawing by Bill Watterson, © 1989 Universal Press Syndicate.

experience the reality of widespread death during a time of war or prolonged catastrophe are likely to develop a more fatalistic attitude toward death, or at least demonstrate greater maturity in their understanding of it, than their counterparts whose experiences with death occur under more benign conditions.[23]

The child as survivor of the death of someone close or as victim of a life-threatening illness is a topic that involves issues beyond those discussed here in connection with the general characteristics of children's socialization. Chapter 8 is devoted to the experience of bereavement and life-threatening illness in children's lives.

In terms of our discussion here, it is important to remember that life experiences, particularly those that involve an intimate encounter with death, may shape an individual's unique beliefs about death. Perhaps only later in life, as an adult, does a person become aware of the real and lasting impact of a childhood experience.

Talking with Children About Death

However tempered they may be by the influence of peers and what is learned in the classroom and elsewhere outside the home, parental attitudes significantly influence the child's attitude toward death. Thus, parents have natural concerns regarding what to tell their children about death. What can be told? What should be told? How can I talk about it? What will the child understand? We have already seen that children develop their own concepts about death, whether or not they receive parental instruction—or even if the topic is considered taboo by parents. Indeed, it seems that children want to learn about death, just as they want to learn about everything that touches their lives. One child wrote, "Dear God, what's it like when you die? Nobody will tell me. I just want to know. I don't want to do it."

Parents explaining death to children should put honesty foremost. Be straightforward. How much to disclose to a child must be based on how willing the parent is to face the consequences of the issues that are raised in the child's mind.

He lived a long way from here
Lew's mother explained.
You never asked
so I never told you
Grandpa died.

I want him to come back.
I miss him, Lewis said.
I have been waiting for him
and I miss him especially tonight.

I do too
said Lew's mother.
But you made him come back
for me tonight
by telling me what you remember.

Charlotte Zolotow,
My Grandson Lew

A parent who sets a ground rule that it's okay to be open and honest in talking about death must be aware that there will probably be times when the child wants to start a discussion and the parent is tired or would rather avoid the subject.

Second, don't put off introducing the topic of death to a child. When the experience of a close death precedes the discussion, the parent is faced with the need to provide an explanation in the midst of a crisis. This unfortunate circumstance arises when a parent puts it off "because it's not really going to happen," only to find that "I'm confronted with it happening right now in my family and the child has to be told something." When a family member is dying or someone has died suddenly and unexpectedly, the explanation to the child is charged with all the emotions the parent is dealing with, making a clear explanation much more difficult to attain.

Third, set the level of explanation to the child's ability to understand. This is determined partly by the child's cognitive stage and partly by his or her unique experience. By using as a guide the child's interest and ability to understand, the parent can provide an explanation that is appropriate to the child's particular circumstances. Such an explanation can help the child cope with his or her general concerns about death as well as with the specific issues that may arise in conjunction with the experience of a close death.

A supportive listener increases the child's openness to dealing with death. Valuing a child's ideas and encouraging his or her candid expression is an excellent way to help a child explore and discuss his or her understanding of death. As their children's mainstay, parents who are open to an interchange on any subject have a number of skills and resources they can use when the discussion turns to death.

When you talk to children about death, it is important to verify what it is they think you've told them. Have them tell you what they learned or what they heard you saying about death. Children tend to generalize from known concepts to make new experiences fit. This may result in a very literal interpretation of new information, especially among young children, who tend to emphasize the concreteness of things. Recognizing this, try to keep your communication free of

The Dead Mouse

We had been out of town and the neighbors had been caring for our various pets. When we returned, we found that our cat had, as cats will, caught and killed a mouse and had laid it out ceremoniously in front of his bowl in the garage. I discovered that that had happened when I heard loud screams from the garage. "Pudley's killed a mouse. There's a dead mouse in the garage!" Loud screams, for the whole neighborhood to hear. I went downstairs. It was the first time that I had a chance to observe how my children dealt with death. I said, "Oh, there is?" "Right here," they said, "Look!" They began to tell me how they had determined it was dead. It was not moving. They had poked at it several times and it didn't move. Matthew, who was five years old, added that it didn't look like it was ever going to move again. That was his judgment that the mouse was dead.

I said to him, "Well, what are we going to do?" I could feel myself being slightly repulsed; my fingers went to my nose. It was obvious to me that the mouse was dead — it had started to decay. Matt said very matter-of-factly, "Well, we'll have to bury it." Heather, seven, climbed on a chair and announced, "Not me. I'm not going to touch it. Don't bring it around here. Aughhh, dead mouse!" At that time, she was intent on being what she thought was feminine, and part of the stereotype involved not getting herself dirty.

So Matt volunteered for the job. "I'm going to need a shovel," he said. I stood back and watched, interested to see what would happen. I noticed that he didn't touch the mouse. From somewhere he already had gotten the idea that it wasn't appropriate to touch dead things. He carefully lifted it with the shovel and took it into the backyard to dig a hole. Heather peered around and watched at a safe distance.

After the mouse was buried, Matt came back and said, "I'm going to need some wood, a hammer, and a nail." I thought, "Oh great! He's going to perform some kind of little ceremony and place a symbol of some kind on the grave." Matt went to the wood-pile and carefully selected a piece of wood maybe two inches long and another piece a bit wider, perhaps three inches wide and about four or five inches long. I thought,

associations that might lead to confusion in the child's mind. Metaphorical explanations about death can help provide a child-sized picture that helps understanding, but unless fact is clearly separated from fancy, the child may grasp the literal details instead of the underlying message the analogy was intended to convey.

A story can illustrate how easily confusion can arise when death is explained to children. A girl of age five was told that her grandfather's cancer was like a seed that grew in his body; it grew and grew until he couldn't live in his body anymore and he died. Her parents didn't notice that ever afterward, all through childhood, she never ate another seed. Not one. Not a cucumber seed or a watermelon seed — no seeds. Finally, at age twenty-one, she was asked, "Why are you avoiding the seeds? Isn't that a little bizarre? What's wrong with the seeds?" Her automatic response was, "You swallow them and you die." After all those years, she finally

"Tombstone?" He got the nail and put the pieces of wood together in the shape of a cross.

I thought, "Oh. A cross, a religious symbol, burial, funeral — all the things I knew about what happens with a dead body." Matt picked up a marking pen and wrote on the front of the cross: "DEAD MOUSE. KEEP OUT!" And he pounded it into the ground in front of where the mouse was buried. I thought, "What's going on in this kid's mind?"

I asked him, "Does that mean that when I die there should be a sign saying, "Dead Mommie. Keep out"? He put his hand on his hip and looked at me with that disgust that five-year-olds can muster for somebody who is *so* dumb, and said, "Of course not. You're going to be buried in one of those places where they have bodies. This is a backyard. Kids could ride their bikes over it. Who would know that there is a mouse buried back here?" I was flabbergasted.

A few weeks later there was a long discussion about what the mouse would look like at that time. My first thoughts were, "Don't do that! You can't dig it up. It's not nice. It's not good. The mouse has to rest his spirit." Then I realized that all those things were coming from that place in me that didn't want to see what a month-old dead mouse looked like.

So I kept quiet. They dug and dug, and I could feel the sweat dripping off me. They dug a huge hole, but could find no remnants of the mouse. I was a bit relieved. But that brought up all kinds of questions about what happened to the mouse. I made this elaborate picture of a compost pile, really a lengthy explanation. Finally I realized that they didn't understand at all and that what I was saying was of no interest to them.

I said, "Well, it's like if you buried an orange." Something safe, I thought, something I can deal with that can be dug up day by day to see how it goes back into the earth.

They buried an orange and dug it up and dug it up and dug it up. And it wasn't an orange anymore.

I came away from that experience thinking, "Where did they learn all that? Matt's behavior, particularly. . . . Where did he get that from?"

saw the fallacy of her compulsion to avoid eating seeds. It would have been useful if someone had asked her when she was five, "What will happen if you swallow that seed?"

We give children a great deal to think about and understand as they learn about death. A child told that her goldfish "went to heaven" may make an elaborate picture of the pearly gates and different sections of heaven. Here is goldfish heaven, this is cat heaven, and over here is people heaven — a very organized concept that makes sense to a child. But we have to be careful that the concepts we convey to a child don't turn out to be dysfunctional.

One woman recalled that when she was three or four a favorite old black dog had to "go away for a long sleep." It wasn't until she was about seven years old that she realized that the dog wasn't just away napping someplace — at the puppy

The most important contribution of an adult talking with a child about death is often to be simply a good listener.

farm having a long sleep. If it had been just "off somewhere to sleep," then the casual goodbye she'd made would have been fine. When, however, she discovered that in fact her beloved dog was dead, she felt angry that she hadn't had the opportunity to give it a proper farewell.

Another woman's first experience with death occurred when she was three-and-a-half and her mother died. It seemed that her mother had just disappeared; she didn't know what had happened to her. Some time later, she began to realize that her mother had died and she started asking questions. Some people told her that her mother had been buried, and her thought was, "Why don't they dig her up?" Others said that her mother had gone to heaven, so she kept looking at the sky, watching for her. With both of these concepts running through her young mind, she did her best to figure out, "How can my mother be buried in heaven?" That's a good example of the concreteness of a child's concepts about death.

A similar confusion is illustrated in the following story about a four-year-old whose brother (nine) told him that daddy had gone to heaven. The four-year-old promptly went and told his mother, "My daddy's on the roof!" She said, "What? Who told you that?" He said, "Andrew did." The older brother then explained, "We were looking out the window and I told him that daddy was in heaven up there." To the four-year-old, the highest "up there" was up on the roof.

If you tell a four-year-old that someone who has died is "up there" and you also say that Santa Claus lands on the roof on Christmas Eve, he may decide that

Santa Claus and the person who has died are great buddies. He might make up stories about how they work together, making toys, feeding the reindeer, and so on.

Children are apt to point out any inconsistencies in what we tell them about death. When one three-year-old's young playmate was killed, his mother explained to him that Jesus had come and taken his friend to heaven. His concrete response was, "Well, that's an awful thing to do; I want to play with him. Jesus isn't very nice if he comes down here and takes my friend from me." In discussing death with a child, it helps if you understand the child's belief system, the kind of thought processes he or she uses to understand the world; and then from your very first statement ask yourself: If I explain death in this way, how will it wind up in the child's understanding?

The most useful approach is to simply talk with the child about what he or she believes, to enter into the child's understanding of what death is. Adults tend to worry about children, especially about their encounters with death. Are they doing all right? Will they be okay? Is death going to be too hard for them to handle? Can they survive this particular loss? (Underlying this concern is worry about ourselves, too.) In general, children do remarkably well. Erik Erikson said, "Healthy children will not fear life if their parents have the integrity not to fear death."

Further Readings

Sylvia Anthony. *The Discovery of Death in Childhood and After*. New York: Basic Books, 1972.

Audrey K. Gordon and Dennis Klass. *They Need to Know: How to Teach Children About Death*. Englewood Cliffs, N.J.: Prentice-Hall, 1979.

Earl A. Grollman, ed. *Explaining Death to Children*. Boston: Beacon Press, 1967.

Edgar N. Jackson. *Telling a Child About Death*. New York: Hawthorne Books, 1965.

Marguerita Rudolph. *Should the Children Know? Encounters with Death in the Lives of Children*. New York: Schocken Books, 1978.

Neil J. Salkind. *Theories of Human Development*. 2d ed. New York: John Wiley and Sons, 1985.

Hannelore Wass and Charles A. Corr, eds. *Childhood and Death*. Washington, D.C.: Hemisphere, 1984.

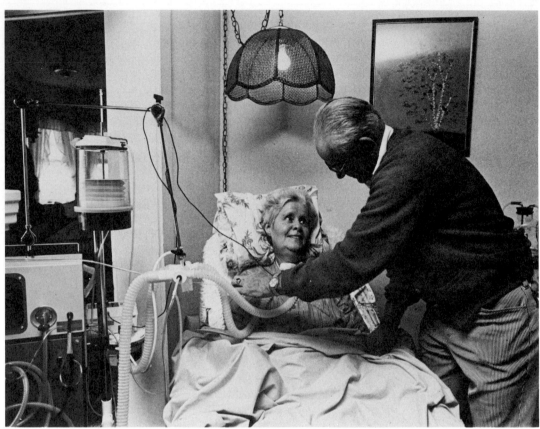

Home care may not come immediately to mind when one thinks of health care systems, yet this centuries-old tradition of care for the ill and the dying is once again emerging as an option for many. Innovations in sophisticated medical life-support equipment often make it possible for the seriously ill to be cared for at a high level of medical technology within the home.

Health Care Systems: Patients, Staff, and Institutions

*T*he struggle to come to grips with the finiteness of physical existence is a constant of human experience. The way we die is not. In the recent past, dying has been significantly altered by technology and the advent of the modern hospital. Most people fear death less than they fear the process of dying. Our medical institutions are designed to soothe and heal; yet it seems that their salve is not always comforting for the dying.

Think about the end of your own life. What do you fear about dying? Many people say they fear dying in pain and loneliness, amid complicated machines that hum softly in an impersonal setting. Oriented toward the goal of preserving life, hospitals have sometimes been remiss about meeting the specific needs of dying patients and their families. In the hospital setting, death may be treated as an anomaly.

An Overview of Modern Health Care

The first hospitals were established centuries ago to aid the homeless and the hopelessly ill. (The word *hospital* derives from the Latin *hospitium*, meaning a place that receives guests.) A distant relative of modern hotels, hostels, and hospices, early hospitals aided sick travelers and victims of disaster. Physicians generally functioned independently of hospitals; members of religious communities provided the nursing care within them. The close association between physicians and hospitals is a comparatively recent development.

In contrast to the hospital as a place for giving aid to the dying, the modern hospital is primarily devoted to acute intensive care. Highly specialized care is provided to patients who usually stay in the hospital only a brief time. The typical hospital patient expects to regain well-being and return to normal life.

Hospital care accounts for the largest proportion of personal health care costs in the United States, and hospital costs have been increasing rapidly. Annual health care expenditures in the United States totaled $500 billion in 1987, 11 percent of the gross national product, with an average cost per person of $1987.[1] In the last decade, per capita health care costs have almost tripled (see Figure 4-1). The phenomenal growth of hospices as an alternative form of terminal care can be attributed, in part, to concerns about containing health care costs. Charles Rosenberg observes that "we expect a great deal of our hospitals: alleviation of pain, extension of life, management of death and the awkward and painful circumstances surrounding its approach."[2]

Over the last few decades, the way Americans finance their health care has undergone several major changes.[3] In 1965, the federal government created the Medicare and Medicaid programs in an effort to extend the benefits of health care to more people. During the 1980s, radical changes were made in the methods used to reimburse hospitals, physicians, and other health care providers. Leading the way was legislation pertaining to DRGs (diagnosis-related groups), which provided for "prospective payment" to such providers. According to this payment system, reimbursement is made not on the basis of costs incurred, but on the basis of a set fee per case, as determined by the type of diagnosis. One result of this change was that patient care began to be viewed in terms of standardized "products," thereby reinforcing the image of hospitals as factories.

While the institution of DRGs gave the federal government what Rosemary Stevens calls a "strong beachhead" to enforce further changes in the health care system through regulation of prices, hospital policies, length of stay, and specific procedures to be followed, many private health insurers began adding to their own requirements, forcing patients to obtain a "preadmission utilization review" to confirm their need for a particular medical service before being admitted to a hospital. In the wake of these developments, Stevens says, "The patient often seems forgotten."[4] The trend toward standardized treatment is also a matter of concern to physicians. Peter Dans notes that, under the impact of the recent changes in health care financing, questions about the quality of care have taken a back seat to questions about "dollars saved," which in many cases "appears to be the only measure of outcome."[5]

Related to financing health care are questions about the adoption of ever more costly medical technologies. There is a growing sentiment, both within and outside the medical community, that we cannot afford an "endless parade of fabulously expensive new lifesaving or lifemaking technologies" and that we must decide where to draw the line.[6] Increasingly, the consensus seems to be that society is not obligated to provide every life-sustaining intervention that the patient or provider believes might be beneficial. At the same time, arguments have been put forward to the effect that a great many physicians tend to rely too heavily

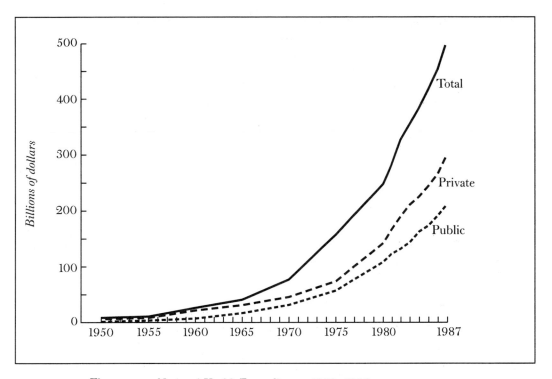

Figure *4-1*   *National Health Expenditures: 1950–1986*

on expensive medical tests — some of which may be less accurate than one would wish, partly because of overworked lab technicians.[7]

To alleviate these pressures on the health care system, some commentators suggest that the available resources ought to be rationed. Rationing involves "the allocation of scarce health care resources among competing individuals," and it occurs "when not all care expected to be beneficial is provided to all patients."[8] The present and prospective scarcity of health care resources is driven by an aging society as well as by an expanding population of "potentially salvageable" patients. We are faced with a situation in which technology generates demand.

Some have suggested that if rationing is to occur, or is occurring, a yardstick of one kind or other should be implemented to measure the outcome of health care choices as they relate to available resources. For example, one such measurement involves the use of "quality-adjusted life years" (or QALYs) to "ascertain the appropriate balance between length of life and quality of life."[9] Using a fairly complicated formula, the notion seems to be that individuals and societies might be willing to work out a "trade-off between length of life and health status." For example, an individual might equate the prospect of living *fewer* years in *perfect* health to the prospect of living *more* years in *less than perfect* health.

The only way to avoid rationing, it seems, is to change either the supply or the demand side of the health resources equation. Some observers suggest that the demand for critical services could be reduced by educating physicians and patients about the limits and consequences of such care. Daniel Callahan advocates what he terms a "principle of symmetry" that acknowledges the inherent limits of medical progress.[10] In stating this principle, Callahan says that "a technology should be judged by its likelihood of enhancing a good balance between the extension and saving of life and the quality of life." Conversely, "A healthcare system that develops and institutionalizes a life-saving technology which has the common result of leaving people chronically ill or with poor quality of life ignores the principle of symmetry."

While Callahan's principle of symmetry can be applied across the board with respect to modern medical technologies, it has particular application to technologies used during the terminal phase of life. Decisions about the allocation of medical resources are not solely in the hands of public policymakers. The choices made by individuals have a significant impact on the health care system and can, in fact, ultimately determine its direction and emphasis. For example, rather than undergoing expensive and ultimately futile treatments at the end of life, individuals might choose to use living wills and similar directives that provide a way to make known their desires regarding the use of such life-sustaining medical technologies when death is near. In any case, many observers believe that the current crisis of limited resources and unlimited demand cannot long endure. As Daniel Callahan says, "Medicine overreaches itself when it sets as its implicit goal that of curing all diseases and infinitely forestalling death."

Care of the Dying

A person entering a health care facility does so to receive medical and nursing care appropriate to a particular malady. The kind and quality of care provided depends largely on the nature of the relationships among three fundamental aspects of institutional health care: (1) the patient; (2) the institution's administrative and organizational patterns; (3) the medical and nursing staff and their attitudes and methods in carrying out the institution's goals. Each side of this triangle—the patient, the institution, and the staff—contributes to the overall shape of health care.

Consider first the patient's relationship to the structure of the institution and to its personnel. What causes many people to fear the possibility of dying in an institutional setting? Why do institutions designed to provide care and comfort often seem impersonal and unfeeling?

The patient's experience is influenced by the hospital's rules, regulations, and conventions, both written and unwritten. Because providing health care for many people requires maximally efficient use of facilities and staff, hospital procedures may be standardized and routine. Thus, the capacity to meet the needs of each individual patient is limited. When the elderly aunt did her dying at home, as was common during the last century, she could be spoon-fed her favorite homemade soup by a member of her family. Today, in the hospital or nursing home, she is more likely to receive a standardized diet, perhaps served imper-

"I think in the next 10–20 years we'll have 'warehouses' with patients on life support systems, if the American public and physicians don't come to grips with and resolve the inherent conflicts involved in the present 'common' method for handling the terminally ill patient." *General practitioner*

"I do not think anybody should have the right to be God and decide death. In view of age and circumstances life may be prolonged to the benefit of patient and family." *Orthopedic surgeon*

"I am a doctor and I feel I should do all in my power to diagnose disease and sustain life." *Internist*

"We should not prolong misery when it's not indicated for other reasons. Everyone has a time to die and should be allowed to die with some dignity." *Urologist*

"The Physician Speaks,"
The Newsletter of Physician Attitudes

sonally by an overworked and harried aide. The trade-off for more sophisticated health care may be less personal comfort.

The patient's family, instead of taking an active role as caregivers, may be relegated to maintaining a deathwatch in the hospital corridor or the waiting room down the hall, with one family member at a time squeezing into the patient's room to keep the bedside vigil. Often there is little or no private space where relatives can gather to discuss their concerns with hospital staff. Hallway meetings between staff and family symbolize for many the impersonality of the hospital. To alleviate such problems, some advocate that hospitals make available a "grief room," where family members can feel more comfortable expressing their emotions without fear of upsetting hospital routine. Such a facility could also be used for meetings between family members and medical personnel.

Unwritten rules, no less faithfully executed by staff, may also contribute to this sense of alienation. For example, a medical institution may follow the convention that only a physician can respond to a patient's or family's questions concerning treatment or prognosis; nurses are expected to reply to such queries with the statement: "Ask your doctor." Because of changes in the doctor-nurse relationship during the last two decades, this conventional "image of nurses as handmaidens is giving way to that of specialty-trained and certified advanced practitioners, with independent duties and responsibilities to their patients."[11] Nevertheless, when convention prevails, the result can be needless fears and unfounded suspicions, which add to the anxiety of patients and their families.

Death may seem taboo. A patient near death may be given medication so that the schedule is not disrupted or the staff or other patients upset. Family members, too, may be urged to accept tranquilizers to subdue their emotional reaction to a loved one's death. Rather than encouraging the expression of natural emotional responses, the emphasis is frequently on subduing, controlling, and restricting any reaction that might jeopardize institutional decorum. Citing the practice of urging drugs on family members to keep emotional disruption to a minimum, Robert Blauner says that hospitals have tended to exhibit the features of a "mass-reduction system, undermining the subjecthood of its dying patients."[12]

When death occurs in the institutional setting, it is often treated so secretly that one would hardly be aware that sometimes patients die. Aside from the few staff members charged with the task of preparing the body and trundling it off to be picked up by the mortician, even those who work in hospitals are sheltered from direct confrontation with death. The false-bottom gurney, which transports the corpse to a nondescript exit, camouflages its odious human cargo. Death is compartmentalized, shut away from public view.

This bureaucratization carries over to public announcements of death. Rarely do newspaper obituaries or death notices name the hospital or nursing home where death occurred, referring instead to a nameless "local hospital." Apparently this evasiveness is meant to confirm the message that hospitals are in business to effect cures and to save lives; acknowledging that patients sometimes die might be deleterious to a hospital's image in the community.

To educate the interns in a large urban hospital about the special needs of the dying, Dr. Elisabeth Kübler-Ross decided to let the patients speak their own case. However, she was initially told by staff members that no one was dying on their ward—there were only some patients who were very critically ill.[13] Even when death is a common reality in one's environment, the operative response may still be denial. Kübler-Ross's pioneering work in educating hospital personnel about the dying became a springboard for the current movement toward increased awareness of the special needs of the dying patient.

Dedicated to saving lives, those who work in hospitals may suppress the feelings of helplessness that arise when they are unable to prevent death. The physician who relates to a dying patient in a cold, detached manner may be compensating for underlying feelings that are painful to acknowledge. The nurse who recognizes that death will soon sever a relationship with a patient may respond in a way that is predicated on the fear of becoming too personally involved. Moreover, because medicine is primarily devoted to meeting patients' physical needs, the emotional and psychological side of patient care may be neglected.

Despite this bleak description of the hospital as a place where death is taboo and the dying patient an anomaly, there are signs of positive change that deserve to be acknowledged and encouraged. Increasingly, hospital personnel are becoming aware that meeting the emotional needs of patients and their families can be as important as caring for bodily needs (see Figure 4-2). Contact that spans the usual professional distance reduces the sense of alienation between patients and medical staff. A nurse who steps into the room, sits down by the patient's bed, and demonstrates a willingness to listen is more likely to be successful in providing comfort than one who merely breezes in, remains standing, and quips, "How're we today? Did we sleep well?" Skillful communication is a key to providing health care for the whole person.

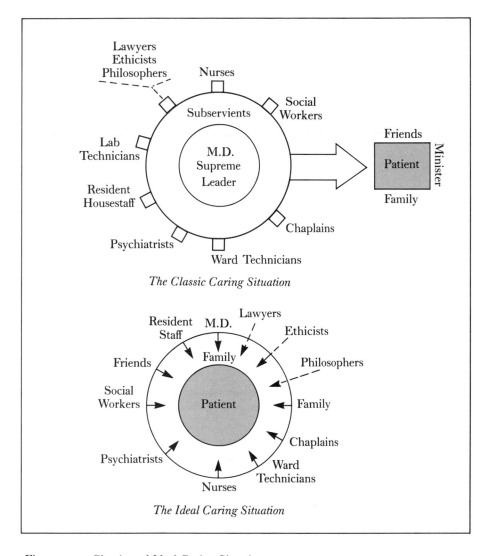

Figure 4-2 *Classic and Ideal Caring Situations*
Source: David Barton, ed., *Dying and Death: A Clinical Guide for Caregivers* (Baltimore: Williams & Wilkins, 1977), p. 181.

A century ago, physicians did perhaps as much to console as to cure the patient. Indeed, consolation and palliative (comfort) measures were sometimes all the medical practitioner could offer the patient. Today, our expectations are such that if a cure is not forthcoming, we feel somehow cheated. Even when treatment is based on sound medical practice, physicians may become scapegoats if it does not result in the desired outcome. Medical malpractice has become a familiar allegation in the nation's courtrooms and a topic debated in state legislatures. Avoiding it may involve clearer and more complete communication between doctors and patients.

When death is made to seem less a natural event than a medical failure, biological death, the cessation of physical functions, may be preceded by *social death*. Eric Cassell writes: "There are two distinct things happening to the terminally ill: the death of the body and the passing of the person."[14] The death of the body is a physical phenomenon, and the passing of the person is a nonphysical (social, emotional, psychological, spiritual) one; yet, these aspects tend to become confused.

Depersonalization and abstraction are part of the scientific method from which come the medical innovations we generally applaud. Yet these mechanisms also tend to make medical care seem unfeeling and lacking in humanness. Depersonalization is most likely to occur when the disease process is not well understood and medical practitioners display what seems greater concern about the disease than about the patient. Additionally, the "power structure" of a medical institution may create a work environment that promotes a defensive reaction among staff members and, thus, an impersonal experience for dying patients.[15] Objectivity and detached concern may become avoidance when a patient clearly begins to die. In a study conducted during the 1960s, Lawrence LeShan found that nurses characteristically took longer to answer the bedside calls of terminally ill patients than they took to answer calls of patients who were less severely ill.[16] Although this particular situation may have changed during the intervening decades, there is still considerable evidence that terminally ill patients experience avoidance in one form or another.

Avoidance of the dying is displayed by the aversion of hospital personnel to discussing death when the topic is raised by the dying patient. Robert Kastenbaum identified five strategies used by staff members in responding to a patient's desire to discuss death: (1) reassurance ("You're doing so well"); (2) denial ("Oh, you'll live to be a hundred"); (3) changing the subject ("Let's talk about something more cheerful"); (4) fatalism ("Well, we all have to die sometime"); (5) discussion ("What happened to make you feel that way?"). The typical response was found to be evasion rather than open discussion.[17]

We cannot expect institutional health care to be as personal as the care the patient's family could give at home. The question remains, however, whether the present model of health care for terminal patients is adequate. Can we do better? Just as many hospitals are instituting new practices in maternity care, is it possible to infuse more human values into care of the dying? We need to investigate the alternatives that might facilitate more compassionate care of the dying.

One such alternative has been proposed by William Buchholz, an oncologist and hospice consultant. Referring to the Greek word *eschaton*, meaning "last things," he suggests that we implement a "medical eschatology," in which the roles of caregiver and scientist are combined to increase our knowledge of a phenomenon that "begins not with death, but when the end first draws into sight."[18]

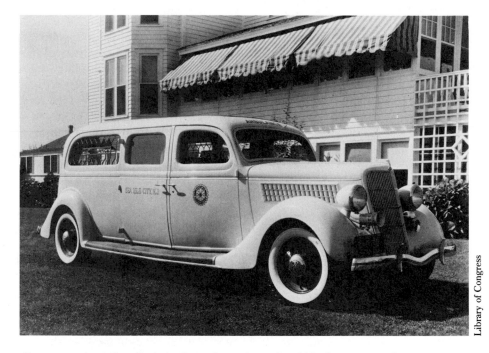

Our expectations of medical care have changed greatly within the past several decades, from a time when ambulance service consisted mainly of transportation—as provided here by the Rotary Club in Sea Isle City, New Jersey—to the present, when sophisticated medical care is provided en route to the hospital by mobile paramedic units outfitted with life-sustaining devices and trained caregivers.

Buchholz says medical eschatology begins when the illusion of immortality is broken and we recognize that all our biographies have an end. This recognition paves the way for us to ask the questions that can lead to a better understanding of the human experience of dying and, as well, better care for the dying person. We need to ask: Which coping mechanisms are most effective, and under what circumstances? What role do psychosocial and transpersonal factors play with respect to life-threatening illness? Prerequisite to answering such questions is the awareness that *caring* is not always synonymous with active *doing*.

There is no single answer to the question of how best to approach the emotional and spiritual care of a person whose body is disintegrating. Some persons counsel disidentification with the body or emphasize the afterlife. But the issue, as Buchholz says, is really whether a caregiver can put aside his or her own beliefs and recognize what is appropriate for the person. Those who care for dying persons need to attend to the clues that can lead to discovery of what is appropriate for a particular person in a given situation. Dying, like birthing, is a natural event, often better witnessed than managed.

Emergency Medical Care

Accidental injury is the leading cause of death for persons under age 35[19]. In 1987, over 95,000 Americans died from injuries sustained in accidents. About half of these accidents involved motor vehicles, with falls, drownings, fires, and accidental poisonings making up most of the remainder. When traumatic injury occurs, time is the enemy. Most victims require immediate surgery, often to stop internal bleeding, and specialists refer to a critical "golden hour" following the injury. Although about half of all deaths from traumatic injury occur within this hour (the first fifteen minutes of which are particularly crucial), the survival rate for those who do receive the appropriate care during this period is 90 percent.[20]

Many advances in emergency medicine that are now commonplace were adapted from techniques used during the Vietnam war. These include the use of the helicopter air ambulance, advances in team surgery and orthopedics, and treatment for burns and shock. The roots of present techniques in trauma care can be traced at least as far back as the Civil War, when Army Major John Letterman developed the "triage" system for evacuating casualties. Designed to reduce the time between injury and care, triage involves assigning priorities based on the seriousness of a patient's injuries. First priority is given to patients whose injuries are serious, but survivable. A lower priority is assigned to patients with little chance of survival as well as to those with less serious injuries.

In 1969, Dr. R. Adams Crowley brought together the Maryland State Police and the Maryland Institute for Emergency Medical Services to form the first civil helicopter medevac program, and, in 1972, the first hospital-based helicop-

Generally, the doctor's announcement of the death was made within the first or first two sentences, usually in the course of one long sentence. An interesting feature of his presentation, more common in the DOA situation than in announcements of the deaths of hospital patients, was that in announcing the death he provided, in some way, that the death be presented as having followed a course of "dying." In nearly every scene I witnessed, the doctor's opening remarks contained an historical reference. . . . This was true in accident as well as "natural" deaths, and true whether or not the physician had any basis for assuming a likely cause of death. . . . Physicians seem to feel in such situations that historicizing their delivery of news, no matter how much their limited knowledge of the case may restrict the range of possibilities, helps not only reduce some of the shock values of "sudden deaths" but aids in the very grasp of the news. The correctness of the physician's supposed cause of death is of secondary significance relative to the sheer fact that he provides some sequential formulation of its generation, some means whereby the occurrence can be placed in a sequence of natural or accidental events. This is felt particularly to be necessary in the DOA circumstance, where many deaths occur with no apparent "reason," particularly the so-called "sudden unexpected deaths," not uncommon among young adults.

David Sudnow,
Passing On: The Social Organization of Dying

ter program was established at St. Anthony's Hospital in Denver. There are now about 150 such trauma centers operating in the United States. Although these specialized trauma centers have helped to reduce the number of deaths from serious injuries, experts say that such care should be even more widely available. Injury — despite being termed "the principal public health problem in America today" by the National Research Council — receives scant public funding compared with other public health problems such as cancer and heart disease. "The lack of a system," says John Grossman, "is killing people."[21]

The Patient-Caregiver Relationship

Physicians — and health care providers generally — have traditionally occupied a special place of honor in society. Aesculapius, the first physician according to Greek legend, was eventually elevated to the pantheon of gods and, along with Hygiea and Panacea, ruled over health and illness in Greek mythology.[22] An activity closely associated with the elemental human experiences of birth, life, and death, the practice of medicine carries high symbolic importance. The concept of *paternalism* is used to describe the assumption of "parentlike" authority by medical practitioners, whose decisions may be made at the expense of the patient's own freedom to choose.

In recent years, however, this "Aesculapian authority" of medical practitioners has been challenged. Concerns have been raised about patients' rights, and an emphasis is being placed on the "patient as person." These concerns stem, says C.D. Bessinger, from the "perception that medicine's science is at odds with medicine's art and with its sense of humanism."[23] There are demands for greater equality, flexibility, and responsiveness in the caregiver-patient relationship. What may ultimately evolve is a social contract between physicians and patients that incorporates some of the qualities of a *covenantal* relationship, which implies a mutuality of giving and receiving between health care providers and patients, and between medical professionals and society.

For caregivers to form relationships with patients that are more human, less mechanistic, and less directed to the patient as an economic unit or as a "case" of this or that disease, Clyde Nabe believes that caregivers need to see their own lives as "acts of grace," as being somehow a gift.[24] The idea of "community" might be used to provide an appropriate context for such transcendental values. The realization that we are all intimately engaged in a "web of interhuman reciprocity" could provide an entryway for bringing covenantal relationships into the health care setting.

Another avenue for resolving the perceived imbalance between the science of medicine and the art of medicine has been described by George Engel, who suggests replacing the conventional "biomedical" model of disease with a "biopsychosocial" model.[25] Such a model would focus not only on an identifiable disease but also on "the patient in the life system," thereby reflecting the ancient view of healing as "restoring wholeness" or, to put it in modern systems terms, "restoring equilibrium." A similar viewpoint is expressed by another medical

> I clearly made Dr. Mueh nervous. He was clearly up to his ears in patients and spread very thin.
>
> He took 90 minutes to talk to me and my wife about my disease. He started out with terminal care and told me I'd get all the narcotics I would need to eliminate pain and that tubes could be used to provide nourishment.
>
> I was amazed that he talked that way, as if I were dying.
>
> Pierre Bowman, Honolulu *Star-Bulletin*

scientist who says that the present methods of training physicians teach them "to think of human beings as machines" when good medicine necessarily "engages the whole human being."[26]

When we bring these concerns to the practical arena of terminal care, we need to ask what happens after a physician diagnoses a patient's illness as life threatening. This is a crucial time in the patient's care that can significantly determine his or her response to treatment, attitude toward the illness, and ability to cope with it constructively. The patient should be given a truthful report of the diagnosis and the proposed course of treatment. The physician should give general information about the disease, with as much detail as the patient desires, so that the patient is informed about what to expect and about any options that he or she can exercise as treatment proceeds.

What is said in this meeting between physician and patient depends on a number of factors, including how the doctor prefers to break the news of a life-threatening illness to a patient, the patient's receptivity to the facts as presented, and the prognosis. Because this initial meeting between the patient and physician can have an important influence on their subsequent interaction and the type of relationships they maintain during the course of treatment, sufficient time should be made available to explore the patient's questions and concerns.

Candace West, a sociologist who conducted a five-year study of how doctors and patients relate to each other, found instances of what she calls a "communications chasm" that may hinder the healing process.[27] In particular, she observed a lack of "social cement" — the introductions, greetings, laughter, and use of patients' names — that are part of ordinary social interactions and that help to bring people closer together. In addition, physicians "advance questions which restrict patients' options for answers," and patients may hesitate to ask questions of their doctors. Other observers have emphasized that physicians need to "listen" with their eyes as well as their ears. Paying attention to the nonverbal communication of gestures and body language can provide evidence of a patient's unease or anxiety about the content of a medical conversation. Sandra Bertman and her colleagues at the University of Massachusetts Medical School have pointed out that "highly technical diagnostic and therapeutic interventions can even become obstacles to effective communication and treatment."[28]

The Patient's Story

In learning to think like a medical scientist, I was forgetting the whole patient. To help the patient in times of suffering, the physician must know the patient: not only as a case but as a person. Each patient has a history, a unique story to tell, which goes beyond the information in the medical history. Different patients have different senses of what makes life important to them, what they want out of life, and how far they are willing to go to preserve it. The patient's full story, like any person's story, includes his or her cultural background, childhood circumstances, career, family, religious life, and so on. It includes the patient's self-understanding, appearance, manner of expression, temperament, and character. In short, it includes those attributes that make the patient a person — and not only a person, but this particular person.

Richard B. Gunderman,
"Medicine and the Question of Suffering"

Dr. Ernest Rosenbaum, an oncologist, provides a helpful model of sensitivity to patients' needs.[29] Once testing is complete and a malignancy indicated, Dr. Rosenbaum arranges for an interview with the patient, encouraging family members to attend as well. Advocating candor and stressing partnership between the patient and the physician, he describes the nature of the diagnosis, proceeding in a way that is mindful of the patient's willingness to learn the medical facts and their implications. The usual progress of the disease is described, as are appropriate forms of treatment, and, finally, the treatment that will be implemented initially.

These meetings, usually lasting about half an hour, are taped so the patient can listen again at home. Dr. Rosenbaum points out that in the office the patient is likely to be upset, anxious, and bewildered — too distracted to listen attentively or really hear much of what is said. Having the interview available on tape allows the patient to listen to it later when there is likely to be a better opportunity to reflect on what was discussed and to take appropriate actions.

Dr. Rosenbaum emphasizes the importance of establishing an atmosphere of openness and trust in order to mobilize the patient's will to live, a key element in any therapeutic effort. To further support this positive approach, Dr. Rosenbaum frequently recommends that patients participate in some type of group counseling program that deals with concerns of importance to patients with life-threatening illness. "Sharing frustrations with others in similar circumstances," says Dr. Rosenbaum, "often relieves the sense of isolation that cancer patients experience."

These sentiments expressed by Dr. Rosenbaum are not limited to situations involving a diagnosis of cancer. Norman Cousins, who experienced life-threatening ailments involving ankylosing spondylitis and a massive coronary, placed a great deal of emphasis on the effect of doctor-patient communication on the patient's well-being and ability to cope with bad news. "A serious diagnosis," said

Cousins in an interview shortly before his death, "can be communicated as a challenge rather than a verdict. . . . If the patient leaves the physician's office in a state of emotional devastation, then the environment for effective treatment has been impaired."[30] Citing recent findings from an emerging branch of medicine called psychoneuroimmunology, which deals with the interaction of the brain and the immune and endocrine systems, Cousins advanced the view that the style of medical communication exerts either a positive attitude, one that promotes faith in the ultimate outcome, or a negative attitude, with corresponding feelings of despondency and despair.[31] In Cousins' experience, both as a patient and as a member of the medical staff at the UCLA Medical Center, good communication between caregiver and patient helps to motivate the patient's own "healing system" and thereby creates the potential for a positive outcome regardless of the ultimate prognosis.

Dealing with the Dying: Stress in the Helping Professions

Nurses, physicians, and other health care professionals work in environments where death is experienced much more frequently than in most walks of life. Although working with dying patients may make death more familiar, it doesn't necessarily make the experience less stressful. Dealing with terminal patients who are suffering intractable pain, or who have young children, or who are manifestly afraid to die adds to the stress associated with providing care.[32] Generally, the most stressful situations are those in which caregivers feel helpless, lacking in power to make the situation better.

Jeanne Quint Benoliel has identified three major areas of concern in the relationship between caregivers and dying patients: (1) the stresses associated with terminal care, (2) the education that caregivers receive for this kind of work, and (3) the influence of the organizational structure and institutional values on providing services to dying patients and their families.[33] In reviewing the literature on how health care providers cope with stress, she notes that "observational studies of nurses have shown that they spend more time with dying patients than with nondying patients," yet they "display more verbal and nonverbal avoidance in spite of the actual greater amount of time spent." This finding suggests that educational programs and health care institutions need to provide more adequate training and assistance to personnel who care for the dying. With regard to the issue of avoidance, Benoliel points out that "open communication does not necessarily mean open talk about death, but it does mean openness to the patient's verbalized concerns."

Besides the ordinary human emotional response to the death of another person, the health professional is exposed to other causes of stress related to the helping role. The inability to produce a cure may be perceived as inadequate care for the patient. The "what ifs" that anyone experiences at a loss may confound helping professionals as well. If not dealt with adequately, these doubts can produce harmful stress.

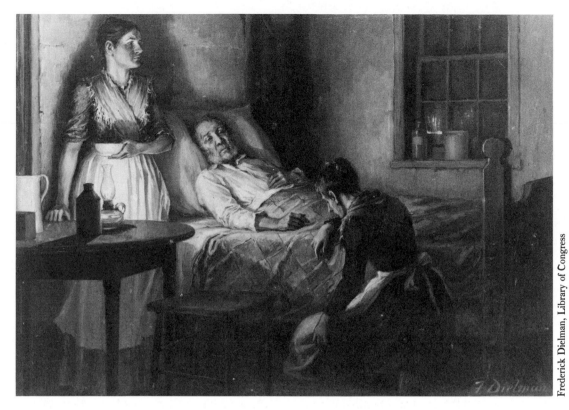

This 1895 illustration captures, in posture and expression, the weariness that accompanies round-the-clock care for the seriously ill and dying. Today's caregivers may feel this burden as much as ever while expecting themselves to put such feelings aside to conform to an image of professionalism.

Consider, for example, the compelling image of the emergency room drama of immediate response to a life-or-death situation. Perhaps at no other place in the hospital is the pressure to perform more intense than in the emergency room or trauma unit. As an ER staffer at one hospital put it, "You can be sitting there almost lulled to sleep during a quiet period, then suddenly everything is happening at once because there's just been a five-car crackup." Medical intervention must be rapidly and efficiently mobilized if life is to be sustained. For some, this kind of pressure is overwhelming. They find the more routine rhythms of patient care in other wards less stressful. Others gain satisfaction from being thrust into situations in which their skills must be quickly brought to bear in order to save lives.

Trauma usually allows little or no opportunity to establish a relationship. Emergency room patients are frequently comatose or incoherent because of shock. In some cases, the ER staff must take action that can make the difference between life and death while receiving little or no feedback from the patient. The patient who survives to be transferred to the intensive care unit may not be seen again by those who labored so energetically to sustain his or her life.

When trauma results in a patient's death, staff members are faced with the task of delivering bad news to relatives and handling their reactions. It has been noted that this task is an "underemphasized part of the work" of trauma care and one for which the staff "may have had no training and little experience . . . [yet] . . . it is a time that the relative will always remember and, if handled badly, will leave lasting scars."[34] Many commentators advise that a private room be made available where relatives and friends can wait and be seen by staff members. Communication of information about a patient's condition or death should be tailored to the situation as well as sensitive to the relationship of the person who is told. Usually, this information is provided by a doctor, perhaps with other staff members also on hand to assist distressed relatives. In this difficult situation, honesty and truthfulness are considered to be imperative, along with genuine understanding and support.

The comparative impersonality of the patient-caregiver relationship in the emergency situation may affect the way ER staffers respond to a patient's death, lessening its impact. Nevertheless, frequent exposure to death is itself stressful. The notion that everyone can be saved may be a desirable objective, but it is not conducive to coping with the realities of the emergency room. When the circumstances surrounding a death elicit the caregiver's own anxieties about death, or when the death seems exceptionally tragic—the death of a child, for example, or the death of a family in an automobile accident on Christmas Eve—hospital personnel are likely to be affected more profoundly than they are by deaths that occur under more routine circumstances.

Health professionals sometimes question what constitutes the proper degree of involvement with a patient. How much should a doctor or nurse personally care about a dying patient? Aside from the professional commitment, what about personal and emotional involvement with the patient? Conflicts between emotions and professional responsibilities can contribute to guilt, confusion, and avoidance behavior—all factors that can increase stress.

If helping is defined as curing, medical personnel are vulnerable to feelings of failure when a patient dies.[35] To avoid such feelings, a caregiver may resort to following hospital routine and standardized policies. The desire to avoid being exposed to the patient's pain and encounter with death may be manifest in delays in administering medication, which adds to the confusion and guilt—all symptoms of the conflicting emotions that arise due to uncertainty about what constitutes "proper and correct" involvement with patients. Such uncertainty may be experienced too with regard to feelings of grief arising from a patient's death.[36]

The professional relationships among members of the health care team may also contribute to stressful situations. Once a terminal diagnosis is made, nurses are likely to come into contact with the patient much more frequently than the patient's physician. Yet the physician's decision about the extent to which life should be sustained, or whether heroic measures should be avoided, influences the type of treatment the patient receives. It is not always possible to simply "follow doctor's orders." For instance, if a doctor has indicated that heroics are to be avoided, who will decide whether a particular procedure is "heroic" or "ordinary" in the circumstances? Should medical measures be taken to sustain life even when not ordered by the doctor? Resentment may arise at being thrust into the position of being what one nursing educator calls "the instrument of death by delegation."[37]

How can medical and nursing professionals deal with these difficulties? The first step involves establishing a supportive environment in which death is discussed openly among those involved in patients' care. Policies should be implemented to meet the special needs of the dying as well as to mitigate the stresses experienced by those who care for them. Procedures can be established that allow flexibility and confidence in responding to the circumstances surrounding a patient's death. Members of the health care team should be given ample opportunity to discuss their feelings and the issues that arise in providing care for the dying.

A study of stress experienced by nurses at a cancer research center in Toronto found that nurses seemed to focus on the problems of caring for the dying patient almost as a displacement of more basic concerns. These concerns included feelings of inadequacy, a sense of isolation from colleagues, questions about the effectiveness of active treatment for dying patients, reluctance to express these concerns openly with colleagues because of fear of criticism and mistrust, and frustration stemming from the failure of physicians to resolve these problems omnipotently. When the nurses asked for and received a series of weekly sessions to facilitate communication and promote understanding of their problems, they reported that their major difficulty was in dealing with patients' feelings about illness, prognosis, and death. They felt "impotent because their training had led them to believe there should be answers where often there are none."[38]

One of the most important avenues for reducing stress among medical and nursing staff involves developing an effective referral system. Such a referral system, along with seminars and regular meetings designed to educate as well as provide opportunities for communication and mutual support, can be potent means whereby the stress experienced by helping professionals can be alleviated.

In one nursing home, for example, staff members' schedules are rotated so that as death nears, someone is with the patient almost constantly. The patient's family is notified and, if desired, a member of the clergy is called to the patient's bedside. If no relatives live nearby, the nursing home's staff assist in making arrangements for the funeral or disposition of the body. Staff members who had developed a close relationship with the patient are given time off to attend funeral services if they wish. Other patients who express an interest are informed of the death.

Staff members who cared for the patient in any way — the nursing staff, housekeeping personnel, dieticians, recreational and special service personnel —

A person's in the room with me and they're very close to dying and afraid. I can feel the fear of death in myself. I'm working through my fear. I give them an opportunity, silent though it may be, to work through theirs. If I come into a room saying, "Oh, there's nothing to be afraid of. We go through death and then into another rebirth," that's not very useful. That's a way of not dealing with the power of the moment — the suffering in that room in the fellow on the bed, and the suffering in the mind of the fellow next to the bed.

Stephen Levine, *A Gradual Awakening*

gather to discuss their responses to the patient's illness and death. Positive aspects of care are noted and encouraged while methods of improving patient care are discussed and plans made for implementation. Thus, staff members are given an opportunity to discuss their professional as well as personal relationship with the patient and their responses to the death. This kind of health care approach, which recognizes the needs of patients, staff members, and surviving family members, is a model of what can be achieved when health care institutions devise methods that allow more personal and human care of the dying.

Those who care for the dying must have confidence in their methods of caregiving and must believe that the care they provide is appropriate and beneficial and in the best interest of the patient. An attitude of caring and support must be communicated to patients to foster trust and feelings of self-worth and value in the patient as well as the caregiver.

Personal care is not limited to the patient's physical needs and well-being; the patient's personality must also be taken into account. According to Jeanne Quint Benoliel, personal care requires continuity of contact between at least one caregiver and the patient, opportunity for the patient to remain informed of his or her condition and treatment, participation by the patient in decisions that affect him or her, and behavior by staff members that elicits the patient's trust and confidence.[39] Someone who has established a supportive and trustful relationship with the patient offers a sense of the familiar amid what might be otherwise strange surroundings. Such a person may be able to act as counselor and advocate, a trusted friend to the patient in possibly difficult times.

Another source of continuity in patient care involves returning the patient to the same hospital or nursing home, perhaps even the same unit, when institutional care is warranted. Seeing familiar faces in unfamiliar surroundings can help the patient feel less emotionally fragmented and can give the comfort that comes from a sense of knowing what to expect. There is less doubt, less anxiety, about what might happen next.

Everyone who confronts the reality of dying — whether as a patient, family member, or health care professional — needs to experience a supportive environment nurtured by openness, compassion, and sensitive listening. The patient's family and friends should be encouraged to participate in the patient's care, as appropriate, thus providing a concrete way to alleviate their feelings of helplessness. Eileen Renear lists some of the ways in which caregivers can help meet the needs of families:[40]

1. Facilitate discussion and the therapeutic flow of feelings by being aware of nonverbal as well as verbal modes of communication. Sensitive, caring communication is an important accompaniment to physical care.
2. Alleviate concerns about pain and discomfort. Share information as well as hope.
3. When death is imminent, this is a special time to emphasize care, both for the patient and for the family. Even if the patient is comatose, he or she can be treated as a person worthy of care and attention. Encourage family members to talk to the patient even though he or she is unconscious or otherwise unresponsive. Inform family members about procedures and prepare them for what to expect.
4. After death, as the focus of caregiving turns to meeting the needs of the survivors, keep the lines of communication open. Simple actions — bringing a cup of coffee, making a phone call, just spending time — can provide a meaningful demonstration of support and loving affection.

Health care professionals are uniquely situated to offer sensitive and caring support for the dying and their families. In most instances, these resources represent an untapped potential that is likely to be realized only when society acts to improve the second-class citizenship of the dying.

Public Health Response to AIDS

What images and feelings do you become aware of as you think about AIDS? For many, AIDS is synonymous with death; a dread disease, contagious and epidemic, a twentieth-century plague. The brief history of AIDS has been marked by questions concerning the allocation of economic, medical, and social resources, as well as by discussions concerning legal and ethical issues in medicine and the delivery of health care to the affected population.

The first cases of acquired immune deficiency syndrome (AIDS), a disease that destroys the body's natural defenses against infection, were reported in 1981.[41] By early 1982, most researchers believed that AIDS was caused by an infectious agent. Discovery of HIV (human immunodeficiency virus) as the cause of AIDS was separately confirmed in January 1984 by Robert Gallo at the U.S. National Institutes of Health and by Luc Montagnier at the Pasteur Institute in Paris.[42] By late 1985, a virus had been identified and linked to the disease, its genetic sequence determined, and a blood test devised to detect antibodies to AIDS.

The criteria for defining cases of AIDS, as established by the United States Centers for Disease Control (CDC), include laboratory evidence as well as the presence of "opportunistic" infections — which are usually the most prominent and life-threatening manifestations of AIDS, although various manifestations of HIV infection in the brain are also common. The complications of HIV infection include fever, diarrhea, severe weight loss, and swollen lymph nodes. When a person infected with the HIV virus does not meet the full criteria for AIDS, the diagnosis of AIDS-related complex, or ARC, is used. This condition is generally considered to be an "asymptomatic" HIV infection that will eventually progress toward AIDS. Individuals infected with the virus may be unaware of it until such time as symptoms become evident, perhaps years later. No cure or preventive vaccine currently exists for AIDS.

The pace of medical discoveries concerning the nature of the AIDS virus was more than matched by the spread of the disease. Some felt that the initial response to AIDS by various public health agencies was slow considering the urgency of the situation, with cases multiplying at an alarming rate. Since the first outbreak of AIDS in the United States predominantly affected homosexual and bisexual men, some people attributed the perceived slow response by the government to bias against the life styles associated with the affected populations. Soon, however, intravenous drug users, hemophiliacs, and recipients of blood transfusions were also recognized as being at risk for AIDS, as were the sexual partners of persons infected with the HIV virus. Although no respecter of persons or life styles, AIDS continued to affect most the population of homosexual and bisexual men. An indication of the suffering caused by AIDS among this group can be seen in the fact that, for single men aged twenty-five to forty-four years old in Manhattan and San Francisco, AIDS was cited as the leading cause of premature mortality as measured by years of potential life lost.[43]

From the first reported cases of AIDS in 1981 through the end of the decade, more than 100,000 cases had been reported in the United States.[44] About 85,000 deaths were attributable to the disease. Of the cases reported in 1989, 89.4 percent involved males and 10.6 percent females. Almost half of AIDS cases occurred in the age group from thirty to thirty-nine years old, and about 90 percent were within the age group from thirteen to forty-nine years old. Nearly 2 percent of diagnosed AIDS cases occurred among children under thirteen years old.

The AIDS "pandemic" is, of course, not limited to the United States. According to estimates made by the World Health Organization, based on reports from 133 countries through February of 1988, about 150,000 cases of AIDS had been reported and between 5 million and 10 million people were HIV-infected.[45] While Asia and Oceania have experienced comparatively few cases of AIDS, Europe, Africa, North America, and South America all have been affected, with the two "epicenters" of the pandemic having been the United States and central Africa. In the United States, according to some estimates, from 10 to 30 percent of confirmed AIDS cases nationwide go unrecorded, and a committee of the National Research Council has called for "increased funding to determine the prevalence of HIV and the behaviors that spread it."[46]

Meeting the goals of treating persons now infected with AIDS and stopping the further spread of the disease requires the investment of money, energy, and talent in programs ranging from fundamental biological research to public

Smithsonian Institution

© Albert Lee Strickland

The making of a memorial quilt was among the elaborate personal and social mechanisms for dealing with grief widely practiced during the nineteenth century, as in this example memorializing a granddaughter who died in infancy. This traditional mourning custom was revived recently to commemorate and remember persons who died from AIDS; in the example shown here, words and symbols express beloved qualities of Joe's life. For survivors, the creation of such memorials provides not only a focus for physically working through grief but also a means of perpetuating the memory of the loved one.

education. Federal funding is concentrated on public education, vaccine develop-ment, and drug testing, but treatment costs—which are reported to be three times the average—are largely the responsibility of the patient. Although insur-ance covers a portion of the cost, the balance has been borne by hospitals and taxpayers. In New York, a state that has the largest proportion of AIDS patients among all the states, it was reported that about two-thirds of the cost of caring for AIDS patients had been paid by local taxpayers. Larry Gostin, a consultant on development of the Federal AIDS Policy Act, has drawn attention to the "politi-cal" dimensions of AIDS, given that "the burden of disease falls predominantly on disfavored populations—intravenous drug users, homosexuals, and prosti-tutes," with racial minorities disproportionately represented among these groups.[47]

The community response to AIDS has been mixed.[48] While some commu-nities have responded with a variety of health and public service programs, others have reacted by narrowing and closing off any sort of outreach. For example, when Elisabeth Kübler-Ross proposed developing a hospice for infants with AIDS at her center in rural Virginia, representatives of the local community acted swiftly to deny the necessary permits. Fear of contagion won out over the desire to help sick and dying infants.

Health care personnel have in some instances voiced similar concerns about AIDS, particularly during the initial period when comparatively little informa-tion about the disease was available. Patients with AIDS were sometimes placed in rooms distant from nurses' stations and told to stay in their rooms. Eventually, the evidence strongly indicated that AIDS could be transmitted only through three primary routes: sexual intercourse (vaginal or anal) with an infected per-son, exposure to infected blood or blood products, and transmission from an infected mother to her child before or during birth.

As hysteria has given way to better information, care, as well as communica-tion between patients and caregivers, has improved. For example, at San Fran-cisco General Hospital, medical and nursing personnel now take care to explain procedures and options to patients, encouraging them to control their own deci-sions. Staff members are encouraged to "talk and touch and hug" AIDS patients, just as they do other seriously ill or dying patients. The hospice model of care—usually with home care as a major component—has been successfully instituted in some areas, especially where the community is close-knit and actively involved and can help to sustain the level of care required for most AIDS patients.

The AIDS epidemic has put considerable pressure on American medical resources and institutions. It is currently estimated that about two out of every one hundred health care dollars are spent on persons with AIDS, with annual costs relative to the disease estimated at nearly $17 billion. Meanwhile, it is esti-mated that 1 to 1.5 million Americans are infected with the virus but haven't yet developed symptoms. Thus, although the frequency of reports and articles about AIDS has dwindled compared with the furor resulting from earlier cases, it is clear that this disease remains a major challenge to the health care system and to society as a whole, as well as a challenge of a more personal sort to the individuals who are directly affected.

© Mal Warshaw and Ross Medical Associates

*Dr. Elisabeth Kübler-Ross, seen here with a patient who has been diagnosed with
a life-threatening illness, is widely recognized for her pioneering efforts toward
increased awareness on the part of the patient, family, and medical staff relative to
the issues that arise in caring for the dying.*

Terminal Care: Alternatives

Patients with life-threatening illness usually receive a combination of both
acute and long-term care. As conditions change, a patient may sometimes need
the acute-care skills and resources provided by a hospital and at other times need
the supportive services of a nursing home or hospice. Institutional care is often
alternated with home care on those occasions when outpatient services are sufficient to meet the patient's needs.

Although 80 percent of terminal patient care in the United States is provided by hospitals and nursing homes, hospice care has become increasingly important. As a comprehensive term, hospice care is distinguished by its orientation specifically toward the needs of the dying patient. Such care may be provided in a setting devoted exclusively to caring for the terminally ill or in a general medical center with a palliative care department. Palliative care refers to treatment that is intended to provide comfort to the patient, although it has no effect on the course of the disease itself. Another form of hospice care is provided by individuals or organizations that offer support services to terminally ill patients living at home or in a conventional health care setting. Each of the three major categories of institutional medical care — hospitals, nursing homes, and hospices — is designed to optimally serve a specific purpose within the health care delivery system.

Hospitals primarily provide short-term, acute care. Aggressive techniques are employed to diagnose symptoms, provide treatment, and sustain life. The most recent data indicate that the average length of a hospital stay has been decreasing and is now about six days.[49] Among the factors contributing to this decline may be increased use of outpatient facilities and home care, as well as advances in treatment. Most hospital patients are discharged back into the community after their well-being has been restored. The hospital's sophisticated equipment and diverse medical and surgical resources combine to emphasize its primary goal: rehabilitation.

Nursing homes (a term that includes convalescent care and extended care nursing facilities) provide a less-sophisticated level of care than do hospitals. Because they are chiefly intended to provide care for the chronically ill, the average length of their patients' stay is substantially longer than that for hospital patients. About three-quarters of nursing home patients eventually return to the community; the remaining one-quarter includes both those who require ongoing nursing care and supervision and those who die while in a nursing home. Nursing homes categorized as skilled nursing facilities have a registered nurse on duty around the clock and a skilled paramedical staff. Homes categorized as intermediate care facilities offer less intensive care and have either a registered nurse or licensed vocational nurse on duty during day shifts.

The hospice, the third type of institutional care, is designed especially for the terminally ill. The goal of hospice care is to allow patients to be free of physical and psychological pain and to provide a comfortable, homelike environment in which dying occurs amid relatively familiar surroundings. Friends and family members often participate to a significant extent in the patient's care. Because the hospice is a relatively new alternative in America, there have been a variety of approaches to this form of care.

Although there are few residential care hospices in the United States, an increasing number of community-based organizations support home care for the dying or supplement care provided by the conventional health care institutions. Hospice care emphasizes keeping the patient as pain free and comfortable as possible while refraining from dramatic medical interventions when death approaches. In fact, many of the advances in pain control, particularly in cases of

The Dying Person's Bill of Rights

I have the right to be treated as a living human being until I die.

I have the right to maintain a sense of hopefulness however changing its focus may be.

I have the right to be cared for by those who can maintain a sense of hopefulness, however changing this might be.

I have the right to express my feelings and emotions about my approaching death in my own way.

I have the right to participate in decisions concerning my care.

I have the right to expect continuing medical and nursing attention even though "cure" goals must be changed to "comfort" goals.

I have the right not to die alone.

I have the right to be free from pain.

I have the right to have my questions answered honestly.

I have the right not to be deceived.

I have the right to have help from and for my family in accepting my death.

I have the right to die in peace and dignity.

I have the right to retain my individuality and not be judged for my decisions which may be contrary to beliefs of others.

I have the right to discuss and enlarge my religious or spiritual experiences, whatever these may mean to others.

I have the right to expect that the sanctity of the human body will be respected after death.

I have the right to be cared for by caring, sensitive, knowledgeable people who will attempt to understand my needs and will be able to gain some satisfaction in helping me face my death.

Marilee Ivars Donovan and Sandra Girton Pierce,
Cancer Care Nursing

advanced cancer, have been stimulated by the approach to terminal care associated with hospices and other palliative care settings. The result has been considerable progress in the development of both pharmacological and psychological means of controlling pain.

In reviewing the phenomenon of hospice care, Inge Corliss observes that a salient feature of such care is its response to the conventional medical message expressed to terminal patients and their families that "nothing more can be done."[50] The hospice response is that, even though no further treatment of the disease may be available, indeed "something more *can* be done." This philosophy of terminal care has "brought the force of modern science to bear on the relief of symptoms" while creating an approach to care that is focused on "a smaller, more intimate pattern of relationships." Corliss notes that, having proved their value and effectiveness, hospices have recently been forced to shift their attention to questions about their ability to survive financially, the uniqueness of the hospice model compared to other methods of delivering terminal care, the impact of Medicare legislation, the integration of spiritual care into the hospice program, and the role of hospice in the care of persons with AIDS.

Whereas the pioneering efforts at hospice care were noted for their "grass-roots" organization and rugged independence, today's hospices function in an environment that is increasingly regulated by government policies and schedules of reimbursement. On this point, Corliss notes that "the politicalization of reimbursement for hospice care has resulted in regulations requiring all programs wishing to obtain Medicare certification . . . to comply with a set of standards based on one model of care."[51]

At the same time, conventional medical institutions have learned from the hospice model and have implemented alternative forms of palliative care. Some governmental agencies as well as private insurers have seen the hospice model as a way to exchange costly institutional care with less-expensive home care staffed by unpaid family members and volunteers. As some commentators have noted, "Home care may sound domestic and low key, but it is quietly bearing massive burdens in the health care system."[52]

These issues have complicated and, to some extent, clouded the original vision of hospice. In the bureaucratic quest to reduce expenditures, individual actions motivated by mercy, sense of community, or desire to serve others may be systematically devalued. This is not to say that persons now involved in hospices have no vision or no sense of continuity with respect to the aims of hospice care. On the contrary, the hospice alternative remains a viable method for providing terminal care, and those involved tend to be highly motivated and often virtually selfless in their enthusiasm and commitment. Yet, at a time when the needs of persons with AIDS are added to the former demands for services provided by hospices, what is required is an even broader implementation of the hospice philosophy and more comprehensive support for its aims of easing the transition of dying patients.

Hospice Care

The hospice movement came about in response to what many people — patients and medical practitioners alike — perceived to be inadequate care for the dying within the conventional hospital. At the sociopolitical level, David Greer and his colleagues note that "hospice care reflects changing societal expectations of the health-care system, from cure to care, extension of life to quality of life."[53] The concept and practice of palliative care, with its emphasis on comfort rather than curing, has been traced by some to religious traditions of care for the sick and dying. In the Judaeo-Christian tradition, for example, we find the concepts of *diakonia* (serving and caring for others), *metanoia* (which conveys the notion of turning within to a deeper self or divine power), and *kairos* (a term that points to the significance of a unique moment of fulfillment).[54]

In tracing the development of hospices, Sandol Stoddard notes that the tradition of such care goes back to the medieval religious orders who kept "places of

> "The hospice movement is a great movement, not because it was legislated by Congress, or mandated by the Federal Government, but because it evolved out of the hearts of people who care."
>
> Senator Edward M. Kennedy (Massachusetts), from his keynote speech at the first annual meeting of the National Hospice Organization, Washington, D.C., October 1978.

welcome" so that pilgrims and travellers could be "cherished and refreshed."[55] Herbs for healing and relief from pain grew in the monastery gardens, and the dying "received special care and honour, for they too were seen as pilgrims, closer than others to God." Hospitals, in contrast, arose along with the later flourishing of science, "built on a military model of efficiency that was invented, originally, by Romans for the quick repair of their gladiators and slaves."

The modern hospice originated in the late 1950s and 1960s; its most notable model is St. Christopher's Hospice in Sydenham, England, organized in 1967 by Dr. Cicely Saunders.[56] St. Christopher's is named for "the patron saint of travelers because it is almost entirely devoted to those whose journey in this life is nearly over."[57] Located in a close-knit neighborhood in southeast London, St. Christopher's has become the model cited most often by those wishing to establish hospice care elsewhere. The patients who come to St. Christopher's are largely drawn from within a six-mile radius of the hospice, an area that contains approximately 1.5 million inhabitants. Of the seventy beds available, fifty-four are allocated to cancer patients, with the remainder occupied by elderly patients who can no longer function independently. On average, the length of stay for a cancer patient is about twelve days.

Filled with flowers, photographs, and personal belongings, the four-bed bays at St. Christopher's create an atmosphere that is cheerful and familiar. Patients are treated as mature, responsible individuals and are given opportunities to discuss their illness or not, depending on their mood and inclination. Patients who are accustomed to smoking or to having a cocktail before dinner are not prohibited from enjoying these familiar pleasures. Visiting hours extend from eight in the morning until eight at night, allowing considerable interaction between patients and their families. Children are encouraged to visit, and even family pets are allowed; a nursery for offspring of the hospice staff is operated on the grounds. The personal approach to patient care at St. Christopher's is accentuated by the parties that are held frequently for patients, staff, and families.

With patient care costing about 80 percent of comparable costs in a British general hospital, the largest percentage of operating costs at St. Christopher's is for staff salaries, reflecting what Dr. Saunders calls a "high person, low technology and hardware" system of health care.[58] Intravenous apparatuses, respirators, and related devices for prolonging life are absent. Instead, St. Christopher's encourages an atmosphere of tranquility and an acceptance of the process of dying.

The highest priority is making the patient comfortable. Painful and distressing symptoms are controlled by skillful use of narcotics and other medications.

Death comes frequently at St. Christopher's. When a patient dies, the curtains are drawn around the bed while nurses and members of the patient's family gather to express their farewells. Relatives can sit with the body for a time if they wish. Afterwards, the body is taken to a private room, where it is bathed and prepared for viewing in a small chapel at St. Christopher's. If the family wishes, a member of the clergy may be invited to come in and speak a few words of comfort regarding the deceased. The family is encouraged to participate to the extent that members desire. Allowing the family to spend time sitting with the body contrasts with the practice of quickly removing the body and handing it over to the mortician as efficiently and as secretly as possible. Death is treated more familiarly at St. Christopher's.

Another feature of the program at St. Christopher's that has been emulated by many hospice groups in this country is the home care program. Through this program, carried out jointly by the nurses at St. Christopher's and various community health practitioners in the vicinity, hospice care is provided to nonresidential patients. Some home care patients have not previously been patients at St. Christopher's; others are patients who have been released from the residential care program to return to their homes. About 10 percent of the patients in the residential program do return home periodically when symptoms are controlled or for a brief visit during holiday periods.

The home care program operates essentially as an outpatient program; medication schedules are planned by the hospice staff, and hospice nurses periodically visit patients at home to monitor their condition. In addition, a nurse is on call around the clock to provide help or answer questions from patients and family members. Knowing that such backup is available is an important source of confidence for the patients and families participating in St. Christopher's outpatient program.

When patients come in for examination or to review their treatment programs, the clinical schedule is so arranged that they need not wait to see the doctor. Discussion time is allowed so that questions from patients or their families can be satisfactorily answered. During these clinical visits, the patient's home care routine or drug maintenance schedule is altered if symptoms warrant. Maintaining the outpatient's comfort receives the same emphasis at St. Christopher's as maintaining the residential patient's.

Augmenting the residential program with a home care program greatly increases the number of persons who can be served by the staff at St. Christopher's. Residential patients can be returned home when their condition makes home care feasible and desirable. Patients from the home care program can be admitted as residents when the family is worn out, emotionally drained, or otherwise unable to provide the patient support necessary. The patterns of health care for the dying practiced at St. Christopher's are now being emulated in varying degrees in this country, both within the conventional medical system and by hospice organizations devoted to making support services available for the terminally ill.

The first American hospice, the Hospice of New Haven in Connecticut, began serving patients through a home care program in 1974 as part of a demonstration program funded by the National Cancer Institute.[59] Its development was stimulated partly by the visit of Dr. Cicely Saunders in the early 1960s to Yale University, where she reported on her efforts at St. Christopher's. When the program in New Haven got under way, Dr. Sylvia Lack of St. Christopher's became its first medical director. Hospice care has grown rapidly since this initial program. Now there are hundreds of hospice programs nationwide, and hospice care is reimbursable under Medicare/Medicaid programs and through some private insurance companies. In addition, within the last few years, a number of hospice programs designed specifically to care for terminally ill children have been inaugurated.[60]

The attractiveness of the hospice concept is reflected in the growth of community organizations designed to put it into practice. Most hospice programs start as relatively informal groups staffed largely by volunteers; later, the organizational structures become more developed. The majority are nonprofit. However, as conventional health care agencies and institutions assume a larger role in hospice care, it is likely that there will be an increase in the number of commercially operated hospice care facilities.

Although a few hospice groups in this country provide residential care for the dying — similar to that provided at St. Christopher's in London — most hospice organizations are composed of volunteers who provide support services to patients who are either at home or in an institutional health care setting.

In brief, then, the philosophy of hospice care includes control of pain and other symptoms (both physical and psychological), accessibility to medical and nursing care, the use of trained volunteers and family members as caregivers, a home care component, and a bereavement program for the survivors. Pain control and alleviation of symptoms are of primary importance in terminal care. It is noteworthy, too, that the emphasis on a "team" approach in hospice care has brought about a new sense of equality among participants in health care.

Home Care

Those who believe that the home is a viable setting for providing terminal care point to a number of possible advantages, including the obvious fact that the patient is simply *at home*, "the center of meaningful activity and connectedness to family, friends, and community."[61] Equally obvious, the home setting offers a greater sense of normalcy than does the hospital or hospice. Home care also offers greater opportunities for sustaining relationships and for exercising self-determination. A characteristic comment from patients as well as family members and friends concerns the fact that home care minimizes the need to "live to a timetable" as would be the case in a hospital, with its designated visiting hours and scheduled routine. Finally, having the patient at home allows for a reciprocity, a mutual sharing of care and concerns, that many families find gratifying.

For these benefits to be realized, however, adequate support must be available not only from the patient's family and friends but also from skilled caregivers who are available to supervise the home care services and to provide guidance or relief when necessary. Home care is essentially a 24-hour-a-day job. Whether family member, friend, or outside volunteer, someone must be available at all times to attend to the various tasks that constitute appropriate patient care.

The main ingredient for successful home care is the presence of a willing and able family member. However, the importance of family caregivers is frequently overlooked or not fully recognized. Support services such as personal care, home-making, and companion sitting can help to alleviate the primary caregiver's workload. Professional services provided by physicians and visiting nurses are essential, particularly those relating to the management of pain and other symptoms. Finally, the physical environment of the home must be suitable for meeting the patient's needs. As one patient said, "You can't always make a home into a hospital."[62]

A number of factors can influence the decision to hospitalize the terminally ill patient. With increasing weakness or loss of mobility, the patient may need more assistance than can be provided at home. An inability to manage elimination needs — loss of bowel or bladder control — may make hospitalization necessary, as may uncontrolled or inadequately controlled pain. Finally, hospitalization may be chosen when families feel "out of control," no longer able to provide the level of care that is necessary.

Hospital-Based Palliative Care

In recent years, a number of hospice or palliative care programs have been instituted within conventional hospitals. Figures from the late 1980s indicate that there are about 2000 hospice programs in the United States, 800 of which are hospital-based.[63] The willingness of hospital administrators and others in the medical community to find innovative ways to care for the dying is an important step toward recognizing and responding to the special needs of the terminally ill and their families. Indeed, hospice-style palliative care is no longer unique to hospices. As Clive Seale points out, in hospitals where nurses have the time to get to know dying patients, where nurses are assigned responsibility for the care of individual patients rather than just given tasks, where supportive relationships exist between staff members, and where a policy of open disclosure of diagnosis and prognosis prevails, "nursing care for the dying approaches the ideals of hospice care."[64]

Broadly speaking, we can distinguish two types of hospice or palliative care within hospitals. In the first, a separate ward is designated for terminal care; in the second, terminal care programs are integrated into the usual hospital organization. Each type has advantages and disadvantages.

Those who favor the creation of a separate ward argue that such a setting allows for a general relaxation of hospital regulations and procedures, thus creating an environment that is more conducive to satisfying the needs and desires of the terminally ill and their families. For example, the age requirements for visitors are often relaxed so that children can be with a dying relative. The rules

I know that, during my own illness in 1964, my fellow patients at the hospital would talk about matters they would never discuss with their doctors. The psychology of the seriously ill put barriers between us and those who had the skill and the grace to minister to us.

There was first of all the feeling of helplessness — a serious disease in itself.

There was the subconscious fear of never being able to function normally again — and it produced a wall of separation between us and the world of open movement, open sounds, open expectations.

There was the reluctance to be thought a complainer.

There was the desire not to add to the already great burden of apprehension felt by one's family; this added to the isolation.

There was the conflict between the terror of loneliness and the desire to be left alone.

There was the lack of self-esteem, the subconscious feeling perhaps that our illness was a manifestation of our inadequacy.

There was the fear that decisions were being made behind our backs, that not everything was made known that we wanted to know, yet dreaded knowing.

There was the morbid fear of intrusive technology, fear of being metabolized by a data base, never to regain our faces again. There was resentment of strangers who came at us with needles and vials — some of which put supposedly magic substances in our veins, and others which took more of our blood than we thought we could afford to lose. There was the distress of being wheeled through white corridors to laboratories for all sorts of strange encounters with compact machines and blinking lights and whirling discs.

And there was the utter void created by the longing — ineradicable, unremitting, pervasive — for warmth of human contact. A warm smile and an outstretched hand were valued even above the offerings of modern science, but the latter were far more accessible than the former.

Norman Cousins, *Anatomy of an Illness*

governing the length of visits and the visiting hours themselves may be made less stringent than elsewhere in the hospital. The supervisory and nursing personnel on the terminal care ward focus their energies on controlling pain and making the patient comfortable rather than on instituting life-sustaining (or death-postponing) interventions.

However, creating a separate ward for the terminally ill usually requires considerable reorganization of hospital facilities and resources, and this can be quite costly. Too, some argue that isolation from the general patient population places a stigma on the dying. Once a patient is admitted to the terminal ward, the message is clear that the prognosis is death — which may have dysfunctional effects on those who prefer not to face death so openly. Also, although terminal care is increasingly recognized as an important part of any total health care program, many practitioners want to work with patients whose odds for recovery are favorable; thus, some believe it would be difficult to recruit staff whose sole duties involved ministering to the terminally ill. In an environment where death is commonplace, even a highly motivated caregiver is exposed to possibly harmful stress.

Because of these potential difficulties, some health practitioners advocate providing the second type of hospice care program: integrating care for the terminally ill into conventional hospital practices and procedures. Because this approach usually requires less reorganization of facilities and personnel, it is typically less expensive to administer. Integrated care of the dying can range from counseling support to specially trained hospital staff members who participate in a comprehensive treatment program for the dying. Hospice volunteers, members of the clergy, or other interested persons may provide supplemental support by visiting patients, discussing their concerns, counseling, and generally assisting in whatever way seems appropriate.[65] Such help is usually made available to both patients and their families.

The presence of someone familiar with the hospital routine and its organization—who can therefore act as an informal liaison between staff and patients and family members—is frequently a source of great comfort to those experiencing the trauma of terminal illness. Staff members who are sensitive to the needs of the dying and volunteers who are adequately trained to provide support for patients and their families can do much to enhance the care provided to the terminally ill. Integrated care of the terminally ill has typically been most successful where someone with persistence and vision has become an advocate for the dying.

Support Groups

Often, institutional health care programs for the terminally ill are supplemented by support groups that focus on specific interests and needs. These groups range from national organizations such as the American Cancer Society to small community-based groups that help to meet the needs of dying patients and their families in a particular locality.

Many of the community groups are composed of volunteers who want to make some of the elements of hospice care available to local patients. A variety of pursuits may be followed in seeking to realize this goal, including patient visiting programs and educational programs for health care professionals as well as laypersons. Some community groups work toward the establishment of a permanent residential care hospice program, while others concentrate on supplementing the programs in conventional health care facilities or in home care.

The Shanti Project was one of the first such programs.[66] Organized by Dr. Charles Garfield in 1974, the project established a central telephone number that interested persons could call in order to be put in touch with volunteers willing to aid the dying. From the beginning, a policy of accepting only firsthand referrals was followed; this allows Shanti to focus its efforts on persons who request help or information for themselves. Shanti provides counseling and companionship for patients and families as well as conducts educational programs for community and medical groups.

Once a referral is made, the Shanti volunteer becomes an advocate for the patient, a role that can include emptying ashtrays and cleaning the patient's room

© Carol A. Foote

Institutional care becomes more personal when the environment reflects something of the patient's own life style and values. Here, surrounded by photographs of her relatives, a nursing home patient is able to reflect on her personal and family connections outside the institutional setting.

as well as consulting on the patient's behalf with medical personnel and health care agencies. Above all, the volunteer acts as the patient's companion and friend. Shanti encourages the use of peer counseling, whereby one patient helps another, and someone who has experienced grief helps another person undergoing a similar experience. Recently, the Shanti Project has focused its efforts on helping patients with AIDS.

Another community-based group providing volunteer emotional support services is Kara in Palo Alto, California. Taking its name from the Gothic root of the word care — meaning to reach out, to care, and to grieve with — Kara works closely with the hospice program of the local Veterans Administration Hospital, as well as with other hospitals and hospices in neighboring communities. In addition to direct volunteer counseling for dying and bereaved clients, Kara provides training and consulting services to professionals and laypersons. A similar pattern of emotional support and educational programs can be found in many places across the country where community-based support groups exist.

At the national level, one of the best-known support services is "I Can Cope," a program originated in 1977 by two oncology nurses at the North Memorial Medical Center of Minneapolis and sponsored by the American Cancer Society.[67] Designed for cancer patients and their families, "I Can Cope" is organized as a learning experience to help participants "develop a better understanding of cancer and various treatments, learn to manage side effects, deal with fears and feelings, and improve their sense of physical and emotional well-being." Educational experiences are provided through lectures, reading materials, and audiovisual media, as well as through the sharing of problems and concerns by the participants. For many, the program decreases feelings of helplessness and passivity and increases self-satisfaction, self-esteem, and confidence.

Another type of support organization is represented by the Elisabeth Kübler-Ross Center. Located in Virginia, the Center coordinates a variety of programs related to life-threatening illness, bereavement, and the "promotion of physical, intellectual, emotional, and spiritual health."[68] In addition to its educational program, the Center is engaged in projects involving the control of chronic pain, the institution of "screaming rooms" in hospitals, and providing care for babies with AIDS.

The Social Role of the Dying Patient

As sociologist Talcott Parsons discovered in the 1950s, a particular social role accompanies illness.[69] Like all social roles — parent, child, student, employee, spouse — the role of the "person who is sick" includes certain rights as well as responsibilities. For example, when we are ill, others exempt us from our usual tasks. We may stay home from work. Someone else may take on our share of housecleaning or child care. Commitments may be neglected. We are granted the right to be sick. We assume a particular social role that causes others to make allowances for our behavior that otherwise might result in social penalties. Whereas taking off from work just to enjoy a day in the sun is likely to be frowned upon, an absence due to illness elicits sympathy rather than reprimands.

The sick person not only enjoys exemptions from many of the usual social obligations but also receives special consideration and care. Others put forth efforts to make sure the patient is comfortable and is receiving adequate treatment and so on. Personal and financial resources may be devoted to the patient's care and treatment. Such care is part of the social role of being sick, of being a patient.

But these rights are balanced by responsibilities. The sick person must want to get well. Malingerers—those who pretend to be sicker than they really are—receive little or no respect from those whose job it is to provide care or help carry the additional burden imposed by their supposed illness. It's okay to receive special treatment when you're really ill or when you've suffered an injury, but the role of the patient demands that you demonstrate that you'd really rather be well. You've got to take your medicine. You're expected to cooperate with those who are prescribing and administering treatment.

At one time or another most people have experienced the role of patient as well as the role of caregiver. The role of the dying patient is quite different. Although sharing some aspects of the curable patient's social role, the dying person's illness does not fit the pattern of a temporary condition allowing eventual return to wellness. Yet, in our society, a social role for the dying is not well defined. The same expectations may be placed on the dying person as on patients whose prognosis is rehabilitation and return to normal modes of living. Even when circumstances are clearly contrary, the dying person may be urged to maintain a hope of recovery, to deny the reality of what he or she is experiencing. If the dying person does not exhibit this cheerful will to live, friends and family may feel angry or rejected.

The person who is dying also assumes a different role in relation to the medical community. When cure is no longer perceived as a medical possibility, supportive and palliative care takes the place of more active intervention and treatment. Typically, the patient's doctor begins to devote less and less time to mapping out hopeful strategies and becomes more supervisory, expecting the patient to assume more responsibility for his or her own care.

The lack of a clear consensus on care of the dying and the role of the dying patient can lead to actions that seem quite incongruous. Consider, for example, the hopelessly ill patient in the final stage of a terminal condition who is rushed into the intensive care unit and subjected to heroic medical attempts to sustain life. Meanwhile, the patient's family may be waiting outside, experiencing a lingering uncertainty or false hopes for the patient's survival. In such circumstances, death may be far from peaceful or dignified. It may be difficult for the patient to deal with the prospect of death in a personally appropriate and comforting way.

Until about the middle of the twentieth century, a social role for the dying person was more or less fixed by custom and circumstance. The rapid and pervasive social and technological changes of recent times have largely eliminated the traditional role of the dying, while offering few guidelines in its stead. What would a newly rediscovered and updated role for the dying look like? It would undoubtedly draw upon historical precedent while also reflecting the social and technological changes in our present modes of caring for dying patients.

Let us imagine some of the attributes of such a newly evolving role for the dying: No longer does the patient need to maintain an appearance of expecting to live forever, of getting well again, of sustaining false hope. At the same time, the patient assumes a more independent role, able to exercise more self-determination and entitled to a greater degree of cooperation from others involved in caregiving. Caregivers, family members, and the patient work together to nurture a sense of "empowerment" that emphasizes the possibility of the patient's "owning" his or her own life.[70]

The patient whose resources had been mobilized in the effort to effect a cure now turns his or her attention to the prospect of death. Relatives and friends, understanding this change of perspective as natural, allow the patient to disengage from the activities and relationships that prevailed before the onset of illness. Such disengagement does not necessarily mean, however, that the terminal patient will display a desire to "separate" from others.[71] In a study of "farewells by the dying," researchers found that most (80 percent) of the terminally ill persons in the sample expressed a desire to communicate their farewells — primarily through the giving of gifts, writing letters, and having informal conversations — and wanted these farewells to take place late in the course of their dying.[72] A "good" death — that is, one appropriate to the person who is dying — is as much anticipated as was the earlier hope of recovery. The dying person is recognized as the protagonist in an important and potentially valuable experience of life.

Further Readings

American Academy of Arts and Sciences. "Living with AIDS: Parts I and II," *Daedalus* 118, nos. 1 and 2 (Spring and Summer 1989).

William Ray Arney and Bernard J. Bergen. *Medicine and the Management of Living: Taming the Last Great Beast*. Chicago: University of Chicago Press, 1984.

Jeanne Quint Benoliel, ed. *Death Education for the Health Professional*. Washington, D.C.: Hemisphere, 1982.

Daniel Callahan. *What Kind of Life: The Limits of Medical Progress*. New York: Simon & Schuster, 1990.

Deborah Chase. *Dying at Home with Hospice*. St. Louis: C.V. Mosby, 1986.

Charles A. Corr and Donna M. Corr, eds. *Hospice Care: Principles and Practices*. New York: Springer, 1983.

Norman Cousins. *The Physician in Literature*. Philadelphia: Saunders, 1982.

Eli Ginzberg. *The Medical Triangle: Physicians, Politicians, and the Public*. Cambridge, Mass.: Harvard University Press, 1990.

Thomas Andrew Gonda and John Edward Ruark. *Dying Dignified: The Health Professional's Guide to Care*. Menlo Park, Calif.: Addison-Wesley, 1984.

Billy Howard. *Epitaphs for the Living: Words and Images in the Time of AIDS*. Dallas: Southern Methodist University Press, 1989.

John F. Kilner. *Who Lives? Who Dies?: Ethical Criteria in Patient Selection*. New Haven, Conn.: Yale University Press, 1990.

James Kinsella. *Covering the Plague: AIDS and the American Media*, New Brunswick, N.J.: Rutgers University Press, 1990.

William F. May. *The Patient's Ordeal*. Bloomington: Indiana University Press, 1991.

Vincent Mor, David S. Greer, and Robert Kastenbaum, eds. *The Hospice Experiment*. Baltimore: Johns Hopkins University Press, 1988.

Anne Munley. *The Hospice Alternative: A New Context for Death and Dying*. New York: Basic Books, 1985.

Therese A. Rando. *Grief, Dying, and Death: Clinical Interventions for Caregivers*. Champaign, Ill.: Research Press, 1984.

Stanley Joel Reiser. *Medicine and the Reign of Technology*. New York: Cambridge University Press, 1978.

Charles E. Rosenberg. *The Care of Strangers: The Rise of America's Hospital System*. New York: Basic Books, 1987.

Paul Starr. *The Social Transformation of American Medicine*. New York: Basic Books, 1983.

Anselm Strauss, Shizuko Fagerhaugh, Barbara Suczek, and Carolyn Wiener. *Social Organization of Medical Work*. Chicago: University of Chicago Press, 1985.

Mary L.S. Vachon. *Occupational Stress in the Care of the Critically Ill, the Dying, and the Bereaved*. Washington, D.C.: Hemisphere, 1986.

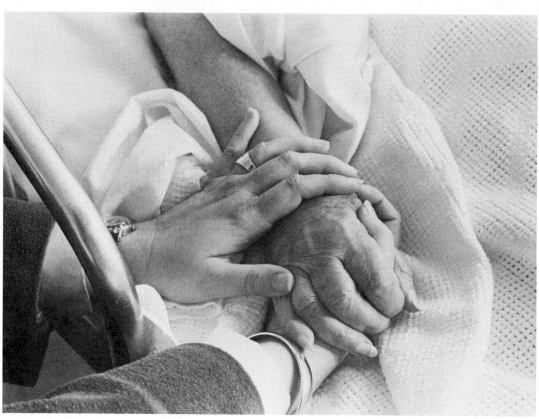

Total care for the patient with a life-threatening illness includes warm, intimate contact with caring persons who are able to listen and share the patient's concerns.

C H A P T E R 5

Facing Death:
Living with
Life-Threatening Illness

*C*ancer. Heart disease. AIDS. For most of us these words send frightening thoughts echoing through the corridors of our mind. The famous as well as the not famous, our friends, and our relatives die from these illnesses. To many people, cancer seems virtually synonymous with death and dying, though in fact the prognosis for a cancer patient is not always death.

In this chapter, we examine life-threatening illness and discuss various ways of responding to it, both medically and personally. Although cancer is preeminent in many people's minds as *the* long-term, life-threatening illness, the circumstances faced by individuals with other life-threatening diseases are much the same. Patients diagnosed with heart disease, cerebrovascular disease, acquired immune deficiency syndrome (AIDS), and other serious illnesses encounter similar kinds of medical and nursing care, methods of coping, and support systems. What is said here about cancer or heart disease, therefore, applies generally to other life-threatening illnesses as well.

The Taboo of Terminal Illness

A patient with acute leukemia compared her experience to that of someone with the Black Death during the fourteenth century in Europe. The origin of the disease in one's body is somewhat mysterious, the result of factors not easily discernible or completely understood. Nature seems somehow to have gotten out of control, and, though not fully comprehending the chain of events that led to such bleak fortunes, the patient feels a responsibility to put things right.

163

When I first realized that I might have cancer, I felt immediately that I had entered a special place, a place I came to call "The Land of the Sick People." The most disconcerting thing, however, was not that I found that place terrifying and unfamiliar, but that I found it so ordinary, so banal. I didn't feel different, didn't feel that my life had radically changed at the moment the word *cancer* became attached to it. The same rules still held. What had changed, however, was other people's perceptions of me. Unconsciously, even with a certain amount of kindness, everyone — with the single rather extraordinary exception of my husband — regarded me as someone who had been altered irrevocably. I don't want to exaggerate my feeling of alienation or to give the impression that it was in any way dramatic. I have no horror stories of the kind I read a few years ago in the *New York Times*; people didn't move their desks away from me at the office or refuse to let their children play with my children at school because they thought that cancer was catching. My friends are all too sophisticated and too sensitive for that kind of behavior. Their distance from me was marked most of all by their inability to understand the ordinariness, the banality of what was happening to me. They marveled at how well I was "coping with cancer." I had become special, no longer like them.

> Alice Stewart Trillin,
> "Of Dragons and Garden Peas:
> A Cancer Patient Talks to Doctors"

Magical thinking — assuming oneself responsible for the illness though not knowing just how — places a great burden on the patient with a life-threatening illness: "What did I do to bring this condition upon myself? If I had done this, or not done that, maybe I wouldn't be in this predicament." Throughout this self-questioning the patient may feel a pervasive sense of helplessness, a sense of trying to combat unknown natural forces that have gone awry, forces that seem bent on destroying one's body.

Besides self-deprecation, the patient is likely to feel the effects of the social stigma associated with the disease. Many people tend to avoid the person who has a life-threatening illness, almost as if they feared it might be catching even when they know it is not. More likely, we catch a sense of the confrontation with death. This confrontation with death exposes our fear of loss and separation from all that we love, our fear of pain, and the imagined horror of dying. It shatters our image of ourselves and our plans for the future.

Heart disease is often thought of as a disease of superachievers, persons who are goal-oriented and whose lives are active and filled with accomplishments. Cancer, on the other hand, is often portrayed as the uncontrollable madness of the body's cells gone wild, the body devouring itself from within. The cancer patient is seen as passive and powerless. In fact, both heart disease and cancer affect all manner of people. Both illnesses are found at all strata of income and in all occupations, among people of widely divergent life styles. AIDS, too, which first came to public attention in this country mainly in populations of homosexual men and intravenous drug users, is a disease that affects people in all walks of life.

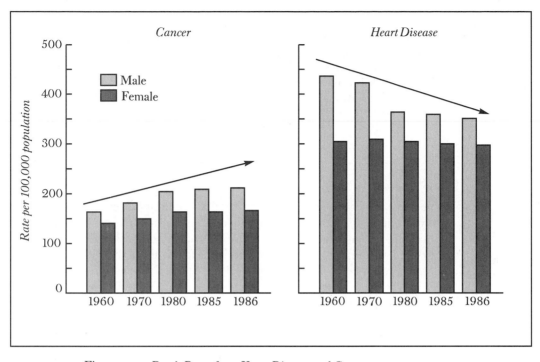

Figure *5-1*   *Death Rates from Heart Disease and Cancer*
Source: U.S. National Center for Health Statistics, *Statistical Abstract of the United States,*
1990, pp. 83–84.

Personal and Social Costs of Life-Threatening Illness

Although the mortality rate from cardiovascular diseases (which includes diseases of the heart) has been declining, it remains the leading cause of death in the United States, accounting for about 970,000 deaths in 1988, or nearly half of all deaths (see Figure 5-1). Cancer, the second leading cause of death in the United States, caused about 490,000 deaths in 1988. Whereas in 1900 about one of every twenty-seven deaths was attributable to cancer, it now accounts for roughly one in five. Although the rate of "cure" (meaning a patient has no evidence of cancer and has the same life expectancy as a person who never had cancer) has been increasing, the mortality rate from cancer has also been rising. It is noteworthy that the increase in cancer mortality has been accompanied by a rise in the average age at death from the disease, suggesting progress in deferring death. At the same time, with a declining rate of death due to cardiovascular disease (CVD), it seems that some of the "younger" persons saved from CVD are now succumbing to cancer.[1]

In addition to costly medical care, patients with life-threatening diseases such as heart disease and cancer are typically faced with loss of earnings, repeated and sometimes lengthy hospitalization, and prolonged rehabilitation. There are also personal and social costs. Emotional havoc accompanies the discovery that

I remember her as she lay in her hospital bed in July. Unable finally to deny the pain. And for the first time in our relationship of 21 years forced to allow someone else to take care of her. My father could not stand the sight and so he stayed outside, pacing up and down in the hallways. I could not help staring at her. Disbelief that this person with tubes running in and out like entrances and exits on a freeway was the same woman who just six months before had laughed gaily and danced at my wedding.

Ruth Kramer Ziony,
"Scream of Consciousness"

one has a life-threatening illness: mental and emotional anguish, pain and discomfort, fear, a sense of hopelessness, depression and anxiety, feelings of loneliness. The patient's family shares this burden. Indeed, looking at the family as a "system," we see that, as the illness affects the family life of the patient, the changed family circumstances have a reciprocal impact on the physically ill patient.[2]

Society also pays a high price. Public as well as private funds are allocated to programs of research, education, prevention, and care. There are indirect costs as well. The patient's relinquishment of employment and other social responsibilities levies social costs resulting from decreased productivity and the retraining of workers.

For the patient, fears excited by the prospect of undergoing treatment may compound the anxieties related to the disease itself. Patients with a life-threatening illness may fear the loss of their sexual functioning or attractiveness, either as a direct result of the disease or as a side effect of the treatment. Self-concept is intimately related to sexual identity. Consider, for example, the importance of the face in interpersonal relationships. Facial cancer patients confront anxieties related not only to the disease but also to their interactions with others, including their intimate, sexual relationships. In learning to live with a clearly visible mutilation, such patients may particularly need the support of others in adapting to a new self-image.[3] The possibility of disfigurement or a reduction in physical abilities raises concerns about the integrity of the body that must be considered within the context of a person's whole psychosocial sexual role.

For instance, a man who derives his sense of virility and masculinity from his work role may become sexually dysfunctional if illness precludes continuing his usual employment. A feeling that he is "less of a man" in one area of his life may become generalized to other parts of his life, including his sexual identity. Or a woman whose breast is removed because of cancer may worry that she is less of a woman — less able to adequately fulfill her role as a wife or mother, or indeed to function in business or social settings. Conversely, a patient who has been diagnosed as having a terminal condition may become compulsively preoccupied with sex, feeling that within the limited time remaining it is all the more important to produce offspring or to maximize sexual experiences. Whether problems

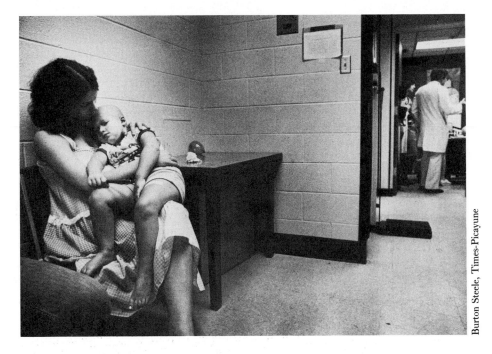

With her seriously ill daughter, this mother waits for the test results that will help determine the next step in care and treatment.

with sexual identity are manifest in avoidance or in compulsive activity, they can have a tremendous effect on the patient's self-concept and his or her relationships with others.

Self-concept encompasses our attitudes, beliefs, thoughts, feelings, goals, fears, fantasies, personal history, sense of self-worth, body image, and psychosexual roles. Although self-concept is learned, and thus changeable, the least flexible aspects of self-concept are those relating to body image, sexuality, and work. The presence of terminal illness dramatically affects each of these aspects of a person's self-concept.

Few patients are ever completely free of the fear that the disease may someday return, even when a cure is apparently successful.[4] The conflict and stress, and indeed panic, arising from the confrontation with death that a life-threatening illness causes, the adjustments in life style and psychosocial role necessitated by such an illness and its treatment — such experiences are common to most seriously ill patients. Nevertheless, much can be done to alleviate the stress, anxiety, and uncertainty that typically accompany life-threatening illness.

Therapeutic tools — including education, counseling, support groups, and communication skills — can be brought to bear on the experience of life-threatening illness. Gaining information about the disease and its treatment, sharing experiences with others in an atmosphere of mutual support, using counseling services to clarify personal and emotional issues, and developing ways of communicating more effectively with caregivers as well as family members and friends — all these are examples of positive approaches to dealing with life-threatening illness. Although these techniques will not necessarily make a serious illness less traumatic, they can promote an understanding that places the crisis in a more affirmative context, making one's experience less confusing and melodramatic, and restoring a sense of personal control over the situation.

The Experience of Life-Threatening Illness

Imagine one day you wake up and notice symptoms in your body that you associate with cancer. What goes through your mind? Perhaps you just barely admit to yourself the possibility that you're sick. Then you quickly push away such thoughts and go about your day's activities. "After all," you say, "there's no reason to suspect it's anything serious; it's probably just some minor infection."

You forget about it for a while. But, more and more persistently, the symptoms you noticed become more demanding of your attention. "This better not be anything serious," you tell yourself, "I've got too much to do." Yet, part of you recognizes that it really might be serious. You admit your concern, starting to feel a bit anxious about what the symptoms might mean.

So you make an appointment with your doctor, describe your symptoms, submit to an examination, and wait for the results. Perhaps right away, or maybe only after additional tests are ordered, you learn the diagnosis. Your doctor informs you that you have a tumor, a malignancy. Cancer.

Now your thoughts and emotions really become agitated. "What will the doctors do for me? How are they going to treat this illness? What kind of changes will I have to make in my life? Should I postpone the trip I've been planning? What about the pain? What course of treatment should be followed? Are there side effects? Can they even cure this kind of cancer? Will I die?"

As the intense drama unfolds, you begin to find ways of coping with this new crisis. Your earlier fears about the symptoms are transformed into concerns about the diagnosis, treatment, and outcome of the illness. You wonder how your life will be affected and what kind of adjustments you will have to make.

As time passes, perhaps you experience a remission: The tumor seems to have stopped growing. The doctors give you optimistic reports. Still, you wonder whether the cancer is really gone for good or just temporarily. You feel like someone in limbo. You're happy that things seem to be going well, but your optimism is mixed with uncertainty and fear. Perhaps after a while you begin to relax and feel less anxious about the cancer's returning. It seems "your" cancer was curable.

On the other hand, you may sooner or later again notice the onset of symptoms. If the cancer is declared incurable, you may fear metastasis, the spreading of the cancer to other areas of your body. Now you wrestle with the questions, "Is

Drawing by Mankoff, © 1987. The New Yorker Magazine, Inc.

*"Oh, darn, and just as I was beginning
to take charge of my life."*

it going to be painful? What organs will eventually be affected? How long do I have to live?"

This scenario, though in many ways typical, is experienced differently by different patients. Some cancers can be cured by relatively minor forms of treatment. Other cancers persist for a time and then, with treatment, diminish or become stabilized. The prognosis in other cases offers little hope for survival. To whatever degree cancer is perceived as a threat to one's well-being, this scenario is likely to resemble the cancer patient's actual experience and, by extension, the experience of anyone with a life-threatening illness.

Once the disease is judged incurable, the patient's fears may focus on the uncertainty surrounding dying and death. These fears probably have been present from the first, underlying the changing concerns about symptoms, diagnosis, and treatment. Yet, when cancer was nothing more than a possibility represented by a particular set of symptoms, attention was directed to what the symptoms might mean. After the diagnosis is learned and as treatment progresses, the fear of death becomes more present, though it is still mitigated by the

I'm forty. So, obviously things happened to me before I came in here. . . . I was married—I had a wife, and I had a son. But my wife divorced me. I was served with the papers the day I went to the hospital for the operation. My son will be twelve this October, I guess. I've never seen him since.

In the beginning, I was bewildered-like. I didn't know what the hell was happening to me. I didn't know what was wrong. And I kept going from doctor to doctor—and getting worse all the time. Slipping and slipping. I was like up in a cloud—and I was cross then. And bitter. I couldn't see why God had made such a big decision on me. I saw my brothers and sisters walking around so healthy-like—and I couldn't understand why it had happened to me and not to them. Things like that. . . . But, after a while, I decided you've got to take what the Lord decides, and make the best of it. . . .

Quoted in Renee Fox,
Experiment Perilous

need to carry out all the various activities that accompany the role of being a patient with a life-threatening illness. Fear is balanced by hope.

As death confronts us squarely, we may yet hope for some last-minute remission, some change for the better that the doctors haven't foreseen. We may fight to the end, thinking, "I've always outwitted the percentages. Why not now?" Or we may cope with the end of life in a very different way, taking charge as much as possible of the remaining time, surrounding ourselves with those closest to us, and accepting our dying. The way each of us copes with dying will likely reflect the ways we've coped with living, the ways we've coped with other losses and changes in our life.

Patterns of Coping with Life-Threatening Illness

Undoubtedly the best-known description of the emotional and psychological responses to life-threatening illness is the one recorded by Elisabeth Kübler-Ross on the basis of her work with dying patients.[5] Although these responses do not occur in a static, progressive manner, they may include denial, anger, bargaining, depression, and acceptance. In an idealized model, an early period of shock, disbelief, and denial eventually gives way to some degree of acceptance. A variety of coping mechanisms, however, may be used to prevent a full recognition and acknowledgment of the truth. When confronted by death or loss, a person may respond with avoidance or denial of the truth, or by suppressing or excluding it from consciousness. Setting oneself apart from thoughts or actions that might bring a recognition of the truth—that is, dissociating oneself from it—is another coping mechanism that may come into play when a person faces an unwelcome reality.

Even after the predicament has been acknowledged, however, there is generally considerable anger, vulnerability, and dependency. The anger is often

"Bloom County," drawing by Berke Breathed, © 1985 by Washington Post Writers Group

manifest as displaced hostility: "Okay, maybe I could've done something to keep this from happening to me, but, damn it, if it isn't safe, why doesn't the government put a stop to it!" Caregivers often become the object of such displaced hostility. The patient's anger at being ill might be displayed in complaints about food or other aspects of care: "Why can't you fix me a good cup of tea? You know I can't do it for myself!" Such coping mechanisms, difficult and possibly painful for patient and caregiver alike, serve to mask the underlying problem, the confrontation with the illness itself and what it portends.

Bargaining, or attempting to strike a deal with fate or with God, is yet another common response. The patient tries to discover some way to enter an agreement that may postpone the inevitable. Perhaps "good behavior" may be exchanged for an extension of life. Whatever the particulars of the attempt to bargain, such efforts represent a quest to alleviate suffering and to postpone the dreaded outcome.

As the symptoms of illness become stronger and the body weakens, the sense of numbness and the endeavors to remain stoic in the face of the reality may be replaced by a sense of loss and depression. The sense of loss engendered by the prospect of death may be made heavier by the burdens of treatment and hospitalization, as well as by the financial costs resulting from the illness and the many disruptions that occur in one's personal life, including the areas of job and family. Kübler-Ross differentiated two kinds of depression: the first, a *reactive* depression to the kinds of issues just described; and the second, a *preparatory* depression that "the terminally ill patient has to undergo in order to prepare himself for his final separation from this world."

After the initial responses—"Oh, no, it can't be me! I don't want to hear about it! Those test results must be for someone else; they got mixed up!"— comes acknowledgment of one's situation: "Yes, I am seriously ill, and I've got to deal with that fact in the best way I can." After a time, many patients come to some acceptance of their situation. They are able to explore more dispassionately its inherent issues and possibilities, and they begin to establish productive ways of dealing with the changed circumstances of their lives. When ready to discuss

There are some people who really can't deal with being told the truth about their illness. If you tell them at the wrong time or in the wrong way, it's too devastating for them.

First of all, get to know the patient. Sit down and talk with him, not about his illness particularly, but general topics. Very soon you get a feeling as to whether or not the patient wants to know. There are two groups: those who want to know and don't mind knowing, and those who very plainly don't want to know. There are some patients who have been told they have cancer, hear doctors discussing it, see their charts, and will still turn around and deny that they have cancer. And, of course, that's a gray area. You're not sure if they want to know. If they want to know, tell them. Don't hide the fact.

Quoted from *Death and Dying: The Physician's Perspective*, a videotape by Elizabeth Bradbury

these concerns, the patient needs a good listener, someone who can be present without judging or trying to persuade the patient to think or feel otherwise.

If the patient is able to confront the fact of illness and find ways of coping with the eventuality it represents, then chances are he or she will experience some resolution of the crisis. Acceptance does not mean giving up or losing hope; rather, it implies coming to an essentially positive, personally satisfying adjustment. Each such adjustment is unique, determined by such factors as the patient's personality, the kind of helping resources available in his or her environment, and the specific nature of the illness (see Figure 5-2).

These stages of coping with illness should not be thought of as strict categories that occur in a fixed sequence. A variety of emotions — anger, resentment, sadness, acceptance — may be experienced at any time during the process of dealing with illness and the prospect of death. Although there does tend to be movement from initial shock and anger toward eventual acceptance of the situation, a patient who has exhibited great acceptance of his or her death may die raging against the inevitable. Conversely, the angry fighter may find quiet resignation in the final moments of life, dying a peaceful death.

Although it is often said that one's style in dying will resemble his or her style in living, coping strategies employed in confronting death are likely to present some *modification* of the way a person copes with other life stresses. Moreover, the range of adaptive responses to loss may vary widely as circumstances change (see Figure 5-3). As Herman Feifel recently noted: "Coping with a life-threatening illness or death threat varies in significant fashion not only among differing groups but among situations."[6] Most dying patients, says Feifel, "do not expect 'miracles' concerning their biological condition. Their essential communication is the need for confirmation of care and concern."

You may find it useful to frame the psychological process of dying in terms of the three stages categorized by Avery Weisman: (1) from the time symptoms are

```
Dear Friends,

     In company with our dear Mother Earth, I have arrived at the time of
autumn in my worldly life, that time of transition between life and death.
Before long, just as the leaves drop from the trees to continue Life's cycle
of generation and regeneration, so will my body be shed and become part of
the muttering earth.  Like the tree gathering in energy to prepare itself
for winter, I feel a need to gather energy for the process of dying.  Also,
I want to share a last celebration with you dear friends.  To do this, I
have planned a ritual of transition to take place on Sunday, November 3, at
2:30 p.m. here at my home.

     I would love it if you can participate with your presence; and if
you cannot, I would appreciate your joining us in spirit with loving energy
via the ethers that afternoon.

     If you can come, please bring a pillow to sit on  and a symbolic gift of
your energy and blessing for me in this process I am going through--something
from nature (rock, shell, feather, etc.); a poem, picture or song; something
written or drawn; or whatever you are inspired to bring.  Please also bring
a casserole, salad or dessert or beverage to contribute to our potluck
supper following the ritual.

     There is a new joy that is beginning to be realized in me as I
acknowledge the prospect of having my spirit float free of my tired body.
I look forward to sharing this with you too.

                              Love and blessings,


                              Joan Conn
```

Figure 5-2   *Invitation to a Going-Away Party*

Ritual and companionship can assist in dealing with impending death. This celebration was attended by close friends and family, who said the occasion was an extremely moving experience. Knowing that she would soon die from cancer, Joan created a ritual that involved drawing a line on the floor and, in her weakened condition, she was helped across it by her ex-husband and her children while members of the gathering played music and sang. Although such an event would not be appropriate for everyone, Joan's farewell party aptly reflected her life style and values. She died seven months later.

66—Real Estate Wanted

FORMER President — Major Manufacturing Company, age 56, with possible terminal disease interested in lease purchase of old home. Reasonably large. Farm house with property, condos, land with run down cabin or home in total disrepair. Probably in foothills between Santa Cruz and Castroville. Option period 18 months or final diagnosis — whichever is first. Any remodeling by permission of owner in his name. Will arrive from Seattle on Tuesday evening. Please leave number at Box 9, c/o this newspaper.

Figure 5-3   *Life Change with Life-Threatening Illness: Real Estate Want Ad*
The confrontation with a life-threatening illness may activate desires to accomplish in the present plans that previously had been visualized as occurring in the future.
Source: Register-Pajaronian (Watsonville, Calif.), March 11, 1981.

noticed until the diagnosis is confirmed, (2) between diagnosis and the final decline, and (3) the stage of final decline.[7] Throughout the process of coping with the changes caused by life-threatening illness — from the moment one notices the symptoms and wonders what they mean to the final moments lying in the deathbed anticipating death — hope and honesty exist in a delicate balance unique to each person: honesty to face reality as it is, hope that the outcome is positive. It is interesting to note how the object of hope changes. The initial hope that nothing is really wrong gives way to hope that there will be a cure. If the disease seems incurable, then one hopes for more time. When time runs out, one hopes for a pain-free and comfortable death, a good death.

Unfortunately, this hope is not always fulfilled by the actual events leading up to death. In a recent study, Robert Kastenbaum and Claude Normand compared deathbed scenes as *imagined* by the young and *experienced* by the old.[8] The young people (students of college age) imagined themselves living into old age and then dying at home, with the companionship of loved ones, quickly, and without pain or other symptoms, while remaining alert and lucid until the end. The researchers found that the respondents tended to substitute "desired" for "most likely to happen" in imagining the end of their lives. The presence of pain, nausea, constipation, pressure sores, and insomnia — all too often part of the dying experience — were virtually absent from the imagined deathbed scenes. Moreover, the expectation of a "quick" death is not borne out by the reality experienced by most terminally ill people, who typically live with their condition for weeks or months. Although the researchers caution that this study is exploratory and tentative, its findings suggest that our picture of dying and death may be influenced more by images portrayed in the media than by what is likely to actually take place. If the deathbed scene imagined by these respondents is to become a reality,

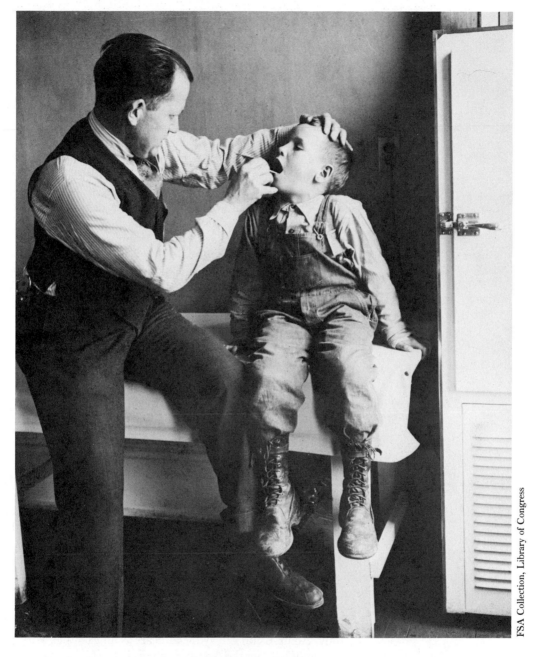

In 1935, medical care in Reedsville, West Virginia, seems less formal than that received in the urban clinics and hospitals of today. Although the practice of medicine has been enhanced by new methods of diagnosis and treatment, most people still believe that the relationship between physician and patient is central to the outcome of an illness.

continued attention will need to be devoted to creating situations akin to hospice, where pain management and the participation of family and friends are seen as important elements in a comprehensive program of terminal care.

Treatment Options and Issues

The treatment options for life-threatening illness depend on the nature of the disease and the patient's particular situation. As new medical technologies become available, treatment options may change drastically. Typically, however, medical advances occur gradually, steadily increasing the choices available to patients. For example, among the new technologies for diagnosing heart problems is an advancement in computer tomography that takes stop-action photos of the beating heart. This device allows cardiologists to measure and analyze data about the heart's functioning that otherwise could be obtained only through invasive and expensive procedures such as catheterization.

The options available for treatment depend not only on the nature of the disease and the medical technologies available to treat it but also on decisions made by society at large. The treatment for sudden cardiac death, a subset of coronary heart disease, is a case in point.[9] Of the 1.5 million heart attacks suffered by Americans each year, about three-quarters of the victims are admitted to hospitals where they receive advanced care; of these patients, more than 80 percent survive and are discharged. Often, however, a heart attack is the first indication of any coronary problem. The key to life-saving intervention in cases of sudden heart attack and similar emergencies is a rapid and coordinated medical response. In communities that have placed a high priority on providing this kind of response and where emergency personnel are equipped with cardiac care units, fatalities have declined. Such care can be costly, however. Thus, a community's ability or willingness to pay for this kind of care can affect a patient's options for treatment.

Ethical issues must sometimes be resolved before a new therapy can be applied widely. The artificial heart is an example of such a therapy. Although artificial hearts and heart-assist devices have been implanted in more than 200 patients worldwide, many of them as "bridges" to a heart transplant provided by a donor, serious questions remain concerning the fairness of the selection process and whether such patients can understand what is in store for them sufficiently to give their informed consent to the procedure.[10] Although proponents say the artificial heart could extend the lives of many people, critics respond that it does not really save patients' lives — it only changes the way they die.

Economic questions also must be considered in making decisions about a proposed therapy. Again using the artificial heart as an example, with perhaps 35,000 potential candidates for the device each year in the United States, at a cost of $150,000 per implant, the procedure could add $5 billion to the nation's health bill. While critics argue that this money could be better spent on health education aimed at preventing heart disease, proponents point out that this cost is not any greater than the amount Americans spend each year on video games. Thus, innovative therapies often bring with them questions that are not amenable to easy or quick resolution.

Current research in cancer treatment suggests promising roles for recombinant DNA technology and for "monoclonal antibodies" that can be tailored to attack selected targets on cancer cells. With greater understanding of disease processes and improved diagnostic procedures, there is increasingly better "staging" of the disease to determine its precise characteristics and when to apply appropriate therapies. In the management of serious illnesses, emphasis is being placed on individualized treatment. Although different illnesses require forms of treatment specific to each, the options available to patients can be illustrated by focusing on the treatment modalities associated with cancer. (Key terms used in conjunction with the treatment of cancer and other diseases are defined in Table 5-1.)

As a general term, *cancer* encompasses many different types of malignant, or potentially lethal, growths that occur in many parts of the body. Because cancerous cells reproduce in a manner unregulated by the body's normal controls on cell growth, over time there is the possibility of unlimited expansion. First affecting tissues in one part of the body, cancer may spread either by invading adjacent tissues or by *metastasis*, a process whereby diseased cells travel in the blood or lymph system or through body tracts to more distant parts of the body.[11] Successful treatment of cancer requires the destruction or removal of all cancerous tissue; without such treatment, the disease recurs.

A number of therapies — primarily surgery, radiation therapy, and chemotherapy — have been applied to the management of cancer. But none is effective for all of the forms in which cancer may appear in the body. A treatment with a high rate of success with one type of cancer may be ineffective with another. Frequently, a combination of therapies is recommended, each designed to accomplish a particular aim within a comprehensive treatment program. Some treatments of life-threatening illness create the need for adjunctive therapies to counteract the side effects of the primary mode of treatment. As we discuss the various methods of treating cancer, the benefits and disadvantages of each type of therapy will be emphasized, along with its effects on the patient's experience.

Surgery

The greatest percentage of cancer cures has been due to the use of surgery. Indeed, most of the progress in cancer survival has come about because of improvements in surgical techniques and in preoperative and postoperative care, especially in control of infection. At present, surgery has no peer in the cure of cancer, although with some forms of cancer it is not successful.

Although surgery is a routine modern medical practice — and surgery to remove diseased tissues or organs is one of the earliest types — many people fear surgery as a violation of the body and the loss of some part of it; often they fear possible disfigurement, disability, or loss of bodily function. In cancer surgery,

T A B L E 5-1   *Medical Treatment Word List*

Alkylating agents: A family of chemotherapeutic drugs that combine with DNA (genetic substance) to prevent normal cell division.

Analgesic: A drug used for reducing pain.

Antimetabolites: A family of chemotherapeutic drugs that interfere with the processes of DNA production, and thus prevent normal cell division.

Benign: Not malignant.

Biopsy: The surgical removal of a small portion of tissue for diagnosis.

Blood count: A laboratory study to evaluate the amount of white cells, red cells, and platelets.

Bone marrow: A soft substance found within bone cavities, ordinarily composed of fat and developing red cells, white cells, and platelets.

Cancer: A condition in which there is the proliferation of malignant cells that are capable of invading normal tissues.

Chemotherapy: The treatment of disease by chemicals (drugs) introduced into the bloodstream by injection or taken by mouth as tablets.

Cobalt treatment: Radiotherapy using gamma rays generated from the breakdown of radioactive cobalt-60.

Colostomy: Surgical formation of an artificial anus in the abdominal wall, so the colon can drain feces into a bag.

Coma: A condition of decreased mental function in which the individual is incapable of responding to any stimulus, including painful stimuli.

Cyanotic: A blue appearance of the skin, lips, or fingernails as the result of low oxygen content of the circulating blood.

Diagnosis: The process by which a disease is identified.

DNA: Abbreviation for deoxyribonucleic acid, the building block of the genes, responsible for the passing of hereditary characteristics from cell to cell.

Hodgkin's disease: A form of tumor that arises in a single lymph node and may spread to local and then distant lymph nodes and finally to other tissues, commonly including the spleen, liver, and bone marrow.

Immunotherapy: A method of cancer therapy that stimulates the body defenses (the immune system) to attack cancer cells or modify a specific disease state.

Intravenous (IV): Describing the administration of a drug or of fluid directly into a vein.

Leukemia: A malignant proliferation of white blood cells in the bone marrow; cancer of the blood cells.

Lymph nodes: Organized clusters of lymphocytes through which the tissue fluids drain upon returning to the blood circulation; they act as the first line of defense, filtering out and destroying infective organisms or cancer cells and initiating the generalized immune response.

Malignant: Having the potentiality of being lethal if not successfully treated. All cancers are malignant by definition.

Melanoma: A cancer of the pigment cells of the skin, usually arising in a preexisting pigmented area (mole).

Metastasis: The establishment of a secondary site or multiple sites of cancer separate from the primary or original site.

Multimodality therapy: The use of more than one modality for cure or palliation (abatement) of cancer.

Myelogram: The introduction of radiopaque dye into the sac surrounding the spinal cord, a process that makes it possible to see tumor involvement of the spinal cord or nerve roots on X-ray.

T A B L E *5-1*   *(continued)*

Oncologist: An internist (specialist in internal medicine dealing with nonsurgical treatment of disease) who has subspecialized in cancer therapy and has expertise in both chemotherapy and the handling of problems arising during the course of the disease.

Parkinson's disease: Degenerative disease of the brain resulting in tremor and rigid muscles.

Prognosis: An estimate of the outcome of a disease based on the status of the patient and accumulated information about the disease and its treatment.

Prosthesis: An artificial structure designed to replace or approximate a normal one.

Regression: The diminution of cancerous involvement, usually as the result of therapy; it is manifested by decreased size of the tumor (or tumors) or its clinical evidence in fewer locations.

Relapse: The reappearance of cancer following a period of remission.

Remission: The temporary disappearance of evident active cancer, occurring either spontaneously or as the result of therapy.

Sarcoma: A cancer of connective tissue, bone, cartilage, fat, muscle, nerve sheath, blood vessels, or lymphoid system.

Subcutaneous cyst: A cyst located beneath the skin; usually benign.

Symptom: A manifestation or complaint of disease as described by the patient, as opposed to one found by the doctor's examination; the latter is referred to as a sign.

Terminal: Describing a condition of decline toward death, from which not even a brief reversal can be expected.

Therapeutic procedure: A procedure intended to offer palliation (abatement) or cure of a condition or disease.

Toxicity: The property of producing unpleasant or dangerous side effects.

Tumor: A mass or swelling. A tumor can be either benign or malignant.

Source: Excerpted and adapted from Ernest H. Rosenbaum, M.D., *Living with Cancer: A Guide for the Patient, the Family and Friends* (St. Louis: C.V. Mosby, 1982).

not only is the organ or tissue with the malignancy removed, but a wide margin of the adjacent tissue, possibly including adjacent organs, may also be removed to prevent spread of the cancer. In the case of breast cancer, for example, radical mastectomy (breast removal) has been a common method of treatment. In radical surgical procedures, even if nearby lymphatic nodes appear normal, they are removed to prevent the persistence of any malignant cells that might cause a recurrence of the cancer. Such radical techniques have achieved a high percentage of cures in such diseases as breast cancer, although many practitioners are now seeking less disfiguring methods of successfully removing the cancerous tissue.

Reconstructive techniques are also important to the overall success of surgery. For example, patients who undergo surgery for cancer of the colon or rectum can now be supplied with relatively simple devices for waste elimination. Improvements in such reconstructive and rehabilitative techniques have lessened the impact of radical surgery on the patient's life style and have shortened recovery time.

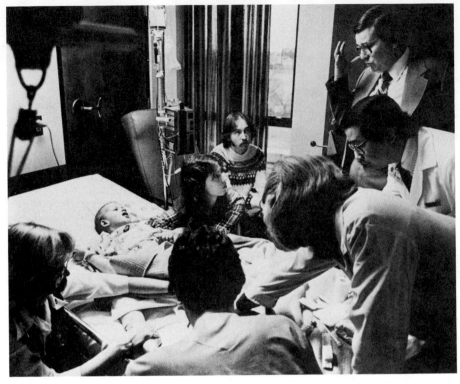

Burton Steele, Times-Picayune

*Family members and consulting physicians gathered around the bedside of a
seriously ill child discuss the impending brain surgery that everyone hopes will bring
a favorable prognosis.*

Despite the progress achieved by surgery, however, fewer than 50 percent of
cancer patients can be cured by this procedure alone. Therefore, great effort has
gone into discovering auxiliary therapies that can be given following surgery.

Radiation Therapy

One of the most widely employed of these auxiliary therapies is *radiation*,
which is used to treat more than half of the cancer patients in the United States.
The potentialities of radiation for treating cancer were recognized soon after the
discovery of radium in 1898. Radiation therapy uses ionizing radiation to destroy
cells, thus preventing further cellular division and growth. Radiation affects both
normal and cancerous tissues, but since cancer cells usually grow more rapidly
than normal cells, they are more seriously damaged. Not all forms of cancer respond to radiation therapy. Some growths and tissues are quite sensitive to radiation; others are relatively resistant.

Radiation does seem to be effective in at least slowing the growth of many types of malignancy. Remissions, though sometimes lasting for a year or less, frequently occur after radiation therapy. Even when a cure is not achieved or the growth arrested, however, a palliative effect often occurs, lessening the severity of the symptoms.

Conversely, radiation therapy can cause uncomfortable side effects. Most patients who receive radiation therapy are scheduled for frequent, intense treatments, commonly as often as three or four times a week over a period of several months. The radiation dose is prescribed on the basis of the stage of the disease and the patient's ability to withstand the side effects. Nausea, vomiting, tiredness, and general weakness often accompany treatment, and patients undergoing radiation therapy often express dread of additional treatments. Because the side effects are so frequently debilitating, many patients must curtail their activities in order to get necessary bed rest.

Although the successes with radiation therapy tend to be less dramatic than those possible with surgery, its continued achievement of at least moderate successes with many patients makes radiation therapy one of the most commonly practiced methods of treating cancer, either alone or in concert with other modes of therapy. As with surgery, however, radiation by itself is not a cure for most cancers since the dosage required to eradicate all the cancer cells would also kill the patient.

Chemotherapy

Chemotherapy is the use of toxic drugs to kill cancer cells. It originated from the observation that the toxic effects of mustard gases during World War I included damage to the bone marrow. Following World War II, clinical trials with chemotherapy began and the early results were encouraging. Today, many different chemotherapeutic agents are employed, in various combinations, for treating cancer. Chemotherapy has been called the leading weapon in the fight to increase the number of patients who can be cured of cancer. To be effective therapeutically, the dose must be strong enough to kill the malignancy or slow its growth but not so potent that it might seriously harm the patient. Ideally, a chemical agent of this kind would attack only the cancerous cells in the body without affecting normal, healthy tissue. As yet, however, there is no such "magic bullet."

All the diverse chemotherapeutic agents basically work by blocking the metabolic processes involved in cellular division. Because cancer cells divide more rapidly than do most normal cells, the agents used in chemotherapy are designed to preferentially affect the cancerous cells.

A patient's chemotherapy program is continually evaluated in light of the stage of malignancy and the patient's response to therapy. A typical treatment program might entail six weeks of intensive chemotherapy, followed by a respite from treatment, then another cycle of chemotherapy.

Like radiation therapy, chemotherapy brings discomforting side effects to many, though not to all, patients: loss of hair, sleeplessness, nausea, difficulty in eating and digestion, bleeding sores around the mouth, ulceration and bleeding in the gastrointestinal tract, and various other toxic effects. Sometimes the visible side effects can be quite alarming to the patient's family and friends.

Whether the particular drug used in chemotherapy is an alkylating agent, which prevents cells from making genetic material (DNA); an antimetabolite or antibiotic, which blocks nucleic acid synthesis; or an alkaloid, which stops cell division and induces other cellular changes, chemotherapeutic agents owe their effectiveness to the fact that they are poison. As a result, they damage normal as well as diseased tissue. In addition, some cancer cells eventually become resistant to the drugs. To overcome these limitations, and because chemotherapeutic agents generally destroy only the portion of the cell population that is currently undergoing division, several drugs that act on cells in different ways are usually administered in combination.

Although chemotherapy does not usually result in a cure, it has been used successfully with some forms of cancer. It has produced long-term, disease-free remissions in many children with acute leukemia, for example, and in many patients with advanced stages of Hodgkin's disease. Some of these patients have been in remission for five years or more and may, in fact, be cured. In certain forms of malignant diseases, such as leukemia, which cannot be treated by surgery, the palliative effects achieved by chemotherapy have allowed patients to lead a comparatively normal, even prolonged, life. Some skin cancers have also responded favorably to applications of certain chemotherapeutic ointments.

Interestingly, chemotherapy appears to be most effective with the less common forms of cancer and least effective with the more prevalent forms—cancers of the breast, colon, and lung. Nevertheless, with many cancers, chemotherapy does bring about a partial or temporary remission or some palliation of symptoms. Often, a more comfortable life, if not a cure, is achieved for the patient.

Other Therapies

Because the orthodox, or conventional, forms of treatment for cancer—surgery, radiation, and chemotherapy—are not always sufficient to bring about a cure, patients sometimes pursue experimental or unconventional therapies that seem to offer hope. Within the medical establishment, a perennial search is under way for more effective methods of treating disease; and, as new discoveries are made, the response from patients is often dramatic. When the National Cancer Institute announced the possibility of using Interleukin-2, a protein produced by the immune system, to boost the body's own natural defenses in attacking some forms of cancer, within a week's time the Institute logged over a thousand calls from people wanting to know how to avail themselves or a family member of the new therapy. Although researchers emphasized that the discovery was a "first step" and "not a cure for cancer," many of the callers were desperate and felt they had "nothing to lose" from trying an experimental treatment.

Unconventional or unorthodox therapies also encompass methods of treatment that the medical establishment considers unproven or potentially harmful.

Those who advocate such remedies may be branded as quacks and their methods characterized as contemporary editions of Dr. Feelgood's Medicine Show, a form of snake oil medicine that, even if intrinsically harmless, diverts patients from conventional medical programs where they might receive help.

What comes to mind when you hear the word *unorthodox?* Not accepted? Outside of the establishment? Ineffective? That a supposed cancer cure derives from the pits of apricots or almonds may push the limits of credibility; and, indeed, such "cures" may actually be harmful. Yet many of our most common medications are derived from such seemingly unlikely sources. Such medications — whether in natural or synthetic form — comprise a significant portion of the armamentaria of conventional medicine. Penicillin is naturally produced from molds. Digitalis, prescribed for some heart ailments, derives from the plant foxglove. The active ingredient of common aspirin is close kin to a substance found in the bark and leaves of the white willow. Clearly, the source of a proposed medicinal substance ought to concern us less than the question, Does it work?

Some of the methods banned from use in conventional medicine are unproven simply because of insufficient research to determine their possible validity. Interferons, for example, are considered by many to be among the most promising of the unproven therapies. Simply put, interferons are a family of proteins produced by the body's cells when in the presence of viral infection. Although it is not entirely clear just how interferons work, they seem to activate an immunologic response similar to the body's own defenses against disease. At present, interferon therapy is still experimental and the results are tentative. Preliminary results tend to cast doubt on whether interferons represent a dramatic breakthrough in cancer therapy, but there are indications that they can beneficially affect some cancers. It is not yet clear how interferons might eventually fit into the total scheme of cancer therapies.

Most patients prefer orthodox therapies, but others distrust or lose faith in the conventional approach and choose unsanctioned alternatives as their course of therapy. Some patients try to find a comfortable balance between medically approved therapies and innovative but unproven approaches. For example, they may follow their doctor's prescription for radiation therapy or chemotherapy while at the same time pursuing techniques such as biofeedback, meditation, or visualization, designed to mobilize the body's own resources. Some alternative approaches to treatment can be combined with an orthodox medical approach; others cannot and require a radical departure from conventional medical practices.

Anson Shupe and Jeffrey Hadden have proposed the term *symbolic healing* to identify the varied therapies known under such names as "faith healing," "supernatural healing," and "folk healing."[12] Accepting the validity of symbolic healing is to acknowledge the reality that "human beings do not live in the physical world alone but also in a world mediated for them by symbolic meanings provided by their culture" and that "symbols cue and prompt responses, not just in brains but in glands as well." In short, what we take to be meaningful — what we believe — about the way of the world potentially affects the functioning of our bodies. The concept of symbolic healing places the human organism within a series of overlapping environments: biological, social, and cultural.

When one looks at concepts of illness and health cross-culturally, say Shupe and Hadden, we find that "human understandings of illness, or dis-ease, usually posit an imbalance among different realms of a patient's life." At its most basic, therefore, healing "consists of restoring balance." This traditional understanding is in essential agreement with the integrated mind/body model now being advocated by a growing number of physicians and medical scientists. The brain has been called "the major organ of adaptation," and Shupe and Hadden remark that "the function of the brain is to seek a stable health homeostasis through the integration of emotions, cognitions, and socio-symbolic relationships with the chemistries of immune, cardiovascular, and endorphin systems, among others."[13] In other words, the brain naturally seeks to bring about a healthy state of functioning.

Now, what meaning does all this talk of symbolic healing have for patients and caregivers? Perhaps most significantly, it reinforces the importance of attending to the dynamics of the healer-patient relationship. Shupe and Hadden cite several elements that are critical in this regard: First, the patient must have confidence in "the legitimacy and credibility of the medical system, even if the details of its technology are not understood." Second, the patient must trust "in the wisdom and expertise of the healer." Third, the healer must have "confidence in the validity of his or her medical intervention." Fourth, the context of healing must employ "culturally consistent myths and symbols" that actively involve the patient.

These insights from cross-cultural studies of the physician-patient relationship can be usefully applied to situations involving persons diagnosed with a terminal illness. As Norman Cousins said shortly before his death, "The great tragedy of life is not death but what dies inside us while we live."[14] The shock of a terminal diagnosis and the reality of living with serious illness can "kill" or wreak damage on the human spirit, that part of the person which is the reservoir of zest for life and positive accomplishment. Despite the statistical probabilities of an illness or the incapacitation it brings into a person's life, healers and patients can join together in encouraging (giving heart to) the inner human spirit while acknowledging the grim reality.

Conventional doctors are beginning to accept the notion that the orthodox form of treatment may not be sufficient for all cases and that confronting patients with an "either/or" situation — forcing them to choose between orthodox or alternative treatments — may at times do more harm than good. With the increase over the last few decades of persons with cancer being cured or surviving longer, there has come greater public attention to the possibility of "beating" cancer by assuming an attitude of "heroic self-healing" through the use of positive thinking, healing imagery, and personal growth techniques.[15] Even though the empirical, or scientific, support for such a psychospiritual influence on illness is considered by most researchers to be tenuous, the psychological implications of belief in such influences may be important in their own right. For some patients, identifying with the notion of "heroic self-healing" offers a method for coping with illness that enhances their quality of life, if not its duration. To be sure, some alternative or unorthodox treatments are harmful to patients. Yet, other alternative or unorthodox therapies may not only empower patients and give them renewed hope but in some cases also serve as useful adjuncts to conventional methods of treatment.

Infection

Because life-threatening illnesses typically lower the body's resistance to microorganisms, patients with such diseases tend to be extremely susceptible to infection. Some believe infection to be the most significant cause of mortality and manifest ill health, or wasting away, in cancer patients. Similarly, the diminished immune response associated with AIDS renders persons with this disease vulnerable to opportunistic infections and tumorous growths. Pneumocystic carinii pneumonia is frequently the first infection to occur with AIDS and is the most common cause of death. In addition, many AIDS patients develop cancers, the most common of which include Kaposi's sarcoma, non-Hodgkin's lymphoma, and Hodgkin's disease.

Infection can result from both endogenous, or resident, organisms and exogenous, or external, organisms. All three of the primary modes of treating cancer — surgery, radiation therapy, and chemotherapy — carry risks of infection. While surgery always involves some risk of infection, cancer patients' risk is increased significantly because resistance to infection tends to be lower and because malignancies tend to be conducive to the growth of microorganisms. Radiation therapy and chemotherapy increase the risk of infection because they work by suppressing the body's natural immune system. That hospitals are poor environments for avoiding infection is an additional argument against unnecessary hospitalization.

Treating infection is often difficult because the use of antibiotics to combat the infection may disturb the balance of normal microbial flora. Those who care for patients with cancer and other such diseases need to be aware of the various preventive and therapeutic measures that are available for reducing the threat of infections.

Pain Management

In discussions about the experience of life-threatening illness, one of the frequently mentioned phenomena is that of pain. Indeed, pain is the most common symptom of terminally ill patients.[16] The effective management of pain is a chief goal of palliative care and a hallmark of the comfort-oriented focus associated with hospice care. Although we often speak of pain as if it were a well-defined entity, the fact is that the experience of pain is "subjective in nature and ultimately unshareable." Linda Garro points out that "pain cannot be directly measured or observed; it is a perceptual experience that can only be communicated through verbal means and/or by behavior interpreted as indicating pain."[17]

In an article on culture and pain, Garro goes on to discuss the way that languages differ in their "lexicon" for talking about pain. For example, English speakers use several basic terms when describing pain: *pain, hurt, sore*, and *ache*. To these basic terms, qualifiers are added to make the description of pain more specific to the actual experience. We talk about having a "burning" or "stabbing" pain, or about having an "unbearable ache" or "soreness in the shoulder." In this way, a particular experience of pain is further defined in terms of temporal, spatial, thermal, pressure, and other qualities. Notice that the tendency is to treat pain as an object: "I have a pain." For a Thai speaker, on the other hand, "the basic pain terms are verbs and refer to the active perception of sensations." Pain is perceived not as an object, but as a process. As these differences in language usage illustrate, the response to pain is to some extent culturally shaped.

Although home care for dying patients is considered by many to be a highly desirable method for providing terminal care, effective pain and symptom control is not always possible in the home setting.[18] Families and friends may encounter relatively few difficulties in supplying adequate nursing care, but pain management typically requires attention by skilled professionals. Yet physicians with experience in home care and a willingness to exercise the needed flexibility for a workable program are in short supply.

Michael Levy notes that pain can be technically defined as an "unpleasant sensory and emotional experience associated with actual or potential tissue damage or described in terms of such damage."[19] More practically, however, he asserts that "pain is what the patient says it is and occurs when he or she says it does." Levy points out that the two main goals of caring for the terminally ill are "to optimize the quality of their remaining life and to alleviate the distress of their survivors." Pain control is crucial to achieving both of these aims.

The three basic approaches to reducing pain — modifying the source of the pain, interfering with its transmission, and altering perception of the pain — can be implemented by a number of methodologies. These include palliative surgery, radiation therapy, and hormonal therapy, as well as a wide variety of drug therapies.

The "politics of pain management" is cited as an important factor relating to the delivery of pain-reducing techniques to terminally ill patients. In some instances, for example, highly addictive but nonetheless effective drugs are withheld or given only sparingly despite the fact that a patient's limited prognosis makes concerns about possible addiction irrelevant. The consensus within the medical community appears to be that, despite considerable advances in recent years, pain control remains inadequate for a large number of patients.

Hospice and palliative care programs have taken a leading role in advocating greater attention to pain management, especially as applied in cases of terminal illness. Interdisciplinary approaches, combining both conventional and innovative techniques, are endorsed by many in the field as offering a way to address the "total pain" — physical, psychological, social, and spiritual — experienced by the terminally ill person. These approaches often use techniques that enhance a patient's ability to maintain a positive attitude and a feeling of greater control over his or her situation. When effectively managed, this combination of conventional medical wisdom and innovative techniques intended to elicit the body's own powers of healing can result in an easing of physical, as well as mental and emotional, discomforts arising out of the experience of life-threatening illness.

Coping Mentally and Emotionally with Life-Threatening Illness

It has long been a truism in medicine that hope and positive attitudes play a key part in the patient's ability to cope with illness. Indeed, some physicians have withheld all of the facts about a serious illness, fearing that a full, open disclosure might lessen the patient's chances of recovery or survival. However well intended, this approach may harm a patient. When the patient is seen as a passive participant who merely follows the program outlined by the physician, options that rightfully belong to the patient may be subtly taken away. There is a difference between glossing over the facts to protect the patient and giving an account of the situation in a manner that corresponds with the patient's willingness to learn the truth. The second course of action is based on cooperation and a sense of partnership between physician and patient.

The distinction between these two models of how the patient is perceived is important, for it can determine whether or not the patient has available the range of resources that he or she finds necessary for coping with the realities of serious illness. When a patient is treated as a whole person and his or her preferences are respected, a sense of self-worth and dignity is elicited in the patient. He or she is empowered to make choices that demonstrate a sense of purpose resulting from a healthy self-concept.

The capacity to maintain a sense of self-worth, to set goals and strive to meet them, to exercise choice out of an awareness of one's power to meet challenges, to engage in active interactions with one's environment — all of these reflect a "coping potency" that sustains the will to live in the face of death. It is said, for example, that both John Adams and Thomas Jefferson managed to live until July 4, 1826, the fiftieth anniversary of the signing of the Declaration of Independence; and, according to Jefferson's physician, his last words were, "Is it the Fourth?"

The role of the emotions in influencing physical well-being has received considerable attention in recent years.[20] In his book *The Will to Live*, Arnold Hutschnecker cited clinical observations to support the thesis that the chief cause of death is illness traceable to emotional disorders. Cardiologists Meyer Friedman and Ray Rosenman established a relationship between certain patterns of behavior and the onset of heart disease, which they reported in their book, *Type A Behavior and Your Heart*. The role of emotional factors in the progress of cancer was dealt with in Lawrence LeShan's *You Can Fight for Your Life*. Oncologist Carl Simonton, in the book *Getting Well Again*, described certain predisposing factors in the development of tumors.

What are some of the common themes in these accounts? They are: loss of sense of purpose in life; inability to express anger or resentment; self-dislike and self-distrust; despairing and hopeless outlook on life; impatience with the pace at

Mike Stevens

71

Figure *5-4*   *Good Cells and Bad Cells: A Child's Drawing*
In this drawing by a child with cancer, the health-giving good cells are depicted as being victorious over the diseased bad cells. Such imaginative techniques can be ways of enlisting the patient's internal resources as an adjunct to conventional therapies.
Source: Center for Attitudinal Healing, *There Is a Rainbow Behind Every Dark Cloud* (Millbrae, Calif.: Celestial Arts, 1978), p. 71.

which events occur; striving to do more in less time; inability to relax; preoccupation with having, rather than being; inability to forgive; tendency toward self-pity; inability to develop and maintain meaningful relationships; and poor self-image. Taken together, these attitudes and behaviors are characterized by intense stress.

A variety of techniques are used for treating the emotional and physical aspects of illness, the best known of which is *visualization*. Here, the patient creates a mental state in which he or she takes control of bodily processes by imagining the diseased parts of the body becoming well again. Affirmations that one already exists in a state of wellness and creative fantasies directed toward wholeness are also used to generate a sense of well-being (see Figure 5-4). These methods originated in the discovery that cases of spontaneous remission shared a common factor: The patient viewed himself or herself as being well again. The

Your Caring Presence: Ways of Effectively Providing Support to Others

1. Be honest about your own thoughts, concerns, and feelings
2. When in doubt, ask questions:
   - How is that for you?
   - How do you feel right now?
   - Can you tell me more about that?
   - Am I intruding?
   - What do you need?
   - What are the ways you can take care of yourself?
3. When you are responding to a person facing a crisis situation, be sure to use statements such as:
   - I feel _____
   - I believe _____
   - I would want _____

   Rather than:
   - You should
   - That's wrong
   - Everything will be ok

   which are statements that may not give the person the opportunity to express his/her own unique needs and feelings.
4. Stay in the present as much as possible: How do you feel RIGHT NOW? What do you need RIGHT NOW?
5. Listening is profoundly healing. You don't have to make it better. You don't have to have the answers. You don't have to take away the pain. It's his pain. He needs to experience it in his own time and in his own way.
6. People in crisis need to know they have decision-making power. It may be appropriate to point out alternatives.
7. Offer any practical assistance that you feel comfortable giving.
8. If the situation warrants it, feel free to refer individual to appropriate agency.

The Centre for Living with Dying

results suggest that the belief systems of the patient, the patient's family, and the physician must all be considered if emotional influences are to help in effecting a cure.

Studies have also been done on the effects of personality patterns and life histories on the outcome of disease processes. Stephanie Matthews Simonton reports that the stress of chronic depression and low self-esteem is a significant problem for many people with cancer.[21] A major focus of providing emotional support relates to helping patients learn to cope more effectively with the stress in their lives. Often, this means encouraging them to express their feelings and to give more attention to satisfying their own needs.

Imaginative techniques, such as visualization, may be practiced in conjunction with conventional cancer therapies. With chemotherapy, for instance, the patient visualizes the chemical agent inside the body, working to diminish the cancer and to restore well-being. At Shibata Hospital in Japan the usual treatments for cancer are accompanied by a psychotherapeutic technique called *ikigai ryoho*, or meaningful-life therapy.[22] David K. Reynolds explains that "the theory of meaningful-life therapy is that it is in our control over our behavior that hope lies." Despite fears or the quirks of our own personality, it is possible to "take responsibility for what to do in the time remaining to us." The cancer patients at Shibata Hospital begin with acknowledgment of their own private suffering and gradually proceed, first, to the recognition that others are also suffering, then to an acceptance of the reality of the illness and the fight that must be carried on, and, finally, to "an ability to live fully and deeply within the realistic limits posed by the illness." A four-part outline summarizes the approach taken in meaningful-life therapy:

1. We must accept the inevitability of dying.
2. It is impossible to eliminate our basic dread of death; we must live alongside it.
3. Behind our fear of death is the strong desire to live fully, realistically.
4. Our fear need not pressure us unconditionally; we can live each day doing well what needs to be done.

Essential to maintaining a positive attitude under the stress of life-threatening illness is the patient's own positive self-image. Others who interact with the patient can be crucial as well. Their expressed fears and misconceptions about serious illness can have a significant bearing on how the patient perceives both his or her physical condition and sense of self-worth.

The late Orville Kelly, founder of the support group Make Today Count, described his response and the reactions of others when he learned that he had cancer.[23] Kelly's first awareness that something was wrong led him to quit his job as a newspaper editor and seek a change of climate. Soon afterwards he discovered a swelling that was diagnosed as a malignancy. Given a prognosis of from six months to six years to live, Kelly was depressed and contemplated suicide, fearing that he might become a burden to his family.

Friends and relatives acted uncomfortable in his presence. One woman asked his wife, "How is he?"—despite the fact that Kelly was no more than a few feet away. Though yet alive, he was being subjected to a kind of social death, his full humanity already being written off by uneasy friends and relatives.

Despite his frightening prognosis, Kelly began to realize that in fact he was still alive. He recognized that the mortality of every generation is ultimately 100 percent. All of us die, and each of us faces the challenge to make each day count, whether or not we live with a terminal diagnosis. He could still love and be loved. No matter how short a time he might have to live, he could make the best of each day. He began talking openly about his feelings, expressing the kinds of concerns experienced by someone with a terminal illness. An article he wrote for the local newspaper elicited such a response that it eventually led to the formation of the Make Today Count organization, a support group for the terminally ill.

But You Look So Good

It's with me each day.
I wake, thinking
Today it will go away.
But the pain seems to stay . . .
Persistent, resistant, consistent.
People say,
But you look so good.
If only I could
Feel like I look.
Or, should
I look bad?
So they'll know
How I feel
is real.
Do they doubt?
I wish the pain
Was on the outside —
something you see.
Not only the pain
Do I need to survive,
But also my
Paranoid imaginings
Of others' disbelief.

Judy Ellsworth

The purpose of support groups like Make Today Count is to offer terminal patients and their families a comfortable and supportive environment where they can feel free to express themselves concerning the impact of life-threatening illness in their lives. These informal meetings may also be attended by nurses, members of the clergy, oncologists, social workers, and others who wish to learn about and share the concerns of the terminally ill and their families.

Being with Someone Who Is Dying

Most of us feel somewhat uncomfortable in the presence of a person who has been diagnosed with a life-threatening illness. What can we say? How ought we to act? It seems that anything we might think of to express our feelings is little more than a stale platitude. So perhaps we stay away or, when visiting, avoid eye contact, shying away from real communication. We let ourselves off the hook while still managing to acknowledge our concern by directing our questions to a member of the patient's family rather than directly to the ill person. Perhaps feeling a little foolish and afraid, we find ourselves wanting to make the situation

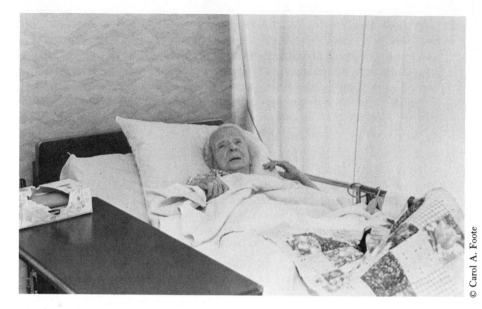

© Carol A. Foote

Being with a loved one who is dying confronts us with the fact of our own mortality as well as the losses associated with that person's death. Even when communication is hampered by physical disability, such times can be precious opportunities for sharing our deepest feelings with someone we love whose presence will be missed in our lives.

something other than it is—something more comfortable, less distressing. Our discomfort and uncertainty may be demonstrated by excessive sympathy or by obsessive avoidance. Neither response is satisfactory, for ourselves or for the patient.

We want to show our concern and to make meaningful human contact. We want to listen, to understand our friend's or relative's concerns, feelings, and thoughts. Life review, a well-known counseling tool used with aged persons, has been suggested as a means whereby a dying person can "complete the last chapter of his or her life with some choices of his or her own."[24] By reviewing past relationships and events, "the person is given the opportunity to make things right or to finish up unfinished business."

Eventually it becomes evident that it is all right not to know how to respond or what to say. What we can offer is ourselves as we are, with our uncertainty and fear and anxieties. Indeed, we need not *do* anything. Being there for the other person means being sensitive to what is going on in the moment and simply responding as our heart dictates. If we are preoccupied with what we should do or say, or with wondering whether we are going to blunder somehow, our minds are full of confusion. The heart's simplicity is crowded out.

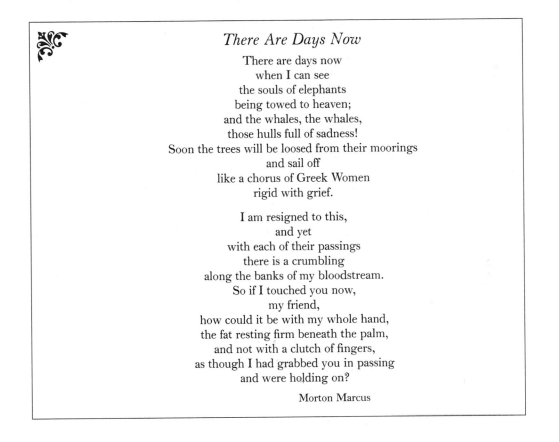

There Are Days Now

There are days now
when I can see
the souls of elephants
being towed to heaven;
and the whales, the whales,
those hulls full of sadness!
Soon the trees will be loosed from their moorings
and sail off
like a chorus of Greek Women
rigid with grief.

I am resigned to this,
and yet
with each of their passings
there is a crumbling
along the banks of my bloodstream.
So if I touched you now,
my friend,
how could it be with my whole hand,
the fat resting firm beneath the palm,
and not with a clutch of fingers,
as though I had grabbed you in passing
and were holding on?

Morton Marcus

There are no pat formulas for how to behave. Neither is there any special qualification for being sensitive. Because there is no correct way to behave, we can simply be ourselves, uncertainty and all. Accepting our doubt, our fear, allows us to do what we can, to be with the other person without trying to rely on some special program. To do otherwise results in a kind of partial death for the patient at a time when social support may be especially needed.

Both medical professionals and laypersons need to foster an awareness of accommodations that can be made to aid a person with life-threatening illness. Treatment schedules, for example, often can be adjusted so that the patient can continue working or going to school or caring for his or her family. Some medical centers make an effort to schedule chemotherapy for cancer patients early on a weekend so that side effects will be diminished by the beginning of the workweek on Monday. Modifying job patterns may allow the patient to continue working, thus encouraging his or her sense of self-worth.

We should also note that the patient is not alone in manifesting various "stages" in coping with terminal illness. Family and friends, too, experience times of denial, anger, guilt, acceptance, and so on. The entire family unit is affected when one of its members requires supportive care. The results of a Canadian study by Betty Davies and her colleagues indicate that families experience a "transition of fading away" as the death of a family member becomes imminent.[25] As the patient's condition worsens, the inevitable ending can no longer be denied. This perception of the patient's "fading away" is accompanied by a task of redefinition, during which individuals and families begin to deal with the burden of letting go of the old before picking up the new. Among the families studied, a period of chaos, confusion, fear, and uncertainty characterized what Davies and her colleagues term the "neutral zone." During this time, the experience was "essentially one of emptiness in which the old reality looked transparent and nothing felt solid anymore." Family members encountered the paradox of caring for a dying loved one while having to carry on with the normal business of living. Eventually, in a style that was generally consistent with coping styles used in the past, individuals and families began to focus on "living day-to-day and preparing for death."

Being with someone who is dying, or who is facing death, we confront our own mortality. It brings us to our senses, and we appreciate just how precious life is and just how uncertain. In that shared humanity, there is a recognition that each of us faces a similar predicament.

In such a context, being with someone who is dying can be a rare opportunity to share the deepest part of ourselves. What is shared may well be anger, frustration, pain, guilt, blame, denial. But there are few opportunities in life to be so vulnerable that we can touch those parts of ourselves usually kept hidden. Being with someone who is dying does not mean that we must become comfortable, but that we learn to accept our discomfort. We learn that we cannot expect ourselves to have all the answers.

Further Readings

Robert Buckman. *I Don't Know What to Say . . .: How to Help and Support Someone Who Is Dying*. (Boston: Little, Brown, 1989).

David Carroll. *Living with Dying: A Loving Guide for Family and Close Friends*. New York: McGraw-Hill, 1985.

Norman Cousins. *Anatomy of an Illness as Perceived by the Patient: Reflections on Healing and Regeneration*. New York: W.W. Norton, 1979.

Ted Eidson, ed. *The AIDS Caregiver's Handbook*. New York: St. Martin's Press, 1988.

Judylaine Fine. *Afraid to Ask: A Book for Families to Share About Cancer*. New York: Lothrop, Lee & Shepard, 1986.

Charles A. Garfield. *Stress and Survival: The Emotional Realities of Life-Threatening Illness*. St. Louis: C.V. Mosby, 1979.

Earl Grollman. *In Sickness and in Health: How to Cope When Your Loved One Is Ill*. Boston: Beacon Press, 1987.

Lawrence LeShan. *Cancer as a Turning Point: A Handbook for People with Cancer, Their Families, and Health Professionals*. New York: E. P. Dutton, 1989.

Stephen Levine. *Healing into Life and Death*. Garden City, N.Y.: Anchor Press/Double-
 day, 1987.
Leonard J. Martelli, Fran D. Peltz, and William Messina. *When Someone You Know Has
 AIDS: A Practical Guide*. New York: Crown, 1987.
Lon G. Nungusser and William D. Bullock. *Notes on Living Until We Say Goodbye: A
 Personal Guide*. (New York: St. Martin's Press, 1988).
Robert Ornstein and David Sobel. *The Healing Brain: Breakthrough Discoveries About
 How the Brain Keeps Us Healthy*. New York: Simon and Schuster, 1987.
E. Mansell Pattison. *The Experience of Dying*. Englewood Cliffs, N.J.: Prentice-Hall,
 1977.

Familiarity with the choices available in funeral services can help us appreciate our many options, perhaps alleviating some of the stress of making such choices in the midst of crisis. The roles of the funeral director and others who can provide assistance in coping with the practical matters of death may also be better understood.

CHAPTER 6

Last Rites: Funerals and Body Disposition

A young musician describes the ceremony he would choose to mark his death: "My body would be cremated and the ashes put into an Egyptian urn. My friends would place the urn on stage at a rock concert and, as the band plays on, everyone will dance and celebrate the changes that we all must pass through eventually."

Some people find the musician's choice lacking in solemnity. "That's not a funeral," they might say. "It's a party." The friends of the musician, however, might respond that his death style is consistent with his life style. Our choices regarding last rites tell something about our attitudes and beliefs about death. The ceremonies that a community enacts to mark the passing of one of its members express, through symbol and metaphor, how death is perceived within that particular social group.

The musician's funeral, for instance, bespeaks an emphasis on celebrating the joys of life. His preference for cremation may reflect a belief that existence is transitory, as if to say, "Life is a passing show. When the movie's over for me, why should I want to preserve my body?" The urn in which the ashes are placed may symbolize the musician's hope that he is somehow part of a historical continuity that transcends even death. In short, each component of the musician's death ceremony tells us something about his concept of death.

A society's attitude toward death, as well as toward the meaning and purpose of life, is revealed in its funeral customs. Examining the death customs of the ancient Egyptians, for

Metropolitan Museum of Art, Rogers/Harkness Funds, 1920

The presence of mortuary goods helped ensure a pleasant afterlife for the ancient Egyptians. Dating from the Eleventh Dynasty, about two thousand years before the present era, this funerary model of a paddling yacht comes from the tomb of Meket-Re.

example, we see a culture preoccupied with acquiring mortuary goods and preparing for the afterlife.[1] A dominant theme in Egyptian religion was belief in life after death. If adequate preparations were made, there was no reason to fear death. The body was mortal. Yet within it were immortal elements: the *Ba*, a soul or psychic force, and the *Ka*, a spiritual double representing the creative and preserving power of life. At death, the *Ka* flew to the afterlife while the *Ba* lived on in the body.

As the permanent dwelling place of the *Ba*, the body was preserved by mummification and protected by wooden coffins, sometimes placed within stone sarcophagi; and the tomb was built to resemble one's earthly home. By providing a home for the *Ba* (often depicted in the form of a bird hovering above the mummy of the deceased), continued enjoyment of the afterlife was ensured. On the other hand, if the *Ba* were destroyed, one would suffer "the second death, the death that really did come as the end." It would be as if the person were annihilated, as if he or she had never come into existence. Preservation of the physical form, either as mummy or as statue, was necessary for survival. This relationship between the identity of the person and the body lying in the tomb, which may in some sense be universal, is found in the feeling of connection with the deceased that one has at graveside.

Likewise, the customary American funeral contains a wealth of information concerning how we relate to death in our society. Consider, for example, the practice of cosmetically restoring the corpse to a more or less "lifelike" appearance. Some believe that this effort at disguise reflects the modern tendency to deny death. Lavish displays for the dead have aroused criticism at least since the time of the Greek philosopher Herodotus in the fourth century B.C.E. (before the common era). But, as some writers have observed, ours is the first society that apparently wishes to do away with all traces of death by quickly disposing of the corpse.

In considering whether contemporary funeral practices encourage death to be denied rather than accepted, we must consider these questions: Who does the funeral serve — the living or the dead? What is the purpose — socially and psychologically — of last rites? What are the essential elements of ceremonies that mark the passing of a member of the community?

In contrast to cultures in which the funeral is primarily a vehicle for preparing the dead to successfully migrate to the afterworld, the American funeral is focused on the welfare of the survivors. Socially, the funeral provides a setting wherein the bereaved family makes a public statement that one of its members has died. The wider community uses the occasion to respond with sympathy and support for the bereaved. Psychologically, the funeral provides a framework within which survivors confront the fact of their loss. By enacting the funeral ritual, survivors move toward resolving the crisis and accepting the loss.

Social Aspects of Last Rites

Funeral ceremonies and memorial services are rites of passage that reflect a community's acknowledgment that one of its members has died. Often termed *last rites*, they mark the final transition or passage of an individual in his or her status as a member of the larger social group. Just as a community convenes to commemorate the other major social transitions in a person's life, the funeral facilitates a gathering together of the survivors to commemorate the deceased's participation as a former member of the community and his or her passage from the group by death.

Notification of Death

A death occurs. First to learn about it, besides the attending medical team, are usually members of the immediate family. Then, in a gradually widening network, other relatives and friends of the deceased are notified. David Sudnow observed that notification occurs generally in a consistent pattern from the immediate family to the wider community (see Figure 6-1).[2] Those with closest relationships to the deceased are notified first, followed by those with less intimate relationships. Sudnow also found that such notification generally takes place between persons in a peer relationship. For example, a bereaved mother first calls

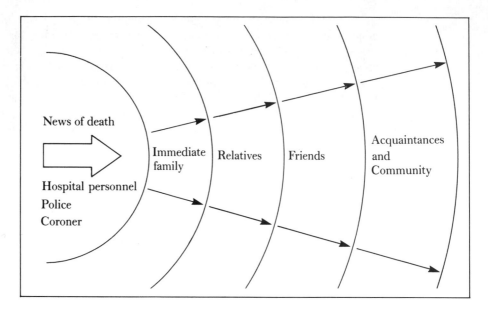

News of death

Hospital personnel
Police
Coroner

Immediate family

Relatives

Friends

Acquaintances and Community

Figure *6-1*   *Widening Circles of Death Notification*

the sibling who had been closest to the deceased, and that person then calls the other brothers and sisters. They, in turn, notify more distant kin.

A similar pattern of notification occurs among those who were not directly related to the deceased. For instance, a coworker or neighbor told about the death notifies others who had a similar relationship with the deceased. This process of notification — taking in a gradually widening circle of relatives, friends, and ac-quaintances — continues until virtually everyone affected by the death is notified.

Death notification also takes place by means of notices that appear in the newspaper (see Figure 6-2). We expect death announcements to appear in a timely fashion. When they do not, the results can be upsetting. The following complaint is typical: "The obituary did not appear in the newspaper until the morning of the funeral. . . . We had a number of calls and letters from people who didn't know about the funeral until it was too late to attend."

When the deceased person is well known, news of the death is broadcast more widely because it affects more people. Thus, notification about the deaths of public figures is carried out on a grand scale. The death of President John F. Kennedy, for example, was known by about 90 percent of the American people within an hour of its official pronouncement at Parkland Hospital in Dallas.[3]

Human beings feel the need to respond to the death of someone who is significant to them. The actual response depends on many factors, including the relationship with the deceased. The person who learns the news of a death only

---

Obituaries

Spirit Bird Benton

Hayward—Spirit Bird Benton, 17, Rt. 5, Hayward, died Friday, April 19, 1991, in Albuquerque, N.M. in an automobile accident.

Spirit Bird was born August 22, 1973 in St. Paul, Minn., the son of Edward J. and Delma (Arrow) Benton. He was a student at Lac Courte Oreilles High School.

He is survived by his father, Edward, Hayward; his mother, Delma, Tama, Iowa; three brothers, John Wedward and Ramon, both of Hayward and Eddie, Green Bay; four sisters, Marilyn, Nancy and Sherrole, all of Hayward and Natalie, Oneida; and a grandmother, Elizabeth Arrow, White River, S.D.

Tribal rites were held on Tuesday, April 23 at the Eagle Lodge, Hayward. Burial was in the Hayward Indian Cemetary in Historyland.

Anderson-Nathan Funeral Home of Hayward was in charge of arrangements.

Figure 6-2   *Newspaper Obituary*
Source: The County Journal
(Bayfield County, Cable, Wis.),
April 25, 1991.

---

after the final disposition of the body may regret not having been able to participate in the final ceremonies marking that person's death. Since the mutual support of the community of bereaved persons is not likely to be as available after the initial period of mourning has passed, the belatedly notified person may feel alone in dealing with grief.

The process of death notification also helps to set apart the bereaved during the period of mourning. In some societies, the black armband, mourning colors and garb, as well as various other signs and symbols, distinguish the bereaved person from those not in mourning. Those traditional signs of mourning have almost vanished from American life. Yet most people still feel that the bereaved deserve special consideration during their distress.

A woman who became involved in an automobile accident several days after the death of her child said later that she wished she could have had a banner proclaiming her status as a "mother whose child has just died." With no outward symbol of her bereavement, she was subjected, as any of us would be, to the strain of waiting around and filling in seemingly endless accident report forms. Had she

> In an earlier time, when society was more agrarian, the whole community could pause from the daily round and rally to the support of the family at the funeral. In this urban age, however, when families live anonymously and work miles from their bedroom communities, and when approximately 60 percent of the women are in the work force, it is increasingly difficult for people to attend daytime funerals unless the deceased is a close relative. The policy of many companies is to give released time to employees only for the funeral of an immediate family member. Consequently, the tendency is for acquaintances to call at the parlor during evening visitation hours and for only the closest friends and relatives to attend the funeral itself. Many clergy feel this deprives the family of a powerful support system and renders impossible a corporate celebration of the life of the deceased.
>
> Frank Minton, "Clergy Views of Funeral Practice"

lived in a small town, the process of notification itself might have set her apart in such a way that the task of completing the paperwork would have been made easier and more convenient.

Though often taken for granted, the process of death notification is important. It can elicit support that is helpful to survivors in dealing with their loss, and it provides the impetus for coming to terms with the fact that a significant loss has taken place.

Mutual Support of the Bereaved

When people learn about the death of someone significant to them, they tend to gather together, closing ranks to provide support and comfort in their mutual bereavement. Generally, this emotional and social support is directed primarily toward the bereaved family. When a small child asked her mother why they were going to visit a bereaved family, the mother replied, "It's important for people to know that you care." What we think we can or cannot do for the bereaved family matters little. What counts is that somehow we demonstrate our care and concern. J.Z. Young says, "Probably the very act of coming together symbolizes communication. A symbol is a sign that points to some state that is of emotional importance. The very fact of assembly gives reassurance that we are part of a larger whole and the individual life is strengthened thereby."[4]

Those who gather at the home of the bereaved participate in a unique social occasion. Unlike other social interactions, this one is not by "invitation only"; generally speaking, anyone who wishes may come. Some persons stay only a short while, expressing their condolences and then leaving. Others, usually relatives or close friends, stay for a longer time, perhaps assisting with the preparation of food, caring for children, helping with funeral arrangements, greeting visitors, or doing whatever else needs doing during the crisis.

Gathering together to support and comfort the bereaved continues throughout the events of the funeral. This pattern of social interaction has important psychological implications for the bereaved as well. It serves to corroborate the fact that a loved one has died. It expresses the notion, "Our community of family and friends has undergone a significant change of status; one of our members is dead." The coming together of the community members to support one another confirms the significance of that loss.

Bereavement as Social Change

Death is a change of status for the person who dies, and it brings a change of status for the survivors. Funeral rituals embody the rhythms of separation and integration. The survivors come together as a community to let go of the dead person and to acknowledge that their situation is no longer the same. This change of status is sometimes reflected in language, as when we refer to someone as a widow or widower. The use of a special term to designate a surviving husband or wife calls attention to the social and psychological impact that is associated with a spouse's death.

Funerals as a Coping Mechanism

Death must be confronted not only within the social setting in which it occurs but within the psyche of the bereaved person. While the processes of death notification and visitation are forms of social interaction, they also provide a potent psychological means for coming to terms with a death.

When death occurs, the most immediate need of the survivors is the disposition of the corpse, which involves both a mental process (deciding what is to be done) and a physical activity (carrying out the course of action decided upon). Making arrangements for disposition of the body engages the survivor in a process that helps to reinforce the recognition that the deceased is really dead. This gradual realization of the loss occurs whether the survivor simply talks with someone about funeral arrangements or actively constructs the coffin and digs the grave.

As with people of other times and other cultures, survivors today frequently choose to bury funerary artifacts or "grave goods" with their dead.[5] Jewelry, photographs, rosaries, Bibles, favorite hats, military medals, stuffed animals, and organizational emblems are among the items most commonly placed in the casket or buried with the deceased. Tobacco, alcohol, and articles related to a favorite activity such as golf or fishing are also frequently mentioned by morticians as examples of grave goods placed with the deceased. The personal sentiment expressed by such placement represents yet another way that survivors deal with the crisis of loss through funeral ritual. Surrounding the final disposition of the body is a complex of social, cultural, religious, psychological, and interpersonal factors that determine the ritual form in which this basic task of body disposition is accomplished. These ceremonies give significance to the events that lead to the final disposition of the deceased's body.

Thousands of American citizens joined in the funeral observance honoring the Unknown Serviceman of the Vietnam Era. Here the procession is crossing Memorial Bridge between a Marine honor cordon, on its way to Arlington National Cemetery. Replete with full military honors, the funeral was an occasion for expressing national gratitude and grief in response to the ultimate sacrifice of those who died in the wartime service of their country.

William E. Rosemund, U.S. Army Photo

The American Funeral

The criticisms sometimes voiced about funeral practices have obscured the fact that most Americans give the funeral service trade positive marks. In surveys of public opinion, about nine out of ten Americans rate the performance of funeral homes as good to excellent.[6] What, then, accounts for the persistence of criticism against American funeral practices? To answer this question, we briefly review both the main objections raised by critics and the evolution of funeral practices during the last century.

Criticisms

The American funeral has been criticized on several grounds: from general objections to what a funeral represents to criticisms of particular funeral practices. Bertram Puckle's *Funeral Customs: Their Origin and Development*, published in 1926, was of the first type — a general polemic against lavish concern for the dead. To Puckle, the funeral represented a vestige of the superstitious fear of the dead characteristic of the pagan and the primitive.

In 1959, LeRoy Bowman, in *The American Funeral: A Study in Guilt, Extravagance, and Sublimity*, documented the commercialism and conspicuous display connected with funerals while investigating the social and psychological value of funerals. Bowman concluded that funeral practices were overlaid with such ostentation that the fundamental meaning and dignity of the funeral rite had all but disappeared. The American funeral, he said, "appears to be an anachronism, an elaboration of early customs rather than the adaptation to modern needs that it should be."[7] Bowman urged Americans to become more aware of the essential social, psychological, and spiritual functions of funeral rituals in order to avoid the potential for exploitation associated with the materialistic features of contemporary practices.

To Bowman, the funeral director was not a professional, but a tradesman, often selling wares that were unnecessary and unwanted. The function of the funeral director, Bowman said, should be to help the family fulfill its own wishes. In this, Bowman urged considerably more flexibility in our last rites. "The uniformity of present usage should give way to individually adapted procedures, whatever they may be." A balanced and sober inquiry, Bowman's book continues to have value to anyone wishing more participation in the design of funeral rituals.

In 1963, two books appeared that brought criticism of the American funeral to the attention of the public: Jessica Mitford's *The American Way of Death* and Ruth M. Harmer's *The High Cost of Dying*. Both books cited the materialism of the contemporary funeral and called for reforms.

Mitford said that conventional funeral practices were not only bizarre but morbid. In the attempt to disguise and prettify death, it becomes more grotesque. She took issue with the euphemisms employed to soften the reality of death: the metamorphosis of coffins into "caskets," hearses into "coaches" or "professional cars"; flowers become "floral tributes," and cremated ashes are "cremains." The corpse, meanwhile, lies in state in the "slumber room." The undertaker, now a

If you have an uncomfortable feeling about funerals, which are the accepted social pattern for confronting death in our culture, if you try to avoid or eliminate them, that might be a sign that you're dealing with major residual death anxiety. That's one of the things that shows up in our culture: the way people delude themselves and retreat from the major therapeutic resources that are provided culturally. There's a notion that if we have a mini-funeral, we'll have mini-grief. But we know that the exact opposite is true.

The more you reduce your emotional acting out at the time of the event, the more you prolong the pain of grief and postpone the therapeutic work of mourning.

That's why in a culture such as ours, where you have an unwise management of grief, you have a very large proportion of illness responses after the death experience. People act it out physically, rather than doing it psychologically or socially. That's a very heavy weight.

But in primitive cultures, such as the aboriginals in Australia, where you have almost a two-week funeral process, where there are all kinds of acting out of deep feelings, you come to the end of that two weeks and a major portion of the grief work has been done, and the survivor is ready to move into the period of resolution through the mourning process, which takes quite a bit longer usually.

Edgar N. Jackson,
from an interview with the authors

"mortician" or "funeral director," offers the solid copper "Colonial Classic Beauty," replete with a "Perfect-Posture" adjustable innerspring mattress, in a choice of "60 color-matched shades." Within this handsome arrangement, the deceased wears "handmade original fashions" from a "gravewear couturiere" and "Nature-Glo, the ultimate in cosmetic grooming."[8]

Mitford's satiric criticisms sparked concern among those in the funeral trade and also increased the public's awareness of alternatives, such as memorial societies. Once the initial furor lessened, most funeral directors responded to the criticisms by earnestly working to offer a wider range of choices in funeral service. A 1967 survey of funeral directors by Robert Fulton indicated a trend toward more individualized services.[9]

Some clergy members have voiced concerns about the expanding role of funeral directors into areas that previously came under the jurisdiction of the religious community. In earlier times the clergy fulfilled a significant role in dealing with the bereaved family and in making preparations for the disposition of the corpse. Now funeral services are seldom held in churches, having been moved to the chapels that are part of the modern funeral establishment. Many clergy would like to reverse this trend, particularly in the case of funerals for their church members.[10] Although many clergy do advocate simpler and less costly funerals, even those most critical of present practices did not fault funeral directors for a lack of professional integrity.

A study conducted as part of the Federal Trade Commission (FTC) investigation into funeral practices found substantial approval of present funeral prac-

The funeral director is caught between ambivalent demands: On the one hand, he is encouraged to disguise the reality of death for the survivors who do not possess the emotional support once provided by theology to deal with it; on the other hand, he is impelled to call attention to the special services he is rendering. Thus, he both blunts and sharpens the reality of death.

Robert Fulton and Gilbert Geis,
"Death and Social Values"

tices.[11] In general, respondents said they were shown an adequate range of caskets, understood what was included in the price, and received sufficient information to make a satisfactory decision. Most believed that the funeral director had been helpful in selecting the kind of service desired, without deprecating less expensive caskets or services. Indeed, they expressed the view that the funeral director had helped them keep costs down. Few believed there was any attempt to manipulate the purchase of funeral services by taking advantage of their grief.

Nevertheless, there is a widespread feeling that funeral directors are in a position to take advantage of their customers since the activities and costs of funeral services are unfamiliar to most people. The funeral industry is viewed as a "mystery business," about which the average person knows little. Thus, despite what appears to be general satisfaction with funeral service, there is some concern about whether a consumer would know if he or she were being ripped off.

Perhaps because of this concern, the Federal Trade Commission implemented its "Trade Regulation Rule on Funeral Industry Practices" in 1984. The Funeral Rule, as it is called, stipulates that funeral providers give detailed information about prices and legal requirements to persons who are arranging funerals. It requires disclosure of itemized price information, both over the telephone and in writing. Misrepresentations about the disposition of human remains are prohibited, as are certain unfair practices, such as embalming for a fee without prior permission, requiring customers to purchase caskets for a direct cremation, or making the purchase of any funeral good or service conditional on the purchase of any other funeral good or service.[12]

History

The detailed regulations promulgated by the FTC can be viewed as the natural outcome of a historical process that removed death from the purview of family and friends and placed it in the hands of professional morticians. When families themselves took care of the disposition of their dead, any criticism of their manner of performance would have been irrelevant. And, of course, it was not designed to produce a profit. Disposition was simply a human task to be carried out in a spirit of compassion, kindness, and respect. Even though we are now accustomed to giving over the care of our dead to the undertaker, we may yet

Figure 6-3   *City Directory Listing for a Cabinet Maker and Supplier of Funeral Furnishings, circa 1850*

carry residual feelings that realizing a profit from performing these services is somehow macabre.

Another source of our discomfort about the commercialization of funeral service arises from our own anxiety about death and our aversion to touching or being in the presence of a corpse. (Such aversion can perhaps be attributed to our unfamiliarity with personal care of the dead—an effect, rather than a cause, of current practices.) Yet when the corpse is of someone we loved, our aversion may be mixed with guilt; we are pulled in opposing directions, and feel uncomfortable about the dead. We may unconsciously resent the funeral director who handles the body of our loved one. Thus, we feel a confusing range of emotions regarding the dead: aversion, guilt, resentment, affection, and anxiety.

Formerly, the family's ceremonial occasions were held within the home. The undertaker was a tradesman, a merchant who supplied the materials and funeral paraphernalia: such items as the casket and carriage, door badges and scarfs, special clothing, memorial cards and announcements, chairs, robes, pillows, gauze, candles, ornaments, and so on—items used to equip the home for the mourning ritual (see Figure 6-3).

By the end of the nineteenth century, however, the undertaker had assumed a much larger role. No longer merely a tradesman who furnished goods to the bereaved family, the undertaker had become a provider of services. He was being asked to take more control and to assume a larger role, actually taking part in the disposition of the dead: laying out the body for the wake, transporting it to the church for the funeral, and finally to the cemetery for burial.

Embalming the dead came into use in the years after the Civil War. President Lincoln's funeral procession, which traveled from Washington, D.C., to Springfield, Illinois, was a public event that increased awareness of the new practice of embalming.[13] Still, other means of temporarily retarding decomposition of the corpse continued in use (see Figure 6-4).

(There is evidence that embalming was performed on some of the soldiers killed during the Civil War, which allowed their bodies to be returned home.

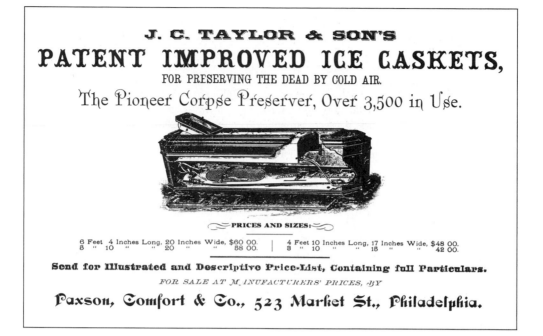

Figure *6-4* *Refrigerated Casket Advertisement,* 1881
Undertakers of the 1880s could keep a body for viewing over a longer period of time by using an ice casket such as the one shown in this advertisement. When embalming became widespread, these cold-air preservation devices became obsolete.
Source: Atheneum of Philadelphia Collection; from Paxton, Comfort, and Company, *Undertakers' Supplies Catalog,* 1881.

Through World Wars I and II and down to the Korean conflict, however, battle-field dead were typically buried in the particular theater of operations in which they had been killed, with a possibility of final disposition to the United States after the end of hostilities. The Vietnam conflict was the first in which battlefield dead were returned from a foreign battle zone for stateside burial as a matter of course. The military services have their own mortuary officers who may be given specialized training to help them carry out their duties.)[14]

With the coming of smaller houses and increased urbanization, the place where the dead were prepared for burial changed: The viewing of the body moved from the parlor of the family home into a room reserved for such use by the tradesman-undertaker. The funeral "parlor" in town gradually substituted for the ceremonial room that people no longer had in their own homes. This one-room funeral parlor was the forerunner of the present-day funeral home or mortuary.

"Now, Mr. Barlow, what had you in mind? Embalmment of course, and after that incineration or not, according to taste. Our crematory is on scientific principles, the heat is so intense that all inessentials are volatilized. Some people did not like the thought that ashes of the casket and clothing were mixed with the Loved One's. Normal disposal is by inhumement, entombment, inurnment or immurement, but many people just lately prefer insarcophagusment. That is *very* individual. The casket is placed inside a sealed sarcophagus, marble or bronze, and rests permanently above ground in a niche in the mausoleum, with or without a personal stained-glass window above. That, of course, is for those with whom price is not a primary consideration."

Evelyn Waugh, *The Loved One*

The last quarter of the nineteenth century in America saw the growth of trade and professional organizations. The trend away from ceremonies in the home was also having an effect on undertakers themselves. By the late nineteenth century, they had already become "morticians" and were starting to think of themselves as "funeral *directors*." The Funeral Directors' National Association, established in the 1880s — now the National Funeral Directors Association (NFDA) — was among the first of these new trade organizations designed both to promote business and to establish minimum standards for service. Trade publications, such as *The Casket* and *Sunnyside*, provided a means of communication among funeral directors. In 1917, the National Selected Morticians was formed as a limited-membership group dedicated to the ideal of service. A more recent organization, the National Foundation of Funeral Service, was formed in 1945 to conduct research, establish a comprehensive library of funeral service information, and sponsor an institute providing professional education for funeral directors. Today, most states require that funeral directors be certified by state licensing, and all states require that embalmers be licensed.

Looking back on the debate between those who claimed that abuses existed and the funeral service industry, which responded that such abuses were the exception, we can conclude that perhaps both sides were right. Most funeral directors apparently conduct business honestly and are sensitive to their customers' needs. Surveys of the public's attitudes — even those taken before institution of the FTC's rule — have generally confirmed satisfaction with funeral service practices. As with purchases made in other areas, however, the customer who winds up with the least regrets is likely to be one who has taken time beforehand to fully explore his or her options.

Selecting Funeral Services: Awareness and Alternatives

The purchase of funeral services is a transaction unique in commerce. Most people give it little or no thought until they find themselves in the midst of an emotional crisis. When arrangements for funeral services are made during a time

The funeral has traditionally been a time when family and friends come together to pay respects and to say farewells. It is a time of mutual support for the bereaved and of tribute to the deceased. The display of flowers surrounding this coffin bespeaks the affection felt for the deceased while she was alive and the sense of loss at her absence from the community.

Library of Congress

of crisis and confusion, the customer is confronted with the need to make an on-the-spot decision about a purchase that cannot be returned. Caskets do not bear a notice saying, "Return in thirty days if not completely satisfied." Once made, the decision is final. Lack of information, coupled with lack of any forethought about funerals or body disposition, may lead to decisions that will be regretted later. For instance, unaware that a casket is not required for a body that is to be cremated, the bereaved may be inclined to buy the best available, thinking that there is no real alternative.

The choices involved in selecting funeral services tend to be quite different from those involved in other purchases. When purchasing a new car, for example, you can shop around and test-drive various makes and models. If you encounter a

"Doonesbury" drawing, © 1986 by G. B. Trudeau, Universal Press Syndicate

salesperson who uses high-pressure techniques, you can either submit to such tactics or walk away: You have a clear choice. Yet, rarely do the emotional conditions in which funeral services are purchased allow for such coolheadedness or presence of mind that the bereaved can simply walk away and go elsewhere to compare prices. In some localities, there may be only one mortician to serve the entire community. Even in the best of circumstances, the customer may be hard put to find suitable alternatives. When a death has already occurred, it can be too late to start investigating the options.

The funeral is a setting for private sorrow and public loss in which the burden of grief is reduced by sharing with others. It effects the disposition of the corpse while acknowledging that indeed a life has been lived. The funeral is a statement from the family to the community: "We have lost someone, and we are grieving." Ideally, it is a personal statement based on felt needs and values.

Unfortunately, the funeral may become an occasion for an expensive or lavish display as survivors attempt to assuage guilt or to compensate for some unresolved conflict with the deceased. Spending a huge sum of money on a funeral, under such circumstances, may thwart the real purpose of last rites: namely, to acknowledge publicly that a member of the community has died and to effect closure on that person's life for the bereaved. The purpose of the funeral can be realized whether it is garnished with diamonds and rubies, or with poetry and a song.

Funeral Service Charges

The National Funeral Directors Association has distinguished four categories of charges that together make up the cost of a conventional American funeral. The first category includes the services provided by the funeral director and mortuary staff, the use of mortuary facilities and equipment, and the casket and related funeral merchandise selected by the customer.

The second category pertains to the actual disposition of the body. Depending on the method of disposition chosen, this can include the purchase of a gravesite and costs for opening and closing the grave; or, if above-ground entombment is chosen, the cost of a mausoleum crypt; or, if the body is cremated, the cost of cremation and the subsequent interment, entombment, or scattering of the cremated remains, as well as the cost of an urn to hold the ashes, if desired.

The third category is made up of costs related to memorialization, which may include a monument or marker for the grave, or, for cremated remains, a memorial niche in a columbarium with an inscription or plaque.

The fourth category involves miscellaneous expenses either paid directly by the family or reimbursed to the undertaker. These may include a clergy member's honorarium, the use of limousines and additional vehicles (if not included in the funeral services category), flowers, notices of the death that appear in newspapers, and transportation outside the local area.

In summary, then, the total cost for the final disposition of the deceased includes funeral service charges, body disposition costs, memorialization expenses, and miscellaneous or supplemental expenses.

Until recently, the funeral director's portion of these expenses might be quoted to customers in a variety of ways. The most widespread form of pricing, and the simplest, was the single-unit method: A single price was quoted for a standard funeral; the specifics of the service and the total price depended on the type of casket selected. A more expensive casket thus would become the centerpiece of a correspondingly more ornate and elaborate ceremony.

As consumers wanted more detailed information about costs, many funeral directors turned to functional or multi-unit pricing: A separate price would be quoted for each of the several components of the total service provided. For example, using a bi-unit method of pricing, there would be one charge for funeral services and another for the casket. Tri-unit pricing further broke out costs by quoting one charge for the funeral director's services, another for the use of facilities and equipment, and a third for the casket. Multi-unit pricing methods thus exemplified the trend toward itemizing funeral costs in ever greater detail.

With the advent of the Federal Trade Commission's "Funeral Rule" in 1984, itemized price information became a requirement for *all* funeral providers. The rule requires, at minimum, that prices be itemized for seventeen specified goods and services, if those items are offered by the funeral provider (see Table 6-1). These goods and services must be specified on the provider's General Price List, which has been called "the keystone of the Funeral Rule," so that customers can compare prices or choose only those elements of a funeral they want. It is important to note that the FTC requirements do not prohibit funeral directors from also offering package funerals, as discussed earlier.

The average cost of funerals, excluding cemetery costs, is now about $3500. A mid-1980s survey of nearly 700 firms revealed that the charges for individual funerals ranged from a low of $100 to a high of $23,560.[15] With about 2 million Americans dying each year, the annual expenditure for funerals and body disposition in the United States is over $6 billion.[16] Although most mortuary firms are operated as small businesses, taken in the aggregate, disposition of the dead is clearly big business.

T A B L E 6-1   *Funeral Rule Itemization Requirements*

Forwarding of remains to another funeral home [1]
Receiving remains from another funeral home [1]
Direct cremation [1,2]
Immediate burial [1]
Transfer of remains to funeral home
Embalming [3]
Other preparation of the body
Use of facilities for viewing
Use of facilities for funeral ceremony
Other use of facilities [4]
Hearse
Limousine
Other automotive equipment
Acknowledgment cards
Casket prices [5]
Outer burial container prices [6]
Charge for professional services of the funeral director [7]

1. Any fee for professional services must be included in the price quoted for this item.
2. If a provider offers direct cremations, consumers must be allowed to provide their own container if they desire, as long as it meets state or crematory requirements. Also, if direct cremations are offered, the provider must make available either an unfinished wood box or alternative container for consumers who request it. A disclosure to this effect must be included in conjunction with the price for direct cremations.
3. In addition to the quoted price for embalming, there must be an affirmative disclosure stating, in part, that "except in certain special cases, embalming is not required by law."
4. Other facilities might include, for example, a tent and chairs for a graveside service.
5. Casket prices must be disclosed either on the General Price List or on a separate Casket Price List.
6. Prices for Outer Burial Containers may be listed on the General Price List or on a separate price list. Also, a disclosure must be made to the effect that "in most areas of the country, no state or local law requires you to buy an outer burial container; however, many cemeteries ask that you have such a container so that the grave will not sink in. Either a burial vault or a grave liner will satisfy these requirements."
7. As noted above, charges for services entailed in forwarding and receiving remains, direct cremations, and immediate burials are not involved here, since the FTC rule requires that service costs be included in the prices for those items. The fee for professional services may be listed separately from other items, or it may be included in the price of caskets. Whichever method is chosen by a funeral provider, a disclosure to that effect must appear on the General Price List.

When criticized for what some have called the high cost of dying in America, funeral directors point out that they have significant operating costs which must be recovered.[17] Personnel, equipment, and facilities are kept available to the public twenty-four hours a day. Indeed, a timely response to the family's call is a matter of professional pride to most funeral directors—a sign of willingness to assist the bereaved in a time of crisis.

Typically, the funeral business is located in a rather large, possibly colonial-style, building, the floor plan of which may be adapted or designed especially for its function as a funeral home. Ronny Turner and Charles Edgley have compared funerals to theatrical presentations, with certain activities taking place, as it were, off stage.[18] The backstage area, hidden from the public's gaze, is where the body is prepared by embalming and application of cosmetics for its eventual role in the funeral drama. There is generally no hint of these backstage regions to those who enter by the front door. Turner and Edgley describe the funeral chapel as "a model of theatrical perfection" that might well "make a Broadway star envious." Usually arranged in such a way that there are several entrances and exits, it "may be served by back doors, halls, tunnels, and passageways that lead from the preparation room without ever trespassing frontstage areas."

Funeral directors regard themselves as professionals who provide services to people who are in crisis. Although funeral directors have been criticized by some for taking on the role of "grief therapists," the fact is that many funeral directors consider this function essential to meeting the needs of the bereaved. Indeed, many participate in seminars and courses designed to impart counseling skills specifically for working with bereaved persons.

Comparing the Costs

Comparing the costs of competing funeral establishments may be difficult even when costs are itemized. Different funeral providers do not always offer the same goods and services, and they may choose different methods of presenting prices. Thus, the comparison shopper may be trying to compare what seems like apples and oranges, with confusing results. Nevertheless, it is useful to distinguish among the charges that may be assessed. (As you read the following discussion of funeral goods and services, you may find it useful to refer to Table 6-2, which shows the relative costs of various items that are typically part of mortuary services; actual prices will vary from region to region and generally increase on a par with rises in the Consumer Price Index.)

Charge for Professional Services

Essentially, this is a basic charge for the services provided by the funeral director and his or her staff. It is payment for arranging the funeral, consulting with family members and clergy, directing the visitation and funeral ceremony, and preparing and filing necessary notices and authorizations related to body disposition. This latter service may include filing the death certificate and certain claims for death benefits.

The fee for professional services covers a pro rata share of the overhead expenses required to maintain facilities and staff around the clock. The method of arriving at this charge is, of course, left to the discretion of each funeral provider, and it varies according to a number of factors, including the clientele served and the prices charged by competitors.

Cemetery or crematory services, flowers, and placement of newspaper notices are generally not covered in this basic service charge. Those items are usually billed separately, and there may be a charge for the funeral director's services in purchasing such items on the customer's behalf.

According to the Funeral Rule, if direct cremation or immediate burial is chosen, any fee charged for professional services must be included in the price quoted for those methods of disposition. Similarly, this fee must be *included* in

T A B L E 6-2   *Sample Funeral Service Prices*

Forwarding of remains to another funeral home	$600
Receiving remains from another funeral home	$485
Direct cremation	
with container provided by purchaser	$500
including alternative container	$545
including cloth-covered wood casket	$825
Immediate burial	
with container provided by purchaser	$470
including cloth-covered wood casket	$790
including oak-finished pine casket	$1,340
Transfer of remains to funeral home	$60
($60 additional for nighttime transfer)	
Embalming	$135
Other preparation of the body	
Cosmetology	$50
Hairstyling	(included)
Dressing and placing remains in casket	$50
Disinfection and sanitation	
(preparing for closed-casket funeral)	$90
Use of facilities for viewing (per day)	$55
Use of facilities for funeral ceremony	
Chapel	$225
Smaller stateroom	$140
Other use of facilities	
Staff conducting graveside service	$55
Scattering cremated remains at sea or in mountains	$55
Holding remains (per day / applies only to immediate burial or	
cremation when body is not embalmed)	$20
Hearse	$75
Limousine	$50
Other automotive equipment	$45
Acknowledgment cards (box of 25)	$20
Memorial folders or prayer cards (first 100)	$35
(Add $10 for every additional 100)	
Register book	$20
Burial clothing	$80-$200
Cremation urns	$20-$325
Casket prices	$325-$7,000
Outer burial container prices	$55-$1,650
Charge for professional services	$400

prices quoted for forwarding remains to another funeral home or receiving remains from another funeral home.

As an alternative method of pricing, the FTC rule allows funeral providers to incorporate a fee for professional services into the prices of caskets. When casket prices include a fee for professional services, however, a description of those services must be placed on the casket price list.

Intake Charges

This is the charge for transporting the remains from the place of death to the mortuary. There may be a surcharge for a nighttime pickup to cover additional costs of staff.

Embalming

Nowhere in the United States is embalming required by law, except in certain circumstances. Yet embalming is such an accepted mortuary practice in America that hardly anyone questions it. Embalming involves removing the blood and other fluids in the body and replacing them with chemicals to disinfect and temporarily retard deterioration of the corpse. This procedure is usually considered a practical necessity when a body will be viewed. With few exceptions, however, the new FTC rule requires that mortuaries obtain express permission to embalm from the family in order to charge a fee for the procedure.[19] Furthermore, the price list must include the following disclosure next to the price for embalming:

> Except in certain special cases, embalming is not required by law. Embalming may be necessary, however, if you select certain funeral arrangements, such as a funeral with viewing. If you do not want embalming, you usually have the right to choose an arrangement which does not require you to pay for it, such as direct cremation or immediate burial.

Embalming laws vary from state to state. In Connecticut, for instance, embalming is required only when a body is to be transported across state lines by common carrier (bus, train, plane, or commercial vehicle). In Kentucky, embalming is not mandatory under any circumstances. The District of Columbia requires that a body be embalmed only when death results from communicable disease. In Louisiana, a body must be embalmed if it is held longer than thirty hours before final disposition. California requires embalming only when the body is to be transported by common carrier. In summary, then, according to the specific requirements of each state, special circumstances involving transportation, disease control, and the final disposition of the body may make embalming mandatory.

If refrigeration is available, a mortuary may offer the alternative of storing a body for a short time without embalming. A refrigerated, unembalmed body will remain relatively preserved for about three days, although some mortuaries stipulate that they will not hold an unembalmed body for longer than forty-eight hours. The cost of refrigeration is likely to be somewhat less than for embalming.

Some mortuaries have a combined charge for embalming and body preparation; others itemize each of the procedures involved in readying a body for viewing and for the funeral. Thus, in addition to embalming charges (or, if embalming is not done, in lieu of such charges), separate fees may be charged for each of the procedures performed in the preparation room.

Other Body Preparation Charges

Body preparation includes minimal antiseptic hygiene procedures, such as washing the body. One funeral establishment lists separate charges for embalming; for cosmetology, hairstyling, and manicuring; and for dressing the body, placing it in the casket, and composing it for viewing.

Casket Prices

Of all funeral costs, people usually feel the most important is that of the casket because of its symbolic and emotional value in honoring the deceased. The customer is faced with a wide range of options, and, whereas many other items of the funeral service are based on a standard fee, the price of a casket is highly variable. The latitude in choice ranges from inexpensive cardboard containers all the way to solid mahogany, copper, or bronze caskets costing thousands of dollars. Depending on the socioeconomic status of their clientele, most funeral homes can provide a variety of caskets in a wide range of prices. Since funeral homes are free to determine their own methods of pricing their caskets, the customer may discover that a casket selling for $1000 in one funeral home costs twice as much in another. This price difference may be due to a higher markup designed to increase the profit margin; or, as mentioned earlier, it may result from the fact that the funeral provider has chosen to include the fee for professional services in the casket price rather than charging for it separately.

Because of this variability, prices of caskets can be discussed here only in general terms, with the aim being to describe the types and qualities of caskets available. A relatively inexpensive, conventional casket could range in cost from several hundred to a thousand dollars. These caskets are typically made of plywood and covered with cloth, and contain a mattress that is likely to be made of straw covered with an acetate sheet.

At the next pricing level, refinements appear. Although these are also made of wood, they may be covered with copper or bronze sheathing. Gasketed steel caskets are available at prices ranging from about a thousand to several thousand dollars. The mattress, too, exhibits refinements, being constructed with springs, over which is a layer of foam rubber and a covering of acetate material. In this range, some caskets are available with devices designed to ensure an airtight environment within the casket. (Although a solace to some people, any added protection is debatable; critics contend that such devices actually hasten decomposition.)

The price tag on a top-of-the-line casket ranges upwards to $10,000 or more. For this sum, one obtains a casket constructed of mahogany, copper, or bronze and fitted out with all the accoutrements of the casket manufacturer's art. Deluxe models feature an adjustable boxspring mattress that can be tilted to enhance the display of the corpse.

Marketing analysis indicates that the gasketed steel casket is most popular with Americans. Based on the number of caskets shipped to funeral directors, this type of casket holds a 44 percent share of the market, trailed by nongasketed steel (19.1 percent), cloth-covered (17.5 percent), hardwood (13.4 percent), copper or bronze (2.3 percent), and stainless steel caskets (0.8 percent).[20]

Our choices for displaying and disposing of the dead are regulated less by the force of law than by custom and by ignorance of alternatives. For example, many people are surprised to learn that there is no law requiring a body destined for cremation to be placed in a casket. Most crematoria require only that the body be delivered in a rigid container. Most mortuaries can provide a cardboard box, which suffices for this purpose, at a small charge. The FTC rule now prohibits funeral providers from telling consumers that state or local law requires them to purchase a casket when they wish to arrange a direct cremation (that is, a cremation that occurs without formal viewing of the remains or any visitation or ceremony with the body present). For firms that do arrange for direct cremations, the rule stipulates that the following disclosure be made to customers:

> If you want to arrange a direct cremation, you can use an unfinished wood box or an alternative container. Alternative containers can be made of materials like heavy cardboard or composition materials (with or without an outside covering), or pouches of canvas.

Finally, as regards caskets, the FTC rule requires funeral providers to supply customers with a list of the prices and descriptions of available caskets. This may be handled in one of two ways: either on the General Price List or on a separate Casket Price List.

Facilities Charges

The use of a visitation or viewing room is a common component of most funerals. In the itemized listing of prices, the funeral director may use whatever method of pricing is preferred or follow common practice for that particular area. For example, various settings in the funeral home might be listed, along with the charges for each by day, half day, or hour. Similarly, if a funeral ceremony is held at the mortuary chapel, a charge for the use of that facility will be specified by the funeral provider. When other facilities are made available to customers (for example, a tent and chairs for graveside services), the charges for their use must be stated on the funeral provider's price list.

Vehicles

As with other aspects of funeral service, mortuaries may follow quite different price schedules for the use of vehicles. According to the FTC rule, charges for the use of a hearse, limousine, or other automotive equipment must be itemized separately on the General Price List. Sometimes additional vehicles are requested for the use of pallbearers, family members, or other participants such as clergy. A "flower car" may be used to transport floral arrangements to the cemetery. If a motorcycle escort is desired, there is a charge for each escort.

Outer Burial Container Prices

If outer burial containers are offered by the funeral home, their prices must be listed, either separately or on the General Price List. In addition to listing prices, the following disclosure must be made:

In most areas of the country, no state or local law makes you buy a container to surround the casket in the grave. However, many cemeteries require that you have such a container so that the grave will not sink in. Either a burial vault or a grave liner will satisfy these requirements.

Since many funeral homes do not sell burial vaults or grave liners, this item may not appear on the price lists of the mortuaries in your area. Further information about the types of outer burial containers is given in our discussion of burial and entombment costs later in this chapter.

Miscellaneous Charges

Under this category, we include charges for goods or services provided directly by the funeral home as well as those obtained from outside sources on behalf of the customer. This latter category could include such "cash-advance" items as floral arrangements and newspaper notices. The customer may be billed for the actual amounts of the items, or the funeral provider may add a surcharge for arranging these cash-advance items. If an additional charge is made, a notice to that effect must be shown on the General Price List.

The FTC rule specifically mentions that acknowledgement cards must be itemized if the funeral provider sells those items or performs the service of filling out and sending them for customers.

Other items that come under the heading of miscellaneous costs include any fees or honoraria for pallbearers, an honorarium for the clergyperson who conducts the funeral service, and the cost of any burial garments purchased from the mortuary.

Direct Cremations and Immediate Burials

Not all funeral homes offer direct cremations and immediate burials to consumers, although the number of those that do is increasing. These methods of body disposition usually occur without formal viewing of the remains or any visitation or ceremony with the body present. (Some mortuaries are responding to consumer requests for viewing and for informal ceremonies by placing the body on a cloth-covered gurney.)

If direct cremation or immediate burial is offered by a funeral home, the charge—including the fee for professional services—is shown on the General Price List. When direct cremation is selected, the customer must be given the option of providing the container or of purchasing an unfinished pine box or alternative container (such as canvas pouch, or a box made of cardboard, plywood, or composition material). Similarly, for immediate burials, the customer has the option to provide a container or purchase a simple casket, such as one made of wood and covered with cloth. (If a funeral home offers immediate burials but does not offer direct cremations, the FTC rule does not require the firm to make available an alternative container or unfinished wood box, although a funeral director might choose to do so.)

> Assume that we are confronted with the dead body of a man. What disposition shall we make of it? Shall we lay it in a boat that is set adrift? Shall we take the heart from it and bury it in one place and the rest of the body in another? Shall we expose it to wild animals? Burn it on a pyre? Push it into a pit to rot with other bodies? Boil it until the flesh falls off the bones, and throw the flesh away and treasure the bones? Such questions provoke others which may not be consciously articulated, such as: "What do men generally think this body is?" And, "What do they think is a proper way of dealing with it?"
>
> Robert W. Habenstein and William M. Lamers,
> *The History of American Funeral Directing*

Body Disposition

Think for a moment about the manner you would choose for the disposition of your body after you die. When Americans are asked their preferences, responses usually fall into one of three categories: burial, cremation, or donation to science. Corpses must be disposed of for sanitary considerations, though it is unlikely that a person's choice of method is influenced by that fact. It is more likely that preferences are based on social, cultural, and philosophical reasons. Although bodies can be disposed of in ways other than the three mentioned, most of us probably would consider them improper.

The decomposition of the body is hastened in some societies by the flesh being washed from the bones when the corpse is partially decomposed; parts of the body are then retained as a memorial. In other societies the body is left to the elements and generally decomposes quite rapidly (except in very dry, desert climates, where the heat removes the moisture from the body, acting thereby to preserve it). Some Indian tribes of the American plains constructed platforms on which the corpse was left, exposed to the effects of the sun, wind, and rain. In some societies, the remains of the dead are consumed by birds of prey or other animals. In India, for example, one can still view the Towers of Silence on Bombay's fashionable Marabar Hill, where the Parsi community disposes of its dead by leaving corpses to be devoured by vultures. As followers of Zoroaster, they regard earth, fire, and water as sacred, not to be defiled by the dead. Their beliefs are not shared, however, by the residents of high-rise luxury apartments whose windows look out upon what they consider an improper and grotesque method of body disposition.

Burial can be in a single grave dug into the soil or entombment in a multi-tiered mausoleum. With soaring real estate prices, a "high-rise condominium cemetery" was recently erected in Tokyo as a "concession to modern living."[21] With many temples running out of space, finding a reasonably priced final resting place anywhere near urban areas has become difficult. (Similar problems have beset "pet cemeteries" in this country, where the side effects of urban change have led

Burial at sea is a naval tradition the world over, particularly during times of war. Here the body of a seaman is committed to the deep during burial services aboard the USS Ranger in 1963.

to animal cemeteries suspending operations or even closing burial grounds that were once intended to be a beloved animal's final resting place.)[22]

The phrase "burial at sea" might connote a corpse slid ceremonially off the side of a ship, or it could refer to a corpse placed inside a boat that is set aflame and then adrift.

Cremation causes rapid dissolution of the body by intense heat and has been carried out by means ranging from a simple wood fire to sophisticated electric retorts.

Another method of body disposition is donation to science. The person who chooses this method may gain satisfaction from the notion that a contribution is being made to the advancement of knowledge: "My body will serve a useful function even after I'm gone." However, most medical schools and similar institutions usually have an adequate supply of cadavers, making donation an option that may be difficult for most people to exercise.

Elmer Ruiz: Gravedigger

Not anybody can be a gravedigger. You can dig a hole any way they come. A gravedigger, you have to make a neat job. I had a fella once, he wanted to see a grave. He was a fella that digged sewers. He was impressed when he seen me diggin' this grave—how square and how perfect it was. A human body is goin' into this grave. That's why you need skill when you're gonna dig a grave.

The gravedigger today, they have to be somebody to operate a machine. You just use a shovel to push the dirt loose. Otherwise you don't use 'em. We're tryin' a new machine, a ground hog. This machine is supposed to go through heavy frost. It do very good job so far. When the weather is mild, like fifteen degrees above zero, you can do it very easy.

But when the weather is below zero, believe me, you just really workin' hard. I have to use a mask. Your skin hurts so much when it's cold—like you put a hot flame near your face. I'm talkin' about two, three hours standin' outside. You have to wear a mask, otherwise you can't stand it at all. . . .

The most graves I dig is about six, seven a day. This is in the summer. In the winter it's a little difficult. In the winter you have four funerals, that's a pretty busy day. . . .

The grave will be covered in less than two minutes, complete. We just open the hoppers with the right amount of earth. We just press it and then we lay out a layer of black earth. Then we put the sod that belongs there. After a couple of weeks you wouldn't know it's a grave there. It's complete flat. Very rarely you see a grave that is sunk. . . .

I usually tell 'em I'm a caretaker. I don't think the name sound as bad. I have to look at the park, so after the day's over that everything's closed, that nobody do damage to the park. Some occasions some people just come and steal and loot and do bad things in the park, destroy some things. I believe it would be some young fellas. A man with responsibility, he wouldn't do things like that. Finally we had to put up some gates and close 'em at sundown. Before, we didn't, no. We have a fence of roses. Always in cars you can come after sundown. . . .

A gravedigger is a very important person. You must have hear about the strike we had in New York about two years ago. There were twenty thousand bodies layin' and nobody could bury 'em. The cost of funerals they raised and they didn't want to raise the price of the workers. The way they're livin', everything wanna go up, and I don't know what's gonna happen.

Can you imagine if I wouldn't show up tomorrow morning and this other fella—he usually comes late—and sometimes he don't show. We have a funeral for eleven o'clock. Imagine what happens? The funeral arrive and where you gonna bury it? . . .

There are some funerals, they really affect you. Some young kid. We buried lots of young. You have emotions, you turn in, believe me, you turn. I had a burial about two years ago of teen-agers, a young boy and a young girl. This was a real sad funeral because there was nobody but young teen-agers. I'm so used to going to funerals every day—of course, it bothers me—but I don't feel as bad as when I bury a young child. You really turn. . . .

This grief that I see every day, I'm really used to somebody's crying every day. But there is some that are real bad, when you just have to take it. Some people just don't

continued

continued from previous page

want to give up. You have to understand that when somebody pass away, there's nothing you can do and you have to take it. If you don't want to take it, you're just gonna make your life worse, become sick. People seems to take it more easier these days. They miss the person, but not as much.

There's some funerals that people, they show they're not sad. This is different kinds of people. I believe they are happy to see this person — not in a way of singing — because this person is out of his sufferin' in this world. This person is gone and at rest for the rest of his life. I have this question lots of times: "How can I take it?" They ask if I'm calm when I bury people. If you stop and think, a funeral is one of the natural things in the world. . . .

I believe I'm gonna have to stay here probably until I die. It's not gonna be too bad for me because I been livin' twelve years already in the cemetery. I'm still gonna be livin' in the cemetery. (Laughs.) So that's gonna be all right with me whenever I go. I think I may be buried here, it look like.

Quoted in Studs Terkel, *Working*

A few years ago, cryonics became attractive to some people. Cryonics is a method of subjecting a corpse to extremely low temperatures — in effect, keeping the body frozen — until some time in the future when it is envisioned that medical science will have advanced to a point where the body could be resuscitated. Thus, strictly speaking, this is not a method of body disposition in the sense used so far. Although most people view cryonics more as a curiosity than as a realistic alternative to conventional methods of body disposition, it is a practice that has a small number of dedicated adherents.

From the burials of prehistoric cave dwellers to cryonics, human beings have practiced a wide range of alternatives for disposing of the dead. Although many of us may give little thought to the subject of body disposition, it is nonetheless fraught with emotional and psychological importance. When Major Edward Strombeck was killed in a plane crash while on duty in Vietnam, the military cremated his body and then forwarded the ashes, by mail, to his home in Hawaii. The protests of his mother and other family members gained the attention of U.S. Senator Daniel Inouye, who helped bring about a change in policy which ordered that the ashes of military personnel be escorted home with dignity and honor.[23] What do your own preferences regarding body disposition tell you about your attitudes and beliefs toward death?

Burial and Entombment Costs

The prices for cemetery plots vary widely among cemeteries and often according to location within a cemetery. The cost of a burial plot is generally about

Burial vaults, such as those seen here in Oaxaca, Mexico, represent an alternative to underground burial that is found in many parts of the world. When space is at a premium, bodies may be removed from the vaults after a certain period of time and given underground burial.

$500, although one can spend more than $5000 or less than $100. (In one small rural cemetery, limited to the township's residents, a burial plot can be purchased for $25.) In addition, although burial vaults are not required by law, most cemeteries require that the casket be placed inside a grave liner or vault to support the earth around and above it. A grave liner costs about $200–$300 and a vault about $300–$450, although some types of vaults designed (but not guaranteed) to seal out moisture cost substantially more.

The cost of entombment in a mausoleum or outdoor crypt generally ranges from about $1500 to $3000, although again prices vary considerably. The most expensive crypts are typically those at eye level, with the least expensive crypts at the top and bottom.

Whether burial or entombment is chosen, additional charges are levied for opening and closing the grave or crypt. These charges range from about $75 to $350, largely depending on the area of the country.

❧ Requiem

Under the wide and starry sky
Dig the grave and let me lie
Glad did I live and gladly die
    And I laid me down with a will.

This be the verse you grave for me
Here he lies where he longed to be
Home is the sailor, home from the sea
    And the hunter home from the hill.

        Robert Louis Stevenson
        (his epitaph)

Memorials and Endowment Costs

A bronze or stone grave marker is likely to cost upwards of about $200. The average cost for a simple, flat-on-the-ground grave marker is about $250, the name plate for a mausoleum crypt somewhat less. More elaborate memorials can cost from a few hundred to many thousands of dollars.

Most cemeteries also assess a "perpetual care cost" or endowment to subsidize upkeep of the cemetery. These costs range upwards of $100 and may be quoted as part of the cost for burial or entombment.

Cremation Costs

In the United States, the practice of cremation extends back into the nineteenth century (cremation had long been practiced by the original inhabitants, of course). In Europe, the practice is considerably older, going back at least to the Bronze Age. Cremation is the most common method of body disposal in such countries as India and is required by law in Tokyo and (except for rural communities with no crematories) also in China.

Although a relatively small percentage of Americans choose to be cremated, it is a method of body disposition that is growing in acceptance. In 1986, cremation was the disposition of choice in about 14 percent of the total number of deaths, almost double the rate of ten years previously. It is projected that by the year 2000, cremation will become the method of body disposition in nearly one-quarter of all deaths in the United States, a proportion that Canada reached in 1985.[24]

The laws regulating the disposition of cremated remains vary among states and localities. For example, until recently a California law prohibited the scattering of ashes by private citizens. The person scattering the ashes could have been charged with a misdemeanor, punishable by a fine or imprisonment; if two or more persons participated, it was considered a conspiracy, and a felony could have been charged against them. This law has been removed from the books.

The process of cremation involves subjecting the corpse to extreme heat, approximately 2000 to 2500 degrees Fahrenheit. In the United States, natural gas is the most commonly used fuel. An average-size body takes about one and one-half hours to be reduced to *ashes* weighing from five to seven pounds. (The

A coffin is about to be placed inside the retort at this crematory in Japan. The remains of the deceased will be reduced by fire to a few handfuls of ashes and bits of bone.

term ashes leads some people to believe that the cremated remains will look and feel like wood or paper ashes. In reality, the "ashes" are composed of pieces of bone, which look and feel like coarse coral sands whose shell-like components are worn by the wind and waves.) Cremated remains can be buried in a cemetery plot, placed in a columbarium niche, interred in an urn garden, kept by the family, or scattered at sea or on land, in accordance with state and local laws.

The Cremation Association of North America encourages memorialization in conjunction with cremation just as with traditional burials. Urns to hold cremated remains can be purchased at prices from about $25 to $300, though a substantially more expensive urn can be purchased if the customer wishes. If the ashes are to be entombed, columbaria niches (a small vault in which the urn is placed) are available, with the cost depending on the size and location of the niche.

Promoting cremation as a means of body disposition are the growing number of memorial and cremation societies. Typically, these societies aim to provide body disposal services to members at a lower cost by contracting with a mortuary or crematorium to provide services based on a volume purchase. In many communities across the country, conventional funeral providers now compete with such organizations, thereby increasing the range of options available to consumers.

As with other areas of funeral service since the FTC rule, the customer is usually able to select exactly the services he or she wants. Whereas the conventional mortuary offers a wide range of services related both to the funeral and to the disposition of the body, the typical memorial or cremation society's services deal solely with disposition of the remains. The cost of cremation is generally less than a thousand dollars, although optional services — such as viewing the body — add to the basic cost. In some instances, cremation and memorial societies provide an option allowing family and friends to attend the scattering of the ashes. Generally, however, these organizations take a minimalist approach to funerals and body disposition.

Judging by their rapid growth, cremation and memorial societies are meeting a need felt by many people, and the widespread offering of similar options by conventional funeral establishments provides corroboration of this assessment. It is perhaps easier now than at any time since funerals were moved from the family parlor to the mortuary to compare the costs of funeral and body disposition options among competing establishments. In most cases, a telephone call is all you need to obtain relevant pricing information for your locality.

Making Meaningful Choices

The funeral has been defined as "an organized, purposeful, time-limited, flexible, group-centered response to death."[25] If this definition can be applied to our modern approaches to caring for the dead, then, in view of the varied styles of funeral service now available, can we identify any single set of values to guide our actions in memorializing the dead and providing for the needs of the survivors? Probably not. Increasingly, the choices that are made relative to funerals and body disposition reflect individual rather than community judgments. Each of us has to make up his or her own mind. If funeral rituals provide closure on the deceased's life for survivors and allow the community to affirm the timeless rhythms of separation and integration, then what should our feelings be when the social elements of the funeral are lacking or absent, as with "take-out-and-cremate" practices? Can the emotional and psychological issues that accompany bereavement be resolved satisfactorily? Many would say no; yet there is a paucity of hard data to establish the conventional funeral as the most effective vehicle of psychological resolution.

Commenting on the changing attitudes toward the funeral and traditional methods of body disposition, Robert Fulton and Greg Owen observe that the obligations — religious, emotional, and economic — that a funeral imposes on a family have come to be seen by many people as both burdensome and inappropriate.[26] In surveying the contemporary situation, they note that:

> Advocacy of a memorial service, with the body absent, and medical donation of the body or its parts are attempts within the context of contemporary values to resolve the different problems associated with the disposition of the dead. Other attempts to contain or limit the social impact of a death upon the family or community can be seen in the decline of public obituaries, the dramatic rise in immediate

disposition and/or cremation of the body, the increasing formalization of rules governing an employee's time off for bereavement, and the direct implementation of Federal Trade Commission guidelines on the business practices and procedures of American funeral directors.

Yet, according to Edgar Jackson, despite the changes that have occurred in American funeral practices over the past decades, funeral directors receive more expressions of gratitude from the people they serve than do the members of any other helping profession. Jackson notes that the funeral director is there at a time when the family is experiencing an acute crisis. The immediate response and help in sorting out the events of the days following the death of a loved one provide stability and reassurance for the bereaved family.[27] Robert Fulton corroborates this view, adding that funeral directors are in a unique position to assist the bereaved and are potentially a valuable part of a community's mental health resources and helping network.[28]

In a pluralistic society, there are many ways of dealing meaningfully with death. Some may choose a minimal role in caring for their dead loved ones; others will seek more active participation. Becoming aware of the available alternatives enables us to make more meaningful choices. The experience of a couple following the death of their young son is illustrative. Initially, they had planned no formal funeral ceremony. They intended that the body would simply be cremated and the ashes scattered. On the day before the body was released from the coroner for cremation, however, they found themselves experiencing the acute grief that comes with such a sudden and intimate loss. They were having difficulty coming to terms with their emotions and the loss of their son.

Someone in their circle of friends suggested they could direct their energy into building a coffin. Soon, friends and members of the family, including the five-year-old brother of the child who was killed, were busily engaged in the task of constructing a coffin. Later they expressed a sense of relief at being able to "do something" (see Figure 6-5). For the participants, building the coffin became a meaningful way to honor the dead child as well as a means of working through some of their own feelings, allowing them to get a better handle on their experience. This, then, is the real value of learning about and considering our options: finding the response that is meaningful to us personally.

The social support that accompanies meaningful ritual need not be limited to the period immediately following a death. In traditional Hawaiian culture, for example, the bereaved community held a memorial feast on the first-year anniversary of the day of death for any person—man, woman, child, even a newborn baby.[29] For the extended family group, this was considered "one of the three greatest occasions, the others being the feasts of rejoicing for the first-born and the marriage festival." Although this occasion was called the *'aha'aina waimaka* or "feast of tears," because it embraced everyone who had shed tears out of respect and love for the deceased, it was really "a happy occasion, a joyful reunion of all who had previously shed tears together." As one participant described it, "There was drinking, eating, singing and dancing. We had a *lu'au* when all the grief was done."

Figure 6-5 *Three Views of a Child's Coffin*

Top View: When the wooden coffin constructed by the family and friends had
been completed, the surviving child ran his hand over the surface and voiced his
approval but said that it "needs something more." He gathered his marking pens
and began to ornament the coffin with drawings. The inscriptions on the outer
surface of the lid show the child's interest in identifying by name and by picture
the fact that this coffin was built for his brother. His own participation in the
making of the coffin is also connoted by the inclusion of his name and by the
demonstration of his newly developed skills with the use of numerals and letters.

   Detail of Lid Interior: In this detailed closeup of a portion of the interior lid,
viewed from left to right, one can see a chrysalis—indicating a transition from
caterpillar to butterfly—along with some of the younger brother's favorite
television characters: Big Bird, Oscar the Grouch, and the Cookie Monster.

Interior of Lid: In contrast to the matter-of-fact inscriptions placed on the outer surface, the inside of the coffin lid is filled with representations of experiences, events, and objects that brought joy into the life of the child's younger brother. Many of the dead child's favorite activities, such as listening to the stereo with headphones and sitting on a horse at grandma's house, are depicted. The surviving child depicts himself as sad because of his brother's death yet also as happy because of the shared experiences he enjoyed with his brother. It is interesting to notice the degree of detail and the variety of images placed on the interior of the coffin lid.

Further Readings

Robert W. Habenstein and William M. Lamers. *Funeral Customs the World Over*. Rev. ed. Milwaukee: Bulfin Printers, 1974.

Robert W. Habenstein and William M. Lamers. *The History of American Funeral Directing*. Milwaukee: Bulfin Printers, 1962.

Paul Irion. *A Manual and Guide for Those Who Conduct a Humanist Funeral Service*. Baltimore: Waverly Press, 1971.

Edgar N. Jackson. *The Christian Funeral: Its Meaning, Its Purpose, and Its Modern Practice*. New York: Channel Press, 1966.

Ernest Morgan. *Dealing Creatively with Death: A Manual of Death Education and Simple Burial*, 11th ed. Burnsville, N.C.: Celo Press, 1988.

Gay Petrillo. "The Distant Mourner: An Examination of the American Gravedigger," *Omega: Journal of Death and Dying* 20 (1989–1990): 139–148.

Vanderlyn R. Pine. *Caretaker of the Dead: The American Funeral Director*. New York: Irvington Publishers, 1985.

Joe Marquette, UPI/Bettmann Newsphotos

Grief encompasses a wide range of emotions in survivors. Bereavement is often a time of turning inward, of clutching to the reminders of the deceased and to the memories they evoke.

C H A P T E R 7

Survivors: Understanding the Experience of Loss

We are all survivors. Not everyone has experienced the loss that occurs with death, but everyone has experienced losses of some kind. Reflect for a moment on something — material or nonmaterial — that you have lost. You may recall the loss of a job, a friend's moving away, misplacing an important letter, the death of a pet, any number of things. Whether such losses seem big or small, they are a fact of life for everyone.

Endings are another way to think about loss: The end of summer vacation, graduating from school, leaving a familiar neighborhood, confronting the prospect of retirement — all these endings typify changes that arise in the course of living, changes that often occasion feelings of grief. Some writers call such experiences "little deaths." As you recall some of the "little deaths" in your own life, notice how you have responded. Shock, disbelief, resentment, sadness, and relief are natural reactions. Generally, the more valuable or emotionally charged an experience or relationship, the greater a person's reaction to its loss.

As you read these words, you are alive. You are a *survivor* of the many changes that have taken place in your life up to the present moment. Keeping this fact in mind as you learn about bereavement, grief, and mourning will increase your awareness of the issues related to surviving the death of someone close to you.

For many people, grief has negative connotations. They say, "Oh, don't talk about that subject, it's too depressing," or "I'd rather just think positive thoughts, not dwell on all

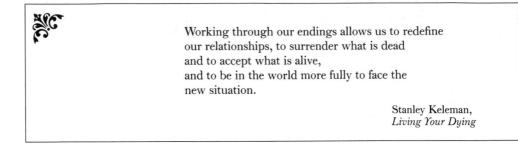

> Working through our endings allows us to redefine
> our relationships, to surrender what is dead
> and to accept what is alive,
> and to be in the world more fully to face the
> new situation.
>
> Stanley Keleman,
> *Living Your Dying*

that negativity." Expanding our knowledge of survivorship allows us a more encompassing and accurate picture of what grief and mourning represent in human experience. Among the most impressive facts is the vast continuity and essential unity in the human experience of bereavement, grief, and mourning.

Bereavement, Grief, and Mourning

The word most often associated with loss by death is grief. We hear that someone is bereaved, is grieving, or has "grief work" to do. We say that the person is mourning. Understanding the definitions of bereavement, grief, and mourning broadens our understanding of what it means to be a survivor.

Bereavement comes from a root word meaning "shorn off or torn up" — as if something had been suddenly yanked away. The word thus conveys a sense of a person's being deprived, of having something stripped away against one's will, of being robbed. Bereavement signifies a force that comes from outside as a violent, destructive action taken against us. Obviously, if we think about bereavement only as a violent event, our understanding will be different from that of a person who defines bereavement as a change that is natural, a normal event in human experience. Thus considered, bereavement can be defined simply as the objective event of loss.

Grief is a person's emotional response to the event of loss. Like bereavement, grief is often thought of in negative terms: heartbreak, anguish, distress, suffering — a burdensome emotional state. Yet grief really encompasses the *total* emotional response to loss. Among the full range of emotions that might be present in a survivor's grief are not only sorrow and sadness, but also relief, anger, disgust, and self-pity. Limiting our definition of grief reduces the chances of accepting all of the emotions that may be present.

Mourning refers to the process of incorporating the experience of loss into our ongoing lives. This process deals with the questions: How does one carry on? How does one survive a loss? Reflecting as it does the patterns of a particular culture, mourning can be understood as the outward acknowledgment of loss. Certain behaviors are socially or culturally defined as appropriate for making known the fact that a person is mourning. The cultural "rules" for mourning behavior are manifested in such remarks as "That family is in mourning — the

> Comparing the extent and form of emotional responses to announcements of death in various circumstances, I found a considerable amount of variability. On some occasions there was no crying whatever; the doctor's mention of the death was responded to with downward looking silence. On other occasions, his utterance "passed away" or "died" spontaneously produced hysterical crying, screaming, moaning, trembling, etc. . . . In numerous instances I have seen men and women tear at themselves, pulling their hair, tugging at their garments, biting their lips.
>
> David Sudnow,
> *Passing On: The Social Organization of Dying*

father died recently — and they aren't going out socially." Seclusion enforces on the survivors a period of abstinence from the social relationships and pleasures of life. Philippe Ariès traced the practice of seclusion back to the Middle Ages and noted that it serves two purposes: First, it allows the truly unhappy survivors to shelter their grief from the world, and, second, it prevents survivors from forgetting the deceased too quickly.[1]

Conventional forms of mourning behavior have also included wearing black armbands or clothes of subdued colors and, if the deceased was a public figure, flying the national flag at half-mast. Following the death of George Washington, Congress led the nation in a thirty-day period of mourning, during which some citizens wore black bands on which were stamped in white letters the inscription that appeared on the president's coffin plate: "General George Washington — Departed this life on the 14th of December, 1799."[2] In some places in the world, widows commonly dress in black for many years following the death of a spouse, outwardly acknowledging their loss and their mourning. The veiled woman dressed in black, a *mater dolorosa*, arrived on the scene in the nineteenth century, emphasizing how nearly impossible it was for the living to forget the departed.

In modern societies, mourning behavior is generally much less formal than it is among some traditional cultures or than it was in our own past. Because we lack rigorous social definitions of what constitutes appropriate mourning behavior, there may be conflict between conventional notions of mourning and the ideas of the deceased or the survivors, as illustrated by the following anecdote: A young girl wrote to an advice columnist about a "sweet sixteen" party that her dying father had asked the family to celebrate for her, even if the party should occur on the day of his funeral. The girl said she had not felt like having a party, but the family decided to honor the promise to her father. The party was held two days after her father's death, and it turned out to be a good experience for all who attended. The problem arose when several relatives became horrified because, in their model of the world, enjoying a party was inappropriate behavior during a time of mourning. It is useful to suspend our judgments about what constitutes appropriate mourning behavior and to recognize that a broad spectrum of behaviors is appropriate in today's pluralistic and multicultural society.

The Experience of Grief

The questions asked most frequently about grief concern the attempt to define *normal* grief and mourning. How long should a person grieve? What kinds of behavior are appropriate during a period of mourning? To frame adequate answers to such questions, we need to consider many factors, including personality and values, social and cultural influences, and the relative importance of the deceased to the survivor. These factors affect the duration of grief, the physical and psychological responses, and the disruption of and subsequent reorientation to satisfactory life patterns. As with most attempts to define a norm, a definition of what constitutes normal grief and mourning will allow for wide latitude according to time, place, circumstances of the death, and the particular survivor's experience.

Duration of Grief

Research suggests that the most acute and intense experience of grief, immediately following a loss by death, usually lasts about four to six weeks. However, during the first year following bereavement, the survivor is likely to experience anniversaries, birthdays, holidays, and other special occasions that previously had been shared with the deceased in ways that involve coming to grips with the deceased's absence. Although the most acute phase occupies a comparatively brief time, the death of a close relation typically results in a reaction that is measured in years rather than in weeks. During this period, the survivor gradually comes to accept the loss and reorient his or her life without the deceased.

Prolonged grief or unresolved grief is described not so much in terms of duration but in terms of its effect on the survivor. Determinations of behaviors that are truly "abnormal" are best made by professionals who have been exposed to a broad range of grief responses. Severe, persistent problems with sleeplessness or loss of appetite may be symptomatic of difficulties in resolving a loss, as may such medical complaints as ulcerative colitis, rheumatoid arthritis, or asthma. Depression — especially when accompanied by serious emotional problems, alcohol or drug abuse, or suicidal behavior — may be a correlate of unresolved grief, signaling the need for professional intervention to help deal with the underlying reasons for difficulty in coming to terms with the loss.[3]

The attempt to make a sharp distinction between normal and *pathological grief* has been largely replaced, however, by a greater awareness of individual and cultural differences in the expression of grief. In short, the "gradual erosion of categorical thinking" about grief has resulted in a more cautious attitude toward labeling particular manifestations of grief as pathological or abnormal.[4] For example, the onset of intense pain years after a loss may in fact be the response to a "new" death or loss and, thus, a time-appropriate rather than delayed response.[5] To illustrate, a young woman whose husband had died nearly four years earlier reported a bout of intense grief. Bewildered by the experience, she said, "I don't understand myself; it feels almost like the day he died." In conversation with her counselor, she discovered the event triggering her pain: Within a few days, the

Edward V. Gillion

© Albert Lee Strickland

The nineteenth-century Romantic view of death is reflected in the Lawson memorial, which characterizes both the devotion of the bereaved to the deceased and the belief that loving relationships continue beyond the mortal framework of the human lifespan.

Contemporary memorial stones often reflect a similar emphasis on the unending love felt by survivors for the deceased and on the faith that bonds forged during a person's lifetime can remain strong despite death.

couple's seven-year-old daughter would be celebrating her first communion. Although happily remarried, successfully back to work, and obviously healing from her loss, this devoutly religious woman grieved the absence of her child's father from a celebration that had been discussed and anticipated since the child's birth. Even in cases where the issue seems to be prolonged or pathological grief, through appropriate therapeutic means it is possible to restore abnormal grief reactions to normal ones, even years after a death.

With a major loss such as death, the survivor's overwhelming experience is the sense of finality. For this reason, and because the loss is so important, the survivor may experience a recurrence of grief for that loss at various times throughout his or her lifetime, although with decreasing intensity and frequency. Nevertheless, certain incidents that arise naturally in daily life will again bring to mind that what once was is no more. For example, it is now recognized that, although most widows and widowers are not actively mourning after the turmoil of the first one to three years, the loss nevertheless remains a part of them, and feelings of grief never cease entirely. A longitudinal study of widows and widowers, none of whom were older than forty-five years, found that the forces of

> All that day I walked alone. In the afternoon I looked for a church, went into a cafe, and finally left on the bus, carrying with me more grief and sorrow than I had ever borne before, my body in tatters and my whole life a moan.
>
> Oscar Lewis,
> *A Death in the Sanchez Family*

bereavement and adjustment usually operate over a period that is more appropriately termed a period of "life transition" than a "life crisis," with bereaved spouses continuing the psychological work of mourning for the rest of their lives.[6]

In our own lives we can recognize the recurrence of mourning for earlier losses. We may mourn the loss of childhood and its experiences. A woman told about visiting her parents after some years of living on her own. One day, while poking around in the attic, her mother opened a trunk and pulled out a collection of dolls that had belonged to the daughter when she was a child. Seeing the dolls elicited feelings of grief for the childhood that was now lost to the past. She said, "I looked at those dolls and their tiny clothes, and I got in touch with the loss of that time in my life when my mother had taken care of me and had made clothes for my dolls. There I was, sitting in the attic, just bawling."

Each of us has undoubtedly experienced similar situations in our own lives. Some event, picture, place, melody, or other stimulus has provoked feelings of grief related to something or someone no longer present in our lives. In a landmark study of grief published in 1944, "The Symptomatology and Management of Acute Grief," Erich Lindemann identified three primary tasks necessary for satisfactorily managing grief: first, *letting go* of the deceased, accepting the fact of the loss; second, *adjusting* to a life without the deceased; third, *forming new relationships*.[7]

Symptoms of Grief

The research done by Erich Lindemann and others has provided a fairly detailed picture of the range of somatic symptoms, or body reactions, that may be present with normal grief. Somatic disturbances can include tightness of the throat, choking, shortness of breath, the need for frequent sighing, an empty feeling in the abdomen, muscle weakness, chills, and tremors. These bodily sensations may be accompanied by intense mental distress: tension, loneliness, and anguish.

The survivor's perceptions may be disorganized. Events may seem unreal, sensory responses undependable and erratic. Survivors describe periods of hallucination or even euphoria. During such times, they experience a heightened perceptual and emotional sensitivity to persons and events in the immediate environment. It is common for survivors to be preoccupied with images of the deceased. Often, survivors are highly irritable or even hostile. They may talk incessantly about the deceased. Or they may talk about everything but their confrontation

Bereaved persons in most cultures may dream that a beloved person has come back. In the early stages of bereavement, this, as well as hallucinating the dead, is a normal manifestation of grieving. However, Hawaiians usually see the dead in dreams more often, for more reasons, and for longer periods after a death than do, for example, Western Caucasians. In modern Western culture, when dreams (or hallucinations) of the dead continue too long, they are usually symptoms of pathological grief: the process or "work" of grieving has not progressed through the normal stages.

For the Hawaiian who is emotionally close to his ethnic roots, such prolonged dreaming or envisioning of the dead may or may not be a sign of blocked grief work. In the Hawaiian tradition, the dead do return: in dreams and visions, in sensations of skin, in hearing the voice or smelling the perfume or body odor of the one who has died.

The difference between what is culturally normal and what may be pathological is only partly spelled out by the dream content. We must also know what is going on in the life and family life of the dreamer; we must know how much and what kind of emotion the dream aroused. Especially, we must know what were the relationships in life between the one who died and the survivor who dreams.

Mary Kawena Pukui, E. W. Haertig, and
Catherine A. Lee, *Nana I Ke Kumu (Look to the Source)*

with loss and the circumstances of the death. Survivors often manifest a general restlessness.

In addition to feelings of sadness, longing, loneliness, and sorrow, there may be feelings of guilt or anger. The survivor may feel anger and outrage at the apparent injustice of the loss and tremendous frustration and a sense of impotence at the inability to control events. As survivors, we may feel that if we could arrange the world more to our liking, we would not have included loss as part of the human experience.

The symptoms and behaviors appropriate to normal grief clearly make up a broad range of responses. But no particular survivor will necessarily experience all of them, nor must all be present if grief is to be considered normal. If a person has mental images of the deceased and says, "Oh no, I shouldn't be thinking like this," the denial can create additional conflicts and greater difficulties in coming to terms with loss. In contrast, if a survivor is aware that many kinds of feelings are acceptable, the experience of grief is likely to be much more easily managed.

When loss occurs, the usual patterns of living are disrupted. People stop doing the things they ordinarily do. Their actions may be so unlike their usual behavior that an outsider, or even an acquaintance, might judge it bizarre or aberrant. In an early study of grief, "Mourning and Melancholia," Sigmund Freud addressed this concern from the psychoanalytic perspective.[8] According to this view, although grieving behavior may be quite different from a person's usual behavior, normal grief is not a pathological condition nor is its presence a cause for medical treatment. Grief is the normal reaction to loss. In its application to grief, the *attachment theory* postulated by Freud, John Bowlby, and others can be briefly summarized:[9] When the bereaved perceives that the love object no longer exists, grief arises, along with a defensive demand to withdraw libido (energy) from the object to which it had been attached. This demand may meet with opposition, causing the survivor to temporarily turn away from reality in an attempt to cling to the lost object. Normally, the libido eventually becomes detached from the love object, and the ego (personality) becomes free of its clinging attachment to the deceased.[10]

This basic model has been criticized by some because of its apparent assumption that attachment objects can be replaced. As Colin Murray Parkes points out, "Each love relationship is unique, and theoretical models which assume that libido can be withdrawn from one object in order to become invested in another similar object, fail to recognize this uniqueness."[11] Bereavement, says Parkes, is revealed as one category of "psychosocial transition," a concept that is highly relevant to the study of loss and change. This transition was described by the father of a dead child who said, "Living without my son has meant adding another room onto the house in my mind; not so I can shut the door on his death, but so I can move in and out of the experience of my loss." As this father recognized, the psychosocial transition resulting from loss requires space and attention.

Studies have led to the conclusion that acute grief possesses the qualities of a definite syndrome, with both psychological and somatic symptomatology. However, the signs of grief may either appear immediately or be delayed; they may even appear to be absent. Symptoms may be distorted, exaggerated, or highly variable — differing among individuals and according to circumstances. In short, grief is seen to be a complex, evolving process with multiple dimensions.[12] As Dennis Klass wisely observes, "Bereavement is complex, for it reaches to the heart of what it means to be human and what it means to have a relationship."[13]

Phases of Grief

In an attempt to understand and delineate the various processes associated with grief, researchers have devised a number of models that present these processes within a framework involving a theory of stages (see Figure 7-1).[14] Some models postulate three stages, others seven or ten. To outline the stages of grief work in this manner seems to suggest a linear progression from the first stage, through the second, and so on, until the process has been completed. Although this notion might provide comfort to those who wish to evaluate a survivor's journey toward reintegration after loss, it is important to place these theories in their intended context.

The theories concerning stages of grief represent an effort to specify various aspects of a process that occurs in highly individualistic ways. Thus, although models of grief can be very helpful in increasing our understanding, we should not superimpose a particular structure on the actual grief experience of a particular survivor. Furthermore, although each of the phases of grief may be considered as distinct emotional states, they are not necessarily separate; they will invariably intertwine and overlap.

Theorist	Onset ◄ – – – – – – – – – – · GRIEF · – – – – – – – – – – ► Resolution						
Gorer	Shock		Intense grief work			Reestablishing physical and mental balance	
Kavanaugh	Shock	Disorganization	Volatile emotions	Guilt	Loss and loneliness	Relief	Reestablishment
Raphael	Shock, numbness, disbelief		Separation pain		Psychological mourning process		Reintegration
Weizman and Kamm	Shock, disbelief, denial		Undoing		Anger	Sadness	Integration
Worden	Accepting the reality		Experiencing the pain		Adjusting to a changed environment		Withdrawing and reinvesting emotional energy

Figure 7-1   *Grief Models by Theorist*

The earliest phase of grief is typically characterized by *shock* and *numbness*, usually lasting from the time the survivor learns of the death until the final disposition of the deceased's body. *Disbelief* and *denial* are components of the grief experienced at this time. Confused and bewildered by the impact, the bereaved may feel vulnerable and seek protection by isolation and withdrawal. During this period the survivor is occupied with activities surrounding the disposition of the deceased's body, such as arranging for burial or cremation and sorting out the deceased's personal and family affairs. This is the time when sympathy cards arrive and the survivor accepts the condolences of friends and relatives. There may be feelings of *disorganization*, which Robert Kavanaugh has likened to the bereaved person, motionless and helpless, being stranded in the middle of a fast-flowing stream while water and debris rush about him or her. Mourning rites during the period of shock help reintegrate the family following the disruption caused by the death of one of its members. The initial phase of grief fades as the bereaved moves through the funeral rites and the reality of the death is gradually acknowledged.

The middle phase of grief is a period of *intense grief work* and *separation pain*. During this time the bereaved experiences intense yearning for the person who has died. Then, as the finality of the loss is increasingly accepted, the bereaved begins to review and sort through all the bonds and "bits" of interaction that built the relationship. There is an intense reexperiencing of the whole history of the relationship, and the bonds of attachment are slowly relinquished. This is also a time of *undoing*: the bereaved wishes to undo the calamity, to make everything as it was before. Fantasies of alternatives that would have prevented the death are characteristic of this phase. Varying considerably among survivors,

Grief may indeed range the gamut. It may be shrill and maniacal; it may be subdued and reflective; it may be philosophical. The recording of grief and of the response to it, of the sadness that is virtually physiological and is certainly deeply mysterious in its fullest psychological character, serves, as Aristotle and the later students of tragic catharsis have suggested, as a kind of purgation, as a means of releasing the terrible suppressed tensions, fears, anxieties, deeply fearsome in their potential for still greater unknown effect. Identifying the full range and depth of the symptoms must always come first, must be the basis on which understanding, management, and assimilation of grief into the totality of living rests.

Morris Freedman, "Notes on Grief in Literature"

this phase generally lasts from several weeks to several months. During this period the bereaved's attention is withdrawn from external events, and many of the physiological symptoms associated with intense grief may be present. For example, the survivor may experience restlessness and disturbed sleep, perhaps with dreams in which the deceased figures prominently. Lack of appetite and weight loss are also common. Paradoxically, at a time when grief is often most intense, the survivor usually receives relatively little support from family, friends, or the community, or by way of formal rituals, for the funeral, memorial service, or the like have already passed. This stage is often a time when the bereaved is left alone with his or her grief. As survivors, and as caring persons, we should remember that a lack of support at this crucial time can limit opportunities for the bereaved to express feelings of grief, with the possible result that these feelings are suppressed and normal readjustment is delayed or thwarted.

This middle phase of grief is characterized by *volatile emotions*, which suggests the image of boiling water, intermittently giving off steam, like a volcano, while at other times appearing relatively dormant. *Anger* is commonly experienced, with the object of the anger being the deceased loved one ("How could you abandon me?"), God ("How could you let this happen?"), or the situation itself ("How could this happen to me?"). Anger is sometimes displaced toward persons in the bereaved's environment, such as family members or friends. *Guilt*, too, may be experienced, as well as a sense of *longing and loneliness* as needs and dependencies that previously were satisfied by the deceased become painfully apparent to the survivor. This is a time of "if onlys" and "what ifs," as the bereaved comes to terms with issues of responsibility and power relating to changing the reality that is: The person is dead. As the reality of the death begins to be absorbed, the predominant feeling becomes one of *sadness*. During this *psychological mourning process*, the world at first seems disorganized and chaotic; eventually, as the bonds of the relationship are undone, the emotions are freed for reinvestment in life once more.

The last phase of "active" grief is a period of *reintegration*, of *reestablishing physical and mental balance*; the survivor no longer constantly experiences acute

FLORENCE MAY
DIED
JUNE 14, 1884
AGED 6 DAYS

MARY MAUD
DIED
JUNE 18, 1884
AGED 10 DAYS

CHILDREN OF
J. & A. A. LOCKINS

© Albert Lee Strickland

This tombstone in a Canadian cemetery records the brief lives of twin sisters and bears silent witness to the loss felt by survivors.

physical or emotional turmoil at being bereft. Although sadness doesn't disappear completely and may be stimulated when a reminder or memory is especially poignant, it recedes into the background. Sleep and appetite return to normal, and the survivor is again an interested participant in the outside world. *Relief* may be felt as the pain subsides and the attachment diminishes, bringing a new freedom to the bereaved's life (which may be difficult to admit to others). The bereaved person begins to move ahead with his or her life, and the present concerns of life become the foreground on which to focus.

Keeping in mind that the model of grief discussed here represents an outline or synthesis of the responses that may be experienced when one is confronted with a loss, the *tasks* of mourning described by William Worden may prove helpful in providing an overall view of the grieving process.[15]

The first task of mourning, says Worden, involves *accepting the reality* of the loss. Even when a death is anticipated, the reality may be difficult to accept fully. "Denying the facts of the loss," says Worden, "can vary in degree from a slight distortion to a full-blown delusion." One signpost at this point in the journey is the survivor's choice of words when talking about the deceased person. Most significant is the transition from present to past tense, from *is* to *was*, as, for example, from "Randy is a wonderful carpenter" to "Randy was a wonderful carpenter."

The second task involves *experiencing the pain* of grief. This includes both the physical pain that may be experienced as well as the emotional and behavioral pain of loss. As Worden says, "Not everyone experiences the same intensity of pain or feels it in the same way, but it is impossible to lose someone you have been deeply attached to without experiencing some level of pain." A significant danger for survivors at this point involves the misuse of "pain killers" such as alcohol and drugs (prescription or not). Experiencing the pain does not mean "deadening" it. Support groups for survivors are helpful at this point in the journey of grief.

The third task involves *adjusting to a changed environment* in which the deceased is missing. It may take considerable time to make this adjustment, especially when a relationship was of long duration and exceptional closeness. Often, the many roles fulfilled by the deceased in one's life are not fully realized until after the loss occurs. The term "changed environment" encompasses the physical, emotional, and spiritual dimensions of life. For some people, adjustment is related to making physical changes (for example, rearranging the furniture or changing the place settings at the dining table). It is important to understand that the changes undertaken may intensify grief. For instance, one family decided to travel to a foreign country during the first holiday season following the death of their daughter. Although they were not sitting around the fire at home crying, their sorrow was experienced while on the tour. Later, they acknowledged that the urge to radically alter their usual holiday rituals arose from a desire to adjust to the changed environment in which one of the family members was no longer present. Yet their grief traveled with them. As it happened, because the surviving family members were aware of their own feelings and open with each other, the trip did prove to be healing.

Finally, the fourth task of mourning involves *withdrawing emotional energy from the relationship that has ended so that the energy can be reinvested*. Worden remarks that people sometimes have difficulty with this task, either because of a feeling that it somehow involves a dishonoring of the deceased's memory or because they fear investing emotional energy into another relationship that could also end in loss. The successful completion of this final task of grieving is hindered when the bereaved holds onto past attachments and refuses to form new ones. This task may be the most difficult of all. Yet to leave it undone is be stuck in a condition of not loving. The completion of mourning involves the recognition that, although one does not love the deceased person any less, there are also other people to be loved.

Keep in mind that models of mourning as a process distinguished by specific phases are intended to help us comprehend the functioning of grief and its effect on survivors. But we should not mistake the map for the territory. Although "stage theories," descriptions of phases of grief, are useful in defining certain aspects of grief that may be encountered by a survivor, the actual experience resembles a series of dance steps more than it does a cross-country walk.

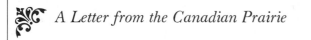
A Letter from the Canadian Prairie

Heather Brae, Alberta
January 12, 1906

Miss Jennie Magee
Dear Sister:

You will be surprised to hear from me after so many years. Well I have bad news for you. My Dear little wife is Dead and I am the lonelyist Man in all the world. She gave Birth to little Daughter on the 27th of December three Days after she went out of her mind and on the 7th of January she took Pnumonia and Died about half past three in the afternoon. We buried her tuesday afternoon in a little cemetary on the Prarry about 15 miles from here. I am writing to you to see if you will come and keep house for me and raise my little Baby. I would not like to influence you in any way as I am afraid you would be lonely when I have to go from home as I will now and again. You are used to so much stir in the city. I have 400 acres of Land and I have 9 or ten cows and some hens. If you come you can make all you can out of the Butter and eggs and I might be able to Pay you a small wage . . . Write and let me know as soon as Possible what you think about the Proposition. I am writing to the rest tonight to let them know the bad news. I think this is all at Present from your affectionate Brother.

William Magee

Linda Rasmussen, Lorna Rasmussen,
Candace Savage, and Anne Wheeler,
A Harvest Yet to Reap: A History of Prairie Women

When you recall a loss in your life, you may remember the elements of shock, intense emotions, and becoming reestablished, but not in such a neat and clearly delineated sequence of mutually exclusive states. Sometimes it may have felt as if all the feelings were present at once. Part of you may have been feeling shock while another part was calm. We are capable of experiencing many emotions, even conflicting ones, at the same time.

The Mortality of Bereavement

To be a survivor is to experience not only symptoms of physical disease but dis-ease of a psychological and social nature as well. We have already enumerated some of the observable symptoms that may arise in the body with the onset of grief: tightness of the throat, loss of appetite, difficulty in breathing, and a host of others. These body responses constitute one aspect of the biology of grief.

However, there is another aspect of the biological response to grief that can have more serious consequences for the survivor. W.D. Rees and S.G. Lutkins examined the mortality of bereavement and found that the death rate among survivors during the first year of bereavement was nearly seven times that of the general population.[16] And research by Arthur C. Carr and Bernard Schoenberg has shown that some chronic diseases have a higher incidence among the recently bereaved.[17] These diseases include cancer, tuberculosis, ulcerative colitis, asthma, obesity, rheumatoid arthritis, congestive heart failure, leukemia, and diabetes. In a recent study conducted by Marvin Stein at Mount Sinai School of Medicine, diminished immune response was found among a group of widowers during the first few months following bereavement.[18] Other studies have produced similar results showing a significant depression of lymphocyte (T-cell) function during the early period following bereavement.[19] Although no direct cause-and-effect link has yet been established between bereavement and the onset of disease, the evidence does suggest that reaction to loss can contribute to the epidemiology of certain diseases, especially those related to stress.

Hans Selye's studies point to the existence of an acute alarm reaction, or mobilization of the body's resources, in situations of high emotional stress.[20] According to Selye, the alarm reaction is a "generalized call to arms" of the body's defenses that manifests itself in various physiological changes that prepare the organism to cope with the agent or situation that elicited the alarm reaction. If this reaction is not followed by some form of adaptation or resistance to the agent eliciting it, severe damage or even death can ensue. In addition, the stress associated with bereavement appears at times to aggravate a physical condition that may have been latent, causing symptoms to become manifest or to develop more rapidly. Stress is a component of the grief process that plays a crucial role in the survivor's ability to cope with loss.

One researcher, George Engel, compiled a number of case reports indicating a relationship between stress and sudden death.[21] He then classified the various stressful situations into eight categories, four of which can be considered as either a direct or an indirect component of grief and mourning: (1) the impact of the death of a close person, (2) the stress of acute grief, (3) the stress that occurs with mourning, and (4) the loss of status or self-esteem following bereavement.

On first thought, loss of self-esteem may not seem to be corollary of experiencing bereavement. Guilt, however, tends to lower self-esteem, and guilt *is* a common component of grief. Consider the bereaved person who says, "If only I had tried harder, if I had done something differently, my friend might not have died." In addition, situations in daily life may work to lower a survivor's self-esteem following the death of a spouse, close friend, or family member. For instance, a widower who used to attend social functions with his spouse may find that he is now left off the guest list. A widow may decline invitations or avoid situations that she considers activities for couples. The financial status of the bereaved person often changes. If self-worth has depended on a certain income level, then less money and tighter finances may lower self-esteem. The loss of status enjoyed because of a deceased mate's professional or community standing can have a similar effect.

During the fifteenth century, grief was a legal cause of death and could be listed on death certificates. Can a bereaved person indeed die of a "broken heart"? Although the idea that severe grief can somehow damage the heart has persisted since ancient times, Colin Murray Parkes notes that "the fact that bereavement may be followed by death from heart disease does not prove that grief is itself a cause of death."[22] When stress is not dealt with adequately, however, disease can result. The determinant is not so much the presence of stress as the ability to cope with it. How a person copes with catastrophic losses—such as the death of a mate, close friend, or family member—tends to be consistent in many respects with how that person copes with the everyday stresses and small losses of daily living. It is important, therefore, to be aware of stress and its potentially harmful effects, and to take constructive steps to manage the level of stress in one's life. Social support may well be the key to helping the bereaved mitigate the potentially harmful effects of grief with respect to heightened mortality or morbidity following loss.[23]

Variables Influencing Grief

Just as no two persons are alike, no two experiences of grief are alike. The circumstances of a death, the personality and social roles of the bereaved, his or her relationship with the deceased—these are among the factors that influence the nature of grief. An understanding of these factors can provide not only knowledge about the processes of grief but also clues about why some deaths seem especially devastating to survivors.

A major influence on the experience of grief is whether the circumstances of a death classify it as a *high-grief* or *low-grief* death.[24] A high-grief death is characterized by the intense emotional and physical reactions to loss usually associated with normal grief; a low-grief death, although emotionally affecting, is less devastating, and thus the reaction is less severe and the bereaved is able to cope more readily. The death of a child is often cited as the classic example of a high-grief death, whereas the death of a person in old age, someone we think of as having lived a long and varied life, is likely to be a low-grief death. It is the circumstances of a particular death and its effect on a particular survivor, however, that really determines whether the emotional response is of high or low grief. The survivor's age may also be a determining factor. For example, the death of a parent may be more catastrophic to a young child or an adolescent than to a grown child who has lived apart from his or her parents for many years.

The experience of grief also varies according to the amount of social support available. For instance, after the death of an unborn child, whether through miscarriage or induced abortion, a survivor is likely to receive little support from the social conventions that comfort other survivors in their grief. Often, no funeral or other ceremony is observed, and the loss may not be acknowledged at all by the larger community. Thus, the usual processes that allow a survivor to confront a loss and to take leave of the deceased are greatly hampered. These kinds of losses have been termed *disenfranchised grief*—that is, grief experienced in connection with a loss that is not socially supported or acknowledged through the usual rituals.[25]

Grief may also be less than fully recognized not because of the circumstances of the loss, but because of certain qualities that others may wittingly or unwit-

Many people believe the death of a young child to be the most heartrending of all bereavement experiences—what researchers term a high-grief death, because it tends to elicit a tremendous sense of loss.

tingly associate with the bereaved himself or herself. For example, as Darlene Kloeppel and Sheila Hollins point out, significant complications may occur when a death in the family is combined with a family member having a mental handicap.[26] These complications may affect both the family's functioning and the retarded person's grieving process. It is important to recognize, write Kloeppel and

Hollins, that "death and mental retardation are both taboo subjects in our society," and that "taboos elicit fear and avoidance." Specific interventions designed to alleviate the potential difficulties inherent in such situations may be needed to assist both the family and its mentally handicapped member on their journey through grief.

When grief is disenfranchised, either because the significance of the loss to the survivor is not recognized or because the relationship between the deceased and the bereaved is not socially sanctioned, the person suffering the loss has little or no opportunity to mourn publicly. The surviving same-sex mates of persons who die from AIDS face this situation. Although AIDS affects people in all walks of life, the homosexual partners of persons with AIDS may find comparatively little support from the wider community as they cope with their loss. How many community resources, such as spousal support groups, are welcoming of persons with a differing sexual orientation? The answer to this question undoubtedly varies depending on the community and the mind-set of a particular support group. For example, in one medium-sized community, a support group composed of parents who experienced neonatal loss successfully integrated a lesbian couple whose baby had died, thus providing a measure of community support. When a high-grief death is treated by society as if it were not a significant loss, the process of adjustment is unnecessarily made more difficult for survivors.

The Survivor's Model of the World

A survivor's experience of loss and grief is conditioned to a large extent by his or her model of the world—that is, by his or her perception of reality and judgment about how the world works. In considering how a person's model of the world applies to the experience of bereavement, we look at four factors identified by Edgar Jackson as particularly important in conditioning a person's emotional reaction to bereavement.[27]

The first factor is the individual's personality. Personality, of course, influences how we relate to life experiences generally. Some people seem to ride easily over large bumps, but may receive quite a jolt from a small shock; for others, the situation is reversed. In this respect, self-concept is an important determinant of how a person responds when death occurs. An immature, dependent personality will be more vulnerable to the loss of a person in whom a large amount of emotional capital has been invested. Such an investment may represent an attempt to compensate for feelings of personal inadequacy by projecting part of one's self-identity onto another person. When bereavement occurs, more of this projected self is involved in the loss. In contrast, the person with greater self-esteem and a stronger self-concept is not so prone to such overcompensation, with the result that grief is likely to be less devastating. Similarly, it has been found that persons who report a high degree of purpose in life tend to cope with bereavement more effectively than do persons who report a low purpose in life.[28]

The second conditioning factor identified by Jackson relates to social roles, which provide the framework wherein the survivor copes with grief. Again, it is the way in which a person incorporates social roles into his or her model of the world that influences the response to death. This response is determined in part by answering the question, What does society say should be a particular survivor's response to death in general or to a particular death? A soldier in combat is expected to perform his duties despite any personal feelings of grief or loss when comrades die. Among some primitive societies a widow knows in advance what kind of behavior is expected, and the members of her society gather to ensure that grief is expressed in quite specific ways. In most modern societies, on the other hand, people generally have greater freedom to determine for themselves what kind of behavior is appropriate. Even so, the social and cultural environment is important in shaping a person's grief and mourning. For example, in a study of the effect of ethnicity on death attitudes, over half of the Japanese-Americans and Mexican-Americans in the population studied felt that at least one year (and preferably two or more years) should pass before a widowed spouse remarries; among blacks and Anglos, only one-fourth of the sample held such a position.[29]

The third factor that conditions a grief reaction is the survivor's perception of the relative importance of the deceased. Was the deceased an important person in my life? Will my life be changed greatly by this death? Importance may also be considered in terms of the survivor's *perceived similarity* to the deceased. The hypothesis here is that the more similar to the deceased a survivor believes he or she is, the greater is the grief.[30]

The deaths of family members and close friends usually cause the deepest grief, but the deaths of others who have been significant in our lives can also cause strong grief reactions. Americans grieved for the deaths of President John F. Kennedy, Robert Kennedy, Martin Luther King, and the *Challenger* astronauts, even though the vast majority had never met any of them personally. In the case of President Kennedy's death, for example, researchers found a tendency for individuals to react to the assassination in terms of personal grief and loss rather than in terms of a more generalized concern for the future or of political or ideological concern.[31] A similar outpouring of grief on a nationwide scale occurred when Abraham Lincoln was killed by an assassin's bullet.

The fourth conditioning factor identified by Jackson is the person's value structure — that is, the relative worth assigned to different experiences and possible outcomes. For example, we sometimes hear people say something like, "Of course, his wife misses him terribly, but she is also relieved that he is no longer enduring such pain and suffering." In other words, the knowledge that her husband's suffering is over helps mitigate her grief at his death. Jackson cites an example of a husband who, knowing that he will soon die from a terminal illness, prepares his wife for the time when he will not be present to manage their financial affairs. Again, the value that this couple placed on being prepared was a conditioning factor relative to their experience of facing the husband's dying and the wife's subsequent grief.

More generally, value structures that allow death an appropriate place in a person's philosophy of life can be a significant determinant of how he or she experiences loss and grief. For example, religious beliefs can influence the way individuals relate to the meaning of death and, thus, can shape to a significant extent the experience of loss and grief. Even when such belief offers the bereaved hope of an eventual reunion with the deceased loved one, however, the individual's present response to grief is nonetheless a reality that must be recognized. As Richard Leliaert says: "To suggest that faith itself can drive out the pain of bereavement is to counsel badly."[32] Although religious faith can indeed offer consolation and comfort during a time of mourning, the path of grief must nevertheless be trod. Leliaert notes that "good spiritual caregiving for bereaved persons needs a fine balance between the human need to grieve adequately and the spiritual grounds for hope provided by formal religions or spiritual belief systems." The spiritual or philosophical underpinnings that can give death an appropriate place in our view of human existence need also to embrace the processes of grief and mourning.

Mode of Death

How a person dies affects a survivor's grief. The type of death — be it natural, accidental, homicide, or suicide — influences the grief experience as does the survivor's previous experience with that type of death.[33] In a recent address before a group of death educators and counselors, Yvonne Ameche described her experience on the night two policemen came to her door with news of her son's unexpected death. Despite having experienced the deaths of her grandparents during her childhood and, later, the deaths of both her parents, Mrs. Ameche said, "I don't know if anything prepared me for the knock on the door the night Paul died. . . . I remember reeling back [and feeling] like I had been physically assaulted."[34] The sense of overwhelming shock caused by the unexpected nature of her son's death was accompanied by feelings that her own familiar sense of self had been "lost" as well. The journey of survivorship from head to heart, as Mrs. Ameche describes it, "where I started to internalize what I had so carefully intellectualized," took a long time. And, she added, "It was a long time before I felt like myself."

The phenomenon of *anticipatory grief* can be understood as a response to prior knowledge of an impending death, with the result that the survivor has time to contemplate its effect before it actually occurs. Some researchers believe that if a death has been anticipated, perhaps as a result of chronic illness, this knowledge modifies the experience of grief; the event of the death itself may not be as difficult to cope with in comparison with a death that occurs suddenly, without warning.[35] Others, however, say that anticipatory grief does not significantly diminish the grief experienced when the loss becomes an objective fact. This is not a question to be resolved easily, but there is general agreement that the element of shock is more intense and overwhelming when death occurs suddenly and is unanticipated.

A phenomenon that can be associated with anticipatory grieving is *secondary morbidity*, which refers to "difficulties in the physical, cognitive, emotional, or social spheres of functioning that may be experienced by those closely involved with the terminally ill person."[36] For example, the burden of caring for a dying relative may cause a caregiver to pay inadequate attention to his or her own health care needs, with the result that the caregiver becomes sick or feels "run down."

The manifestation of such difficulties can extend to professional or volunteer caregivers as well as to family members and friends of the dying person.

Consider the various ways in which people die. We think of the aged grandmother, dying quietly in her sleep; the young child pronounced DOA after a bicycle accident; the innocent bystander caught in the crossfire of a terrorist attack; the chronically ill person dying a lingering death; the despondent executive who commits suicide. Our minds (not to mention the evening news) can provide us with many such examples — powerful, heart-wrenching images. Each mode of death, each set of circumstances in which death occurs can uniquely affect the survivor's ability to integrate the loss. War, for example, results in a particular set of circumstances surrounding death, and this constellation of circumstances affects how survivors deal with the loss.[37]

Or, again, consider some of the qualities that are unique to suicide. Survivors are often left with a numbing feeling of, "Oh, my God, he did it to himself!" If someone close to us was in such pain that he or she chose suicide, we may be burdened with guilty questions: "Why didn't I see the predicament and do more to help? What could have been done to respond to the cry for help?" The impact of suicide can intensify survivors' feelings of blame and guilt. That someone we know has willingly chosen to end his or her life adds an element of personal confrontation. Besides guilt and self-questioning, survivors may direct strong feelings of anger and blame toward the person who committed suicide. Suicide is seen as the ultimate affront, the final insult — one that, because it cannot be answered, compounds the survivors' frustrations and anger.

Moreover, feelings of guilt and blame may be made more difficult to cope with because of societal attitudes toward suicide and related perceptions of the bereaved family members. Survivors are, to some degree, more likely to be "held responsible" for a death by suicide than for a death by illness. This negative reaction to suicide survivors may be especially directed toward the parents of a child who dies by suicide.[38] As Gordon Thornton and his colleagues point out, one result of such societal attitudes may be a comparative lack of social support for individuals who are bereaved by suicide.[39] Counselors and others who are aware of this unfortunate result must make corresponding allowances in providing the necessary support.

Furthermore, a suicide is typically unexpected. Its suddenness and surprise can only magnify the survivor's sense that death was wrong or inappropriate. Like the death of a child, a death by suicide goes against the grain of our intrinsic belief that people should live on into old age. The death of a child or a suicide, then, may leave the survivor with an additional, burdensome feeling that the death was premature.

Notwithstanding the circumstances that surround a sudden unnatural death, the elementary tasks of bereavement — letting go of the deceased, maintaining supportive relationships with others, and promoting a positive self-image — are the same as must be undertaken for any type of bereavement. Although some researchers and clinicians believe that individuals who have been bereaved as a result of suicide tend to be especially vulnerable to unusually severe grief or other

> The other day I heard the father of a boy who had committed suicide say, "Everyone has a skeleton in their closet. But the person who kills themselves leaves their skeleton in another's closet." The grief and guilt that arise in the wake of suicide often leave a legacy of guilt and confusion. Each loved one wracks the mind and tears the heart questioning, "What could I have done to prevent this?"
>
> Stephen Levine, *Who Dies? An Investigation of Conscious Living and Conscious Dying*

adverse effects, it is important to recognize that the survivors of such deaths do not necessarily exhibit more pathological reactions or a more complicated and prolonged grief process than do other survivors.[40]

Persons who have survived a disaster in which others died also have special concerns in grieving.[41] They have become survivors twice over — survivors of a catastrophic event that could have ended their own lives, and survivors of the deaths of others, perhaps friends or relatives. In studies of survivors of the Holocaust, researchers often found a deep sense of guilt about having survived the camps and the torture while others were not as fortunate.[42] Although there is evidence that such feelings tend to be intensified by disasters or events such as the Holocaust, this sense of guilt at still being alive can affect any survivor.

If the deceased was a victim of homicide, the survivor's predominant emotions may be anger and fear. For a time, the world may be experienced as dangerous and cruel, unsafe and unfair. As with a suicide or the death of a young child, the suddenness and apparent injustice of the circumstances of death affect the experience of grief. Furthermore, as Lula Redmond points out, "The raw wound of the grieving homicide survivor is overtly and covertly affected by the performance of law enforcement officials, criminal justice practitioners, media personnel, and others after a murder."[43] Dealing with the criminal justice system extends the normal grieving period, as the case drags on with no assurance that the result will give the survivor a sense that justice was done. Among the "trigger events" that Redmond cites as restimulating grief are:

1. identification of the assailant
2. sensing (hearing, smelling, etc.) something that elicits recollection of an experience acutely associated with the traumatic event
3. anniversaries of the event
4. holidays and other significant events in the life of the family (such as birthdays)
5. hearings, trials, appeals, and other criminal justice proceedings
6. media articles about the event or about similar events

Relationship of Survivor to Deceased

The experience of bereavement is profoundly influenced by the relationship between the deceased and the survivor. Think for a moment about the various kinds of relationships in your life. As you name them, you will notice that a variety of labels come to mind—parents, children, pets, neighbors, coworkers, teachers, friends, and lovers. The *form* of a given relationship is one determinant of a survivor's experience of grief. Generally speaking, the death of a family member or other close relative requires a greater adjustment by the survivor than does the death of a coworker or neighbor. But the outward form of relationship is not the sole determinant of a survivor's experience of grief. The grief resulting from the death of a close friend may parallel the bereavement patterns associated with surviving a death within the family unit; indeed, with respect to the sense of loss experienced by survivors, close friendship can be viewed as a dyadic partnership similar in many respects to a conjugal partnership.[44]

Whatever the outward form may be—kin, friend, neighbor, or mate—relationships vary according to the degree of intimacy involved, the perception of each other's roles, the expectations of the other person, and the feelings about the quality of the relationship itself. In Bali, for example, family members and other kin are rarely referred to by their *personal* names, but rather by the *degree of relationship*, thus placing emphasis on the social roles. In our culture, most people do refer to siblings and other relatives by their personal names, yet how many refer to a parent by his or her given name?

A person's relationship with his or her parents may reflect more the socially defined roles of "parent" and "child" than it does feelings of friendship or personal intimacy. For some, however, a parent may occupy additional roles of business associate, neighbor, and close friend. These differing roles and expectations are likely to result in a very different experience of grief when the parent dies.

As we see, then, a number of factors influence whether a particular relationship is *central* or *peripheral* to a person's life. A death involving someone central to the survivor's life generally will be much more affecting than the death of someone felt to be on the periphery. The degree of relationship, level of intimacy, and the roles and expectations associated with the relationship all influence whether we categorize a particular relationship as central or peripheral to our lives.

The severity of the grief response may be predicted to some extent by relating a survivor's relationship to the deceased (categorized as central or peripheral) with the survivor's *belief* about the circumstances of the death (whether preventable or unpreventable).[45] In other words, a survivor's attachment to the deceased and his or her sense of the appropriateness of the death will generally determine the response. For example, given a *central* relationship between the survivor and the deceased and the belief that the death was *preventable*, one would expect the grieving process to be both intense and prolonged. On the other hand, if the survivor had a *peripheral* relationship with the deceased and believed the death was *not preventable*, one might expect the grieving process to be mild as well as relatively brief.

Ambivalence is another factor influencing relationships and subsequent grief. Such feeling about the quality of a relationship, reflecting a push-pull struggle between love and hate, may be subtle or dramatic. Perhaps no relation-

David Des Granges, Tate Gallery, London

This portrait of the Saltonstall family, painted in 1611 by David Des Granges, provides a record of living family members and their relational links with the deceased, whose influence is still felt. The husband and father, Sir Richard, is portrayed as if standing at the bedside of his dead wife whose arm reaches toward their two children. Seated in the chair and holding her baby, the newest member of the family, is Sir Richard's second wife, whom he married three years after the death of his first wife.

ship is entirely free of ambivalence or of questions about its quality. But when feelings of ambivalence are intense and prolonged, grieving can be complicated by unresolved emotions.

Unfinished Business

Unfinished business can be aptly termed "business that goes on after death." Something remains incomplete at the time of death. The content of unfinished business, how it is handled, and how the survivor is affected by it all have an impact on the experience of grief. Unfinished business can be thought of in one or both of two ways relative to its effect on survivors: first is the fact of death itself; second is the relationship between deceased and survivor. As to the first, perhaps an earlier death of a parent, child, sibling, or someone else close continues to be a vivid reminder of the survivor's uncertainty and fears about death. Regardless of an individual's particular beliefs or values, the more "finished" is the business of death — that is, the more a survivor feels resolved within himself or herself toward it — the easier it is to accept death and to cope with grief and mourning. If a person rails against death, denying it and refusing to accept it, the experience of grief is more likely to be difficult and perhaps prolonged. Accepting death, giving it a place in our lives, allows us to be finished with otherwise unresolved issues about death itself.

Second, and probably more crucial in alleviating the stress and pain of grief, is the unfinished business between the deceased and the survivor. Something in the relationship was left incomplete — perhaps some longstanding conflict was never resolved during the deceased's lifetime, and now the survivor feels it is too late. Such unfinished business can include things that were and were not said, things done or not done. Unfinished business may give the survivor feelings of unfulfillment. The work of Elisabeth Kübler-Ross and others points up the importance of finishing business between the person who is dying and his or her survivors. Open and uninhibited discussion at the time of an impending death can yield significant benefits both for the person who is dying and for the survivor.

Persons who have experienced the death of someone close often say that the things left unsaid or undone seem to come back to pain them, to give them bad times in the night. The sense of never being able to resolve the conflicts left by unfinished business is what amplifies the suffering. Consider the image of a son standing over his father's grave saying, "If only we had been closer, Dad. We ought to have taken more time to visit each other."

It may be possible to resolve some unfinished business even after the person's death by working through it with the help of counseling and therapeutic intervention. But it is easier and clearer to work toward resolving unfinished business daily, in all our relationships and especially our intimate ones. Perhaps the key to taking care of unfinished business is forgiveness: accepting the situation as it is.

Deathbed promises constitute a particular kind of unfinished business, and they affect more people than we might at first imagine. Consider the classic scene in which the person who is dying elicits some promise from the survivor to perform some particular action after the person dies. Most survivors agree to enact the promise, whether or not they really want to comply with the deathbed request. Thus, a deathbed promise can later cause considerable conflict for the survivor, who may be torn between fulfilling the promise and taking a contradictory course of action. Some people carry through a deathbed promise and find it to be a gratifying choice; others find that a deathbed promise needs to be reevaluated in the light of their own wishes and circumstances.

Intellectual Versus Emotional Responses

When there is a marked difference between the survivor's emotional and intellectual responses to death, and the survivor believes that only one response can be right, the result is conflict. To expect the head and the heart to react the same to loss is unrealistic; there is often disparity between feelings and thoughts.

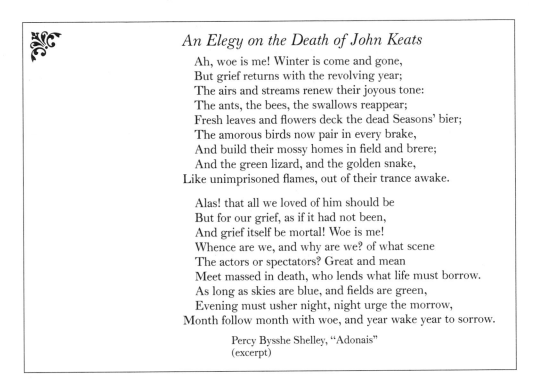

An Elegy on the Death of John Keats

Ah, woe is me! Winter is come and gone,
But grief returns with the revolving year;
The airs and streams renew their joyous tone:
The ants, the bees, the swallows reappear;
Fresh leaves and flowers deck the dead Seasons' bier;
The amorous birds now pair in every brake,
And build their mossy homes in field and brere;
And the green lizard, and the golden snake,
Like unimprisoned flames, out of their trance awake.

Alas! that all we loved of him should be
But for our grief, as if it had not been,
And grief itself be mortal! Woe is me!
Whence are we, and why are we? of what scene
The actors or spectators? Great and mean
Meet massed in death, who lends what life must borrow.
As long as skies are blue, and fields are green,
Evening must usher night, night urge the morrow,
Month follow month with woe, and year wake year to sorrow.

Percy Bysshe Shelley, "Adonais"
(excerpt)

During the process of working through grief, many different emotions will be felt, and many different thoughts will arise. By allowing them all and withholding judgment as to the rightness and wrongness of particular emotions or thoughts, the survivor is much more likely to experience grief as healing.

One must give oneself permission to experience feelings of loss. Survivors often have rigid rules about what kind of feelings can be expressed in grief, and when — such as where and when it is acceptable to be angry or to open to the pain and release an intense outburst of sadness.

Permission to have and express feelings is immensely important in dealing with the issues of survivorship. Intellectually, we may think, "How can I be mad at someone for dying?" Yet anger may indeed be a component of grief; consider the example of someone who died because of driving while intoxicated, or of the suicide. On the other hand, anger may be present even if death was seemingly unavoidable and beyond the victim's control. One young mother told of walking past a photograph of her recently deceased child and noticing, amid the grief and pain, a small voice within her blurting out, "Brat! How could you die and leave me as you did!" In a purely intellectual sense, we might be tempted to think this mother's behavior quite out of place. How could she be angry at her child for dying? Yet that sense of rage, that frustrated anger, is typical in the experience of survivors.

Advice for the Bereaved

Realize and recognize the loss.

Take time for nature's slow, sure, stuttering process of healing.

Give yourself massive doses of restful relaxation and routine busy-ness.

Know that powerful, overwhelming feelings will lessen with time.

Be vulnerable, share your pain, and be humble enough to accept support.

Surround yourself with life: plants, animals, and friends.

Use momentos to help your mourning, not to live in the dead past.

Avoid rebound relationships, big decisions, and anything addictive.

Keep a diary and record successes, memories, and struggles.

Prepare for change, new interests, new friends, solitude, creativity, growth.

Recognize that forgiveness (of ourselves and others) is a vital part of the healing process.

Know that holidays and anniversaries can bring up the painful feelings you thought you had successfully worked through.

Realize that any new death-related crisis will bring up feelings about past losses.

The Centre for Living with Dying

Survivors must permit themselves to experience those feelings, to feel anger at the person for having died and anger at themselves for not having been able to prevent the death—indeed, giving themselves permission to experience all the feelings that arise. Thus, they need not judge themselves as uncaring or bad.

Coping Mechanisms for Survivors

From the dawn of human consciousness, survivors have used a variety of activities, rituals, and social institutions to help them cope with the fact of loss. We saw in previous chapters how funeral rites and other ceremonies surrounding disposition of the body have served this purpose by providing an orderly and acceptable framework for dealing with the initial shock of loss. However, because the process of coming to terms with a loss continues beyond the brief period taken up with such rituals, many survivors seek additional sources of support.

In the past, much of this support was provided within the family and the close-knit community of friends and relatives. However, with the changes in patterns of social life, such as smaller families and greater geographic mobility, some of these traditional sources of support may be unavailable or insufficient to meet the particular needs of survivors. Thus, many bereaved persons have sought support by sharing their concerns with others who have had similar bereavement experiences. Such survivor support groups extend communal support beyond the initial period of the funeral rites and provide supportive resources that may be otherwise lacking in the survivor's milieu.

In addition to funeral rituals and survivor support groups, coping mechanisms for survivors include gaining an understanding of how best to proceed

Tears stream down the face of accordian player Graham Jackson as the body of President Franklin Delano Roosevelt is carried to the train at Warm Springs, Georgia, the day after his death — a poignant example of how bereaved persons express their loss in public as well as private.

with the practical management of life's affairs. We will look briefly at how each of these coping mechanisms for survivors can aid in the process of coming to terms with bereavement and grief.

Funerals and Other Leave-Taking Rituals

Funerals and other leave-taking rituals can help provide a sense of closure on the deceased's life and thereby help survivors integrate the loss into their ongoing lives. Sociologist Glenn Vernon notes that such rituals typically represent an opportunity for a "controlled expression of anger and hostility, and also for a lessening of guilt and anxiety."[46] The role of the wake among traditional Hawaiians illustrates these remarks. Everyone in the *ohana*, or extended family, came to the wake, including children. With each new arrival, a relative would say — as if telling the dead person — "Here comes Keone, your old fishing companion," or "Tutu is coming in now; remember how she used to massage you when you were

The upper middles would probably drink themselves silly at the funeral. Although a few years ago this would have been frowned on. When my husband in the sixties announced that he intended to leave £200 in his will for a booze-up for his friends, his lawyer talked him out of it, saying it was in bad taste and would upset people. The same year his grandmother died, and after the funeral, recovering from the innate vulgarity of the cremation service when the gramophone record stuck on 'Abi-abi-abi-abi-de with me', the whole family trooped home and discovered some crates of Australian burgundy under the stairs. A rip-roaring party ensued and soon a lower middle busy-body who lived next door came bustling over to see if anything was wrong. Whereupon my father-in-law, holding a glass and seeing her coming up the path, uttered the immortal line: 'Who is this intruding on our grief?'

Jilly Cooper, *Class*

sick." The mourners then addressed the dead, recalling their memories and perhaps describing their feelings of abandonment, even scolding the deceased for dying. A fishing companion might exclaim, "What do you mean, going off when we had planned to go fishing! Now who will I fish with?" Or a wife might say, "You had no business to go. You should be ashamed of yourself. We need you."[47]

Although these customs were not consciously planned to vent grief, they nevertheless facilitated it. The practice of scolding the corpse, for instance, provided an opportunity for survivors to vent hostility toward the dead who had abandoned them. What a contrast to the Western cultural notion that one should "not speak ill of the dead," which may deny feelings of anger at the deceased.

Of course, not all funeral rituals are alike. Some survivors express their grief with intense fervor, others adopt a nearly stoic expression. In one culture funerals are occasions for weeping and wailing, even literally "tearing one's hair out," magnifying the emotional response to provide catharsis; another culture emphasizes keeping emotions subdued, not demonstrating grief, not "breaking down." There may even be discrepancies between expressed norms and observed grief behaviors.[48] Still, whatever the particular characteristics, as a culturally condoned vehicle for expressing grief behavior, the mourning rituals that surround death can facilitate closure by providing survivors with a social framework for coping with the fact of death.

Indeed, funeral rituals as an impetus for social support may be especially important in societies like the United States, which is typified by loose social networks. Whereas dense social networks — the small or medium-sized Israeli kibbutz, for example — have social structures that allow mourning to take place within an intimate circle of family, friends, neighbors, and coworkers, comparatively loose networks may use explicit forms of funeral ritual to generate an adequate sense of social support for the bereaved.[49]

Other forms of leave-taking ritual have been inspired by traditional mourning rituals such as funerals. Various forms of "directive mourning therapy" can allow the grieving survivor to take symbolic leave of the deceased.[50] This kind of

Pam Price, UPI/Bettman Newsphotos

Family members leave the church after attending the funeral of a son and brother. As a focus of familial and community support for the bereaved, the funeral ceremony performs a unique function among the social rituals devised to mark significant events in the lives of members of a community.

ritual can also be used to assist individuals in moving from a maladaptive to an adaptive style of grieving.[51] Such leave-taking typically makes use of *linking objects* that are symbolic in some way of the survivor's relationship to the deceased.[52] An example is the writing of a farewell letter to the deceased and its subsequent burial or burning. A leave-taking ritual can be followed by a "reunion" ritual, perhaps in the form of a ceremonial dinner with family and friends. In this way, the movement of separation and joining found in traditional rituals can be adapted to the circumstances of a particular survivor.

Survivor Support Groups

By offering opportunities for bereaved persons to share their concerns and empathy with one another, support groups provide important help to survivors in coping with grief and mourning. Such groups are usually based on the concept of *perceived similarity*. Members of a group usually have experienced similar losses and meet together to support one another as they work toward understanding and integrating those losses into their lives. Probably the best known of these groups are the many organizations of widows (often known as widow-to-widow groups) within which widows can congregate to share their experiences of being a woman alone and to encourage one another in coping with the death of a spouse. Other support groups exist as well, each ministering to the needs of a particular group of survivors.

Just as survivor support groups differ in emphasis, they also differ in approach and methodology. The meetings of some support groups resemble an encounter session, the rule being to accept and express feelings. Others function more as social groups, providing a place for the survivor to come and be with others who have had similar experiences. Some groups are composed entirely of peers, whereas others are facilitated by a trained professional or lay counselor.

Many hospice and palliative care programs provide specially trained volunteers to assist families in coping with their grief.[53] The coming of a greater openness about death has been accompanied by growing attention to bereavement care in many countries.[54] In Britain, for example, the organization Cruse has a national network of trained volunteer bereavement counselors who are supported by social workers, psychiatrists, and other professionals. Israel provides support services to war widows. And, in the United States, groups such as the Widow-to-Widow program have spurred the development of widespread mutual help groups and other forms of bereavement support.

Practical Management of Life's Affairs

Survivors are sometimes urged to take a hand in the practical management of their everyday affairs as soon as possible following bereavement. During the early period of bereavement, however, there is a need for finding a balance between the *bridging* activities that will lead the survivor to a future without the deceased and the *linking* activities that give the survivor familiar ties to the past.

The survivor must deal with the impact of change, which may affect every detail of life: The family unit is different; the social realties have changed; there are legal and financial matters that require attention. The survivor must face these issues and answer the question, "How can I make the adjustment in each of these areas?" Because the loss of someone close brings tremendous change, it is usually helpful if, in the management of life's affairs, the survivor limits the number of other changes that occur at the same time.

So each shall mourn, in life's advance,
    Dear hopes, dear friends, ultimately killed;
Shall grieve for many a forfeit chance,
    And longing passion unfulfilled.

William Makepeace Thackeray,
"The End of the Play"

Bereavement as an Opportunity for Growth

Survivors are better able to cope if they are aware that death and bereavement can be an opportunity for growth. This perspective allows movement toward resolving the loss. One can begin to reformulate the loss, thus freeing up energy that had been bound to the past. As John Schneider says, "There is a change in perceptual set from focusing on limits to focusing on potential; from coping to growth; and from problems to challenges."[55] The tragic event of the loved one's death is reformulated in a way that offers new opportunities. The reframing of this experience can carry over into other areas of the person's life, so that beliefs and assumptions that were once limiting may be reassessed with greater self-confidence and self-awareness. The process of resolving loss and working through grief provides incentives that make possible significant life changes.

In this way, the loss is transformed. The intensive focus on self-awareness gives way to a new sense of identity whereby the loss is placed within a context of growth and life cycles. Grief becomes a unifying rather than alienating human experience, and the lost relationship is viewed as changed but not ended. Transforming the loss involves integrating what was lost into one's own life energies. Being a survivor may allow changes in beliefs and values, understanding about death and about life, that might not otherwise have been possible. Recollecting their grief, bereaved individuals have described themselves as stronger, more competent, more mature, more independent, and better able to face other crises; for many, bereavement led to positive experiences with their social support systems of family and friends.[56]

As we have seen, the process by which a survivor integrates a loss into his or her life varies. In many cases, turning to inner sources of creativity gives form to the experience of grief. Creatively responding to loss can lead to remarkable results. Those who work with the bereaved can spark a grieving person's creative response, as in the case of a young woman who had experienced the sudden, unexpected death of her son at birth. Overwhelmed by feelings of sadness, depression, and inability to do anything other than grieve the death of her baby, she was despairing of words to communicate her feelings. In a counseling session six months after her son's death, she remarked, "I haven't touched a lump of clay since Justin died." The obvious question was, what had she done with clay before his death? She said that her sculptures of whales and seals had sold at a local

Figure 7-2(a)   *Anguish of loss*

Figure 7-2(b)   *Sharing the grief*

Figure 7-2(c)   *Collapsing*

*"The anguish of loss is overpowering and vast,"
begins the prose accompanying the sculpture by
Julie Fritsch pictured here, part of the series created
following the death of her son. "Sharing the grief"
states the theme of the second sculpture,
acknowledging that "together we must comfort and
be comforted." The third sculpture portrays the
bereaved artist "collapsing from the weight of
emotions I cannot control." The prose accompanying
this sculpture continues: "Drained of any ability to
cope or carry on, I must collapse now. And feel
myself overcome by absolute grief."*

seaside crafts shop. The counselor pointed out that the reason for her inability to
return to her art might lie in the source of her creative energies. Although whales
and seals might one day reemerge from the lumps of clay, her creativity at present
might take a different form. The client agreed to find a quiet moment when she
would put her hands to the lump of clay as an experiment to see what might emerge.

Both the bereaved mother and the counselor were amazed at the results (see Figure 7-2). Over the course of twelve months, a series of some twenty-two figures emerged. The earliest were naked, later works were draped with blankets, and, with the final pieces, the fabric of the blankets had been turned into clothing. The mother's creativity not only gave form to her loss but also manifested an unconscious understanding of the process of recovery and the integration of her loss. Subsequently, the sculptures were photographed and published, along with her prose, giving comfort to other survivors.[57]

Death is a community event. Death does not end the survivor's membership in family, community, or nation. Attitudes toward the dead are largely a continuation of the natural affections and styles of relationship that hold for the living in any given culture. Bereavement, grief, and mourning are complementary threads in the fabric of life, part of the warp and weft of human experience.

A survivor's response to death is complex, encompassing a multitude of personal, family, and social factors. It is influenced also by the circumstances surrounding the death. By becoming aware of the vast range of responses that can be present in the experience of loss and grief, we increase our choices for dealing with loss. By understanding the issues involved in survivorship, we offer ourselves greater opportunity to cope successfully with loss and to use the experience of loss as a means of becoming more fully human.

Further Readings

Kenneth J. Doka, ed. *Disenfranchised Grief: Recognizing Hidden Sorrow*. Lexington, Mass.: Lexington Books, 1989.

Julie Fritsch with Sherokee Isle. *The Anguish of Loss*. Maple Plain, Minn.: Wintergreen Press, 1988.

Edgar N. Jackson. *The Many Faces of Grief*. Nashville: Abingdon Press, 1977.

C. S. Lewis. *A Grief Observed*. New York: Seabury Press, 1961.

Marian Osterweis, Fredric Solomon, and Morris Green, eds. *Bereavement: Reactions, Consequences, and Care*. Washington, D.C.: National Academy Press, 1984.

Colin Murray Parkes. *Bereavement: Studies of Grief in Adult Life*, 2d ed. Madison, Conn.: International Universities Press, 1987.

Colin Murray Parkes and Robert S. Weiss. *Recovery from Bereavement*. New York: Basic Books, 1983.

Therese A. Rando. *Grieving: How to Go on Living When Someone You Love Dies*. Lexington, Mass.: Lexington Books, 1988.

Therese A. Rando. *Loss and Anticipatory Grief*. Lexington, Mass.: Lexington Books, 1985.

Beverly Raphael. *The Anatomy of Bereavement*. New York: Basic Books, 1983.

Catherine M. Sanders. *Grief, The Mourning After: Dealing with Adult Bereavement*. New York: John Wiley and Sons, 1989.

Judy Tatelbaum. *The Courage to Grieve: Creative Living, Recovery and Growth Through Grief*. New York: Harper and Row, 1982.

Jill Truman. *Letter to My Husband: Notes about Mourning and Recovery*. New York: Viking Penguin, 1987.

A child feels the death of a parent or other close family member or friend as deeply as do adult survivors of a close death. This young girl finds solace and a means of coming to terms with the death of her father by bringing a favorite drawing to the gravesite and spending some time alone with her thoughts and memories of her father and what his loss represents in her life.

CHAPTER 8

Death in Children's Lives

*C*hange is pervasive in the lives of children. Families move. Children leave familiar playmates, their neighborhood, school, and the people and places they have come to know and to which they feel attached. A parent may say, "But, dear, it's only for a year," or, "We'll come back to visit next summer." To a child, however, a year or next summer is a very long time indeed. Concepts related to time and distance may lie outside the young child's frame of reference. Change can represent a very real loss.

Changes in family relationships — divorce or separation, for instance — may be experienced as a kind of death. The child senses that the known relationship has changed, but exactly what kind of relationship the future may hold is uncertain and possibly bewildering. Even though such changes may not connote the sense of finality that adults reserve for death, the child may experience a lingering uncertainty, a kind of "little death." Separation from one's parents is usually painful for a child whether the separation is due to death, divorce, or some other reason.

Change is also experienced as older brothers and sisters grow up and move away from home. As the composition of the family shifts, the child is faced with the need to adjust to new and unfamiliar situations. Perhaps the child delights in the change insofar as it means the thrill of having his or her own room. On the other hand, with the departure of an older sibling, the child may be losing an advocate or a confidant who provided support and understanding. Change brings both gains and losses.

An addition to the family, a new baby brother or sister, is a change that the child may experience with both excitement and trepidation. The new family member may represent an intrusion upon the child's place in the family, a loss of attention from parents and other family members. Yet the child may also enjoy the adventure and the more mature responsibilities that accompany change.

Changes, like all those given, require readjustments in the child's life. In addition, a child may encounter other significant losses: the death of a brother or sister, a parent, or a friend; or confrontation with an illness that threatens his or her own life. As much as we may wish it would be otherwise, children also are exposed to events of change and loss, experiences of bereavement and grief. In this chapter, we examine issues of life-threatening illness and bereavement as they affect children; we also look at the means for helping children cope with the experience of change and loss.

Major Causes of Death in Childhood and Adolescence

The most difficult death for many people to face is the death of a child. Death is often viewed as appropriate only when it comes in old age, at the end of a person's lifespan. It is not easy to accept that death occurs during childhood, that a person's lifespan is brief. Confronting the death of a child uncovers our uneasiness about death in a more dramatic way than a death that is seen as the culmination of a long life. Yet the fact that death does end a child's life underscores the truth that no one is immune to death.

With the dramatic decline in deaths from infectious diseases, the relative importance of injury as a cause of death has increased. As the most prominent cause of death during the first half of the human lifespan, injury has been characterized as "the last major plague of the young."[1] When we review the main causes of death among children and adolescents, we find that accidents top the list, followed by cancer, heart disease, homicide, and suicide. (The incidence of suicide among young persons is discussed in Chapter 13.)

Of all the deaths resulting from accidents in the age groups just mentioned, a significant number involve motor vehicles. Many of these accidents further involve the use and abuse of alcoholic beverages, which have been found to influence not only motor vehicle accidents but other types of accidents as well. The death and disability of children and young adults in America due to injury is bringing about a growing recognition that the magnitude of the problem demands a coordinated program of public education and research. Injury is devastating to a young person, emotionally as well as physically. Whether or not death results, injury involves significant losses, and when a young person bears responsibility for a peer's injury or death because of an accident, as in alcohol-related and drug-related incidents, the felt loss can be severe.

If a person feels that he or she has played a role in the events that led to the disability or death of a friend or other loved one, guilt may predominate among

> When I am dead, and laid in grave,
> And all my bones are rotten,
> By this may I remembered be
> When I should be forgotten.
>
> On a girl's sampler, 1736

the emotions experienced after the loss. For example, in one situation that involved three brothers playing with a loaded gun, the youngest pushed the oldest, who held the gun, as the bullet was discharged, killing their sibling. "I have always struggled with myself about whether my brother would have died if I hadn't tried to push my other brother away," said a thirty-year-old man, recalling events that had taken place more than a quarter of a century earlier. "I always thought I did the right thing, but no one ever told me or even talked with me about my feelings. For years, I cried myself to sleep alone in my bed at night." Because accidents occur suddenly and unexpectedly, allowing no time to prepare for the outcome, their aftermath is especially shocking and devastating to survivors.

Children with Life-Threatening Illness

Although more children and adolescents die from injuries received in accidents than from the effects of disease, the situation confronting the child with a life-threatening illness is one of special poignancy. Perhaps we feel, justifiably or not, that an accident is something that just "happens" and is, therefore, unpreventable, whereas we expect medicine to provide a cure for disease. In this section, we turn our attention to the ways children perceive an experience with life-threatening illness and how they cope with that reality in their lives.

The Child's Perception of Illness

The terminally ill child's inquisitiveness about dying may be painful for a parent to adequately confront. The child's desire to understand his or her illness and its prognosis may be met with silence. Despite this silence, however, children are often able to interpret the behavior of those around them in order to gain insight into their condition.

In her study of a children's ward, Myra Bluebond-Langner observed that children typically were able to guess their condition by interpreting how people behaved toward them.[2] For example, children interpreted behaviors such as crying or avoidance as indicating the seriousness of their illness and their nearness to dying. These children, most of whom were between the ages of three and nine, could assess the seriousness of their illness even though no one had told them that they were very sick or that they were going to die. Although the children some-times discussed their illnesses with their peers, they refrained from doing so with adults. Apparently perceiving that their conversations made adults uncomfort-able, the children on the ward talked about the taboo topic among themselves, much as children discuss other forbidden topics: out of range of an adult's hearing.

Bluebond-Langner also observed that the children's interpretations of their conditions changed over time; the illness was first perceived as acute, then chronic, and finally fatal. Similarly, medications were first "healing agents," then "something that prolongs life." As their perception of drugs progressed from something that was "always effective" to "effective sometimes" to "not really ef-fective at all," their behaviors toward taking medication changed likewise. The children generally knew a great deal about the world of the hospital, its staff and procedures, and the experiences of leukemic children. Most were aware of the condition of other children, making comments like "Jeffrey's in his first relapse," and noticing when other children died. Again, they shared these experiences among themselves. Although many children did not know the proper name for their disease, they typically exhibited considerable knowledge about its treat-ment and prognosis.

Fears and Anxieties

Most researchers who have studied seriously ill and dying children report that the sick child's primary concern is related to fears of pain and separation. The three main sources of stress for hospitalized dying children can be summarized as: (1) separation from the mother (or mother figure), (2) painful or traumatic procedures, and (3) the deaths of other children. Development of the concept of death during successive stages of childhood (discussed in Chapter 3) is reflected by the sequence of major concerns experienced by the sick child. For example, children under five years old tend to be most distressed by separation from the mother. Children in the middle group, roughly ages five to nine, tend to be most concerned about the discomforting and possibly disfiguring effects of the disease and related medical procedures. The older child is more likely to experience anxiety caused by awareness of other children's deaths. These findings are essen-tially consistent with the developmental model: Separation anxiety is typical of the young child; a personification of death, with fears about mutilation and pain, becomes predominant during the middle years of childhood; and the older child's anxieties resulting from the deaths of other children correspond to a more mature understanding of death as final and universal. Studies indicate, however, that terminally ill children experience a greater awareness of death than do their healthier counterparts. Also, they typically have greater awareness of the hospital experience and the accompanying medical procedures.

Children who are dying as a result of perinatally acquired HIV infection are especially heartrending. (Often referred to as "AIDS babies," some infants with AIDS survive into early childhood.) Their lives are subjected to extraordinary disruption, accompanied by the loss of any sense of security. As Sara Dubik-Unruh says, such dying children are often members of "dying families."[3] These

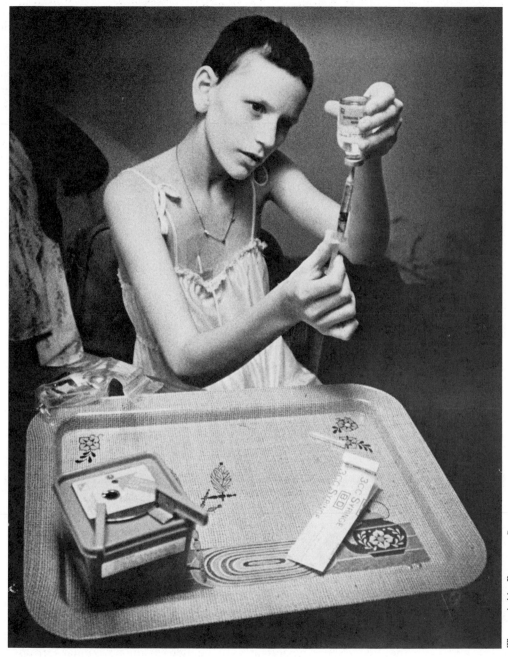

Theresa Aubin, Bremerton Sun

Adolescents and older children with life-threatening illnesses may take on increasing responsibilities for their daily treatment regimes. Here, a young cancer patient flushes her venous access catheter, the route used to administer chemotherapy, which must be cleaned nightly.

families may be affected by a multitude of crisis situations, such as incarceration, addiction, illness, abandonment or court removal of children, hospitalization, separation from parents and siblings, and homelessness. It has been estimated that between one-fourth and one-third of infants with AIDS will not be cared for by their biological parents. Nor have community support services consistently been available. On the contrary, at times public agencies as well as private companies have refused to provide care for these children. Dubik-Unruh points out, "The situation of a child who is already ill, who loses one parent, moves from one temporary placement to another, experiences multiple changes in caretakers, and ultimately loses the remaining parent and/or siblings, is staggering to imagine." Negative attitudes expressed by the wider public community can also have a harmful impact on the emotional well-being of these children. Although many, perhaps most, of these HIV-infected children will die while still quite young, some are expected to survive. Dubik-Unruh concludes that the care of these children "must include their emotional well-being as well as their physical health, to enable those children who do survive to face the future with strength, and to allow those children who do not survive to live the remainder of their lives with their innocence and childhood intact, and their personal integrity respected."

Hospital and Home Care

Illness separates the child from the people and the surroundings that are familiar and loved. Besides physical pain, there may be anguish resulting from the child's inability to engage in the activities and pursuits of healthy children. The sick child misses school, is restricted from playtime activities, and becomes enmeshed in a more or less alien world of hospitals and medical paraphernalia.

Even when a child has grown somewhat accustomed to life in and out of the hospital, new forms of treatment and new medical settings are unfamiliar and may be upsetting. Change of routine brings added fears and anxieties. As the illness changes, the child's need to deal with new, unfamiliar doctors and other medical personnel may be quite disturbing. This reaction occurs regardless of how friendly the hospital setting is or what efforts are made by the staff to create a special environment for sick children.[4] Thus, parents and health care personnel must continually be helping a child to deal with new aspects of illness and hospitalization. As nursing educator Donna Juenker points out, "Each time a child returns to the hospital he is literally a different person. He is at a wholly new stage of development with correspondingly different fears and expectations."[5]

For children whose illness reaches the stage of a terminal prognosis, care may shift from the hospital to the home. Active measures intended to provide a cure are replaced with palliative care designed to increase comfort and to allow the child to spend what remains of the time left among familiar surroundings. As in the case of terminally ill adults, various programs exist to provide care for terminally ill children, including some hospice-based programs. More common is the practice of home-based palliative care, which many caregivers believe provides substantial practical and emotional benefits for terminally ill children, their parents, and their siblings.[6] Whatever the setting — hospital, hospice, or home — families who are in the midst of experiencing a child's death need appropriate and adequate professional and lay support.[7]

The Child's Coping Mechanisms

The seriously ill child is not simply a passive participant in the medical and social circumstances surrounding the illness. A child experiences psychosocial concerns related to absence from school, changes in family patterns, the threat of increased dependency on others, and the financial or emotional strain on his or her family. Medical concerns relate to the visibility of the illness, physical discomfort, and the symbolic significance attached to the part of the body affected. How a child perceives the illness and the manner in which he or she responds to it depends on age, the nature of the illness and its treatment, family relationships, and past experience.

Like everyone else, the sick child uses various coping mechanisms to deal with the anxiety and confusion that accompany life-threatening illness. Of course, the child's age and developmental stage determine the level of awareness and the kinds of coping mechanisms available. Yet even a very young child may exhibit a surprisingly wide range of resources for coping with the possibility of death.

Children with life-threatening illnesses may use distancing strategies to limit the number of persons with whom they have close relationships. This reduces the risk of a distressing interaction because there are fewer opportunities for such an occurrence. Using such a strategy, a child selects from the total situation only those aspects or those persons that he or she finds least threatening. In this way, the child attempts to construct as safe and secure an environment as possible within the circumstances.

At various times, a child may avoid stress by attempting to deny the reality of the situation or by withdrawing from a potentially stressful situation. The child may cope with a painful procedure by rationalizing that it will help effect a cure. Or the child makes a deal that, in his or her own mind, balances the painful treatment with some desire that will be fulfilled once the pain is endured. For example, a child asks, "After I get my shot, can I play with my toys?" Some children cope by regressing to a pattern of behavior that reflects a less demanding, more comfortable time in their lives. For example, a child may regress to the use of baby talk or "forget" his or her toilet training.

Sublimation or goal substitution may be an effective means for the child to cope with the infringements of a serious illness. For example, a child who is prevented by illness from engaging in a competitive sport may find a substitution for the desired activity by playing board games in a highly competitive fashion. One might envision scenes of sick children racing through the hospital corridors, IV bottles swinging from their wheelchairs, in a spontaneous competition.

These and other coping mechanisms enable the child to deal with the uncomfortable and frightening aspects of the illness. How a child copes with illness depends not only on the circumstances, but also on the child's *perception* of its meaning and consequences.

Children as Survivors of a Close Death

Nearly all parents would wish to spare their children the pain of bereavement. Sometimes rather grand attempts are made to minimize the effects of a loss when it occurs in a child's life. The death of a pet, for example, may be swiftly followed by its replacement with another animal. At best, such a course of action has limited usefulness. Death is a fact of life that eventually cannot be ignored. A more constructive approach when such losses occur is to help the child explore his or her feelings about death and develop an understanding of death that is appropriate for the child's ability to comprehend.

In this section, the bereaved child's expression of grief is examined, with particular emphasis on the child as survivor of the death of a parent or sibling.

The Bereaved Child's Experience of Grief

Children are capable of experiencing grief. A bereaved child may experience the same kind of physical and emotional symptoms as adults, including lack of appetite, insomnia, nightmares, and nausea. Although children tend to exhibit considerable resiliency in coping with tragedy, adults can nevertheless contribute by being willing to listen to the child's expressions of mourning and to communicate and demonstrate support for the child's well-being.

A child's response to loss is similar in many respects to that of adults, but a particular child's experience will reflect the influence of such factors as age, stage of mental and emotional development, patterns of interaction and communication within the family, degree of relationship with the person who has died, and previous experiences with death. Sudden, unexpected death or death as a result of suicide can bring added factors that the child must face in coming to terms with the loss.[8]

Among children of the same age, significant differences may be observed in their abilities to comprehend death and cope with its effects on them as survivors. For example, one five-year-old might appear quite devastated by the death of a parent. Another child of the same age and in similar circumstances might seem comparatively unaffected. The first child may put forth intense effort in trying to come to terms with the loss. The second child, on the other hand, may seem satisfied with the brief explanation that "Daddy's gone and he won't ever be coming back." Which of these children do you believe exhibits the healthier response to loss?

As you may have guessed, such a question is inappropriate, because not enough is known about each child to allow framing an adequate reply. Suppose, however, that the first child's pattern of coping involves a period of acute grief, succeeded by a satisfactory resolution of the loss. Suppose, further, that the sec-

Suddenly the feeling that this was all just a dream ended. Christopher was angry. It wasn't fair. Why did that dumb man have to hit Bodger?

"I ought to run *him* over with a truck."

"Oh, honey, Bodger ran right in front of him. The man didn't have time to stop."

They took Christopher home to bed where he relived the accident over and over in his mind. He tried to pretend that the truck had missed the dog, or that he hadn't called and Bodger had stayed on the other side. Or he pretended that they hadn't left the dirt road where there were hardly ever any cars. Or that they had stayed home and waited.

But the bad dream always rolled on out of his control until the moment when Bodger was lying in the road.

Carol and Donald Carrick, *The Accident*

ond child's indifference is only transitory, a temporary state of mind that is succeeded by a protracted and possibly difficult process of coming to terms with the death — a process that may continue into adolescence or even adulthood before the loss is satisfactorily resolved. As this example suggests, it is not always possible to rely on appearances to assess how well a child is coping with loss.

A child may cope with the pain of a loss by selectively forgetting, or by reconstructing reality in a more desirable and comfortable way. For example, a child may not recall how frightened he was by the sight of a sibling lying in a hospital bed surrounded by awesome medical paraphernalia, or the child may reconstruct the memory of a sibling's protracted illness that included long stays in the hospital so that it seems as if the sibling was only away from home briefly for a few tests. The forgotten details or the reconstructed images allow the child to think about the experience without being overwhelmed with painful memories. On the other hand, as Richard Lonetto states, "An actual death experience for the child also can stimulate the development of more mature concepts about death that do not follow a prescribed pattern."[9] So, although it is reasonable to expect that age and cognitive development affect a child's response to loss, many other variables are at work, not least of which are the attitudes exhibited by the significant adults in the child's life.

The Death of a Pet

Often, a child's first experience with death involves a pet, a situation that is not surprising considering that about 63 million cats, 55 million dogs, and 25 million birds are kept as pets in the United States. When a pet dies, parents may wonder how best to help their child cope with the loss. Should one try to minimize the child's loss? Or should the death be seen as a natural opportunity for the child to consider what death means and to explore his or her feelings about the loss?

One mother described the responses of her daughters to the deaths of a new litter of baby rabbits.[10] Upon learning the news, the seven-year-old burst into tears and howled, "I don't want them dead." The five-year-old at first stood silently and then asked to call her father at work. She told him, "If you had been here, Daddy, you could have been the rabbits' doctor," reflecting a belief, appropriate for her age, that it should have been possible somehow to save the baby rabbits or restore them to life. Later, when the children began to dig a grave to bury the dead rabbits, the seven-year-old stopped crying for the first time since learning the news, while the five-year-old kept repeating, "The baby rabbits are dead, the baby rabbits are dead," in a monotone.

In the days following the rabbits' deaths, the girls asked many questions. The seven-year-old was particularly interested in questioning a widowed family friend about her dead husband. How often did she think about him and why did people have to be taken away from those who loved them, she wanted to know. The five-year-old, meanwhile, continued to mourn silently until her mother encouraged her to express her feelings. Then she began to sob. Finally, she said, "I'm glad I'm only five, you only die when you're old."

The younger child's first concern was for herself, the fear that she herself could die. The older child, on the other hand, worried about the durability of relationships. Although each child had a distinctive response to the loss, both children showed a need to be close to their parents during the days following the deaths of the rabbits, and they told the story of the rabbits' deaths again and again as they dealt with their experience.

Of course, it is not just children who are affected by the death of a pet. A woman described the reaction of her husband to the death of Iggy, a desert iguana.[11] When the iguana died, she reported, her husband "cried throughout the shoebox burial in the backyard." He later said that he was crying "for every pet he had ever loved and lost."

Attachments between humans and pets can be very strong. Yet mourning the loss of a pet sometimes elicits ridicule. Some may say that the bereaved pet owner is overreacting. After all "it was only an animal, a mere pet." However, those who counsel individuals who are grieving over the loss of a pet emphasize that feelings should be expressed by adults as well as children. As for replacing a pet, sufficient time should be allowed to mourn the loss before a new animal is acquired. This may take weeks or months, perhaps longer. The bonds of attachment to the pet that has died may jeopardize a healthy transition of affections to another animal if the natural process of grief has been prematurely curtailed or ignored.

A sign of the increasing attention given to mourning the loss of a pet can be seen in the growth of pet cemeteries. The International Pet Cemetery Association reports a total of 400 pet cemeteries in the United States, with the oldest dating back to the 1800s.[12] The appropriateness of grief over the death of a pet has also been acknowledged by veterinarians, some of whom send a contribution to pet care research institutions as a memorial to a deceased pet. A major greeting card company recently introduced sympathy cards expressing condolences over

Jack Delano, FSA Collection, Library of Congress

Children can feel strong attachment to their pets. Involving a child in the experience of a pet's death through ritual or discussion provides a means of coping with the loss.

Small boy. 'Where do animals go when they die?'
Small girl. 'All good animals go to heaven, but the bad ones
    go to the Natural History Museum.'

Caption to drawing by E. H. Shepard, *Punch*, 1929

the loss of a pet. When the bond between a pet and its owner is broken by death, the significance of that loss is increasingly recognized as a natural occasion for mourning, by adults as well as children.[13]

The Death of a Parent

Of all the deaths that can be experienced in childhood, the most affecting is generally considered to be the death of a parent. A parent's death is perceived as a loss of security, nurture, and affection — a loss of the emotional and psychological support upon which the child could formerly rely.

Because the relationship between parent and child is seldom free from conflict, whether or not openly exhibited, a parent's death may also elicit feelings of guilt. What child has not at some time directed angry thoughts — "I wish you were dead!" — toward his or her parents? Recalling such feelings, the bereaved child may feel responsible somehow for the parent's death.

Sometimes feelings of guilt result from what the child imagines to be actions that in some way contributed to a parent's death. For example, a child whose parent died of a terminal illness might remember particular instances when she was noisy and her sick parent needed rest. "Perhaps if I had been less noisy," the child thinks, "Mom would have gotten well." As proof of this imagined connection between the child's behavior and the parent's death, the child may cite the fact that "Mom went away and never came back to us." Such feelings are typical of the responsibility that children may assume as they try to understand their experience of a close death.

When the death of a parent affects a very young child, there subsequently may occur emotions related to mourning the years of relationship that were lost as a result of the parent's premature death. This is a common occurrence, for example, when the parent's death happened in connection with war. There can be a lingering sense of "never having known" the deceased parent. Conflicting emotions may lie relatively buried for a considerable time until some stimulus — perhaps the discovery of the parent's military papers or a visit to a memorial for the fallen combatants — brings the unresolved loss to the surface. Sharing the loss with others who find themselves similarly situated can help bring healing, even many years later. Some of the sons and daughters of parents who died in Vietnam have found solace by joining together in a national organization, Sons and

George Willard became possessed of a madness to lift the sheet from the body of his mother and look at her face. The thought that had come into his mind gripped him terribly. He became convinced that not his mother but someone else lay in the bed before him. The conviction was so real that it was almost unbearable. The body under the sheets was long and in death looked young and graceful. To the boy, held by some strange fancy, it was unspeakably lovely. The feeling that the body before him was alive, that in another moment a lovely woman would spring out of the bed and confront him, became so overpowering that he could not bear the suspense. Again and again he put out his hand. Once he touched and half lifted the white sheet that covered her, but his courage failed and he, like Doctor Reefy, turned and went out of the room. In the hallway outside the door he stopped and trembled so that he had to put a hand against the wall to support himself. "That's not my mother. That's not my mother in there," he whispered to himself and again his body shook with fright and uncertainty. When Aunt Elizabeth Swift, who had come to watch over the body, came out of an adjoining room he put his hand into hers and began to sob, shaking his head from side to side, half blind with grief, "My mother is dead," he said. . . .

Sherwood Anderson, *Winesburg, Ohio*

Daughters in Touch, where they find a common bond in their efforts to come to terms with loss.[14] Frequently, these efforts include talking to other veterans, thereby filling in the picture of a deceased parent whom the child was never able to fully know. "The surviving kids," said the mother of one young woman whose father died in Vietnam, "are the last casualties of the war, because they're just now reaching an age where they comprehend the impact."[15]

A child's experience of himself as a survivor may also give rise to feelings of guilt or uncertainty. A drawing made by a four-year-old whose father died of leukemia illustrates this (see Figure 8-1). Some time after his father's death, as the child was playing with his pencils and drawing paper, he asked his mother how to spell various words. Attracted by the child's activity, his mother noticed that he had drawn a picture of his father. In the drawing the father was saying to the child, "I am mad at you!" Surprised at this depiction of her husband's anger toward her son, the mother asked, "Why should your father have been mad at you?" The child explained, "Because you and I can still play together and Dad can't be with us anymore." Amid the confusing feelings resulting from his father's death, the child was attempting to come to terms with the fact of his own survivorship.

Now, in working with this child as a survivor, his mother had done a very wise thing. She said, "Tell me about this picture." In other words, she began to ask specific, open-ended questions that would elicit descriptions of the child's feelings. By doing this, she was able to respond directly to the child's concerns.

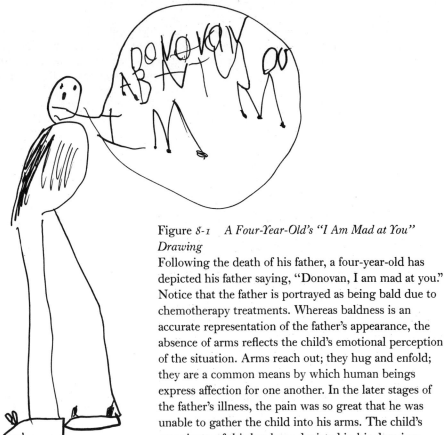

Figure 8-1   A Four-Year-Old's "I Am Mad at You" Drawing

Following the death of his father, a four-year-old has depicted his father saying, "Donovan, I am mad at you." Notice that the father is portrayed as being bald due to chemotherapy treatments. Whereas baldness is an accurate representation of the father's appearance, the absence of arms reflects the child's emotional perception of the situation. Arms reach out; they hug and enfold; they are a common means by which human beings express affection for one another. In the later stages of the father's illness, the pain was so great that he was unable to gather the child into his arms. The child's experience of this has been depicted in his drawing. Also notice that the drawing shows the father's body facing the viewer, yet his feet are drawn at an angle as if they are walking off the page. Again, the drawing reflects the child's experience, this time showing the father's movement out of his life. Importantly, the child's mother used the occasion of this drawing as an opportunity to talk with the child about his present feelings regarding his father's death.

Spontaneous drawings and other methods of art therapy are excellent methods for working with young children to help them explore and express feelings that otherwise might remain hidden, yet disturbing to them.[16] Using art with bereaved children helps them to work through grief by providing a safe, focused environment for expressing their concerns and feelings.[17]

The Death of a Sibling

Unlike a parent's death, a sibling's death rarely represents a loss of security for the surviving child. Still, the effect of such a close death may increase the surviving child's sense of vulnerability to death, especially when siblings are close to one another in age. The surviving child may experience a variety of responses to the death of a sibling. Perhaps the brother or sister was a protector, a caregiver as well as a playmate. The surviving child may be sad that this unique relationship has ended, worried that the protection and care given by the sibling is no longer available, and yet relieved or even pleased that, with the sibling's absence, he or she is now more the center of attention in the family. Such a mixture of emotions may produce guilt and confusion in the child who is trying to come to terms with the death of a sibling.

The child looks to the parents for help in understanding the significance of the sibling's death and in coping with its effects on both the family and himself or herself. The parents' methods of coping can play a large part in determining how the surviving child copes.

For the adolescent survivor of a sibling's death, the struggle to come to terms with the loss may be intertwined with the developmental task of formulating a personal sense of the meaning of life, a task that typically involves intense questioning about the value of religious beliefs and the existence of God. As David Balk points out, the death of a sibling shatters "trust in a benign, innocent universe" and "questions about the nature of life and death, about good and evil, and about the meaning of life become personal."[18] The normal developmental struggles over religion become sharper-edged when an adolescent's sibling dies. Coping with a sibling's death can bring about a greater maturity in cognitive development, social reasoning, moral judgment, identity formation, and, says Balk, religious understanding. Indeed, many bereaved youth consider religion to be an important resource for coping with loss, a source of meaning that aids in the search for significance in the face of tragedy.

Sometimes the parents' response to a child's death sets into motion dysfunctional family patterns that impair the surviving child's ability to cope. Such dysfunctional responses may range from resentment of the surviving child to an attempt to recreate in that child some of the qualities of the deceased child. The surviving child's feelings of rejection may be further complicated by feelings of guilt concerning a sibling's death.

Obviously, this scenario describes a "worst case" situation. Yet such parental responses may be present to some degree even among families that seem to be coping very successfully with the loss of a child. As a parent tries to come to terms with the experience of a child's death, he or she may unintentionally minimize contact with the surviving child. The living child may be a painful reminder of the child now lost. Conversely, a parent may become overprotective of the surviving child.

The bereaved child must be given opportunities to acknowledge and express his or her feelings of bereavement. Feelings of guilt as well as sadness need

Siblings enjoy a special relationship, one conjoining both rivalries and mutual affection and love. The death of a brother or sister thus severs a unique human relationship. The surviving child may feel the loss more intensely because of an identification with the deceased brother or sister. The surviving child recognizes that he or she is also not immune to dying at an early age.

to be explored and resolved in a loving and supportive atmosphere. When a child expresses guilt, one can ask, "What would it take to forgive yourself?" An open exploration allows the child to find personally satisfying ways of coping with a loved one's death. A surviving child's feelings of guilt are related to normal sibling rivalry. The sister at whom I angrily yell, "I hate you!" in the morning may be lying dead at the morgue in the afternoon, the victim of a bicycle accident. To a young child, the coincidence of anger directed toward a person and that person's subsequent death may be viewed as a cause-and-effect relationship.

A child's assumption of responsibility may be characterized by a preoccupation with the "should haves." One five-year-old whose younger brother was run over by a truck while they were outside playing told his mother later, "I should have . . . I should have." He saw himself as his younger brother's protector, responsible for his safety. His mother asked him, "You should have what?" He replied, "I just should have!"

His mother then asked, "What do you mean, you 'should have'?" The boy answered, "I should have looked, I should have known, I should have—": a flood of "should haves" about being his brother's guardian and protector. Taking the child into her arms, his mother said, "I understand, honey. Daddy's got the 'should haves.' Mommy's got the 'should haves.' We all have them. It's okay to have them. And it's okay to know that everybody could have done something differently, and that they *would* have if they'd had a choice."

When a sibling dies, the surviving child usually tries to fit together what he or she has understood about death up to that time with what is observable in the present. For instance, if a child believes that death is something that happens in old age, and then experiences the death of a younger brother, how can the child reconcile the difference between concept and experience? The primary means by which a child constructs a bridge between earlier notions about death and present reality is simply to observe how parents and significant others respond to the bereavement and express grief. Also important in resolving the conflict between the concept and the experience of death is the parent's ability to listen to the child's concerns and to help fit the experience to the child's ability to comprehend the meaning of death.

That allowing a child to participate in the family's experience helps the child cope with crisis is aptly demonstrated in a drawing by the five-year-old who saw his younger brother killed. The drawing represented "the day my brother was killed"; the point of greatest stress was shown to be the period of time when he was left at a neighbor's house while his parents were at the hospital (see Figure 8-2). Even more frightening than seeing the wheel of the truck roll over his brother's head was the feeling of being left alone, being separated from the rest of his family, not knowing what was happening with his parents and his younger brother.

This child's parents not only encouraged the child to express his feelings, they also sought out therapeutic resources in the community as an added support for coping with tragedy. Just as the child's work with spontaneous drawings

Figure 8-2   *A Five-Year-Old's "Crooked Day" Drawing*
In this drawing of "The Crooked Day," a five-year-old boy depicts his experience
of the events that transpired on the day his brother received fatal injuries in an
accident. Contrary to what might be assumed about this drawing, the places on
the line where the greatest stress is indicated occurred after the accident itself.
The sharp dip in the line at the lefthand side of the drawing represents the
accident; the point at which the line crosses back on itself denotes the time when
the surviving child was left with a neighbor while his parents were at the hospital
with his brother. This was a period of uncertainty and confusion, and the child
was angry about not being with the other members of his family. The point at
which his parents returned and informed him of his brother's death is indicated
by the vertical slash marks, which were literally stabbed onto the paper. The
jagged line connoting the remainder of the day represents the emotional upheaval
that occurred as the child and his parents together focused their attention on
coping with the initial shock of their loss. Importantly, the drawing ends with
an upward slanting line that is indicative of an essentially positive attitude — the
child's ability to deal constructively with his experience of loss. This drawing
demonstrates that even a simple artistic expression, such as a line depicting the
chronology of events, can reveal a wealth of detail about a child's experience of
a traumatic event such as death.

helped bring to light his disturbance at being left out, the parents gained support
by sharing their experience with others who had survived similar experiences.

Helping Children Cope with Change and Loss

As we have seen, change sometimes brings painful experiences into a child's
life. The death of a parent or sibling is a significant loss, as is a personal confrontation with life-threatening illness. How can a parent — or any caring person — help
a child who must come to terms with the experience of loss? In the aftermath of a
close death, what kind of assistance can be offered to a bereaved child? How do
family patterns and styles of communication influence a child's ability to cope
with change and loss?

The Lesson

'Your father's gone,' my bald headmaster said.
His shiny dome and brown tobacco jar
Splintered at once in tears. It wasn't grief.
I cried for knowledge which was bitterer
Than any grief. For there and then I knew
That grief has uses — that a father dead
Could bind the bully's fist a week or two;
And then I cried for shame, then for relief.

I was a month past ten when I learnt this:
I still remember how the noise was stilled
In school-assembly when my grief came in.
Some goldfish in a bowl quietly sculled
Around their shining prison on its shelf.
They were indifferent. All the other eyes
Were turned towards me. Somewhere in myself
Pride, like a goldfish, flashed a sudden fin.

Edward Lucie-Smith

Consider what it feels like for an adult to face the terminal illness or death of someone close. Now, how does this person explain these painful circumstances to a child? Because of the nature of the crisis, perhaps coupled with notions about a child's limited ability to understand, the child's feelings and concerns may be inadvertently dismissed or ignored. Even an adult who recognizes the child's interest or need to know may be uncomfortable about exposing the child to what might be painful and disturbing news. Adults are often concerned that knowing the truth might cause a child more harm than good.

In any event, a child's natural curiosity effectively removes the option of withholding information. Simple concern for the child's feelings dictates that he or she be included in matters affecting emotional well-being. Still, adults find it difficult to talk to children about death until they have had some time to sort out their own feelings and thoughts.

Children seem to cope more easily with their feelings about a close death or the serious illness of a family member when they are allowed to participate in the unfolding experience of grief and bereavement. When they are excluded, or when their questions go unanswered, the resulting uncertainty in the child's mind generates additional anxiety, confusion, and pain. Sharing the reality of what is happening allows a child to begin to understand and cope with the experience.

Being sensitive to a child's natural inquisitiveness and concern about death and dying does not mean that one should overwhelm the child with excessive detail, nor does it mean talking down to the child as if he or she were incapable of comprehending at all. Rather, it implies an openness in responding to the child's concerns within the context of his or her ability to understand. In talking to a child about death or some other crisis, it is important to keep the explanation simple, to stick to basics, and to verify what the child has understood.

Although a child's experience of change and crisis is similar in some respects to an adult's, there are also significant differences. These differences in a child's manner of perceiving, experiencing, and coping with change need to be considered by parents and others who wish to be helpful to children in crisis.

Guidelines for Sharing Information

Recognizing that children are individuals and that their methods of coping with loss may differ, it is possible to suggest guidelines that parents and others can use to advantage. First, it is necessary to acknowledge and accept the child's feelings. Crying, for instance, is a natural response to the loss of someone significant. Admonishing a fearful child to "Be brave!" or "Be a little man and buck up!" denies the validity of the child's spontaneous emotion.

Second, to help a child cope with loss, the adult must strive, as much as possible, to answer the child's questions honestly and directly. Explanations should be truthful to the facts and should be as concrete as possible. Don't overwhelm the child with information that is beyond his or her developmental level.

Religious beliefs can be an important part of a family's understanding of death. If they are, it is only natural that parents will want to share these beliefs with their children. But the child deserves to be told that these are *beliefs*. Care should be taken to express such beliefs in a manner that does not lead to misunderstanding or confuse the child. An adult's religious concepts of an afterlife, for example, may be quite different from what the listening child is able to understand. A child who is told that "God took Daddy to be with him in heaven" may not feel very kindly toward a being who could be so capricious and inconsiderate of the child's feelings. Religious and philosophical concepts of death may confuse and frighten young children whose emphasis on "concreteness" is not well suited for grasping abstractions. (Older children, on the other hand, may gain value from such conceptions, provided these are added to their concrete understanding rather than offered as a replacement for their already-developed death awareness.) Similarly, fairy tales, metaphors, and the like should be avoided or else used with care. Young children tend to take such explanations of death literally.

Foremost among the guidelines for helping children cope with crisis is a willingness to listen. Sometimes we assume that our own experience of the world is shared by others. In fact, though, each of us perceives the world in our own way. Understanding another person's experience requires the art of listening. The aim is to discover what the other person thinks, feels, and believes: What does he or she think is important about this situation? What are the person's concerns, fears, hopes, and anxieties? If a need for support or assistance is expressed, then what specific kind of help is being asked for?

Lament

Listen, children:	Anne shall have the keys
Your father is dead.	To make a pretty noise with.
From his old coats	Life must go on,
I'll make you little jackets;	And the dead be forgotten;
I'll make you little trousers	Life must go on,
From his old pants.	Though good men die;
There'll be in his pockets	Anne, eat your breakfast;
Things he used to put there,	Dan, take your medicine;
Keys and pennies	Life must go on;
Covered with tobacco;	I forget just why.
Dan shall have the pennies	
To save in his bank;	

Edna St. Vincent Millay

These questions are especially important in the case of children. Sometimes children are required to be "unseen and unheard," thus thwarting their natural tendency to explore and grapple with the emotions and thoughts generated by change. Particularly when it disrupts familiar patterns of living, change can result in much confusion and conflict, creating a tangle of emotions and thoughts that is difficult to sort out. Paying attention to a child's behavioral changes is a way to gather information about his or her experience of crisis. Helping a child to know what is happening goes a long way toward providing a basis for coping with change.

When children are asked about their experiences with crisis, many say that the most difficult times came when they did not know what was actually happening. A child whose diagnosis of life-threatening illness was withheld from her by her family said later, "We'd always done everything with each other knowing what was going on. Suddenly that was different. That scared me more than what was happening to my body. It felt like my family was becoming strangers."[19] A sudden change in family communication patterns can be alarming to a child and actually heighten anxiety about the crisis itself.

Even in families that encourage openness, crisis may precipitate breakdowns in communication, as the following story illustrates: A young girl whose mother refused to discuss her illness told a hospital staffer, "I know I'm going to die. I want to talk to Mother, but she won't let me. I know she's hurting, but I'm the one who's dying." When told of this conversation by the staff member, the girl's mother replied angrily, "She wouldn't be thinking of dying if you hadn't made her talk about it."

As the communication between mother and daughter continued to deteriorate, the daughter became increasingly withdrawn. Still refusing to allow her daughter to discuss her feelings about the illness, the mother's communication style finally degenerated into baby talk: "Her doesn't feel goody today . . . her doesn't want to talk." Clearly, the communication style exhibited by this mother and daughter wasn't helping either to cope with the predicament. Because of lack of openness, the normal human needs for affection and reassurance could not be satisfactorily met.

We can picture communication styles occupying a continuum that ranges from encouraging the child's participation in all facets of the crisis to trying to keep reality hidden from the child. The best gauge of a child's readiness to be informed about a potentially painful situation is the child's own interest, usually expressed through questions. Using the child's own questions as a guide, we can give straightforward and honest answers without burdening the child with facts irrelevant for his or her understanding of the situation. Above all, the child needs to be reassured that he or she is loved.

Using Books as Tools for Coping

One way for adults to explore the subject of death with children is through books. In recent years, publishers have brought out an increasing number of children's books concerned with dying, death, and bereavement. Of the books for children and young adults dealing with these topics, about two-thirds are works of fiction featuring death or dying as a primary theme.

Books for children deal with various losses involving significant relationships — parents, grandparents, siblings, other relatives and friends, as well as pets. Books can even be found dealing with the seldom seen topic of the death of a child's mother. Bibliotherapy — that is, the use of books as an aid to coping — can facilitate communication between an adult and a child and create an opportunity to talk about feelings and experiences. For example, a four-year-old whose father has died can view a picture book such as *Everett Anderson's Good-Bye*, which depicts a young boy's feelings about his father's death, and be encouraged to talk about his or her own feelings. An adult might ask, "What else do you think someone like Everett might do or say when feeling angry about his father's death?"

The therapeutic value of reading books describing how a protagonist successfully faces death is not limited to younger children. Stories can suggest additional choices for readers of any age, adults as well as children. In situations wherein death has recently occurred or is expected, the selection of an appropriate book may give adults and children an opportunity to begin talking about each other's experiences (see Figure 8-3).

When a Family Member Has a Life-Threatening Illness

When a member of the child's family is seriously ill, family routine will be disrupted. If the family's style of communication is closed, or if a child is kept from learning the truth about a parent's or sibling's illness, the well child may become confused as to the reasons for changes in the family's usual patterns of interaction. It may seem to the child that he or she is rejected, left out of family

Bibliographies

Hazel B. Benson. *The Dying Child: An Annotated Bibliography*. Westport, Conn.: Greenwood Press, 1988.

Joanne E. Bernstein. *Books to Help Children Cope with Separation and Loss*. New York: R. R. Bowker, 1977.

Marian S. Pyles. *Death and Dying in Children's and Young People's Literature*. Jefferson, N.C.: McFarland, 1988.

Hannelore Wass and Charles A. Corr, eds. *Helping Children Cope with Death: Guidelines and Resources*. Washington, D.C.: Hemisphere, 1982.

Books for Children

Chana Byars Abells. *The Children We Remember*. New York: Greenwillow, 1986. Combines text and photographs from the Yad Vashem Archives to chronicle the story of Jewish children during the Holocaust.

Alice Bach. *Waiting for Johnny Miracle*. New York: Harper and Row, 1980. The story of a teenager's experience with cancer and the emotional reactions of the patient, her family, and her friends.

Marion Dane Bauer. *On My Honor*. New York: Clarion, 1986. The story of a boy's feelings of guilt over the role he played in the death of his best friend.

Joanne Bernstein and Stephen Gullo. *When People Die*. New York: E. P. Dutton, 1977. An explanation of the feelings and behaviors associated with grief.

Eve Bunting. *The Empty Window*. New York: Frederick Warne, 1980. The young protagonist's experiences with and reactions to a dying friend.

Eve Bunting. *Face at the Edge of the World*. New York: Clarion, 1985. A boy reflects on his friend's last week of life to discover why he committed suicide.

Eve Bunting. *The Happy Funeral*. New York: Harper and Row, 1982. The funeral of a child's Chinese-American grandfather.

Leo Buscaglia. *The Fall of Freddie the Leaf: A Story of Life for All Ages*. Thorofare, N.J.: Charles B. Slack, 1982. The passage of a leaf through the seasons.

Mary Carey. *A Place for Allie*. New York: Dodd, Mead, 1985. A girl comes to terms with her father's death and her mother's resulting concerns with security.

Carol Carrick. *The Accident*. Illustrations by Donald Carrick. New York: Seabury/Clarion, 1976. A young child copes with the death of a pet.

Lucile Clifton. *Everett Anderson's Good-Bye*. Illustrated by Ann Grifalconi. New York: Holt, Rinehart and Winston, 1983. A young boy explores his feelings about the death of his father.

John B. Coburn. *Anne and the Sand Dobbies: A Story About Death for Children and Their Parents*. New York: Seabury Press, 1964. This classic tells how a father answers the questions of his son who has lost both his dog and his younger sister.

Eleanor Coer. *Sadako and the Thousand Paper Cranes*. Illustrations by Ronald Himler. New York: Putnam, 1977. The story of a Japanese girl's illness and death from

continued on next page

Figure *8.3*　*Books for Helping Children Cope with Loss*

continued from previous page

leukemia resulting from the Hiroshima bomb, her courage, and the memorial to her by her classmates and community.

Miriam Cohen. *Jim's Dog Muffins*. Illustrations by Lillian Hoban. New York: Greenwillow/William Morrow, 1984. A friend and a teacher help a boy cope with the loss of his dog.

Elizabeth Corley. *Tell Me About Death, Tell Me About Funerals*. Illustrations by Philip Pecorado. Santa Clara, Calif.: Grammatical Sciences, 1973. Information about funerals is presented in a comforting manner to a girl whose grandfather has died.

Tomie DePaola. *Nana Upstairs and Nana Downstairs*. New York: Penguin, 1978. A boy learns to face the eventual deaths of his grandmother and great-grandmother.

Elfie Donnelly. *So Long, Grandpa*. New York: Crown, 1981. A Viennese boy learns to cope with the illness and death of his grandfather.

Carol J. Farley. *The Garden Is Doing Fine*. New York: Atheneum, 1975. A girl learns to accept the reality that her father is dying.

Jason Gaes. *My Book for Kids with Cansur: A Child's Autobiography of Hope*. Aberdeen, S.D.: Melius and Peterson, 1987. A boy's gift to other children with cancer.

Mordicai Gerstein. *The Mountains of Tibet*. New York: Harper and Row, 1987. Inspired by the Tibetan Book of the Dead, this illustrated tale uses the theme of reincarnation to tell the story of a Tibetan woodcutter who, after dying, is given the choice of going to paradise or living another life anywhere in the universe.

Barbara Girion. *A Tangle of Roots*. New York: Charles Scribner's Sons, 1979. A mother's sudden death and the daughter's readjustment following the loss.

Charlotte Graeber. *Mustard*. Illustrations by Donna Diamond. New York: Macmillan, 1982. A young boy deals with the increasing infirmity and eventual death of a cat that had been part of the family since before he was born.

Earl Grollman. *Talking About Death: A Dialogue Between Parent and Child*. 3d ed. Boston: Beacon Press, 1990. A nonfiction explanation about death.

Bernice Hogan. *My Grandmother Died*. Illustrations by Nancy Munger. Nashville: Abingdon, 1983. A young boy learns to cope with the finality of his grandmother's death by maintaining his memories of her.

Lyn Littlefield Hoopes. *Nana*. New York: Harper and Row, 1981. A grandmother's death.

Hadley Irwin. *So Long at the Fair*. New York: McElderry-Macmillan, 1988. Joel Logan, a high school senior, finds that he must remember and work through the past to come to terms with the suicidal death of his girlfriend.

Nancy Jewell. *Time for Uncle Joe*. New York: Harper and Row, 1981. Memories of a deceased uncle.

Mary Kate Jordan. *Losing Uncle Tim*. Niles, Ill.: Albert Whitman, 1989. When a young boy's uncle dies of AIDS, he strives for reassurance and understanding and finds that his favorite grown-up has left him a legacy of joy and courage.

M. E. Kerr. *Night Kites*. New York: Harper and Row, 1986. A teenage boy grapples with the discovery that his older brother is dying of AIDS.

Jill Krementz. *How It Feels When a Parent Dies*. New York: Knopf, 1981. A photographic essay with children's descriptions of their experiences.

Matthew Lancaster. *Hang Tough*. New York: Paulist Press, 1985. The experiences of a ten-year-old boy dying of cancer.

Madeleine L'Engle. *A Ring of Endless Light*. New York: Farrar, Straus & Giroux, 1980. A teenage girl copes with the experience of loss, grief, and terminal illness by discovering underlying spiritual and moral dimensions.

Eda LeShan. *Learning to Say Goodbye: When a Parent Dies*. New York: Macmillan, 1976. Nonfiction.

Wendy Lichtman. *Blew and the Death of the Mag*. Illustrated by Diane Mayers. Albion, Calif.: Freestone Publishing, 1975. A beautifully written story that describes a young girl's experience of grief resulting from the death of her closest companion.

Norma Fox Mazer. *After the Rain*. New York: William Morrow, 1987. The after-school visits of fifteen-year-old Rachel with her dying grandfather begin as a chore and gradually become a central part of her life as she shares his final days.

Gloria H. McLendon. *My Brother Joey Died*. Photographs by Harvey Kelman. New York: Simon & Schuster, 1982. The issues surrounding a sibling's death as told from the perspective of a nine-year-old.

Miska Miles. *Annie and the Old One*. Illustrations by Peter Parnall. Boston: Little, Brown, 1971. The story of a Navajo girl's efforts to prevent the inevitable by unraveling each day's weaving on a rug whose completion she fears will bring her grandmother's death.

Jane Mobley. *The Star Husband*. Illustrations by Anna Vojtech. New York: Doubleday, 1979. This adaptation of a Native American myth affirms the natural cycle of life, death, and rebirth.

Walter Dean Myers. *Fallen Angels*. New York: Scholastic, 1988. The gritty and heart-rending story of Richie Perry, just out of high school, who enlists in the Army and spends a devastating year in Vietnam.

Herbert Neiberg and Arlene Fisher. *Pet Loss: A Thoughtful Guide for Adults and Children*. New York: Harper and Row, 1982.

Linda Peavy. *Allison's Grandfather*. Illustrations by Ronald Himler. New York: Charles Scribner's Sons, 1981. A young child reflects upon her friend's grandfather's death.

Joan Phipson. *A Tide Flowing*. New York: Atheneum, 1981. A boy finds means to cope with crises despite his mother's death and his father's rejection.

Barbra Ann Porte. *Harry's Mom*. Illustrations by Yossi Abolafia. New York: Greenwillow/Morrow, 1985. A story for young children about a mother's death.

Elizabeth Richter. *Losing Someone You Love: When a Brother or Sister Dies*. New York: G. P. Putnam's Sons, 1986. The experience of sibling loss as related in interviews with young people.

Ann Rinaldi. *Term Paper*. New York: Walker and Company, 1980. A father's sudden death and a child's subsequent feelings of responsibility for the death.

Fred Rogers. *When a Pet Dies*. New York: G. P. Putnam's Sons, 1988. Portrays a family whose dog dies and another family whose cat dies; the grieving children ask questions of their parents and adjust to their losses.

continued on next page

continued from previous page

James Shott. *The House Across the Street*. Nashville: Winston-Derek, 1988. A young girl befriends an elderly neighbor whose daughter died twenty years before, and the resulting encounter helps in resolving the unresolved grief of her newfound friend as well as her grief at losing her grandmother.

Anne Warren Smith. *Sister in the Shadow*. New York: Atheneum, 1986. During a summer job as a mother's helper, a young girl is confronted by the effects of an earlier experience of crib death on the family's patterns and relationships.

Sara Bonnett Stein. *About Dying: An Open Family Book for Parents and Children Together*. New York: Walker and Company, 1974. A story about death composed of parallel texts providing basic information for children and supplemental information for adults.

Yukio Tsuchiya. *Faithful Elephants: A True Story of Animals, People, and War*. Boston: Houghton Mifflin, 1988. A poignant story of the horror of war and its effect on animals and people.

Susan Varley. *Badger's Parting Gifts*. New York: Lothrop, Lee and Shepard, 1984. The story of an old dog's dying and the grieving of those who loved him.

Judith Viorst. *The Tenth Good Thing About Barney*. Illustrations by Erik Blegvad. New York: Atheneum, 1971. A boy thinks of the ten best things about his pet cat, who has died.

Isle-Margret Vogel. *My Twin Sister Erika*. New York: Harper and Row, 1976. The death of a sibling.

E. B. White. *Charlotte's Web*. Illustrations by Garth Williams. New York: Harper and Row, 1952. This classic story describes the grief experienced at the death of a close friend—Charlotte, a spider—and the continuing of life through her offspring.

Paul Zindel. *The Pigman's Legacy*. New York: Harper and Row, 1980. The memory of a dead friend.

Charlotte Zolotow. *My Grandson Lew*. New York: Harper and Row, 1974. Lew learns the value of memories of his deceased grandfather.

Charlotte Zolotow. *If You Listen*. New York: Harper and Row, 1980. A mother reassures a child of her father's love.

activities, or ignored for no apparent reason. The well child may wonder, "Why are my parents so nice to my sister, but they ignore me all the time!" or "Geez, I get into trouble about every little thing while my brother gets off scot-free no matter what he does!"

Although openness is an important condition for helping a child to cope with the crisis, once again, explanations must be suited to the child's cognitive abilities. For example, a very young child whose parent is seriously ill might be told simply that "Mommy has an ouch in her tummy which the doctors are trying

Mark Boster, AP/Wide World Photos

These young girls pay a final vist to a slain classmate, who died at age twelve because of a senseless act of violence. Feelings of grief may be mixed with feelings of dread and fear, the recognition that death can come at any time and to anyone, regardless of age. Whether caused by an abrupt act of violence or by prolonged illness, the experience of death in children's lives may elicit this awareness of mortality.

to fix." A school-age child, on the other hand, might be given a more complex explanation to the effect that the parent needs medical treatment because something is growing in her stomach that doesn't belong there.

A child who is aware of a parent's or sibling's illness will probably feel anxiety, which may be manifest in various ways. For example, a child may be angry because "Mommy isn't here," yet feel guilty because of imagined notions about "causing the illness." To help balance these conflicting feelings, the child can be urged to participate in comforting the sick person in ways that are appropriate. A child might pick a bouquet or make a small drawing as a gift. This activity allows affirmation and expression of love and kindness despite possible feelings of anger or guilt.

Siblings who feel neglected because the family's attention is devoted more and more to a sick brother or sister may resent the adjustments they have to make in their lives. They may also experience sadness, anger, denial, and fear. The well child can be helped to balance such conflicting emotions by being accepted as a participating family member, given information about the crisis, and encouraged to be part of the family's process of dealing with the sibling's illness.[20] When the well child is included in these ways, there is a greater likelihood that family communication will be maintained and that the family routine will seem more normal. Myra Bluebond-Langner has aptly said: "The well siblings of terminally ill children live in houses of chronic sorrow."[21] Although children cannot be protected from the reality of death, their experiences of it can be made less traumatic when they receive sensitive, caring support from those closest to them.

Support Groups for Children

Many of the organizations dedicated to providing support during crises of serious illness and bereavement emphasize caring for all members of a family, including the children. The Compassionate Friends, for instance, not only provides support to bereaved parents but has related programs designed to help their surviving children cope with the loss of a sibling. Other support groups, such as the Center for Attitudinal Healing, have a primary focus on the ill child, although typically there are auxiliary programs involving other family members. Organizations such as these may be local or national in scope.

Another type of support organization for children with life-threatening illness involves volunteers, numbering from a few individuals to several hundred, who seek to grant the wishes of children with a limited prognosis. The Sunshine Foundation, founded in 1976, along with the Brass Ring Society and the Starlight Foundation, both formed in 1983, are examples of such organizations.[22] Through the efforts of such groups, children and their families may be given the opportunity to take a vacation together or to fulfill some wish that otherwise seems impossible.

Community support represents an important adjunct to the family's own support system. Organizations like those mentioned help not only the child who is seriously ill or bereaved but also the parents and other adults who are experiencing corresponding losses.

Further Readings

Sol Altschul, ed. *Childhood Bereavement and Its Aftermath*. Madison, Conn.: International Universities Press, 1988.

Erma Bombeck. *I Want to Grow Hair, I Want to Grow Up, I Want to Go to Boise: Children Surviving Cancer*. New York: Harper and Row, 1989.

John Bowlby. *The Making and Breaking of Affectional Bonds*. London: Tavistock, 1979.

Robert W. Buckingham. *Care of the Dying Child: A Practical Guide for Those Who Help Others*. New York: Continuum, 1989.

Center for Attitudinal Healing. *There Is a Rainbow Behind Every Dark Cloud*. Millbrae, Calif.: Celestial Arts, 1978.

Charles A. Corr and Joan N. McNeil, eds. *Adolescence and Death*. New York: Springer, 1986.

Erna Furman. *A Child's Parent Dies: Studies in Childhood Bereavement*. New Haven, Conn.: Yale University Press, 1974.

Robert A. Furman. "The Child's Reaction to Death in the Family," in *Loss and Grief: Psychological Management in Medical Practice*, edited by Bernard Schoenberg, et al., pp. 70–86. New York: Columbia University Press, 1970.

Karen Gravelle and Charles Haskins. *Teenagers Face to Face with Bereavement*. Englewood Cliffs, N.J.: Julian Messner, 1989.

Jo-Eileen Gyulay. *The Dying Child*. New York: McGraw-Hill, 1978.

William J. Kay, ed. *Pet Loss and Human Bereavement*. Ames: Iowa State University Press, 1984.

Tolbert McCarroll. *Morning Glory Babies: Children with AIDS and the Celebration of Life*. New York: St. Martin's Press, 1988.

Chris Oyler, Laurie Becklund, and Beth Polson. *Go Towards the Light*. New York: Harper and Row, 1988.

Helen Rosen. *Unspoken Grief: Coping with Childhood Sibling Loss*. Lexington, Mass.: Lexington Books, 1985.

John E. Schowalter, et al., eds. *The Child and Death*. New York: Columbia University Press, 1983.

Holding their dead baby, this Harlem couple finds comfort in the sharing of their memories and their grief as they acknowledge the death of their firstborn child. Of all the losses that can be experienced during adult life, most people feel that the death of a child is the most painful.

C H A P T E R 9

Death in the Lives of Adults

*J*ust as human development does not stop with childhood's end, the patterns of coping with loss continue to evolve throughout a person's lifespan. Even when the circumstances of bereavement are outwardly similar, a person's response to loss depends on many factors, not least of which is age. Although the *event* of a parent's death, for example, may occur during childhood or adulthood, the *experience* will differ at each developmental period. Furthermore, adult life entails losses that happen only during maturity. The death of a spouse occurs in the context of marriage, the death of a child in the context of family and the childbearing and child-rearing years.

If we define stress as any stimulus that requires an organism to adapt, surviving the death of someone close to us clearly fits within that framework. Thus, loss can be viewed as a type of environmental stress affecting human beings. Although the death of a loved one is the most obvious loss we are likely to experience, stress also results from losses that occur in connection with other major life changes — such as marriage, divorce, the birth of a child, moving to a new home, graduation from school, or getting a new job. Just as we can associate distinct developmental tasks and abilities with children of varying ages, so, too, we can distinguish distinctive phases and transitions during adult life.

Psychosocial Stages of Adulthood: A Developmental Perspective

In Chapter 3, we discussed the first five stages of psychosocial development proposed by Erik Erikson—namely, those pertaining to the years of childhood and adolescence. The last three stages of psychosocial development, according to this model, occur during adulthood. As in childhood, each stage of adult life requires a particular developmental response, and each stage builds upon previous ones.

Young adulthood, the first of these adult stages, is represented by the conflict between intimacy and isolation. This stage involves various forms of commitment and interaction, including sex, friendship, cooperation, partnership, and affiliation. Because mature love takes the risk of commitment, as contrasted with the self-absorbed and self-reflective love of adolescence, the death of a loved one may be most devastating during this stage and the next.[1] In a study conducted by Louis LaGrand of losses experienced by college students, more than three-quarters involved the loss of a significant other either by death or by separation resulting from the end of a friendship, the dissolution of a love relationship, or divorce.[2]

The next psychosocial stage, says Erikson, is *adulthood*, which involves the crisis of generativity versus stagnation. This stage is characterized by a widening commitment to take care of the persons, things, and ideas one has learned to care for. This emphasis on care helps explain why the death of a child is so painful. Symbolically and actually, a child's death is opposed to the nurturitive psychosocial task of adulthood.

When we reach the stage of *maturity*, the eighth and final stage of the life cycle, according to Erikson, the turning point or crisis to be resolved is that of integrity versus despair. Viewing all the developmental phases as connected, with each building on the ones before, the crisis of this stage is especially powerful. This last phase is marked by the end of our "one given course of life." Successfully negotiating this last developmental task gives us the strength of wisdom, which Erikson describes as "informed and detached concern with life itself in the face of death itself."[3]

Loss Experiences in Adulthood

Keeping this developmental perspective in mind, the remainder of this chapter will focus on specific loss experiences occurring during adult life. You may find it useful to consider the losses that have occurred in your own life, both as a child and as an adult. How have they differed, and in what ways are they similar? Have others responded to your experiences of loss in supportive ways? What coping mechanisms were you able to bring into play to move through the experience successfully? Questions of this kind can form a framework for examining typical losses in adult life.

Mickey Sanborn, U.S. Air Force Photo

Among the most poignant losses that can be experienced in adult life are those related to war. The Vietnam Veterans' Memorial in Washington, D.C., is a focal point for coping with the grief of individual as well as national losses. For many who fought the war, as well as for other survivors, the effects are pervasive and felt daily. Here, visitors reflect on the names of individuals engraved on the face of the black wall of the Memorial, following its official dedication in November 1982.

Last Words

Goethe's mother (1808): (To a servant girl bringing an invitation to a party) "Say that Frau Goethe is unable to come, she is busy dying at the moment."

Beethoven (1827): "I shall hear in Heaven."

Hegel (1831): "Only one man ever understood me . . . And he didn't understand me."

Palmerston (1865): "Die, my dear Doctor? — That's the last thing I shall do!"

Gertrude Stein (1946): "What is the answer?" After a short silence she laughed and added, "Then what is the question?"

Gide (1951): "I am afraid my sentences are becoming grammatically incorrect."

The Oxford Book of Death, edited by D. J. Enright

Individual Differences in Meaning of Death and Coping Styles

Studying losses experienced by college students, Louis LaGrand found that events some students considered to be major losses — such as course failure, death of a pet, or suspension of a roommate from school — were viewed by others as less significant. This disparity does not mean that students in the first group were wrong, that their losses weren't so important after all. Neither does it indicate that the other students were insensitive and unfeeling. It does underscore the fact that a person's *interpretation* of loss, its personal meaning in his or her own life, determines its relative significance.

The aspects of death that make us fearful or anxious also differ among individuals. For instance, even though a butcher and a funeral director are both involved in jobs with death-related implications, they may each feel comfortable with their own, but not the other's, work.[4] Similarly, the attitudes a person has toward the prospect of his or her own death reflect individual differences, and these attitudes change over the course of life and depending upon circumstances. If death seems a remote possibility, an event not expected to occur for many years,

T A B L E 9–1   *Some Reasons Given by Aged Persons for Accepting Death*

Death is preferable to inactivity.

Death is preferable to the loss of the ability to be useful.

Death is preferable to becoming a burden.

Death is preferable to loss of mental faculties.

Death is preferable to living with progressively deteriorating physical health and concomitant physical discomfort.

Source: Adapted from Victor W. Marshall, *Last Chapters: A Sociology of Aging and Dying* (Monterey, Calif.: Brooks/Cole, 1980), pp. 169–177.

What Personnel Handbooks Never Tell You

They leave a lot out of the personnel handbooks.
Dying, for instance.
You can find funeral leave
but you can't find dying.
You can't find what to do
when a guy you've worked with since you both
    were pups
looks you in the eye
and says something about hope and chemotherapy.
No phrases,
no triplicate forms,
no rating systems.
Seminars won't do it
and it's too late for a new policy on sabbaticals.

They don't tell you about eye contact
and how easily it slips away
when a woman who lost a breast
says, "They didn't get it all."
You can find essays on motivation
but the business schools
don't teach what the good manager says
to keep people taking up the slack
while someone steals a little more time
at the hospital.
There's no help from those tapes
you pop into the player
while you drive or jog.
They'd never get the voice right.

And this poem won't help either.
You just have to figure it out for yourself,
and don't ever expect to do it well.

James A. Autry

the thought may cause little alarm or concern. When a medical checkup reveals the presence of a life-threatening illness, however, the response may be otherwise. The meaning of death is also usually interpreted differently as a person ages. Failing health, for example, is among the reasons given by some aged persons for preferring death to continued existence (see Table 9-1). A study by Gesser, Wong, and Reker found that "fear of death/dying was relatively high among the young, peaked during middle age and fell to its lowest point among the elderly."[5] Although the old generally appear to fear death less than do younger people, individual differences remain important throughout the lifespan. Also, although death is perceived as normal and acceptable in old age, *choosing* death is less acceptable for the aged than for younger persons.[6] Thus, the relative absence of death anxiety, or fear of death, among the old should not be interpreted as an acceptance of euthanasia, or of actively taking steps to shorten one's life.

In addition to interpreting the significance of losses and the meaning of death in distinctive ways, individuals use various ways of coping. Variability in coping styles—from acceptance to drug intoxication—was noted as one of the most revealing features of student reactions to loss in the study mentioned. Social support, especially talking about the loss with others, was typically important in resolving grief. Successfully handled, the experience of loss can result in meaningful learnings and positive changes of attitude.

Think about the experiences of your life and those of other adults you know. Notice the range of losses that come to mind. Some of these losses may be associated with the major causes of death among adults. Among the middle-aged, for instance, deaths from accidents, suicides, and homicides take a significant toll; for the older population, death usually results from weakened physiological defenses.

Aging and the Incidence of Loss

Although many illnesses and disabilities are most common among persons in the seventh or eighth decade of life or older, the probability of dying increases steadily as we grow older. Aging doesn't begin at fifty, or sixty-five, or eighty-five. Already, at this very moment, we are all aging.

Besides the experience of nearing our own death, the usual order of nature dictates that our experiences of others' deaths also increase as we grow older. Children become seriously ill, and some die. Relationships come to an end, suddenly or perhaps over a long period due to chronic illness. Growing older also increases the chances that an individual will experience the death of his or her parents, and, conversely, that a parent may experience the death of an adult child. Eventually, we may find it impossible to care adequately for ourselves. Leaving one's own home to live with strangers, sharing the surroundings of institutional care, may bring a loss of virtually everything familiar acquired over a lifetime.

"Bloom County," drawing by Berke Breathed, © 1984 by Washington Post Writers Group

Parental Bereavement

What is the difference between a child's death and that of an adult? Think about a child being diagnosed as terminally ill, or suddenly dead. What makes the loss of a child a high-grief death? To most of us, the death of a child connotes the unfinished, the untimely loss of a potential future. Perhaps the parents envisioned the child playing on the local youth soccer team, graduating from school, getting married, raising children—all the various milestones and occasions that comprise a sense of continuity into the future. Plans and hopes for the child's life are ended by death. We expect that a child will outlive his or her parents. A child carries something of the parent into the future, even after the parent's death. In this sense, a child's very existence grants a kind of immortality to the parent, and this is taken away when the child dies.

If parenting is defined as the task of raising a child to the age of self-sufficiency, a bereaved parent may feel that he or she has failed. The special interdependency between parent and child makes the death of a child a deep experience of loss. Mourning may be focused on issues of parental responsibility. People generally define parenting as protecting and nurturing a child until he or she can act independently in the world. If mourning parents hold such a definition, the death of a child is experienced as the ultimate lack of protection and nurture, the ultimate breakdown and failure in being a "good parent."

Among the Cree of North America, infants were often given "ghost-protective" moccasins to wear. Holes were cut in the bottom of the moccasins as a means of safeguarding the baby from death. If the spirit of an ancestor appeared and beckoned, the infant could refuse to go, pointing out that his or her moccasins "needed mending."[7] Such feelings about the parental role of safeguarding a child are universal, and parents expend considerable effort in seeking to guarantee a child's safety and welfare.

Many of the issues of parental bereavement span the life cycle. They are present for forty-year-old parents and for eighty-year-old parents. They are experienced by parents of grown-up children as well as by parents of babies. A parent's fantasies and plans can be just as strong for an unborn infant as for an older child. But to understand completely the nature of parental bereavement and the range of losses involved, both the age of the parent and the age of the child are significant. A sixty-five-year-old divorced or widowed mother may feel considerable loss of security when her thirty-five-year-old child dies suddenly. One such woman said repeatedly: "He was going to take care of me when I got old; now I have no one." Whether or not her son would have indeed taken on the responsibility she envisioned, his death represented the loss of *her* imagined future.

Parental bereavement is a powerful experience that relates to both socio-biological and psychological explanations of human grief. Studies of human bonding and the dynamics of family systems, as well as psychoanalytic notions about the presence of "inner representations" that exist between parents and children, all contribute to a comprehensive model of parental grief.[8] It is in appreciating the uniqueness of the parent-child relationship that we begin to understand the unique grief that is experienced at the death of a child. Given the biological, social, and psychological dynamics that form the bond between parent and child, resolving the grief experienced at the loss of a child is truly a family affair.[9]

Coping with Parental Bereavement as a Couple

In counseling bereaved parents, clinicians often note the presence of a kind of "general chaos." Frequently, a directionlessness sets in, part of a pervasive sense that the parents have been robbed of a past and a future. The prevailing attitude may be one of "do it now." Sexual acting out is not uncommon during parental bereavement. The attitudes and behaviors of parents after a child's death reflect the reality of being overwhelmed, which helps explain the incidence of marital disruption and divorce among bereaved parents.

With such a traumatic event, parents are expected to provide support to each other. But the energy expended by each partner in dealing with his or her own grief may deplete the emotional resources needed to provide mutual support. Some bereaved parents report that, in addition to losing a child, they felt they had lost their spouse for a time. In her study of marital couples who experienced the fetal or infant death of a child, Kathleen Gilbert noted that, for many couples, the available social support outside the marriage was directed toward the wife, while the husband was expected to be strong: "Men spoke of the stress of maintaining the family, facing financial worries, going to work, and being expected 'to produce one hundred percent' while at the same time facing the prospect of serving as the only support for their wives."[10] In a study by Bach-Hughes and Page-Lieberman focusing specifically on fathers who had experienced a perinatal loss, the fathers described the period following bereavement "as an intensely active time involving confirmation of the death, managing the physical process of labor and delivery, notifying the extended family and friends of the death and delivery event, and managing the mother's psychological state as well as their own feelings as fathers."[11] Many fathers spoke of suppressing or "storing" their own feelings as they helped their wives through the experience and attended to other details of the initial period following the loss. They tended to describe what they saw and did rather than what they felt.

As individuals, parents likely have different grieving styles, which can leave each of them feeling isolated and unsupported by the only other person in the world who shares the magnitude of the loss. Some data as well as clinical accounts suggest that bereaved spouses may grieve "out of synch" with one another, although a recent study by Bohannon found "no evidence that husbands and wives grieve in an obvious asynchronous or roller coaster pattern."[12] Nevertheless, even though they share the same loss, individual beliefs and expectations give rise to conflicts in styles of coping with the loss, possibly reducing the sense of "commonality" in a couple's grief experience.[13]

For example, in some way, each parent experiences a different "symbolic loss." In the case of fetal or infant death, a mother has a stronger physical attachment to the child and, based on the reality of daily contact with the developing child, is likely to begin making plans for the child sooner than does a father. The individual *experience* of loss also differs. Mothers who lose a child during pregnancy or near birth have to deal with the related changes occurring in their bodies. Another factor affecting the sense of commonality in a couple's grief experience has to do with their view of themselves as a *couple*. The marital roles previously enacted may prove inadequate in the face of the disruptions caused by traumatic grief.

A number of factors having to do with what each partner perceives as "appropriate" or "incongruent" grieving can be important in how couples are able to provide mutual support. Gilbert found that "in a majority of couples the partners could not agree on the most appropriate way to regain a sense of stability and meaning in life" following the loss. There was also disagreement about how to handle emotions. Indeed, this sense of incongruent grieving is generally acknowledged to be the primary source of conflict among bereaved couples. Despite the desire and expectation of each partner to "go through grief" together, differences in grieving styles may give rise to questions about whether one's partner is behaving appropriately. In this regard, a particular source of conflict centers on each partner's *interpretation* of the other's behavior. For example, a father who tries to contain his grief so as to "be there" for his spouse may be perceived by the spouse as cold and unfeeling. The intention to be caring and protective may be misinterpreted, causing mistaken notions about the meaning of the behavior and leading to conflict rather than comfort. Disagreements arise not only about the emotional manifestations of grief and the methods for coping with it, but also about what constitutes correct mourning behavior, the public display of grief.

There are also factors that work to reduce conflict between grieving couples and help promote positive interactions. Foremost among these is the ability to engage in open and honest communication. Based on the responses in her study, Gilbert reports that "exchanging information increased a sense of mutuality and understanding," and notes that "the ability to convey accurate information was useful in answering immediate questions as well as those that occurred later as the couple attempted to make sense of the death." Furthermore, "the ability to cry together and display deep emotions in each other's company" was frequently perceived as helpful toward resolving the loss. Each partner's emotional expression of loss can aid in validating the reality of the other's perceptions of loss. The ability to simply listen to a spouse's expression of deep emotion is very meaningful, as is the ability to express support through nonverbal cues and signals.

One of the most distinctive characteristics of couples who reported little conflict was the positive view that each held of the other and of their relationship. The ability to accept individual differences and to be flexible about their role relationships were among the factors that contributed to sharing each other's grief. Gilbert notes that an extremely helpful method for coming to terms with a spouse's behavior is "the ability of partners to reframe each other's behavior in a positive light." For example, a father who had previously experienced his mate's sobbing as "breaking down" can come to see it as emotionally cleansing. Rather than judging a spouse's behavior as unhelpful or inappropriate, reframing makes it possible to explain the behavior in more positive terms. Seeing a behavior as

The items placed around the grave of this infant in Hawaii—balloons, flowers, and jars of baby food—bespeak the parents' loss and acknowledge the enduring bonds of even a short-lived relationship.

providing emotional release allows a mate to support the expression instead of trying to curtail it by urging the spouse to "get it together." As always in relationships, it is often the "little things" that spouses do that make their partners feel supported and important.

Childbearing Losses

Pregnancy represents a major life transition for adults. The expected result is the birth of a viable, healthy baby. Miscarriage, induced abortion, stillbirth, and neonatal death are not the anticipated outcomes of pregnancy. Yet, during 1986, nearly 68,000 fetal and infant deaths were recorded in the United States, with about 43 percent of these deaths having been stillbirths, another 37 percent neonatal deaths, and the remaining 20 percent post-neonatal deaths.[14]

According to medical definition, *stillbirth* refers to fetal death that occurs between the twentieth week of gestation (pregnancy) and the time of birth, resulting in the delivery of a dead child. *Neonatal* deaths are those that occur during the first four weeks following birth. In the statistics given above, *post-neonatal* deaths include those that occur after the first four weeks and up to eleven months following birth.

The statistics cited above do not include fetal deaths in connection with *miscarriage*, which occurs prior to the twentieth week of gestation. Miscarriage, also termed *spontaneous abortion*, is defined as "loss of the products of conception before the fetus is viable."[15] The distinction between miscarriage and stillbirth is based on the logic that most fetuses are viable — that is, able to survive outside the mother's body — after the twentieth week of pregnancy. It is estimated that about 20 percent of all pregnancies end in miscarriage, with about three-quarters of these ending before twelve weeks.[16] In contrast to spontaneous abortion, which occurs naturally, *induced abortion* (sometimes called artificial or therapeutic abortion) is brought about intentionally, with the aim of ending a pregnancy by mechanical means or drugs.

Although this section focuses primarily on pregnancy and perinatal losses, reproductive loss also occurs as a result of infertility and sterility. Whereas *infertility* refers to "diminished or absent capacity to produce offspring," *sterility* denotes "complete inability to produce offspring," due either to inability to conceive (female) or to induce conception (male).[17] Although most couples are able to produce children without undue difficulty, it is nonetheless true that "some manage only after years of disappointment and some not at all."[18] Despite the quite considerable advances in medical treatment for infertility, a substantial number of couples must ultimately face the fact that they will remain childless, their biological and social urges to reproduce thwarted by forces beyond their control.

Giving up a child for *adoption* is yet another example of reproductive loss. Releasing a child to be raised by other than the biological parents might not initially be thought of as a childbearing loss since this circumstance results from choice. Nevertheless, grief accompanies such a decision. Unrecognized, unsupported, and unresolved, the grief from such a loss can have a deep emotional effect on the birth parents. For such parents, seeing a child at play or walking down the street may spur a reaction of wondering what one's own child might be like at that age. In a very real sense, it is mourning an unlived life in that the birth parent has no relationship with the child as he or she grows to maturity. Recognizing adoption as a type of childbearing loss, some communities now offer grief support for birth parents.

All these reproductive or childbearing losses involve the reality of mourning unlived lives. Judith Savage says: "Childbearing losses are mourned not only for what was, but also for what might have been."[19] Grief is felt not only for the physical loss, but also for symbolic losses. In the process, survivors mourn "the child of the imagination, that part of themselves which seems now to have no possibility of embodiment in the world." Writing from the perspective of a Jungian psychologist who, by the age of thirty-three, had experienced multiple losses (her adoptive and biological parents, her two brothers, and her infant son), Savage reports that she chose "to examine the intrapsychic, symbolic rule of the unconscious in bereavement," for "it is in the unconscious that attachments endure." She says:

> By unraveling the mystery of the imaginative relationship, that is, the projections of the self onto the unborn child, it becomes clear that primary relationships are not composed merely of interchangeable functional attributes and roles but are uniquely personal bonds that are generated from deep within and are as much a reflection of the individual soul as they are an accurate reflection of the other.[20]

Thus, within the mourning process, it is important to become aware of two distinct yet related realities: the *actual* relationship and the *symbolic* nature of the parent-child bond. Grieving parents often talk about lost companionship, lost dreams — all the ways in which a particular child would have enriched their lives. Such talk is concerned with the actual loss. The symbolic loss relates to the meaning attached to the relationship, as when an individual, by parenting a child, becomes a nurturing, supportive guide. As one bereaved father said, "Not only have I lost a son who might follow in my footsteps, but, without him, I have no feet." As his recovery progressed, it was important for him to acknowledge and mourn both the loss of his son and the loss of meaning and purpose in his life.

When a person's identity as a nurturing parent has been thwarted, healing the grief requires honoring the archetypal bonds of parent and child. Simply put, an archetype is a basic form that takes shape from our experiences as human beings. Myth, legend, and history shape our understanding of such archetypal forms. In the context of parental bereavement, the archetypal child occupies polar opposites: the divine child (one who is all good) and the terrible child (one who is all bad). Within the experience of childbearing loss, the image of the lost child activates powerful associations. Apprehending the archetypal meaning is essential to recovery.

Therefore, following the model suggested by Savage, the task of mourning involves merging the "archetypal child" with the actual child. This frees up psychic energy and transforms the search for the "external object" into an inner search whereby "the meanings attached to the child are made conscious," with the result that "those attributes which were feared permanently lost are regained and the parent can return to life with hope, imagination, trust, and an openness toward experience."[21] In this way, the loss is neither denied nor minimized; instead, it becomes part of a natural psychological process that guides one's own journey toward wholeness and expansion.

The grief and mourning that parents experience following a perinatal loss is as devastating as the loss of an older loved one.[22] Furthermore, the grief experienced when such a loss occurs may be influenced by the parents' perceptions that their loss is not understood or really acknowledged by others.[23] Parents report insensitive comments, such as "It must be easier since you didn't get too attached." Self-esteem suffers when a parent is unable to complete the act of sexual reproduction. Blame for this failure can be turned inward as well as directed outward. Questions about the cause of the tragedy abound: Was it that glass of wine, the aspirin, or, as one mother asked in desperation, "Was it the nutmeg I put on my oatmeal?" The most inconsequential actions may be evaluated in this manner.

Anger is a common response of the newly bereaved. Physicians, nurses, and other health personnel are blamed. Anger may be directed toward the other parent with the accusation, "You never wanted this baby anyway!" Anger may also be focused on the baby, resulting in confusing emotions for parents. After all, what kind of person could be angry at an innocent infant? Yet anger of this kind is a valid response to such a loss. As one woman said of her stillborn daughter, "Why did she just drop in and out of my life? Why did she bother coming at all?" This range of emotional responses may be accompanied by auditory or kinesthetic hallucinations: A baby cries in the night, waking parents from sleep; the baby kicks inside the womb, yet there is no pregnancy, no live child.

Postpartum depression may be intensified by the loss. Absent a baby, the mother may be confronted by physical reminders of the loss, such as the onset of lactation. One bereaved mother said, "I wanted to go to the cemetery and let my milk flow onto my daughter's grave." Meanwhile, the father may feel culturally constrained to "be brave" so that he can give support to the mother who is recuperating physically as well as emotionally. In the process, the father's need to grieve may go unmet, and his emotions may be pushed below the surface until long after the event.

Well-intentioned family members and friends may attempt to minimize the death in an effort to console the bereaved parent. They may say, "You're young; you can have another baby," unaware that such a comment, though possibly true, is inappropriate. No other baby will replace the one who has just died. Advice such as this is especially difficult for couples who postponed having children because they may feel an added constraint of time that compounds the experience of loss. Compared to other types of bereavement, the grieving parents may find social support for their loss lacking.

A positive example of perinatal bereavement care is found in the comprehensive program sponsored by the Reuben Center for Women and Children at the Toledo Hospital in Ohio.[24] Established in 1980, the program now has numerous bereavement protocols, including guidelines on how staff and volunteers can offer bereavement support, photographic techniques (photos are taken of all deceased infants and are given to parents either at the time of the death or at whatever time they may want them), use of trained support group volunteers, distribution of printed materials on bereavement and grief (including a brochure written expressly to educate relatives and friends of the bereaved about what they can do), use of hospital chaplains, various funeral options, and the availability of support groups for families who do not live near the hospital. The hospital hosts regular monthly meetings of a bereavement support group; if desired, home visits are also made. In addition, educational programs and other forms of support are provided for perinatal staff members who deal with the primary care of the newly bereaved families. Outreach of various kinds is also offered to the community at large, including a "service for remembrance" held annually in October in conjunction with National Pregnancy and Infant Loss Awareness Month. Programs like this demonstrate that comprehensive support for perinatal loss can be provided to families, staff, and the community. Although caregivers have become more aware of the importance of ritual leave-taking and bereavement support when perinatal loss occurs, losses due to miscarriage, induced abortion, infertility, and adoption still receive comparatively little acknowledgment or social support.

Miscarriage

Many people assume that the loss of a baby during the early stages of pregnancy evokes feelings of disappointment, but not grief. To parents who have dreamed about the baby even before its conception, however, miscarriage is a shock that brings pain and confusion. The sense of anticipation experienced during pregnancy can reflect both positive and negative qualities, and this ambiguity can be a source of doubt and guilt when miscarriage unexpectedly ends the pregnancy. A parent may ask, "Didn't I want this baby enough?" When parents experience a series of miscarriages, grief is further compounded. Women who have this experience express horror or dismay at being labeled by the medical term "habitual aborters." Parents may be told that miscarriage is simply "Nature's way" of weeding out genetic anomalies. To the grieving parents, this remark provides little or no consolation since it was *their* baby that Nature decided to sort. Platitudes that minimize or deny the loss are decidedly unhelpful.

Parents may have difficulty identifying their loss precisely or making sense of what has happened.[25] One young mother's grief was complicated after a miscarriage early in her pregnancy because she had no remains to be buried. "I didn't know where my baby was," she said. She was able to begin resolving her grief when she returned to the hospital and asked for the remains of her baby. Taking them home, she buried them in her backyard. She takes comfort in looking out the window and knowing her baby is there.

 "My husband was understanding but couldn't know what this did to my whole sense of myself," said Karen following her miscarriage. "After months of my moping and lack of interest, he wondered if I wasn't prolonging things and overreacting. I started resenting him for having escaped the full emotional burden of the loss. It was a difficult time for us. I think it is impossible for a man to understand miscarriage on anything but an intellectual level."

Rochelle Friedman and Bonnie Gradstein,
Surviving Pregnancy Loss

Finally, even though a miscarriage may have occurred many years ago, grief for the unborn baby can reappear during other significant life events — for example, at the birth of a subsequent child or the onset of menopause. A particular marker, such as reaching age forty or age sixty-five, can reawaken feelings of grief.

Induced Abortion

Statistics indicate that about three to four out of ten pregnancies end in abortion, resulting in a total of about 1.6 million abortions conducted annually in the United States.[26] Although it might be assumed that women who elect to voluntarily terminate a pregnancy would not experience a grief reaction, this hypothesis is certainly not universally true. On the contrary, the results of a study conducted by Larry Peppers indicate that there is a grief reaction to elective abortion, and it is "symptomatically similar to that experienced following involuntary fetal/infant loss."[27] Additional findings from this study indicate that: (1) the grief reaction may be initiated when the decision is made to terminate the pregnancy, (2) some women experience a minimal grief reaction while others suffer considerable emotional trauma, and (3) the intensity of the grief is associated with the length of the pregnancy. The grief reaction may also be influenced by the woman's perception of the pregnancy: Does she perceive herself as "simply" pregnant, or does she see herself as a potential mother?

In Japan, at places like Hase Temple in Kamakura and Shiun Jizo Temple north of Tokyo, thousands of tiny stone statues called *mizuko* represent children conceived but never born.[28] Some of these "water children" wear bibs and stocking caps. Placed alongside them are toy milk bottles, dolls, and twirling pinwheels, along with memorials written by their sponsors — women who chose to have an abortion rather than give birth. The statues, each one costing several hundred dollars, are erected as repositories for the souls of unborn babies. At Hase Temple, the more than 50,000 *mizuko* are watched over by a thirty-foot-tall wooden statue of the "Goddess of Mercy," who is also the patroness of safe birth. Although abortion is quite common in Japan due to government restrictions on birth control, the popularity of "mizuko worship" bears witness to an intense desire felt by many women to somehow acknowledge the unborn fetus.

Even when the decision for an abortion is based on information about the baby's health, this choice can be a source of conflict that adds to the parents' grief. Many genetic diseases can now be identified by tests during the early phases of pregnancy; and, when the results are unfavorable, terminating the pregnancy may seem the best or only choice. Some tests can be done only well into the pregnancy, after the mother has already felt the baby moving. The predominant feature of this type of loss is guilt, and there is little social support, including support groups, available to help. Parents who decide in favor of a therapeutic abortion fear that no one will understand their "choice" and that they will be judged harshly. Couples who terminate pregnancies may face not only the death of a particular baby, but also the possibility of a childless future; biological considerations or genetic risk may preclude the choice to conceive again. Caring and sensitive counseling for couples who face this tragedy is essential.

Elective abortion when considerations other than fetal health are involved represents a loss that is difficult to grieve. The repercussions of such decisions may not be felt until later. One woman, who had chosen to abort a pregnancy as a young adult because she and her husband felt their relationship could not withstand the added pressures of raising a child at that time, experienced considerable remorse later when she and her husband found themselves unable to have other children. "That may have been our only chance," she lamented. When losses of this kind occur, individuals may experience subsequent pregnancy loss as "retribution" for an earlier abortion.

Furthermore, persons who are significant in one's life may not sanction the act, or they may not recognize that a loss has occurred. Kenneth Doka points out how the differing viewpoints concerning abortion may place the bereaved in a dilemma: Those who believe a loss occurred may not sanction the act, whereas those who sanction the act may not recognize that grief in response to the perceived loss needs to be expressed and legitimized. As with other forms of disenfranchised grief, the problems of grieving may be exacerbated when the usual sources of solace and social support are not available or helpful.[29]

Stillbirth

"Instead of giving birth, I gave death," said a mother whose daughter died in childbirth. Instead of a cradle, there is a grave; instead of receiving blankets, there are burial clothes; instead of a birth certificate, there is a death certificate. The world is turned upside down, the confusion endless. Although parents do appear to "recover" from the effects of a stillbirth, this journey does not mean that one ends up where one began. After a stillbirth, "a family's wishes and hopes and dreams — the individuals' illusions about what life *ought* to be — are quickly shattered by the reality of what life really *is*."[30]

Those who have worked with the newly bereaved parents of a stillborn baby stress the importance of acknowledging the child's birth. Rather than whisking away the stillborn infant as quickly as possible, hospital staff can encourage the parents to see and hold their baby. Working through the experience of grief is facilitated by acknowledging the reality of the baby's life and death. A postmortem photograph of the child may prove helpful to the process of grieving.[31] When the parents are involved only to the extent of signing the death certificate, the aims of healthy grieving are thwarted. Many parents decide to hold a funeral or memorial service for the stillborn baby, a practice that not only acknowledges the reality of what has happened, but that also allows an opportunity for finding meaning and solace in the face of a confusing situation.

Support groups dealing with issues of pregnancy loss encourage hospitals to use information packets that include a "Certificate of Stillbirth," which acknowledges the birth as well as the death of the child. Linking objects, such as a lock of hair, a photograph, and the receiving blanket, can provide immense support to parents — if not at first, then later, when they want to hold onto every precious memory. Nearly 90 percent of the parents included in a study by John De Frain

Small Son

They have gone.
The last mourner,
the last comfort,
last cliche.

I wrap a pillow
in your blanket.
Lie burying my face
to hold your fading
milk sweet smell.

The silence swells.

    I run

to where the stand
of saplings wait
for clearing.

Chopping, slashing,
small limbs
dragged and pulled
and piled for burning

I turn away
consumed,
the taste of ashes
in my mouth.

        Maude Meehan

named their stillborn baby in recognition that it was indeed part of the family, no matter how briefly: "Naming seemed to help show others that the baby really existed and was important, not just something to be thrown away and forgotten."[32] Most of these parents concluded that, even though the hurt may fade as time passes, the memories do not.

Neonatal Death

When a baby is born alive but with life-threatening disabilities due to prematurity, congenital defects, or similar causes, the ensuing period of waiting for a seriously ill baby to die can be a nightmare for parents. Frustration and a sense of futility may be overwhelming as surgery or other interventions are attempted and fail. These feelings can be especially severe when the hospital has no facility where the parents can be with their baby, even if only briefly.

Sometimes a baby born with one or more life-threatening conditions embarks on a life-or-death struggle that lasts weeks. Parents may be confronted with the need to work through ethical choices that could result in their baby's death. Meanwhile the costs incurred in keeping the baby alive and comfortable continue to accrue. After the death of the baby, parents may express resentment toward the medical institution and its personnel, feeling as if they have survived the painful ordeal only to be billed for the medical expenses.

In circumstances involving a critically ill newborn, *any* decision may haunt parents. They may ask themselves over and over whether they made the right choice. Often, letting the baby die is the only choice. As one young neonatologist remarked, "One of the most difficult and important things for me to learn was to hand over the baby to the parents so it could die in their arms."

Loss of the "Perfect" Child

When a child is born with disabilities, such as congenital deformities or mental retardation, parents can find it difficult to accept the reality that the child is not as they had wished for and dreamed about. Coming to terms with this loss is not easy. In such instances, parents need to grieve for lost expectations. Coping means finding ways to help themselves and their child lead the most productive lives possible under the circumstances.

Sudden Infant Death Syndrome

Although it is not, strictly speaking, in the category of pregnancy loss, Sudden Infant Death Syndrome (SIDS) carries with it many of the same consequences in terms of bereavement. SIDS victims are usually under the age of one year; the death is sudden, and often comes at night. Parents are often left angry, and with a tremendous amount of guilt. Although medical researchers now have some indication of possible causes, SIDS remains largely unexplained. The suddenness of death, the age of the child, and the uncertainty about the cause of death all combine to make such a death a high-grief experience for survivors.

In the past, the parents of an infant whose death was attributed to SIDS were often subjected to criminal investigation. Concerns about child abuse prompted law enforcement officials to question whether the parents might be responsible. Investigation into SIDS deaths is now generally handled with greater sensitivity, partly as a result of information disseminated by support groups concerned with both SIDS and the effects of misdirected questioning and accusations on grieving parents. Still, parents who survive the death of a child due to SIDS often question themselves just as sternly, wondering if the death was in any way due to something they did or to something they left undone. Could it have been prevented in some way? Parents may also be concerned that SIDS could have a genetic basis, thus raising questions about the conception of subsequent children.

The Critically Ill or Dying Child

For the parent whose child is critically ill or dying, the experience represents many losses. Many of the issues discussed in connection with pregnancy loss, neonatal death, and the death of an infant also pertain to the death of an older child or adolescent. The meaning of such a death is more complex, however, because the relationship between parent and child has been of longer duration, with a correspondingly larger store of memories. A child may represent many different things to a parent. As Beverly Raphael reminds us, a child is "a part of the self, and of the loved partner; a representation of generations past; the genes of the forebears; the hope of the future; a source of love, pleasure, even narcissistic delight; a tie or a burden; and sometimes a symbol of the worst parts of the self and others."[33]

A parent's attachment to a child begins before birth. As experiences are shared, the bond between parent and child takes on increasing complexity. As a

Käthe Kollwitz, Library of Congress

The overwhelming grief of parental bereavement is expressed in the soft-ground etching Überfahren (Passing Over), *by Käthe Kollwitz, whose art became a means of working through her own sorrow following the death of a child. The dead child is carried by adults bent with the burden of grief; other children look on.*

child develops his or her own personality during the years of childhood and adolescence, the relationship between parent and child at times may include feelings of ambivalence, no matter how strong the bonds of affection and love. The emotional complexity of this relationship can make the threatened loss or death of a child an especially difficult type of bereavement.

When a child's life is threatened by illness, it affects the entire pattern of family life. Parents and siblings are all involved in coping with the fact of the illness, which gradually becomes integrated into overall family patterns. When the prognosis of the disease is death, the impact of such an announcement is likely to be devastating, setting into motion a need to adapt to the unpleasant reality.

Patterns of Family Involvement

Added to the physical isolation that accompanies illness, as the child grows closer to death there is often a psychic separation, a distancing from the child by parents, relatives, and even members of the health care team. For the dying child, this psychic distancing can be the most severe pain of all.

If the significant adults in the child's life find it difficult to witness the physical disintegration caused by the disease, they may avoid situations that elicit painful feelings. Visits with the child become shorter, less frequent. Sometimes, parents exhibit their unwillingness to discuss the reality of the situation by taking long absences from the child's room or by keeping their interactions with the child as brief as possible. They may create excuses for interruptions whenever the situation becomes too painful or may avoid altogether any topics related to the child's illness. In these and similar ways, parents can subtly signal their limits about what they feel comfortable discussing with the child.

Established family patterns also play an important part in determining the kind of emotional and psychological support that is provided for the dying child. Members of an extended family, with a large network of relatives, may be able to pace themselves, arranging visits to the hospital on a schedule that allows support for the child to be shared in such a way that no one is physically or emotionally overwhelmed. Members of a smaller family, on the other hand, may be unable to spend as much time with the child as they would like. Parents who work, for example, may want to be with the child more and yet have to earn money to cover medical expenses. Perhaps whatever action is taken, the resulting neglect of its opposite will bring feelings of guilt at "not having done enough."

A family's communication patterns also shape how parents and other family members relate to a child's illness. Few families can sustain complete openness to the reality of a child's terminal illness throughout what may possibly be a very lengthy process from diagnosis of the disease to the child's death. Indeed, usually the illness itself varies in the intensity of debilitating or disrupting symptoms. At times, the sick child may function quite normally and the routine of special medical care becomes simply another aspect of family life. At other times, the disease may require that the family deal very specifically with the changes in the child's condition. Families must learn to adjust to the fluctuations between hope for recovery and acceptance of terminal illness, while always supporting the child in the best way possible.

In observing family interactions that occur in response to life-threatening illness, Barney Glaser and Anselm Strauss noted four basic ways in which individuals establish the context of awareness with regard to the dying patient.[34]

These modes or contexts of awareness include both the content and the style of interpersonal communication about death. It will be instructive to consider briefly each of these patterns of awareness and communication.

In the *closed awareness* context, the dying person does not recognize that death is impending, although other persons may know. In general, closed awareness does not allow for communication about the illness or the probability of death.

In the *suspected awareness* context, the patient suspects that the prognosis is death, but is not told so by those who know. The dying person may try to confirm or deny these suspicions by testing family members, friends, and medical personnel in an effort to elicit information known by others but not openly shared with the patient. Despite others' secrecy, however, the patient may observe that the illness is severely disrupting the family's usual style of relating, and may sense others' fearfulness or anxiety about his or her condition, thus confirming the suspicions in the patient's mind.

The *mutual pretense* context can be likened to a dance in which the participants sidestep a direct confrontation about the patient's condition. Typically, this involves complicated, though usually unspoken, rules of behavior designed to sustain the illusion that the patient is getting well. With mutual pretense, everyone — the patient included — recognizes the fatal prognosis, but all act as if the patient will recover. Mutual pretense may be practiced right to the end, despite any violation of the unspoken rules that might have prompted disclosure of the patient's true condition.

Underlying mutual pretense is the notion that everyone should strive to avoid "dangerous" or "threatening" topics, such as details of the child's disease and prognosis, the child's appearance, medical procedures, another child's illness or death, and future plans and events. Obviously, this eliminates from discussion a considerable portion of the child's current experience.

The pattern of mutual pretense usually begins early; subtle signals are communicated among parents, caregivers, and the child that the method being used to cope involves pretending that things are really normal. Thus, caregivers may substitute "possible WBC disease" — a shorthand reference to white blood cells — for the more explicit "fourth-stage leukemia."

If something happens that threatens to break the fiction and disclose the reality of the situation, the parties to mutual pretense simply act as if the threatening event did not occur. Various distancing strategies may be called upon to preserve the illusion that the child is not seriously ill — most often by avoiding any interaction that threatens disclosure of the truth. Children may respond to the risk of disclosure by becoming angry or withdrawn; adults may excuse themselves by saying they need to go out for a smoke or a walk or to make a phone call. In the short term, such strategies can be useful ways of coping with a difficult and painful situation.

Glaser and Strauss's fourth designation, the context of *open awareness*, describes the situation in which the likelihood of death is acknowledged and discussed. Such openness does not necessarily make death easier to accept, but it

Last year, a fourteen-year-old boy who suddenly collapsed on the street was rushed to our hospital emergency room. Even though there were no clinical signs of life, at least six physicians frantically attempted resuscitative measures. In the hallway outside the emergency room, I came upon two stunned parents who were standing absolutely alone. None of the physicians wanted to leave the dramatic scene to obtain a history, let alone provide any solace. I did not want to either, the boy was dead (possibly from a cardiac conduction defect — even the autopsy later was unrevealing); but I forced myself to sit down in an adjoining room and listen while they talked of their hopes and their son's aspirations. I am used to talking with parents whose children die of sudden infant death syndrome; this was different and I was overwhelmed. Afterward, I went to my office and cried. I later thought that I should have let my interns and residents witness me cry to learn that professionalism does not preclude expression of human feeling.

Abraham B. Bergman, "Psychological Aspects of Sudden
Unexpected Death in Infants and Children"

does offer the possibility of sharing support in ways that would not otherwise be available.

The awareness context is a crucial element in determining the interaction among staff, family, and patient. As new information is presented to the patient or to family members, the awareness context may change. For example, a context of closed awareness or mutual pretense may prevail throughout a succession of medical procedures. Then, perhaps with the news of yet another series of tests or treatment program, the illness may be acknowledged as life threatening. At that point, the awareness context may shift from closed or suspected to open.

Caring for the Terminally Ill Child

Perhaps one of the clearest messages to come out of the current interest in death and dying is the need to redefine the meaning of caregiving for patients whose prognosis is death. It is essential that caring for the terminally ill child take into account not only physical needs but also emotional and psychological needs as well.

Seriously ill children may need "mental first aid" to help them cope with their thoughts and emotions. This may simply mean comforting the child and being supportive through a difficult or painful procedure. A child who is severely disturbed by his or her illness, however, may require more substantive intervention to deal successfully with anxiety, guilt, anger, and other possibly conflicting or unresolved emotions. Some children seem to cope with traumatic experiences without requiring much outside help; others need considerable support to cope successfully with relatively minor crises. Whatever the case, working with children requires a flexible approach.

Attempting to protect a child from confronting disturbing feelings may result in even greater anxiety and conflict. A child who feels unsupported or unsure about what is happening can experience fantasies that are more frightening than the truth. An atmosphere of support and encouragement in which the child and the parents feel free to express their fears and concerns can help to alleviate anxiety as well as diminish the child's feelings of separation and loneliness.

As much as possible, family members should be encouraged to participate in the child's care. Although professional caregivers are equipped by training and experience to provide for the child's medical needs, a parent's special expertise lies in the nontechnical aspects of child care. Activities such as bathing the child, helping the child get dressed, assisting at meal times, tucking the child in at night, and providing emotional support are all tasks wherein a parent can be involved to the benefit of everyone concerned.

On the other hand, parents should be wary about performing procedures that might cause the child pain. The parent who helps with the IV or similar painful procedure may be seen by the child as someone who is causing or intensifying pain. The parent's role is to devote attention to providing comfort and support to the child. As Shirley Steele says, "Parents should be helped to participate in the role of a parent rather than trying to play the role of a nurse."[35]

Confronting the Reality That a Child Is Dying

To move from avoidance to acceptance in confronting the reality of a child's terminal illness requires that those persons close to the child agree to be honest with themselves and with others. A decision must be made to be candid but with compassion and kindness toward everyone affected by the child's illness. Truth without compassion is destructive. Compassionate communication of truth acknowledges the reality in a spirit of loving kindness.

Families that deal openly with a child's illness are typically those in which the parents do not derive their personal identities solely from their role as parents. In other words, although parenting is an important part of their lives, it does not constitute the totality of their self-image, which encompasses other significant accomplishments and values as well. Thus, even though they are in the midst of a painful and frustrating predicament, their own survival is not an issue.

Creating a context of open awareness does not make the situation easier or mean that one will cope more successfully. At times, it may become more difficult, because the option to distance oneself from the experience by avoiding or denying it is less available. However, open awareness is not a condition that is static and unchanging; there may be a shift from comparative openness to being closed or to mutual pretense, depending on the intensity of the immediate experience and the ability or desire of the persons involved to cope with that reality.

Congruency of—that is, agreement between—beliefs and actions is an important determinant of how a crisis is experienced. The more your beliefs and actions are congruent, the more likely you are to cope successfully with a crisis. Suppose, for instance, that in your value system a style of pretense is seen as a useful way to deal with situations that are threatening or discomforting, and that such a style of communication is typical of your family's interactions. Then pretense may be an effective means of coping with painful circumstances such as those surrounding a dying child. Suppose, on the other hand, that you value openness and honesty, and your family has always been scrupulously honest with one another. If a child is dying, yet everyone is pretending that the crisis really doesn't exist, that the child is getting well, then your anxiety is likely to be made even more unbearable by the conflict between your beliefs and actions.

Crisis, though unsettling and painful, is also an opportunity for turning one's attention to the essentials of life and relationship with others. Some persons who are confronted by the reality of a seriously ill child not only survive, but grow from the experience. Jerome Schulman writes: "Rather than simply coping — in the sense of merely surviving — many parents and children respond to a severe illness by making a more mature reevaluation of their lives and achieving a truer vision of what counts. Their lives become more significant, more basic, more meaningful. They live one day at a time . . . but they learn to make each new day more enriching."[36]

The Death of an Adult Child

Although there is scant research on parental bereavement in situations involving the death of an adult child, Beverly Raphael points out that the "older parent who experiences the death of an adult child is likely to be deeply disturbed by it."[37] Although there is likely to be a degree of separation between an adult child and his or her parent, the parent's grief may be intense. Such a death may be difficult for the bereaved parent to resolve. Indeed, it has been suggested that the death of an adult child may be the most difficult of all griefs. The death is not only untimely, as are deaths of children generally, but may result in a form of "survivor guilt" particularly distressing for parents. For a young or middle-aged adult to die while his or her parents live on seems unnatural. It goes against what we think of as the proper order of things. A study conducted in Israel of bereaved parents who had lost an adult son during military service found that the parents experienced a deep sense of "existential vacuum" that was expressed through lack of meaning and purpose in life.[38]

The older parent who survives the death of a middle-aged child may also suffer the loss of a caregiver. The child represented a source of comfort and security that is now gone. Parental bereavement also can be complicated by a parent's sense of "competing" with the child's spouse for the role of "most bereaved." In situations where all of those who have been bereaved by the child's death need and seek comfort, who has priority in receiving the attentions of others? Sometimes, too, the loss of an adult child results in circumstances that require parents to assume care of their grandchildren. Meeting such an unforeseen need may be emotionally disruptive as well as economically difficult. The death of an adult child, happening as it does "out of sequence" and unexpectedly, can present an especially difficult form of parental bereavement.

Peer Support Groups for Specific Parental Bereavements

Many kinds of support groups exist to offer information and help to parents who are coping with the serious illness or death of a child. One such group, Compassionate Friends, focuses primarily on the needs of parents who have experienced the death of a child. A group known as the Guild for Infant Survival is composed of parents who have lost children to "crib death" or Sudden Infant Death Syndrome (SIDS). Another group, Candlelighters, is made up of parents of children with cancer. From a child's initial diagnosis with cancer, through his or her treatment and long-term survival or death, there are specific programs for the child, his or her parents, and other family members. These programs range from offering emotional support in coping with the reality of childhood cancer to providing practical information for dealing with problems related to treatment, nutrition, interruption in school attendance, disruption of family patterns, and so on.

Besides providing emotional support for the grief experienced at the loss of a child, some organizations for bereaved parents also engage in political advocacy designed to remedy the situation that precipitated the death. Examples of these peer support groups include Mothers Against Drunk Driving and Parents of Murdered Children. The grief resulting from losses such as those reflected in the names of these two organizations is complicated by the violent circumstances of a child's death, circumstances that may be accompanied by intrusions on the family's grief by media coverage of the event as well as by subsequent criminal investigation and judicial proceedings.

There are innumerable ways of offering support to bereaved families: listening, sending cards and letters of condolence or making phone calls, bringing food, doing housework, caring for other children in the family, helping with chores, sharing one's own grief over the loss, letting the parents grieve, giving the parents time to be alone, and touching with one's eyes, arms, and heart.[39] Such support can be offered by relatives, friends, and neighbors who are not afraid to talk about the issues of death and life that follow in the wake of parental bereavement.

Spousal Bereavement

Of all the transitions in the life cycle, the death of a spouse is considered the most disruptive crisis. The ties between two persons in a paired relationship are usually so closely interwoven that, as Beverly Raphael says, the death of one partner "cuts across the very meaning of the other's existence." Although some part of us recognizes the likelihood that one spouse will die before the other and that the survivor will be left to carry on alone, such thoughts are kept in the background. The pressing activities of daily life occupy our attention until one day the possibility becomes a reality that can't be ignored.

The aftermath of a mate's death has been described as follows: "Everyday occurrences underscore the absence of your mate. Sitting down to breakfast, or dinner, opening mail, hearing a special song, going to bed, all become sources of

Mr. and Mrs. Andrew Lyman, Polish tobacco farmers living near Windsor Locks, Connecticut, exemplify some of the qualities that contribute to a close relationship. When such a bond is severed by death, the effect is felt in every area of the survivor's life.

pain when they were formerly sources of pleasure. Each day is full of challenges and heartbreaks."[40] Although a spouse's death always requires an adjustment from being a couple to being single, the transition may be especially hard for the survivor who is also a parent. With children to care for, there is an added burden of making a transition to single parenthood.

Factors Influencing Spousal Bereavement

Although the loss of a spouse has been the most intensively studied of all loss experiences during adulthood, most of this research has focused on a relatively brief time span following bereavement; studies of enduring effects are comparatively rare.[41] Thus, questions remain: How common are cases of severe difficulties among surviving spouses, and how long do such problems usually last? How do factors such as age and gender affect styles of coping with the death of a mate? What role does social support play in coming to terms with such a significant loss?

It is noteworthy that studies of spousal bereavement tend to focus exclusively on heterosexually paired relationships; homosexual couples who have made a lifelong commitment to each other are virtually ignored in the literature as well as in the wider community, where grief experienced at the death of a partner in a same-sex relationship is often poorly understood and acknowledged only minimally. Grief may be exacerbated by conflict with a mate's parents who never made peace with their son's or daughter's unconventional life style. "If I was effectively nonexistent to them before," one surviving mate said, "I really vanished after my partner died. For years, they denied our commitment to each other; now they acted as if they could completely erase me! They claimed everything: the body, our home, and, seemingly, my right to grieve." In reading and thinking about spousal bereavement, notice that the experience of such a loss pertains to the bonds formed by the partners that are broken by death. Even though the automatic reaction is to think of a "marital" bond as signifying a legally sanctioned heterosexual relationship, it is important to recognize that the reality of grief over the loss of a mate is essentially independent of any legal or social sanctions about the nature of relationships.

When a man to whom you have been married for more than thirty years dies, a piece of you that you will never know again goes out the door with him. Sitting dry-eyed in a chair watching the rescue-squad men load him onto the stretcher and strap him in, I was mercifully numb. Yes, I said obediently, I would await a call from the coroner; yes, his doctor could be reached at the hospital; yes, I would be all right alone.

And then they were wheeling him out the door, casting uneasy backward glances at me. Thirty years of being us was suddenly transformed into just me.

Elizabeth C. Mooney, *Alone: Surviving as a Widow*

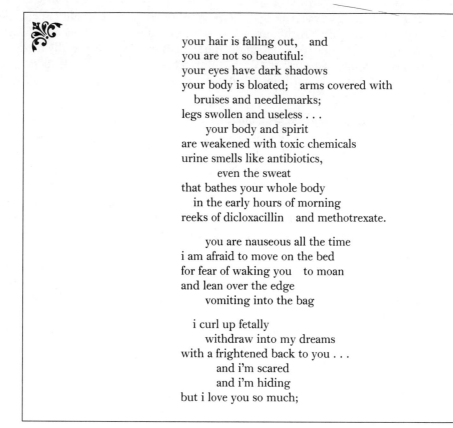

your hair is falling out,   and
you are not so beautiful:
your eyes have dark shadows
your body is bloated;   arms covered with
     bruises and needlemarks;
legs swollen and useless . . .
          your body and spirit
are weakened with toxic chemicals
urine smells like antibiotics,
          even the sweat
that bathes your whole body
     in the early hours of morning
reeks of dicloxacillin   and methotrexate.

     you are nauseous all the time
i am afraid to move on the bed
for fear of waking you   to moan
and lean over the edge
     vomiting into the bag

     i curl up fetally
          withdraw into my dreams
with a frightened back to you . . .
          and i'm scared
          and i'm hiding
but i love you so much;

It is not easy to tease out the various factors that contribute to problems in coping with the death of a spouse.[42] Financial problems and adjusting to living alone clearly play a role. In addition to those discussed in Chapter 7, three major factors seem particularly to affect the outcome of spousal bereavement: age, gender, and the survivor's patterns of interaction with the deceased.

The patterns of intimacy and interaction between spouses are an important determinant of how the loss of a partner will be perceived by a survivor. Whereas one couple derives primary satisfaction from shared activities, another prefers separateness. In some relationships, the focus is on children; in others, the adult partners take precedence. The patterns of a relationship are in flux as the partners themselves develop and as circumstances change over time. Thus, the loss of a mate can have many different meanings.

Consider, too, the difference in outlook between a young couple, together only a short time, and an older couple whose lives have been shared for many years. Although the death of a spouse may occur at any time, it occurs most often among older couples, after the children are grown and perhaps have children of

this truth does not change . . .
        years ago,
when i met you, as we were falling in love,
your beauty attracted me:
    long, golden-brown hair
clear and peaceful green eyes
high cheekbones   and long smooth muscles
    but you know — and this is true —
i fell in love with your soul
    the real essence of you
and this cannot grow less beautiful . . .

        sometimes   these days
even your soul is cloudy
    i still recognize you

we may be frightened
        be hiding our sorrow
it may take a little longer
to acknowledge the truth,
but i would not want to be   anywhere else
    i am here   with you
you can grow less beautiful to the world
    you are safe
            i will always love you.

A young widow

their own, and after other transitions common to the later years of life, such as retirement, have been experienced. Spousal bereavement in old age may follow a lifetime of mutual commitment and shared experiences. In contrast, a young couple just setting out to build a world together is engaged in what Charles Brice characterizes as an "ongoing creative dialogue which, in turn, defines the mature love relationship."[43] When one of the partners dies, the survivor is left alone to reconstitute previously shared aims. Although an older person must also come to terms with such a loss and reorganize his or her life accordingly, the reevaluation of aims and goals is not likely to be as thoroughgoing. During the years from youth to old age, a person's standard of living and overall quality of life are also likely to change, thus affecting the meaning and reality of loss. Finally, youth and age involve differing expectations about mortality.

Age also influences a person's style of coping.[44] Although bereaved spouses of all ages report depressive symptoms during the first year of bereavement, younger people seem to experience more physical distress and they tend to rely more on drugs to counter this distress than do older persons. On the other hand, aged persons may have health problems that were neglected while they cared for an ailing spouse. In the first year following the loss of a mate, there appear to be increases in the morbidity and mortality rates of widows and widowers, with aged persons particularly at risk. While caring for a dying spouse, the survivor's ties to the outside world may have been curtailed, thus increasing feelings of loneliness following bereavement.

Relief following the death of a spouse, although little discussed, is an emotion experienced by many women and men who have cared for an ailing spouse over a long period of time or when the death prevents further suffering for the deceased. Less socially accepted, or even acknowledged, is relief experienced when a mate's death is welcomed as the end to an unsatisfactory relationship.

Although spousal bereavement involves experiences that are common to both men and women, it also elicits distinct behaviors related to culturally sanctioned gender roles. In one culture, a widower might avoid crying publicly since to do so would be viewed as "weak" and shameful. A widower in another culture, however, might express his grief through many tears and loud crying since not to do so would suggest a "weakness" in ability to love.

Spousal bereavement can be devastating for either sex, and individuals who have lived out traditional sex roles may find the transition especially hard. Learning to manage unfamiliar role responsibilities in the midst of grief can be a formidable task, intensifying feelings of helplessness. The widow who has never written a check or the widower who has never prepared dinner is confronted not only with grief at the loss of a loved one, but also with major role readjustments. New skills must be learned simply to manage the needs of daily life. A recent study found that an individual's involvement in multiple roles was a better predictor of adjustment following bereavement than was gender, age, time elapsed from the spouse's death, educational attainment, income level, or degree of religiosity.[45] In other words, widowed individuals whose life styles included multiple roles — such as parent, employee, friend, student, hobbyist, or participant in community, political, and religious organizations — experienced a better adjustment to bereavement than did those with fewer role involvements. The researchers also found that the number of role involvements was positively correlated with an individual's sense of purpose in life. These findings seem to be corroborated by another study, the results of which suggest a relationship between a widow's adjustment to loss and "behavioral flexibility as reflected in sex-role identity."[46]

Both widowers and widows appear to have a less happy life than their married counterparts. But adverse effects appear to be more prevalent among widowers, perhaps because those who have lived out traditional sex roles find it difficult to manage the domestic matters that previously had been left to the now-deceased spouse. Widowers also may be less likely than widows to seek help from others, again a trait that may be associated with a traditional sex role. As Judith Stillion points out, men who care for an ailing partner over an extended period of time may be at a disadvantage in coping with the onset of normal physical and psychological problems of bereavement if "their socialization prohibits them from asking for help, showing strain, or even, in some instances, recognizing and

Of America's more than one million nursing home patients, women outnumber men by about three to one. The majority are white, widowed, and disabled. Few have visitors and only about 20 percent return home; the vast majority will die in the nursing home.

discussing their feelings with helping professionals."[47] A study by Ann Bowling, which followed more than five hundred elderly widows and widowers over a period of six years following their bereavement, found that there was "excess mortality" for males over age seventy-five as compared with males of the same ages in the general population.[48]

Gender also influences the experience of spousal bereavement in another way. Because women statistically live longer than men, it is estimated that three out of every four married women will be widowed at one time or another. Of the 13.5 million widowed persons living in the United States, more than 11 million are widows.[49] Those widows who want to remarry may be faced not only by social pressures but with a situation wherein there are few eligible men. One study, reported by Stillion, found that widowers were significantly better adjusted than were widows, even when such factors as income, level of education, age, and amount of forewarning of death were considered. To account for this, three reasons were suggested: First, women have tended traditionally to shape their identities around their husbands, whereas this has not been true of men in our culture. Second, the fact that men tend to die earlier than women and that men who survive their wives tend to marry women younger than themselves decreases the likelihood that women will remarry; knowing this, widows are less optimistic about their chances of future intimacy than widowers. Third, widows are often concerned about making decisions and handling finances alone, as well as about their physical safety and their children.

On the other hand, some have suggested that widowhood is less difficult for women than retirement is for men. This is because there are many other widows with whom to share leisure time and activities, so that a woman's status actually increases with widowhood, whereas a man's status decreases at retirement. Education and social class, Stillion says, appear to "play a major role in the way in which a widowed woman reconstructs her identity and her world after the death of her husband."

Social Support for Bereaved Spouses

The availability of a stable social support network seems to be crucial in determining how bereaved spouses adjust to their changed status. The death of a mate results in the loss of a primary source of one's social interactions, and it alters a person's social role in the community. It appears from recent studies, however, that most widowed persons report considerable stability in both the structural and qualitative aspects of their social support networks, at least during the initial years after bereavement.[50] Maintaining the continuity of social support networks can potentially be important in smoothing the process of adjustment to loss and alleviating disruptions caused by attendant role changes following the death of a spouse.

Relationships with friends, neighbors, and family appear to result in lower levels of loneliness and worry and higher feelings of usefulness. Maintaining relationships with nonrelatives appears to be especially important, since friendships are based on common interests and life styles. Family relationships, in contrast, may pose a potential psychological threat to the widowed elderly since they contain elements of "role reversal" between the adult child and the aging parent that suggest or demand dependency from the aged widow or widower. Furthermore, an adult child's experience of the loss differs from that of the bereaved spouse, who is likely to value the loss as more significant than does the child and to feel the effects of the loss more intensely with respect to physical and emotional health.[51] The bereaved spouse's social network, therefore, is of considerable importance in helping make the adjustment to newly bereaved status.

One of the most valuable resources for the recently widowed is contact with peers — that is, other bereaved persons who have lost a mate and who can serve as

"Widow" is a harsh and hurtful word. It comes from the Sanskrit and it means "empty." I have been empty too long. I do not want to be pigeon-holed as a widow. I am a woman whose husband has died, yes. But not a second-class citizen, not a lonely goose. I am a mother and a working woman and a friend and a sexual woman and a laughing woman and a concerned woman and a vital woman. I am a person. I resent what the term widow has come to mean. I am alive. I am part of the world.

If fate had reversed its whim and taken me instead of Martin, I would expect him to be very much part of the world. I cannot see him with the good gray tag of "widower." He would not stand for it for one moment. And neither will I. Not anymore.

But what of love? The warmth, the tenderness, the passion I had for Martin? Am I rejecting that, too?

Ah, that is the very definition of bereavement. The love object is lost. And love without its object shrivels like a flower betrayed by an early frost. How can we live without it? Without love? Without its total commitment? This explains the passionate grief of widowhood. Grief is as much a lament for the end of love as anything else.

Acceptance finally comes. And with it comes peace. Today I carry the scars of my bitter grief. In a way I look upon them as battle stripes, marks of my fight to attain an identity of my own. I owe the person I am today to Martin's death. If he had not died, I am sure I would have lived happily ever after as a twentieth-century child wife never knowing what I was missing. . . .

But today I am someone else. I am stronger, more independent. I have more understanding, more sympathy. A different perspective. I have a quiet love for Martin. I have passionate, poignant memories of him. He will always be part of me. But—

If I were to meet Martin today. . .?

Would I love him?

I ask myself. Startled. What brought the question to my mind. I know. I ask it because I am a different woman.

Yes. Of course I would. I love him now. But Martin is dead. And I am a different woman. And the next time I love, if ever I do, it will be a different man, a different love.

Frightening.

But so is life. And wonderful.

Lynn Caine, *Widow*

role models during the subsequent period of adjustment. Successful contact of this kind can make other intervention unnecessary. The widowed person acting as role model does not try to minimize the painful or difficult feelings of grief. Rather, exposed to the helper's accepting attitude, the newly widowed person learns to live with these feelings and to gain perspective on them. Many "widows" groups now include widowers as well, and separate widower-to-widower support groups also exist.

The Widowed Persons Service (WPS), whose parent organization is the American Association of Retired Persons (AARP), began implementing its concept of mutual help to widowed individuals in 1973, following the pioneering work of Phyllis Silverman at Harvard University Medical School.[52] By the end of 1988, more than 200 chapters were functioning across the United States. As a one-to-one outreach program offering peer support, WPS provides mutual help to newly widowed people by trained volunteers who themselves have been widowed. In some areas, meetings are held to give widowed people the opportunity to talk and be with friends in an environment that is "accepting of the widowed person no matter what the circumstances."[53] Those who have taken part in support groups such as those offered by the Widowed Persons Service generally report that the experience proved to be beneficial in helping them understand their grief and move toward resolving the loss.

The Death of a Parent

The death of a parent usually represents the loss of a long-term relationship that has nurtured and provided much support to the surviving child. The love between parent and child is associated with such qualities as unconditional and absolute; parents are often described as "accepting" and "always there when the chips are really down, no matter what." Thus, a parent's death confronts the surviving child with issues peculiar to that relationship. A recent study of changes that occurred following parent death in midlife adults found that the loss of a parent typically preceded a time of upheaval and transition, and "the event of parent death was an important symbolic event for midlife adults."[54] Most people reported that the death of a parent had changed their outlook on life, often spurring them on "to examine their lives more closely, to begin to change what they didn't like, and to appreciate more the relationships they had."

Any death can remind us of our own mortality, but the death of a parent may force a person to realize, perhaps for the first time, that he or she has become an adult. When parents are alive, they usually provide moral support for their children; there is a sense that if real trouble comes a child can call on his or her parents for at least psychological comfort. For many people, these feelings provide a great sense of security. With a parent's death, that security is diminished or no longer available. The bereaved child may feel there is no one who would answer a call for help unconditionally. With the knowledge of his or her own transitory nature may come feelings of insecurity and fear of being alone.

There is some evidence that the death of our parents results in a "developmental push," which "may effect a more mature stance in parentally bereaved adults who no longer think of themselves as children."[55] When both parents have died, there is a subtle role change for the adult child, who no longer has his or her parents to "fall back on," even if only in one's imagination. One woman who had survived the deaths of both her parents said that, although she knew that friends and other family members loved her and cared about her, she felt that the love from her parents was unique, unconditional, and irreplaceable.

The death of a mother is considered a harder loss to sustain than the death of a father. This may be due partly to a mother's traditional status as the primary nurturing caregiver. Another reason, however, may lie in the fact that, statis-

> We have been so long accustomed to the hypothesis of your being taken away from us, especially during the past ten months, that the thought that this may be your last illness conveys no very sudden shock. You are old enough, you've given your message to the world in many ways and will not be forgotten; you are here left alone, and on the other side, let us hope and pray, dear, dear old Mother is waiting for you to join her. If you go, it will not be an inharmonious thing . . . As for the other side, and Mother, and our all possibly meeting, I *can't* say anything. More than ever at this moment do I feel that if that *were* true, all would be solved and justified. And it comes strangely over me in bidding you goodbye how a life is but a day and expresses mainly but a single note. It is so much like the act of bidding an ordinary good night. Good night, my sacred old Father! If I don't see you again — Farewell! a blessed farewell!
>
> Your
>
> William
>
> William James, to his father, Henry James, Sr., during the latter's final illness in 1882

tically, fathers die before mothers. Thus, when the mother dies, her death represents the loss of "having parents," and the bereaved adult child may experience reactive grief over the death of the other parent as well.

When a family relationship has been dysfunctional, the death of a parent brings to an end the hope of creating a better, more functional relationship. Upon the death of her alcoholic mother, one middle-aged woman lamented, "With her death, dead also is the dream that she would eventually go into treatment and that we would finally heal the wounds our family has suffered. Although I am relieved that I can no longer be hurt by her drinking, I do wish it could have turned out differently."

The typically low level of grieving associated with the death of a parent during adult life is sometimes related to the fact that the adult child is generally involved in his or her own life, and feelings of attachment have been largely redirected toward others, such as spouse and children. Nevertheless, the loss of a parent may continue to have an impact as the bereaved child recalls the relationship that had existed.

Illness and Aging

The expectations most people have about aging or being old differ from the actual experience. Young adults typically expect problems among older people to be more serious than they are for those who experience them. Bernice Neugarten reports that when she first developed a course on Adult Development and Aging, "It was generally assumed that you reached a plateau simply called adulthood and you lived on that plateau until you went over the cliff at age sixty-five."[56] The stereotyped image of an aged person is marked by such outward signs as dry and wrinkled skin, graying hair, baldness, failing eyesight, loss of hearing, stiff joints, and general physical debility. Indeed, the physical signs of *senescence*, or the process of becoming old, are rightly associated with the aging of the human organism. (Senescence can be thought of in terms of vulnerability; the risk that an illness or an injury will prove fatal increases with age.)[57]

But, as various observers have pointed out, in fact the old tend to be more individually distinct than any other segment of the population: They have had more years to create unique life histories. As Neugarten says, "People are 'open systems,' interacting with the people around them. All their experiences leave traces." Thus, the physical manifestations of aging ought not cloud the fact that mutual respect, faith, communion with others, and concern with the basic existential issues of life are essential to the well-being of the aged.[58] As a recent study of older community residents showed, despite indications of physical decline during the final year of life, most (82 percent) of these people experienced a majority of "positive quality" months in their last year.[59]

As a society we have undertaken to provide for the physical care of our aged through such programs as Social Security and Medicare. We appear to have been less interested, however, in providing a "place" for the aged in society. It seems that the societal wish is only that the old "age gracefully." As Daniel Callahan observes, the conscientious desire to rid ourselves of stereotypes about old age may have also "led us away from fruitful and valid generalizations about the elderly and fresh efforts to understand the place of old age in the life cycle."[60] Callahan points out that, while acknowledging the individual *differences* among the aged, we can also attend to the "*shared* features of old age, the features that make it meaningful to talk about the aged as a group and about old age as an inherent part of individual life." Rather than thinking about old age solely in terms of retirement from the community or about the aged as an ever-growing segment of the population with medical "needs" that must be met by other members of society, Callahan argues that we need to search out "an interpretation of the social reality of old age that will provide a moral foundation for public policy," a policy that would do away with "the pretense that the elderly are just individuals who happen to be old." In seeking what Callahan terms a "public meaning" of aging, important questions need to be discussed:

1. Since aging is often accompanied by "private suffering" caused by physical and psychological losses, how can such suffering become a meaningful and significant part of life?
2. What are the moral virtues (e.g., patience, cultivation of wisdom, courage in the face of change) that properly should be associated with preparing for and living old age?
3. What are the characteristic moral and social obligations of the elderly? Is old age a time for devoting one's life to pleasure and well-being, or is it a time for active involvement in the civic life of society?
4. What medical and social entitlements are due to the elderly? If we cannot meet every medical need or pursue every possible line of medical research, how can we arrive at an equitable level of support?

While There Is Time

I carry the folding chair
for my mother
I carry the shawl
the large straw hat
to shield her from the glare
She leans her small weight
on my arm   Frail legs unsteady
feet now cramped with pain

Each day we sit for hours
at the ocean   The sun is hot
but she is wrapped and swathed
her hands are icy cold
they hide their ache
beneath the blanket

Her eyes follow the
movement that surrounds us
the romp of children
flight of gulls
the strong young surfers
challenging the sea

When the visit is ended
when my mother leaves
I will burst from the house
run empty-handed to the beach
hold out my arms
and swoop like a bird
my hands will tag children
as I pass

I will run and run
until I fall
and weep
for the crushed feet
the gnarled fingers
for her longing
I will run for both of us

Maude Meehan

As Callahan suggests, in considering and discussing these issues, our answers need to reflect both "what kind of elderly person we want ourselves to be and what ideal character traits we would like to promote and support." In considering one's own future status as an elder, it is worth noting that any attempt to meet all the "needs" of the elderly must fail, especially if those needs are defined as the avoidance of disease and frailty. The obvious truth is, says Callahan, "it will *always* be impossible to meet such needs" despite an implicit social ideology that apparently "seeks to neutralize any inevitability about the process of aging and decline."

Some have characterized the crisis of aging as a "crisis of meaning." Despite medical and technological progress that has extended human longevity, there are haunting questions about the meaning and purpose of life. Melvin Kimble observes that our culture "appears to lack symbols of transcendence and rituals that would give meaning to the experience of growing old," with the result that "an irrational and anxious dread about aging has begun to manifest itself at much earlier stages of the life cycle than one would normally expect."[61] What used to be called the prime of life is, for some people, being experienced as decline. The positive images and meanings of growing old, says Kimble, are eroded when we regard old age as a pathological state or as an avoidable affliction. The suffering that befalls the elderly person may be subject to an "oppressive judgment," as if he or she is somehow irresponsible, unenlightened, or otherwise manifesting a defective personality structure. But, growing old is not essentially a "medical problem." As Robert Butler states, "None of us knows whether we have already had the best years of our lives or whether the best are yet to come. But the greatest of human possibilities remain to the very end of life — the possibilities for love and feeling, reconciliation and resolution."[62] The latter part of life has its own distinct challenges and opportunities, the foremost of which is the question of human mortality. Facing death has been called "the final developmental task of old age."

As the culminating phase of a human life, the period of old age or maturity is an appropriate time to focus on the tasks specific to that part of the human journey. Hannelore Wass suggests that older persons are entitled to become familiar with information about the processes of aging and with the subject of dying and death.[63] Practical death education for aged persons could include discussions of patients' rights, support groups, legal matters, funerals, facing one's own mortality, helping a dying or bereaved family member or friend, and learning to cope with loss and bereavement. Robert Butler says:

> After one has lived a life of meaning, death may lose much of its terror. For what we fear most is not really death but a meaningless and absurd life. I believe most human beings can accept the basic fairness of each generation's taking its turn on the face of the planet if they are not cheated out of the full measure of their turn.

With improvements in nutrition and health care, the debilitating effects of aging are being steadily pushed toward the end of the human lifespan. In developed societies, most health promotion activities are devoted to improving the quality of life while "compressing" morbidity and extending "active" life expectancy.[64] In other words, shortening the period of debilitating illness associated with old age enables people to remain relatively active until quite near the end of their lives. (It should be noted that, in developing countries, recent declines in infant mortality have brought about a growing population of older persons, with corresponding increases in the costly burden of chronic disease morbidity.)[65] While the maximum *lifespan* has remained relatively static at about eighty-five to ninety years of age, *life expectancy* has steadily increased, with the result that most individuals in modern societies now enjoy comparatively good health and active life styles until nearly the time of death. Recognizing the changing health status of older people, the National Council on Aging uses the terms "young-old" for people ages sixty to seventy-five, "middle-old" for those seventy-five to eighty-five, and "old-old" for those over the age of eighty-five.

With respect to life expectancy, there is a widening gap between the sexes, with women enjoying an increasing advantage over men in terms of longevity; in many industrialized countries, the age-adjusted total mortality is 60 percent higher in men than in women.[66] Still, the cumulative effect of the physical, mental, and cultural factors related to aging is that the older person eventually experi-

> The worst fear of people who are at risk for Huntington's disease is that they will eventually get the disease and life will become meaningless for them. For most people, death itself is not nearly as fearful as the possibility of years of meaningless suffering. . . . The meaning of life is not, after all, the same for everybody. It varies from person to person according to a multitude of circumstances. And for each person it varies from day to day, even from hour to hour. The meaning of life constantly changes but *never ceases to exist*. It exists even in suffering. Often it exists especially in suffering. That is fortunate, because suffering is an inevitable part of life.
>
> Dennis H. Phillips, *Living with Huntington's Disease: A Book for Patients and Families*

ences loss on a daily basis. These losses may include diminished physiological functions, changes in self-esteem, inability to continue as a materially productive member of society, and increasing helplessness and vulnerability in all aspects of life.

Chronic and Debilitating Illnesses

The most obvious of the losses experienced by older people are those that occur in connection with diseases common to the second half of life. These diseases include atherosclerosis, hypertension, and stroke syndrome, which are often found in interrelationship, each condition influencing the onset of the others. *Atherosclerosis*, a buildup of fatty deposits in the arteries that eventually constricts the flow of blood, has been singled out as a nearly universal health problem, posing a barrier to any appreciable prolongation of life. *Hypertension*, or high blood pressure, frequently accompanies or contributes to a variety of other illnesses, and it can lead to death from stroke or heart failure. *Strokes* are caused by a sudden blocking or rupture of the cerebral arteries, which interferes with the circulation of the blood in the brain. Even when a stroke is not fatal, its aftermath may include loss of memory, defects in speech, emotional problems, paralysis, or loss of control over bodily functions. Although conditions precipitating these illnesses may begin at an early age, the threat to well-being is generally cumulative, thus increasing the likelihood of ill effects as one gets older.

Some cancers also have age-specific mortality rates. Cancers of the lungs, breast, or cervix, for example, are more frequent at younger ages, whereas cancers of the stomach, intestinal tract, prostate, skin, or kidney are more common among aged persons.

In addition to the major causes of death—diseases of the heart, cerebrovascular disease, and cancer—other illnesses may either be fatal or, if not, result in severe, incapacitating losses. Arthritis and rheumatism, for example, although seldom identified as causes of death, can nevertheless be debilitating and limit normal activities.

It is hard for me to speak of the regression that I watch. At first, there was a groping to express herself, along with the intense frustration at her every attempt. And then her moments of expression became less frequent, until eventually the struggle stopped. This disease has invaded her brain to such a depth that a state of passivity and helplessness has set in. One scene that is forever impressed on my memory took place in my apartment a little over two years ago. My mother was unable to achieve the simple motion of entering a room to sit in an armchair. She fearfully clung to the door frame, her eyes darting back and forth from chair to door, door to chair. Ultimately, she remained at the door until help came. Today, two years later, I wish I could at least see her standing unassisted.

Princess Yasmin Khan, daughter of Rita Hayworth

Degenerative diseases such as Alzheimer's and Parkinson's also bring specific losses in their wake, as do hereditary diseases such as Huntington's and amyotrophic lateral sclerosis (ALS). When Alzheimer's disease affects a middle-aged or an old person, for example, losses occur not only for the affected individual but also for family and friends who can no longer relate in the same way to the person they once knew. As the husband of one Alzheimer's patient said, "My wife is standing next to me, but she's not really there; what's standing there is a memory." The symptoms of Alzheimer's include declines in learning, attention, and judgment; disorientation in time and space; difficulty in finding words and communicating; and changes in personality. Conversely, with a disease like ALS, the body is rendered an increasingly useless shell while the mind remains intact and functioning.

The physiological signs of aging itself may be accompanied by *psychological disorders*, such as emotional distress (sometimes resulting from stressful and anxiety-provoking conditions) and disorders related to personality, mood, and depression, as well as *psychosomatic symptoms* that affect such physical processes as sleep, appetite, bowel movements, and fatigue. The old may also exhibit a variety of neuroses, psychoses, and brain syndromes. Each of these conditions, in varying degrees and according to their seriousness, involves significant change, transition, and loss.

Besides specific diseases, a variety of dysfunctions can have an impact on the older person's quality of life. For instance, sensory and cognitive impairments may result in loss of hearing or sight, or in a diminished sense of taste and smell. Oral and dental problems may make eating difficult, with the result that nutrition suffers, thus compounding the cycle of poor health. Deficient reaction times and psychomotor responses may increase the chance of accidents. Although any of these illnesses or disabilities could represent a significant loss by itself, a number of these conditions may be present at once.

Consider for a moment the effect of even a relatively minor injury on your usual functioning. As you think about the limitations this injury poses, you may gain insight into what multiple losses may mean in the lives of those who experience them. Such limitations clearly involve confrontations with loss: What was once possible is now gone.

Because patients with debilitating diseases such as those discussed require long-term care to manage the symptoms associated with the disease, there is also a significant impact on families. As a result, support programs for both patient and family members have developed, including home care, day care, respite care, patient groups, family groups, dedicated nursing home units, and other group living facilities. The issues that arise in the context of caring for persons with chronic and debilitating illnesses are perhaps most pronounced in situations that involve the very old.

Caring for the Chronically Ill and Aged Adult

Listen to conversations about care of the chronically ill and the old. Notice how many times individuals describe the need for care in language like this: "She couldn't live by herself so her son took her in," or "He was failing and had to be put in a nursing home." A question like, "What will we do with Dad when he is too old to manage by himself?" reflects both genuine concern and inadvertent disregard for the aged relative. It is perhaps not surprising, in light of remarks like these, that many aged persons report feelings of being put away, taken in, done to, and otherwise manipulated, their integrity ignored. What is the reality?

Historically, the family has been a haven for ill and aged relatives. Many families do care for aged members of the household, and a high value is placed on such care by some cultural groups. Although most chronically ill and aged persons live in their own homes or with their families, a significant number need more assistance than they or their family members can provide. Concern has grown as families find it increasingly difficult to provide for ill and aged relatives. In the United States, social service programs on behalf of the aged can be traced to the Depression of the 1930s and passage of the Social Security Act of 1935. It was not until 1950, however, with enactment of the Old Age Assistance Act, that the first federal program designed specifically to relieve problems among the aged was implemented. Following implementation of the Medicare and Medicaid programs in the mid-1960s, widespread federal assistance became an accepted means of providing care for America's elderly. The question of how to provide adequate, as well as economical, care for the aged remains one of intense public concern. These issues become more important as life expectancy increases. Over the next several decades, aged persons will not only increase in number, but also constitute a larger share of the total population.

Institutional and Community Programs of Care

The types of institutions in which older people find themselves are of several types. *Domiciliary care homes* provide custodial care to residents who need minimal supervision in a sheltered environment and who are able otherwise to take care of their own needs. For persons with more serious illnesses or disabilities who need medical attention, there are *personal care homes*. Depending on whether residents can manage their own medical regimes, these facilities may or may not provide nursing care. Retirement communities and residential hotels or apartments generally fall into these two categories, which comprise about one-fourth of the institutional choices available.

Skilled nursing facilities, offering either intermediate or comprehensive levels of care, furnish round-the-clock nursing services based on personal need as well as medical and dietary supervision. Such institutions may operate as extended care or convalescent facilities associated with a general hospital, or they may be independent facilities that admit residents without prior hospitalization.

Alternatives to institutional care also exist. These programs are not available in all areas nor can they always provide the degree of support required. Nevertheless, they demonstrate that it is possible to provide care in ways that maintain an appropriate balance between support and independence. *Home health care*, for example, assists persons who are able to continue living in their own homes. Depending on the resources available in a community, this assistance is provided by one or more agencies and in a variety of ways, ranging from medical and nursing visits to preparation of meals, help with exercise and other maintenance needs, and simple (but important) visitation. It is estimated that as many as 40 percent of aged persons now living in institutions could remain in their own communities, in familiar surroundings if adequate home health care services were available to them.

Day hospitals and *elder daycare centers* represent another form of alternative care for the aged. Typical programs include health maintenance, financial and general counseling, meals, and other services designed to increase independence, such as housekeeping, shopping, and transportation.

Halfway between institutionalization and independent living is a form of care known as *congregate housing*. This is usually a large residence with individual apartments or a series of structures within a small neighborhood. The distinguishing feature of this form of care is its organizational structure, which, like a series of concentric circles or graduated steps, provides the particular level of care needed by each resident. In such a community, some individuals are essentially living independently, preparing meals in their own apartments or eating in the dining room when they wish. In this way, they enjoy a sense of security, knowing that help is available when it's needed, without giving up their independence.

Losses Through Institutionalization

Institutional care is depersonalizing. Despite even the best intentions on the part of staff members, the emotional needs of residents may suffer. Residents often feel deprived of their self-esteem and integrity as well as their personal property. Rules and regulations, which seem unavoidably to increase depersonalization,

There are a variety of options for care of the frail elderly. The wide veranda and rocking chairs of the "rest home," however, are fast disappearing from the American scene.

abound. Even a cherished picture of a loved one may find no place in the resident's room: not the bed stand (that's for bed pans), not the wall (patients are frequently moved); so where? Often the answer is, "Nowhere." Gerontologists — those who study the aged and the processes of aging — have found that the "psychological railroading" associated with highly routinized environments can lead to *institutional neurosis*, the symptoms of which include "a gradual erosion of the uniqueness of one's personality traits so that residents become increasingly dependent on staff direction for even the most mundane needs."[67]

Although institutional care must be oriented toward providing adequate, efficient services to residents — often including extensive medical care — there is

> In Europe the availability of domiciliary homes for the elderly goes back to sixteenth-century "alms houses" for the indigent old in England and on the continent. During the Middle Ages, care of the elderly was sporadic, generally perceived of as a moral obligation of the church. In England, the Poor Law of 1601 settled the responsibility of caring for the poor and infirm on the shoulders of each community.
>
> Jon Hendricks and C. Davis Hendricks, *Aging in Mass Society*

general agreement that much could be done to increase flexibility. Favoring institutional expediency over the unique needs of residents cannot, finally, be justified.

Institutional Care for the Frail Elderly

The older a person is, the more likely he or she is to become institutionalized. Despite the image of aged persons being "dumped" in a nursing home by uncaring family members, this is rarely the reality. On the contrary, families may delay obtaining adequate care for their elders because of reluctance to face the need for more intensive care than they can provide at home. Institutionalization is often viewed as the ultimate personal failure for both the aged person and his or her family. Perhaps two-thirds of the elderly view institutions as the least desirable alternative possible, "a sort of confession to final surrender, a halfway stop on the route to death."[68] When institutional care becomes the only reasonable course open to the family of an aged relative, a more satisfying outcome ensues when necessary information is gathered before a decision is made for a particular facility (see Table 9-2).

In the coming years, our prospects for the future also include changes in the patterns of disease as well as the technology of health care. New alternatives to both institutional and home-based care for the aged will be explored. And, perhaps most important, we will continue to see and create new social attitudes about being old.

T A B L E 9–2   *Steps in Choosing a Nursing Care Facility*

1. Make a list of local facilities offering the type of services needed.
2. Find out whether the facilities are licensed and certified.
3. Visit the facilities.
4. Prepare a checklist of desirable features and evaluate each facility in light of the needs of the person who would be moving in.
5. Determine the costs.
6. Make your decision.

Source: Adapted from Colette Browne and Roberta Onzuka-Anderson, editors, *Our Aging Parents: A Practical Guide to Eldercare* (Honolulu: University of Hawaii Press, 1985), pp. 204–209.

Further Readings

Susan Borg and Judith Lasker. *When Pregnancy Fails*. Boston: Beacon Press, 1981.

Stanley Brandes. *Forty: The Age and the Symbol*. Nashville: University of Tennessee Press, 1985.

Colette Browne and Roberta Onzuka-Anderson, eds. *Our Aging Parents: A Practical Guide to Eldercare*. Honolulu: University of Hawaii Press, 1985.

Committee on an Aging Society. *Health in an Older Society*. Washington, D.C.: National Academy Press, 1985.

Robert C. DiGiulio. *Beyond Widowhood: From Bereavement to Emergence and Hope*. New York: Free Press, 1989.

Ken Dychtwald. *Age Wave: The Challenges and Opportunities of an Aging America*. Los Angeles: Jeremy P. Tarcher, 1989.

Rochelle Friedman and Bonnie Gradstein. *Surviving Pregnancy Loss*. Boston: Little, Brown, 1982.

Jean Golding, Sylvia Limerick, and Aidan Macfarland. *Sudden Infant Death: Patterns, Puzzles, and Problems*. Seattle: University of Washington Press, 1985.

Dennis Klass. *Parental Grief: Solace and Resolution*. New York: Springer, 1988.

Ronald J. Knapp. *Beyond Endurance: When a Child Dies*. New York: Schocken, 1986.

Louis E. LaGrand. *Coping with Separation and Loss as a Young Adult*. Springfield, Ill.: Charles C Thomas, 1986.

Kathleen O'Connor and Joyce Prothero, eds. *The Alzheimer's Caregiver: Strategies of Support*. Seattle: University of Washington Press, 1986.

Therese A. Rando, ed. *Parental Loss of a Child*. Champaign, Ill.: Research Press, 1986.

Marty Richards, et al. *Choosing a Nursing Home: A Guidebook for Families*. Seattle: University of Washington Press, 1985.

Harriet Sarnoff Schiff. *The Bereaved Parent*. New York: Crown, 1977.

Jerome L. Schulman. *Coping with Tragedy: Successfully Facing the Problem of a Seriously Ill Child*. Chicago: Follett, 1976.

Sallie Tisdale. *Harvest Moon: Portrait of a Nursing Home*. New York: Henry Holt, 1987.

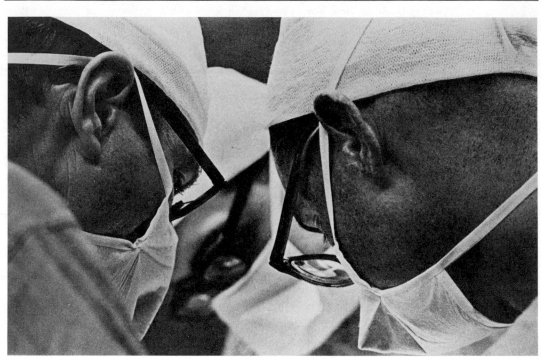

At the Hospital for Special Surgery physicians use medical techniques that call for teamwork and expertise. Life-sustaining interventions made possible by advances in medical technologies require physicians and society as a whole to consider difficult issues of medical ethics.

CHAPTER 10

Medical Ethics:
Dying in a Technological Age

Grandpa was born before Henry Ford put his first automobile on the road, and he died shortly after Neil Armstrong set his foot on the moon. From Michigan to outer space, he experienced an unprecedented advance in the technological capacities of our society. At the time of his death, he was surrounded by technological innovations. The canvas-topped, hand-cranked two-seater car he hand-built in 1922 had been replaced by a factory-built, vinyl-topped four-door automatic, with power steering and power brakes. A retired auto worker, he had begun to question the consequences of the automobile on the quality of his life. If he had been conscious as he lay dying, he might have talked about the consequences of the machines sustaining his life on the quality of his death.

Advances in biomedical technology present us with new and sometimes confusing choices. Surgery can repair physical dysfunctions that once were fatal. When repair is not possible, replacement of the defective organ may be. Medical centers regularly perform major organ transplants. According to the American Council on Transplantation, we have transplanted more than 86,998 kidneys, 6282 hearts, 5044 livers, and 271,900 corneas.[1] Bone, liver, pancreas, lung, and skin are also listed as bodily organs that have been successfully transplanted. The most dramatic of transplant procedures, the heart transplant, has been performed more than 4000 times, with a present survival rate of about 86 percent.

343

It has been said that the great advances in medicine came about because physicians have taken seriously the Hippocratic obligation to keep people alive.[2] But the practice of this worthy maxim can lead to confusing consequences. Techniques for cardiopulmonary resuscitation (CPR) and respiratory assistance have progressed to the point that physicians can interrupt the "normal" dying process; unfortunately, some of the patients saved by the use of such techniques "have their cardiac and respiratory functions restored, but remain with irreversible damage to the brain."[3] The average person might question the obligation to keep people alive in certain instances, such as when a person is maintained in a hopelessly comatose condition, or when heroic medical procedures are undertaken to keep a seriously deformed baby alive. The sophisticated and innovative technologies, which now have unprecedented impact on the way we die, present a great challenge to us as we confront the prospect of our own or another's death.

Most deaths in modern societies are anticipated, the result of a malady that may linger months or even years. Yet even irreversible, debilitating ailments that are ordinarily expected to result in death are being actively combatted. Now that infectious diseases of the past have been largely controlled, the medical community is waging war against the diseases that threaten us today.

The human organism can often be kept going despite the cessation of normal heart, brain, respiratory, or kidney function. When medical technologies spare patients' lives and enable them to resume more or less normal functioning, the results are gratifying. But, paradoxically, the very technologies designed to prolong our lives may prolong our dying as well. When life is sustained artificially, while the person shows no signs of personality or consciousness and there is no likely chance of recovery, ethical questions arise.

When death mercifully does come in such instances, who or what finally "dies"? Put another way, what in fact is death? When does it occur? Until quite recently, cessation of breathing and heartbeat defined death. In our time, the definition of death is less clear.

Better health care, improved sanitation practices, proper nutrition, reduction in infant mortality and deaths in early childhood, and other such factors have contributed both to the expectation of a longer lifespan and to enhanced well-being generally. Assuming that you represent the statistically average person, you can look forward to living for a total of about seventy-five years. If you follow a typical progression, the chances are that your death will occur in an institutional setting: a hospital or similar facility offering care for terminal patients.

The social and technological advances that have brought about improved health care and greater choices in medical services have also resulted in questions concerning how best to make use of these choices and improvements. When these questions impinge on the ethical realm of decision making, the choices are difficult for both individuals and social institutions. Ethical decision making becomes even more complicated in a climate of medical economics in which traditional "virtue-centered" ethics are being eroded by growing self-interest and the "busi-

The Oath of Hippocrates

I swear by Apollo the physician, and by Aesculapius [god of medicine], Hygeia [goddess of health], and Panacea [goddess of healing], and all the gods and goddesses, that, to the best of my ability and judgment, I will keep this oath and agreement: to regard my teacher in this art as equal to my own parents; to share my living with him and provide for him in need; to treat his children as my own and teach them this art if they wish to learn it, without payment or obligation; to give guidance, explanations, and every other kind of instruction to my own children and those of my teacher, and to students who subscribe to the Physician's Oath, but to nobody else.

I will prescribe treatment to the best of my ability and judgment for the benefit of my patients and will abstain from whatever is harmful or pernicious. I will give no poisonous or deadly medicine, even if asked to, nor make any suggestion; neither will I give any woman a pessary to produce an abortion. I will both live and work in purity and holiness. I will not operate, not even on patients suffering from the stone, but will leave this to specialists who are skilled in this work. Into whatever houses I enter, I will make the patient's good my principal aim and will avoid all deliberate harm or corruption, especially from sexual relations with women or men, bond or free. Whatever I see or hear about people, whether in the course of my practice or outside it, if it should not be made public, I will keep it to myself and treat it as an inviolable secret.

While I abide by this oath and never violate it, may all people hold me in esteem for all time on account of my life and work; but if I break this oath, let the reverse be my fate.

nessification" of medical care.[4] Although judicial intervention by the courts in an attempt to sort out what is ethically proper in bioethics cases has become relatively commonplace, the burden of such decision making ideally rests with individuals, families, and caregivers who, acting together, form a community of interest, with firsthand knowledge about a particular case and the will to make moral decisions.[5]

In reviewing the rapidity with which issues of medical ethics have come to the forefront of discussion during the past three decades, Leon Kass observes that "today the ethics business is booming," with medical schools offering courses in medical ethics, hospitals establishing ethics committees, courts adjudicating ethical conflicts, and blue-ribbon commissions analyzing and pronouncing upon ethical issues.[6] Yet, Kass argues, much of this "action" is really talk — philosophical theorizing and rational analysis — with comparatively little time devoted to "what genuinely moves people to act — their motives and passions." This is not to say that rational analysis and abstract problem solving are not relevant, but that the "morality of ordinary practice" must also receive attention. As Kass says, "Every human encounter is an ethical encounter, an occasion for the practice (and cultivation) of virtue and respect, and, between doctors and patients, for the exercise of responsibility and trust, on both sides."

Fundamental Ethical Principles

To provide a framework for discussing such issues as informed consent, euthanasia, and withdrawing or withholding medical treatment, it is worth examining what is meant when people talk about behaving ethically or morally. Although the definitions of such terms are often taken for granted, understanding how they are applied in the context of medical care provides a foundation for the ensuing discussion.

Ethics refers to the investigation of what is good and bad, especially as these concepts relate to moral duties and obligations. Ideally, the outcome of this investigation will be a set of moral principles or values that can serve to guide proper behavior. When we think of *morals,* or moral principles, we are dealing essentially with notions of right and wrong. Although the two terms — morals and ethics — are closely related, one way to distinguish them is to note that morals generally involves conforming to established codes or accepted notions of right and wrong, whereas ethics suggests grappling with subtler or more challenging questions of rightness, fairness, or equity. Briefly stated, then, ethics is concerned with what are usually difficult issues relating to value and obligation. The ethical pursuit is characterized by attempts to answer the question, "What is the good?" along with its corollary, "What is to be done?"

In applying ethical principles to the realm of medicine, we must become familiar with several concepts. The first of these, *autonomy*, refers to an individual's right to be self-governing — that is, to exercise self-directing freedom and moral independence.[7] Personal autonomy may be limited by the corresponding rights of others to exercise their autonomy, and it may be limited by society, which may exercise countervailing rights in the name of the community at large. A common example of this last is the requirement that a traveler obtain inoculations before being granted a visa to enter certain countries; the traveler's autonomy or personal choice is subject to restrictions relating to public health that are imposed by the larger community.

In discussing the principle of autonomy in health care ethics, we are really talking about "respect" or regard for the autonomy of others.[8] Personal autonomy is complex and often ambiguous. Although it is wrong to subject a person's actions or choices to coercion, autonomy does not imply that an individual cannot willingly yield to decisions proposed by others. For example, a patient may not wish a detailed presentation of the pros and cons of a particular treatment, preferring to trust in the relationship established with his or her physician. Of course, determining a person's choices or preferences is not always simple — such choices may be ambivalent or even contradictory, and they can change over time.

Furthermore, respect for autonomy does not mean forcing individuals to arrive at decisions independently of their social support networks. Among the elderly, for example, a relationship seems to exist between a sense of control over one's decisions and positive outcomes as one ages. Yet, as Marshall Kapp points out, this "empowerment" of the elderly should not be used to impose a burden of self-determination on individuals who prefer guidance from others or even want physicians, family members, or close friends to take on primary responsibility for medical decisions.[9] In other words, an individual has the right to choose the degree to which his or her capacity for autonomy will be exercised. Respect for autonomy does not mean that we abandon people in their decision making.

Family members and others close to the patient may have a legitimate voice in determining the kinds of choices that patients make. John Hardwig refers to the fact of human connectedness, particularly the interconnectedness of the family, as a basis for balancing respect for individual autonomy and respect for the values of others with whom one has significant relationships[10]. While acknowledging that the ill deserve special consideration, Hardwig rejects the notion that they deserve exclusive consideration. That is, the effect that an individual's decision is likely to have on others must also be considered. And, in advocating a role for "intimate others" in medical decision making, Nancy Jecker argues that, if decisions are made without considering their effect on the "family commons," those choices may rightfully be overridden to prevent harm to the commons.[11]

Despite the limits inherent in the principle of autonomy, it is an important constraint on actions by others. The concept of autonomy supports the "respect for persons" needed in the patient-provider relationship.

Another term important to medical ethics is *beneficence*, which can be understood as doing good or as conferring benefits that support personal or social well-being. This principle of beneficence as applied to medical care is sometimes expressed by its counterpart, *nonmaleficence*, or the injunction to "do no harm."

Finally, medical ethics is concerned with the principle of *justice*, a term that, like "the good," is difficult to define simply. Justice embraces the qualities of impartiality and fairness, as well as right and proper action. In relation to fairness, justice implies going beyond one's own feelings, prejudices, and desires in an effort to reach a balance between conflicting interests. You will find it helpful to keep these three fundamental principles of medical ethics — autonomy, beneficence, and justice — in mind as you explore the specific issues discussed in the remainder of this chapter.

Truth Telling and the Terminal Patient

If you were diagnosed as having a life-threatening illness, would you want to know about it? Some people answer quickly: "Of course, I want to know about everything that's going on with me!" Others answer as readily: "If there's any way that I could be spared the truth, I'd rather not know that I'm about to die." Whatever our response, it's likely to be conditioned by the attitude that we assume in the more casual situations of our daily lives. Our life style influences our death style. A perennial fighter against the odds and a person who believes that "ignorance is bliss" and shuns stress are likely to have very different responses to terminal illness.

The doctor who fears being subjected to a malpractice suit if he doesn't tell the worst, and who tells the worst, may actually help to bring on the worst. . . . A serious diagnosis can be communicated as a challenge rather than as a verdict. The physician who volunteers a terminal date, for example, or allows himself to be pressured into offering a terminal date may actually be putting a hex on the patient.

Norman Cousins, "Tapping Human Potential"

Surveys indicate that most people would want to be told if they were diagnosed with a life-threatening illness. Yet the questions of *when* and *how* they should be told are often difficult to answer. Physicians must present such news in a way that serves the best interests of each patient. Factors of personality, emotional constitution, and capacity for continued function under stress must be considered anew in each instance. There are few guidelines. Most doctors are guided by their experience.

A diagnosis of life-threatening illness affects not only the patient but also members of the patient's family. Indeed, sometimes it is a member of the family who learns the truth first. Those who know then have a burden of responsibility, for they must decide what to tell the patient.

Most physicians now feel a responsibility to inform a patient about the facts of his or her life-threatening condition, and they try to do so sensitively and in appropriate ways. But this has not always been the case. A study conducted by Donald Oken in 1961 revealed that most doctors demonstrated a "strong and general tendency to *withhold* this information."[12] None of the doctors reported having a policy of telling every patient. Only about 12 percent said that they would usually tell patients of a diagnosis of incurable cancer. When they did inform patients, descriptions of the disease were often couched in euphemisms. They might tell a cancer patient that he or she had a "lesion" or a "mass." Some used a more precise description such as "growth," "tumor," or "hyperplastic tissue." But often the description was phrased to suggest that the cancer was benign. Adjectives were used to temper the impact of the cancer diagnosis. The tumor was "suspicious" or "degenerated." Treatment was advised because the tissue was "precancerous" or the tumor was "in the early curable stage." In short, these physicians explained the medical situation in the most general terms while still eliciting the patient's cooperation in the proposed course of treatment.

Some of the factors that motivated the physicians in this early study are just as important today. Physicians may fear that unadulterated knowledge of the prognosis could adversely affect the patient's ability to cope. Thus, they believe they are acting in the patient's best interest by minimizing the patient's sense of the threat of the illness. Doctors generally believe that it is crucial to give reassurance and support to the patient, to make sure that the patient maintains hope.

Nonetheless, the climate of truth telling among physicians has changed in more recent decades. A 1977 study by D. H. Novack designed to replicate Oken's earlier study found a reversal of attitude, with about 97 percent of the doctors indicating that they would usually tell cancer patients the diagnosis.[13] As was true of the 1961 study, however, the doctors in Novack's study said that the determining factor in revealing a diagnosis was their own clinical experience and personal conviction. A more recent study by Novack focusing on the attitudes of physicians toward using deception to resolve difficult ethical problems found that most physicians were willing to engage in some forms of deception, although such deception was dependent upon the specific circumstances involved.[14] It was noted that physicians "appear to justify their decisions in terms of the consequences and to place a higher value on their patients' welfare and keeping patients' confidences than truth telling for its own sake."

With the coming of a greater general freedom to discuss death, a terminal patient is more likely to learn the truth about his or her illness, and to learn sooner, than was usual in the past. Still, despite doctors' greater forthrightness, the full extent of an illness may be withheld unless the patient or a family member exhibits a readiness to be told. Although the general facts of an illness may be disclosed voluntarily by the physician, details that might be depressing to the patient are generally withheld unless the patient takes the initiative. The most direct way of expressing the desire to receive such information is to ask specific questions.

Informed Consent to Treatment

The relationship between patient and physician implies the existence of a contract whereby each party agrees to perform certain acts designed to achieve the desired results. Fundamental to the contract are self-determination and informed consent. It is generally acknowledged that patients have the right to self-determination regarding a proposed plan of treatment. In practice, we usually rely on the physician's judgment, accepting the diagnosis of an illness and acceding to the proposed course of treatment; we follow the doctor's advice and expect a more or less speedy recovery. We see our doctor to obtain medication to cure the flu or to mend a broken arm and give little consideration to possible alternative treatments. The etiology, or cause, of the disease or injury generally concerns us less than obtaining relief from its symptoms.

More complex, however, is the question of the patient's consent to treatment when the illness is serious or life threatening. Not only has life-threatening illness vastly greater consequences for the patient, but the physician's role is fraught with greater ambiguity. Frequently, several different treatment plans are available, each with its own set of potential risks and benefits. Medical practitioners may be uncertain about what might be the most promising treatment. Too, with diseases like cancer, the side effects of surgery, radiation, and chemotherapy may be nearly as frightening or as discomforting as the disease itself.

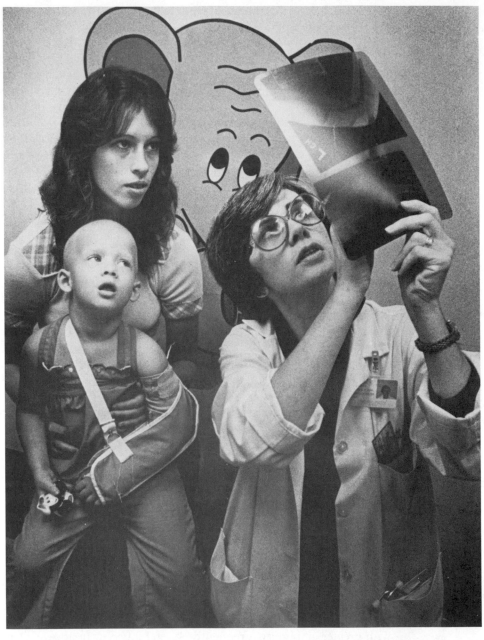

Burton Steele, Times-Picayune

Informed consent is a fundamental ethical principle in medicine. Even fairly routine procedures, such as mending a small fracture, may become complicated when the patient is leukemic, as is this child: Alternatives must be weighed more carefully before a course of treatment is chosen.

Clearly, then, the patient's *informed consent* to a plan of treatment is crucial. Informed consent is based on three principles: First, the patient must be competent to give consent. Second, consent must be given freely and voluntarily. Third, consent must be based on an adequate understanding of what is involved in the treatment program. In an ideal model, the physician informs the patient about the risks of the proposed therapy, about alternative methods of treatment, and about the likely outcome of undertaking no treatment.

The antecedents of informed consent go back hundreds of years in English common law. Although the phrase "informed consent" did not achieve legal definition until 1957, the doctrine of informed consent has been recognized in case law or statute in nearly all American jurisdictions. The President's Commission for the Study of Ethical Problems in Medicine noted that "the legal doctrine of informed consent imposes on physicians two general duties: to disclose information about treatment to patients and to obtain their consent before proceeding with treatment."[15]

Decisions about medical care involve values and goals as well as methods and behavior. The values underlying informed consent include serving the patient's well-being and respecting his or her right to self-determination. To make these values a reality, attention must be paid not only to the patient's capacity to make decisions about his or her care, but also to the communication process between patient and practitioner.

Although it has substantial foundations in law, the doctrine of informed consent is essentially an ethical imperative. It cannot be equated with a formal recitation of the risks of a particular treatment but involves instead a process of shared decision making based on mutual respect and participation. Because people differ in their attitudes toward autonomy and choice relative to medical care, the process of informed consent must be flexible. Despite this variability, the Commission said that informed consent is "ethically required of health care practitioners in their relationships with all patients, not a luxury for a few."

A survey conducted for the Commission found "a universal desire for information, choice, and respectful communication about decisions," yet many people have only a vague notion of informed consent. When asked, "What does the term *informed consent* mean to you?" 21 percent of those surveyed said they did not know. About half said that informed consent meant "agreeing to treatment" or "letting the doctor do whatever is necessary or best." Only 10 percent mentioned having information about risks, and less than 1 percent mentioned being told about alternatives.

Among physicians, about half described informed consent as "generally informing patient about condition and treatment," while somewhat fewer added that it included "disclosing treatment risks to patient." Only 14 percent mentioned telling patients about treatment alternatives.

Informed consent requires that patients *and* caregivers be prepared for shared decision making. Despite a tradition emphasizing the individual's right to self-determination, medical practitioners from the time of Hippocrates have frequently been skeptical of this sentiment. Hippocrates' advice to physicians includes the admonition to do one's duties "calmly and adroitly, concealing most things from the patient while you are attending to him" and to reveal "nothing of the patient's future or present condition."

Informed consent becomes increasingly important when medical care is provided by teams of highly specialized professionals whose responsibilities may be defined less by the overall needs of the patient than by particular diseases or organ systems. There may be no single individual charged with responsibility for the entire care of the patient, no one with whom the patient is familiar enough to turn to for information, advice, and comfort. The Commission noted that the threat such a situation poses to the patient's autonomy cannot be remedied by "formal disclosure of remote risks on informed consent forms." Nor can legal prescriptions alone ensure or enforce compliance with the ethical imperative of informed consent.

Although some have argued that patients cannot fully understand medical information relevant to their health care, the majority of physicians surveyed by the Commission reported that virtually all of their patients could understand most aspects of their condition and treatment, if sufficient time and effort were given to explanation. The Commission noted that "questions of patient capacity in decision making typically arise only when a patient chooses a course — often a refusal of treatment — other than the one the health professional finds most reasonable."

Although forced, coercive treatment is rare, caregivers can — unwittingly or not — exert undue influence on patients by means of subtle or overt manipulation. The Commission remarked that "a good deal of routine care in hospitals, nursing homes, and other health care settings is provided . . . without explicit and voluntary consent by patients." Once the patient is in a health care institution, cooperation with those who provide such routine care is generally expected. The tacit communication may be that the patient has no choice.

Thus, the communication process itself may be the key factor in determining whether informed consent is present. When medical information is presented by caregivers, the facts and possible outcomes must be tailored so as to facilitate a discussion attuned to the needs, capabilities, and emotional state of a particular patient. In the Commission's survey, 97 percent of the public said "patients should have the right to all available information about their condition and treatment that they wish," with 94 percent reporting that they would "want to know everything." When asked who could judge best the amount of information that should be divulged, however, the public's responses were nearly evenly divided between patient (45 percent) and physician (44 percent).

When physicians were asked about how they treated the issue of informed consent, slightly more than half (56 percent) said they always discussed their diagnosis and prognosis with patients, and another 42 percent said it was their usual practice. When asked what they would tell a patient who had a fully confirmed diagnosis of advanced lung cancer, however, only 13 percent said they would give a straight statistical prognosis. A third said they would tell the patient

Nurse: Did they mention anything about a tube through your nose?

Patient: Yes, I'm gonna have a tube in my nose.

Nurse: You're going to have the tube down for a couple of days or longer. It depends. So you're going to be NPO, nothing by mouth, and also you're going to have IV fluid.

Patient: I know. For three or four days, they told me that already. I don't like it, though.

Nurse: You don't have any choice.

Patient: Yes, I don't have any choice, I know.

Nurse: Like it or not, you don't have any choice. (laughter) After you come back, we'll ask you to do a lot of coughing and deep breathing to exercise your lungs.

Patient: Oh, we'll see how I feel.

Nurse: (emphasis) No matter how you feel, you have to do that!

President's commission for the Study of Ethical Problems in Medicine and Biomedical and Behavioral Research, *Making Health Care Decisions: A Report on the Ethical and Legal Implications of the Patient-Practitioner Relationship*

that they didn't know how long he or she might live, "but would stress that it could be for a substantial period of time"; 28 percent would say that they "couldn't tell how long, but would stress that in most cases people live no longer than a year"; and 22 percent would "refuse to speculate on how long the patient might live."

To the degree that a proposed course of treatment is elective, the outcome uncertain, and the procedure experimental, the patient's informed consent becomes correspondingly more important. For example, drawing a blood sample is a widely known and commonplace procedure and entails little risk to the patient. Consequently, we do not expect to receive a detailed explanation of risks when we roll up our sleeve for the insertion of the needle. However, a complicated surgical procedure, one that involves a nearly equal proportion of risks and benefits, makes the matter of the patient's informed consent crucial. Although informed consent is mandated by law when medical experiments are conducted on human subjects, truly informed consent may be difficult to attain, particularly when such research is highly esoteric or technical in nature.

Another gray area involving informed consent relates to the use of *placebos* in medical practice. A placebo is an "inert substance made to appear indistinguishable from an authentic drug," with an inactive component such as sugar substituted for the active drug.[16] Placebos are commonly given to patients when new drugs are being tested so the drugs can be evaluated by comparison, and such use is not ethically questionable. On the other hand, the prescribing of placebos by doctors in routine medical practice does raise questions related to deceiving patients, even though it can be argued that the aim is worthy. Typically, placebos are prescribed when no organic cause for an ailment is found, and it is believed that the placebo will have a beneficial psychological effect. Some authorities estimate that 35 to 45 percent of all prescriptions are essentially placebos. David Towle says that "those physicians who use placebos argue that the end, curing the patient, takes precedence over the means: in this case, the deception of the patient."[17]

As can be seen from the examples of experimentation with human subjects and the use of placebos, the ideal of informed consent is not always easy to attain. Even in cases involving conventional medical practice, it may be difficult to clearly determine what constitutes sufficient information on which the patient can base a decision. Too, patients, as noted, differ in how much they want to be told. Some patients take an active role in their treatment, even suggesting to their physician alternative methods of treatment; they are eager to receive a full disclosure of the medical facts, and insist on understanding the various options. Other patients prefer simply to follow the program outlined by their doctor; they do not want to know about potential risks or the percentage of failures.

Patients devise different strategies for coping with their illnesses; full disclosure may be a help to some patients, a hindrance to others. This difference can present a dilemma to the medical practitioner. Required to obtain the patient's informed consent before proceeding with treatment, the physician must also be sensitive to the patient's preferences for the amount and kind of information given.

In addition, physicians must safeguard themselves against the threat of malpractice suits that may arise when patients do not adequately understand the possible consequences of a course of treatment. Unfortunately, given the current climate of malpractice litigation, some physicians may view the concept of informed consent as a nonmedical legalistic and bureaucratic intrusion that interrupts the practice of medicine. Such a viewpoint is not likely to result in physicians providing information in a way that truly meets the needs and desires of patients. As Howard Brody suggests, informed consent should not be interpreted as merely reciting "an exhaustive list of risks of any particular medical procedure."[18] On the contrary, if informed consent is to become an integral part of patient care, doctors must make their reasoning about a proposed course of treatment "transparent" to the patient. In Brody's view, "Adequate informed consent is obtained when a reasonably informed patient is allowed to participate in the medical decision to the extent that the patient wishes." To this end, the physician must disclose the basis for choosing a proposed treatment and provide opportunities for the patient to ask questions and have them answered to his or her satisfaction. In sum, Brody says, the doctor must "share his thinking, answer questions, and determine how participatory the patient wishes to be and facilitate that level of participation." In this way, informed consent becomes more than simply a laundry list of risks recited to avoid potential complaints or legal problems; it facilitates true patient-physician cooperation in working toward a common goal of optimal health care.

The issues surrounding informed consent undoubtedly will be among the chief concerns of medical practitioners for some time. To ensure compliance with the requirements of informed consent, some have suggested linking payment for medical services to assurance of the patient's consent.[19] The great advances in medical care have simultaneously raised our expectations of what can be achieved and made medical practices more esoteric — a paradoxical situation, given that the patient must sufficiently understand the medical realities to make informed decisions about the proposed plan of treatment.

Choosing Death: Euthanasia and Allowing to Die

Ethical questions about the "right to die" have become prominent since the landmark case involving Karen Ann Quinlan. On April 15, 1975, at age twenty-one, she was admitted to the intensive care unit of a New Jersey hospital in a comatose state. Soon her vital processes were being artificially sustained via a mechanical MA-1 respirator. When she remained unresponsive, in a so-called "persistent vegetative state" with no known hope of recovery, Karen's parents asked to have the respirator disconnected so that nature might take its course. This request was opposed by the medical staff responsible for Karen's care, and their refusal resulted in a suit before the New Jersey Superior Court to determine who should have the right to act on Karen's behalf: her parents or the medical staff. Although the Superior Court ruled in favor of the medical staff, thereby keeping Karen on the respirator, this decision was overturned by the Supreme Court of New Jersey in March of 1976.[20]. Artificial respiration was discontinued, and Karen was eventually transferred to a nursing care facility, where she died in June 1985 at age thirty-one, having become a focal point for issues pertaining to "death with dignity," which continue to be intensely debated.

Throughout most of the history of medicine, the Hippocratic obligation of physicians to care for patients has been interpreted to mean, "Thou shalt not kill, but needst not strive officiously to keep alive." This traditional understanding of the Hippocratic obligation acknowledges that in some circumstances medical treatment is futile, offering no further benefit to the patient. With the advent of modern medical technologies, however, the slogan of the medical practitioner has often seemed to be: "Keep the patient alive at all costs." This fundamental change in the aims of medical care not only affects the dying and their relatives, it also presents a burdensome paradox to physicians. What is the proper balance between preserving life and preventing suffering when further treatment is likely to be futile? Although today's medical technologies offer tremendous possibilities for sustaining life, what effect do these life-sustaining technologies have on the *quality* of patient's lives?

When suffering outweighs the benefits of continued existence, some would argue that individuals have a "right to die," whether or not that right is exercised. Patients themselves often make last-ditch attempts to end their lives. Joseph Fletcher reports that patients may "swallow Kleenex to suffocate themselves, or jerk tubes out of their noses or veins, in a cat-and-mouse game of life and death which is neither merciful nor meaningful."[21] Surrounded by an array of machinery and tubes, the patient may seem less a whole human person than an objectified extension of medical technology.

When I was a junior physician in a hospital, we were once called urgently to the bedside of a lady of ninety. The nurse had used the term "cardiac arrest"—the old lady's heart had stopped (as hearts are apt to do, around ninety!). But because the cardiac arrest alarm was raised, I and the other houseman launched into a full-scale resuscitation. With violent drugs injected directly into the heart, blasts of electric current through her chest, noise and chaos, she had anything but a peaceful death. On reflection we realized that all this had been inappropriate, but nothing in our medical student training gave us any guide. Indeed once the emergency is in the air, there is not time to weigh up the pros and cons. The decision is rarely a doctor's anyway, because usually the only person on the scene when an emergency occurs is a nurse—probably a relatively junior one if it is night time—and she decides whether or not to resuscitate. Needless to say, it is a very courageous nurse who decides not to. Once things have started, it is very difficult for the doctor when he arrives to stop everything, particularly if the patient is showing signs of reviving.

Richard Lamerton, *Care of the Dying*

Even when a patient is deemed to be irreversibly comatose or in a persistent vegetative state—that is, profoundly unconscious, lacking any sign of normal reflexes controlled by the brain stem or spinal cord, unresponsive to all external stimuli, and with no reasonable hope of change for the better—medical personnel are duty bound to render beneficial treatment.[22] But what constitutes beneficial treatment in such cases? Is preserving life the only ethical choice, regardless of the circumstances? Should useless treatment be withheld or withdrawn even though such a decision is virtually certain to result in the patient's death? When confronted with the case of an irreversibly comatose patient or an end-stage terminal patient in great suffering, should a physician consider actively *hastening* a patient's death?

Such questions are central to the debate concerning *euthanasia*, a word that comes from the Greek. Euthanasia is defined as the act of bringing about a gentle, painless death. In practice, the term is usually understood as "intentionally taking the life of a terminal patient who requests it in order to end a painful dying."[23] In discussions of euthanasia, a distinction is often made between *active* euthanasia (that is, actively bringing about death by, for example, administering a lethal injection), and *passive* euthanasia (allowing death to occur as a result of withdrawing or withholding some treatment that might otherwise sustain life). This distinction is sometimes characterized as the difference between "killing" and "letting die."

Some ethicists argue that the term *passive euthanasia* is a misnomer, since it tends to confuse the generally unacceptable (and unlawful) practice of actively causing death with the fairly well-established and accepted practice of withholding or withdrawing useless treatments.[24] In the United States, taking active measures to end someone's life is a capital crime. In contrast, it is widely considered to be good medical practice not to artificially prolong the life and suffering of a person whose disease is inevitably fatal.[25] Forgoing life-sustaining treatment (that is, doing without a medical intervention that would be expected to extend life) encompasses both *withholding* (not initiating) treatment and *withdrawing* (discontinuing) an ongoing treatment.

Reviewing the range of today's medical technologies, the President's Commission for the Study of Ethical Problems in Medicine reported: "For almost any life-threatening condition, some intervention is capable of delaying the moment of death. . . . Matters that were once the province of fate have now become a matter of human choice."[26] Antibiotics and artificial nutrition, as well as respirators, kidney machines, and other technologies of modern medicine are examples of therapies that sustain life.

When a patient is hopelessly ill, most people would question the appropriateness of such heroic attempts to preserve life as sustaining the breathing and heartbeat with sophisticated equipment. There is a pervasive feeling that when a person is without hope of regaining consciousness or the semblance of normal human activity, he or she should be allowed to die as peacefully as possible. A patient whose case is utterly without hope may be designated "Code 90," or "DNR" (Do Not Resuscitate), or "CMO" (Comfort Measures Only), each a message to the medical and nursing staff that, when death appears to be imminent, extraordinary life-saving measures are not to be applied. Efforts are directed toward easing pain and making the patient as comfortable as possible until death comes.

When a patient is hopelessly ill or irreversibly comatose, medical ethicists delineate three "treatment" options that can be considered: (1) active treatment to forestall death; (2) active intervention to terminate life; and (3) passive management, a middle course involving neither extraordinary life-saving measures nor active hastening of death. In practice, active intervention to intentionally terminate a patient's life is quite rare. It is much more likely that the choice will be made to pursue either active intervention (using extraordinary measures to sustain life) or a course of passive management (using only "ordinary" or "essential" means of treatment).

Ordinary care includes the use of conventional, proven therapies that are maximally effective with minimal danger. *Extraordinary measures*, on the other hand, usually entail significant risks and unpredictable results. Typically, such treatment is intended as a temporary measure designed to sustain life artificially until the patient's own restorative powers can take over. Of course, given the particulars of a situation, a treatment considered by some as ordinary or essential may be considered by others as extraordinary or even intrusive. The use of antibiotics to combat pneumonia in an end-stage cancer patient is an example of how a normally ordinary and essential treatment may be viewed as extraordinary because of the circumstances.

Although there now appears to be general agreement among medical practitioners as well as among the public that extraordinary measures need not be used when a patient is hopelessly ill, it is nonetheless true that many areas of uncertainty remain. For example, in the absence of a physician's written DNR (Do Not Resuscitate) order, most hospitals require the active initiation of cardiopulmonary resuscitation (CPR) in the event of cardiac or respiratory arrest. Yet, when such resuscitation is clearly futile, some observers believe it should be withheld, as would other forms of treatment that offer no benefit to the patient.[27]

In the United States, most of the discussion in recent years has concerned the issue of withholding or withdrawing treatment. In the Netherlands, however, physicians report taking *active* steps to end the lives of patients who request a "dignified death."[28] It is estimated that between 2000 and 10,000 terminally ill patients in the Netherlands, most with cancer, die as a result of voluntary active euthanasia each year, their deaths typically hastened by lethal doses administered by sympathetic physicians. As a result of decisions during the 1970s and 1980s by the Dutch courts, euthanasia is no longer prosecuted in certain circumstances. Consonant with prevailing medical ethics in the Netherlands, the criteria established by Dutch courts include the presence of a confirmed terminal diagnosis; the patient's unwavering desire, confirmed in writing, of his or her wish to die; the presence of unbearable and incurable physical suffering; and a second medical opinion. Although the current Dutch penal code states that anyone who takes another person's life — even at their explicit request — can be punished, it also states that such an act is not punishable if "driven by an overwhelming power, a sudden conflict of duties or interests in a situation in which a choice must be made." Based on this situation, physicians and health care institutions have established guidelines to be followed when a patient requests euthanasia.

Some argue that euthanasia is morally permissible when it prevents an even greater cruelty — namely, preventing someone who is in pain and wishes to die from obtaining the release offered by death. According to this view, both the patient and the physician ought to be free to pursue the course indicated as in the patient's best interests, given his or her terminal condition.

Critics of this argument respond by emphasizing the dangers of allowing euthanasia to become an acceptable and routine policy. Objections to euthanasia include the difficulty of obtaining a patient's clear consent, the risk of incorrect diagnosis, and the uncertainty whether an innovative treatment might have become available in time to offer a cure. Another objection has been characterized as the "wedge" or "slippery slope" argument: One should not permit acts that, although possibly moral in themselves, might eventually pave the way for acts that would be immoral. If we were to permit euthanasia in cases of irreversible terminal illness today, tomorrow the practice might well be expanded to situations that are far less justifiable, leading to acts of killing motivated by caprice or whim, or perhaps darker motives.

(Another argument that can be made against euthanasia relates to the notion held by some Buddhists, for example, that the period surrounding dying offers an extraordinary opportunity for awakening or enlightenment. That there may be a biochemical basis for this belief is suggested by recent research on endorphins,

Dying of a prolonged disease is less an event than a difficult process, which, like birth, requires understanding help.

Medicine should prolong life, not the process of dying. There comes a point in a degenerative disease when further "aggressive" treatment would intensify the patient's suffering without substantial benefit. Then concern for the patient should become concern for a dignified death, for palliative care for symptoms and needs. This point is difficult to determine, because much is unknown about the behavior of advanced malignant disease. But the point must be determined.

Hospices . . . are an answer to demands for euthanasia (meaning not the patient's legal right to demand withdrawal of life-support treatment, but the right to demand a killing act). Support for euthanasia legislation derives, in part, from the mistaken fear that doctors are obligated to prolong life with all available technologies, however severe the ordeal and cost, and the mistaken fear that unremitting pain in terminal diseases, especially cancer, is unavoidable. With hospice care as an alternative, there would be little demand for euthanasia.

George F. Will, *The Pursuit of Virtue & Other Tory Notions*

which are natural products of the body that seem to relieve pain while enhancing clarity of thought during the dying process.)

Elisabeth Kübler-Ross and Dame Cicely Saunders, the founder of modern hospice care, have both argued strongly against voluntary euthanasia for the terminally ill. Such a practice, they say, is unlikely to remain voluntary; soon, the irreversibly sick will be made to feel guilty for not agreeing to end it quickly. Others involved in palliative care concur with the notion that permitting euthanasia to become an accepted policy is not only morally dangerous, but also unnecessary since the suffering of dying patients can be treated. In summary, their argument states:[29]

1. There is an inherent risk that a legally sanctioned "right" to euthanasia might come to be experienced by the patient as an obligation, with a subtle pressure to "end it all" so as to lessen the burden on loved ones.
2. Where would one draw the line once the slippery slope of euthanasia has been embarked on?
3. When the pain and depression are treated and the sources of anxiety addressed, the infrequent request for euthanasia may disappear.

Most people who endorse the philosophy of hospice or palliative care would agree that the provision of adequate treatment for pain and depression essentially does away with any reason for considering active measures to prematurely end a terminal patient's life. Furthermore, as Richard Gula argues, when the character of a community is shaped by qualities of interdependence, care, and hospitality, it results not in abandonment of the dying, but, rather, "accompanying in a faithful and loving way those whom medicine cannot cure."[30]

Nevertheless, there are those who wish to legally institute a "right to die," or, as some prefer to phrase it, to legalize the possibility of choosing *when* to die.[31] Joseph Fletcher argues that "it is vacuous to distinguish between direct and indirect means, or between active or passive means."[32] He says, "The only real question is whether human beings may ever take their dying into their own hands." In Fletcher's opinion, as well as the opinion of organizations such as the Hemlock Society and Americans Against Human Suffering (which placed an initiative on the 1988 California ballot that sought to make it legal for doctors to end the lives of terminal patients who want to die), it is only a matter of time until active euthanasia is decriminalized.

However accurate that forecast, many ethicists and medical practitioners express concern about blurring the distinction between "allowing to die" by withholding or withdrawing treatment and actively "helping to die." In an article published in the *Journal of the American Medical Association*, Charles Sprung says that, even though active euthanasia is considered by many people as "unconscionable" and unlikely to be accepted, "the seeds of active euthanasia have already been planted in our country."[33] Prominent physicians have voiced the belief that "it is not immoral for a physician to assist in the rational suicide of a terminally ill patient." An example of acting on such a belief was the controversial case of "Debbie," a twenty-year-old woman with terminal ovarian cancer who was killed by her physician because he "wanted to help put her out of her misery."[34] Even if the medical profession or society as a whole disavows such actions, individual physicians may act without ethical sanction.

The premise of "what is useful is right" has infected society, says Sprung, including the medical arena. Sounding a warning against taking medically sound and ethically appropriate practices to the point that they become inappropriate or devaluing of human life, he recounts the "aberration of the physician" in Nazi Germany, where "direct medical killing and systematic genocide" became conceivable partly because people accepted the concept of *lebensunwertes leben*, "a life unworthy of life." In such a context, "physicians were providing healing treatment by destroying the life unworthy of life."

Calling attention to the fact that attitudes and practices have changed dramatically over the past couple of decades, Sprung says: "We have evolved from situations in which it was a deviation from the medical and ethical standard to withdraw a respirator, nutrition, or intravenous fluid from a non-brain dead patient to the present environment in which it is accepted practice and becoming the norm to withdraw such medical treatments in certain groups of patients."

In a commentary on Sprung's article, Robert Carton grants that a change in attitudes has indeed taken place but argues that to condemn the blurring of moral issues and a casual attitude about the termination of life does not necessarily mean that one supports "biologic life under all circumstances."[35] Such a strategy, says Carton, "can lead us into grotesque situations in which mere cellular life persists in bodies from which all personality has irretrievably fled." The ethical problem regarding the termination of life support is, as Carton rightly observes, "entirely new," and "any satisfactory solution will defend the dignity and integrity of individual humans."

David Roy, director of the Center for Bioethics in Montreal and editor of the *Journal of Palliative Care*, believes that the distinction between euthanasia and allowing to die must be maintained: "This distinction is a recognition of the limits of modern medicine's power, and of the limits of the medical profession's mandate; a recognition also that horrible and intolerable abuse is as much a possibility for us today as it has already proved to be a reality in the past."[36] The challenge of civilization to our societies, he says, is not to legalize euthanasia, but rather to transform our care of the suffering and dying.

Nutrition and Hydration

In several states, families of irreversibly comatose patients have recently sought and obtained court rulings allowing removal of artificial feeding tubes. In Florida, for example, a District Court of Appeals said that artificial feeding is similar to other extraordinary means of sustaining life, such as the respirator. It ruled that the right of privacy includes the right to remove nasogastric tubes from persons who are in persistent vegetative states with no prospect of regaining cognitive brain function. In a unanimous decision, the court said that when the use of medical technologies results in a situation where all that remains is the forced function of bodily processes, including artificial sustenance of the body itself, "we recognize the right to allow the natural consequences of the removal of those artificial life-sustaining measures."[37] Concurrence in such decisions is reflected in a policy announced by an ethics panel of the American Medical Association stating that artificial feeding and the infusion of water can be stopped in cases of irreversible coma.

Some commentators, however, have condemned judicial decisions authorizing the withdrawal of nutrition from a "preservable unconscious patient," even going so far as to characterize such actions as the intentional killing of a human being. Others, holding to the distinction between active euthanasia and forgoing a medical intervention, contend that the withdrawal of artificial nutrition is consistent with traditional medical and legal doctrines.[38] Among those who believe that removal of artificial nutrition is tantamount to intentional killing, some argue that the symbolic significance of nourishment justifies the continuation of artificial nutrition and hydration even when all other medical treatments have been stopped. Feelings about the provision of food and drink and about the specter of "starving" a patient to death are deeply rooted in the human psyche. On the other hand, those who believe it is indeed moral to withdraw artificial nourishment argue that these everyday sentiments about the symbolic meaning of food and water "cannot be transferred without distortion to the hospital world," and that, indeed, "authentic sentiment may demand discontinuance of artificial feeding."[39]

This "conceptual ambiguity" about the artificial delivery of food and fluids, say James McCartney and Jane Trau, "derives from the traditional consideration

© Carol A. Foote

Assistance in providing nutrition to chronically ill and dying patients ranges from help with eating, as seen here in the case of these nursing home residents, to total reliance on artificial feeding. The issue of artificially providing nutrition to comatose, hopelessly ill patients is one of the newest ethical issues in medicine.

of nourishment as simple care."[40] When such nourishment is withheld, it brings up images of burdening the patient with "the pain of death by starvation." But the invasive nature of delivering such nourishment and the skills required to administer it, as well as the pain and discomfort experienced by many patients, argue against the perception that such artificial delivery of sustenance is merely providing care. Contrary to the view that artificial provision of nourishment is simple care, McCartney and Trau find that, in actuality, these procedures more closely resemble palliative or even therapeutic treatment. As Dena Davis remarks in the context of a case involving whether or not to implant a permanent feeding tube into the body of an eighty-year-old woman, the issues relating to providing nourishment are highly charged emotionally, and "we need to be very careful to sort out the physiological aspects of providing nutrition from the social phenomenon of 'feeding.'"[41]

In 1987, the New Jersey Supreme Court ruled on cases involving the removal of feeding tubes from two patients in that state. Nancy Ellen Jobes, thirty-one years old, was four months pregnant in April 1980 when she was in a car accident, and she had fallen into a coma when doctors removed the fetus (which died). The other patient, Hilda Peter, sixty-five years old, had suffered a stroke in

1984 and had been in a coma since that time, a condition that her physicians said could continue indefinitely. In deciding the cases, the court stated that it recognized that "the state has an interest in preserving life," but that those interests "weaken — and the individual's right to privacy becomes stronger — as the degree of bodily invasion (affected by the medical treatment at issue) increases and the prognosis dims."[42]

The opinions of the Florida and New Jersey courts relative to the removal of artificial feeding devices are not universally shared, however. This fact was clearly illustrated by the June 1990 decision of the United States Supreme Court regarding the case of Nancy Beth Cruzan. As a result of injuries sustained in an automobile accident in January 1983 when she was twenty-five, Cruzan had been in a persistent vegetative state. Although paramedics restored her breathing after the accident, her brain had been deprived of oxygen for so long that she never regained consciousness. In February 1983, doctors implanted a feeding tube in Cruzan's stomach, the only form of life support she was receiving. Prior to the Supreme Court's deliberations, the Missouri Supreme Court had denied her parents' petition to end artificial feeding, a treatment that Nancy's physicians said could prolong her life for as long as thirty years. As Nancy's guardians, her parents claimed legal standing to assert her right to be free from "unwarranted bodily intrusions." However, absent Nancy's express consent to remove life-sustaining artificial nutrition and hydration, the state court held that her guardians could not exercise her right to refuse treatment and that the state's "unqualified" interest in preserving life should therefore prevail.[43]

As the case went before the U.S. Supreme Court, the American Medical Association and other groups, including Concern for Dying, filed *amicus curiae* briefs in support of the Cruzans' position. Other groups, including the Association of American Physicians and Surgeons, filed opposing briefs, arguing that a physician's obligation to patients who are comatose or in a persistent vegetative state "does not depend upon the prospect of recovery."

In its 5–4 decision, the Supreme Court ruled that Missouri could enforce the standards expressed in its statute by reason of the state's interest in protecting life. Although the Court affirmed a patient's right to refuse medical treatment, including artificial nutrition and hydration, it said that states are justified in requiring that only the patient — in a clear and competent expression of his or her wishes — can decide to withdraw treatment. Here is a synopsis of the Court's decision:[44]

> The scope of the Court's considerations was quite narrow. It sought to determine whether Nancy Cruzan had a right under the United States Constitution that would require the hospital to withdraw life-sustaining treatment. The Court answered in the negative. While acknowledging that a competent person has a constitutional right to refuse life-sustaining medical treatment on the basis of "liberty interests" (not privacy) protected by the 14th Amendment, the Court held that there is nothing in the United States Constitution that forbids Missouri from establishing the procedural requirements it did (that is, clear and convincing evidence) for decision making by surrogates for incompetent patients.

Thus, despite the Cruzans' insistence that they were in a position to voice their daughter's wishes (as her court-appointed guardians), the Court's decision hinged on the fact that Nancy had not formally made her wishes known by executing a living will or similar advance directive stating her preferences. (Advance directives such as living wills and durable powers of attorney are discussed in the next chapter.) Although the motives of the Cruzans were not questioned by the Court, which found them to be "loving and caring parents," its ruling reflected the opinion that the motives of family members in other cases could be "not entirely disinterested." Thus, in the majority opinion of the Court, "A state is entitled to guard against potential abuses in such situations." The Cruzan case highlights the importance of leaving written instructions for relatives and doctors to follow in the event of incapacitating and terminal illness. Notice, if you will, how the principles of autonomy, beneficence, and justice were applied in this case.

The Supreme Court's decision effectively returned further consideration of the case back to the Missouri courts. In December of 1990, a Missouri judge reconsidered the case in light of the Supreme Court's decision and new testimony from three of Nancy's friends who claimed to have had conversations with her to the effect that she would not want to live "like a vegetable." The attorney general of Missouri had, in the meantime, asked the court to drop the state as a colitigant, saying that the state no longer had a "recognizable legal interest" in the case and would not contest the Cruzans' attempts to end their daughter's life. In addition, Nancy Cruzan's court-appointed guardian recommended that the feeding tube be removed. A doctor who had previously testified against removing the feeding tube now reversed himself and testified that he believed it would be in Cruzan's best interest to end her "living hell." At this point, the state court ruled that the "clear and convincing evidence" standard had been met and granted permission for removal of the tube supplying food and water. Thirteen days later, while anti-euthanasia protesters congregated outside the hospital, Nancy Cruzan died. "She remained peaceful throughout and showed no sign of discomfort or distress in any way," the Cruzan family said in a statement. "Knowing Nancy as only a family can, there remains no question that we made the choice she would want."

Following Nancy's death, columnist Ellen Goodman wrote: "The Cruzan case, like that of Karen Ann Quinlan, became a story that made America talk publicly and at length about death in the technological age."[45] As the first case of its kind to come before the Supreme Court, the Cruzan case focused national attention on "right to die" issues and helped prompt legislation requiring that patients be informed of their right to refuse treatment.[46] Ethicists found the legal resolution of the case to be less notable than its "educative and symbolic value." As Daniel Callahan said, "It signals the fact that laws on this issue differ from state to state, and it has called to attention the anguish that families have when they are faced with a confusing legal situation." Arthur Caplan said: "The family was put through seven years of bureaucracy, courtrooms, hearings, second-guessing, and media exposure for a decision that I always felt they should have had the ability to make privately and with dignity."[47]

A number of years ago, before all the discussion about defining brain death and maintaining life on a respirator and so on, a patient of mine, a young pregnant woman at term, suddenly developed extremely high blood pressure. Then she had a stroke and the baby's heartbeat stopped, so we supported her by artificially maintaining blood pressure and other vital functions, including breathing. But she had had a complete brain death immediately. And she had lost the baby. We got an EEG [electroencephalogram], and it was completely flat. We repeated it twenty-four hours later, and again it was completely flat.

It was the worst tragedy I've ever seen, because in just a few minutes she was gone and the baby was gone—just within moments. I talked with her husband, her mother, and her father. (Now, this was long before the issues surrounding definition of death had become so contentious that the lawyers got involved.) I told them that the thing to do was turn off the machine. Just as I had not read about all this, they as a family had not read about it. It seemed quite logical to me.

So we picked a time when we were going to do it, and they all came and waited outside the door. I told them again what I was going to do, and they said to go ahead and do it. I went in and turned off the machine. The nurse and I watched her, and in five minutes her pulse rate had stopped. I think this is the proper way to handle this sort of situation when brain death is involved. I think it has a negative effect to continue life support systems for weeks and months. It was a tragedy, and given the tragedy, what options do you have? Continue the life support system or don't continue it. To me, there's no argument whatsoever to continue the life support system.

Quoted from *Death and Dying: The Physician's Perspective,* a videotape by Elizabeth Bradbury

While the Cruzan case caused many people to think about formally expressing their wishes while still able to do so, the recent case of Carrie Coons, an 86-year-old New York stroke victim may give some of them pause.[48] For more than four months following her stroke, Mrs. Coons showed no signs of alertness. Doctors, lawyers, and family members believed her to be in a persistent and irreversible vegetative coma, and so petitioned the court for the right to disconnect her life support—an action previously approved of by Mrs. Coons. This permission was granted. Two days later, Mrs. Coons began to stir, eventually eating small portions of food and saying a few words. When her physician asked what should now be done about her case, Mrs. Coons replied, "These are difficult decisions," and fell asleep. Permission to disconnect her feeding tube was withdrawn.

Ethical issues involving forced feeding of *noncomatose* patients became prominent in the California judiciary when the decision of Elizabeth Bouvia, a quadriplegic, to refuse such treatment was upheld by that state's Supreme Court. The ruling said that mentally competent, informed patients have the right to refuse any medical treatment, including life support provided by mechanical or artificial means. This historic ruling allowing Elizabeth Bouvia to refuse forced feeding was hailed by some as a victory for individual liberties; others called it "legal suicide."[49]

Given the degree of uncertainty currently surrounding many ethical issues in medicine, who should make decisions about forgoing life-sustaining treatment? In the final report of its studies, the President's Commission emphasized the importance of: (1) respecting the choices of individuals who are competent to decide to forgo even life-sustaining treatment; (2) providing guidelines and procedures for making decisions on behalf of patients who are unable to do so on their own; (3) maintaining a presumption in favor of sustaining life; (4) improving the medical options available to dying patients; (5) providing respectful, responsive, and supportive care to patients for whom no further medical therapies are available or elected; and (6) encouraging health care institutions to take responsibility for ensuring that adequate procedures for decision making are available for all patients.[50] Probably no other topic of death and dying generates as much debate as do the ethical issues related to the hopelessly ill.

Seriously Ill Newborns and Neonatal Intensive Care

The ethical issues that arise from the dilemma of whether to sustain life or to allow death are perhaps most sensitively realized in the case of infants. Throughout this century and especially within the past few decades, the mortality rate among infants and children has been reduced, largely through advances in both the knowledge and techniques of neonatal care. In hospitals with specialized infant intensive care units, for instance, the neonatal mortality rate is roughly half that of hospitals not having such special care nurseries. Neonatal treatment now includes "the use of respirators, sensitive monitoring of blood pressure, oxygenation, blood flow and biochemical parameters, and other evolving nursing and medical technologies," and "new techniques have been developed in heart, intestine, liver, kidney, and brain surgery to correct congenital anomalies."[51]

The special care nursery, which can make the crucial difference in an infant's chances of survival, is an innovation in medical practice that virtually everyone can applaud. As Marie McCormick reports, "Neonatal intensive care continues to be effective in saving lives" and "the majority of survivors do not suffer from severe to moderate handicap."[52] Unfortunately, some of the infants whose lives are spared will never be capable of living what is considered a normal human life. They may suffer from cardiopulmonary ailments or brain damage, or they may be severely handicapped by some congenital malformation. Formerly, such dysfunctional conditions in infancy would almost surely have resulted in death. Now that many such infants survive because of the specialized care they receive, we are confronted by ethical questions concerning the quality of their lives and the guidelines that should be followed in determining whether or not medical intervention is the best course of action.

Should the life of an infant with intestinal blockage be spared by surgical intervention? Is the answer always "Yes, life should be saved," or does the answer change according to circumstances? What if the infant is brain-damaged or severely retarded?

Consider the following case: An infant was born with his entire left side malformed, with no left eye, and practically without a left ear; his left hand was deformed, and some of his vertebrae were not fused. Being also afflicted with a tracheo-esophageal fistula (an abnormality of the windpipe and the canal that leads to the stomach), he could not be fed by mouth. Air leaked into his stomach instead of going to the lungs, and fluid from the stomach pushed up into the lungs. One doctor commented, "It takes little imagination to think there were further internal difficulties as well." In the ensuing days, the infant's condition steadily worsened. Pneumonia set in; his reflexes became impaired; and, because of poor circulation, severe brain damage was suspected. But despite the seriousness of all these factors taken together, the immediate threat to his survival, the tracheo-esophageal fistula, could be corrected by a fairly easy surgical procedure.

The debate began when the parents refused to give their consent to surgery. Some of the doctors treating the child believed that surgery was warranted and took the case to court. The judge ordered surgery, ruling that "at the moment of live birth, there does exist a human being entitled to the fullest protection of the law. . . . The most basic right enjoyed by every human being is the right to life itself."[53]

In another case, which provides some contrasts to the one just cited, the mother of a premature baby overheard the doctor describing her infant as having Down's syndrome with the added complication that the intestines were blocked. Ordinary surgery can correct this kind of blockage; without correction, the child cannot be fed and will die. The mother felt that "it would be unfair" to her other children if a retarded child were brought into the home. Her husband supported this decision, and they refused their consent for surgery.

One of the physicians argued that the degree of mental retardation in children with Down's syndrome cannot be predicted; and, in the physician's words: "They're almost always trainable. They can hold simple jobs, and they're famous for being happy children. They're perennially happy and usually a great joy. When further complications do not appear, a long life can be anticipated." However, in this case, the hospital staff did not seek a court order to override the parents' decision against surgical intervention. As a result, the child was placed in a side room and, over the following eleven days, it starved to death.

The differences between these two cases are instructive. The severely malformed infant in the first case seemed to have less chance of survival or of living a normal life than the afflicted infant in the second example. Yet the hospital staff in the first case chose to seek a court order granting treatment, whereas the staff at the second hospital chose to abide by the parents' wishes, even though the child could probably have been saved.

In commenting on the second case, James Gustafson argues that the child's right to life was not adequately explored, either by the physicians or by the parents.[54] From the doctors' point of view, once the decision was made not to proceed with the operation, the child became terminal, and thus further means of sustaining life were unwarranted. Gustafson, however, argues that the subsequent withholding of ordinary means of treatment was in actuality an *extraordinary* nonintervention.

Whatever our feelings may be about the decisions just described, a distinction between cases involving infants and those involving terminal patients with a prolonged illness is worth noting. Generally, in the latter case, all procedures that might prolong life have been tried or at least presented to the patient as options. But in cases involving infants, Gustafson says, the withholding of treatment results from a "decision not to act at all."

In the past several years, controversy has arisen over the question of using anencephalic infants as potential donor sources. The medical condition of anencephaly is generally stated as "the congenital absence of skull, scalp, and forebrain (cerebral hemispheres)."[55] Infants with this condition are born with all but a small portion of their brain missing. Since this condition is fatal, some ethicists believe that anencephalics could provide a source of organs and tissues for other infants. However, the laws regarding organ donation require that death be pronounced using brain death criteria or the cessation of heart and respiratory functions. Anencephalic infants do not meet the regulatory requirements because they can exhibit spontaneous breathing and, "if physicians were to wait until all electrical activity from the small portion of the brain present in such infants ceased, there is grave concern that the vital organs and tissues of the infant would be severely damaged."[56] Opponents of using anencephalic infants as organ sources argue that the death of "infant organ donors should be declared with no less certainty than that of adult donors," and, in any event, such transplants may well be unethical.[57]

The difficulty inherent in making decisions about the treatment of seriously ill newborns was highlighted in the study by the President's Commission. While affirming that parents should have the power of decision in most instances, the Commission also stated that medical institutions should pursue the best interests of an infant "when those interests are clear."[58] Using as an example the situation of an otherwise healthy Down's syndrome child whose life is threatened by a surgically correctable condition, the Commission said that such an infant should receive surgery since he or she would benefit. While stating that therapies expected to be futile need not be provided, the Commission added that, even in cases when no beneficial therapy is available, action should be taken to ensure the infant's comfort. Based on a review of current neonatal care technologies and present standards for determining treatment, medical ethicist Arthur Caplan concludes that decisions regarding disabled newborns ought to be based on a standard that combines "the best interest of the child," an infant-centered approach, as well as considerations about the "relationship potential" of such a child, an approach that "allows the interests of others — for example, the family or society — to weigh in the decision about whether to treat."[59]

Organ Transplantation

Of recent innovative medical techniques for saving patients formerly considered hopeless, probably the best known is the transplantation of human organs. Acceptance of organ transplantation, as well as the number of such procedures,

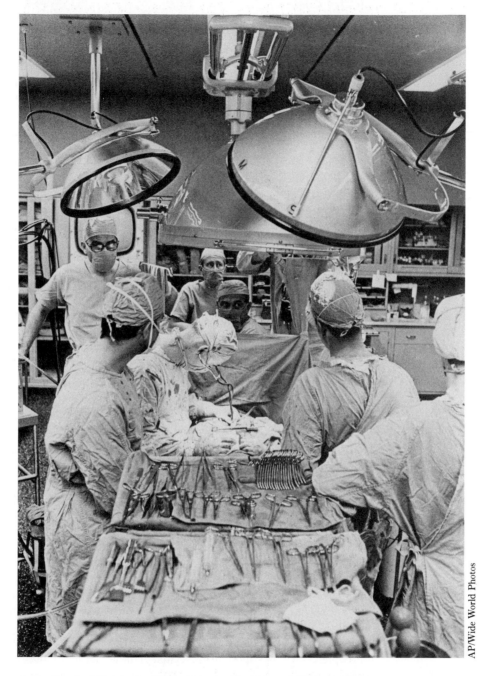

At the Stanford University Medical Center, Dr. Norman Shumway and his colleagues perform open-heart surgery. Advances in transplantation procedures and related medical therapies make such operations more feasible, yet they also raise questions that are difficult, at times quite painful, to resolve.

has been growing at a steady pace since the first kidney transplant, from one identical twin to another, in 1954 at the Peter Bent Brigham Hospital in Boston. Early transplant efforts were not always successful and, as Leonard Bailey observes, "cadaveric organs were virtually unavailable in the 1950s and most of the 1960s because we did not know how to define death appropriately."[60] The establishment of new criteria for defining so-called brain death in 1968 (discussed in the next section) and the discovery of the immunosuppressive drug cyclosporine in 1976 advanced transplantation science, transforming the 1980s into what Bailey calls "a halcyon decade of organ transplantation." During 1988, the most recent year for which statistics are available, 9123 kidneys, 1644 hearts, and 1682 livers were transplanted, in addition to nearly 37,000 cornea grafts and over 300,000 bone and skin grafts.[61]

In some cases — kidney and skin transplants, for example — the donor is a living person. Donor and recipient may even be members of the same family. The transaction involved in the gift of an organ from one's own body into the body of another by transplantation can generate feelings of altruism and a sense of pride. In a very real way, such a gift allows another person to live.

Yet the donor's decision may also involve feelings of masochism or guilt. Perhaps a donor feels "backed against the wall" by other family members who want the transplant operation to take place. At the same time, the potential recipient of an organ may experience conflict concerning the transaction. The recipient may feel guilty that another person has to give up an organ to the possible jeopardy of the donor's health; there may be anxiety about the outcome: "What if we all put ourselves through this procedure and my body rejects the donated organ? I'll feel responsible for ruining someone else's life, and we'll all be losers." Thus, both donor and recipient may have mixed feelings. Generally, the medical team responsible for the transplant operation tries to make sure that the psychological issues are resolved just as successfully as those related to the physiological concerns.[62]

When a living donor is unavailable, or when the needed organ — a heart, for example — cannot be removed from a living human being, an alternative must be found. The organ may be removed from the body of someone who agreed before death to allow organs to be taken for transplantation. Sometimes the deceased's next of kin give permission. As with living donors, intense feelings can surround the decision to give a gift of such importance to another human being.

Because fewer organs are donated than are needed, physicians must choose among prospective recipients. Thus, the physician or the medical team becomes a "gatekeeper."[63] Once a prospective recipient has been certified as physically suitable for a transplant, other factors are considered. Emotional stability, age, and ability to withstand stress all influence the chances of achieving a successful outcome. The ideal candidate for a transplant is a patient whose condition is deteriorating despite the best conventional medical treatment available and for whom a transplant offers a reasonable likelihood of recovery — in other words, someone who is likely to die in the absence of radical intervention. Thus, the alternative — death — makes the risks associated with a transplant procedure acceptable.

Because organ transplantation has become an important part of current medical interventions, there is a constant need for replacement body parts — liver, kidney, heart, and so on. Many of these organs come from cadavers. In the case of an organ such as the heart, cadavers obviously represent the only source. The practice of medicine now routinely includes the transplantation of organs from the body of a person who has been declared dead into the body of a living person who can continue to receive the life-giving benefits of the transplanted organ.

Even though organ transplantation has become relatively routine, it has nonetheless caused quite dramatic changes in the way we think about death — in particular, about the moment of death. Current medical technologies allow doctors to maintain the viability of body organs by sustaining certain physiological functions in the body of a person who has been declared dead. When artificial life-support systems are used to maintain breathing and heart action, the definition of death is blurred. The determination of death in such cases proceeds from methods of defining death that were only recently formulated.

The Need for a New Definition of Death

On the face of it, the definition of death might seem quite obvious: A person dies, is dead, and the corpse is disposed of. But as soon as someone asks, "What do you mean by 'a person dies'?'" the whole matter begins to unravel. What at first may seem simple turns out to be amazingly complex. Indeed, there are many historical accounts of persons being thought dead who in fact were in a state that only mimicked biological death.

Not too many years ago, one could hear horror stories about bodies lying in a morgue coming back to life, as it were, and startling the bereaved family, not to mention the mortician. A state of unconsciousness, perhaps, or an extreme slowing of body functioning resulted in the appearance of death. To provide a safeguard against the threat of being buried alive, some people gave instructions that their bodies be placed in coffins with bells or some other attention-getting device that the "corpse" could activate even after burial should consciousness return after a mistaken determination of death (see Figure 10-1).

Think for a moment. When would you consider yourself to be dead? How would you know that death had occurred in someone else? The answers to these questions range from the definite, "when decay and putrefaction have set in," to the more subjective: "when I can no longer take care of myself." A person using the first answer as a way of determining death would hardly be pleased to be judged dead by the standards of the second.

The present concern with defining death is, of course, more sophisticated, taking into account complex scientific data. Although we still must make determinations of death from observable indications that life has ceased, these observable signs can be interpreted differently, depending on how death is defined. In other words, how we define death establishes the empirical procedures we use to determine that a person has died. To better understand the issues relating to defining and determining death, some writers distinguish five levels at which decisions are made with respect to the death of a human being: First, a conceptual understanding of what constitutes death must be established; second, general criteria and procedures for determining that a person has died must be selected; third, these criteria must be applied in a particular case to determine if the patient meets the criteria; fourth, if the criteria are met, the person is pronounced dead; and fifth, the death is attested on a certificate of record.[64]

The Traditional Signs of Death and the New Technology

Historically, the death of the human organism has been ascertained by the absence of heartbeat and respiration. With the cessation of these vital signs, and as the cells and tissues of the body die, advanced signs of death become evident: the lack of certain reflexes in the eyes, the fall of body temperature (algor mortis), the purple-red discoloration of parts of the body as blood settles (livor mortis), and the rigidity of muscles (rigor mortis). Even today, most deaths are determined by the absence of these vital signs.

However, respirators and other sophisticated devices, which sustain vital processes artificially, render the traditional means of determining death inadequate. Using traditional criteria, a patient in an irreversible coma with no brain wave activity could be termed alive on the basis of *artificially* maintained breathing and heartbeat. Efforts to expand the criteria for determining death have fo-

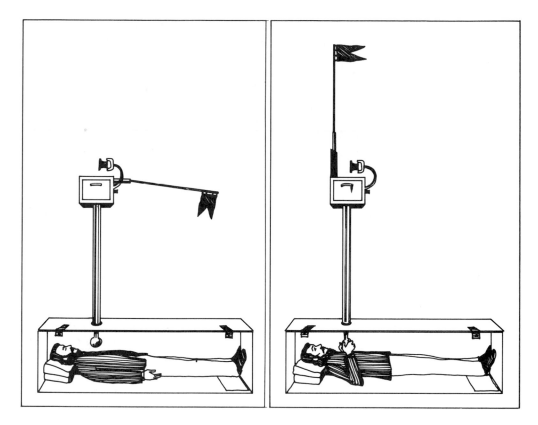

Figure *10-1 Coffin Bell-Pull Device*
To prevent premature burial in cases of doubtful death, devices such as this
French "life-preserving" coffin were invented and patented. If activated, the box
above the ground opened to let in air and light, the flag raised, a bell rang, and a
light came on to signal that the buried person was still alive. The person who had
been mistaken for dead could also call out, and his or her voice would be
amplified by the device. The fear of being buried alive stemmed from the period
of great plagues and epidemics when, in the hasty disposition of the dead, a
mistaken determination of death might result from a state of illness that only
mimicked death.

cused on "brain" death or, in some instances, cerebral death (that is, cessation of
activity in the upper part of the brain, the cerebrum, which is regarded as the
locus of conscious mental processes). As a result, medical practitioners have
adopted a definition of death that equates it with irreversible coma, as determined
by a flat electroencephalogram (EEG) reading. Confirmatory signs of irreversible or "terminal" coma include unresponsiveness to all external stimuli and lack
of any sign of normal reflexes controlled by the brain stem or spinal cord.[65]

As pointed out in an editorial in the British medical journal *Lancet*, the problem of defining brain death arises only when a patient is put on a respirator and is thus sustained artificially; indeed, the editorial stated bluntly that the resulting dilemma about brain death is of the doctor's own making.[66] In fact, the dilemma is one that relates to a host of medical, legal, ethical, moral, and religious concerns. The debate about new definitions of death and how they should be applied has become a public policy issue of interest to both professionals and laypersons, much like the debate over nuclear armaments. Like the nuclear debate, the history of which can be traced to a particular event — the development of the atomic bomb — the debate concerning how death should be defined and determined can also be traced to a particular event — the development of the respirator. Thus, the current situation is the result of a technological innovation. Clyde Nabe says:[67]

> Technology seldom presents itself in a value-free way. There are usually trade-offs involved; the respirator saves lives and allows many human beings to continue productive lives that would otherwise be lost. But it also presents us with situations wherein we are uncertain we are dealing any longer with a human life; the morality of continuing to respirate a body that may or may not be a human being is unclear.

Rather than replacing the traditional clinical means of diagnosis — pulse, heartbeat, and respiration — the new criteria for determining death supplement them, being applicable to instances that arise from the new technology. The widespread use of organ transplantation procedures has been an important impetus to recent efforts to arrive at a new definition of death. In many cases, transplanted organs are taken from donors who have suffered brain death but whose heartbeat and breath are maintained artificially. With regard to organ transplantation, two issues are central: (1) determining when death can be said to have occurred, and (2) deciding when it is permissible to remove the deceased's organs. Even when the second of these issues is not relevant to a particular patient's situation, however, the determination of death can still present a dilemma. As the *Lancet* editorial emphasized, once a patient is placed on devices that artificially sustain vital functions, a variety of complex medical, legal, and ethical questions may impinge on how death is defined.

If alternative definitions of death are to be assessed, the distinction between *clinical death* and cellular death must be understood. As we have seen, clinical death is determined by a set of criteria imposed on a particular array of vital signs (such as blood flow and breathing). Thus, when a patient's breathing or heartbeat stops — even if temporarily, as during certain surgical procedures — it can be said that the patient was clinically dead during the time these vital functions had ceased. However, it can be argued that when the state of cessation of vital functions is reversible, it would be imprecise or unwarranted to term such a cessation clinical death.

Cellular death, on the other hand, refers to a process that is gradual and that involves complex variables, including such vital signs as blood flow and breathing, but also encompassing physiological processes within the body's cells. Death is defined biologically as "the cessation of life resulting from irreversible changes in cell metabolism."[68] Since the living cell is an unstable system, it requires a continuous input of energy; otherwise, "it will degrade into a nonliving collection of molecules." Without oxygen, body cells vary in their survival potential. The cells of skin and connective tissues may survive for several hours; the neurons of the brain can last only five to eight minutes. When there is a loss of neurons in the midbrain and medulla, the brain center that controls breathing is destroyed; the death of neurons in the cerebral cortex destroys intellectual capacity.

As cellular death proceeds, the body's major systems and organs undergo an irreversible process of deterioration. The breakdown of these metabolic processes, the sum of which we call life, results in a loss of organic functions — that is, death. We have already seen how, as death progresses at the cellular level, such phenomena as algor mortis, livor mortis, and rigor mortis occur in the body.

Medical science now allows for the manipulation of the dying process so that while cellular death causes irreversible breakdown of some organs of the body, other organs can be maintained indefinitely by artificial means. This ability of modern medicine to alter the natural sequence and process of cellular death has brought about a need to redefine the physiological meaning of death and to institute new procedures for making a clinical determination of it.

Conceptual and Empirical Criteria

What is death? How can it be determined that a person has died? These questions, though closely related, involve separate issues. As Clyde Nabe points out, to untangle the complexity of these issues, we must "make plain the distinctions between the *clinical criteria* for determining when death has occurred, and the *decision* as to what *constitutes* death, and what we mean by 'death.'"[69] Definitions of death involve conceptual issues; methods of making a determination that death has occurred involve empirical and procedural issues.

Robert Veatch has outlined four levels that must be addressed in the inquiry concerning the definition and determination of death.[70] The first level involves formally defining *death*, an essentially conceptual or philosophical endeavor. Veatch supplies a formal definition: "Death means a complete change in the status of a living entity characterized by the irreversible loss of those characteristics that are essentially significant to it." This definition encompasses the deaths not only of human beings but also of nonhuman animals, plants, cells, and indeed can even be understood metaphorically as applying to a social phenomenon such as an organization or a society or culture. Whatever the instance, however, it is clear that death is a dramatic change in the status of the entity.

To give content to this formal definition, we must address Veatch's second level of inquiry, again a conceptual or philosophical question: What is so essentially significant about life that its loss is termed *death?* Some answers have included: the flow of vital bodily fluids (breath and blood, for example), the soul, the capacity for bodily integration, and in more recent definitions, consciousness. We will examine each of these in greater detail shortly.

The third level distinguished by Veatch concerns the question of the *locus* of death: Where in the organism should one look to determine whether death has occurred? With this question, we move from conceptual issues to an empirical enquiry—although the answer to this question depends upon the conceptual basis used to define death.

At Veatch's fourth level of inquiry, the criteria of death must be formulated: In other words, what technical tests must be applied at the locus to determine if an individual is living or dead?

To summarize these four levels: We must first establish a general definition of death; then give that definition content by stating what is essentially significant about the change of status from life to death; then locate where in the organism one can observe the signs of this change; and finally describe the tests that should be applied to determine whether a person is alive or dead. Veatch believes that it is the confusion of these four levels that has confounded much of the current debate and efforts to establish new standards for determining death.

Four Approaches to the Definition and Determination of Death

Veatch then identifies four "plausible approaches" to defining and determining death. Whereas the formal definition of death applies to all of these approaches, the subsequent levels of inquiry—that is, those involving a particular concept of death, the locus of death, and the criteria for determining death—are distinctive for each approach. Each approach relates death to a loss: the first, of the flow of vital fluids; the second, of the soul by the body; the third, of the capacity for bodily integration; the fourth, of the capacity for social interaction. As you read about each approach, you can see how death is determined in accordance with the way it is defined.

Irreversible Loss of Flow of Vital Fluids

The first approach pertains to the cessation of the flow of vital bodily fluids. With this conceptual understanding of death, one looks to the heart, blood vessels, lungs, and respiratory tract as the locus of death. To determine whether an individual is alive or dead, one observes the breathing, feels the pulse, and listens to the heartbeat. The more sophisticated modern methods of electrocardiogram and direct measurement of oxygen and carbon dioxide levels in the blood could be added to these traditional tests because they focus on the same loci and criteria for determining death.

This approach to defining death is adequate for determining death in most cases, even today. When vital functions are artificially sustained by machines, however, no unambiguous determination of death can be made by this definition. For instance, a patient is connected to a heart-lung machine that keeps the vital fluids of blood and breath flowing through the body. According to this definition, the patient is alive. If the patient is disconnected from the machine, these vital functions cease and, by this definition, the patient is dead. Yet during open-heart surgery, these circulatory systems are interrupted—making it possible to consider the patient clinically dead under this definition. But we know the patient is not dead, because such temporary cessation is simply part of the surgical procedures.

The ambiguity of this first approach results from defining death on the basis of physiological criteria that, although intimately related to life processes, do not seem to constitute those most significant for identifying human life.

Irreversible Loss of the Soul from the Body

In the second approach to defining death — one used in many cultures worldwide and from time immemorial — the criterion is the presence or absence of the soul in the body. Within this framework, as long as the soul is present, the person is alive; when the soul leaves, the body dies. Indeed, some traditions define death in precisely this way. The *Tibetan Book of the Dead*, for example, presents the view that life is terminated in a series of gradual steps, from a state of life to the state we call death. Christian theologians and other religious ethicists also grapple with this question.

This second conceptual definition of death, then, involves the irreversible loss of the soul from the body. The locus of the soul has not been scientifically established (nor has its existence), although some believe the soul is related to the breath or the heart, or perhaps, as seventeenth-century philosopher René Descartes believed, to the pineal body, a small protrusion from the center of the brain. Thus, for those who hold this concept, the criteria for determining death would presumably involve some means of ascertaining death at the particular locus where the soul is thought to reside. For example, if the soul is thought to be coincident with the breath, then absence of breath would indicate the loss of the soul and, hence, death. In a study conducted in 1907, dying persons were placed on a very sensitive scale to determine whether any weight loss occurs at the moment of death. Researchers noted a loss, averaging from 1 to 2 ounces, leading to speculations about whether the loss indicated the departure of the soul from the body at death.[71]

To most persons living in modern, urban-technological societies, in which secular beliefs are prominent, this approach to defining death is simply not relevant. Our first difficulty would be to adequately define the soul. Even if this difficulty could be surmounted, we would need some way to ascertain whether the soul was present or absent at a given time. Moreover, this definition of death forces an examination of whether death occurs because the soul departs from the body, or, conversely, whether the soul departs from the body because death has occurred. In other words, does the soul "animate" the body, giving it life, or do the physiological processes of vitality in the body provide a vessel wherein the soul resides? Such questions may elicit fascinating speculations, but they bear little relevance to the dilemmas posed by modern medical practice in a scientific age.

Irreversible Loss of the Capacity for Bodily Integration

In the third approach, death can be defined as the irreversible loss of the capacity for bodily integration. This approach is more sophisticated than the first, because it refers not simply to the traditional physiological signs of vitality

Knowing What a Human Being Is

Rolling Thunder often repeated, "We do so many unnatural things, we don't know what's natural anymore." One day he and I were sitting on the ground out in the desert. He was describing a young Indian apprentice from another tribe and making designs in the sand with a stick. Suddenly he said, "You people don't even know what a human being is!" I did not see the connection between the subject at hand and that sudden exclamation, but I had learned to understand what he meant by "you people." It was not a judgmental finger-pointing to be taken personally, but a sort of generalized identification to be applied wherever it fit. "You can look right at someone's empty body and think that you're lookin' at the person when they're not even there. Time and time again, you people speed to the scene of an accident, pick up an empty body and take it down the highway at eighty miles an hour, leaving the person miles behind, not knowing what the heck is going on!"

As an example, he then described to me an episode in which he went into the hospital to assist a young lady—a friend of friends—who had been in a head-on collision and was a long time in a coma.

"But the moment I took a good look at the body, I could see she wasn't even there. I had to find her—go get her—and she was way out in the field where the car'd flipped over the cliff, and she was sittin' on a rock. Her friend who was driving was killed. And this one sittin' on the rock, she didn't even know where she was. But, boy, she was determined to stay there. She was totally disoriented. I had to pull her, nearly force her back. Only time we can do that is when we know their own will isn't working—otherwise we always leave it up to their own choice.

"Well, in the early days, most everyone could tell when a person wasn't in their body. That was just natural to see that. That's been lost now, mostly. Only thing I can say is, until you learn to understand these things, you should never, never move an unconscious body. Unconscious means the person is not in there. So treat the body on the scene and never, never move it. Not until you learn how. People can't find their own way back to the body—not when they've been pulled loose that way by some accident or something. Time and time again, traumatized people get abandoned that way. Time and time again, people die in a coma because of that."

Quoted in Doug Boyd, *Mystics, Magicians, and Medicine People: Tales of a Wanderer*

in the body (the flow of breath and blood), but to the more generalized capability of the body to regulate its own functioning. This approach recognizes the fact that a human being is an integrated organism with capacities for internal regulation through complex homeostatic feedback mechanisms.

This definition at least partly resolves the ambiguity of the first definition, for a determination of death would not be made merely because a person's physiological functioning was being maintained by a machine. A determination of death could be made when the organism itself was no longer capable of bodily integration. In other words, artificial life support would not constitute the determining factor; rather, only with the irreversible loss of the capacity for bodily integration could there be a determination of death. The locus for such a determination is currently considered by clinicians to be the central nervous system — more specifically, the brain. The determination of death that results from this definition is often characterized as "brain death" (although this term is somewhat misleading because it focuses attention on the death of a part of the organism, not the whole organism).

In 1968, the Harvard Medical School Ad Hoc Committee to Examine the Definition of Brain Death proposed criteria for determining death by this new definition. The Harvard committee identified four essential criteria for brain death: (1) lack of receptivity and response to external stimuli; (2) absence of spontaneous muscular movement and spontaneous breathing; (3) absence of observable reflexes, including brain and spinal reflexes; and (4) absence of brain activity, signified by a flat electroencephalogram (EEG). [The Harvard criteria call for a second set of tests to be performed on the patient after twenty-four hours have elapsed. They also specifically exclude cases of hypothermia (body temperature below 90 degrees Fahrenheit) as well as situations involving the presence of central nervous system depressants such as barbiturates.] Notice that these criteria incorporate the traditional means of determining death — heartbeat and blood flow. Procedures for applying these criteria have been adopted widely, particularly when the traditional means of determining death are inconclusive.

Irreversible Loss of the Capacity for Consciousness or Social Interaction

Although the Harvard criteria have gained wide acceptance in clinical settings, some argue that they fail to specify what is *significant* about human life. Veatch, for example, says that it is the higher functions of the brain — not merely reflex networks that regulate such physiological processes as blood pressure and respiration — that define the essential characteristics of a human being. Thus, the fourth approach to defining death emphasizes the capacity for consciousness and social interaction. The implicit premise of this approach is that for a person to be fully human, not only must certain biological processes operate, but the social dimension of life — consciousness or personhood — must be present. Being alive implies the capacity for conscious interaction with one's environment and with other human beings. According to this definition, when the capacity for social interaction is irreversibly lost, a determination of death follows.

Using this approach, where should one look to determine whether an individual is alive or dead? Current scientific evidence points to the neocortex, the outer surface of the brain, where processes essential to consciousness and social interaction are located. If the supposition is correct, the EEG alone would provide an adequate measure for determining death.

In the theoretical debate regarding how death should be defined, this fourth approach is known as a "higher-brain" theory, in contrast to the "whole-brain" theory advocated by those who define death as the irreversible loss of function of the organism as a whole. As Karen Gervais points out, however, "By emphasizing the brain's integrating role in the human organism the whole-brain theory of death reduces to a lower-brain theory of death."[72] Observing that human beings

Modern medicine raises a thicket of difficult social and ethical issues. We have grown used to seeing members of the medical community try to resolve them in the courtroom. Sometimes they're there as expert witnesses, sometimes as defendants in malpractice suits. At other times they come seeking the protection of a judicial ruling, for example, on the circumstances in which a gravely ill patient has "the right to die" and "heroic" life support can be withdrawn. Once in a while it's a criminal matter. . . .

Moral uncertainties will continue to abound in medicine. No hospital rule book can do justice to the ambiguous circumstances in which lower-level line staff must translate institutional policy to humane practice. This is true, incidentally, not only for a licensed practical nurse at the bottom of a hospital pecking order, but for a policeman or social worker or a member of a dozen other occupations whose members deal daily with humanity's most painful contradictions. This is often underrespected, underpaid, emotionally draining work with impossibly complex multiple objectives: How simultaneously to follow a rulebook, get the job done and be humane?

> Excerpts from an
> editorial in the *Boston Sunday Globe*,
> November 8, 1981

are "ontologically unique and complex organisms," Gervais says that "it is loss of consciousness and not loss of biological functioning that should determine when human life is over." According to this view, the death of a *person* is synonymous with the death of a human being. In commenting on the search for a more precise definition of human death, Gervais concludes that we are left with a basic choice about the definition of human life — namely, whether we consider a human being as an organism or as a person.

Legislation Defining Death

The responsibility of determining whether or not death has occurred in a particular case usually rests with the attending physician. Yet, as we have just seen, the philosophical and moral issues that impinge so greatly on deciding exactly what is meant by death must concern everyone. The definition of death touches upon many aspects of social life. Criminal prosecution, inheritance, taxation, treatment of the corpse, and mourning are all affected by the way society "draws the dividing line between life and death."[73] Many states have recognized that the traditional definition of death — that is, the cessation of the flow of vital bodily fluids — is sometimes inadequate in the present technological setting.

In 1970, Kansas become the first state to adopt brain-based criteria for determining death. A number of other states subsequently adopted similar statutes. Because the Kansas-inspired statute contained dual definitions of death (one based on cessation of vital functions and the other on brain functions), it did not provide a unitary description of death and therefore was criticized as potentially confusing.

In 1972, Alexander Capron and Leon Kass proposed an improvement on the Kansas statute that related the two standards for determining death.[74] This proposal was governed by the following five principles:

1. The statute should concern the death of a human being, not the death of cells, tissues, or organs, and not the "death or cessation of his role as a fully functioning member of his family or community."
2. It should move incrementally, supplementing rather than replacing the older cardiopulmonary standards.
3. It should avoid serving as a special definition for a special function such as transplantation.
4. It should apply uniformly to all persons.
5. It should be flexible, leaving specific criteria to the judgment of physicians.

With various modifications this proposal was adopted by several states. The proposal was criticized by some, however, because it did not address the issues raised by organ transplantation procedures; that is, it did not require at least two physicians to participate jointly in determining death, nor did it stipulate that the physician who pronounces death not be a member of the medical team seeking organs for transplantation. Capron and Kass responded to this criticism by asserting that transplant considerations ought to be dealt with in separate legislation dealing specifically with that subject, such as the Uniform Anatomical Gift Act (a topic discussed in Chapter 11).

Another model statute was proposed in 1975 by the American Bar Association. It was designed to provide a definition of death "for all legal purposes." This proposal virtually ignored traditional cardiopulmonary criteria for determining death, focusing instead on the "irreversible cessation of total brain function." As with the earlier statutes, the ABA proposal, verbatim or with modification, was adopted by a number of states. These proposals were followed in 1978 by the Uniform Brain Death Act and, in 1979, by a model proposed by the American Medical Association. Several states adopted statutes based on either one or more of the proposed models or on their own individual standards for determining death.

Finally, in 1981, the statute recommended by the President's Commission, known as the Uniform Determination of Death Act, was adopted by Colorado and Idaho, making them the first states to do so; and, by 1988, the number of states adopting the Act totaled twenty-five (see Figure 10-2). This proposal was designed to be broadly acceptable, thus easing the enactment of uniform law for defining and determining death throughout the United States. It has been widely endorsed by political and professional groups, including the American Bar Association and the American Medical Association, both of which approved the proposal as a substitute for their own earlier models. Recommending enactment of uniform statutory law, the Commission also said decisions about such a law should be left to the individual states, rather than imposed by the federal government.

Uniform Determination of Death Act

1. [*Determination of Death.*] An individual who has sustained either (1) irreversible cessation of circulatory and respiratory functions, or (2) irreversible cessation of all functions of the entire brain, including the brain stem, is dead. A determination of death must be made in accordance with accepted medical standards.

2. [*Uniformity of Construction and Application.*] This act shall be applied and construed to effectuate its general purpose to make uniform the law with respect to the subject of this Act among states enacting it.

Figure 10-2   *Uniform Determination of Death Act*
Source: President's Commission for the Study of Ethical Problems in Medicine and Biomedical and Behavioral Research, *Defining Death: A Report on the Medical, Legal and Ethical Issues in the Determination of Death* (Washington: Government Printing Office, 1981), p. 73.

According to the report of the Commission, the Uniform Determination of Death Act "addresses the matter of 'defining' death at the level of general physiological standards rather than at the level of more abstract concepts or the level of more precise criteria and tests," because these change over time as knowledge and techniques are refined.[75] Since irreversible circulatory and respiratory cessation will be the obvious and sufficient basis for diagnosing death in the vast majority of cases, the statute acknowledges that fact by setting forth the basis on which death is determined in such cases — namely, that breathing and blood flow have ceased and cannot be restored or replaced. When a patient is not supported on a respirator, the need to evaluate brain functions does not arise.

The Commission also said that a statutory definition of death should be kept separate and distinct from any provisions concerning organ donation and the termination of life-sustaining treatment. In contrast to most of the earlier proposals, which stated that a person would be "considered dead" when the criteria were met, the language of the Uniform Determination of Death Act is clearer and more direct. It states simply that a person who meets the standards set forth in the law "is dead."

Confusion about the definition of death has arisen, the President's Commission said, "because the same technology not only keeps heart and lungs functioning in some who have irretrievably lost all brain functions but also sustains other, less severely injured patients." The result has been a "blurring of the important distinction between patients who are *dead* and those who are or may be *dying*." The Commission concluded that "proof of an irreversible absence of functions in

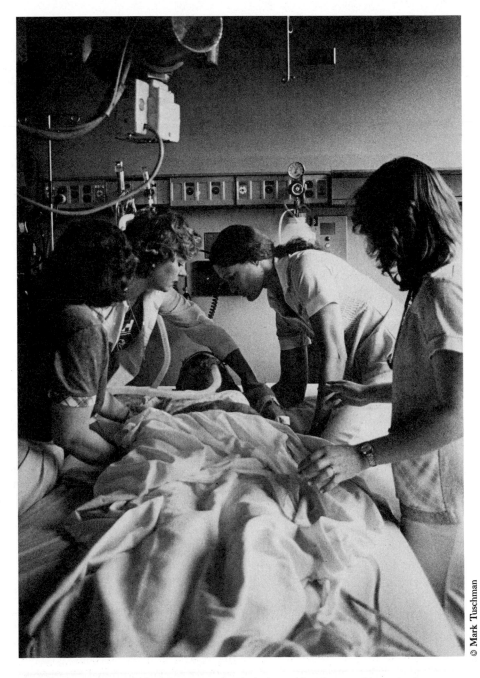

© Mark Tuschman

In the intensive-care unit both human and technical considerations combine to make necessary the evaluation of ethical questions regarding the meaning of life and death.

the entire brain, including the brain stem, provides a highly reliable means of declaring death for respirator-maintained bodies."

The Commission noted that the 1968 "Harvard criteria" for making a determination of death have been reliable, adding that "no case has yet been found that met these criteria and regained any brain functions despite continuation of respirator support." It pointed out, however, that although the criteria are intended to define a state of "irreversible coma," or death, the phrase is misleading since the word coma refers to a condition of a living person, whereas "a body without any brain functions is dead and thus *beyond* any coma." Irreversible loss of functions of the whole brain is generally the result of: (1) direct trauma to the head, such as from a motor vehicle accident or gunshot wound, (2) massive hemorrhage into the brain from a ruptured aneurysm or from complications of high blood pressure, or (3) anoxic damage from cardiac or respiratory arrest or severely reduced blood pressure.

The Commission argued that it would radically change the meaning of death to expand our definition to include persons who have lost all cognitive functions but still are able to breath spontaneously. Death is an absolute and single phenomenon, the Commission said. Thus, even terms such as "brain dead" are misleading. When brainstem functions remain—for example, when respiration occurs naturally but there is no cognitive awareness—the condition of such a patient can be described as "persistent vegetative or noncognitive state." (This was the case with Karen Ann Quinlan, cited earlier.) Although one may observe involuntary movements and unassisted breathing in a person's body, the lack of higher brain functions indicates an absence of awareness of self and the environment. Sustained by medical and nursing care, including artificial feeding through intravenous or nasogastric tubes and antibiotics to fight recurrent infections, such patients may survive for years without a respirator. (The longest such survival, according to the Commission's report, was over thirty-seven years.)

The Commission emphasized a "whole-brain" formulation in preference to a definition based on functions of the so-called "higher brain." In doing so, it cited the nearly universal acceptance of the "whole-brain" concept by both the medical community and the general public. A "higher brain" formulation, on the other hand, would require agreement on the meaning of personhood, a concept that does not enjoy such consensus. If "personhood" is made to depend on a certain state of awareness or consciousness, then the severely senile or retarded individual could be excluded. Likewise, according to some proposed definitions, a person whose higher brain functions have been permanently damaged but whose lower brain continues to function might lack the qualities of "personhood." At the present level of understanding and technique, said the Commission, "the 'higher brain' may well exist only as a metaphorical concept, not in reality."

The rise of modern medical technologies has created a need to define more specifically the locus of death when the traditional criteria prove insufficient to make a determination of death. Despite considerable progress toward a working definition of death, our legal definitions are inadequate when applied in certain circumstances that arise during the process of dying. In short, our guidelines for determining death require further refinement as we fashion public policy with regard to prevalent medical practices.

Yet perhaps the precise moments of both our entry into and exit from life will prove to be elusive. The search for scientific criteria that allow a definite determination of death may provide ever more precise, but not absolute, definitions. This is not to suggest that the search is futile. But ultimately there is no alternative to the human responsibility for making ethical decisions on matters of life and death in circumstances of fundamental ambiguity.

Further Readings

Renee C. Fox and Judith P. Swazey. *The Courage to Fail: A Social View of Organ Transplants and Dialysis*. Chicago: University of Chicago Press, 1974.

Karen Grandstrand Gervais. *Redefining Death*. New Haven: Yale University Press, 1986.

Rasa Gustaitis and Ernle W.D. Young. *A Time to Be Born, A Time to Die: Conflicts and Ethics in an Intensive Care Nursery*. Reading, Mass.: Addison-Wesley, 1986.

Frank Harron, John Burnside, and Tom Beauchamp. *Health and Human Values: A Guide to Making Your Own Decisions*. New Haven: Yale University Press, 1983.

Albert R. Jonsen, Mark Siegler, and William J. Winslade. *Clinical Ethics: A Practical Approach to Ethical Decisions in Clinical Medicine*. New York: Macmillan, 1982.

Jay Katz and Alexander M. Capron. *Catastrophic Diseases: Who Decides What? A Psychosocial and Legal Analysis of the Problems Posed by Hemodialysis and Organ Transplantation*. New York: Russell Sage Foundation, 1975.

Ruth Macklin. *Mortal Choices: Bioethics in Today's World*. New York: Pantheon, 1987.

Stanley Joel Reiser, Arthur J. Dyck, and William J. Curran, eds. *Ethics in Medicine: Historical Perspectives and Contemporary Concerns*. Cambridge, Mass.: MIT Press, 1977.

Earl E. Shelp. *Born to Die? Deciding the Fate of Critically Ill Newborns*. New York: Free Press, 1986.

Robert M. Veatch. *Cross Cultural Perspectives in Medical Ethics: Readings*. Boston: Jones and Bartlett, 1989.

Robert M. Veatch. *A Theory of Medical Ethics*. New York: Basic Books, 1981.

Robert N. Wennberg. *Terminal Choices: Euthanasia, Suicide, and the Right to Die*. Grand Rapids, Mich.: William B. Eerdmans, 1989.

William J. Winslade and Judith Wilson Ross. *Choosing Life or Death: A Guide for Patients, Families, and Professionals*. New York: Free Press, 1986.

This drawing by William A. Rogers, Reading the Will, *humorously depicts some of the emotional responses heirs may experience during probate. Besides issues involving wills and probate, the judicial system touches on many other aspects of death and dying; these range from trying homicide cases to settling questions involving the continuance of life support to a hopelessly comatose patient.*

C H A P T E R II

The Law and Death

*F*rom the relative simplicity of filing a death certificate to the settling of a complicated estate, the law and legalities impinge upon our experiences of death and dying. In some cases, laws serve to increase our options; in other cases, they restrict them.

We examine first the legalities involved in advance directives, such as living wills and natural death directives, and then the process of organ donation as formalized by the Uniform Anatomical Gift Act. Both of these legal developments are directly related to the material covered in the previous chapter on ethical decisions in medicine.

We then examine administrative and institutional concerns, including the death certificate, the role of the coroner and the medical examiner, and the procedures involved in autopsies. We also discuss how these institutions reflect societal interests in the circumstances surrounding and following death. The remainder of the chapter deals with making a will, probating an estate, paying estate and inheritance taxes, and claiming insurance and other death benefits.

Advance Directives

Living wills, natural death directives, and durable powers of attorney — known collectively as advance directives — are widely acknowledged to be increasingly important in medical decision making. The concept of a "living will" was initially developed in support of the argument that individuals should not be kept alive by artificial means against their will. Advance directives indicate the desire that medical heroics be avoided when death is imminent, that life-sustaining devices and extraordinary medical procedures not be used when there is no realistic chance of recovery. By providing written evidence that an individual does not want to be artificially kept alive when terminally ill, advance directives also represent an effort to protect doctors and hospitals from accusations of malpractice and from civil liability or criminal prosecution.

Originally, living wills had no force in law. They were understood merely as an expression of an individual's wishes. During the late 1970s, however, state legislatures across the country considered various "right to die" bills intended to require physicians to honor patients' desires at the end of life. By 1989, thirty-eight states and the District of Columbia had enacted some type of living will, durable power of attorney, or "natural death" legislation.[1] As the letters in Figure 11-1 indicate, however, living wills and other advance directives have been a source of controversy. Whereas opponents argue that living wills represent a step toward society's acceptance of active euthanasia, possibly leading to abuses such as arbitrarily withdrawing treatment from patients close to death, proponents argue that living wills safeguard the rights of patients to determine the manner of their own dying.

Despite the widespread adoption of living will legislation, considerable differences exist among the states regarding such issues as "the assessment of penalties for either disobeying the directive of a properly executed instrument or preventing the transfer of a patient seeking to come within the provisions of the law to another physician who will respect and follow the patient's wishes," and "the triggering mechanisms of the legislation are often cumbersome and self-defeating."[2] In short, even in states where natural death legislation exists, a patient's wishes about the prohibition of life-sustaining treatment may be impeded. Living wills are not always legally binding. There may be few, if any, guarantees to ensure that a patient's wishes will be carried out. Thus, whether the wishes expressed in a living will or natural death directive are followed may depend upon the policies of a given health care institution and standard practices within a community or jurisdiction.

Living will legislation typically stipulates that such a directive can be executed at any time by an adult and that it remains in force — unless amended by the signer — for a specified period of years (in one instance, for five years; in another, for seven). Executing a living will may require certification of its authenticity by witnesses who are not relatives or beneficiaries of the signatory. In some cases, before a living will is presumed to be valid, a person must be declared a "qualified patient" (that is, he or she must be in a terminal condition) before executing the directive. Otherwise, the attending physician will not be bound by the directive and may consider other factors — such as information from the patient's family and the nature of the illness, injury, or disease — before deciding whether the directive should be implemented.

Uncertainty about the projected course of an illness or a disease may cause doctors to be wary of committing themselves to the declaration that a patient is

Editor: If the governor signs the bill currently before him, this will become the first state to legalize suicide.

I believe this measure is immoral, bizarre, and tainted with Mephistophelian connotations.

Legislators, at all levels, should legislate laws pertaining only to life, as we know it. Death, in any manner, is nature's absolute domain, and no one should attempt to trespass on that domain.

I trust the governor is wise enough and sane enough to veto the bill presently lying heavily and cadaverously on his desk.

Editor: We have explored this bill and its implications in death and fully support the right of an individual, who wishes to do so, to be allowed to make a legally recognized written directive requesting withdrawal of life-support systems when these procedures would serve no purpose except to artificially delay the moment of death.

We reiterate our belief in the basic human right of an individual to control his destiny. We have communicated our support of this bill to the legislature and to the governor.

Editor: This bill, and all other natural-death or death-with-dignity bills, is based on a faulty premise. For when we react to tubes, oxygen and other paraphernalia, our concern is with daintiness, not dignity.

Dignity is the quality of mind having to

do with worth, nobility, and forbearance. The dying, with the help of the living, can have dignity — no matter what functions of control are lost.

Instead of unplugging and abandoning our dying patients, we should work to achieve truly compassionate care for them in hospices like those in London, England, and New Haven, Connecticut.

Editor: No physician is required by law to use extraordinary means of preserving life, and none has ever been convicted for failing to do so.

So the real purpose of death-with-dignity or natural-death bills must be to set the stage for letting doctors take positive action: giving lethal injections or denying ordinary means of care to patients who may be handicapped or burdensome to society.

We must be suspicious of any trend which offers death as a solution to problems, no matter how heart-rending those problems may be.

Editor: The bill allowing an adult of sound mind to refuse extraordinary life-preservation measures reaffirms for me the value of life. Life is active choosing toward greater fulfillment and reduced suffering, not the beating of a heart in a pain-wracked and hopeless body. This bill is a public and legal recognition of that principle.

Figure *11-1   Letters in Response to Proposed Living Will Legislation*

hopelessly terminal. Too, a patient having reached such a stage may be incapable of signing a natural death directive or of ensuring that its provisions are followed. Indeed, whether or not a natural death directive is followed may in some instances depend largely on the nature of the relationship between patient and physician and, specifically, on the physician's willingness to abide by the patient's wishes. Gender has sometimes been a factor, with the treatment preferences of women being viewed as less reflective, mature, or rational than the treatment preferences of men.[3] In effect, an advance directive may be less a directive than a request.

Statement of Wishes

TO MY FAMILY, MY PHYSICIAN, AND MY ATTORNEY:

    If the time comes when I can no longer take part in decisions for my own future, let this statement stand as my wishes.

    If there is no reasonable expectation of my recovery from physical or mental disability, I request that I be allowed to die and not be kept alive by artificial means or heroic measures. Death is as much a reality as birth, growth, maturity, and old age — it is the one certainty. I do not fear death as much as I fear the indignity of deterioration, dependence, and hopeless pain. I ask that drugs be mercifully administered to me for terminal suffering even if they hasten the moment of death.

    This request is made after careful consideration. Any physician or any other person following these wishes shall be released from any liability whatever as a result of following said wishes.

Dated: _____

Signature: _____

Figure *11-2*   *Statement of Wishes for Optional Use with California's Durable Power of Attorney for Health Care*

    Recognizing this limitation, California enacted legislation in 1985 providing for a Durable Power of Attorney for Health Care (see Figure 11-2). Any individual who is at least eighteen years old and of sound mind can now complete a document that *does* have the force of law in the state of California. This document allows a person to designate an agent who is empowered to make health care decisions, particularly with respect to the withholding or withdrawal of life-sustaining treatment. An agent must act consistently with a patient's wishes as specifically stated in the document itself or as otherwise made known. In addition, a court may take away the agent's power to make decisions if he or she: (1) authorizes any illegal act; (2) acts contrary to the patient's known desires; or (3) where those desires are not known, does anything clearly contrary to the patient's best interests. Unless revoked orally or in writing by the person making it, the Durable Power of Attorney for Health Care is effective in California for seven years from the date of its execution; and, if the person is unable to make health care decisions at the end of that period, the power of attorney remains in force until he or she can make such decisions. The California statute illustrates the evolving nature of living will legislation and of support for the idea that individuals have the right to make decisions about their own health care even as they approach death. By 1990, some eighteen states had enacted similar legislation allowing for health care proxies.

Completing an *advance proxy directive*, or durable power of attorney, provides an additional safeguard that an individual's preferences about life-sustaining treatment will be followed. Such a proxy enables an individual to "nominate another whose express duty it will be to make *all* decisions regarding health care in the event the principal becomes incapacitated or otherwise unable to make decisions of that nature."[4] The nominated person might be a spouse, adult offspring, or friend with whom one has discussed treatment preferences. The durable power of attorney for health care does not usually require an attorney's assistance, and appropriate forms can be obtained from the state medical association or even from a local stationery store.

Studies indicate that patients are less worried about receiving unwanted treatment and doctors less worried about the legal consequences of withholding treatment when the patient has executed some type of advance directive expressing his or her wishes.[5] Although advance directives appear to both safeguard a patient's autonomy and minimize conflict in a critical care situation, it is important to recognize that they are virtually useless if doctors and hospitals do not know of their existence. To meet this difficulty, some advocate the implementation of policies whereby hospitals would routinely ask patients whether they have completed an advance directive. Such a policy would not only bring all existing documents to light, it would also give the patient an opportunity to revise those portions of the directive that no longer accurately express his or her treatment preferences.[6] The suggestion has also been made that wallet cards and bracelets (similar to those used for "Medic Alert") be developed to signify that an individual has completed an advance directive. Such an innovation might be especially worthwhile in cases when life-sustaining treatment is routinely initiated (as with paramedics at an accident scene) or when an individual is unable to express his or her wishes about the desirability of such treatment.[7]

According to the provisions of a law passed by Congress just prior to its recess in 1990, health care providers who receive federal Medicare funds — including hospitals, skilled nursing facilities, home health agencies, hospice programs, and health maintenance agencies — will be required to: (1) provide adult patients with information about their rights under state law to accept or refuse treatment, and their right to make advance directives for health care decisions; (2) maintain written policies and procedures to ensure that patients receive such information in written form; (3) document in the patient's medical record whether the patient has executed an advance directive; (4) ensure compliance with requirements of state law with respect to advance directives; and (5) provide staff and community education about advance directives.[8] Information about advance directives is to be provided to patients at the time of their admission to the health care facility or when an individual comes "under the care of the agency" (as in the case of care provided by a home health agency or hospice). It is important to note also that this law allows a health care facility to express its own beliefs about providing (or not providing) care to the patient before admission. Some nursing homes, for example, insist on the right to follow their conscience in providing nutrition by tube-feeding and are legally allowed to do so by state law. If a

© Albert Lee Strickland

Designed to increase public awareness of organ donation, this billboard on a Florida highway calls particular attention to donations that can save the lives of children.

facility has a policy that is contrary to a person's own wishes, he or she can choose another facility.

This measure, the Patient Self-Determination Act, has been described as a "medical Miranda warning" (referring to the requirement that police officers advise arrested suspects of their rights) in its insistence that patients be advised of their rights regarding advance directives and life-sustaining treatment.[9] It has been reported that only about 10 percent of mentally competent adults have signed a living will, and that a far smaller number have designated someone else to make decisions by means of a health care proxy. Although some believe the new requirements will help people decide their own fate, others believe that the law will promote the death of patients by devaluing the goal of sustaining life. Another concern is that patients may become unduly alarmed about the state of their health if they are questioned about whether or not they have executed an advance directive. The elderly widow, for example, who enters a nursing home following the death of her husband may be frightened by what she perceives as a warning that she, too, is about to die, thus adding to the anxiety and depression caused by disruptions in her life.

With respect to how the Patient Self-Determination Act is eventually assessed, there is considerable agreement that much depends on how the law is implemented through state regulations and at the local level, where health care services are delivered to patients. As the case of Nancy Beth Cruzan (discussed in Chapter 10) has made abundantly clear to many people, advance directives offer a relatively simple and easy means of providing the requisite "clear and convincing evidence" as to one's wishes concerning life-sustaining medical treatment. Larry Churchill points out that advance directives emphasize a "procedural ethics" that is concerned with fairness in process, but gives little regard to the quality of trust.[10] People write advance directives not so much to express their autonomy or self-directed choice, but because of fear born of mistrust. When the social and communal dimensions of life are lacking, trusting relationships suffer. Advance directives, rather than being viewed solely as an expression of autonomy, can be responded to as an opportunity for conversation that helps rebuild trust. Respect for autonomy is not to be eliminated, but the good that people seek through advance directives is not autonomy per se, not an abrogation of the communal dimensions of life, but a "good death."

Organ Donation

The Uniform Anatomical Gift Act, approved in 1968 by the National Conference of Commissions on Uniform State Laws and enacted in some form in all fifty states, provides for the donation of the body or specific body parts upon the death of the donor. Because of the chronic shortage of donor organs, the Act was revised in 1987 to simplify organ donation by removing requirements that the document be witnessed and that next of kin give their consent. The major provisions of the Uniform Anatomical Gift Act are presented in Table 11-1.

Many people find it gratifying to know that, by making an organ donation, they can give help to others even after their own death. Organs can be donated by completing a form such as the donor card shown in Figure 11-3. A donor may specify that only certain body parts or organs be available for donation or may state that *any* needed organs or body parts may be taken. Besides specifying how one's body may be used after death, the donor may also specify the final disposition of his or her remains once the donation has been effected. Although polls indicate that virtually all Americans are aware of organ transplants and that the overwhelming majority say they would be willing to make an organ or tissue donation, only a small percentage of the adult population carry donor cards. Studies indicate that individuals who are less anxious about death are more likely

T A B L E *11-1* *Major Provisions of the Uniform Anatomical Gift Act*

1. Any person over eighteen may donate all or part of his or her body for education, research, therapeutic, or transplantation purposes.
2. If the person has not made a donation before death, the next of kin can make it unless there was a known objection by the deceased.
3. If the person has made such a gift, it cannot be revoked by his or her relatives.
4. If there is more than one person of the same degree of kinship, the gift from relatives shall not be accepted if there is a known objection by one of them.
5. The gift can be authorized by a card carried by the individual or by written or recorded verbal communication from a relative.
6. The gift can be amended or revoked at any time before the death of the donor.
7. The time of death must be determined by a physician who is not involved in any transplantation.

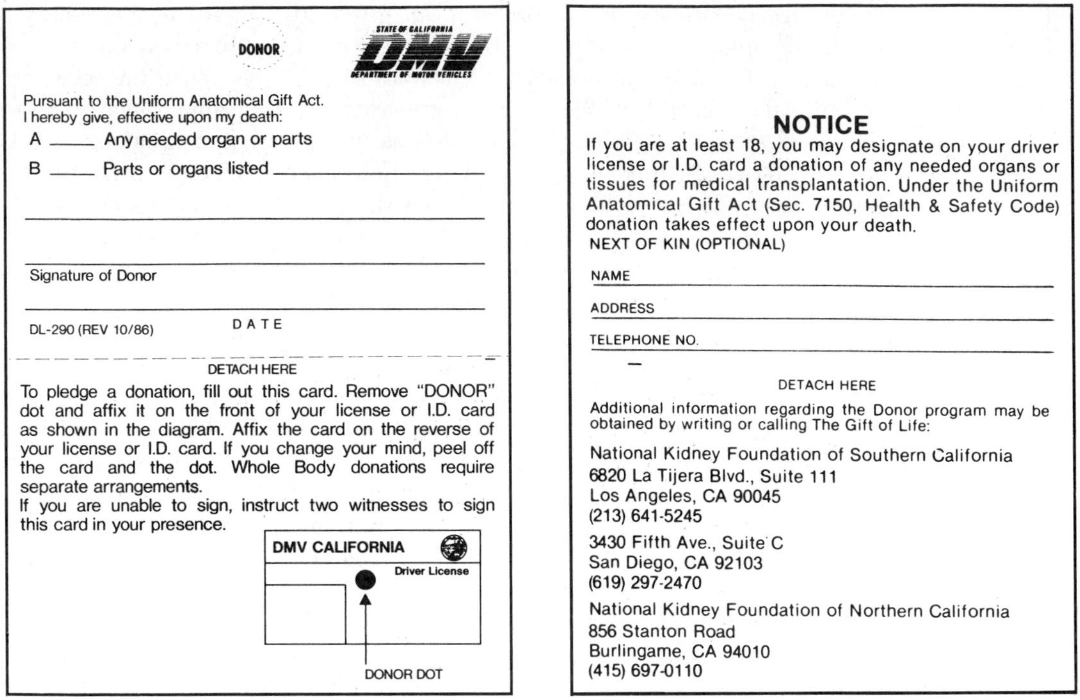

Figure *11-3*   *Donor Card*
Source: California Department of Motor Vehicles.

to sign organ donor cards.[11] In any case, many donations are made by relatives at the time of a loved one's death.

Despite the fact that donor cards are legal in all states, a donor's wishes may be thwarted when there are strong objections from relatives. Since most hospitals also obtain consent from the next of kin, a hospital is unlikely to insist on organ donation if close family members adamantly disagree with the deceased's wishes. Thus, as with other provisions that one intends to have carried out after his or her death, plans for organ donation should be discussed with family members to ensure that their feelings are considered in the final decision.

The success achieved with organ transplants has given hope to the seriously ill, and it has also created a waiting list of patients seeking donor organs. The National Organ Transplant Act was enacted by Congress in 1984 "to provide for a comprehensive review of the medical, legal, ethical, economic, and social issues presented by human organ procurement and transplantation, and to strengthen the ability of the nation's health care system to provide organ transplants."[12] The Division of Organ Transplantation was established in the Health Resources and Services Administration of the Public Health Service, and a National Task Force on Organ Transplantation conducted a two-year study of the issues involved in organ procurement and transplantation. The Act also provided for establishment of a central office to help match donated organs with potential recipients. The United Network for Organ Sharing (UNOS), located in Richmond, Virginia, maintains lists of persons waiting for transplants and tracks the status of all donated organs in the United States to ensure both the fairness of distribution and the competence of medical centers where organ transplants are performed. Interest in such a network was spurred partly by the potential for abuses resulting from commercialization of donated organs.

Because the demand for donated organs is larger than the supply, most states have enacted "required request" (also known as routine inquiry) laws requiring hospitals to institute policies and procedures for encouraging organ and tissue donations. In 1986, Congress established similar requirements for hospitals participating in the Medicare and Medicaid programs. According to these laws, hospitals must develop a protocol for identifying potential organ and tissue donors and to notify and cooperate with organ procurement centers when organs have been donated.

At or near the time of death, hospital personnel must ask whether the deceased had agreed to be an organ donor; and, if not, the family must be informed about the option to donate organs and tissues. Hospitals are to exercise reasonable discretion and sensitivity to the family circumstances in discussing organ donation with surviving family members. In many hospitals, a "transplant coordinator," typically a member of the nursing staff, contacts family members and makes the request for organ and tissue donation.[13]

Under the provisions of the Uniform Anatomical Gift Act, organ donation is entirely voluntary. Many ethicists and medical practitioners believe, however, that a voluntary approach is woefully inadequate given the number of people waiting to receive donated organs. While some observers think the answer lies in better public education about organ donation, thereby increasing the pool of voluntary donors, others advocate enactment of a national law that would *require* organ donation unless an individual specifically "opts out" by signing an objection on the back of his or her driver's license or on some other designated document. Such advocacy reflects the view that individuals have an *obligation* to consent to the removal and transplantation of their organs after death. David Peters, for instance, argues that using terms such as "gift" and "donation" imply that what is taking place is an "act of human kindness beyond the call of duty," but, he says, consenting to transplantation of one's organs after death is a moral duty, "the duty to attempt an easy rescue of an endangered person."[14] David Thomasma, taking a theological approach, bases his support for obligatory organ removal on the premise that "human beings own each other" and that organ donation is not merely a "good deed," but is a profoundly religious, even sacramental activity between human beings.[15] In reviewing the impact of organ transplantation on social attitudes and practices, Robert Fulton and Greg Owen point out that "the harvesting of cadaver kidneys and other organs of the body" has achieved a significance for our society that would have been impossible to anticipate just a few short decades ago, and they note that legislation related to organ donation "has the potential to take from the family survivors the right of decision with respect to the deceased's body, a right that has been integral to family life since before the Christian period."[16]

Another area of recent controversy among medical scientists, ethicists, and other groups concerns the use of fetal tissue transplants to treat such clinical disorders as Parkinson's disease, diabetes, and immunodeficiency and metabolic disorders.[17] Despite the potential good that might result from using fetal tissue for transplantation research, some fear that the procurement of fetal tissue, which is made available as a result of abortion, could lead to serious abuse. Advocates of fetal tissue transplants believe that the Uniform Anatomical Gift Act's stipulations with respect to the use of cadaverous tissue are sufficient to ensure ethical practices.

The Death Certificate

The death certificate constitutes legal proof of death. The official registration of death is considered the most important legal procedure following a death, and death certificates are required by all jurisdictions in the United States. The causes of death usually recognized by law include natural causes, accident, suicide, and homicide. Although death certificates vary somewhat from state to state, most generally follow the format outlined by the United States Standard Certificate of Death.[18]

On the face of it, the document used to certify the facts of death is quite straightforward, a concise summary of the pertinent data regarding the deceased and the mode and place of death. As Edwin Shneidman and others have shown, however, this seemingly simple document has much broader implications than one might at first imagine.[19] In addition to its value and purpose as a legal document that affects disposition of property rights, life insurance benefits, pension payments, and so on, the usefulness of the death certificate extends to such diverse matters as aiding in crime detection, tracing genealogy, and gaining knowledge about the incidence of disease and other aspects of physical and psychological health.

Death certificates reflect both a private and a public function. The typical death certificate now in use (see Figure 11-4) allows for only four different *modes* of death: accidental, suicidal, homicidal, and natural. Shneidman is among those who argue that certification of death ought to be concerned with the facts of death, not only as experienced by the person who died but also as experienced and accounted for by witnesses. As Shneidman points out, the *cause* of death isn't necessarily the same as the *mode* of death. For example, if a death were caused by asphyxiation due to drowning, should such a death be classified as an accident, a suicide, or a homicide? Any of these modes might apply.

Underlying the distinction between mode and cause is the more complex issue of untangling the intentions and subconscious factors, the states of mind and actions, that may have contributed, directly or indirectly, to the death. For

CERTIFICATE OF DEATH
STATE OF CALIFORNIA
USE BLACK INK ONLY

STATE FILE NUMBER

LOCAL REGISTRATION DISTRICT AND CERTIFICATE NUMBER

DECEDENT PERSONAL DATA

1A. NAME OF DECEDENT—FIRST (GIVEN) | 1B. MIDDLE | 1C. LAST (FAMILY) | 2A. DATE OF DEATH—MO, DAY, YR | 2B. HOUR | 3. SEX

4. RACE | 5. SPANISH/HISPANIC—SPECIFY YES____ NO | 6. DATE OF BIRTH—MO, DAY, YR | 7. AGE IN YEARS | IF UNDER 1 YEAR MONTHS | DAYS | IF UNDER 24 HOURS HOURS | MINUTES

8. STATE OF BIRTH | 9. CITIZEN OF WHAT COUNTRY | 10A. FULL NAME OF FATHER | 10B. STATE OF BIRTH | 11A. FULL MAIDEN NAME OF MOTHER | 11B. STATE OF BIRTH

12. MILITARY SERVICE? 19___ TO 19___ NONE | 13. SOCIAL SECURITY NO. | 14. MARITAL STATUS | 15. NAME OF SURVIVING SPOUSE (IF WIFE, ENTER MAIDEN NAME)

16A. USUAL OCCUPATION | 16B. USUAL KIND OF BUSINESS OR INDUSTRY | 16C. USUAL EMPLOYER | 16D. YEARS IN OCCUPATION | 17. EDUCATION—YEARS COMPLETED

USUAL RESIDENCE

18A. RESIDENCE—STREET AND NUMBER OR LOCATION | 18B. CITY | 18C. ZIP CODE

18D. COUNTY | 18E. NUMBER OF YEARS IN THIS COUNTY | 18F. STATE OR FOREIGN COUNTRY | 20. NAME, RELATIONSHIP, MAILING ADDRESS AND ZIP CODE OF INFORMANT

PLACE OF DEATH

19A. PLACE OF DEATH | 19B. IF HOSPITAL, SPECIFY ONE: IP, ER/OP, DOA | 19C. COUNTY

19D. STREET ADDRESS—STREET AND NUMBER OR LOCATION | 19E. CITY | TIME INTERVAL BETWEEN ONSET AND DEATH | 22. WAS DEATH REPORTED TO CORONER? REFERRAL NUMBER YES___ NO

CAUSE OF DEATH

21. DEATH WAS CAUSED BY: (ENTER ONLY ONE CAUSE PER LINE FOR A, B, AND C)

IMMEDIATE CAUSE (A) | 23. WAS BIOPSY PERFORMED? YES NO

DUE TO (B) | 24A. WAS AUTOPSY PERFORMED? YES NO

DUE TO (C) | 24B. WAS IT USED IN DETERMINING CAUSE OF DEATH? YES NO

25. OTHER SIGNIFICANT CONDITIONS CONTRIBUTING TO DEATH BUT NOT RELATED TO CAUSE GIVEN IN 21 | 26. WAS OPERATION PERFORMED FOR ANY CONDITION IN ITEM 21 OR 25? IF YES, LIST TYPE OF OPERATION AND DATE.

PHYSICIAN'S CERTIFICATION

I CERTIFY THAT TO THE BEST OF MY KNOWLEDGE DEATH OCCURRED AT THE HOUR, DATE AND PLACE STATED FROM THE CAUSES STATED. | 27B. SIGNATURE AND DEGREE OR TITLE OF PHYSICIAN | 27C. PHYSICIAN'S LICENSE NUMBER | 27D. DATE SIGNED

27A. DECEDENT ATTENDED SINCE MONTH, DAY, YEAR | DECEDENT LAST SEEN ALIVE MONTH, DAY, YEAR | 27E. TYPE ATTENDING PHYSICIAN'S NAME AND ADDRESS

CORONER'S USE ONLY

I CERTIFY THAT IN MY OPINION DEATH OCCURRED AT THE HOUR, DATE AND PLACE STATED FROM THE CAUSES STATED. | 28A. SIGNATURE AND TITLE OF CORONER OR DEPUTY CORONER | 28B. DATE SIGNED

29. MANNER OF DEATH—specify one: natural, accident, suicide, homicide, pending investigation or could not be determined | 30A. PLACE OF INJURY | 30B. INJURY AT WORK YES NO | 30C. DATE OF INJURY MONTH, DAY, YEAR | 31. HOUR

32. LOCATION (STREET AND NUMBER OR LOCATION AND CITY) | 33. DESCRIBE HOW INJURY OCCURRED (EVENTS WHICH RESULTED IN INJURY)

FUNERAL DIRECTOR AND LOCAL REGISTRAR

34A. DISPOSITION(S) | 34B. PLACE OF FINAL DISPOSITION—NAME AND ADDRESS | 34C. DATE MO, DAY, YEAR | 35A. SIGNATURE OF EMBALMER | 35B. LICENSE NUMBER

36A. NAME OF FUNERAL DIRECTOR (OR PERSON ACTING AS SUCH) | 36B. LICENSE NO. | 37. SIGNATURE OF LOCAL REGISTRAR | 38. REGISTRATION DATE

STATE REGISTRAR

A. | B. | C. | D. | E. | F. | CENSUS TRACT

VS-11 (REV. 3-89) | MAKE NO ERASURES, WHITEOUTS, OR OTHER ALTERATIONS

Figure 11-4   *Certificate of Death in Use in California*
Source: California Department of Health Services, Vital Statistics Branch.

instance, if an intoxicated person jumps into a swimming pool with no one else present and drowns, is the death accidental or suicidal? Does it make a difference whether the impetus for alcohol abuse resulted from emotional distress and feelings of despondency? Or what is the mode of death if the cocktails were served by a too-generous host? What if the person serving the excessive alcohol were also an heir of the person who dies?

Obviously, intentions can be far more complex than allowed for by the relatively elementary distinctions concerning mode and cause of death now listed on

© Carol A. Foote

When death occurs under suspicious or uncertain circumstances, the coroner or medical examiner usually directs an investigation to determine the cause of death. If foul play is suspected, a police or sheriff's department investigation is undertaken.

most death certificates. A study done in Marin County, California, to assess the conventional classifications of mode of death as well as the lethality of the deceased's intention revealed that some deaths classified as natural, accidental, and homicidal were also precipitated by the deceased's own actions; the deceased had lethal intentions against himself or herself. The use of a *psychological autopsy* as an investigative tool for reconstructing the events leading up to a death is discussed in Chapter 13.

The Coroner and the Medical Examiner

Most deaths in the United States result from disease. Usually in such cases, the physician attending the patient at the time of death completes and signs the death certificate. When death is sudden or occurs in suspicious circumstances, the cause of death must be determined by a coroner or medical examiner. Suspected homicides and suicides are investigated, as are accidents, deaths that occur on the job, deaths that occur in jails and other government institutions,

> The office of coroner developed in England approximately 800 to 900 years ago. Coroners were originally referred to as "crowners," the name deriving from the fact that they were officially appointed by the Crown to represent the King's interests in the investigation of violent, unexplained, and suspicious deaths, and more importantly, in the disposition of any personal or real property that became available under the existing laws following a homicide or suicide. The Latin word for crown is *corona*, and hence in later years the name of the office came to be called coroner.
>
> Cyril H. Wecht, "The Coroner and Death"

deaths that occur in hospitals or similar facilities when negligence is suspected or the death was unexpected, and deaths that occur at home when there is no attending physician who is able to sign the death certificate attesting to the cause of death.

The cause of death is determined by use of various scientific procedures, possibly including an autopsy, toxicology and bacteriology tests, chemical analyses, and other studies that are necessary to arrive at adequate findings. The results of such a postmortem examination may play a crucial role in court cases or insurance settlements. Too, the outcome of such proceedings may be important not only to law enforcement agencies but also to the families involved: Whether a death is due to foul play, negligence, suicide, accident, or natural causes can have a significant emotional effect on survivors. Unlike autopsies performed as part of medical training or at a family's request, investigations that come under the purview of the coroner or medical examiner are required by law.

It should be noted that usually the coroner is an elected official and the medical examiner is most often appointed. The major difference between these two positions, however, has to do with training. Whereas the coroner may not need any special background or training, the medical examiner is a qualified medical doctor, generally with advanced training and certification in *forensic pathology* (that is, the application of medical knowledge to questions of law). In addition to responsibilities for investigating the cause of death in questionable circumstances, the medical examiner plays a key role in community health programs such as suicide prevention, drug abuse education, and research.

Autopsies

An autopsy (from the Greek *autopsia*, meaning "seeing with one's own eyes") is a medical examination of a body after death to determine the cause of death or to investigate the extent and nature of changes caused by disease. An autopsy may be performed for legal or official reasons (as mentioned in connection with the role of the coroner or medical examiner), or as part of a hospital's teaching or research program. As a method of conclusively establishing the cause of death, autopsies increase our understanding of disease, thereby resulting in

© Carol A. Foote

When a coroner's preliminary investigation reveals the need to scientifically determine the cause of death, the corpse is brought to the morgue, where it is held until an autopsy can be performed.

   The autopsy, or medical examination to determine the cause of death, is conducted under the coroner's direction when the circumstances of a death are violent, suspicious, or unexplained, or when a death is medically unattended and a doctor is unable to certify the cause of death. All homicides, accidents, and suicides come under the coroner's or medical examiner's jurisdiction.

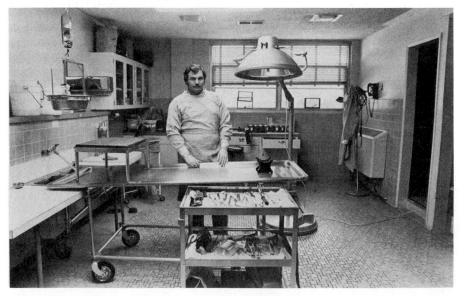

© Carol A. Foote

improved therapy. Autopsies are used to confirm diagnoses, train doctors, and conduct research. Hospitals that aspire to official status as teaching institutions must perform a relatively high percentage of autopsies. In the United States, the number of autopsies has dropped to about 14 percent of all deaths, a rate that limits the number of studies that could potentially result in medical benefits.

Autopsies involve detailed examination of both the exterior and interior of the body.[20] Once the abdominal cavity is exposed, organs are removed for examination of their internal structure, and small samples may be taken for later analysis. After the autopsy is completed, organs not needed for further study are replaced in the body cavity and all incisions are closed.

Sometimes, the deceased's family will request an autopsy to determine whether genetic or infectious conditions led to death or to help resolve questions about possible malpractice. Except when required by law, an autopsy can be performed only after the next of kin's consent is obtained or when the deceased has previously donated his or her body for autopsy under the provisions of the Uniform Anatomical Gift Act.

Within the past decade, forensic science has achieved noteworthy results relative to investigating human rights violations. In Argentina, for example, a team of forensic scientists helped to identify remains of the *desaparecidos*, the "disappeared," who had been buried in mass graves during a period of military rule and terrorism in that country. The families of the disappeared had often been helpless in their attempts to determine the fate of loved ones. Aided by the techniques of forensic science, including the use of autopsies to determine the cause of death, many families were able to learn the fate of their missing relatives and to give them a proper burial. Furthermore, during the ensuing trials of several former military leaders, forensic scientists presented expert testimony that helped convict those responsible for the deaths. Members of the team later expressed hope that "the knowledge that litigation and forensic documentation can hold governments accountable for their actions may help deter state-sponsored killings in the future."[21]

Laws Regulating Body Disposition

In most states, the deceased's next of kin are responsible for disposition of the body. When the deceased has provided for donation of the body or body parts, the final disposition of the remains is often left to the discretion of the hospital, medical school, or other medical institution that has possession of the body. Even in these instances, however, once the medical purposes have been achieved, the next of kin usually has a say in the final disposition of the remains. Whether or not the next of kin requests return of the remains, medical schools report their own concern for the ethical treatment of cadavers as well as their proper disposal, perhaps including some form of memorial service that acknowledges the human gift represented by the donation of bodies to science.[22]

The responsibility of the next of kin to arrange for the final disposition of the body is circumscribed by laws governing the manner in which disposition may

Many of the legal issues surrounding death can be clarified with the help of a competent attorney who is versed in the options available to clients.

be effected. For example, some communities have enacted ordinances prohibiting burial of a corpse within city limits. Although the general policies regulating body disposition are more or less uniform throughout the United States, laws and ordinances do vary among states and localities.

Wills

A legal document expressing a person's intentions and wishes for the disposition of his or her property after death, the *will* is a valuable tool for planning one's estate and for conveying property to one's beneficiaries. Conferring a kind of immortality on the *testator* (the person making the will), a will can be thought of as the deceased's last words. The will can become a focal point for powerful emotions, embodying as it does the testator's feelings and intentions toward his or her survivors. A glossary of terms relating to wills and probate can be found in Table 11-2.

Many people think of a will as simply a tool for financial planning, perhaps overlooking its important comforting effects on testator and survivors. Barton Bernstein, a lawyer who has written widely on this point, says that the attorney who assists in drawing up a will and in executing it can perform a valuable service

T A B L E *11-2* *Terms Related to Wills and Probate*

Administrator: A person appointed by the court (in the absence of a will, or if no executor is named in one) to carry out the steps necessary to settling an estate. When an administrator is to be appointed, state law requires the drawing up of a preferential list of candidates. Assuming that the necessary qualifications are met, the order of preference typically begins with the spouse of the deceased and continues successively through the deceased's children, grandchildren, parents, siblings, more distant next of kin, and a public administrator.

Attestation Clause: A statement signed by the persons who witness the testator's making of the will.

Codicil: An amendment to a will.

Conditional will: A type of formally executed will that states that certain actions will take place provided that a specified future event occurs. For example, suppose a testator wishes to bequeath money or property to a potential beneficiary who is incapable of self-care, but who has a reasonable chance of recovery. With a conditional will, the money or property could be held in trust for that person until the conditions specified in the will (e.g., recovery) have been satisfied. A problem of conditional wills lies in the difficulty of stipulating with exactitude the nature of events and circumstances that might occur in the future.

Executor: A person named by the testator in his or her will to see that the provisions in the will are carried out properly.

Holographic will: A will written entirely by the hand of the person signing it. Some states do not recognize holographic wills as valid, and those that do generally have stringent conditions for such a document to be deemed valid. Not considered a substitute for a formally executed will.

Intestate: The condition of having made no valid will.

Mutual will: A type of formally executed will that contains reciprocal provisions. May be used by husbands and wives who wish to leave everything to the other spouse with no restrictions, although it limits the range of choices that are available when a will is executed individually.

Nuncupative will: A will made orally. Many states do not recognize a nuncupative will, or do so only under extremely limited circumstances. A few states admit an oral will if the person makes it in fear of imminent death or expectation of receiving mortal injuries, and the peril does result in death. A nuncupative will may also be valid when made by a soldier or sailor engaged in military service or by a mariner at sea; in these instances, the individual need not be in immediate peril. Generally, an oral will must be witnessed by at least two persons who attest that the will is indeed a statement of the testator's wishes.

Probate: The process by which an estate is settled and the property distributed. This process generally occupies an average of nine to twelve months, though it may be longer or shorter depending on circumstances and the complexity of the estate.

in helping survivors deal with bereavement and handle their affairs during the period of mourning.[23]

Many terminally ill patients and their families seek the help of counselors and other mental health professionals as a means of exploring their fears, uncertainties, and conflicts as well as devising a plan to meet the prospects that lie ahead. Bernstein believes that lawyers should be included as part of that inter-disciplinary team. Otherwise, although the help obtained from such professionals can be a tremendous aid in clarifying concerns, opening communication channels, and enhancing interpersonal relationships, the task of planning for a future that will not include the dying family member may be neglected. The death of a major breadwinner can be especially devastating. Estate planning not only optimizes survivors' financial security but also helps ensure peace of mind to survivors and to the terminally ill person, who can be confident that his or her affairs have been put in order. Additionally, the service of a lawyer may be effectively used to ensure that the dying person's wishes regarding organ donation or the terms of a natural death directive are carried out.

Bernstein outlines three basic legal stages that apply in cases of terminal illness when death follows expected medical probabilities.[24] The *first* stage involves long-range planning, in which the terminally ill person arranges his or her legal and financial affairs for the eventuality of death. During the *second* stage, which occurs shortly before death, the survivors gather pertinent legal papers, obtain sufficient funds to cover immediate expenses, and notify the attorney and insurance representative so they will be ready to make a smooth transition of the deceased's legal and financial affairs. Also at this time, if the dying person intends to make an anatomical gift, the appropriate medical personnel are alerted.

In the *third* stage of legal activity, which follows the death, preparations for burial are made, the will is delivered to an attorney for probate, and various other legal and financial professionals come into the picture. The effort that went into planning is now rewarded in the survivors' greater sense of security and certainty that affairs have not been left to chance. The survivors can confront their loss without the distraction and worry of complex legal and financial entanglements.

Definitions and Elements of Wills

In many early legal systems, all property belonged to the family, clan, or tribe. The right to make a will is an acknowledgment of the rights of private property rather than communal ownership. The right or privilege to determine how one's property will be distributed following death is not available in all societies, nor is it without limitations. In some countries, the government automatically assumes control over the settlement of a person's affairs; in the United States, the individual has considerable liberty in determining how property will be distributed. Still, depending on the laws of a particular state, enforcing and carrying out the provisions of a will may be restricted by circumstances that affect one's heirs. For example, someone may try to avoid willing anything to his or her spouse, but if the will is contested it may be overturned by a court. State statutes usually stipulate that a surviving spouse cannot be disinherited. Some statutes require that dependent children be provided for in the will. The rule of thumb is that anything in a will that clearly conflicts with ordinary standards of social policy may be abrogated or made invalid if the will is contested.

The person who makes a will must have the mental capacity to understand the nature of the document and the consequences of signing it. He or she must

> "What would you like for breakfast, Jack?" I asked my son-in-law on Sunday, the day of the funeral.
>
> "A fried egg, over," he replied.
>
> Such a simple thing. Yet, I'd never fried an egg.
>
> Oh, we often had them on weekends; but my husband was the breakfast cook, while I dashed up and down the steps putting clothes in the washer, running the vacuum, and all the other tasks always awaiting a working wife.
>
> I stood there, the frying pan in one hand, the egg in the other.
>
> How many times in the future would I find myself standing the same way? How many things had I never done? How many things had I taken for granted?
>
> Maxine Dowd Jensen,
> *The Warming of Winter*

understand the nature and extent of the property being bequeathed by the will and be able to identify the persons who, by convention, ought to be considered when making a will, whether or not they actually become beneficiaries. Given these conditions, and in the absence of any significant delusions, the testator is said to be of sound mind, capable of executing a legal will. State laws generally specify a minimum age at which a person can make a legal will—usually eighteen, though in several states as young as fourteen—and various other requirements, such as the presence of witnesses and execution of the document in a proper form.

In addition to standard information such as the testator's identification and a declaration that the document constitutes the person's last will and testament (along with a statement revoking previous wills, if applicable), a will may include information regarding the property to be distributed, the names of children and other heirs, specific bequests and allocations of property, as well as information concerning the establishment of trusts, the granting of powers to a trustee and/or guardian, other provisions for disposition of property, and payment of taxes, debts, and expenses of administration.

Not all these items are necessarily part of every will, nor is a will limited to the items listed here. For instance, an additional provision may delineate how property is to be distributed when simultaneous accidental deaths occur. Many wills contain a provision spelling out the lines of succession should the primary beneficiary die before the estate can be settled.

Most attorneys encourage people making their wills to involve spouses in the process to prevent problems that can arise when each spouse makes out a separate will or makes a will without the other's knowledge. When survivors find out after the testator's death that things are not as expected, an added burden of pain and confusion makes coping with the death that much more difficult. There is no requirement, however, that one's mate be involved in the making of a will.

Keeping in mind these general principles regarding wills, we now proceed to an examination of some nuts-and-bolts issues that pertain to making a will.

Will of Tomás Antonio Yorba

In the name of the Holy Trinity, Father, Son, and the Holy Ghost, three distinct persons and one true God, Amen.

1st Clause. Know all [men] who may read this my last will and testament: that I — Tomás Antonio Yorba, native born resident of this department of California, legitimate son of Antonio Yorba and Josefa Grijalva — being sick, but, by divine mercy, in the full enjoyment of my reason, memory and understanding, believing, as I firmly do, in all the mysteries of our holy Catholic faith, which faith is natural to me, since I have lived in it from my infancy and I declare that I want to live in it as a faithful Christian and true Catholic, trusting that, for this reason, his divine Majesty will have mercy on me and will pardon all my sins, through the mysteries of our Lord Jesus Christ and the intercession of his most holy mother, who is my protector and benefactress in these my last moments, so that together with my guardian angel, with St. Joseph, my own name's saint, and all the other saints of my devotion and all the other hosts of heaven, they will assist me before the grand tribunal of God, before which all mortals must render account of their actions — make and decree this my last will and testament as follows, in ordinary paper because of lack of stamped paper.

2nd Clause. Firstly, I commend my soul to God who created it, and my body to the earth, from whence it was fashioned, and it is my wish that I be buried in the church of the Mission of San Gabriel in the shroud of our father St. Francis, the funeral to be according to what my executors and heirs consider that I deserve and is befitting.

3rd Clause. Item: In regard to the expenses of the funeral and masses, these should be drawn from the fifth of my estate, according to the disposition of my executors, and I leave the residue of this fifth to my son Juan.

4th Clause. I declare that with respect to my debts, my heirs and executors should collect and pay any legal claims that may turn up or be due according to law. Item: I declare to have been married to Doña Vicenta Supúlveda, legitimate daughter of Don Francisco Sepúlveda and Doña Ramona Supúlveda, of this neighborhood, by which marriage I had five children named: (1) Juan; (2) Guadalupe, deceased; (3) José Antonio; (4) Josefa; (5) Ramona. The first being 10 years old, the second died at the age of three, the third six years old, the fourth four years old, and the fifth two years old. Item: I declare to have given my wife jewels of some value as a wedding present, but I do not remember how many, nor their value; but they must be in her possession, since I gave them to her. Item: According to my reckoning I have about 2,000 head of cattle, 900 ewes and their respective males, three herds of about 100 mares and their stallions, and three donkeys; about 21 tame horses, 7 tame and 12 unbroken mules; and lastly, whatever cattle, horses or mules may turn up with my brand which may not have been legally sold. Item: I declare to have the right — through inheritance from my father — to part of Middle Santa Ana and Lower Santana, known to be of the Yorbas. I have in Middle Santa Ana an adobe house, its roof being part timber and part thatched, consisting of 18 rooms, including the soap-house. Item: I declare that I have two vineyards with wooden fences which are now planted with bearing vines and some fruit trees; also a section of enclosed land.

5th Clause. I declare that it is my wish to name as executors and guardians of my estate, first, my brother, Don Bernardo Yorba, and second, Don Raimundo Yorba, by joint approval, to whom

continued

continued from previous page

I give all my vested power, as much as may be necessary, to go in and examine my property for the benefit of my heirs in carrying out this will, and I grant them the power to procure another associate [executor] to expedite its due execution, whom I consider appointed as a matter of course, granting him the same authority as those previously named.

6th Clause. I name as my heirs my children and my wife, in the form and manner indicated by the laws, following the necessary inventory.

7th Clause. In this my last will, I annul and void whatever will or wills, codicil or codicils, I may have previously made, so that they may stand nullified with or without judicial process, now and forever, since I definitely desire that the present testamentary disposition be my last will, codicil, and final wish, in the manner and form most legally valid. To this effect I beg of Don Vicente Sanchez, Judge of 1st *instancia*, to exercise his authority in probating this will.

To which I, the citizen Vicente Sanchez, 1st constitutional Alcalde and Judge of the 1st *instancia* of the city of Los Angeles, certify; and I affirm that the present testamentary disposition was made in my presence, and that the testator, Don Tomás Antonio Yorba, although ill, finds himself in the full command of his faculties and natural understanding, and, to attest it, I do this before the assistant witnesses — the citizens Ramon Aguilar and Ignacio Coronel — the other instrumental witnesses being the citizens Bautista Mutriel and Mariano Martinez; on the 28th day of the month of January, 1845. The testator did not sign because of physical inability, but Don Juan Bandini signed for him.

Figure *11-5*   *Historical Will*
Social custom plays a significant part in the making of a will. The will of Don Tomás Antonio Yorba, dating from the period of Mexican rule in California, presents an illuminating contrast to the modern will with its emphasis on the distribution of the testator's property. Although Yorba's estate was among the largest of the time — consisting of a Spanish land grant of 62,000 acres known as the Rancho Santiago de Santa Ana in Southern California — only a small fraction of his will relates to matters affecting the distribution of the estate to his heirs.
Source: Huntington Library. Translation by H. Noya.

The Formally Executed Will

The *formally executed will* is the conventional document used for specifying a person's wishes for the distribution of his or her estate after death (see Figure 11-5). If carefully and sensitively prepared, it not only has sufficient clarity of purpose and expression to withstand a court's scrutiny, but can help ease the burden and stress on survivors while demonstrating the testator's affection for those who were close during life.

To make a formally executed will, it is usually necessary to consult an attorney. A comprehensive review of an estate may require that various records and

And in a decade or two or more when death taps at the door, your estate may be far larger than you now envisage. It may be so already. One tends to think in terms of a few principal segments of one's estate. For purposes of planning, your "estate" includes everything of monetary value: your home and other real estate; all bank and savings accounts; usables including *objets d'art* and hobbies, such as a stamp collection; your carefully planned investment portfolio; life insurance; rights under a pension plan, if you enjoy that umbrella; as well as growing protection from social security. All must be arranged so as to afford maximum benefit to the beneficiaries.

Paul P. Ashley, *You and Your Will*

other information be gathered.[25] During the meeting with the attorney, the nature of the property and the testator's wishes for its distribution are discussed. Several meetings may be required to carefully plan and consider the ramifications of various alternatives.

Once the will's content is finally determined and its provisions set, the attorney has it typed and an appointment is made for its formal execution. On that occasion, two (in some states, three) disinterested persons are brought in to serve as witnesses, the will is reviewed, the testator acknowledges that the document accurately reflects his or her wishes, and signs it. Although preparation of the will may involve weeks or even months of thoughtful consideration and planning, the actual signing can take less than five minutes. Once the will is signed and witnessed, the testator is assured that the distribution of the estate according to his or her wishes is protected by a valid legal document.

Amending or Revoking a Will

A will is not unchangeable. It can be revoked and replaced by a new will or amended. Amending a will is a means of adding new provisions without having to rewrite it entirely. For instance, a testator who, after the will has been executed, acquires valuable property, such as an art collection, might want to make a specific provision for the new property without disturbing other parts of the estate plan. A codicil, which is executed in the same manner as the original will, would accomplish that objective. Wills should be reviewed periodically to determine if changed circumstances call for revision.

When the addition of codicils makes the will unwieldy or potentially confusing, it is time to review the entire will and make a new one. States vary in their requirements for legally revoking a will. Generally, the testator's *intent* to revoke the will must be demonstrated; the accidental burning of a will, for instance, does not imply revocation. On the other hand, if someone turns up with an earlier will, it may be difficult to prove that it was revoked if a subsequent will does not explicitly say so. When in doubt about the validity of a will, seek competent legal advice.

> The clock wound by Elizabeth still ticked, storing in its spring the pressure of her hand.
>
> Life cannot be cut off quickly. One cannot be dead until the things he changed are dead. His effect is the only evidence of his life. While there remains even a plaintive memory a person cannot be cut off, dead. A man's life dies as a commotion in a still pool dies, in little waves, spreading and growing back towards stillness.
>
> John Steinbeck, *To a God Unknown*

Probate

During the course of probate, the validity of the will is proved; an executor or administrator of the estate is appointed; the necessary matters for settling the estate are carried out; and, with the probate court's approval, the decedent's property is distributed to the beneficiaries. If the deceased left a valid will, property is distributed in accordance with its terms. If there is no will (that is, the person died *intestate*, having left no valid will), the probate court usually names an administrator and the property is then distributed according to the laws of intestate succession in that particular state.

Essentially, the probate period allows time for the deceased's affairs to be resolved, debts and taxes paid, arrangements made to receive monies due the deceased at the time of death, and finally distribution of the deceased's property. Notices to creditors are generally published in newspapers so that claims outstanding against the estate can be paid prior to distribution of the property to beneficiaries. In addition, the period of probate includes an opportunity for any interested persons to contest the validity of the will.

The Duties of the Executor or Administrator

Someone has to be responsible for carrying out all the steps necessary to settling an estate through probate. Whether an *executor* named in the will or an *administrator* appointed by the court, this person must generally meet certain minimum requirements stipulated by the law of the state in which probate occurs. Once approved by the court, the executor takes an oath to perform all duties faithfully. Some states require the posting of a bond to protect beneficiaries from any potential mismanagement of the estate during the probate period. Once these legalities are in order, then the actual job of settling the estate begins.

The prospective executor's or administrator's first duty is to notify interested parties of the testator's death. This is typically accomplished by placing a notification of death in appropriate newspapers (see Figure 11-6). Such a notice serves three purposes: (1) It announces that someone is ready to prove the validity of the

**NOTICE OF DEATH OF
LEE D. WILLIAMS
AND OF PETITION TO
ADMINISTER ESTATE
Case Number: 11111**

To all heirs, beneficiaries, creditors, contingent creditors, and persons who may be otherwise interested in the will or estate of LEE D. WILLIAMS.

A petition has been filed by JANE DOE, in the Superior Court of Santa Cruz County requesting that JANE DOE be appointed as personal representative to administer the estate of the decedent.

A hearing on the petition will be held on March 22, 1982, at 8:30 a.m. in Dept III, located at 701 Ocean Street, Santa Cruz, California 95060.

IF YOU OBJECT to the granting of the petition, you should either appear at the hearing and state your objections or file written objections with the court before the hearing. Your appearance may be in person or by your attorney.

IF YOU ARE A CREDITOR or a contingent creditor of the deceased, you must file your claim with the court or present it to the personal representative appointed by the court within four months from the date of first issuance of letters as provided in section 700 of the California Probate Code. The time for filing claims will not expire prior to four months from the date of the hearing noticed above.

YOU MAY EXAMINE the file kept by the court. If you are a person interested in the estate, you may file a request with the court to receive special notice of the filing of the inventory of estate assets and of the petitions, accounts and reports described in section 1200 of the California Probate Code.

s/ JOHN P. SMITH
Attorney for the Petitioner

JOHN P. SMITH
9999 Pacific Avenue
Santa Cruz, CA 95060
March 7, 9, 14

Figure 11-6
Newspaper Notice to Creditors

decedent's will; (2) it acknowledges that someone is petitioning to be appointed by the court to begin probate; and (3) it gives notice of the death to creditors so that any outstanding claims against the estate can be submitted for settlement.

The executor makes an inventory of the estate, including all personal and real property owned by the decedent. Names and addresses of all beneficiaries are compiled. Bank accounts, stocks, bonds, and other assets are inventoried, as are the contents of the deceased's home and his or her safe deposit box, if any. When a surviving spouse is the estate's primary or sole heir, the inventory of personal and household goods can be less meticulous, though items that have special worth, such as paintings, jewelry, and antiques, are specified. Important papers are gathered, including insurance policies, social security and pension information, military service records, and other documents that will require review and possibly action. Several copies of the death certificate are obtained to facilitate claims for payment of insurance benefits and the like.

The executor is also responsible for properly managing the estate pending its final disbursement to heirs. Tax returns may need to be filed on behalf of the decedent and the estate. The executor may be charged with paying an allowance to the surviving spouse or to minor children for their support during the period of

> When it comes to divide an estate, the politest men quarrel.
>
> Ralph Waldo Emerson
> *Journals* (1863)

probate. If the decedent was in business or was a stockholder in a corporation, the executor must skillfully execute a smooth transition that benefits the estate.

An executor or administrator who is not knowledgeable in the law usually enlists the aid of an attorney to make certain that legal requirements are satisfied. Both the executor or administrator and the attorney are entitled to compensation for their services to the estate. These fees are usually a percentage of the value of the estate's assets, the percentage being computed according to fee tables established by state legislatures.

After all the information is compiled about payments due the estate and claims against it, the executor or administrator takes the necessary steps to have the debts paid and to receive monies due. If an estate's funds are not sufficient to pay all creditors, disbursement is usually made according to guidelines established by state law.

Finally, a schedule for distributing the estate's property to the beneficiaries is prepared and submitted for the approval of the probate court. Once the court's approval is obtained, the property is distributed, final accounting is prepared for the court's review, and receipts are obtained to certify that the distribution has been made correctly. Assuming that everything has been carried out properly, the court then discharges the executor or administrator. The estate is settled.

Avoiding Probate

Because probate involves delays and can sometimes be expensive, many people try to avoid it. Books purporting to explain how to avoid probate appear from time to time on the bestseller lists, demonstrating the widespread appeal of this kind of financial advice. Sensible, legal steps can be taken to avoid or at least minimize probate costs. For example, a husband and wife may own their house and other assets in joint tenancy, a form of property ownership that allows a spouse to take full legal possession of the property upon the other's death without probate.

Some approaches to avoiding probate, however, can have serious pitfalls, particularly the do-it-yourself approach taken without obtaining qualified legal counsel. Suppose, for example, that an elderly couple would like their house to go to their grandson after their deaths. Intending to avoid probate, they might visit a local stationery store, purchase the appropriate form to file a change of ownership, add the grandson's name to the property deed, and record this document with the county recorder. So far, so good. But now suppose that several years later they decide to sell the house, or they change their minds about making the grandson their beneficiary and want to remove his name from the deed. To make this desired change, they must obtain the grandson's signature, much as if he were "selling" his right of ownership in the house. Placing a minor's name on a deed may require going into court and requesting that a legal guardian be appointed to act on behalf of the minor should a change of ownership be desired.

Given careful consideration and the benefit of competent legal and financial advice, many options are available for setting up one's estate so that the chance of probate is minimized or eliminated. Arranging that fewer assets fall under probate can make procedures briefer and less complex. Such actions may offer significant savings of legal fees and erstwhile probate costs. However, all such plans to avoid or minimize probate should be adopted only after careful consideration.

Laws of Intestate Succession

It is estimated that seven out of ten Americans die without leaving a will. Perhaps so many of us fail to make a will because death makes us uncomfortable. Or perhaps, overwhelmed by busyness, we neglect this aspect of financial planning with the questionable excuse that we are not yet at the age when death is statistically probable. Considering the consequence that can result when one dies intestate — that is, without a will — we would do well to give this matter more than passing thought.

One of the chief reasons for making a will is to ensure that property will be disbursed according to one's wishes. In the absence of a will, property is distributed according to general guidelines established in state law. The state generally tries to accomplish what it believes the deceased would have done had he or she actually made a will. The laws that dictate the disbursement of property, the care of minor children, and all the matters that pertain to settling the estate reflect society's ideas of fair play and justice. Thus, the values of society, rather than the deceased's personal values, determine the outcome.

If any heirs are minors, their share of the estate will be held in trust for them. Their guardian, even when it is the surviving parent, may be forced to periodically report to the court on management of the children's trust. The complications that may arise from dying intestate make a solid argument for taking steps to execute a will.

Whereas an executor named by the testator is permitted to act more or less independently in the management of the estate provided that he or she acts prudently, the court-appointed administrator may be required to obtain the court's approval before proceeding with sensible and necessary decisions. When an estate is sizable or is otherwise complex, the difference between management of the estate by an executor and management by the court-appointed administrator may be significant.

Although the laws of intestate succession differ among states, some general patterns prevail. In community-property states, for example, any property held in common goes automatically to the surviving spouse. If there are no children, separate property also goes to the surviving spouse. When there is only one child,

© Chronicle Features, 1984

"The Far Side," drawing by Gary Larson, Chronicle Features

3-9

"Aaaaaaaa! . . . It's George! He's taking it with him!"

the estate will probably be divided equally between child and surviving spouse. If there is more than one child, usually one-third of the estate goes to the surviving spouse and the remaining two-thirds is divided equally among the children.

If there is no surviving spouse, property is divided among the children; if no children, disbursement is made to the deceased's parents; if they are not living, property is likely to be divided among the deceased's surviving siblings; if there are none, the estate may be divided among the late siblings' children. In attempting to settle an estate, the court will make a determined effort to locate surviving heirs. If none can be found, however, the proceeds from the estate go to the state.

Because the laws of intestate succession are designed to protect the interests of the surviving spouse and children of the deceased, some people find it convenient to let the state decide how their property is distributed after death. The major flaw in this view, however, is that the decisions made by the state may be quite other than those the person would have made. Paul Ashley observes that the distinction between intestate succession and distribution according to the terms of a formally executed will is fundamental: Who would you rather have make the rules and decide the outcome of your estate — the legislature and public officials, or you, the testator?[26]

Estate and Inheritance Taxes

Estate and inheritance taxes have the same rationale as other forms of taxation: the redistribution of wealth. Equality of opportunity is a cornerstone of American society, and taxation is seen as a method of breaking up concentrations of wealth and providing greater economic benefits for a greater number of citizens. Although there may be dissent about *how* wealth is thus redistributed, it is presumed that there is consensus among the American people about the desirability of redistribution. Nevertheless, few people enjoy paying taxes, and many feel that so-called death taxes are among the most abhorrent. Although a case can be made for the philosophical view that inheritance taxes should be 100 percent — "Empty we come into the world, empty we leave" — this notion goes against the grain of human nature.

Estate Taxes

The estate tax, imposed by the federal government, is not a tax on property but rather a tax paid on the *transfer* of property from the decedent to his or her beneficiaries.[27] Estate taxes are assessed on the total value of the taxable estate before it is divided. Like individual income tax returns, estate taxes are calculated on the basis of assets less allowable deductions. The estate's assets are those items included on the inventory taken by the executor or administrator, and the value of these assets is generally determined by court-appointed appraisers. Once the gross value of an estate is determined, allowable deductions are computed. Typical deductions include expenses incurred during a terminal illness; funeral costs; administrative expenses; debts, mortgages, and liens against the estate; net losses that occur during administration of the estate; charitable and public bequests; several categories of tax credits, if applicable to a particular estate; and the marital deduction.

First enacted in 1948, the *marital deduction* was designed to extend to everyone in the United States the same opportunity for tax savings that had been provided to those living in community-property states. Whereas earlier laws placed a limit on the deduction allowed on transfers of property between spouses, current law provides an unlimited marital deduction. This means that no tax need be paid on the death of the first spouse if the entire estate is left to the surviving spouse. In some cases, however, particularly those involving large estates, it may not be advantageous to use the unlimited marital deduction since it is designed to allow a postponement of tax until the death of the surviving spouse, not an avoidance of tax.

Although the marital deduction provides an opportunity to avoid taxation on transfers of estates between spouses, it limits a testator's freedom of choice

Inheritance

When I was ten years old, my father died. And at that time, of course, I thought my father was the best and finest man there ever was. And some years later when I was eighteen and I began to mingle in the adult community, I introduced myself to strangers and they would ask me if John Estrada was my father. When I said yes, they would say, "Well, let me shake your hand. He was a fine man and a good friend of mine." And then they would tell me wonderful stories about him. Since that time, I have hoped that when I am gone, some people might meet my children and say to them that I was a good man and a good friend. To me that is a finer inheritance than any material possession.

Fred Estrada

with respect to the distribution of his or her estate. Thus, some people choose to incur larger taxes as a trade-off for retaining greater control over how an estate will be distributed.

Inheritance Taxes

Whereas estate taxes are levied by the federal government, inheritance taxes are imposed by the states. The tax is assessed on each heir according to the amount of property received. Taxation rates and regulations vary among the states. Inheritance tax has generally been smaller than the federal estate tax. However, many estates now exempt from federal estate taxes may remain subject to state inheritance taxes.

Inheritance taxes are levied according to the relationship between the decedent and the beneficiary: As the relationship grows more distant, the exempt amount is decreased and the tax rate on the excess is increased.

Some states tax insurance benefits, others do not, and yet others provide exemptions calculated according to the relationship of the named beneficiary to the insured. Some states have made efforts to abolish inheritance taxes. Information about the specific inheritance tax rates and regulations that apply in your state can be obtained from a local attorney, the state's inheritance tax department, or reference books such as *The World Almanac*.

Trusts

A *trust* can be defined simply as the holding of property by one person for the benefit of another. The many kinds of trusts constitute extremely valuable tools of estate planning. Common forms of trusts include arranging for the financial security of minor children and providing funds for college or similar expenses.

Although we usually think of trusts as a financial planning tool that benefits others, it is possible to set up a trust for oneself. In fact, the person making the trust can serve as both its trustee and beneficiary. A *living trust*, for example, can be established whereby a husband and wife hold their property in trust for themselves. Such a trust differs from a *testamentary trust*, which becomes effective upon the testator's death.

One wise use of the living trust is to provide funds for medical care in the event that the trustor is unable to act in his or her own behalf because of senility or some other incapacity. One instance of the wisdom of planning before need is described by Paul Ashley. An eighty-year-old man established a living trust, designating his attorney to handle his affairs if he should not be able to do so himself. Shortly after setting up this trust, the man suffered a stroke that incapacitated him for nearly three years, making it impossible for him to conduct necessary business and financial transactions. Because he had the foresight to institute a living trust for just such a contingency, he and his wife were assured of receiving every care and comfort that could be made available during the term of his disability.[28]

Trusts can be designed to serve many different kinds of purposes. Trusts are often an excellent means to avoid or minimize the complexity and duration of probate procedures, thus saving time and money.

Life Insurance and Death Benefits

In the United States, the first life insurance company was established in 1759 by the Presbyterian Synod of Philadelphia for Presbyterian ministers. Although life insurance did not become common until the middle of the nineteenth century, it is now a huge industry whose assets grew from $207 billion in 1970 to $1167 billion in 1988.[29] Most of us own some type of life insurance, even though it is estimated that less than half of us have arranged for someone to handle the affairs of our estate following our death and less than one-third of us have made a will. Recent statistics indicate that over 80 percent of American households include at least one member who owns life insurance.[30]

Policies and Considerations

Life insurance offers a convenient and relatively inexpensive means of providing at least a basic estate for our beneficiaries after we die. It may represent a fairly small portion of a comprehensive estate, or the major portion of a smaller estate. The distinguishing feature of life insurance in estate planning is that it offers a means whereby many people join together to share a potential risk that each could not bear alone. Insurance plans can be designed in a wide variety of ways and to suit many purposes. Some policies are part of a total investment portfolio that can be drawn upon during the insured's lifetime. Other policies provide for benefit payments only after the death of the insured. Table 11-3 presents a glossary of insurance terms. The insurance company generates its profit from carrying out the administrative duties that are necessary in bringing together the large number of participants required for such a cooperative venture. Companies licensed to sell insurance must conform to state laws regulating insurance practices.

"My husband, dead, at just 37."

If your husband dies you could still get money to help raise your family.

social security protects your family now.

Ask about disability and survivors benefits at any social security office.

U.S. DEPARTMENT OF HEALTH, EDUCATION, AND WELFARE
Social Security Administration
DHEW No. (SSA) 74-10807

Yanker Poster Collection, Library of Congress

Aimed at informing the public about survivor benefits available through Social Security, this poster addresses an age group that may give little consideration to the possibility of a spouse's death and its financial consequences.

Those who favor including insurance as part of estate planning argue that life insurance may offer some advantages not available from other forms of investment. For example, unlike some other assets, life insurance benefits are not subject to attachment by creditors. Too, benefits usually become available immediately following death, unlike assets that must be processed through probate. Thus, insurance benefits can have impotant psychological and emotional value as well. Such funds may provide relief and a sense of security to a surviving spouse and other dependents during the period immediately after bereavement. Knowing that money is available to cover anticipated expenses may help to reduce the stress associated with this period of crisis. On the other hand, a hasty or ill-informed decision concerning how insurance benefits are spent may ultimately

TABLE 11-3   *A Brief Glossary of Life Insurance Terms*

Annuities: Closely related to life insurance, annuities are designed to ensure that a person's accumulated funds will last for the remainder of his or her life by guaranteeing a specified income for as long as he or she lives. The price of an annuity is based on the average life expectancy for persons of a given age; those who die earlier than the average are, in effect, paying to support those who live longer.

Beneficiary: The person (or other entity, such as an institution or a charitable organization) named to received the proceeds of a life insurance policy that are payable at the death of the insured.

Chartered Life Underwriter (CLU): A designation awarded to agents who complete a college-level course of study in insurance and financial planning.

Endowment: An insurance policy that provides for the payment of the face amount of the policy after a specified number of years, or at a specified age of the insured, or to the beneficiaries of the insured at his or her death. Typically used to accumulate savings, such as for education or retirement, an endowment policy offers less protection in the event of early death than does a whole life policy.

Face amount: The amount of insurance protection under a given policy as stated on the first page, or face, of the agreement; this amount may be increased by dividends or decreased by loans against the policy.

Group life insurance: An insurance agreement covering a group of people, often the employees of a company or, in some cases, the members of a voluntary-membership organization; the premiums may be paid either exclusively by the employer or jointly by the employer and employees.

Insured: The person whose life is insured under the terms of an insurance agreement, often the person who takes out the policy.

Life insurance policy: A written agreement between an insurance company and the insured that provides for payment of a stipulated sum of money to the beneficiary or beneficiaries named in the policy or to the estate of the deceased upon the death of the insured.

Mutual company: An insurance company owned by the policyholders and managed by a board of directors chosen by the policyholders. After administrative expenses are paid, the profits from operating the firm are returned to policyholders in the form of dividends.

Nonparticipating policy: A policy on which no refunds or dividends are paid and which bears a relatively low guaranteed premium.

Paid-up policy: An insurance policy on which no further payments are due and under which there remain outstanding benefits as provided by the terms of the policy.

Participating policy: An insurance policy in which the insured shares in the distribution of dividends resulting from the surplus earnings of the insurance company.

Premium: The amount paid to an insurance company by the insured in exchange for the benefits provided under the terms of the policy.

Stock company: An insurance company owned by its stockholders. Generally, the policies are nonparticipating; that is, no dividends are paid to those who are insured by the company. Instead, profits are shared by the company's stockholders. Although insurance premiums are usually lower with a stock company, when dividends paid over a period of time are taken into account, one may find that costs are ultimately less with a mutual, or participating, company.

Term insurance: The simplest type of policy. Provides protection for a stated period of time (usually from five to twenty years) and expires without value if the insured survives

T A B L E *11-3 (continued)*

longer than the stated period. Term insurance provides maximum protection for a minimum outlay at a given time.

Underwriter: The insurer, or a person acting on behalf of the insurer, who accepts and classifies the life insurance risk; also, the person who solicits insurance as an agent of the insurer and who assumes the obligation on behalf of the insurer by signing the insurance agreement.

Whole life insurance: A policy that continues throughout the insured's lifetime. The premium remains constant since it is based on the expectation that the policy will be held for the person's lifetime. The younger a person's age when the policy is taken out, the lower the premium. In early years, the premium paid is more than the true cost of the insurance; in later years, it is less. Thus, the policy builds up a cash value based on the difference between the premium paid and the true cost of the insurance. This cash value can be "captured" by borrowing on it or by discontinuing the policy and getting a refund. Upon the death of the insured, the policy provides for payment of the stated amount of insurance as increased by any dividends that have been retained and reduced by any loans against the policy. Also called ordinary life and straight life. This type of policy requires a lower cash outlay than other types of policies over a person's lifetime.

increase the survivor's stress rather than alleviating it. Issues like this, so important for the well-being of one's survivors, need to be carefully considered during the making of a comprehensive estate plan.

Other Death Benefits

Many survivors qualify for various lump-sum and income benefits from government programs and institutions such as Social Security and the Veterans Administration. The dependents of Civil Service employees may be entitled to similar benefits. To obtain current information about any of these government death-benefit programs, one can call or write the government bureau administering them. It is important to realize that a person entitled to benefits under one or more of these programs will receive such benefits only if a claim is filed. Moreover, delays in filing may result in a loss of benefits.

When death results from accident or negligence, various kinds of insurance settlements or other death benefits may become payable to survivors. Such benefits are often related to court cases that involve the attempt to place a "value" on the deceased person's life and what that loss represents to his or her survivors. Although settlements of this kind may indeed be helpful to survivors as they pick up the pieces and try to go on with their lives following such a loss, the monetary amount of a settlement, no matter how large, is poor compensation for the loss of a loved one (see Figure 11-7).

Actions taken by a survivor may affect eligibility to receive some forms of benefit payments. For example, a spouse who remarries or has income that exceeds specified limits may lose entitlement to Social Security benefit payments. A

Burial in a national cemetery, such as the Black Hills National Cemetery in South Dakota, is a benefit made available to veterans who have served in American military forces during wartime. Such cemeteries have been established across the United States. Other death benefits for veterans include a lump-sum payment to help defray burial expenses and, under certain circumstances, direct payments to survivors.

© Albert Lee Strickland

well-conceived and adequate estate plan will include consideration of benefits that may accrue from government programs such as those mentioned as well as benefits that may be due from employee or union pension programs. Further, some states have passed laws requiring that a surviving spouse and any dependent children be given the choice of whether to continue group health insurance policies that were held by the deceased spouse. Having an understanding of such benefits and knowing how to get them can help alleviate feelings of anxiety and vulnerability that accompany bereavement.

"I'm not happy because I no more my son already. . . . I miss him. Even if I get my money, I no more my loved one, my son. I'm not interested in money. Every day, after work, even if I feel tired, I no miss to go visit my boy. Sometimes I cry. Sometimes I give food (for his grave). Soda. His favorite — Kentucky Fried Chicken. Sometimes fried saimin. Then I give an orange. Ice cream. . . . One day after the crash, my boy, he come my house in spirit. He tell me, 'Daddy, I miss you. I no more hands. I no more eyes.' Ho, I cry."

Figure *11-7*   *Death of a Son*
Jovencio Ruiz of Molokai, responding to a question about the six-figure insurance settlement for the death of his 14-year-old son, Jovencio, Jr. in the Aloha IslandAir crash in October 1989.

Further Readings

George J. Annas. *The Rights of Patients: The Basic ACLU Guide to Patient Rights*. 2d ed. Clifton, N.J.: Humana Press, 1991.

Paul P. Ashley. *You and Your Will: The Planning and Management of Your Estate*. Rev. ed. New York: New American Library, 1985.

Joseph M. Belth. *Life Insurance: A Consumer's Handbook*. 2d ed. Bloomington: Indiana University Press, 1985.

Robert N. Brown, Clifford D. Allo, Alan D. Freeman, and Gordon W. Netzorg. *The Rights of Older Persons: The Basic ACLU Guide to an Older Person's Rights*. New York: Avon Books, 1979.

Ronald Chester. *Inheritance, Wealth, and Society*. Bloomington: Indiana University Press, 1982.

Jack Goody, Joan Thirsk, and E.P. Thompson, eds. *Family and Inheritance*. New York: Cambridge University Press, 1978.

Charles F. Hemphill, Jr. *Wills and Trusts: A Legal and Financial Handbook for Everyone*. Englewood Cliffs, N.J.: Prentice-Hall, 1980.

Charlotte Kirsch. *A Survivor's Guide to Contingency Planning*. Garden City, N.Y.: Anchor Press/Doubleday, 1981.

William J. Moody. *How to Probate an Estate: A Handbook for Executors and Administrators*. Rev. ed. New York: Cornerstone Library, 1977.

Oceana Publications, Inc. *How to Make a Will, How to Use Trusts*. 4th ed. Dobbs Ferry, N.Y.: Oceana Publications, 1978.

Frank Smith. *Cause of Death: The Story of Forensic Science*. New York: Van Nostrand Reinhold, 1980.

Marvin B. Sussman, Judith N. Cates, and David T. Smith. *The Family and Inheritance*. New York: Russell Sage, 1970.

Edward F. Sutkowski. *Estate Planning: A Basic Guide*. Chicago: American Bar Association, 1986.

S. Department of Energy

The thermonuclear warhead presents a new kind of encounter with death; such warheads, and such encounters, have become pervasive since the first detonations of atomic weapons during World War II. This ominous mushroom cloud rises from a surface blast at Enewetak Island in 1952. Today's nuclear devices are many times more powerful.

Environmental Encounters
with Death

*T*he essayist E.B. White said, "To confront death, in any guise, is to identify with the victim and face what is unsettling and sobering."[1] Though we are often insulated from death in modern societies, we nevertheless encounter it in many guises. In news reports and in our entertainment, death is a staple item. Consciously or not, we risk subtle, and sometimes dramatic, encounters with death as we engage in our life's pursuits — on our jobs and in our recreational activities. Fatal accidents and disasters are other experiences in which the tragedy of death is present. Violence, war, and nuclear catastrophe, which threaten us not only as persons but also as a society, overshadow and influence our plans and activities. Is it surprising, then, that this inventory of potential encounters with death contributes to the high incidence of stress which affects so many people and becomes yet another potential threat to life?

Mostly, we ignore or give only passing thought to these encounters with death. Seldom do we contemplate death in a way that shakes us emotionally or gives us pause. Yet our environment furnishes us with opportunities for encountering death at almost every turn. In Chapter 1 we saw how the mass media — newspapers, television, movies — as well as art, literature, and music all present images that can affect our own attitudes toward death. In subsequent chapters we examined other encounters with death, such as life-threatening illness and surviving the deaths of those close to us. Here we look at some of the encounters with death that are part of

I stared in a horrified trance as a figure appeared, frozen in the air for the briefest moment, its arms outstretched above its head as if in utterly hopeless supplication. Then it continued its relaxed, cart-wheeling descent, with only the thundering crashes attesting to its frightening impacts on the rock. It disappeared into a gully.

"Don't look!" I screamed to my wife, who was, of course, as helplessly transfixed as I was. And the sounds continued. After a time, the figure came into view at the base of the gully and continued down the pile of rubble below. My last view of it is frozen in time. The figure's arm was curled easily over its head, and its posture was one of relaxation, of napping. It drifted down that last boulder field like an autumn leaf down a rippling brook. Then it disappeared under the trees, and only the pebbles continued to clatter down the rock. Suddenly it was very, very still.

I looked down to Debby and had to articulate the obvious: "That was a man," I said quietly, numbly.

William G. Higgins, "Groundfall"

life in modern societies. Some, such as natural disasters, have been part of human experience since life began; others, such as the nuclear threat, represent a wholly new dimension of death's presence in our lives.

Risk Taking

The images communicated by the media and other forms of popular culture can influence the kinds of risks we are willing to take in our lives. Often, risks accompany the actions we take in pursuit of the "good life." Indeed, all life involves risk, though the degree of risk we are willing to assume is typically subject to our personal choices as to how we live our lives.

Think about your own life. What kinds of risk do you face in your employment, your leisure activities, your style of living in general? Are any of the risks life threatening? Do you take "calculated" risks? Can you exercise choice about assuming these risks, or do some seem to be unavoidable?

In some areas of our lives we can exercise considerable choice about the nature and degree of risk we take. For example, smoking, drinking, taking drugs, and driving habits typically involve risks that can be controlled. Similarly, we can usually exercise choice in our occupation and recreational activities.

The risks associated with various jobs are sometimes quite dramatic, involving dangers that most people, given a choice, would very likely avoid. Certain occupations come readily to mind: explosives expert, high-rise window washer, movie stuntperson, test pilot, as well as police officer and fire fighter. Such a list could be continued almost indefinitely. We might add scientists and researchers working with hazardous materials, mine workers, electricians, heavy-equipment operators, and farm workers using toxic pesticides. As you add your own exam-

UPI/Bettmann Newsphotos

To keep from tumbling through space at 125 miles per hour, this mile-high skydiver spreads his arms and legs to control his freefall before opening his parachute. Although risks are ever present in our lives, we expose ourselves to many of them by personal choice.

ples to this list, notice whether they involve the risk of sudden death — as from an explosion or a fall from a high-rise building — or of long-term death, such as that resulting from exposure to hazardous conditions. Some jobs involve health risks that are identified only after many years of continual exposure to the harmful condition.

An occupation may increase the risk of death by increasing the worker's level of stress. No doubt all work involves stress; whether stress becomes a threat to the worker's health, however, depends on both the nature of the work and the worker's attitude. A U.S. government report, *Work in America*, states, "Satisfaction with work appears to be the best predictor of longevity — better than known medical or genetic factors — and various aspects of work account for much, if not most, of the factors associated with heart disease."[2]

Death can also be encountered in our recreational activities and sports: mountain climbing, parachuting, scuba diving, motorcycle racing, and the like. Some people might characterize such activities as thrill seeking, though this term suggests motives that some participants in these activities would not ascribe to themselves. Often, part of the pleasure derived from such activities is the fact that there is an element of risk; thus, the activity presents an opportunity to test limits and develop confidence in our ability to accept the risk and deal positively with fear. On the other hand, the thrill may come from successfully achieving the goal of a particular activity. Mountain climbers, for instance, might willingly accept the risk because climbing provides both physical conditioning and the aesthetic pleasure of reaching the heights and surveying the expanse of uncluttered nature.

Although mountain climbing involves obvious risks, two different climbers can relate to these risks in vastly different ways. One climber may display an attitude of abandon that could only be characterized as foolhardy or death defying. The other may devote many hours to obtaining instruction, preparing equipment, conditioning for the climb, and asking advice from more experienced climbers before deciding to set foot on a mountain. In short, steps can be taken to minimize the risks. An activity, then, may be attractive to some persons *because* of its inherent risks, whereas others accept the risks as inseparable from the other attractive features of the activity. When behavior involves doing dangerous things simply for the thrill of it, or as a way to "laugh in the face of death," such behavior may represent an attempt to deny death or to deny one's fear of death.[3]

No one is immune to risks. At home, on the job, or at play the risk of death confronts us in one way or another. After a classroom discussion about the risks involved in various activities, one student said, "It seems we're coming around to the point that everything we do involves risks. You could even stab yourself with your knitting needle!" Perhaps, but usually when we consider activities involving risk, we think of pursuits about which there is a direct acknowledgment of the risk. The possibility of falling backward from a rocking chair while knitting strikes most people as less risky than, say, driving a formula race car or embarking on an expedition to the Himalayas.

Sometimes the risks we face are not known. However, more often, we can exercise options that allow us to control or manage the element of risk. What automobile driver has not chosen at some time to drive just a bit faster in order to arrive at the destination sooner? Accident statistics, as well as common sense, tell us that exceeding the speed limit increases the risk. Yet one makes a trade-off; the added risk is exchanged for the expected benefit of arriving at the destination sooner.

A death resulting from a high-risk sport or similar activity may have a special impact on other individuals who engage in the same activity. In addition to the impact upon those who are involved most immediately (for example, persons who had rented equipment or given instruction to the deceased), the death also affects the larger community of participants in the sport by challenging "the underlying assumption of the sport that careful, cautious practice insures safety."[4] To cope with this challenge, and with the death itself, rumors may circulate that the deceased failed to take necessary precautions or followed an unwise or ill-considered course of action. These rumors may represent an attempt to fit what has happened into a manageable scheme and to mitigate any feelings of guilt about having been unable to prevent the death. As a means of coping with such a death, this tendency to "blame the victim" may facilitate the resolution of grief and allow other participants to feel comfortable continuing the activity despite the risks.

Accidents

Accidents are the fourth most common cause of death among the total population in the United States and the *leading cause* of death among persons ages thirty-four and younger.[5] Often, accidents are viewed as happening by "chance" or because of "fate" or "bad luck." From that view, it follows that little if anything can be done to prevent accidents. But the definition of an accident as an event that occurs "by chance or from unknown causes" can be refined, as the dictionary reflects, to encompass the understanding that an accident may indeed be "unavoidable," or it may result from "carelessness, unawareness, or ignorance." Thus, accidents are typically events over which individuals do have varying degrees of control. For example, suppose a gun is brought into the household. The presence of the gun increases from zero the chance that there may be an accidental firing of the weapon. Of course, such an accident may never happen. But if a gun were *not* in the home, there would be *no* chance of an accidental firing.

In other words, the choices we make affect the probabilities of various kinds of accidents. It is an established fact that drivers who have been drinking tend to take greater risks than do sober drivers. It has also been determined that a driver's judgment and performance are inversely related to the amount of alcohol imbibed, whereas a driver's tendency to overrate his or her driving abilities is directly related to the amount imbibed. The effect of alcohol on driving is evident in the fact that, statistically, almost half the drivers involved in fatality accidents are under the influence of alcohol.

Are such accidents the result of mere chance or fate? If not, then steps can be taken to reduce their probability. Unfortunately, the notion that accidents are chance events contributes to the neglect of such problems as drinking and driving. For example, even though the percentage of young people involved in alcohol-related motor vehicle accidents has recently declined, alcohol is still a factor in about one in five fatal crashes involving young people ages sixteen and seventeen and more than a third of the fatal crashes involving young people between the ages of eighteen and twenty-one.[6]

A better understanding of accident causes — one that considers such factors as carelessness, lack of awareness, and neglect — might well result in constructive actions toward the prevention of these kinds of accidents.

Sometimes we call certain persons *accident prone* because they seem to become involved in accidents with an unusually high frequency. The term is often used jocularly, and there is not sufficient evidence to scientifically define a personality type that would be described as accident prone. However, certain known factors can affect the type of accident that may occur and the individual's probability of being involved in it. Such accident proneness is usually based on factors such as age and experience.

For example, insurance rates reflect the degree of risk of motor vehicle accidents: Policies cost more for both the young driver and the elderly driver. A large percentage of accidental deaths among teenagers is related to automobile use. Because the elderly also incur an increased risk, it is interesting to compare the reasons. The young driver's increased risk results largely from inexperience and youthfully impulsive driving habits. The elderly person's increased risk, on the other hand, is due to slower reaction time and physical impairments that make driving more hazardous.

When accidents of all types are considered, adolescent and young adult males are at greatest risk. It is unclear whether the high accident rate for this age group and sex reflects this group's greater willingness to assume risks (to assert masculinity, perhaps?) or cultural attitudes that tend to encourage males more than females to engage in risky activities. Perhaps as we reach the point where as many women as men engage in activities once considered the exclusive province of men, the group at greatest risk may contain as many women as men.

So far we have emphasized intrinsic factors that influence accidents — that is, factors having to do with a person's own physical and mental qualities. Another set of factors — extrinsic factors, or conditions that exist within the environment — also influences the occurrence of accidents. Unsafe conditions present in the environment are sometimes called "accidents waiting to happen." Often such conditions are the result of negligence or of ignorance about the threat they pose to safety. For example, say a swimming pool is left unattended and easily accessible to young children; if a toddler happens by and falls into the pool and is drowned, the owner of the pool might be judged negligent.

Typically, unsafe conditions in the environment reflect the attitudes and value systems of the person or group responsible, or of society as a whole. For instance, a landlord who refuses to correct unsafe conditions on the tenant's premises apparently does not value others' safety. Accidents caused by drunk driving occur because of choices made by both the drinking driver and society. Societal neglect is also partly responsible for many of the fire disasters that occur in the United States. Fire safety remains a serious national problem, though actions could be taken to improve unsafe conditions that contribute to fire deaths.

Examples like these could be multiplied many times over in various areas of environmental health and safety. Indeed, it seems that unsafe conditions are ubiquitous. It would be naive to believe that the risks we encounter could be eliminated completely. Still, in many areas of our lives, risk can be minimized (see Figure 12-1). The lack of attention — perhaps one should say the lack of resolve — to take the necessary steps toward correcting unsafe conditions prompts Robert Kastenbaum and Ruth Aisenberg to ask: "How negligent must a society be before its 'accidental' deaths are tantamount to homicide?"[7]

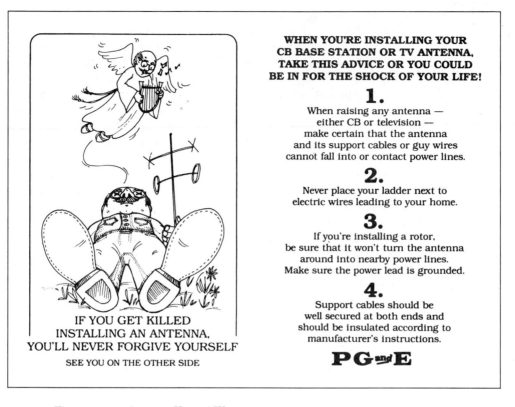

WHEN YOU'RE INSTALLING YOUR
CB BASE STATION OR TV ANTENNA,
TAKE THIS ADVICE OR YOU COULD
BE IN FOR THE SHOCK OF YOUR LIFE!

1.

When raising any antenna —
either CB or television —
make certain that the antenna
and its support cables or guy wires
cannot fall into or contact power lines.

2.

Never place your ladder next to
electric wires leading to your home.

3.

If you're installing a rotor,
be sure that it won't turn the antenna
around into nearby power lines.
Make sure the power lead is grounded.

4.

Support cables should be
well secured at both ends and
should be insulated according to
manufacturer's instructions.

PG and E

IF YOU GET KILLED
INSTALLING AN ANTENNA,
YOU'LL NEVER FORGIVE YOURSELF

SEE YOU ON THE OTHER SIDE

Figure *12-1* *Antenna Hazard Warning*
The threat of death may be used to warn consumers and employees of risks
to safety. Here, the threat of death is presented with a touch of humor, being
represented as a transition to an angelic state complete with stereotypical harp.
Source: Pacific Gas & Electric Company.

Disasters

Some encounter death from disaster vicariously, through news reports.
Others vividly recall disaster as a frightening event, occurring suddenly and
bringing destruction and loss. For everyone, the possibility of disaster is a constant threat, the end result of a sequence of events that ultimately leads to catastrophe. Globally, deaths due to natural disasters are said to constitute up to 4
percent of the total deaths in the world each year.[8]

Disaster can be defined as a life-threatening event that affects many people
within a relatively brief period of time, bringing sudden and great misfortune.
Disasters result from natural phenomena—floods, earthquakes, and other "acts

of God"—as well as human activities. Included in the latter category are fires, airplane crashes, chemical spills, and nuclear contamination.

In the United States, the incidence of disasters has increased in recent years. One reason for this increase is that more than half the U.S. population now lives within fifty miles of the coastline, an area that, in the West, is vulnerable to fires, floods, earthquakes, and landslides, and, in the Southeast, is prey to storms, hurricanes, and tornadoes. The growth in population and the rise of industrialization have themselves brought increased exposure to disasters related to human activities—for example, fires, explosions, and chemical pollution.

These factors have increased the risk of disaster worldwide. In 1984, the world's worst industrial accident occurred when gaseous methyl isocyanate escaped from Union Carbide's pesticide plant in Bhopal, India, bringing death to 2500 people residing near the plant. The unprecedented magnitude of this accident was followed by what was reported to be the largest human-caused, mass disaster lawsuit ever, with claims totaling more than $100 billion in damages.

In recent years, an increasing number of disasters have been related to environmental pollution, as happened in Bhopal. The accidental contamination of livestock feed with the chemical PBB in Michigan and the emergency shutdown of the nuclear reactor at Three Mile Island are other examples.[9] In 1986, radioactivity was released over a large area of eastern and northern Europe when a nuclear power plant at Chernobyl in the Soviet Union suffered catastrophic failure, an accident termed the worst in the history of nuclear power generation. Dangerous levels of radiation contaminated the area surrounding the plant, causing death and serious injury and damaging the food supply. The proliferation of technology requires that attention be given to the potential for such catastrophes. Although the number of disasters affecting the U.S. population has increased, this area of death awareness and study has mostly been neglected. Robert Kastenbaum has cited this neglect as an example of "our society's selective attention to death even when it does choose to pay any attention at all."[10]

Communities can decrease the risk of injury and death by taking measures designed to lessen the impact of a potential disaster, but the effects of a disaster are difficult to anticipate fully. In September 1985, a devastating earthquake hit Mexico City, without warning, killing almost 10,000 people. Previously, the city had enacted building codes that took into account the possibility of low-frequency earthquake waves associated with the ancient lake beds on which Mexico City is built. But these codes did *not* include a specification for the number of shaking cycles that buildings should be constructed to withstand, a factor that seismologists later determined contributed to the large number of fatalities.

People often submit themselves to the risk of disaster because of considerations that make the risk acceptable. Employment opportunities, for example, may prove the deciding factor. Perhaps many people who live in areas where disaster is a likely event rationalize the danger, if they give it any thought at all, as simply "playing the percentages."

Yanker Poster Collection, Library of Congress

Adequate warnings of an impending disaster can save lives. Yet necessary information may be withheld because of greed or political expediency, or simply because of uncertainty about the nature and extent of the threat, or because of concern about causing panic.

The tragedy that followed the eruption in 1902 of the Mt. Pelee volcano, on the island of Martinique in the West Indies, is instructive of how information that could warn potential disaster victims is sometimes mismanaged with disastrous

consequences. The officials of the nearby community of St. Pierre were alerted to
the likelihood that the volcano would erupt. But, concerned that the population
would panic if notified and thus thwart their plans for an upcoming local election,
the St. Pierre officials withheld any warning of the danger from the populace. As
a result, virtually the entire population of the small community was incinerated.
When news of an impending disaster is managed in such a way, it demonstrates
what Robert Kastenbaum describes as the "enormously powerful threat [of] a
tightly controlled information network."[11] The May 1980 eruption of Mount St.
Helens provides an instructive comparison. Even though this eruption was
larger, only sixty lives were lost compared with 30,000 casualties resulting from
the eruption of Mount Pelee. This dramatic difference is attributable partly to
adequate warnings of the hazard and the timely establishment of a restricted zone
of access.[12]

Even with an adequate warning system and a reliable, efficient information
network, people do not always respond to such threats in a prudent fashion. Just
as some people ignore the risks associated with smoking or drug abuse, individuals may feel they are immune to disaster. Predictions of potential disasters are
often met with the response: "I've never been affected before. Why should I start
worrying now?" The same attitude is exhibited when people who learn of a
chemical spill or a fire nearby decide to travel to the disaster area for a closer look.

What can be done when disaster strikes? What kind of help is needed in its
aftermath? Imagine the situation: People are injured, some are missing, others
are dead. Homeless survivors are likely to be in a state of shock and uncertainty
about the whereabouts of loved ones and about the future. Each type of disaster,
of course, creates particular problems that need attention.

Meeting the immediate needs of survivors — providing food and shelter, caring for medical needs, and restoring vital community services — is essential. Yet
even as attention is given to responding to these immediate needs, the emotional
needs of survivors should not be neglected (see Figure 12-2). Ministering to
these needs might include forming a missing persons group to help alleviate the
anxieties of survivors who are worried about the safety of relatives. Locating and
caring for the dead is also an important aspect of helping survivors cope with the
trauma of disaster. The comment of one relief agency worker, "It doesn't really
make too much sense to dig up the dead and then go and bury them again,"
reveals an unfortunate ignorance of the human emotions that surround disposition of the dead. Perhaps what survivors of a disaster need most is compassion.
Although efforts directed toward coping with disaster tend to be focused on the
emergency period, the return to both financial and emotional stability may take
years. Unfortunately, the "therapeutic community" that comes together to assist
in recovery from disaster is usually "short-lived, dissipating rapidly with the end
of the emergency period and the start of reconstruction, when highly charged
community development issues begin to resurface."[13]

Those who come to the aid of the survivors of a disaster may also become
"survivors" in the sense that their work of *postvention* (a term coined in the early

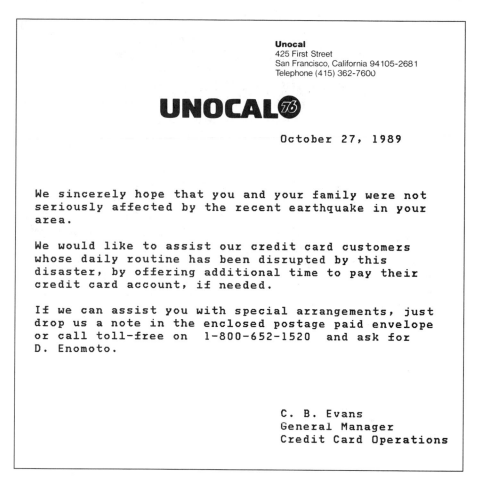

Unocal
425 First Street
San Francisco, California 94105-2681
Telephone (415) 362-7600

UNOCAL⑦⑥

October 27, 1989

We sincerely hope that you and your family were not seriously affected by the recent earthquake in your area.

We would like to assist our credit card customers whose daily routine has been disrupted by this disaster, by offering additional time to pay their credit card account, if needed.

If we can assist you with special arrangements, just drop us a note in the enclosed postage paid envelope or call toll-free on 1-800-652-1520 and ask for D. Enomoto.

C. B. Evans
General Manager
Credit Card Operations

Figure *12-2   Disaster Letter from Unocal*
Even a computerized corporate response to the disruption of normal living patterns can assist and comfort survivors as they cope with the devastation wrought by a natural disaster.

1970s by Edwin Shneidman to denote help given in the aftermath of a disaster) involves an intense encounter with human suffering and tragedy. Consider the experience of a Kansas City doctor who arrived at the scene of the Hyatt Regency Hotel disaster in 1981 to find among the debris bodies chopped in half, decapitated, and maimed. He watched as a critically injured man's leg, trapped under a fallen beam, was amputated with a chain saw. He worked sensitively and professionally as one of the first caregivers to force his way to where the victims were trapped. In the aftermath of the disaster, when things returned more or less to normal, he told officials that he felt the need to spend some time away from reminders of the disaster and take time to cope with his own experience as a survivor. Often, those who provide care and support are themselves given little support in coping with their own needs. Providing effective care to the survivors of critical incidents or disasters requires a comprehensive approach that includes "predisaster preparedness, early intervention using psychological first aid, and postdisaster treatment" using a range of counseling and therapeutic resources.[14]

When a storm dumped 20 inches of rain in one night on a coastal community in California, residents awoke the next morning to the news that twenty-two people had been killed, more than a hundred families had lost their homes, and another three thousand homes had been severely damaged. Within a few days, an impromptu organization was set up to help survivors deal with the psychological trauma of their losses. Known as Project COPE (Counseling Ordinary People in Emergencies), it provided immediate counseling to disaster victims and coordinated the services of more than a hundred mental health professionals.[15] Counselors found that people who had lost loved ones or property were experiencing grief reactions heightened by the sudden, capricious nature of their losses. Some who had lost only material possessions felt guilty for mourning the loss of property when others had lost family members. Some felt guilty for surviving the disaster. Those made homeless by the storm felt isolated and alone. There were feelings of anger at bureaucratic delay and toward uncooperative insurance companies and government agencies. Many of the victims felt anxious, vulnerable, and depressed. In some cases, old problems reemerged related to personal or relationship issues.

COPE set up programs to respond to each of these problems. Survivors were both reassured that their reactions were not unusual and helped to recognize that their grief was legitimate. Victim support groups brought together individuals who could understand and listen to one another's concerns. Counselors helped survivors sort out their priorities so they could begin solving problems created by the disaster. Skills were shared to help victims channel their anger constructively. Emergency crews and relief workers were not left out. COPE recognized that individuals who come to the aid of victims (including those who counsel the victims) are also vulnerable to the emotional impact of a disaster. With its comprehensive response to the psychological needs of survivors, COPE was cited as a model of providing mental health care to disaster victims.

We cannot eliminate the encounter with death that accompanies disaster, but we can take steps to reduce its impact, preserve life, and demonstrate compassion for survivors. And we can implement, when possible, procedures to warn of impending disasters.

In 1721, the novelist Daniel Defoe wrote *A Journal of the Plague Year*, a fictional account of the Great Plague of 1665 that had devastated London. Drawing upon published accounts and his recollection of tales heard during childhood, he vividly depicted the horror of a plague-stricken city and the terror of its help-

Charlie Palmer, UPI/Bettmann Newsphotos

Flowers placed by survivors adorn the coffins of victims who perished in an early New Year's Day fire in Chapais, Quebec. Survivors of a disaster often experience its traumatic effects for a long time after.

less citizens, confronted by a tragedy they could not comprehend. What prompted Defoe to write, in 1721, about a plague that had taken place almost two generations earlier? He knew that a plague again threatened to sweep across Europe, a plague that could cause death and destruction on the scale of the Great Plague of 1665. Defoe wrote to alert a largely indifferent populace to the threat so that precautions could be taken and the catastrophe averted. (Fortunately, the plague of 1721 was far less virulent than had been anticipated.)

Today we no longer fear the Black Death, but when disaster strikes, the effects are no less serious for its victims and survivors. Too often, warnings come too late or go unheeded. Perhaps death seems something that happens only somewhere else, to someone else. Yet in a subtle though pervasive way, those of us now living are confronted by a multidimensioned "plague" that is no less threatening than the more easily distinguishable plague of Defoe's time. Writing about the problem of determining the comparative threat to our well-being from various risks, Harvey Sapolsky observes: "Although it does not carry a warning label, our

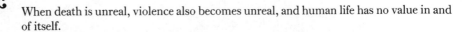

> When death is unreal, violence also becomes unreal, and human life has no value in and of itself.
>
> Vine Deloria, Jr.

political system may be hazardous to our health. It hunts small risks ruthlessly while permitting much bigger ones to exist relatively unmolested."[16] Indifference to the modern forms of plague — violence, war, nuclear catastrophe, environmental pollution, stress — only increases the likelihood of an encounter with disaster.

Violence

Violence, one of the most potent of our encounters with death, can affect our thoughts and actions even though we ourselves have not been victimized. Potentially, if not in actuality, all of us are its unsuspecting victims. Interpersonal violence is now officially recognized as a public health problem, as evidenced by the establishment of a Violence Epidemiology Branch at the Centers for Disease Control, an office charged with studying assaultive behavior and homicide. Of the 18,269 murders that occurred in the United States during 1988, about 35 percent were related to arguments of one kind or another (nearly twice the number related to the commission of a felony).[17] In some urban areas, emergency-room physicians report being "besieged with patients whose injuries are identical to wounds incurred by soldiers in Vietnam."[18] These wounds result from semi-automatic "assault weapons" that fire dozens of bullets per minute at several times the velocity of an ordinary pistol: "Organs that would have been merely grazed or even cleanly pierced by a handgun bullet are exploded by assault weapon fire, requiring massive transfusions of blood." A report by the American Medical Association concludes that firearms injuries and deaths constitute a critical public health issue.[19] Nationwide, firearms are involved in 60 percent of all homicides and 64 percent of all suicides. "One of the most troubling aspects of handgun violence," according to the AMA report, "is the fact that children very often are the victims of fatal gunshot wounds, self-inflicted either intentionally or accidentally, or received as innocent bystanders in scenes of domestic or street violence." The most threatening of violent acts are those that occur without apparent cause, when the victim is selected seemingly at random, thus heightening anxiety at the possibility that violence could unexpectedly confront anyone.

Think about the bystander killed during the commission of a robbery or the victim of what seems a senseless and brutal attack by a mass murderer. A few years ago in California, a number of murders were committed by someone whom the police dubbed the Trailside Killer, because the killings occurred along several

> The deepest grave on earth can never contain the violent death of a single decent soul.
>
> John Nichols, *American Blood*

popular woodland trails. A woman who usually jogged every morning along one of these trails expressed feelings of being personally threatened because these violent acts had taken place "so close to home." In an area where she had previously felt safe and secure, she now felt fearful. Although she had no direct experience of the killings, she was nevertheless victimized by the violence because it occurred in her own familiar environment. Rape and other violent crimes against women have prompted some to examine the role of "femicide" as a motivating factor in a "continuum of terror" that all too often results in death.[20]

One woman described a potential encounter with death that began innocently enough when she answered a knock on her door. Recognizing a former schoolmate whom she hadn't seen in a long time, she invited him in and they began to chat. She began to feel somewhat uneasy, though she could not say why. About two months later, however, she heard on the news that her visitor had been arrested and was subsequently convicted for the brutal murders of several young women. These murders had been committed around the time of his unexpected visit. Recalling the experience, this woman commented, "I sometimes wonder how close we may be to death at times and just not realize it. It seems we really never know."

The possibility of encountering violence seems to be increased by the anonymity and isolation characteristic of much of modern life. Feelings of connectedness to others can generate a sense of safety and security. In small towns and close-knit neighborhoods, there is often a community concern that tends to make random violence less likely. The modern landscape seems to provide fewer of such societal mechanisms. Living life in comparative isolation from our neighbors, many of us experience little comfort from the thought that violence might be averted by warnings or that help is available when a threat becomes real.

Some people believe that violence is endemic in American society. The fact that there were often few legal restraints during the great westward expansion gave rise to attitudes that promoted arbitrary justice and encouraged people to do whatever survival seemed to require, be it inside or outside the law. The treatment of the Native American nations, as well as the history of slavery and prejudice against black Americans, is replete with acts of violence. When such historical examples are combined with current statistical analyses of violence, some argue that American society has in many ways fostered the notion that violence can solve one's problems.

It takes little investigation, however, to recognize that the use of violence in pursuit of personal or political ends is a phenomenon found worldwide. State-

© Patrick Dean

This warning sign, prominently displayed at the entrance to a convenience store in Florida, reflects the age-old tactic of deterring potential violence by making a preemptive threat. Although the law-and-order policy exemplified by this warning may be welcomed by individuals who have been victimized by violent acts, such threatening gestures also promote the message that violence is a means of solving problems.

sponsored terrorism, for example, is a historical as well as modern phenomenon that includes not only the mass deaths brought about by Hitler and Stalin, but also the death-dealing actions of innumerable small-group terrorist organizations in many places around the globe. "Terrorists," as Walter Laqueur says, "seek to cause political, social, and economic disruption, and for this purpose frequently engage in planned or indiscriminate murder."[21] Although it can reasonably be argued that the attention devoted to terrorism by the media and by governments gives undue prominence to what is essentially a "side-show" in comparison with the real dangers facing humanity, this excessive attention may be explained partly by the fact that deaths caused by terrorism occur indiscriminately. Terrorism seems an affront to civilization, an action that occurs outside the boundaries of the social sanctions that we have erected to regulate conduct between individuals and between groups. In this respect, terrorist acts resulting in death are comparable to other acts of homicide that take place between strangers.

Assessing the Homicidal Act

Community standards of morality and justice play a major role in determining how the act of killing is assessed by a society and by its legal-political-judicial system. As Figure 12-3 illustrates, *homicide* — the killing of one human being by another — is separated into two main categories: criminal and noncriminal. These main categories encompass additional distinctions. For example, an act of homicide is considered excusable or justifiable when a person who kills another is found to have acted within certain legal rights, such as that of self-defense, or when the killing is judged an accident involving no gross negligence.

Thus, although a murder is necessarily a homicide, a homicide is not always a murder. The law has traditionally recognized two main distinctions within the category of *criminal* homicide: murder and manslaughter. Murder is associated with acts carried out with deliberate intention ("malice aforethought"), and the category of first-degree murder is used to designate killings that are carefully planned or that take place in conjunction with other serious crimes, such as rape. Manslaughter, on the other hand, is defined as wrongful, unplanned killing, done without malice. An example of *voluntary* manslaughter is that of a person, who after being provoked, kills another person in a fight. Such a person is said to have acted in the heat of passion, without considering the consequences. When homicide results from criminal carelessness but is unintentional, it is termed an act of *involuntary* manslaughter, as in the case of a fatal automobile accident caused by reckless driving or a death caused by gross negligence.

The circumstances surrounding a particular killing, the relationship between the killer and the victim, and the killer's motivation and intention are all considered in determining how an act of homicide is assessed within the American judicial system.

In a study by Henry Lundsgaarde of more than 300 killings that occurred in a major American city, it was found that more than half of the suspects were released before reaching trial.[22] To comprehend the reasons why some homicide cases are not brought to trial, it is necessary to look at how the circumstances of a homicidal act influence its investigation and how the judicial processes determine whether an accused killer is brought to trial.

The medical-legal investigation of an act of homicide generally includes three components: (1) an autopsy to determine the official cause of death; (2) a police investigation to ascertain the facts and gather evidence pertinent to the killing; and (3) various judicial and quasi-judicial procedures, carried out by the district attorney's office and the court system, to determine whether there is sufficient cause to bring a case to trial.

Fundamental to this investigation is the acknowledgment that homicide is an interpersonal act. That is, it involves a relationship between the killer and the victim: They may have had close domestic ties, being members of the same family or otherwise related; they may have been friends or associates; or they may have been strangers. In Lundsgaarde's study, summarized in Table 12-1, it was found

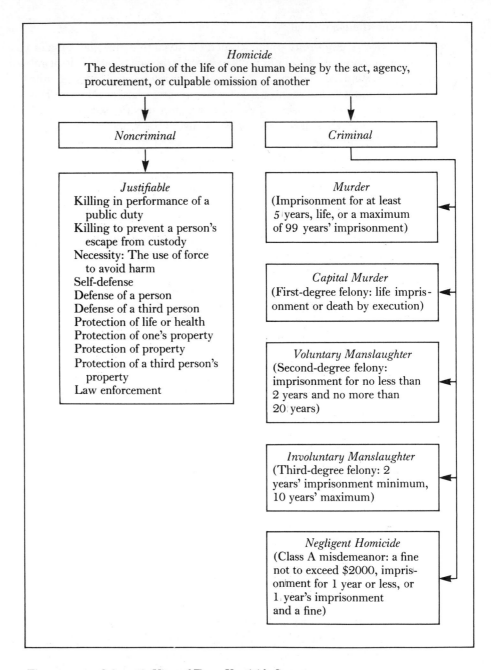

Figure 12-3 *Schematic View of Texas Homicide Statutes*
Source: Vernon's Texas Codes Annotated: Penal Code, 1974. From Henry Lundsgaard, *Murder in Space City: A Cultural Analysis of Houston Homicide Patterns* (New York: Oxford University Press, 1977), p. 213.

TABLE 12-1 *Three Major Killer and Victim Relationships Expressed in Reference to Final Case Disposition*

Case disposition	Relatives (Percent)	Friends/Associates (Percent)	Strangers (Percent)
Offender deceased	3.90	4.41	
No bill			
No charge filed	40.26	36.77	23.64
Nolle prosequi			
Dismissed	3.90	2.94	1.82
Not guilty	6.49	4.41	3.64
Probation	10.39	8.82	7.27
Death penalty			9.09
Outcome undetermined	10.39	2.94	3.64
Charge pending	2.30		7.27
Life sentence	1.29	2.94	1.82
Sentenced	20.78	36.77	41.82
Total	100.00	100.00	100.00

Source: Excerpted from Henry Lundsgaarde, *Murder in Space City: A Cultural Analysis of Houston Homicide Patterns* (New York: Oxford University Press, 1977), p. 232

that "the closer, or more intimate, the relationship is between a killer and his victim, the less likely it is that the killer will be severely punished for his act." In other words, killing a stranger was more likely to result in a stiff penalty than killing a friend or family member.

The response of the criminal justice system to acts of homicide reflects cultural attitudes about killing and what constitutes appropriate punishment. Lundsgaarde says, "What appears so shocking, or understandable as the case may be, about many killings depends upon our personal understandings of and assumptions about the rules that 'should' and 'ought' to govern a particular kind of relationship."

Basing its standards on cultural attitudes, the criminal justice system in a particular community sets about its task of determining whether an act of homicide is lawful or unlawful. If lawful, the killer is released and the case is closed. If unlawful, a further determination is made as to whether the killing in question was an act of murder, manslaughter, or negligent homicide — and there are various degrees of criminal intent within each of these categories as well. In making these determinations, the criminal justice system, including the police investigation, takes into account the intention, motivation, and circumstances surrounding the homicide.

What are the cultural assumptions by which an act of homicide is judged? Lundsgaarde's research showed that the legal outcome for a person who kills his wife's lover is quite different from the outcome for a person who combines killing with theft, robbery, or similar criminal or antisocial acts. Society is reluctant to

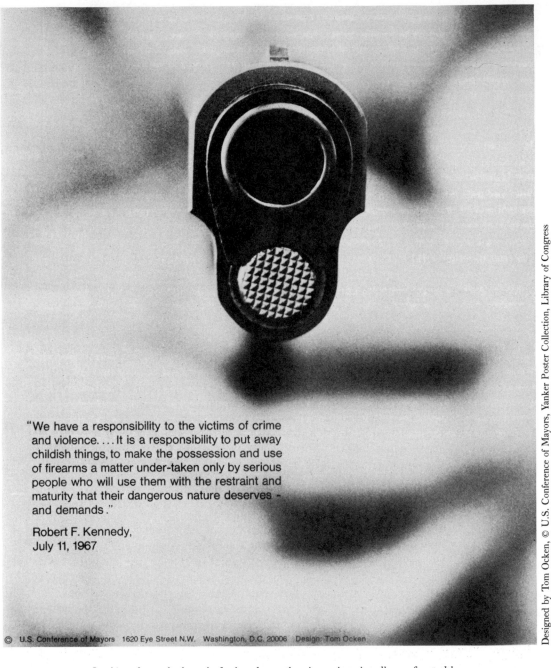

"We have a responsibility to the victims of crime and violence.... It is a responsibility to put away childish things, to make the possession and use of firearms a matter under-taken only by serious people who will use them with the restraint and maturity that their dangerous nature deserves - and demands."

Robert F. Kennedy,
July 11, 1967

© U.S. Conference of Mayors   1620 Eye Street N.W.   Washington, D.C. 20006   Design: Tom Ocken

Designed by Tom Ocken, © U.S. Conference of Mayors, Yanker Poster Collection, Library of Congress

Looking down the barrel of a handgun, the viewer is pointedly confronted by the possibility of death in this poster designed to increase public awareness of the pervasive threat represented by the widespread possession of firearms.

become involved in matters that fall within the domain of the family, even when they involve violence. A close relationship is believed to involve its own set of mutual responsibilities and obligations — its own "code of justice," if you will — that provides social sanctions for acts that occur within the relationship. In contrast, says Lundsgaarde, "The killer who chooses a stranger as his victim overtly threatens the preservation of the social order."

To put it another way, an individual who kills a stranger is not likely to be constrained by personal concern for the victim. Thus, society devotes its attention to acts of homicide that threaten the preservation of law and order within the larger society. Lundsgaarde says: "Intimates form symmetrical social relationships that insulate them within a series of obligations subject to enforcement by social and psychological sanctions. The robber, rapist, killer, or even the self-styled terrorist, is not restrained in his behavior by anything other than criminal sanctions." Killings that occur within the family unit or between persons who know one another tend to be viewed as less of a threat to society at large.

Some people believe that violence is "contagious" in modern American society. This reasoning can be developed along several lines: First, it may be that a violent society creates an environment in which psychotic individuals are encouraged to act out their antisocial behaviors in more harmful ways than they might if alternative ways of releasing such potentially violent tendencies were available. Second, each violent incident may spawn others, thus spreading the contagion of violence. Third, some believe that if an act of violence is not properly resolved, it will be repeated. With regard to this last point, a "proper resolution," according to Fredrick Wertham, is "for society to make clear what it wants. Society must say, *No, this we will not tolerate*," and this must be affirmed and upheld by a judicial process that emphasizes accountability for one's acts.[23]

Capital Punishment

Is capital punishment, then, the strong statement that is needed? In theory at least, capital punishment, which has been termed "planned, timed dying," is supposed to serve a twofold purpose: (1) to punish the offender and (2) to have a deterrent effect on potential offenders. Although the death penalty has been applied to a wide variety of offenses since ancient times, many political philosophers and social reformers have argued that it is needlessly cruel and overrated as a deterrent to murder. According to Glenn Vernon,

> Investigations into the ineffectiveness of the death penalty as a deterrent to murder revealed that some murderers were so busy with other things during the events preceding the murder that they simply did not think of the death penalty, and that others were interacting with their victims in such an extremely emotional manner that the consequences of their murderous acts were not even taken into account.[24]

By the mid-nineteenth century, reforms of the death penalty began to occur in various countries. Today, it is virtually abolished in Western Europe and most of Latin America. In the United States, most capital punishment statutes require that a sentence of death be imposed only after evidence is submitted to establish whether "aggravating" or "mitigating" factors were present in the crime. If the "aggravating" factors prevail and the sentence is death, then the case is reviewed by an appellate court. Apart from certain crimes on which the Supreme Court has not ruled (the most notable being treason), the only capital crime in the United States today is murder.[25] During 1988, 11 persons were executed in the United States, all for murder, and, at year's end, 2124 persons were under sentence of death.[26] According to various public opinion polls conducted in 1990, about 75 percent of Americans favor the death penalty for persons convicted of murder.[27] Hanging, electrocution, the gas chamber, and lethal injection have all been used for executing criminals at various times and places in the United States.

Is it inconsistent for society to try to eradicate or prevent murder by itself engaging in killing? It may be that the effect of capital punishment on violence is to increase its frequency, because it reinforces the notion that killing can solve problems. Citing evidence from psychology and behavioral therapy, which emphasizes the beneficial effects of *positive reinforcement*, Kastenbaum and Aisenberg say "there is little evidence to suggest that imposing massive punishment on one individual will 'improve' the behavior of others"; on the contrary, it may serve as positive reinforcement of hostile fantasies and murderous tendencies. The greatest risk for the potential murderer, they contend, is not the risk of execution, "but the risk of being killed by the police, the intended victim, or some bystander."[28]

If capital punishment is not an effective deterrent to murder, then what alternatives are available to society? Comparing our present system with early Anglo-Saxon and English law and with many non-Western legal systems as well, "Modern criminal law has completely transformed the ancient view of homicide as a wrong against a victim and his family to its modern version that views homicide as an offense against the state."[29] In short, the modern tendency is to view crime as a social problem.

The separation of civil and criminal law — more specifically, the separation of personal obligation and criminal liability — essentially eliminates the killer's liability to the *victim as person*. Instead, the liability is viewed as violence against the public at large. Restoring an element of civil liability for violent acts — for example, by some form of victim compensation program — might more effectively deter homicidal behavior and violent crimes than do present arrangements.

In seeking ways to reduce the level of violence in society, it may be useful to consider some factors that tend to *prevent* violent behaviors. Even if some individuals might have a greater innate potential for violence or aggressive behavior, how that potential is expressed depends to a significant extent on environmental influences. Kastenbaum and Aisenberg suggest that adopting the following guidelines lessens the potential for violence:[30]

1. Avoid the use of prejudicial, dehumanizing, or derogatory labels, whether applied to oneself or to others.
2. Avoid or eliminate conditions that underlie dehumanizing perceptions of oneself or others.
3. Promote communication and contact between potential adversaries, emphasizing similarities and common goals rather than differences.
4. Refrain from using physical punishment as the primary means of discipline.
5. Champion the good guys.
6. Teach children that violence is not fun, cute, or smart. Emphasize that they are responsible for their behavior.
7. Identify and foster the human resources that can provide alternatives to violence. For example, promote sharing among children, and encourage them to think before engaging in impulsive and possibly hostile actions against others.
8. Reduce the attractiveness of violence in the mass media.

Courting Death

Victims sometimes play a significant part in encouraging violent acts against themselves. Indeed, some homicide investigators have concluded that the victim is not always as innocent as might initially be assumed. Consider the example of a husband who has been repeatedly threatened by his angry wife wielding a loaded revolver. His response to this threat is, "Go ahead, you might just as well kill me." What can be said about his role as a victim in such circumstances? Or consider another such incident: A daughter, overhearing her parents arguing, tries to intercede, but is told by her mother, "Never mind, honey, let him kill me." After the daughter leaves the house to seek assistance, her father obtains a revolver from another room and shoots and kills the girl's mother.

Investigators have found that, during domestic strife, wives have made statements like, "What are you going to do, big man, kill me?" coupled with dares like, "You haven't got the guts." Kastenbaum and Aisenberg remark that such statements "strike us as combining elements of seduction and lethality." At least in some cases, they conclude, there are indications that the victim not only seemed to be "asking for it," but was the one actually responsible for escalating the conflict to the level of physical violence.[31]

While recognizing that victims do sometimes help to bring violence upon themselves, we should also be cautious about placing a stigma of blame on victims indiscriminately. Lula Redmond underscores the fact that labeling victims as bad, careless, seductive, "with the wrong crowd," or as somehow "asking for it" denies the reality that everyone is vulnerable to victimization.[32] Blaming the victim may be a convenient, albeit erroneous, way to overcome one's own sense of vulnerability and thereby regain a sense of personal security. If suitable "explanations" can be found to account for the victim's demise, they might provide convincing evidence that a similar encounter *could never* happen in one's own life. Far more effective than blaming the victim is to understand the factors that favor violence and to take steps to reduce their presence in our own lives and throughout society as a whole.

Dysfunctional Strategies

Society seems uncertain about how to stem the tide of violence. The judicial system appears to function arbitrarily. Ambivalence toward the notion that violence between individuals is an acceptable means of solving problems or achieving goals makes recourse to violence easier to tolerate. The victim, too, in many cases, may play a crucial role in his or her own demise. Violence results at least partly from social patterns as well as social problems.

These patterns and problems often reveal the presence of "dysfunctional strategies"—factors that increase the likelihood of violence rather than prevent it. The term *psychic maneuvers* has been used to describe the factors that have been determined to facilitate murder and other homicidal acts. A listing of these factors is summarized in Table 12-2. You might review this list three times. First, think about how each of these psychic maneuvers might function in your own life.

T A B L E 12-2   *Factors Favoring Violence*

Anything that physically or psychologically separates the potential killer from the victim. For example, the use of a gun leads to a concentration on the means (pulling the trigger) rather than the end result (the death of a person). Psychological separation occurs when the victim is perceived as fundamentally different from oneself.

Anything that permits the killer to define murder as something else, such as "making an example of the victim," "making the world safe for democracy," "implementing the final solution," or "exterminating the terrorists."

Anything that fosters perceiving people as objects or as less than human. This happens when victims become "cases," "subjects," or "numbers," as well as when the killing occurs from a distance as with high-altitude bombing or submarine warfare.

Anything that permits one to escape responsibility by blaming someone else: "I was just carrying out orders."

Anything that encourages seeing oneself as debased or worthless: "If I'm treated like a rat, I might as well act like one. What have I got to lose?"

Anything that reduces self-control or that is believed to have this effect: alcohol, mind-altering drugs, hypnotism, mass frenzy, and the like.

Anything that forces a hasty decision or that does not permit time for "cooling off." That is, a situation may force one to decide to shoot or not to shoot with no opportunity for deliberation.

Anything that encourages a person to feel above or outside the law: The notion that rank, prestige, wealth, or the like makes it possible for one to "get away with murder."

Source: Adapted from Robert Kastenbaum and Ruth Aisenberg, *The Psychology of Death: Concise Edition* (New York: Springer, 1976), pp. 291–294.

Note that they do violence to ourselves and others even when they function far more subtly than the overt act of homicide. Second, note how these psychic maneuvers function within society, how they contribute to antagonisms between individuals and between groups. The third time, consider how each of these psychic maneuvers represents a dysfunctional strategy that is typically found in the conflicts and wars between nations.

War

Within the context of ordinary human interaction, our moral as well as legal codes stand in strict opposition to killing. In war, killing is not only acceptable and necessary, but possibly heroic. War abrogates the conventional sanctions against killing by substituting a different set of conventions and rules about moral conduct. The expectation that one will kill and, if necessary, die for one's country is a concomitant of war. As Arnold Toynbee says, "The fundamental postulate of war is that, in war, killing is not murder."[33]

In Dalton Trumbo's classic antiwar novel, *Johnny Got His Gun*, we find a veteran "without arms legs ears eyes nose mouth" who devises a means of communicating with the outside world by "tapping out" messages on his pillow with his head. He asks to be taken outside, where he can become an "educational exhibit" to teach people "all there was to know about war." He thinks to himself, "That would be a great thing to concentrate war in one stump of a body and to show it to people so they could see the difference between a war that's in newspaper headlines and liberty loan drives and a war that is fought out lonesomely in the mud somewhere, a war between a man and a high explosive shell."[34]

The present century has seen not only two major world wars, followed by the unprecedented buildup of armaments that characterized the "cold war," but also innumerable regional conflicts in many areas of the world. Historians believe that 7.5 million Russian troops may have perished during World War II. In recent decades, 58,000 Americans died in Vietnam while over 400,000 North Vietnamese and Viet Cong were killed in that conflict. During the Persian Gulf War, while American casualties were few, estimates place the number of Iraqi troops killed at from 40,000 to 100,000.

Genocide, defined as the effort to destroy an entire nation or human group, has also been practiced with dire results during this century.[35] During World War I, the Turkish effort to eradicate Armenians resulted in an estimated 800,000 people killed. Between 1941 and 1945, Nazi Germany exterminated six million Jews in the Holocaust and killed another five million people who were deemed to be political opponents, mentally ill, retarded, or somehow "genetically inferior." With the coming to power of the Khmer Rouge in Cambodia during the mid-1970s, about two million Cambodians died from execution and starvation, an example of "autogenocide," a group killing its own people. Also during the 1970s, the infamous "disappearances" carried out by the military in Argentina resulted in the deaths of as many as 30,000 people. In the aftermath of the Persian

Col. Rex L. Dively, Signal Corps Photo

*At Buchenwald, near Weimar, Germany, a few of the dead are piled in a yard
awaiting burial following the invasion by the Allies. Starvation and disease due to
unsanitary living conditions, as well as the incessant torture of prisoners, caused an
average of two hundred deaths each day at this infamous Nazi concentration camp.*

Gulf War, early reports indicated that the Iraqi regime led by Saddam Hussein
may have killed tens of thousands of the indigenous Kurds in northern Iraq while
causing about two million to flee their homes.

Furthermore, chivalrous notions of combat, with mounted men-at-arms
meeting gallantly to do battle on an uninhabited hill or plain, have been replaced
in modern times by the reality of mass technological warfare. According to figures circulated by the International Red Cross (IRC), nine out of ten casualties in
modern warfare are civilians — men, women, and children who simply "got in the
way of somebody's war." In the so-called postwar period since 1945, says the IRC,
at least 20 million people have died in over 100 conflicts, and another 60 million

have been wounded, imprisoned, separated from their families, and forced to flee their homes or their countries.[36] This human misery goes on even as you read these words.

Think for a moment about your responses when you hear or read about war. What kinds of images are evoked when you think about combat, the atomic bomb, the Nazi Holocaust, Hiroshima, Vietnam, or the Persian Gulf War? Reflect on your own personal experiences and the experiences of those close to you. What makes the encounter with death in times of war different from other encounters with death? War is sanctioned by society as a legitimate means of achieving some desired goal — defending the national interest or protecting the homeland. Nevertheless, as Glenn Vernon says, "Confrontation with wartime killing may be one of the most difficult experiences of those who have been taught to avoid killing."[37]

The Conversion of the Warrior

War activates a special set of conventions designed to make it psychologically possible for individuals to go against the grain of what they have learned about right and wrong — to put aside the ordinary rules of moral conduct. As long as the combatant "keeps more or less faithfully to the recognized rules," Toynbee says, "most of humankind have been willing to alter their moral sense in such a way as to regard the killer in war as 'being righteous.'"[38] One of the conventions of warfare, Toynbee points out, is to dress the part. The psychological effect of the soldier's uniform is that it "symbolizes the abrogation of the normal taboo on killing fellow human beings: it replaces this taboo by a duty to kill them." Sam Keen notes that "the job of turning civilians into soldiers involves a liberal use of propaganda and hate training."[39] The enemy must be dehumanized so that he can be killed without guilt. "The problem in military psychology," Keen says, "is how to convert the act of murder into patriotism." As Vernon puts it, "Human behavior is relative to the situation, and given the right situation man can be taught or can learn to kill: whereas given other situations quite different behavior patterns are followed."[40]

Joel Baruch, a Vietnam veteran, writing about his combat experiences, says, "Changes in personality and mood are rooted in the special climate of the combat zone. These mutations evolve in such a wily fashion that the person who undergoes them is not aware of the alterations himself."[41] This is the crux of the matter. The conventions of war are mind- and personality-altering. It is possible to debate the ethical issues involved in war, its demands on citizens, the meaning of patriotism, and so on, arguing whether or not killing in wartime is intrinsically different from what would be defined as murder under other circumstances. The result is the same; the logic, the intention differs.

Here is Baruch's account of his first encounter with death on the battlefield:

> Stone dead, he was. Eyes wide open, staring at nothing. A thin veneer of blood curling at the corner of his lips. Two gaping holes in his chest. Right leg half gone. My first combat fatality. A lifeless body where only moments before a heart beat its

customary seventy pumps in one orbit of the minute hand. It is one thing to hear about death; to watch it happen is quite another. I went over to the nearest tree and vomited my guts out.

By his next experience of combat death, however, he questioned whether he was becoming callous and unfeeling: "I was becoming impervious to the death of my fellow soldiers, and, in addition, I was negating the possibility of my own . . . demise."

Another Vietnam veteran explains:

Social context is much more important than most people realize. We pretty much live within the boundaries of one social context. If you lived in a different society, you would consider a different set of behaviors as normal. What's bewildering and frightening in the combat situation is how quickly "normal" can change.[42]

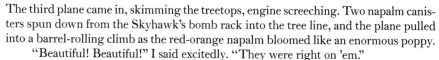

The third plane came in, skimming the treetops, engine screeching. Two napalm canisters spun down from the Skyhawk's bomb rack into the tree line, and the plane pulled into a barrel-rolling climb as the red-orange napalm bloomed like an enormous poppy.

"Beautiful! Beautiful!" I said excitedly. "They were right on 'em."

The napalm rolled and boiled up out of the trees, dirty smoke cresting the ball of flame. The enemy mortar fire stopped. Just then, three Viet Cong broke out of the tree line. They ran one behind another down a dike, making for the cover of another tree line nearby. "Get 'em! Get those people. Kill 'em!" I yelled at my machine gunners, firing my carbine at the running, dark-uniformed figures two hundred yards away. The gunners opened up, walking their fire toward the VC. The bullets made a line of spurts in the rice paddy, then were splattering all around the first enemy soldier, who fell to his knees. Letting out a war whoop, I swung my carbine toward the second man just as a stream of machine-gun tracers slammed into him. I saw him crumple as the first Viet Cong, still on his knees, toppled stiffly over the dike, behind which the third man had taken cover. We could see only the top of his back as he crawled behind the dike. What happened next happened very quickly, but in memory I see it happening with an agonizing slowness. It is a ballet of death between a lone, naked man and a remorseless machine. We are ranging in on the enemy soldier, but cease firing when one of the Skyhawks comes in to strafe the tree line. The nose of the plane is pointing down at a slight angle and there is an orange twinkling as it fires its mini-gun, an aerial cannon that fires explosive 20-mm bullets so rapidly that it sounds like a buzz saw. The rounds, smashing into the tree line and the rice paddy at the incredible rate of one hundred per second, raise a translucent curtain of smoke and spraying water. Through this curtain, we see the Viet Cong behind the dike sitting up with his arms outstretched, in the pose of a man beseeching God. He seems to be pleading for mercy from the screaming mass of technology that is flying no more than one hundred feet above him. But the plane swoops down on him, fires its cannon once more, and blasts him to shreds. As the plane climbs away, I look at the dead men through my binoculars. All that remains of the third Viet Cong are a few scattered piles of bloody rags.

Philip Caputo, *A Rumor of War*

Each of us experiences differences in our behavior according to the social context. How we behave among family members is likely to be different from how we behave among strangers or business associates. Sometimes these differences reveal the presence of contradictory values. Usually, such contradictions remain subtle and rarely meet head on. The contradictory values that exist for the soldier in combat, however, require what the veteran just quoted calls

> . . . a much more total schizophrenia. When you're there you don't really remember what it's like to come back into the social context of a society where killing is abhorrent. And, when you come back home, you don't really remember the context of the combat situation, except perhaps in your nightmares.

When a society reflects on its participation in war, it often speaks in terms of patriotism, the heroism of fighting for one's country, the need to defend the things that are held dear. When we listen to the words of those who have lived through combat, however, we often hear a very different kind of value system at work. We hear about individuals fighting for their lives or fighting because they had no alternative. Heroic intentions and patriotic feelings may be the rationale for donning the uniform, but in combat the emphasis is likely to be on survival.[43]

This is an issue that most of us would prefer to avoid. We do not want to hear what combat is really like, the reality of being in a situation where ordinary standards of conduct are turned topsy turvy and killing another human being becomes necessary and accepted behavior. The bravado and heroics of war may fascinate us. The reality is more difficult to face.

As one writer describes it,

> Combat is filled with potential emotional trauma. There's the constant fear of death. The noise and sights and smells, the firing of weapons, watching other human beings die or disappear in a puff of smoke and explosion of fire. There's blood and body bits and screams of pain. People are maimed and killed and some of them may be close friends. It continues hour after hour after hour.[44]

War is dehumanizing and depersonalizing. Robert Lifton and Eric Olson likened Vietnam to Hiroshima in that both events reflect the progression of modern technological warfare, which results in "unseen victims suffering and dying without ever having met their opponents."[45] Despite the extensive reporting of war, especially since the time of American involvement in Vietnam, the veteran's experience of it remains incomprehensible to most people. The significant losses experienced by veterans are not resolved simply by leaving the combat zone or being discharged from military service. In the aftermath of Vietnam, for example, traumatic events related to the war caused many veterans to experience symptoms such as numbness, irritability, depression, difficulties in relationships, and guilt at having survived when others did not. Nightmares and flashbacks to traumatic scenes were also among the protracted reactions to the war experienced by many veterans. Such symptoms have been termed delayed stress syndrome or post-traumatic stress disorder (PTSD). It might be more accurately said that such reactions to major traumatic experience represent "delayed grief syndrome" or "post-traumatic grief disorder."[46] Known as "shell shock" during World War I and "battle fatigue" during World War II, post-traumatic stress disorder became prominent in the 1970s when many Vietnam veterans experienced postwar readjustment difficulties. Experts say that up to half of those who saw serious, continuing combat suffered symptoms of post-traumatic stress syndrome. The Department of Veterans Affairs reportedly estimated that 800,000 of the more than two million veterans who served in Vietnam were suffering emotional and psychological wounds sixteen years after the war's end.[47]

Although psychotherapy, support groups, and other such approaches to healing have been at the center of efforts to treat PTSD, some veterans find solace and renewed self-respect through innovative means of coming to terms with their experiences. On Memorial Day, 1990, a group of Vietnam veterans began a 700-mile walk from Angel Fire, New Mexico, to the Pine Ridge Indian Reservation in South Dakota. At the end of their journey, the veterans (who called themselves "The Last Patrol") were welcomed by several hundred Oglala Sioux and invited to participate in the traditional ceremonies for returning warriors. After participating in the sweat-lodge ceremonies, honoring dances, and smoking the sacred pipe of the Oglala Sioux, one veteran enjoyed one of his few nights of restful sleep after years of nightmares and said, "This is a new life for many of us. . . . [This] was an opportunity to eliminate the things that have tortured us." Other veterans have participated in meditation retreats led by the Vietnamese monk Thich Nhat Hanh. The Buddhist walking meditation reminded some veterans of "walking point" in Vietnam, and traumatic memories surfaced and were discussed during group sessions. One veteran who participated said that the hours of silent meditation with the Vietnamese Buddhists "dissolved his mistrust of the 'enemy.'"[48] Some veterans have visited Vietnam in journeys that conjoin personal pilgrimage and social outreach, especially to the Amerasian children left as outcasts in their own country as a result of the war.

In contrast to the war in Vietnam, the Persian Gulf War was brief, widely supported at home, and regarded as a victory. Yet, no matter what the outcome of a war, combat can leave haunting memories. After the shooting stops and there's peace, the mind must still "sort out and file the almost incomprehensible facts of war."[49] During the Persian Gulf War, one helicopter door gunner told his friends to stop boasting about high Iraqi casualties after he saw dead Iraqi troops for the first time. "It's different when you see their faces, with blood coming out of their wounds," he said.

Although many veterans experience a feeling of being "unplugged from life," some people come out of the combat experience with feelings of mastery and maturity. The director of a trauma stress service at Georgetown University Medical Center in Washington, D.C. said: "It actually has the potential to be a positive experience."[50] Those who do suffer trauma from their experiences in the Persian Gulf will benefit from the lessons learned as a result of Vietnam. Caregivers, families, and the public as a whole now have a better understanding of the emotional toll that may be exacted by the stress of war. As Paul Recer says, "Medical

Rites of Passage

... As a psychiatrist who has worked with Vietnam veterans, I know all too well the long-term effects of wartime traumas. Ten and fifteen years after the events, there remain nightmares, fears, depression and, most fundamentally, failures of loving in veterans of combat. The timelessness of the unconscious does not bend to political realities. National treaties mark the beginning, not the end, of the psychic work of mastery.

Primitive societies intuitively knew the value of cultural ceremonies that marked the end of hostilities. Rites of passage were provided for the soldiers and the society to make the transition from the regression of combat to the structure of integrated living. These rituals acknowledged and sanctioned the otherwise forbidden acts of war. They thanked the soldier for his protection, forgave him his crimes and welcomed him back to life.

Our failure to provide such a cleansing for our warriors and ourselves has left our culture struggling for closure. It has as well made the task of intrapsychic mastery so much more difficult for the individual soldier.

Harvey J. Schwartz, M.D.

people are learning to reassure veterans that what they are feeling — the nightmares, the deadened emotion, the flashbacks — are all part of the mind's attempt to adjust to horror. Such feelings are not shameful, but merely human." In the aftermath of Vietnam, Lifton and Olson observed that veterans "have much to teach us about our culture and ourselves. We sense in their words and in their experience something that must be faced. As survivors of that experience, they confront us with truth at its source."

Coping with the Aftermath of War

Places like the Vietnam Veterans' Memorial in Washington, D.C., provide a point of encounter with the truth about war and with the healing that can begin as a result of facing it. Since its dedication in 1982, the Memorial has become a kind of "wailing wall" for the families and friends of the more than 58,000 whose names are engraved there as well as for those who served and survived.[51] Many of the visitors have left mementos, ranging from a pair of old cowboy boots first found at the base of the Memorial shortly after its dedication, to childhood teddy bears, baseball caps, newspaper clippings, diaries, and tear-stained letters. One of the first letters was placed by the mother of an Army sergeant whose death had occurred nearly fifteen years before her visit to the Memorial. In the letter, she described finding her son's name for the first time:

> We had been looking for about a half-hour when your father quietly said, "Honey, here it is." As I looked to where his hand was touching the black wall, I saw your name, William R. Stock.
>
> My heart seemed to stop. I felt as though I couldn't breathe. It was like a bad dream. I felt as though I was freezing. My teeth chattered. God, how it hurt.

© Robin Layton Kinsley

Waiting to board the USS John F. Kennedy, *Richard Wille, a Navy computer technician, embraces his three-year-old daughter in farewell. Understanding only that her father was going away, Amanda seemed anxious and bewildered until she found a piece of string on the Norfolk, Virginia, dock. After her father broke the string and tied one piece around his wrist and the other around hers, Amanda cried and hugged him goodbye. Similar scenes of farewell were enacted perhaps a half million times during the Persian Gulf War.*

In the aftermath of Vietnam and the more recent Persian Gulf War, there seems to be a growing recognition of the price exacted by war, not only on those who face the enemy and do the fighting, but also on the individuals and families waiting at home. During the Vietnam war, neither the troops nor their loved ones received much in the way of support or gratitude from society. Efforts have been made since then to distinguish between a much-maligned and unpopular government policy, on the one hand, and the men and women who served in the armed forces, on the other.

When the troops returned from the Persian Gulf war, they were greeted with enthusiastic welcomes at patriotic rallies festooned with yellow ribbons and American flags, a vastly different reception from that given the veterans returning from Vietnam a generation earlier. Mike Marshall, who served two tours of duty in Vietnam, talked about his own experience and expressed gratitude at the homecoming given his paratrooper son:[52]

> I think this reception will be something that he'll remember all his life. And it'll be something I'll always remember. If I had experienced something like this, I wouldn't have the sour taste in my mouth that I do today. All we had was people throwing oranges and tomatoes and stuff at us. I didn't have a town parade or anything. You just kind of drifted back into society. I never really did get a greeting or a handshake or anything like that. I think the American people just wanted to forget it.

A young Army private whose father had served in Vietnam said: "I wish the Vietnam vets would have gotten a reception like this," and a Sergeant Major who served in Vietnam as well as in the Persian Gulf remarked that the support for the troops evidenced by the warm welcome had "healed a lot of wounds."

The sacrifices made by the families of men and women in the military have often gone unnoticed. In recalling her odyssey as the wife of a Marine Corps officer who served in Vietnam, Marian Novak says: "I watched my husband train for war; I waited thirteen months for him to return from it; and then I waited another fifteen years for him to truly come home."[53] We tend to estimate the cost of a war in terms of the men and women who fought or died in it. Yet, war creates a "phantom army" composed of the spouses, children, parents, and friends who serve invisibly at home.[54] In this sense, the euphemistic term "collateral damage" encompasses not only the civilian deaths that occur in the war zone, but also the emotional pain experienced by individuals and families whose lives are disrupted by the loss of loved ones serving in the armed forces.

Over three hundred Americans were killed preparing for or fighting in the Persian Gulf War.[55] Most were young, just starting families or setting down roots. The youngest was an eighteen-year-old private who joined the Army three months after graduating from high school. The oldest was a fifty-five-year-old Air Force reservist who planned to retire at the end of his assignment in the Gulf. Among the last to die was Army Major Marie T. Rossi, a pilot and one of the first women soldiers to be sent into Iraq. She died, along with three crew members, when her Chinook helicopter crashed into an unlit microwave tower during bad weather. As Dana Priest wrote of the men and women who died:

Most died doing their small part in a gigantic military operation. Some were shot out of the sky. Others planted their feet in the wrong patch of ground, only to be felled by mines. Many perished in motor vehicle accidents or when their weapons misfired.

All were drawn from the ranks of men and women who believed the military could bring them closer to the dreams they carried about themselves: to engage their patriotism or fly fast planes for a living; to leave isolated rural townships or crime-ridden inner cities or someday be able to afford to go to college; to stop drifting and find a direction; to supplement their pay as part-time soldiers, many never imagining they would end up in war.[56]

Priest writes: "While the quick allied victory will take a prominent place in history and for many Americans is the source of jubilation and renewed national pride," the families of these men and women "may find it hard to cheer." The lives of these families will be shaped for a long time by their loved ones' deaths. In Kingston, Massachusetts, a twenty-four-year-old Army Sergeant was buried with a picture of the baby daughter he never met. In Decatur, Georgia, a three-year-old girl received a birthday card and roses from her father, a Navy Airman, the day he drowned off the coast of Israel. In the letter, he wrote: "I want to wrap you up in hugs. If anything happens to me before that day, remember Daddy loves you very much." At least 138 children of American military personnel lost their fathers during the Persian Gulf War.

Making War, Making Peace

Various theories have been put forward to account for war. Natural human aggression and the role of special-interest groups in society have been cited as causes of war. Economics, religion, nationalism, and ideology are also commonly cited. According to Karl von Clausewitz, a nineteenth-century military writer whose *On War* is considered a classic study, war is the continuation of political policy by other means. Generally speaking, war is defined as a condition of hostile conflict between opposing forces, each of which believes its vital interests are at stake and thus seeks to impose control on the opposing side through the use of force.

Within a comprehensive definition of war, we can distinguish several categories. *Total war* is "war without constraints."[57] It aims to destroy the enemy's forces and involves not only the military combatants, but also the resources and the civilian population of the warring societies. All-out nuclear war is one possible example of total war. The U.S. Civil War and World War II are also cited as examples of total war due to the widespread involvement of noncombatants and destruction of resources. *Limited war*, on the other hand, is concerned less with the destruction of the enemy than with the achievement of some political end or some immediate strategic result. It is defined as warfare that does not significantly affect the daily lives of most of the civilian population. The concept of limited war also refers to situations in which at least one of the principal combat-

We know, as surely as we know that we are alive, that the whole human race is dancing on the edge of the grave. Yet most of us believe in our hearts that it can never really happen—just as we do not really believe we are going to die . . . It is not a pleasant thought, but it cannot be ignored: the game of war is up, and we are going to have to change the rules if we are to survive. During the last two years of World War II, over one million people were being killed *each month*. If the great powers go to war with each other just once more, using all the weapons they now have, a million people will be killed each minute. Technology has invalidated all our assumptions about the way we run our world.

There is a terrifying automatism in the way we have marched straight toward scientific total war over the past few centuries, undeterred by the mounting cost and the dictates of reason and self-interest. We *do* know what is going to happen, and we are frightened, but we do none of the seemingly obvious things that might let us alter our course away from oblivion. We resemble a column of intelligent lemmings, holding earnest meetings to denounce the inequity of cliffs during halts in the march. Everybody agrees that falling off cliffs is a bad idea, many have noticed that the cliff edge is getting steadily closer, and some have come to the heretical conclusion that the column's own line of march is causing this to happen. But nobody can leave the column, and at the end of each halt it sets off again in the same direction.

Some generation of mankind was eventually bound to face the task of abolishing war, because civilization was bound to endow us sooner or later with the power to destroy ourselves. We happen to be that generation, though we did not ask for the honor and do not feel ready for it. There is nobody wiser who will take the responsibility and solve this problem for us. We have to do it ourselves.

Gwynne Dyer, *War*

ants intentionally places restraints on the use of available weapons or personnel, or limits potential areas of hostilities.

Notice that what one side considers "limited war" could be "total war" for the other side. While the Vietnam war was experienced as a limited war by the United States, it was a total war for the Vietnamese. A similar comparison applies to the Persian Gulf War. Although it is certainly true that individuals and families on both sides of the conflict suffered significant losses, the extent of social disruption and destruction of national resources was much more total for the people of Iraq.

The third category of warfare is *internal war*. This category includes conflicts occurring within a particular political entity, with rebel forces seeking to destroy or replace an existing government. Revolutions, insurrections, rebellions, and civil war are subcategories of internal war. Although internal war may be waged by conventional means, it is frequently associated with guerrilla warfare (efforts to harass and disrupt the established government by means of sabotage, assassination, or propaganda).

Is war intrinsic to the human condition? Many people would respond affirmatively to such a question. If they are correct, then the nature of modern warfare, its tremendous potential for death and destruction, demands that efforts be made to search out ways of minimizing conflict even if it cannot be completely abolished.

Why do nations resort to war as a means of solving problems? A variety of needs and motives may be related to the onset of war (see Table 12-3). Conflicts of interest can give rise to hostility. Such conflicts often involve territory. Feelings of injustice, deprivation, or suffering may be attributed to the actions of others, resulting in the desire to right perceived wrongs. A sense of injured honor may result in efforts to defend it. Feelings of insecurity or fear of being attacked can promote "preemptive" or "preventive" attacks. Whatever the combination of needs and motives that characterizes a particular conflict, joining together with others against a common enemy brings about a sense of connectedness, be-longingness, and community within a warring group — qualities that represent yet another need that may be satisfied by going to war.

Human beings, it seems, have an innate tendency to divide the world into "us" and "them." Seemingly trivial information is used to create ingroups and outgroups, and then to discriminate against members of the outgroup. As Ervin Staub observes, "When people are devalued, they may be seen as objects rather than human beings with feelings and suffering like our own."[58] Sam Keen says:

> In the beginning we create the enemy. Before the weapon comes the image. We *think* others to death and then invent the battle-axe or the ballistic missiles with which to actually kill them. Propaganda precedes technology. . . . It seems unlikely that we will have any considerable success in controlling warfare unless we come to understand the logic of political paranoia, and the process of creating propaganda that justifies our hostility.[59]

Even democratic nations are vulnerable to being manipulated by leaders who create incidents or produce false information in an attempt to stir up patriotic fervor. Ervin Staub notes that, "by generating hostile acts from others, leaders can create psychological readiness for war."[60] Social systems use "propaganda of integration" to promote citizen support for national goals. The result can be a uniform definition of events and lack of critical analysis. The media, wittingly or unwittingly, tend to report in ways that support and maintain the social system. When sensationalistic reporting replaces objective appraisal of the facts, truth is one of the first victims.

As Staub points out, the assumptions we make about human nature or the nature of groups significantly shape realities: "Our perceptions determine how we perceive others' actions." If we see the world and other human beings as hostile, then ambiguous actions may be perceived as threatening. When we act to defend ourselves, others' reactions confirm our initial assumption. "Through a

T A B L E *12-3*   *Motives and Needs that Give Rise to War*

1. To gain power or wealth.
2. To gain territory or physical dominance, or to get others to adopt one's ideals and values.
3. To defend or elevate personal and societal self-concept, self-esteem, or sense of identity.
4. To retaliate and do harm after being provoked.
5. To achieve personal or national glory.
6. To respond to a sense of injustice.
7. To act in self-defense.
8. To fulfill a sense of duty or responsibility.
9. To encourage a sense of personal competence and gain personal power.
10. To gain hope for control over events and renewed faith in the future.
11. To restore or revitalize the comprehension of self and world following chaos, disorder, or other sudden profound changes.
12. To gain a sense of positive social identity by adopting shared ideologies.

Source: Adapted from Ervin Staub, *The Roots of Evil: The Origins of Genocide and Other Group Violence* (New York: Cambridge University Press, 1989), pp. 36–43, 249–250.

cycle, which is often a vicious cycle but can instead be a benevolent one, we create and maintain our realities." When we have a deep sense of community with others and experience benevolent persons and institutions, we enjoy feelings of safety and trust. Staub says: "As heroic self-sacrifice proves, the value of community, caring, and connection can supersede the need for security."

Speaking in Bombay during the first war between India and Pakistan in 1948, the philosopher J. Krishnamurti observed that "the real causes of war are hidden in our unwillingness to keep inwardly, psychologically free." The misery, violence, and "appalling chaos in the world," he said, "is the result of our daily actions in relationship to things, to people, and to ideas." If our minds and hearts are not "burdened by possessiveness, whether of things made by the hand or by the mind," he continued, "we can live extremely simply and wisely, and therefore peacefully."[61]

If putting an end to war is a responsibility of the individual, where might we begin? Scores of organizations exist to promote peace through individual action, education, and structural initiatives that seek to alter the manner in which nations relate to one another in the world arena.[62] In tracing the origin of conflict, Sam Keen says that the first step involves facing the fact of our hostility, our drive to "fabricate an enemy as a scapegoat to bear the burden of our denied enmity." Failing to acknowledge our own hostility and hatred, we engage in "compulsive rituals, shadow dramas in which we continually try to kill those parts of ourselves we deny and despise." To justify ourselves, we portray the enemy as a stranger, an aggressor, a barbarian, an enemy of God. The enemy is seen as greedy, criminal, a torturer or rapist, a desecrator of women and children, subhuman, a beast, or

Yanker Poster Collection, Library of Congress

Yanker Poster Collection, Library of Congress

During World War II, the Russian poster (left) *directed the message to Soviet troops:*
"Soldier of the Red Army, SAVE US" (note the swastika on the bayonet), and the
American poster (right) *appealed to citizens at home to buy bonds to provide*
financial support for the war effort. Though both posters suggest the threat of death to
women and children, unlike the Americans the Russians were faced with the reality
of German troops invading their homeland.

even as death itself. Attempts to assign blame for war to the military or some
other "surrogate for the devil," says Keen, is "no less a denial of responsibility
than laying the blame on an external enemy."

The psychological process of projecting onto the enemy qualities that we
deny in ourselves does not mean, however, that our images of the enemy are
necessarily wrongly placed or that the enemy is innocent of these projections. On
the contrary, "there are aggressors, evil empires, bad men, and wicked women in
the real world." Sometimes the images we hold of the enemy are actually quite
realistic. Keen says, "Hitler was such a perfect devil incarnate, a paragon of evil,
that we have been using him ever since to vilify our enemies."

> Short of utopia there are real enemies. It is a luxury of the naive and sheltered to think
> that right thinking, good intentions, and better communication techniques will turn
> all enemies into friends. . . . If freedom is the basis of all other human values, then
> there are times when men and women will have to choose between killing and sur-
> rendering their humanity.[63]

We must consider both the individual psyche and social institutions in determining the steps to be taken toward civilizing hostilities (see Table 12-4). Addressing the issue of conflict at the social-political level, Ervin Staub argues that reducing the likelihood of war requires "a definition of national security that differentiates essential goals from desirable ones." In this view, relations among nations ought to be guided, at least in part, by the extent to which they fulfill certain essential, "minimal" values, including respect for "the human rights of their own citizens." When a nation does not meet this minimum, other nations should act as responsible bystanders and actively demonstrate their unwillingness "to accept a nation's mistreatment of its citizens." This provision is based on

TABLE 12-4   *Steps Toward Civilizing Hostilities*

1. Replace dehumanizing language with metaphors that dignify the enemy.
2. Become aware of individual and group processes that cause biased perception about others, and learn to test perceptions before acting.
3. Create and use strategies to resolve conflict peacefully.
4. Counteract the human tendency to create us/them distinctions by creating "cross-cutting" relations among groups within society and between nations.
5. Limit armaments to reduce the risk of war.
6. Establish mechanisms for dealing with crisis.
7. Exercise restraint about supplying arms or intervening in regional conflicts.
8. Bridge the knowledge gap between adversaries by encouraging exchange programs, tourism, and other forms of direct communication.
9. View war as an "optional" social institution and work toward eliminating the factors — social injustice, poverty, ignorance — that contribute to conflict.
10. Accept responsibility, for better or worse, for the conduct engaged in by one's community or nation.
11. Be aware of the tendency to glorify past wars.
12. Replace the ancient reverence for the warrior and for heroic sacrifice in war with a new ideal of the kindly, compassionate human.
13. Remember that the human species is young and that the past may not be an adequate mirror in which to find an accurate reflection of human possibilities.
14. Keep in mind that the real enemy is the war system itself, which includes both the political and social institutions through which we educate ourselves and our own psychological defense mechanisms.
15. Go beyond the mind set that convinces us a priori that war is inevitable and that any hope of a world without war is utopian.
16. Explore options other than war for bringing about the qualities of companionship, bravery, devotion to a worthy cause, and honor.
17. Find positive ways of fulfilling the human potential for transcendence.
18. Implement, as a first necessity, a new vision, a new sense of possibility.

Source: Adapted from Sam Keen, *Faces of the Enemy: Reflections of the Hostile Imagination* (San Francisco: Harper and Row, 1986), pp. 157–168; and Ervin Staub, *The Roots of Evil: The Origins of Genocide and Other Group Violence* (New York: Cambridge University Press, 1989), pp. 255–274.

Staub's study of genocide and mass killing. He found that such acts usually do not occur directly; rather, there is a progression toward increasing harm: As earlier, less harmful acts become accepted by the perpetrators as well as bystanders, more harmful acts become possible. Thus, protests voiced by "bystander" nations — backed up if necessary by limits on trade, aid, and cultural exchange — represent a nonviolent means for insisting that nations live up to at least minimal standards of world citizenship.

Sam Keen suggests that the move toward healing conflict begins "when we stop assigning responsibility for war to some mysterious external agency and dare to become conscious of our own violent ways":

> Each of us must begin to demythologize the enemy; cease politicizing psychological events; re-own our shadows; [and] make an intricate study of the myriad ways in which we disown, deny, and project our selfishness, cruelty, greed, and so on onto others.[64]

In Keen's view, movement toward the goal of ending conflict involves "both a heroic journey into the self and a new form of compassionate politics." Accordingly,

> The mystical tradition in religion and its secular equivalent in psychotherapy have always tried to turn warfare inside out, to convert the extroverted aggression of the warrior into the introverted task of destroying the inner Pentagon — the defense mechanisms that isolate and make us hostile toward others. The true holy war is the struggle against the antagonistic mind.[65]

The truism that war and death are intimately linked relates not only to the battlefield loss of life but also, at a deeper level, to the human desire for immortality. Viewed symbolically, war allows us to ritually affirm our own deathlessness by killing the enemy who is Death. This idea is reflected in the promise inherent in some religions that warriors who fall in battle go directly to Valhalla or Paradise. "War as the bringer of death," says Keen, "wears the face of horror, but also of ecstasy."[66] Despite the brutality of war, soldiers often report that it gave them

> the most vivid experiences of their lives. Never were they more filled with awe and the precious, precarious, tragic sense of life. The constant atmosphere of danger, the felt potency of killing, the comradeship of men in arms, create a psychedelic high that releases the warrior from the quiet desperation and boredom of everyday life.[67]

The awareness of death that accompanies combat experience can bring with it appreciation of the fragility of life and a capacity for wonder. "To the extent that we repress the day-to-day awareness of our mortality," Keen says, "our death will go far from us and become hostile." The sense of vivid adventure provided by war is only a "temporary antidote for anomie and meaninglessness."

A central message of the so-called death-awareness movement over the past several decades is that integrating the fact of death into one's life brings a zest for living. A vital society provides opportunities for individuals to fulfill not only basic needs, but also their potential as human beings, including the striving for spirituality or transcendence, "a seeking that goes beyond the material and visible and beyond the boundaries of the self."[68] Community, a sense of connectedness with others, provides a positive context in which transcendence can be sought. Ervin Staub says:

> A vision of the future, ideals that are rooted in the welfare of individual human beings rather than in abstract designs for improving "humanity," small and intermediate goals along the way, commitment and the courage to express ideas in words and actions — all are essential to fulfill an agenda for a world of nonaggression, cooperation, caring, and human connection.

Technological Alienation and Psychic Numbing

When we recall the epic battles of Achilles and Agamemnon, or of the legendary King Arthur and the Knights of the Round Table, or of the samurai in medieval Japan, we find a sense of warfare as heroic. The enemy was seen as a worthy opponent with whom one was engaged in a "metaphysic of struggle" or a "ritual of purification" that encouraged progress or evolution toward a higher form of life.[69] If this sense of chivalry is now largely absent from warfare, leaving "only the abstract virtue of obedience to duty," it is due in significant measure to technological advances in weaponry. Instead of individual initiative and courage, modern warfare emphasizes bureaucratic cooperation and calculation.

"Technological alienation" has been termed the "most characteristic feature of the twentieth-century war machine."[70] Not until World War I did warfare began to involve civilians on a large scale. During the Spanish Civil War, the world was horrified by the German aerial bombing of the Basque town of Guernica on April 26, 1937, an action that indiscriminately slaughtered civilians of both sexes and of all ages. The distinction between combatants and noncombatants had become blurred, if not erased.[71]

In tallying the dead of World War II, civilian victims outnumbered military casualties. Early warfare had limits: the bow and arrow, the bullet from the gun, the artillery shell. The conventional limits of warfare were radically altered with the advent of the atomic bomb, unleashed on Hiroshima on August 6, 1945. The degree of destruction made possible by modern warfare was exemplified during World War II by the mass deaths in Dresden, Hiroshima, and Nagasaki. Gil Elliot says:

> By the time we reach the atom bomb, the ease of access to target and the instant nature of macro-impact [large-scale destruction] mean that both the choice of city and the identity of the victim have become completely randomized, and human technology has reached a final platform of self-destructiveness. . . . At Hiroshima and Nagasaki, the "city of the dead" is finally transformed from a metaphor into a literal reality.

The characteristic human response to such carnage is one of *psychic numbing*. Exposed to such destruction and death, our self-protective psychological response is to become insensitive, unfeeling. Lifton and Olson observe that "jet pilots who cooly drop bombs on people they never see tend not to feel what goes on at the receiving end." They add that "those of us who watch such bombing on TV undergo a different though not unrelated desensitization."

Confronted by the death-dealing potential of modern weaponry, it is worth remembering the story of Dalton Trumbo's veteran who asked to be allowed to become a living exhibit of the ravaging, destructive effects of war. His request was denied, the story explains, because "he was a perfect picture of the future and they were afraid to let anyone see what the future was like."

The Nuclear Threat

Since 1945, the growth of the nuclear weapons arsenal has brought about the possibility of an encounter with death of unprecedented proportions. With the notable exception of the atomic bombs dropped on Hiroshima and Nagasaki, this encounter has been more threat than reality. Still, the fact that nuclear weapons might be used, with little or no warning, has shaped our lives in ways both subtle and dramatic. Studies of high school students indicate that young people are deeply affected by the threat of nuclear war; many are doubtful about the future and about their own survival.[72] Based on interviews with graduating seniors from high schools across the nation over a period of years, a study by Jerald Bachman concludes that "concern with the nuclear issue has been substantial, with the most consistent and steadiest increase in concern of any problem that we asked about."[73] More than a third of all the high school seniors agreed with the statement: "Nuclear or biological annihilation will probably be the fate of all mankind within my lifetime." For some young people, feelings of isolation and insecurity engendered by the threat of nuclear annihilation may result in a pessimistic and fatalistic outlook on life, thereby forming a "shadow" that adds impact to other personal and environmental factors affecting suicidal behavior.[74]

Children and adolescents appear to be deeply concerned about nuclear issues. Yet, when researchers made plans to interview public school students (grades one through nine) in the Boston area, the teachers of these students told investigators that the students "knew nothing about nuclear weapons, did not think about the threat of nuclear war, and would have nothing to say about it."[75] The researchers found that the teachers were wrong. Studies of children in other countries throughout the world, including the Soviet Union, have found a similar awareness of the nuclear threat.

Some believe that the pervasive threat of nuclear war is having a significant effect on the socialization of children. In most societies, war traditionally has served a social function in helping to define the masculine role of "warrior" or protector. Now this historical connection is threatened. Robert Fulton and Greg Owen point out that, whereas "male honor and the traditional perception of masculinity have been based upon acts of bravery or personal displays of courage in

I grew up during the Depression; everything in the country had stopped; there was no work, the factories were cold and empty. People daydreamed about what this country was going to be like when it got going again — the kind of houses people would live in, the kind of cars they would drive, the kind of vacations they'd take, the kind of clothes they'd wear, and all that — and it was a dream for their descendants. I don't find anybody now who gives a damn about what kind of world their grandchildren are going to inherit . . .

All the ads tell you that your own life is short, enjoy it while you can: buy this right now, start drinking really good wines, just take a really swell vacation, drive a really fast car, do it right now. I think it's much more absorbing to plan a world for our grandchildren, but there are no ads that invite you to do that. In a way, the threat of the Bomb may be a boon to wine merchants, restaurateurs, manufacturers of fancy automobiles, salesmen of condos in Aspen. It's all going to blow up — that's part of the sales message.

Kurt Vonnegut, quoted in *Publishers Weekly*

the face of a mortal enemy," nuclear warfare "promises to be an impersonal conflict." They argue that "this challenge to the validity of a central aspect of the male role cannot help but create ambiguity and tension for the present generation of young men."[76] Sam Keen echoes this sense of confusion, pointing out that, "in the old war code, warriors were expendable but women and children were to be protected behind the shield."[77] According to the traditional code of warfare, it was considered wrong to kill women or children, but men were "legitimate candidates for systematic slaughter — cannon fodder." This relationship between masculinity and death is evident in the symbols and occasions that a society devises to honor its warriors. The Congressional Medal of Honor, Arlington Cemetery, the Tomb of the Unknown Soldier, and Memorial Day all serve as modern examples. With the advent of total war in the early decades of this century and, especially, with the more recent development of nuclear weapons, women and children no longer enjoy the "sanctity of innocence" relative to war's devastating effects. Now, as Keen says, women and children are also forced "to live with the deadweight of the threat of annihilation that men have always felt in times of war or peace."

Our vision of what war would be like if fought with atomic weapons is reflected by its changing portrayal in movies. During the first decade after World War II, the bomb was typically portrayed as an instrument for keeping the peace. Beginning in 1959, however, with Stanley Kramer's *On the Beach*, and continuing to the present with films such as *Dr. Strangelove, Fail Safe, War Games*, and the prime-time television drama *The Day After*, viewers have seen atomic weapons portrayed as something to be feared.

The watershed moment for any discussion of nuclear war must be the bombing of Hiroshima on August 6, 1945.[78] The bomb fell near the center of the city, and its explosive force, heat, and radiation immediately engulfed all of Hiroshima:

> Within a millionth of a second of the atomic bomb explosion over Hiroshima, the temperature of the blast center was several million degrees centigrade. A millisecond later, a 300,000-degree centigrade sphere formed, sending out a tremendous shock wave. The wave, losing energy as it expanded, was powerful enough to break windows 15 kilometers from the hypocenter.[79]

Besides the physical devastation caused by the bomb, Robert Lifton says, "The most striking psychological feature of this immediate experience was the sense of a sudden and absolute shift from normal existence to an overwhelming encounter with death."[80] A second atomic weapon was used to bomb Nagasaki on August 9, 1945. For the survivors of Hiroshima and Nagasaki, the awesome effects of the atomic bomb initiated "an emotional theme within the victim which remains with him indefinitely: the sense of a more-or-less permanent encounter with death."

The rationale behind the destruction of Hiroshima and Nagasaki with atomic bombs that killed more than 100,000 people and seriously wounded many others remains a source of controversy. While advocates of the bombing contend that it avoided an invasion of the Japanese islands that likely would have resulted in perhaps one million casualties and massive civilian damage, others argue that, at best, the bombing only hastened Japanese acceptance of an inevitable defeat. The bombing of Hiroshima and Nagasaki with atomic weapons is also viewed by some commentators as the first act of the ensuing cold war, an act that instigated the tremendous arms buildup of the postwar period. Since the end of World War II, the U.S.S.R., Britain, France, and the People's Republic of China have joined the United States as "nuclear" nations, and a number of other countries are believed to have acquired some nuclear weapons capability, including India, Pakistan, Israel, Libya, Egypt, Syria, South Africa, Argentina, and Brazil.[81] Furthermore, many fear that additional countries, as well as some terrorist organizations, may soon come to possess such weapons. (Indeed, Iraq's potential development of nuclear capability was said to have been an important reason for the military action taken against that country and its leader, Saddam Hussein.) The presence of current stockpiles of nuclear weapons and the possibility of further proliferation of such weapons have prompted a search for ways to avert what some believe is a "collision course with disaster."[82]

Modern weapons technology has progressed to the point that a missile can carry its strategic nuclear warhead a distance of 6000 miles in less than half an hour and hit within a few hundred feet of its target. The hydrogen bomb in today's arsenals is about a thousand times more powerful than the atomic bomb, which itself produces an explosion about a million times more powerful than

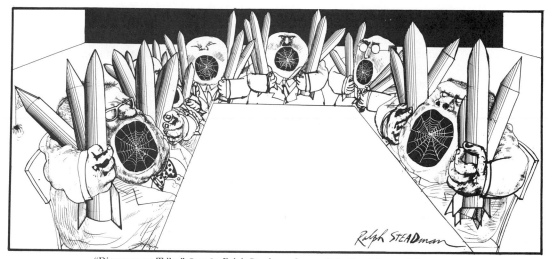

"Disarmament Talks," © 1987 Ralph Steadman, Swann Collection, Library of Congress

comparably sized bombs using conventional explosives such as TNT. The impact of even a small or limited nuclear attack would be enormous. More than three decades ago, then-president Dwight Eisenhower called attention to the changed nature of modern warfare. "We are rapidly getting to the point," he said, "that no war can be won." Unlike conventional warfare, which implies a "contest," said Eisenhower, the outcome of modern conflict could mean both "destruction of the enemy and suicide for ourselves."

The potential destructiveness of modern weaponry and its costs — monetarily and socially — are mind boggling. It has been reliably calculated that existing nuclear weapons represent 18,000 megatons of explosive power, the equivalent of 3.5 tons of TNT for every person on the planet; and that, since the end of World War II, expenditures on the global arms race have totaled more than $17 trillion, nearly twice what has been spent for health.[83] How are we to understand the significance of the fact that six times as much public money goes for research on weapons as for research on health protection? Or that every minute fifteen children die for lack of food and vaccines, while during the same minute the world's military establishment takes nearly $2 million from the public treasury?

Despite its magnitude — indeed, its omnipresence — people nevertheless find it possible to deny the nuclear threat. It has been shown that a high level of death anxiety positively correlates with nuclear war related anxiety and worry.[84] Lester Grinspoon explains that denial is used to cope with the nuclear threat because "people cannot risk being overwhelmed by the anxiety which might accompany a full cognitive and affective grasp of the present world situation and its implications for the future."[85] Table 12-5 describes some of the ways people avoid facing the truth about nuclear war. M. Scott Peck, psychiatrist and author

TABLE *12-5*   *Avoiding the Truth About Nuclear War*

Some commonly used defense mechanisms to avoid facing the truth about nuclear warfare:

Intellectualization: Using knowledge and technical understanding to distance oneself from the facts.

Dogmatism: Maintaining a closed system of beliefs to avoid facts that might be unsettling.

Rationalization: The "ubiquitous defense," exemplified by statements like, "The president knows more about how to prevent nuclear war than we do," or "Nuclear warfare is such a terrifying possibility that no country will ever actually resort to it," or, "Whatever happens will be God's will."

Displacement: An unconscious process by which substitute objects displace the real source of threat. For instance, the superpatriot's concerns about "the enemy" may displace anxieties about the threat to one's own survival represented by nuclear war.

Isolation: Divorcing fact from feeling. One might think about or discuss nuclear war while suppressing the feelings that follow from the possibility of annihilation.

Denial: Ignoring or dismissing facts that would cause pain or anxiety if perceived objectively.

Source: Adapted from Lester Grinspoon, "Fallout Shelters and the Unacceptability of Disquieting Facts," in *The Threat of Impending Disaster*, edited by George H. Grosser et al. (Cambridge, Mass.: MIT Press, 1965), pp. 123–126.

of the best-selling book *The Road Less Traveled*, says that nuclear technology "has brought the human race as a whole to the point at which physical and spiritual salvation are no longer separable. It is no longer possible for us to save our skins while remaining ignorant of our own motives and unconscious of our own cultures."[86]

Lifton and Olson write:

> Nuclearism is a peculiar, twentieth-century disease of power. We would do well to specify it, trace its roots, and see its connection with other forms of religious and immortalizing expression. It yields a grandiose vision of man's power at a historical time when man's precarious sense of his own immortality makes him particularly vulnerable to such aberrations.[87]

Despite the winds of change that have cooled tensions between the world's superpowers, nuclear warfare remains a threat. Political and military conflicts in the Middle East and elsewhere, combined with worsening economic conditions in many places, continue to make peace an elusive quarry. During recent decades, few areas of the world have escaped the impact of war. The threat to survival represented by nuclear weapons has been equivalent to a more or less constant encounter with death for more than four decades.

Stress

We see violence, homicide, war, and nuclear catastrophe clearly as causes of death. Yet a more subtle condition, stress, can be just as much a threat to our

Observer-participants in the Army's exercise "Desert Rock VI" huddle in trenches and attempt to protect themselves seconds before the detonation of an atomic device at Yucca Flats, Nevada, in 1955.

well-being. Many researchers believe that stress plays an important role in such characteristically modern ailments as ulcers, hypertension (high blood pressure), and heart disease. Increased susceptibility to such ailments may result when prolonged stress wears down the body's defenses.

Although the term *stress* in popular usage means different things to different people, it can be defined as any influence that disturbs the natural equilibrium of the body. In the early 1900s, a Harvard physiologist, Walter Cannon, demonstrated that certain emotional responses to stress, such as fear or rage, prepare the body for what is called the "fight-or-flight" response: intense action designed to return the organism to a state of equilibrium, or homeostasis. Thus, stress results when a situation demands that some adjustment or adaptation be made. This adaptation in turn causes certain physiological changes designed to meet the stressful demand.

All of us experience the alarm reaction as we respond to the changing events of our lives. If the stressor is minor and lasts only briefly, the body's defensive mechanisms subside and functioning quickly returns to normal. If the stressor persists or is more intense, the body's adaptive mechanisms continue to function at an elevated level to resist stress. Eventually, the mechanisms are exhausted and vital functions are depleted. The result may be a lowering of the body's resistance to disease. It is this psychosomatic nature of stress — the ability of emotional and mental states to influence physical changes — that is of particular interest to researchers.

Occupational stress is reportedly claiming the lives of more than 10,000 victims a year in Japan.[88] Mostly men in their prime working years, these victims of *karōshi*, or sudden death from overwork, are found in virtually every occupational category. *Karōshi* is characterized as a buildup of fatigue caused by "long hours of work that clearly exceed all normal physiological limitations," disruptions in an individual's normal daily rhythms (often related to travel or lengthy commutes to and from the job), and other job-related strains placed on workers. In some occupations, the rise of global markets (with their corresponding time differences) has forced workers to conduct business far into the night after the normal day's work has been completed. The incidence of *karōshi* in Japan is accompanied by a growing recognition that exhaustion induced by chronic overwork can aggravate preexisting health problems and harm even the healthiest person — possibly causing a life-threatening crisis or death.

Stress is a natural part of human existence. Some believe, however, that the nature of stress has changed markedly since the turn of the century. Whereas in earlier times stress was primarily related to such environmental conditions as the need to obtain food, shelter, and warmth, today stress is related to such factors as more complex life styles, rising expectations, and inner discontent. Thus, the psychological factors influencing stress have become predominant.

Table 12-6 shows a rating scale devised by Drs. Thomas Holmes and Richard Rahe to measure the perceived impact of various life-change events in terms of the degree of social readjustment required.[89] Much as a sound of known loudness

T A B L E *12-6* *The Social Readjustment Rating Scale*

Life Event	Mean Value
1. Death of spouse	100
2. Divorce	73
3. Marital separation from mate	65
4. Detention in jail or other institution	63
5. Death of a close family member	63
6. Major personal injury or illness	53
7. Marriage	50
8. Being fired at work	47
9. Marital reconciliation with mate	45
10. Retirement from work	45
11. Major change in the health or behavior of a family member	44
12. Pregnancy	40
13. Sexual difficulties	39
14. Gaining a new family member (e.g., through birth, adoption, oldster moving in, etc.)	39
15. Major business readjustment (e.g., merger, reorganization, bankruptcy, etc.)	39
16. Major change in financial state (e.g., a lot worse off or a lot better off than usual)	38
17. Death of a close friend	37
18. Changing to a different line of work	36
19. Major change in the number of arguments with spouse (e.g., either a lot more or a lot less than usual regarding child rearing, personal habits, etc.)	35
20. Taking out a mortgage or loan for a major purchase (e.g., a home, business, etc.)	31
21. Foreclosure on a mortgage or loan	30
22. Major change in responsibilities at work (e.g., promotion, demotion, lateral transfer)	29
23. Son or daughter leaving home (e.g., marriage, attending college, etc.)	29
24. In-law troubles	29
25. Outstanding personal achievement	28
26. Wife beginning or ceasing work outside the home	26
27. Beginning or ceasing formal schooling	26
28. Major change in living conditions (e.g., building a new home, remodeling, deterioration of home or neighborhood)	25
29. Revision of personal habits (dress, manners, association, etc.)	24
30. Troubles with the boss	23
31. Major change in working hours or conditions	20
32. Change in residence	20
33. Changing to a new school	20
34. Major change in usual type and/or amount of recreation	19
35. Major change in church activities (e.g., a lot more or a lot fewer than usual)	19
36. Major change in social activities (e.g., clubs, dancing, movies, visiting, etc.)	18

continued

T A B L E *12-6, continued*

Life Event	Mean Value
37. Taking out a mortgage or loan for a lesser purchase (e.g., for a car, TV, freezer, etc.)	17
38. Major change in sleeping habits (a lot more or a lot less sleep, or change in part of day when asleep)	16
39. Major change in number of family get-togethers (e.g., a lot more or a lot fewer than usual)	15
40. Major change in eating habits (a lot more or a lot less food intake, or very different meal hours or surroundings)	15
41. Vacation	13
42. Christmas	12
43. Minor violations of the law (e.g., traffic tickets, jaywalking, disturbing the peace, etc.)	11

Source: T. H. Holmes and R. H. Rahe, "The Social Readjustment Rating Scale," *Journal of Psychosomatic Research*, 11 (1967): 213–218.

can be used as a benchmark for comparing the intensity of other sounds, Holmes and Rahe used marriage — giving it a value of 50 — as a point of comparison for evaluating the perceived impact of other life-change events. In their study of subjects representative of a cross section of socioeconomic and demographic groups, Holmes and Rahe found virtual agreement about the relative intensities of various life events. The life events shown in Table 12-6 are listed in decreasing order of intensity as based on the "mean value" comparisons assigned to them by participants in the study. Significantly, Holmes and Rahe found a correlation between the frequency of life-change events and the onset of illness. People who became sick had generally experienced an increasing number of stressful life changes in the preceding year.

Take a few minutes to review the stress scale to determine how many of these events you have experienced during the past year. When a large number of stress-producing events occur within a brief period, or elicit a high level of stress, there is a greater likelihood that stress may become overwhelming. As you review the changes in your own life that required readjustment, would you give them the same ranking as did the participants in Holmes and Rahe's study?

Before 1900, there was comparatively little heart disease. Most researchers date the marked increase in heart disease from the twentieth century, with the greatest increase occurring since the 1940s. Many believe that the epidemic levels of heart disease in the developed countries can be traced to the effects of life styles that derive from high technology and affluence. Among the most consequential factors of this life style are cigarette smoking, rich and fatty foods, and physical inactivity. The relationship between life style and the onset of heart disease has been confirmed in findings generated from a study, which began in 1948, of the residents in the small Massachusetts town of Framingham. This important study — officially titled the Framingham Heart Disease Epidemiology Study — has singled out stress as the most pervasive of all risk factors for heart and circulatory disease, noting that stress often influences other risk factors such as cigarette smoking and overeating as well.

Another disease that may be influenced by stress is cancer, which some believe could be more appropriately relabeled one of the "diseases of maladaptation."[90] Although a link between stress and cancer is not conclusively proved, many believe that the personality type especially prone to cancer is characterized by loneliness, self-containment, and an inability to express emotions.

It is important to recognize that stress does not invariably lead to bodily deterioration and death. Any change is stressful and creates tension within the individual. But the *presence* of stress is less a determinant of potential problems than the manner in which a person *copes* with stress. Understanding how stress works and its effect on the body is the first step toward coping more effectively with it. As Jean Tache says,

> In each one of us lies dormant a primeval man who in certain situations is aroused and imperiously takes command of the personality. Given the ancient problem-solving options available to him — fight or flight, both requiring physical activity — he can hardly come up with satisfactory solutions to modern problems, for they require reflection, negotiation, and compromise.[91]

Hans Selye, perhaps the foremost investigator of stress, advises that people learn how to deal with stress "without distress."[92] How can this be accomplished? First, Selye recommends that each person find the maximum level of stress that he or she is comfortable with, and that situations that exceed this level be avoided when possible. For example, it may be possible to limit the number of stressful changes that occur at a given time in one's life. Also, situations that elicit potentially harmful levels of stress can be managed in such a way that one makes a positive use of stress rather than succumbing to its negative effects. The stress that may accompany taking a test, for example, can be used to generate mental alertness and preparedness rather than anxiety about the outcome.

Regular physical exercise is another means of coping with stress. Physical exertion provides an outlet for the physiological responses associated with the stress encountered in daily life. In addition, relaxation techniques, such as biofeedback and meditation, offer a means of dealing with stress. Finally, the symptoms of stress can be a signal that we need to reexamine our patterns of living. The symptoms of stress can be recognized as indicators of personal and social problems that need to be confronted and corrected rather than simply treated with drug therapies or other techniques while the root causes are ignored. Some of the social problems that tend to be stressful include community and family disruption, work pressures, lack of close social relationships, rapid social change, war and violence, and inability to relax or enjoy the fruits of one's labors.

Look again at Table 12-6, the social readjustment rating scale devised by Holmes and Rahe. Notice that items ranked as most stressful have in common the element of loss: loss of loved ones, relationships, freedom, well-being, self-esteem. Such losses are inherent in the encounters with death discussed in this chapter. Stress, then, is a concomitant of the encounter with death and loss. Disturbing news, risk taking, accidents, violence and homicide, war, and the potential for nuclear catastrophe — these encounters with death affect us in our daily lives. Sometimes the encounter is subtle, sometimes it is stressful, calling into action our physiological defenses against threat. The failure to find adequate means of coping with these encounters with death and the stress of modern living represents a threat to the survival of the society as well as the individual.

Further Readings

Nancy H. Allen. *Homicide: Perspectives on Prevention*. New York: Human Sciences Press, 1980.

American Academy of Arts and Sciences. "Risk," *Daedalus* 119, no. 4 (Fall 1990).

Committee on Trauma Research, National Research Council. *Injury in America: A Continuing Public Health Problem*. Washington, D.C.: National Academy Press, 1985.

Bruce L. Danto, John Bruhns, and Austin H. Kutscher, eds. *The Human Side of Homicide*. New York: Columbia University Press, 1982.

Terrence Des Pres. *The Survivor: An Anatomy of Life in the Death Camps*. New York: Pocket Books, 1977.

Mary Douglas and Aaron Wildavsky. *Risk and Culture: An Essay on the Selection of Technical and Environmental Dangers*. Berkeley: University of California Press, 1982.

Japan Broadcasting Corporation, eds. *Unforgettable Fire: Pictures Drawn by Atomic Bomb Survivors*. New York: Pantheon Books, 1981.

Sam Keen. *Faces of the Enemy: Reflections of the Hostile Imagination*. San Francisco: Harper and Row, 1986.

John Langone. *Violence: Our Fastest-Growing Public Health Problem*. Boston: Little, Brown, 1984.

Robert Jay Lifton. *The Future of Immortality and Other Essays for a Nuclear Age*. New York: Basic Books, 1987.

Robert Jay Lifton. *Home From the War: Vietnam Veterans, Neither Victims Nor Executioners*. New York: Basic Books, 1985.

Susan D. Moeller. *Shooting War: Photography and the American Experience of Combat*. New York: Basic Books, 1989.

Alan Monat and Richard S. Lazarus, eds. *Stress and Coping: An Anthology*. 2d ed. New York: Columbia University Press, 1985.

Dorothy Nelkin and Michael S. Brown. *Workers at Risk: Voices from the Workplace*. Chicago: University of Chicago, 1984.

Tim Page. *Page After Page: Memoirs of a War-Torn Photographer*. New York: Atheneum, 1989.

Charles Perrow. *Normal Accidents: Living with High Risk Technology.* New York: Basic Books, 1984.

Beverly Raphael. *When Disaster Strikes: How Communities and Individuals Cope with Catastrophe*. New York: Basic Books, 1986.

Eugene Richards. *The Knife and Gun Club*. New York: Atlantic Monthly Press, 1989.

Al Santoli. *Everything We Had: An Oral History of the Vietnam War by Thirty-Three American Soldiers Who Fought It*. New York: Random House, 1981.

Ervin Staub. *The Roots of Evil: The Origins of Genocide and Other Group Violence*. New York: Cambridge University Press, 1989.

Herbert S. Strean and Lucy Freeman. *Our Wish to Kill: The Murder in All Our Hearts*. New York: St. Martin's Press, 1991.

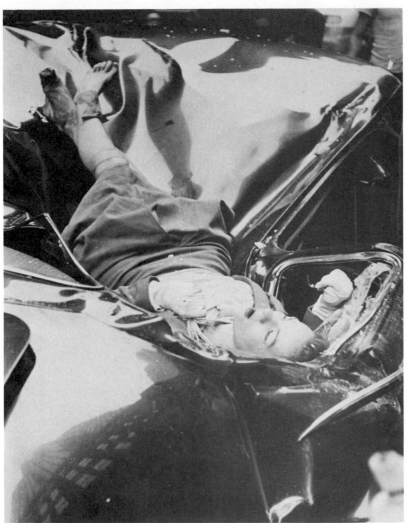

After plummeting eighty-six floors from the observation deck of the Empire State Building — visible in the metallic reflection at lower left — this young woman lies dead, the victim of suicide.

C H A P T E R 13

Suicide

Suicide, the intentional taking of one's own life, encompasses a variety of motives and behaviors. Although suicide has been characterized by some as a "disease of civilization," it is generally agreed that suicide can be found in virtually all societies, both modern and primitive. Altruistic suicide—that is, a person giving up his or her life for others or for a greater good—has likely existed since human beings first banded together in clans.[1] In the context of these early societies, we can imagine situations in which one individual volunteers to draw the attention of a herd of animals to himself, thereby allowing other members of a hunting party to trap them more easily. Although the probability of surviving the onrushing herd was low, the reward for the clan was survival itself. Even in comparatively recent times, some nomadic societies encouraged suicide among the elderly as a way of maintaining the mobility needed for the survival of the group as well as a way of limiting the debility and suffering of old age. Honor was given to the person who, recognizing that the end of life was near, willingly left the community for a certain death. The self-inflicted death of Socrates has stood for over two thousand years as a symbol of dying for one's principles.

Yet these examples of altruistic suicide are not representative of suicides in modern societies. On the contrary, suicide is not a socially sanctioned action, and only rarely does it result from altruistic motives. The modern context for understanding suicide commonly involves such factors

477

as depression, low self-esteem, negative life experiences, and chronic physical pain. When someone commits suicide, we seek to find a cause by turning to psychological, sociological, or biological explanations for the behavior. Suicide is best understood as behavior influenced by personality and culture as well as by the unique circumstances of an individual's situation.

Examining Suicide Statistics

Although the overall suicide rate in the United States has remained fairly constant in the recent past, a significant shift has taken place among certain age groups. Until the late 1960s, suicide rates generally increased directly with age, with the lowest suicide rates among the young and the highest among the aged. More recently, however, a decrease in the rate among older persons has been offset by an increase among adolescents and young adults. Both of these trends are due largely to changes in the behavior of white males. The rising suicide trend among adolescents is associated with a deteriorating state of well-being for adolescents, and the generally declining suicide trend among the aged is associated with an improving state of well-being for elderly persons.[2] The suicide rate for males is almost four times that for females, and this ratio holds generally for all age groups except the elderly, where the male predominance increases.[3]

The white population in the United States commits the majority of suicides and has rates more than twice as high as those for the nonwhite population as a whole.[4] Within the nonwhite population, however, we find a substantially higher rate of suicide among Native Americans than among other cultural subgroups.[5] Taken in the aggregate as a demographic group, the suicide rate among Native Americans is about three times the national average; and, on some reservations, the suicide rate is ten times that of the general population. As these statistics suggest, however, there is considerable variability with respect to suicide rates among Native American groups, a fact that causes some observers to conclude that it is erroneous to attribute one suicide pattern to all Native Americans. Looked at in broad demographic terms, then, statistics indicate that the groups at relatively higher risk for suicide include men, whites, older adults, adolescents, and Native Americans.[6] When one examines suicide statistics, it is clear that suicide is not only a serious public health problem and a leading cause of premature mortality, especially among young people, but that it also causes untold suffering for many thousands of survivors.

Statistical Problems

Despite the losses represented by official counts of suicide, there is general agreement that these figures understate the actual number of suicides, perhaps by as much as half.[7] Suicide among children and adolescents is thought to be especially prone to underreporting. A death is unlikely to be classified as a suicide unless the coroner or medical examiner suspects such a possibility due to the deceased's history of suicidal tendencies or acts of self-injury, or because the deceased left a suicide note, or because the circumstances of death so clearly point to suicide. Glen Evans and Norman Farberow observe that "generally, coroners list suicide as a cause of death only when circumstances unequivocally justify such a determination."[8]

Related to the burden-of-proof issue with respect to classifying a death as suicide is the social stigma of suicide. Suicide is commonly viewed as representing failure — on the part of the individual who commits suicide, his or her family and friends, and society as a whole. Open discussion about suicide remains largely taboo. Neighbors and friends who suspect that a terminally ill husband's death was the result of self-inflicted gunshot wounds may refrain from mentioning the circumstances of the death, engaging instead in a form of polite mutual pretense unless and until the barrier to disclosure is somehow broken through.

Such attitudes can influence the coroner or medical examiner who is charged with determining whether a particular death should be classified as suicide. If the circumstances of a death are equivocal (meaning that the causes are uncertain or unclear) and there is a question about whether the death was a suicide or an accident, it is likely to be classified as accidental. Many automobile accidents, for example, are believed to be suicides in disguise. Indeed, some authorities believe that if these "autocides" were added to known suicides, it would make suicide the number one killer of young people.[9]

Similarly, victim-precipitated homicide may mask the deceased's suicidal intentions. The homicide victim who deliberately provokes others by flashing a knife, or wielding a gun, or by goading others with threats of violence, may be attempting to gain their unwitting help in causing his own death. Victim-precipitated homicide appears to occur with greatest frequency among young black males. As Ezra Griffith and Carl Bell observe, "The black community contends daily with the phenomena of suicide and homicide."[10] Although the rate of suicide among black Americans is lower than that of white Americans, black males between the ages of 25 and 34 bear a disproportionate share of both suicide and homicide. In the view of some psychologists, many young black males consider suicide a weak, cowardly way out of their problems. Thus, rather than inflicting destruction upon themselves, these young people aggressively create violence to get themselves killed, thereby "dying as heroes" and "preserving their definition of masculinity."[11] Since victim-precipitated deaths are classified as homicides, they are not included in suicide statistics.

Because of problems associated with data collection, the social stigma against suicide, and deaths wrongly classified as accidents or homicides, there is good reason to believe that the actual extent of suicide is considerably greater than official statistics suggest. In summarizing these problems, Edwin Shneidman says, "Because of religious and bureaucratic prejudices, family sensitivity,

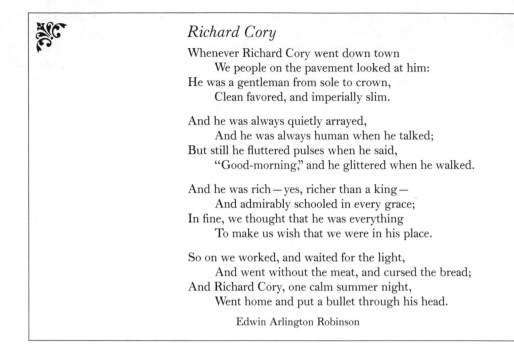

Richard Cory

Whenever Richard Cory went down town
  We people on the pavement looked at him:
He was a gentleman from sole to crown,
  Clean favored, and imperially slim.

And he was always quietly arrayed,
  And he was always human when he talked;
But still he fluttered pulses when he said,
  "Good-morning," and he glittered when he walked.

And he was rich — yes, richer than a king —
  And admirably schooled in every grace;
In fine, we thought that he was everything
  To make us wish that we were in his place.

So on we worked, and waited for the light,
  And went without the meat, and cursed the bread;
And Richard Cory, one calm summer night,
  Went home and put a bullet through his head.

    Edwin Arlington Robinson

differences in the proceedings of coroner's hearings and postmortem examinations, and the shadowy distinctions between suicides and accidents — in short, the unwillingness to recognize the act for what it is — knowledge of the extent to which suicide pervades modern society is diminished and distorted."[12]

The Psychological Autopsy

The investigative methods of the psychological autopsy greatly improve the accuracy of death classification, particularly when the cause of death is uncertain and potentially related to suicidal intent. Initially conceived as a device by which to investigate equivocal cases of suicide on behalf of the Los Angeles County coroner, the psychological autopsy has been called "one of the most significant research tools to come along since the field of suicidology grew into recognition."[13] Developed in 1961 — primarily by Norman Farberow, Edwin Shneidman, and Robert Litman — the psychological autopsy provides a method for determining the thoughts, feelings, and actions of the deceased prior to his or her death.

Information is pieced together by interviewing the victim's friends and relatives as well as other members of the community. Particular attention is paid to learning about current and previous stresses, psychiatric and medical histories, and the general life style of the victim as well as any specifically suicidal communications. The deceased's routine in the days and hours before death is carefully considered, and the investigative team then attempts to "paint an overall picture of the person's character, personality, and state of mind."[14] Based on the data gathered, a judgment is made concerning whether the death was a suicide.

As David Brent points out, the psychological autopsy has been used to study risk factors in suicide for more than three decades, and "the convergent evidence is that the diagnostic information obtained is both reliable and valid."[15] The use of psychological autopsies in cases of adolescent suicide has proved to be helpful in understanding the factors that place young people at risk.[16] There is also evidence that the methods of psychological autopsy may have application as a predictive indicator of individuals who are at risk of suicide because of various "suicidogenic," or suicide-causing, factors in their lives.[17] As both an investigative approach and a research tool, the psychological autopsy holds continued promise for deepening our understanding of suicide.

Comprehending Suicide

It is likely that most people have at some time in their lives fantasized about the possibility of committing suicide. Such thoughts are not uncommon during childhood and adolescence, and they may crop up from time to time in later life as well. Such thoughts occur as a kind of "trying out" or "testing" of the notion rather than as seriously considering suicidal behavior. It is perhaps not too disturbing to fantasize about suicide, but expressing or discussing such thoughts tends to cause embarrassment or discomfort. The subject of suicide may be dealt with by forced humor, uneasy laughter, or a cerebral intellectuality that distances us from any real threat of mortality. We mask our discomfort at the awesome fact that each of us has the power to choose whether or not we continue to exist (see Figure 13-1). Death is usually conceived of as something that "happens" to an individual. "Why," it is asked, "would someone willingly end his or her own life?" Although suicide is often ascribed to a person's despair over a particular set of circumstances, such a description leaves much unanswered.

In considering what might influence a person to commit suicide, you may find yourself thinking, "There's nothing that could cause me to think seriously about ending my own life." To those who believe they have the resources to deal effectively with the demands of life, suicide seems a radical solution indeed. Yet suicide is a complex human behavior, one involving diverse motives and intentions. Thus, our first step toward understanding the dynamics of suicide must be to develop a working definition of suicide that provides a framework for organizing this complexity into more manageable form.

In thinking about the reasons why a person would voluntarily end his or her own life, it becomes apparent that suicide can be studied on the basis of the apparent cause or purpose of the suicidal act, the individual and cultural meanings attached to suicidal behaviors, and the specific populations affected by

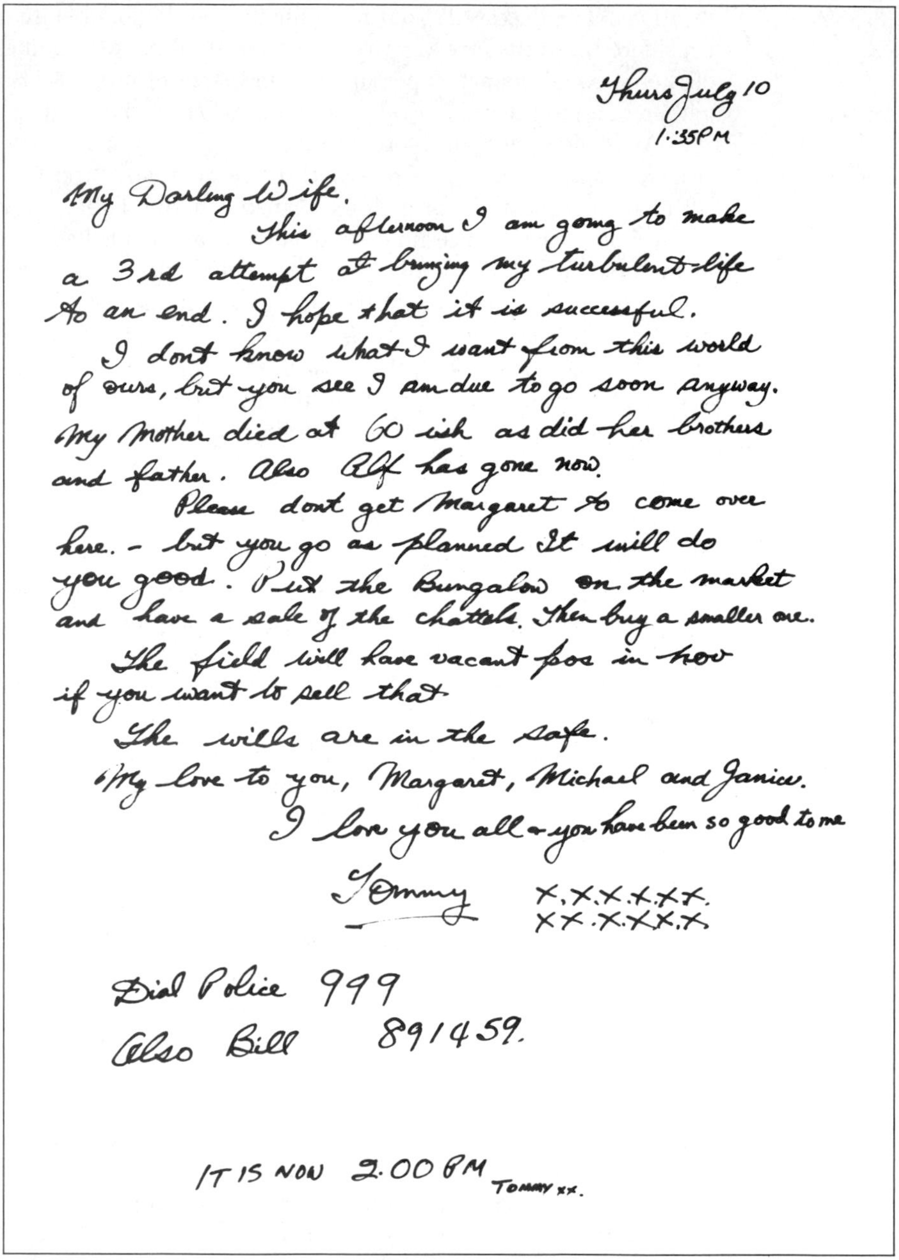

Thurs July 10
1.35PM

My Darling Wife.
        This afternoon I am going to make
a 3rd attempt at bringing my turbulent life
to an end. I hope that it is successful.
    I dont know what I want from this world
of ours, but you see I am due to go soon anyway.
My mother died at 60 ish as did her brothers
and father. Also Alf has gone now.
        Please dont get Margaret to come over
here. — but you go as planned It will do
you good. Put the Bungalow on the market
and have a sale of the chattels. Then buy a smaller one.
    The field will have vacant pos in Nov
if you want to sell that
    The wills are in the safe.
    My love to you, Margaret, Michael and Janice.
            I love you all — you have been so good to me
            Tommy   X.X.X.X.X.
            _____   XX.X.X.X.X

    Dial Police   999
    Also Bill   891459.

    IT IS NOW 2.00 PM
                    TOMMY xx.

Figure 13-1   Suicide Note and Report of Death
Even when a newspaper account is as detailed as this British report (facing
page), the facts of suicide as described in the newspaper may reveal very little of
the intense human factors—the personal and social dynamics—that precipitated
the suicidal act.

Retired man's suicide

A HYTHE man aged 64 killed himself because he could not stand old age, an inquest heard yesterday.

Retired maintenance engineer Aubrey Heathfield Aylmore, who lived at Forest Front, Hythe, was found dead in his car by his wife.

The inquest heard that Mrs. Heathfield Aylmore had been to a WI meeting and returned home an hour later than planned.

She found her husband's body in the garage with a length of hose pipe running from the exhaust into the car.

A note was found in which Mr. Heathfield Aylmore said that this was his third suicide attempt and that he wanted to "put an end to my turbulent life."

Dr. Richard Goodbody, consultant pathologist, said cause of death was asphyxia due to carbon monoxide poisoning.

Coroner Mr. Harry Roe said that Mr. Heathfield Aylmore had been depressed at the thought of growing old.

suicide. The definitions of suicide in Table 13-1 will help us establish a comprehensive working definition that is useful for all of these approaches.

Notice that each definition emphasizes certain aspects of suicidal intention and behavior. Although the basic dictionary definition provides a good starting point for understanding suicide, it is somewhat vague. As you review these definitions, pay particular attention to how each explains the dynamics of suicide. Ask yourself: What kinds of human behavior does the definition include? Is suicide a specific act, or is it a behavioral process? What is the context of suicide?

For example, Ronald Maris's definition focuses on the cause or rationale for suicide. French social scientist Jean Baechler's definition emphasizes suicide as a means of resolving problems. Notice that suicide is defined as a behavior rather than as a specific act. Notice also that suicidal behavior may be immediate or long term. Thus, alcoholism can be considered as suicidal behavior inasmuch as it reflects the attempt to solve an existential problem by making use of something that, over time, can have fatal consequences. Finally, Edwin Shneidman's definition emphasizes the factors of intention and action, and the concept of ending one's conscious existence. From your perusal of these definitions, you can see that suicide involves the mental intention to cause one's own death as well as the actions to carry out that intention.

TABLE *13-1*   *Four Definitions of Suicide*

Suicide is . . .

The act or an instance of taking one's own life voluntarily and intentionally, especially by a person of years of discretion and of sound mind. (*Webster's New Collegiate Dictionary*)[a]

Self-killing deriving from one's inability or refusal to accept the terms of the human condition. (Ronald W. Maris)[b]

All behavior that seeks and finds the solution to an existential problem by making an attempt on the life of the subject. (Jean Baechler)[c]

The human act of self-inflicted, self-intentioned cessation. (Edwin Shneidman)[d]

[a]Used by permission. From *Webster's Ninth New Collegiate Dictionary*, © 1986 by Merriam-Webster Inc., Publishers of the Merriam-Webster® Dictionaries.
[b]Ronald W. Maris, *Pathways to Suicide: A Survey of Self-Destructive Behaviors* (Baltimore: Johns Hopkins University Press, 1981), p. 290.
[c]Jean Baechler, *Suicides* (New York: Basic Books, 1979), p. 11.
[d]Edwin S. Shneidman, editor, *Death: Current Perspectives*, 2nd ed. (Palo Alto, Calif.: Mayfield Publishing Co., 1980), p. 416.

Explanatory Theories of Suicide

The study of suicide has traditionally followed two main lines of theoretical investigation: (1) the sociological model, which has its foundation in the work of nineteenth-century French sociologist Emile Durkheim; and (2) the psychological model, based on the work of the Viennese psychoanalyst Sigmund Freud. Each of these theories offers a coherent framework developed from observations of human behavior within which to understand suicide. More recently, investigators have sought an integrated approach to understanding suicide, one that combines sociological and psychological insights as they apply to individual situations and the way those situations are interpreted.

The Social Context of Suicide

The sociological model, as its name implies, focuses on the relationship between the individual and society. Individual behavior is considered in its social setting and within the group dynamics that influence it. According to Durkheim, these societal dynamics are manifested in the degree of regulation and integration present in a given society.[18] When a society is loosely regulated, individuals experience a sense of chaos and confusion as well as a loss of traditional values and social mores. Rules, customs, and traditions cannot be relied upon as a definitive guide to behavior. Such circumstances are characterized by a sense of *anomie* (meaning "lawlessness"). Because of these broken ties, the individual experiences anxiety, disorientation, isolation, and loneliness. When there is insufficient social regulation, *anomic* suicides result. The classic example of this phenomenon occurs in societies undergoing rapid social change. Set free from traditional moorings, individuals may have difficulty adjusting to a changed environment.

> ### Suicide Note Written by a Divorced Woman, Age 61
>
> You cops will want to know why I did it, well just let us say that I lived 61 years too many.
>
> People have always put obstacles in my way. One of the great ones is leaving this world when you want to and have nothing to live for.
>
> I am not insane. My mind was never more clear. It has been a long day. The motor got so hot it would not run so I just had to sit here and wait. The breaks were against me to the very last.
>
> The sun is leaving the hill now so hope nothing else happens.

The former sense of identity with the social group may be shaken, leaving the individual feeling upset and confused. Among the Aboriginal people of Australia, for example, the rapid pace of social change relative to their traditional life style is being accompanied by signs of behavioral distress, including suicide.[19]

Sudden trauma or catastrophe can also shatter the relationship between an individual and society. The loss of a job, the amputation of a limb, the death of a close friend or family member — any of these losses might constitute an anomic event. Indeed, any disruptive change — whether it is perceived as positive or negative — can precipitate a state of anomie. Durkheim suggested that even sudden wealth might stimulate suicidal behavior if the person felt unable to cope with his or her changed status. Calling attention to the disruptions caused by divorce and by economic hardship, Durkheim argued that anomic suicide is a chronic condition in modern societies.

At the other extreme of regulation we find a society characterized by repressive constraints. Lack of freedom and absence of choice may produce what Durkheim termed *fatalistic* suicide. The inability to engage in an open expression of one's individuality may lead to a sense of fatalism, a sense that one has nowhere to turn. The high rate of suicides occurring in jails and other detention facilities is undoubtedly due at least partly to the intense degree of regulation that characterizes such facilities.

Turning to the effect of social integration, at one extreme we find situations in which the individual feels alienated, separate from the significant institutions and traditions in his or her society. In this instance, the person has few ties to the community and is not integrated into the society but is instead dependent upon his or her own resources and devices. Durkheim termed the suicides occurring in this type of environment *egoistic*. An individual's mental energies are concentrated on the self to such an extent that the societal sanctions against suicide are ineffective. Persons who are disenfranchised or who live at the fringes of society may feel no compulsion to heed life-affirming values because they do not experience themselves as meaningfully related to the wider community. In this sense, anomie (lack of regulation) and egoism (lack of integration) may reinforce each

AP/Wide World Photos

Flames engulf the body of a Buddhist monk, Quang Duc, whose self-immolation before thousands of onlookers in downtown Saigon was a protest against alleged persecution of Buddhists by the government of South Vietnam.

other. In Durkheim's view, when a person is detached from social life, the individual personality takes precedence over the collective personality. Thus, said Durkheim, egoistic suicide is "the special type of suicide springing from excessive individualism."[20]

In the case of *altruistic* or institutional suicide, on the other hand, excessive identification with the values or causes of society may produce such a strong sense of integration with the social group that the individual loses his or her own personal identity. In this case, the group's values predominate over the individual's. "An integrated social situation," says Ronald Maris, "is one in which individuals are strongly attached to society's governing rules."[21] Norman Farberow observes that an overidentification with the values or causes of a society can produce "a too-ready willingness to sacrifice one's life in a burst of patriotism or martyrdom."[22]

For more than 900 Americans who left their home to join a religious fanatic called the Reverend Jim Jones, death came in the jungles of Guyana with these comforting words from the man who engineered the largest mass suicide the world has witnessed:

> What's going to happen here in a matter of a few minutes is that one of those people in the plane is going to shoot the pilot. . . . So you be kind to the children and be kind to seniors, and take the potion like they used to in Ancient Greece, and step over quietly, because we are not committing suicide — it's a revolutionary act.
>
> Everybody dies. I haven't seen anybody yet didn't die. And I like to choose my own kind of death for a change. I'm tired of being tormented to hell. Tired of it. (Applause)

A few cultists protested. Some women screamed. Children cried. Armed guards took up positions around the camp to keep anyone from escaping:

> Let the little children in and reassure them. . . . They're not crying from pain, it's just a little bitter-tasting. . . . Death is a million times more preferable to spend more days in this life. If you knew what was ahead of you, you'd be glad to be stepping over tonight . . . quickly, quickly, no more pain. . . . This world was not your home. . . .

Here the tape runs out. The sound stops before the report of the pistol that killed Jim Jones, presumably fired by his own hand.

Robert Ramsey and Randall Toye, *The Goodbye Book*

In medieval Japanese society, ritual disembowelment, called *hara-kiri* or *seppuku*, was culturally accepted, even demanded in certain circumstances, especially among the warrior, or samurai, class. Occasions when suicide might seem the only socially acceptable course for a samurai included disgrace in battle or the death of a lord, as well as the desire to make a public statement of one's disagreement with a superior. In such cases, *seppuku* or ritual suicide became the necessary act for an honorable warrior, and specific instructions pertained to the manner in which the suicidal act was to be performed.[23]

Similarly, until modern times, certain castes in India were expected to practice *suttee*, which called for the wife of a nobleman to throw herself upon his funeral pyre. Such self-immolation was condoned by the prevailing religious and cultural beliefs, and a widow's reluctance to perform this ritual suicide was met with social disapproval. Indeed, a reluctant wife might find herself "helped" onto the burning pyre.

To these well-known examples of *seppuku* and *suttee* can be added the institutional suicides of the kamikaze pilots of Japan's air attack corps during World War II and the example of the dedicated captain who goes down with the ship. In these examples, suicide is "the self-destruction demanded by a society . . . as a price for being a member of that society."[24] As already alluded to in the case of samurai who committed *seppuku* as a means of protesting policies of their superiors, altruistic suicide does not always involve an acceptance of social norms.

Suicide as protest came to public attention during the Vietnam war when Buddhist monks committed suicide by self-immolation to protest governmental policies.

A highly publicized instance of institutional suicide occurred on November 20, 1978, in Jonestown, Guyana, when more than 900 persons met their death in what has been called the largest mass suicide in history.[25] At a previously little-noticed jungle clearing, which had been the communal settlement of the followers of the Reverend Jim Jones, many of the victims drank cyanide-laced fruit punch and families died together in one another's arms. In hypnotic tones from his throne above the crowd, Jones urged community members to drink the poison. The customs of the social group influenced the individual's decision to commit suicide.

From the social perspective, then, suicide is seen to be the result of a disturbance in the ties between the individual and society. When there is some imbalance or upset with respect to this relationship, the potential for suicidal behavior is heightened. Each form of suicide — anomic, fatalistic, egoistic, altruistic — is related to a particular kind of interplay between the society and the individual.

The Psychodynamics of Suicide

The psychological model of suicide focuses on the dynamics of the individual's mental and emotional life. Drawing upon the psychoanalytic theories originated by Sigmund Freud, the psychodynamic model incorporates the role of both unconscious and conscious motivation, and it assumes that an individual's behavior is determined by past experience and genetic endowment as well as by current reality. In contrast to the Durkheimian view, which looks to external events for an explanation of suicide, the psychodynamic model concentrates on the processes taking place within the individual mind or personality.

Although frustration, hostility, and aggression are central to the psychodynamics of suicide, other factors may also be present, including guilt, anxiety, and dependency, as well as feelings of helplessness, hopelessness, and abandonment. Karl Menninger noted that suicide involves strong, unconscious hostility combined with a lack of capacity to love others.

According to the psychodynamic model, under conditions of enormous stress, the intrapsychic pressures impelling a person toward self-destruction may increase to the point where they overwhelm the defense mechanisms of the ego, or self. There follows a regression to more primitive ego states characterized by powerful forces of aggression. Even with these aggressive forces mobilized, however, the fundamental urge toward self-preservation militates against the ego's acquiescence to its own death.

Thus, another psychodynamic process comes into play. Freudian theory states that the psychological process of identifying oneself with an admired object (that is, another person) characteristically involves a high degree of ambivalence, such that feelings of love may alternate with feelings of hate: "The *conscious* feel-

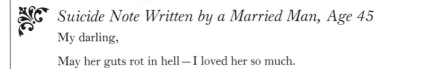

Suicide Note Written by a Married Man, Age 45

My darling,

May her guts rot in hell — I loved her so much.

Henry

ings for the object often reflect one half of the ambivalence, while the other half is kept unconscious, though nonetheless powerful in the individual's mental life."[26]

These psychodynamics are applied to suicide as follows: When the self is frustrated, the aggressive component of the ambivalence is directed against the internalized person — that is, the internal "image" of the person with whom the self has formed an identification. This completes the mental circuit, as it were, so that it is not the self against which aggression is directed, but rather the object of the ambivalent identification. Suicide does away with the source of frustration by eliminating the internalized object that is both loved and hated. Thus, in the psychodynamic model, suicide is linked with homicide. Whereas murder is aggression turned upon another, suicide is aggression turned upon the self. In short, suicide is murder in the 180th degree.

Analysis of suicidal behavior often reveals the presence of conflicting forces that compete for the greater share of the person's mental energies. Thus, *ambivalence* is a characteristic of suicide. At issue is the will to live versus the will to die. Erwin Stengel says, "Most people who commit acts of self-damage with more or less conscious self-destructive intent do not want either to live or to die, but to do both at the same time — usually one more than the other."[27]

Ambivalence toward suicide can be considered in several ways. First, as already suggested, the suicidal individual is likely to experience simultaneously a wish to live and a wish to die. The balance between these opposing polarities may be delicate, with an otherwise minor incident tipping the scales one way or the other. Ambivalence can also refer to a situation in which, although one of these forces is stronger than the other, the weaker one nevertheless continues to affect the person's behavior. Stengel says, "Most suicidal acts are manifestations of risk-taking behavior. They are gambles. The danger to life depends on the relationships between self-destructive and life-preserving, contact-seeking tendencies, and on a variety of other factors, some of which are outside the control of the individual."

Considered as an act of communication, suicide aims to force a change. The suicidal person's situation is such that he or she no longer wishes to continue living in it. For most suicides, however, the goal is not death but the eradication of some problem; suicide seems a means of accomplishing that goal. Much suicidal behavior represents a desperate cry for help, a message to the effect that "something has to change in my life; I can't go on living this way." If a suicide attempt does not bring about a change in the conditions that led up to it, the behavior may be repeated.

Among the valuable insights developed from the psychological model of suicide are the following:

1. The *acute* suicidal crisis is of relatively brief duration; that is, it lasts hours or days rather than weeks or months—though it may recur.
2. The suicidal person is likely to be ambivalent about ending his or her life. Plans for self-destruction are generally accompanied by fantasies that rescue or intervention will occur before the fatal act is completed.
3. Most suicidal events are *dyadic:* They involve both the victim and a significant other in some way.

The insights made available by the psychodynamic model have been usefully applied in constructing a better understanding of suicide and in devising methods of suicide intervention. For example, an analysis of an individual's dreams may help to assess suicidal intent.[28] In this sense, death dreams might be understood as a manifestation of the need for transformation within an individual's personality.

Toward an Integrated Understanding of Suicide

Each of the two major theories of suicide contributes to increased understanding of the patterns of suicidal behavior. Although each model has its roots in a particular methodology, current theories of suicide generally draw upon both in an effort to form a comprehensive understanding of suicide. For example, taking an integrated approach, a disrupted or disturbed home environment (the social context) can lead to feelings of abandonment, loneliness, and low self-esteem (psychodynamics), thereby increasing the risk of suicide.

Both of the major models suggest methods for alleviating the conditions that can lead to suicide. The psychodynamic model points to such factors as low self-esteem; excessive guilt or shame; feelings of isolation, hopelessness, and meaninglessness; a sense of failure or incompetence; and tunnel vision. To counteract these negative influences, this model suggests therapy, emotional support, confidence building, and enhancement of coping skills as deterrents to suicide. The sociological model, on the other hand, calls our attention to particular groups that are at the greatest risk of suicide: the elderly, males, Native Americans, and prisoners, among others. Reducing suicide risk means alleviating the stressful experiences that cause individuals within the at-risk groups to choose suicide.

Some Types of Suicide

In moving toward an integrated model of suicide, we need to draw upon both the sociological and psychological models as well as the individual situation to arrive at a comprehensive understanding of a particular suicidal act. Many classification schemes have been applied to suicide in attempts to better comprehend its personal and social meanings (see Table 13-2). In this section, we examine more closely some of the "types" of suicide, with the aim of providing a more comprehensive picture of suicidal behavior.

Suicide as Release

Suicidal behavior is often entered into as a means of escape or release from some physical pain or mental anguish. For example, a person with a painful terminal illness may perceive suicide as a way out of suffering. The act of ending one's life in such a circumstance is sometimes termed *rational suicide* because the reasoning used — death will bring release from pain — conforms to normal logic.

Although the majority of people with incurable illness continue to have hope that, despite the prognosis, they will live, euthanasia is increasingly being viewed as a personal right in instances of incurable disease.[29] Medical problems tend to be viewed as more acceptable reasons for suicide than are psychological problems, and such attitudes reflect not only on the person who commits suicide but also on his or her family as well.[30] Whereas suicide is usually viewed as an act of violence, euthanasia is more likely to be regarded as a benevolent act ensuing from a decision made by the patient and perhaps enacted with the consent of loved ones. (The term *assisted suicide* can be applied both to advising on methods of suicide and to actually helping someone end his or her life.)

T A B L E *13-2* *Meanings of Suicide*

Some Cultural Meanings of Suicide

Suicide is sinful: A crime against nature, a revolt against the preordained order of the universe.

Suicide is criminal: It violates the ties that exist, the social contract between persons in a society.

Suicide is weakness or madness: It reflects limitations or deviancy ("He must have been crazy" or "He couldn't take it").

Suicide is the Great Death, as in *seppuku, suttee*, and other culturally approved forms of ritual suicide.

Suicide is the rational alternative: The outcome of a "balance-sheet" approach that sizes up the situation and determines the best option.

Some Individual Meanings of Suicides

Suicide is reunion with a lost loved one, a way to "join the deceased."

Suicide is rest and refuge: A way out of a burdensome and depressing situation.

Suicide is getting back: A way of expressing resentment and revenge at being rejected or hurt.

Suicide is the penalty for failure: A response to disappointment and frustration at not meeting self-expectations or the expectations of others.

Suicide is a mistake: The attempt was made as a cry for help and was not intended to be fatal, but there was no rescue or intervention and the outcome was death.

Source: Adapted from Robert Kastenbaum, *Death, Society, and Human Experience*, 2nd ed. (St. Louis, Mo.: C. V. Mosby, 1981) pp. 239–255.

Whereas the type of suicide just discussed might be termed *rational* by some, other forms of seeking escape through suicide result from a destructive logic. In these cases, the victim's self-concept or sense of identity is confused. Problems with self-identity, often coupled with an inability to comfortably relate to others, can lead to the victim's self-perception as a failure. Such suicides have sometimes been termed *referred*, bringing to mind the analogy of physical pain that is experienced at some distance from its source. An injury in the elbow, for example, may be experienced as pain in the little finger; an inflammation of the liver may be experienced as pain in the shoulder. Just as this physical phenomenon is characterized as referred pain, the root causes of referred suicide are likewise only indirectly related to the end result — namely, suicide. Whereas the desire to escape from pain involves a comparatively straightforward logic between intention and action, the logic of referred suicide is ambiguous. The decision to end one's life is not based on a dispassionate assessment of the situation, but instead comes out of an overwhelming sense of anguish and confusion about one's options.

Self-concept is an important factor. Not performing up to expectations or according to certain role definitions may provoke a crisis of self-concept that ultimately leads to the desire to escape the unsatisfactory situation. Expectations may be related to something outside the individual ("If I can't be a good enough daughter to please my parents, I give up!"), or they may be related to inward feelings of frustration ("Everybody thinks I'm doing okay, but I feel rotten"). Evans and Farberow note that "in an age where image is so important (often it appears to be everything), loss of status or identity can prove devastating."[31]

The desire to escape may also arise from the loss of meaning in one's life. Despite significant accomplishments, a person may come to feel, "Now what?" The accumulation of successes one after another may seem a Sisyphean effort, a continual struggle for achievement without a sufficient sense of accomplishment. Or perhaps all of the accomplishments were achieved in the past; there seems nothing more to be gained. Like Alexander the Great, after "conquering the world," one may feel there is nothing to strive for, no reason to live. Conversely, success may be accompanied by feelings of ennui, that "If this is what success is all about, it's not worth the effort." Stress, competition, aggressiveness, and inability to balance conflicting demands can be overwhelming. Being a "superachiever," or taking on more responsibilities than one is comfortable with, can result in a personal crisis that may prove lethal. Low self-esteem coupled with high achievement orientation has been shown to be a dangerous combination of personality characteristics.[32] Roy Baumeister says that the causal chain begins with events that fall short of standards and expectations.[33] Awareness of inadequacy and failure makes self-awareness painful, and the individual wishes to escape from this negative sense of self. Drastic measures may seem acceptable, with suicide becoming the ultimate step in the effort to find a release from self and the world.

Psychotic Suicide and Depression

Psychotic suicide is associated with the impaired logic of a delusional or hallucinatory state of mind related to clinically diagnosed schizophrenia or manic-depressive psychosis. Even though there is no conscious intention to die, the victim may try to eradicate the psychic malignancy or punish himself or herself by self-destruction. According to Evans and Farberow, "The victim suffers a break with reality and loses the ability to distinguish what is occurring and what is imagined."[34] Treatment of the psychotic's suicidal impulses requires that one must first treat the psychosis.

Although most psychiatrically ill patients do not commit suicide, mental illness — especially severe depression — does place individuals at higher risk for suicide. Depressive disorders can and do affect young people as well as adults.[35] In fact, depression is believed to be a factor in roughly one-half of all suicides. Major depression is a syndrome that can be triggered by a wide variety of physical and psychosocial factors, and it is a warning sign that should not be ignored.[36] Differences in how families function may help to explain why a minority of depressed patients attempt suicide while a majority do not.[37] Family members or friends may not realize the depth of an individual's depression or perhaps simply do not wish to admit to the seriousness of the illness.

The depressed person may act out his or her depression in harmful, disruptive, or illegal ways, sometimes involving alcohol or drug abuse. A frequent component of suicide, depression is the disorder most commonly associated with deliberate self-poisoning, often by overdosing with drugs that are available only by prescription.[38] This situation has prompted calls for restricting the use of older, more toxic antidepressants in favor of newer and safer medications.

Subintentional and Chronic Suicide

Subintentional suicide can be viewed as yet another type of life-threatening behavior. As defined by Edwin Shneidman, the subintentioned death is "one in which the person plays some partial, covert, subliminal, or unconscious role in hastening his own demise."[39] Although not usually defined as suicide by official reporting methods, this mode of death does not fit accurately into such categories as natural or accidental either. Some of the fatal events reported as accidents result from the victim's choosing to take an unnecessary and unwise risk. Such behavior might be called careless or imprudent. A deeper probing into causes, however, leads to the conclusion that some accidents are the end result of a pattern of behavior that conforms to the definition of subintentional suicide. Similarly, the investigation of homicide cases sometimes turns up evidence that points to a subintentional factor resulting in the victim's taking certain actions or behaving in some way that served to provoke his or her death at another's hands.

In addition to subintentional death, Shneidman delineates two other characteristic patterns of death-related behaviors: intentioned and unintentioned. Table 13-3 presents an outline of these three patterns. Notice that within each of these

TABLE *13-3*   *Patterns of Death-Related Behavior and Attitudes*

Intentioned Death: Death resulting from the suicide's direct, conscious behavior to bring it about. A variety of attitudes or motives may be operative:

The *death seeker* wishes to end consciousness and commits the suicidal act in such a way that rescue is unlikely.

The *death initiator* expects to die in the near future and wants to choose the time and circumstances of death.

The *death ignorer* believes that death ends only physical existence and that the person continues to exist in another manner.

The *death darer* gambles with death, or, as Shneidman says, "bets his life on a relatively low objective probability that he will survive" (such as by playing Russian roulette).

Subintentioned Death: Death resulting from a person's pattern of management or style of living, although death was not the conscious, direct aim of the person's actions:

The *death chancer*, although in many ways like the death darer, may want higher odds of survival.

The *death hastener* may expedite his or her death by substance abuse (drugs, alcohol, and the like) or by failing to safeguard well-being (for example, by inadequate nutrition or precautions against disease or disregard of available treatments).

The *death facilitator* gives little resistance to death, making it easy for death to occur, as in the deaths of patients whose energies, or "will to live," are low because of their illness.

The *death capitulator* is one who, usually out of a great fear of death, plays a subintentional role in his or her own death, as may a person upon whom a so-called voodoo death has been put, or as may a person who believes that someone admitted to a hospital is bound to die.

The *death experimenter* does not consciously wish to die but lives on the brink, usually in a "befogged state of consciousness" that may be related to taking drugs in such ways that the person may become comatose or even die with little concern.

Unintentioned Deaths: Death in which the decedent plays no significant causative role. However, various attitudes toward death may shape the experience of dying:

The *death welcomer*, though not hastening death, looks forward to it (as might an aged person who feels unable to manage adequately or satisfactorily).

The *death accepter* is resigned to his or her fate; the style of acceptance may be passive, philosophical, resigned, heroic, realistic, or mature.

The *death postponer* hopes to put death off for as long as possible.

The *death disdainer* feels, in Shneidman's words, "above any involvement in the stopping of the vital processes."

The *death fearer* is fearful, and possibly phobic, about anything related to death; death is something to be fought and hated.

The *death feigner* pretends to be in mortal danger or pretends to perform a suicidal act without being in actual danger, possibly in an attempt to gain attention or to manipulate others.

Source: Adapted from Edwin S. Shneidman, *Deaths of Man* (New York: Quadrangle Books, 1973), pp. 82–90.

categories a person might exhibit a variety of attitudes and behaviors regarding death. As you review this table, ask yourself: Where do I stand on this list? What does that say about my own regard for life and death?

Some suicidologists use the term *chronic suicide*, coined by Karl Menninger, to refer to individuals who choose to destroy themselves by means of drugs, alcohol, reckless living, and the like. Often, although such an individual may find the idea of suicide repugnant or unacceptable, an analysis of his or her life style suggests the presence of a "death wish." Marilyn Monroe's death due to a drug overdose is still the subject of debate concerning whether it was accidental or intentionally suicidal. Similarly, although the death of James Dean resulted from reckless speeding in his Porsche, his life style exhibited a level of risk taking that some would say exemplifies chronic or subintentional suicide. Because our ethical standards and laws regarding suicide have evolved from considering it in its "acute" context, many suicidologists believe that we tend to be comparatively insensitive when it comes to the prevalence of chronic suicide in our society.[40]

Cry for Help

Suicidal behavior may be entered into as a form of communication known as a *cry for help*. This is typically the situation of a person who becomes suicidal when the normal avenues for expressing feelings of frustration are blocked. Much suicidal behavior among young people is of this type. Suicidal behavior engaged in as a "cry for help" is associated particularly with persons who threaten or attempt suicide as opposed to those who actually commit suicide. There is often no history of suicidal behavior, and the lethality of the attempt is generally low. The purpose of the behavior seems to be to make significant others aware of how desperate or how unhappy the person feels. As a cry for help, a suicide attempt says, in effect: "I am deadly serious, and you'd better pay attention!" This communication may be directed inwardly to oneself or outwardly to others.

Despite this underlying goal of opening up communication and the usually low order of lethality of the suicidal behavior, death may result nonetheless, even if unintentionally. In responding to the cry for help, it is important to recognize that a serious problem exists and make efforts toward increasing communication and proposing remedies. When low-lethality suicidal behavior is met with defensive hostility or with attempts to minimize its seriousness and make it seem unimportant, the risk of suicide increases along with the possibility that the next attempt will be lethal.

A useful distinction in studying suicidal behavior is the difference between *attempted* suicide and the *fait accompli*. According to Evans and Farberow, attempted suicide "refers to behavior directed against the self which results in injury or self-harm, or has strong potential for injury. Intention in the behavior may or may not be to die, or may or may not be to inflict injury or pain on oneself."[41] Many suicidologists believe that two fairly distinct populations of individuals engage in suicidal behavior: (1) *attempters* (who tend toward repeated, but not lethal, attempts) and (2) *completers* (whose first attempt typically results in death). In this view, attempters and completers may have quite different aims with regard to their suicidal acts.[42] Indeed, the suggestion has been put forward that the study of suicide should focus on attempted suicide as the norm while viewing completed suicide as a failed behavior in which the individual inappropriately died.[43]

Although there is evidence to support the view that some suicides are meant to result in death and others are not, one should nevertheless be careful about assigning a particular instance of suicidal behavior to one or the other of these categories: An attempt can result in death. It should never be assumed that a suicide attempt was meant only as a gesture. Suicidal behavior is life threatening; it can be lethal whether intended to be or not. Psychological autopsies of some suicide victims reveal that they probably thought the attempt would be stopped short of death, but help did not arrive in time. Suicide attempts should always be taken seriously.

Although precise information is impossible to obtain, suicide attempts are known to outnumber committed suicides by a significant margin. A commonly stated, and conservative, estimate for the population as a whole is that for every eight suicide attempts, one is lethal. With respect to suicidal behavior among adolescents, the ratio between attempts and completions has been estimated to be as high as 200 attempts for every completed suicide. It has been pointed out by researchers that in all age groups above age 14, females *attempt* suicide more often than do males, while males *kill themselves* more often than do females.[44] (Among children younger than 14, males both attempt and complete suicide more often than do females.) This gender difference may be explained partly by the methods used, with males using more highly lethal or "aggressive" methods. Whereas females tend to take pills or slash wrists, males tend to use less equivocal means, such as guns. However, the use of aggressive methods by males is only part of the explanation. Stillion and her colleagues point out that "males are more successful than females with every method of committing suicide."[45] Perhaps males consider a failed attempt to be cowardly or unmasculine and thus make a special effort to be successful in their suicidal behavior. In addition to the "suicidal success syndrome" that afflicts males, there is also evidence that males are less likely than females to report suicidal thoughts or seek help (such as from crisis intervention centers). By hiding their feelings of depression or hopelessness, males thereby hinder potential efforts at intervention. These gender differences appear to be especially pronounced among young people.[46]

Of course, some suicide attempts miscarry not because of the person's intention to avoid death but rather because of some outside intervention or some error of execution — for example, an intended drug overdose is not fatal because too little or the wrong kind of drug was taken. Generally, persons who use the most lethal methods in their suicide attempts and nevertheless survive have a lower risk of future suicide attempts than do those who use the less lethal methods. In other words, the person who survives a self-inflicted gunshot wound is less likely to try suicide again than someone who attempted suicide by asphyxiation with a plastic bag.

Perhaps coming very near death somehow purges the suicidal individual of the wish to end his or her life. Some persons who survive a suicide attempt look upon their continued existence as a second chance or a "bonus life." Persons admitted to intensive care as a result of suicide attempts show a relatively low rate of repeat attempts, while the highest rate of repeat suicide attempts is among those who received no treatment for their injuries. Of course, these statistics reflect only general patterns of suicidal behavior. Although such statistics are useful for those involved in suicide intervention and treatment programs, they are not a reliable means for predicting the behavior of a particular individual.

Risk Factors Influencing Suicide

Another way to increase our understanding of suicide involves examining the risk factors that influence suicidal behaviors. Generally speaking, these risk factors encompass four broad areas: culture, personality, the individual situation, and biological factors. When considering particular instances of suicidal behavior, these risk factors typically are found to overlap to varying degrees.

Culture

In this category, we consider sociostructural factors that affect members of a particular social group. Such factors include a society's basic attitude toward suicide as well as the nature of that society. As mentioned in the context of discussing suicide as release from pain, suicide intended to end physical suffering related to terminal disease appears to be more acceptable to many people in our society than is suicide related to escaping the mental pain of less catastrophic life problems. Such messages about the degree of acceptability of various suicidal behaviors can influence the kinds of behavior engaged in by members of a social group.

The acceptability of violence as a solution to problems is another cultural factor that can increase suicide risk. The easy availability of lethal weapons as well as the prevalence of violence in the media can contribute to a sense that violence against oneself is an acceptable alternative when the going gets rough. The apparent acceptance of more violence in our lives can change posturing into deadly deeds.[47] Some suicidologists see a correlation between violence and suicide among the young: As acts of violent aggression have become more widespread and frequent, there has been a corresponding increase in suicide. Some believe that the media also exert influence on suicidal behavior related to the phenomenon of suggestibility or imitation. Although reports of suicides in the media have sometimes been blamed for triggering more suicides, studies generally have not confirmed such an effect. Nonetheless, the idea that suicide can be contagious has a long history. Following the publication of Goethe's *The Sorrows of Young Werther* in 1774, for instance, youthful suicides were frequently attributed to the book's influence. Whether or not attention to suicide in a book, movie, or newspaper report can stimulate an increase in the suicide rate, there is no question about the influence of the sociocultural environment as a potential risk factor in suicide.

Another cultural factor influencing suicide concerns what Brian Barry calls "the balance between pro-life and pro-death forces operating at any given time."[48] Pro-life forces include (1) the belief that problems can promote growth, (2) a perceived ability to solve life problems, (3) a willingness to struggle and suffer if necessary, and (4) a healthy fear of death and its aftermath. Pro-death forces, on the other hand, include (1) the belief that problems are intolerable, (2) a perception that life problems are intractable or unyielding, (3) a sense of entitlement to a rewarding life, and (4) a philosophical stance that sees suicide as a means of obtaining relief. Barry says that individuals in contemporary society, especially young people, have accepted "two fundamental assumptions about life that no previous generation has embraced so massively." The first of these assumptions is the belief that we, as human beings, deserve significant levels of fulfillment in our jobs, marriages, and overall lives. The second assumption is that, "rather than adopting a posture of long-suffering acceptance of unalterable circumstances, the responsible thing to do is to live and die on one's own terms." We live in a culture where we are not only encouraged to aspire to a good life, but we have become convinced that we are entitled to it. Socially tolerant attitudes toward suicide may also help to remove what has traditionally been a powerful constraint inhibiting people from taking their own lives. The modern emphasis on individual freedom may be politically desirable, but it includes the freedom to make irresponsible choices that can be costly.

Personality

Differences in personality may explain why some individuals appear to be at higher risk for suicide than others. Some people have a "basic optimism" while others have a "basic pessimism"—a factor that can be a deciding influence in some suicides.[49] The ability to get along with others and the ability to form meaningful interpersonal relationships have also been cited as possible differences between "suicidal" and "nonsuicidal" people. For example, one of the categories that has been used to describe youthful suicides is that of the loner personality type, which typically emerges during middle adolescence and builds to a high potential for suicide in the later teens. In any case, it appears that the way people relate to others, as well as how they relate to their own problems and difficulties in life, can influence the tendency to feelings of depression and thoughts of suicide. While some people feel devastated when something goes wrong, others exhibit a more easygoing and accepting attitude. Suicides that result from the breakup of a romance, especially among young people, may be influenced to a significant degree by such qualities of personality, with feelings of depression and worthlessness leading to suicidal thoughts.

Another aspect of personality that may represent a risk factor for suicide relates to an individual's fascination with the "mystique" of death, especially self-

> Romeo and Juliet also embody another popular misconception: that of the great suicidal passion. It seems that those who die for love usually do so by mistake and ill-luck. It is said that the London police can always distinguish, among the corpses fished out of the Thames, between those who have drowned themselves because of unhappy love affairs and those drowned for debt. The fingers of the lovers are almost invariably lacerated by their attempts to save themselves by clinging to the piers of the bridges. In contrast, the debtors apparently go down like slabs of concrete, apparently without struggle and without afterthought.
>
> A. Alvarez, *The Savage God*

willed death. Here we find suicidal behaviors that appear to be related to a "poetic" or "romantic" attraction to death. Led by Thomas Chatterton, who killed himself in 1770 at the age of 17, the Romantics thought of death as "the great inspirer" and "great consoler." They made suicide fashionable and felt that "to die by one's own hand was a short and sure way to fame."[50] Death may be approached as a lover to be courted. The poet Sylvia Plath wrote: "I will marry dark death, the thief of the daytime."[51] The novelist Ernest Hemingway and the poets Anne Sexton and Hart Crane are other examples of writers whose fascination with death possibly played a lethal role in their ultimate suicides.

Do such suicides reflect a conscious desire to embrace the mystery of death, or nonbeing? Or do they result from more commonplace human experiences? The suicides of writers and other artists seem to be characterized by much the same frustrations that may affect anyone. Failure to find meaning in life and problems with relationships are common threads. As someone said: "The death of love evokes the love of death." The lack of intimate relationships, low self-esteem, lack of coping skills, loss of dreams and goals, and feelings of stagnation, loneliness, despair, hopelessness, and helplessness are all factors of personality that can contribute to suicidal thoughts and behaviors.

The Individual Situation

The influence of culture and personality creates a unique situation experienced by a particular individual. Environmental factors—including not only the attitudes and social dynamics existing in the broader society but also such particular characteristics as an individual's family patterns and economic situation—can create varying degrees of suicide risk for an individual. A history of abuse and neglect, conflict in relationships, drug or alcohol abuse, the availability of firearms or other ready means of self-destruction, and the like also influence the degree of suicide risk present in an individual's life. The nature of the environment itself can play a crucial role. For example, suicide has been cited as the leading cause of death for persons in jails, with pretrial detainees especially at risk.[52] It has also been found that the suicide rates of juveniles held in adult detention facilities is much higher than that of juveniles held in juvenile detention facilities.[53]

Sociocultural stress appears to be a factor in the comparatively high rate of suicide among some Native American populations. Some Native Americans experience feelings of powerlessness and anxiety because of conflicts between their traditional ways and the ways of the contemporary white society. Forced onto reservations, their religions and cultures undermined, and their children placed in schools where non-Indian traditions are taught, the native peoples of North America have undergone severe cultural and economic dislocation. An additional burden may be experienced by those living in cities, where support systems, such as family ties and traditional customs, are lacking.

An individual's life style may contribute to suicide risk. Substance abuse and other risk-taking activities may come under the category of subintentioned death-seeking behaviors, and they may also contribute to a lessening of psychological barriers between suicidal thought and action.

Specific life events represent another category of experiences that may influence suicidal thoughts or behavior. Researchers have found, for example, that individuals who have been bereaved as a result of suicide may be especially vulnerable to adverse effects, possibly including an increased risk of committing suicide themselves.[54] Persons with AIDS also have been described as prone to suicide.[55]

The typical pattern in *crisis suicide* is that of an adolescent who reaches a point in his or her life involving sudden traumatic changes, such as the loss of a loved one or the loss or threatened loss of status in school. In response, the young person may exhibit sudden and dramatic changes in behavior, possibly including loss of interest in things that were previously important, hostile and aggressive acts (in a previously placid youngster), or signs of confusion, disorganization, and depression.

The influence of peers can also affect an individual's suicide risk. This phenomenon appears to be especially pronounced among adolescents and young adults. A study of suicide among Micronesian males during a twenty-year period confirmed the occurrence of an "epidemiclike" increase.[56] Within the islands of Micronesia, this period was marked by rapid sociocultural transformation as traditional styles of living gave way to reliance upon a cash economy and modern forms of education, employment, health services, and technology. In studying suicide among Micronesians, investigators reconstructed events leading up to a suicide. Using the techniques of psychological autopsy, a significant number of linkages among suicides were found, including two or three suicides occurring among a small circle of friends over several months. There were also cases of suicidal acts in reaction to the suicide of a friend or relative and "suicide pacts" between or among two or more persons. Taken together, these phenomena pointed to the existence of a "suicide subculture" wherein suicide begat suicide. In an environment characterized by a general familiarity with and acceptance of the *idea* of suicide, investigators concluded, suicide had become "a culturally patterned and partly collective response" to personal dilemmas and problems.

Biologic Factors

Recent studies indicate the presence of altered brain neurochemistry in some people who commit suicide.[57] Specifically, biochemical studies of suicide victims and attempters indicate that low levels of serotonin (5-HT) or its neurotransmitter metabolite (5-HIAA) appear to be correlated with suicidal behavior. These findings suggest that biological markers could become important as a means of assessing risk for suicide. Furthermore, a clearer understanding of the role of serotonin and other neurotransmitter systems could lead to the development of comprehensive pharmacologic treatments that would help to reduce suicide risk. Researchers point out, however, that such neurochemical correlates do not fully explain the timing and type of suicidal behavior, nor do they explain why some aggression is directed outwardly toward others and in other cases is directed inwardly toward the self. Thus, although an understanding of biochemical factors will likely play an increasingly larger role in suicide assessment and intervention, known environmental and psychosocial factors retain their importance in helping us gain a comprehensive view of suicide risks.

Lifespan Perspectives on Suicide

Statistically, the level of suicide risk changes throughout the lifespan. The motives for suicide also change as human beings encounter the changing constellation of factors that relate to various periods of human development. In this section, we examine some of the specific risks and motives that have a particular effect on suicidal behaviors at varying ages.

Childhood

Despite a paucity of statistics concerning suicide among young children, many researchers and clinicians believe that suicidal behavior can be found among even very young children and that suicide among children is a growing phenomenon.[58] Evans and Farberow state that children as young as two years old are trying to commit suicide in increasing numbers.[59] They mention reports from clinicians about five- and six-year-olds who have attempted suicide by hanging or by jumping out of a window. One suicidal boy, at age two-and-a-half, was said to be upset over his parents' divorce. In a study focusing on the role of death preoccupations in children aged six to twelve years, Cynthia Pfeffer found that about 12 percent expressed suicidal ideas or actions.[60] Although suicidal behavior appears to be infrequent among school-age children compared with the progressively increasing instances of such behavior observed among junior high, high school, and college students, suicide among young children is nonetheless of real concern. It is sobering to note that between 1980 and 1986 the suicide rate among persons ages 10 to 14 nearly doubled.[61] With suicide attempts being made (or perhaps *recorded*) at younger ages than in the past, and in light of the fact that suicide risk is higher for persons who have made a previous attempt on their lives, those who attempt suicide at a comparatively young age also remain at risk for a longer period of time.

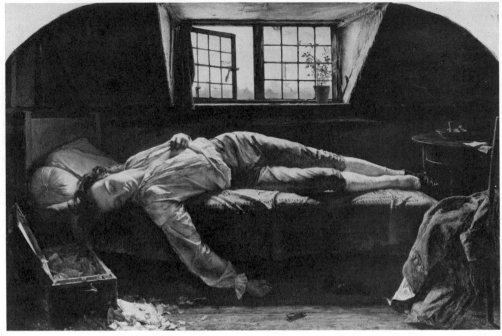

Henry Wallis, Tate Gallery, London

Unable to earn a living by writing and too proud to accept food offered to him by his landlady, this seventeen-year-old killed himself by taking poison. Painted in 1856 by Henry Wallis, The Death of Chatterton *depicts an adolescent suicide that was precipitated by crisis arising out of the developmental transition from child to adult.*

Greater attention must be paid to obtaining accurate and complete statistics as well as to examining the factors that contribute to suicidal behavior by young children. In an early study, five major motivational factors were noted as influencing children's suicide: (1) the desire to escape from a difficult situation; (2) the attempt to assert independence or to punish persons who "interfered" with the child; (3) the effort to gain attention and affection; (4) the wish to achieve reunion with a deceased loved one; and (5) spite.[62]

As mentioned earlier in this chapter, the suicide rate among children might be significantly higher than current statistics indicate if accidents were carefully examined for intent. Some childhood deaths resulting from running in front of cars or plastic bag suffocation might be intentional rather than accidental. Although young children do engage in suicidal behavior and even kill themselves, labeling a death as suicide is especially problematic in the case of a young child who may not yet have formulated a mature concept of death. Nevertheless, there is general agreement that children as young as nine or ten—sometimes even much younger—do threaten, attempt, and commit suicide.

Adolescence and Young Adulthood

In comparison with the amount of statistical data available regarding suicide among younger children, the amount of data on the incidence of suicide among adolescents and young adults is much more complete. This age group has been intensively studied by researchers and reported on by clinicians, especially in recent years, as the suicide rate among youth has increased. In the United States, suicide is cited as the third leading cause of death among persons aged 15–34, following accidents and homicides. René Diekstra has noted that, among countries reporting data to the World Health Organization, the rise in overall suicide rates is due largely to the increase among young people.[63] Furthermore, a study of social indicators and suicide rates suggests that many developing countries will witness a sharp rise in self-destructive behaviors among young people in the near future. In particular, Diekstra cites social disruption (or anomie) and depressive disturbance as factors affecting increased suicide rates.

A survey by Cynthia Pfeffer of risk factors relative to suicidal behavior in children and adolescents cited the influence of both early developmental experiences and current environmental situations.[64] Besides aggression and family violence, factors increasing the risk for suicide among youth included depression, parental suicidal behavior, and family losses. Increased risk has been found among youngsters who have recently lost a parent or who suffer from learning disabilities related to hyperactivity, perceptual disorders, or dyslexia. As with suicide among other age groups, psychiatric diagnosis, dysfunctional personality traits, and psychosocial problems increase the risk of suicide.[65] Although suicide among young people may relate to a variety of problems and diagnoses, generally those who attempt suicide do not differ substantially from other emotionally troubled adolescents.[66] Table 13-4 provides a further listing of specific characteristics that researchers have identified as contributing to increased risk of youthful suicide.

The upheavals in family life during the last few decades are viewed as an important influence on suicidal behavior among the young. New life styles within the family appear to be increasing the pressures upon all family members. Some researchers call for special attention to the needs of children whose parents divorce. Economic pressures and increased mobility add to a sense of upheaval and lessened security. Young people sometimes respond to these changes with uncertainty, fear, and anger. Suicide may seem a way of imposing some control over confusing and upsetting events.

Much youthful suicidal behavior is linked to a life style without goals, direction, or substance. Commenting on the values of the home, the family, and parenting, Michael Peck says that many adolescents "describe what might best be called a narcissistic do-your-own-thing upsurge among parents," with the result that youngsters grow up with "little clear-cut guidance, confused or absent values, and a sense of floating along in time without direction."[67] Evans and Farberow mention social workers' use of the term "throwaway society" to describe troublesome children who are literally thrown out of their homes by their

TABLE 13-4   Risk Factors Contributing to Youthful Suicide

1. Early separation from one's parents.
2. Family dissolution, economic hardship, and increased mobility.
3. Effect of highly conflicted families or families who are unresponsive to the young person's needs, or who are anomic (not accepting of the usual standards of social conduct), or depressed, alcoholic, etc.
4. Increased social isolation as compared to the support previously provided by the extended family, church, and community.
5. Greater awareness of the nuclear threat.
6. Rapidly changing sex roles.
7. Increase in relative proportion of young people in the total population and corresponding increase in competition because of the large youthful cohort population.
8. Pressure for achievement and success, perhaps resulting from parental expectations.
9. Impact of peer suicides and role models of popular entertainers in terms of "copycat" suicide.
10. Media attention given to suicide and the influence of self-destructive themes in popular culture, especially in popular song lyrics.
11. Sense of lack of control over one's life.
12. Low self-esteem and poor self-image.
13. Devaluing of emotional expression.
14. Lack of effective relationships with peers.
15. Easy availability of drugs and alcohol.

Source: Adapted from William C. Fish and Edith Waldhart-Letzel, "Suicide and Children," *Death Education* 5 (1981): 217–220; Michael Peck, "Youth Suicide," *Death Education* 6 (1982): 29–47; and Judith M. Stillion, Eugene E. McDowell, and Jacque H. May, *Suicide Across the Life Span: Premature Exits* (New York: Hemisphere, 1989), pp. 95–100.

parents.[68] One social worker calls this phenomenon the "Kleenex mentality," referring to the practice of using things and just throwing them away.

Many suicidologists also believe there is a relationship between the increase in youthful suicides and the pressures and overcrowding experienced by a large cohort of "baby boomers" passing through the violence-prone years of childhood. This factor, coupled with lack of employment opportunities and other economic factors, has brought about significant life-style and behavioral changes in the experience of the generation now moving up through young adulthood. The result may be too many young people wanting too many things that are not available, thus increasing their feelings of anonymity and alienation.

Some researchers believe that adolescents and young adults are particularly susceptible to an element of "contagion" with respect to suicide, whereby one person's suicide triggers another. Typically, these so-called *cluster suicides* take place within the same locale, with examples having occurred in Clear Lake City and Plano, Texas; New York's affluent Westchester, Rockland, and Putnam counties; Cheyenne, Wyoming; Cherry Creek School District near Denver, Colorado; and Columbus, Ohio.[69] Such mutual influencing of one adolescent by another appears to have the greatest impact on individuals who are especially vulnerable to suicidal thoughts and behavior.

A similar phenomenon is that of *suicide pacts*, a mutual arrangement between or among two or more people who determine to kill themselves at the same time and usually in the same place. Although the victims of suicide pacts are usually older spouses, often with one of the parties seriously ill or debilitated, instances have been cited of suicide pacts between adolescents.[70] In 1987, four teenagers in New Jersey, two boys and two girls, decided to commit suicide together by sitting in a car with the motor running inside a locked garage. Reportedly, they were distraught over the death of a friend. They were discovered dead the next morning. Two days later, another suicide pact took the lives of two teenage girls in Illinois who killed themselves in like manner.

Another instance of adolescents entering into a suicide pact involved a boy and girl who reportedly became obsessed with the possibility of reincarnation after reading Richard Bach's *Jonathan Livingston Seagull*. They crashed their car into their old junior high school building, causing the boy to be killed instantly. The girl, who apparently had last-second doubts about reincarnation, barely survived after diving under the car's dashboard. A final example of this phenomenon involved two teenagers who killed themselves in 1969 to protest the Vietnam War. They asphyxiated themselves after leaving behind a number of suicide notes explaining their political protest against the war. As in the case of the "epidemic" of suicides among young people in Micronesia, which was mentioned earlier in this chapter, the incidence of suicide clusters and suicide pacts can exert a mutual influence on individuals who are vulnerable to suicidal intentions.

The influence of the media as a factor influencing suicide among young people has also been cited by a number of researchers. Following the movie *The Deerhunter*, which contained a scene depicting soldiers playing Russian roulette with a loaded pistol, there were reports of individuals (mostly males in their teens and early twenties) shooting themselves in the head within a few days of watching the movie.[71] Some studies have shown that suicide rates rise after news reports about suicide and after publicity about the death of a prominent person or celebrity. It has been suggested that the media could help reduce suicide risk by promoting healthy coping mechanisms rather than by "normalizing" suicidal behavior by reporting it.[72] The issue of violence in the media, both as news and as entertainment, has also been cited by some as potentially increasing suicide risk by presenting an image of violence as a solution to problems.

Alcohol and drug abuse are widely recognized as comprising a deadly link in the chain of self-destruction. Evans and Farberow state that "almost 50 percent of the adolescents who commit suicide are drunk or high on something shortly before their death, and that figure soars to 75 percent for adolescents who attempt suicide but do not succeed."[73] The paranoia and agitation caused by the "high" associated with crack cocaine reportedly leads in many cases not only to

> ### ✤ Suicide Note Written by a Single Woman, Age 21
> My dearest Andrew,
>
> It seems as if I have been spending all my life apologizing to you for things that happened whether they were my fault or not.
>
> I am enclosing your pin because I want you to think of what you took from me every time you see it.
>
> I don't want you to think I would kill myself over you because you're not worth any emotion at all. It is what you cost me that hurts and nothing can replace it.

violent crime, but also to suicidal behavior.[74] Frank Crumley points out that accumulating evidence supports the hypothesis that substance abuse among adolescents constitutes a risk factor for a range of suicidal behavior, including suicidal ideation, attempted suicide, and completed suicide.[75] Substance abuse appears to be associated with a greater number of repeated suicide attempts as well as more lethal attempts. In addition, the data support an association between alcohol intoxication and suicide by firearms among adolescents. Thus, adolescents who engage in substance abuse, particularly those with any type of depressive disorder, appear to be at higher risk for suicidal behavior.

Much adolescent suicidal behavior occurs with little planning or thought of the potential outcome. A child or adolescent may not fully recognize the danger inherent in his or her self-destructive actions. Sometimes teenage flirtations with death, such as "playing chicken," prove to be more than was bargained for. Adolescence is typically a time of testing the limits. More obviously, suicidal behaviors such as cutting one's wrists or taking a drug overdose may be engaged in as a means of gaining attention or of expressing frustration without fully recognizing the potential for death. Or, again, suicidal behaviors may be engaged in with a kind of lackadaisical attitude about the possible result. Whatever the motive, however, the outcome can be just as deadly.

For young adults (statistically, in the age group 25 to 34), the suicide rate in the United States is somewhat higher than the rate for adolescents, although the rate of increase has not been as great as that for adolescents. Additional risk factors contributing to suicide among this older age group include depression, separation and divorce, occupational stress, and a sense of hopelessness.[76] It should be noted that this is also an age group significantly affected by the AIDS epidemic, which represents yet another risk factor for suicide among those whose lives are touched by this disease.

Although some researchers and clinicians believe that current research into the use of neurobiologic markers holds promise for identifying young people who are at high risk for suicide, at present the most promising approaches for reducing suicide among young people appear to be in two major areas: first, providing treatment for disorders that increase the risk of suicide, such as depression, sub-

Suicide Note Written by a Single Man, Age 51

Sunday 4:45 PM   Here goes

To who it may concern

Though I am about to kick the bucket I am as happy as ever. I am tired of this life so am going over to see the other side.

Good luck to all.

Benjamin P.

stance abuse, and family conflict; and, second, targeting more prevention efforts at high-risk groups, such as affectively disordered young men who exhibit substance abuse and other antisocial behavior.[77]

Middle Adulthood

Middle age, the period roughly between ages 35 and 65, has been termed the "terra incognita of developmental psychology."[78] Developmentally, this is considered a period of "generativity," of giving back to society some of the gifts of nurture and sustenance received during earlier periods of life. It is viewed as a time of shifting from valuing physical capabilities to valuing wisdom, of building new relationships as old ones are changed or lost, and of gaining greater flexibility. Stillion and her colleagues note that some observers have characterized this period as "middlescence," suggesting that "middle age may be as turbulent for many adults as the period of adolescence."[79] This is also a time of coping with the loss of dreams and ambitions, coming to terms with the realization that one may not reach the goal of being a great artist or writer or a company president, or the aim of attaining a perfect marriage or raising perfect children.

Factors influencing suicide among the middle-aged include an accumulation of negative life events; affective disorders, especially major depression; and alcoholism. The suicide rate for middle-aged men is about three times as high as for middle-aged women, even though the suicide rate is highest for women during the latter years of middle age.[80] In studying the contents of a diary left by a 48-year-old woman who committed suicide, Dennis Peck found that the journal indicated that a variety of sociopsychological conditions and emotions may have played a role in the planned course of action leading to her death.[81]

Late Adulthood

In the United States, the suicide rate remains highest among the elderly, and it has been noted that "elderly people have shown high suicide rates relative to other age groups throughout history."[82] Some of the reasons given for suicide among those in later adulthood (generally defined as persons over age 65) are given in Table 13-5. The biological and social changes that accompany old age

T A B L E *13-5*   *Factors Influencing Suicide in Later Adulthood*

1. Social isolation and loneliness.
2. Boredom, depression, sense of uselessness.
3. Loss of purpose and meaning in life after retirement and separation from family and friends.
4. Financial hardship.
5. Multiple losses of loved ones.
6. Chronic illness, pain, incapacitation.
7. Alcohol abuse and drug dependence.
8. Desire to avoid being a "burden" to others or to end one's life with "dignity."

bring losses that may make life seem less worth living. To some elderly, suicide may appear to be a "rational" option for avoiding severe illness or other hardships of old age. Suicide has been found to generate intense feelings among old people domiciled in long-term care facilities.[83] Stillion and her colleagues have noted, however, that old age "can be a period of increased life satisfaction and ego integrity, or one of dissatisfaction, despair, and disgust."[84]

Even though suicide rates among persons over 65 remain the highest of all age groups, there has been a decline in these rates over the past decades. This decline may be due, at least partly, to differential longevity between the sexes. Since more women than men live to older ages, and because women have lower suicide rates, the overall rate of suicide would naturally decline. In addition, the present generation of older adults has maintained reasonably good health as compared to preceding generations, and they are also the beneficiaries of more education and greater social benefits than was previously the case. A third possible reason for the decline has to do with the economic gains and financial security that characterize many older Americans today.

Stillion and her colleagues point out, however, that this decline in suicide rates among older adults may not remain stable as the aging cohort of "baby boomers" moves toward older adulthood. Perhaps because of limited resources and opportunities, "groups that constitute larger portions of the total population tend to have higher suicide rates than groups that constitute smaller portions."[85]

It has been noted that "elderly people complete suicide more often while making failed attempts less often than people in all other age groups."[86] The ratio of attempts to completions among persons over age 65 is reportedly only 4:1. As with other age groups, suicide among the elderly is likely to be underreported. "The cause of death among the elderly is often more difficult to determine. Older people can, for example, take overdoses of prescription medications, mix drugs, fail to take essential medicine, or starve themselves."[87]

Double suicides (also known as suicide pacts), although rare, do occur among the elderly. The typical double suicide involves an older couple, one or both of whom are physically ill. Heavy alcohol use by one or both partners is also common. Such couples tend to be "interdependent and isolated from other

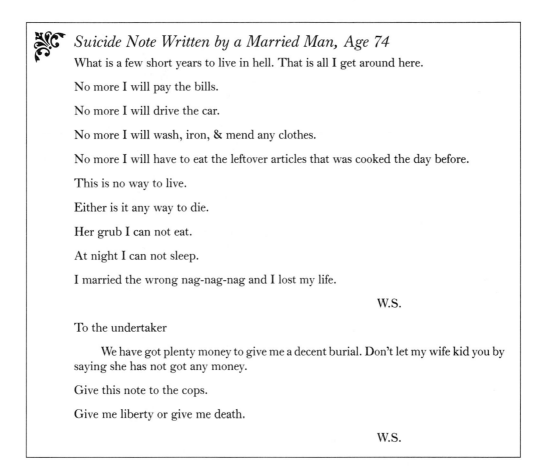

Suicide Note Written by a Married Man, Age 74

What is a few short years to live in hell. That is all I get around here.

No more I will pay the bills.

No more I will drive the car.

No more I will wash, iron, & mend any clothes.

No more I will have to eat the leftover articles that was cooked the day before.

This is no way to live.

Either is it any way to die.

Her grub I can not eat.

At night I can not sleep.

I married the wrong nag-nag-nag and I lost my life.

W.S.

To the undertaker

We have got plenty money to give me a decent burial. Don't let my wife kid you by saying she has not got any money.

Give this note to the cops.

Give me liberty or give me death.

W.S.

sources of support." Stillion and her colleagues state that there seems to be a "special chemistry" between couples who commit suicide together: "Typically, the more suicidal partner tends to be dominant and the more ambivalent partner tends to be passive in the relationship."[88]

Contemplating Suicide

Imagine for a moment the progression of thoughts of someone seriously considering suicide. Assume first that in an untenable situation suicide seems the only recourse, or at the least an option to be considered further. The next step might involve formulating some means of killing oneself. At this point the means have not been actually acquired, but various possibilities are considered.

Many people have reached this stage — perhaps through mere fantasizing, or perhaps with serious intentions. For some, the shock of recognizing that one is harboring such thoughts is enough to force a decision toward a more life-affirming alternative. For others, once the means of suicide is decided upon, the next

Käthe Kollwitz, Library of Congress

Despair, a common component of many suicides, is starkly depicted in this lithograph, Nachdenkende Frau, *by Käthe Kollwitz. If the potential victim's warning signals are observed by persons who take steps to provide crisis intervention, the suicidal impulses may be thwarted.*

step toward suicide is taken, a step that greatly increases the level of lethality with regard to suicidal intention.

This stage involves actually acquiring the means to kill oneself, thus setting into motion the logistics that make suicide a real possibility. As at the earlier steps in this sequence, a change of mind is still possible, and a different solution can be sought. Otherwise, the final step in the suicidal progression comes into play: actually using the means that have been acquired to commit the suicidal act.

These steps toward lethality have been described as occurring in a definite sequence, but to the person involved the process may be experienced as anything but logical and orderly. In actuality, suicide typically involves a complex array of conflicting thoughts and emotions. The predominant experience may be one of confusion. Still, recognizing the particular steps that must be taken to carry out the suicidal act is useful for understanding both the amount of sustained effort involved in completing a suicide and the many decision points at which a change of mind or outside intervention is possible.

Choice of Method

Once a decision is made to commit suicide, a choice must be made concerning the means to be used (see Figure 13-2). Sometimes a particular method of suicide is chosen because of the image it represents to the suicidal individual. One might imagine drowning as a dreamy kind of death, a merging back into the universe. Or one might associate an overdose of sleeping pills with the death of a movie star. Whatever one's image of a particular method, the reality is likely to be quite different. Some persons who overdose on drugs do so expecting a quiet or peaceful death. The actual effects of a drug overdose are usually far from peaceful or serene.

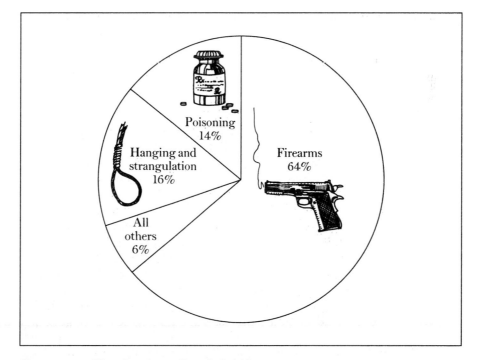

Figure *13-2*   *How Americans Commit Suicide*
Source: National Center for Health Statistics, *Vital Statistics of the United States.*

Resume

Razors pain you;
Rivers are damp;
Acids stain you;
And drugs cause cramp.
Guns aren't lawful;
Nooses give;
Gas smells awful;
You might as well live.

Dorothy Parker

Sometimes a particular method of suicide is chosen for its anticipated impact on survivors. In one study of suicide notes, it was found that persons using "active" methods of suicide more often communicated that rejection was a critical factor in the decision for self-injury.[89] A person who wants survivors to "really pay for all the grief they caused me" might select a means of suicide that would graphically communicate this rage. Someone who did not want to "make a scene" might choose a method imagined as being less shocking to one's survivors.

Experience and familiarity also influence the choice of suicidal method. For example, an experienced hunter well acquainted with rifles might be inclined to turn to such a weapon for suicide because of its accessibility and familiarity. Someone who understands the effects of various drugs might use them to concoct a fatal overdose.

In short, the choice of suicidal method reflects the experience and state of mind of the person choosing it. It may be a spontaneous choice, the person picking whatever lethal devices are readily at hand. Or it may be the result of considerable thought and even research. Either way, the choice of suicide method often reveals significant information about the state of mind that led to the attempt.

The process of making this choice can be likened to making the travel arrangements for a cross-country trip. A person wanting to travel from the West Coast to the East Coast must consider the various kinds of transportation available—automobile, train, airplane, and so on. Some of these are quite rapid; others are relatively slow and deliberate. For example, once you board an airplane and it lifts off the runway, there is no opportunity to change your mind and disembark before touching down at the scheduled destination. On the other hand, someone bicycling from coast to coast would have innumerable opportunities to decide upon a different destination.

Similarly, some methods of committing suicide offer little hope of changing one's mind after the lethal act is initiated. Once the trigger is pulled on a revolver placed next to one's skull, for example, there's virtually no possibility of altering the likelihood of a fatal outcome. On the other hand, the would-be suicide who cuts her wrists or takes an overdose of drugs *might* have time to alter an otherwise fatal outcome by deciding to seek medical help. The potential for death, if help is not forthcoming, may be as great as that for the gunshot wound to the head, but the possibility of intervention is greater. There is, then, an order of lethality among methods used in the suicidal act.

Order of Lethality

The various methods used in suicide attempts are not necessarily equivalent in potential lethality. Some methods carry a greater statistical risk of lethality than others. A recent report issued by the American Medical Association has emphasized the danger of firearms, noting that more than half of all suicides in the United States are committed with guns.[90] In the following listing, eleven methods of attempting suicide are ranked from most to least lethal. Any of these methods is potentially a killer. Ranking is by probability of death from use of the method.[91]

Order of Lethality

1. Gunshot
2. Carbon monoxide
3. Hanging
4. Drowning
5. Plastic bag (suffocation)
6. Impact (from jumping from a high place)
7. Fire
8. Poison
9. Drugs
10. Gas
11. Cutting

Although each method is potentially fatal, how it is applied influences the degree of lethality. For instance, a bullet into the head or the heart is more likely to kill than a gunshot wound to other parts of the body. Likewise, with the least lethal item on this list, cutting, the depth of cut and the location of the wound are significant determinants of the outcome.

Suicide Notes

Suicide notes have been called "cryptic maps of ill-advised journeys."[92] Although it is often assumed that nearly all suicides leave notes behind for their survivors, in fact only about one-quarter of suicides write a final message. As at least a partial record of the mental state of suicides, such notes are of immense interest to the suicidologist. Imagine yourself in circumstances that would lead to your writing a suicide note. What kinds of things would you want to say in your last words to your survivors?

Many people find it difficult to distinguish between genuine and simulated suicide notes.[93] Actual suicide notes represent a wide variety of messages and

Suicide Note Written by a Married Man, Age 45

Dear Claudia,

You win, I can't take it any longer. I know you have been waiting for this to happen. I hope it makes you very happy, this is not an easy thing to do, but I've got to the point where there is nothing to live for, a little bit of kindness from you would of made everything so different, but all that ever interested you was the *dollar*.

It is pretty hard for me to do anything when you are so greedy even with this house you couldn't even be fair with that, well it's all yours now and you won't have to see the Lawyer anymore.

I wish you would give my personal things to Danny, you wouldn't get much from selling them anyway, you still have my insurance, it isn't much but it will be enough to take care of my debts and still have a few bucks left.

You always told me that I was the one that made Sharon take her life, in fact you said I killed her, but you know down deep in your heart it was you that made her do what she did, and now you have two deaths to your credit, it should make you feel very proud.

Good By Kid

P.S. Disregard all the mean things I've said in this letter, I have said a lot of things to you I didn't really mean and I hope you get well and wish you the best of everything.

Cathy — don't come in.

Call your mother, she will know what to do,

Love,
Daddy

Cathy don't go in the bedroom.

intentions. Some notes explain to survivors the decision to commit suicide. Others express anger or blame. Conversely, some notes emphasize that the writer's suicide was "no one's fault." The messages in suicide notes range from sweeping statements of the writer's philosophy or credo regarding suicide to extremely detailed listings of practical chores that will need attention after the writer's death. For example, one note instructed survivors, "The cat needs to go to the vet next Tuesday; don't miss the appointment or you'll be charged double. The car is due for servicing a week from Friday."

Suicide notes may include: expressions of love, hate, shame, disgrace, fear of insanity, self-abnegation, feelings of rejection; explanations for the suicidal act or defenses of the right to take one's life; disavowal of any survivor's responsibility for the suicide; instructions for distributing the suicide's property and possessions. Genuine suicide notes typically display dichotomies of logic, hostility toward others mixed with self-blame, the use of particular names and specific instructions to survivors, and a sense of decisiveness about suicide. A theme of many is that of an intense love-hate ambivalence toward survivors, as expressed succinctly in the following suicide note:

> Dear Betty:
>   I hate you.
>   Love,
>   George

This example of ambivalence also points up the dyadic nature of suicide—here involving husband and wife. Suicide notes often provide clues about the intentions and emotions that led the person to suicide, but they rarely tell the whole story—and they often raise more questions than they answer. The message of a suicide note may come as a surprise to survivors who previously had no hint of the person's feelings.

Suicide notes often have a significant effect on survivors. Whether the final message is one of affection or of blame, survivors have no opportunity to respond. In this sense, suicide represents the ultimate last word.

Suicide Prevention, Intervention, and Postvention

The Los Angeles Suicide Prevention Center, founded in 1958 by Norman L. Farberow and Edwin S. Shneidman, became the prototype for prevention and crisis centers not only in the United States but throughout the world.[94] As Stillion and others have noted:

> The importance of the Los Angeles Suicide Prevention Center cannot be overstated in any history of suicide. The work begun in that center by Shneidman and his associates, and expanded upon later when Shneidman became director of the Suicide Center in the National Institute of Mental Health, changed the nation's view of suicide and suicidal behavior. The most important change was a shift away from seeing suicide as an act committed by an insane person to seeing it as an act committed by a person who felt overwhelming ambivalence toward life.[95]

The ensuing decades have seen a dramatic increase in the number of suicide crisis centers, coupled with the rise of telephone hotlines focusing on suicide prevention among specific groups. For example, during the severe economic crisis affecting American farmers and ranchers, a suicide hotline was established for people in rural areas.[96] The typical suicide prevention center operates primarily as a telephone-answering center with around-the-clock availability to persons in crisis. The services provided are mainly designed to serve as a short-term resource for persons contemplating suicide. The caller's anonymity is respected, and the caller's expressed need of help is unquestioningly accepted. Staff members—some of them professionals, many of them volunteers who have been given special training—make use of various helping strategies to reduce the suicidal caller's stress.

As the incidence of suicide and the problems associated with it have increased, some suicide intervention centers have expanded their services to encompass treatment for a broad range of self-destructive behaviors. For example, the Los Angeles Suicide Prevention Center offers a variety of counseling and community services. Low-cost counseling is available for potential suicide victims as well as for the survivors of a friend's or relative's suicide. Clinics have been instituted to provide treatment for depression and drug abuse. Community-based programs for former offenders who have been released back into society and for troubled youths also have been implemented to assist individuals in overcoming destructive behaviors. The activities of the Los Angeles Suicide Prevention Center exemplify the understanding of suicide as a subset of a larger class of self-destructive behaviors, all of which require attention if tragedy is to be averted.

Prevention

There is little reason to be optimistic about the prospect of preventing suicide, at least in the sense of eliminating it from the repertory of human behaviors. To do so, the sources of human unhappiness and dissatisfaction would have to be eradicated. Unfortunately, efforts to create a social environment that is conducive to the pursuit of happiness inevitably fall short of perfection. Interpersonal problems and social pressures thwart the achievement of universal happiness and satisfaction. This is not to say that efforts to ameliorate human suffering are unavailing, only that they are inherently limited.

Nevertheless, much can be done to reduce suicide risk. Education is considered an essential element in any program of suicide prevention. Many such programs concentrate on providing education about suicide to school-age children and adolescents. The lessons to be learned, however, can be applied for the most part across the lifespan, and they include the following key points: First, it is crucial to acknowledge the reality that life is complex and that all of us will inevitably have experiences of disappointment, failure, and loss in our lives. Second, we can learn to deal with such experiences by developing appropriate coping techniques, including the skills of critical thinking. Individuals "who form a habit early of analyzing situations from a variety of perspectives, of asking appropriate questions, and of testing the reality of their own thinking are far less likely to settle easily into the cognitive inflexibility that focuses on suicide as *the* solution."[97] A corollary of such coping skills involves the cultivation of a sense of humor, especially the ability to laugh at oneself and at life's problems, to see the humor in situations. Finally, education can be directed toward learning how to set appropriate and attainable goals. This last point has special importance for the young person. "Young people who experience a wide gulf between who they are and who they want to become are at risk for low self-concepts, self-hatred, depression, and suicidal behavior."[98] The importance of adequate self-esteem as a preventive against suicide has been stressed repeatedly.[99]

In recent years, a number of school-based suicide awareness and prevention programs have been established.[100] Books about suicide for young people have also become more widely available than in the past.[101] Nevertheless, much remains to be done, in terms of both fine-tuning present programs and expanding current efforts. For example, some educators have made the case that young males require a different kind of suicide awareness program than the one generally provided.[102] They argue that, in comparison to males, females appear to be more sensitive to suicide and its management, especially with respect to their willingness to seek and accept help when in crisis. Males, on the other hand, need to learn how to respond to their own "cries for help," rather than denying them.

Suicide prevention programs also need to be expanded to reach more adequately the populations at greatest risk. Among a group of native Ojibway/Cree communities in Ontario, Canada, for example, the Muskrat Dam community has organized a group known as Helping Hands to confront the "new phenomenon" of suicide in a culture that was previously unaffected by it.[103] Patterning its response to this crisis after traditional spiritual values, the Helping Hands project has as its main objectives instilling a sense of value within the youth and general community population, rebuilding the lives of disturbed youth to enable them to proceed with direction and purpose, restoring pride and a sense of well-being within members of the community, motivating the young people to lead constructive and productive lives, providing life-skills training that can be applied within the family and community, and assisting individuals in the development of good mechanisms for coping with mental health problems. Programs like Helping Hands, which are sensitive to the needs of a particular community or segment of the population at risk for suicide, represent a crucial adjunct to more conventional methods of suicide prevention.

Intervention

Whereas suicide prevention, strictly defined, aims to eliminate suicide risk, the goal of suicide intervention is to reduce the lethality of the individual suicidal crisis. Although in practice many suicide intervention programs are named "suicide prevention centers," such programs generally use the theories and techniques common to crisis intervention. Their emphasis is on providing short-term care and treatment to persons who are actively in a suicidal crisis in order to reduce the inherent lethality of suicide.

As Evans and Farberow point out, the cardinal rule in suicide intervention is to *do something*.[104] Intervention means taking threats seriously; watching for clues to suicidal intentions and behaviors; answering cries for help by offering support, understanding, and compassion; confronting the problem by asking questions and not being afraid to discuss suicide with the person in crisis; obtaining professional help to manage the crisis; and offering constructive alternatives to suicide. A key theme of suicide intervention is that talking is a positive step toward resolving the crisis. Stillion and her colleagues provide the following general principles that can help untrained individuals respond to a person who may be suicidal:[105]

When I was thirteen months old, my mother killed herself. So I eventually learned, as I learned her maiden name, Georgia Saphronia Collier, and where she was born, Sulphur Springs, Arkansas, and how old she was when she ended her life, twenty-nine. (And good lord, writing these words now, all these years afterward, for the first time in memory my eyes have filled with tears of mourning for her. What impenetrable vessel preserved them?) I didn't know my mother, except as infants know. At the beginning of my life the world acquired a hole. That's what I knew, that there was a hole in the world. For me there still is. It's a singularity. In and out of a hole like that, anything goes.

Richard Rhodes, *A Hole in the World:*
An American Boyhood

1. At the outset, determine the seriousness of the suicidal intent. Generally, the quickest method for ascertaining intent involves asking direct questions.
2. Having ascertained the immediate level of danger, ensure that the suicidal person is not left alone, especially when he or she is emotionally upset and may act impulsively.
3. Secure qualified help as soon as possible.

The emotional support of the suicidal person's family is considered essential in limiting the risk that suicidal intentions will be carried through to completion.[106] When family support is inadequate, other sources of support must be sought out and provided.

Postvention

Suicide *postvention*, a term coined by Edwin Shneidman, refers to the assistance given to *all* survivors of suicide, including those who attempt suicide as well as the families, friends, and associates of those who commit suicide. Evans and Farberow state: "It means, simply, extending to suicide survivors the caring support they need immediately after a suicide and, in time, assisting them in their coming to terms with a tragedy that has struck them."[107] As discussed in an earlier chapter on grief, the bereaved survivors of suicide have special needs, for they often experience feelings of guilt and self-blame which need to be adequately confronted. When these feelings are not dealt with or are mismanaged, the likelihood of dysfunctional relationships, emotional problems, and other difficulties in the lives of suicide survivors increases.

Helping a Person Who is in Suicidal crisis

Warnings that an individual is considering suicide may be communicated in a variety of ways. Evans and Farberow point out that suicidal intent may be expressed in four main ways: (1) *verbal direct* ("I will shoot myself if you leave me"), (2) *verbal indirect* ("A life without love is a life without meaning"), (3) *behavioral direct* (for example, a chronically ill person hoarding pills), and (4) *behavioral indirect*.[108] Among the warning signs that fall under this last category, Evans and Farberow mention:

1. Giving away prized possessions, making a will, or attending to other "final" arrangements;
2. Sudden and extreme changes in eating habits or sleep patterns;
3. Withdrawal from friends or family, or other major behavioral changes accompanied by depression;
4. Changes in school or job performance;
5. Personality changes, such as nervousness, outbursts of anger, or apathy about health or appearance;
6. Use of drugs or alcohol

The recent suicide of a friend or relative, as well as a history of previous suicide attempts, also should be considered as warning signs of potentially increased suicide risk.

A number of commonly held beliefs, or myths, have grown up about suicide and about the kind of person who is likely to commit suicide. Unfortunately, many of these beliefs, being false, are harmful, for they have the effect of depriving the suicidal person of needed help. As you review the listing of fallacies about suicide given in Table 13-6, notice which ones you may have believed or unconsciously incorporated into your assumptions about suicide. According to Charles Neuringer, these myths about suicide arise because suicide defies the primary law of nature — survival itself — and raises doubts about the worth of living.[109] By developing a set of false beliefs about suicide, we avoid facing basic issues about life and death and thereby reduce our discomfort. Nevertheless, it is important that we separate fact from fallacy if we wish to understand suicide or help the person who is in a suicidal crisis.

If a person says, "I feel like killing myself," that statement should not be taken lightly or brushed aside with the quick response, "Oh, well, you'll probably feel better tomorrow." To the person in crisis, there may seem little hope of a "tomorrow" at all. It is important to pay attention to the message being communicated. Similarly, responding to such a statement with a provocation — "You wouldn't be capable of committing suicide!" — or with a tone of moral superiority — "I don't want to hear such immoral and unhealthy talk!" — may be damaging, deepening rather than alleviating the suicidal crisis. A response that provides only a litany of the "good reasons" why the person should not commit suicide may also offer little practical assistance to the person in crisis.

More helpful is listening carefully to exactly what the person in crisis is communicating; the tone and context of statements should reveal to the sensitive listener something about the communicator's real intent. Often, remarks about suicide are made in an offhand manner: "If I don't get that job, I'll kill myself!" Perhaps the remark is a figure of speech, much as in the joking statement, "I'll kill you for that!" There is a tendency to discount such statements in a culture where

TABLE 13-6   Myths and Facts About Suicide

Myth: *People who talk about suicide don't commit suicide.*
Fact: This fallacy has been called the "grand old myth of suicide," one that excuses the failure to respond to another person's cry for help. Most people who attempt suicide communicate their intentions to others, as hints, direct threats, or self-destructive actions or preparations for suicide. Unfortunately, these cries for help often go unheeded by friends, family members, co-workers, or health care personnel.

Myth: *Improvement in a suicidal person means the risk of suicide has passed.*
Fact: Improvement may be necessary before a severely depressed person can take the steps necessary to carry out the suicidal intention. Many suicides occur within three to six months following apparent improvement. Thus, an apparently positive change in mood can be a danger signal: Making the decision to carry out the suicidal act can be exhilarating and freeing; the person feels, "Now that I've made the decision, I no longer have to agonize about what I'm going to do." This relief is subject to misinterpretation by others, who may believe the crisis has passed.

Myth: *Once a suicide risk, always a suicide risk.*
Fact: The peak of suicidal crisis is generally brief. The simultaneous conjunction of the thought of killing oneself, possession of the means to complete the act, and the lack of help or intervention is a more or less unusual set of circumstances. If intervention occurs, the suicidal person may well be able to put suicidal thoughts behind and lead a productive life.

Myth: *Suicide is inherited.*
Fact: Although this fallacy gives suicidal behavior an aura of biological fate, the fact is that suicide does not "run in families," in the sense of being a genetically inherited trait. However, dysfunctional family patterns with respect to problem solving or surviving the suicide of a loved one may create beliefs about suicide that influence a person's subsequent behavior. The fear that one has a greater potential for suicide may create a self-fulfilling prophecy. In this sense, the suicide of

"talk is cheap," and "actions speak louder than words."[110] When a suicidal threat is intended seriously, however, it deserves to be taken seriously. To do otherwise is to fall prey to the myth that "talking about suicide means the person will not really go through with it."

These less than helpful tendencies can be counteracted by knowledge of the patterns of suicidal behavior and by the ability to distinguish facts from fallacies. Another way to assist the person in crisis is to become acquainted with the community crisis intervention resources that are available.

Perhaps most important, become aware of your own attitudes about life, death, and suicide. When working with someone who is struggling with suicidal thoughts, you should recognize that no one can take *ultimate* responsibility for

TABLE 13-6, *continued*

a family member may provide an excuse, or make it easier, to contemplate suicide as a means of escape from a difficult situation.

Myth: *Suicide affects only a specific group or class of people.*

Fact: Suicide is not the "curse of the poor" or a "disease of the rich." It occurs among all socioeconomic groups and affects individuals with widely divergent life styles. Social integration is a more important determinant of suicidal behavior than socioeconomic class.

Myth: *Suicidal individuals are insane.*

Fact: Although it is true that some suicides are mentally ill, the planning and carrying out of suicide usually requires careful reasoning and deliberate judgment. Many suicide notes reveal not only ambivalence but also considerable lucidity about the writer's intentions. Despite its devastating effect on the individual's physical being, suicide can be considered as a defensive act or problem-solving technique to preserve the integrity of the self.

Myth: *Suicidal individuals are fully intent on dying.*

Fact: Actually, most suicides are undecided about continuing to live or ending their lives. In their ambivalence, they may gamble with death, leaving the possibility of rescue to fate. Although some attempters do ultimately commit suicide after previously uncompleted attempts, the majority do not. Thus, a suicide attempt may signal that a person's pyschological or interpersonal needs are not being satisfactorily met and a change is desired; it does not necessarily indicate that he or she wants to die.

Myth: *The motive for a particular suicide is clearly evident.*

Fact: People often try to establish a quick "cause" for suicide, attributing it to economic hardship, disappointment in love, or some other immediate condition. Deeper analysis usually uncovers a lengthy sequence of self-destructive behaviors leading up to the act of suicide. The apparent "cause" may be simply the final step of a complex pattern of self-destructive acts.

---

another's decision to end his or her life. Doing what can be done without trying to assume total responsibility may be difficult when one's inclination is to preserve life, yet only so much can be done to assist another person in crisis.

In the short term, it may be feasible to keep someone from taking his or her life. Constant vigilance or custodial care of some kind may be available to prevent suicide during a brief period of intense suicidal crisis. But the decision to assume responsibility for preventing someone else's suicide over a prolonged period is extremely difficult to implement. How much responsibility one feels comfortable assuming for another person must be feasible and consonant with the particular situation. A terminally ill man dying in great pain said to his wife: "You'd better keep my medication out of reach, because I don't want to keep up this struggle

Graffiti

I find a snapshot
buried in my father's drawer.
A picture of the grandfather I never knew.
Small, stooped yet dignified he stands
beside my brother's wicker pram
surrounded by his family.
My mother tells the story, hidden in the past
of the last time she saw him.
She was big with child, and so allowed to sit
while his two daughters served the sons
who gathered at the table.
Grandma who reigned as always at the head
arranged the seating of those sons
not in the order of their age
but of the weekly wage they earned
and without question brought to her.

I learn that you, mild gentle man
never at home in the new language, the new land,
subdued by failure, each passing year withdrew
further into old world memories, and silence.
Rising that evening from the table, as usual
scarcely noticed as you went to lie down
on your narrow bed, there was no sign, no signal.
Only that as you passed, you bent
with a shy unaccustomed show of tenderness
to murmur "*Liebchen*" and to kiss my mother's head.
She tells me that I leaped and struggled in her womb
when from your room you shattered silence
with a shot. Your life exploding
sudden messages across blank walls in bursts of red.

Maude Meehan

any longer." The wife was forced to decide whether she could take responsibility for his choice of either continuing to live with pain or ending his life by an overdose. After much soul searching, she concluded that, although she had great compassion for his predicament and did not want him to suffer, she could not assume the responsibility for safeguarding his medication, doling out one pill at a time, constantly fearful that he might locate the drugs and attempt suicide anyway.

Not taking responsibility does not mean that one must go to the opposite extreme, expressing such an attitude as, "Well, if you're going to kill yourself, then get it over with!" Although one should recognize that there are inherent

Once a person is this close to the suicidal act, the chance of a successful intervention is usually slight. Fortunately, in this dramatic instance intervention was successful.

Stanley Forman, Boston Herald American

limits to how much one person can protect another from that person's own self-destructiveness, one can at the same time offer life-affirming support and compassion.

The suicidal person is probably experiencing considerable ambivalence about acting on his or her thoughts of suicide. The person may seem intent on suicide while hoping for some intervention. It is important to sustain or stimulate that person's desire to live. Plans for self-destruction are likely to proceed apace with fantasies or plans for rescue. The person who happens to be cast in the role of helper in such a drama can try to affirm the individual's beliefs that there are choices other than suicide.

One way to help persons in crisis is to help them discover what about themselves *can* matter, however small or insignificant it may seem. It is important that something be found that matters *to the person*. A useful way to elicit this information is to ask the person to think of something he or she has found valuable about himself or herself in the past. Once it has been found, ask the person what the possibilities are of continuing that sense of value into the present.

Asking the person what is useful, what he or she needs in order to feel valuable and worthwhile, may be a matter of survival. Some people do not survive; others can survive, with assistance from others and commitment from themselves. The sustaining motivation to survive cannot come from without; it has to be generated from within the person's own experience. In the short term, external support can help to ensure survival during the peak period of crisis. But one should be skeptical of the notion that one person can sustain another person's will to live over the long term.

Suicidal thoughts and behaviors indicate a critical loss of a person's belief that he or she is someone who matters. The feeling that nothing matters, in the sense that one's life is in complete disarray, is not by itself the stimulus for suicide. More important to suicidal thoughts and behaviors is the person's belief that "I don't matter." As we have seen, those two streams of thought in combination — the sense that the external situation is unsatisfactory and that one does not matter enough to improve it — can lead to death by suicide. As has been well stated, "Suicide is a permanent solution to what is most likely a temporary problem."[111]

Further Readings

Alfred Alvarez. *The Savage God: A Study of Suicide*. New York: Random House, 1971.

Margaret Pabst Battin. *Ethical Issues in Suicide*. Englewood Cliffs, N.J.: Prentice-Hall, 1982.

Albert C. Cain, ed. *Survivors of Suicide*. Springfield, Ill.: Charles C. Thomas, 1972.

David Chidester. *Salvation and Suicide: An Interpretation of Jim Jones, the Peoples Temple, and Jonestown*. Bloomington: Indiana University Press, 1988.

Jacques Choron. *Suicide*. New York: Charles Scribner's Sons, 1972.

Fred Cutter. *Art and the Wish to Die*. Chicago: Nelson-Hall, 1983.

Norman L. Farberow, ed. *Suicide in Different Cultures*. Baltimore: University Park Press, 1975.

Larry Gernsbacher. *The Suicide Syndrome: Origins, Manifestations, and Alleviation of Human Self-Destructiveness*. New York: Human Sciences, 1985.

Sidney Goldstein. *Suicide in Rabbinic Literature*. Hoboken, N.J.: KTAV Publishing House, 1989.

Earl A. Grollman. *Suicide: Prevention, Intervention, Postvention*. 2d ed. Boston: Beacon Press, 1988.

Corrine Loing Hatton and Sharon McBride Valente, eds. *Suicide: Assessment and Intervention*. 2d ed. Norwalk, Conn.: Appleton-Century-Crofts, 1984.

Lee A. Headley, ed. *Suicide in Asia and the Near East*. Berkeley: University of California Press, 1983.

Herbert Hendin. *Suicide in America*. New York: W.W. Norton, 1982.

Syed Arshad Husain and Trish Vandiver. *Suicide in Children and Adolescents*. New York: SP Medical & Scientific Books, 1984.

Norman Linzer, ed. *Suicide: The Will to Live vs. the Will to Die*. New York: Human Sciences Press, 1984.

Ronald Maris, ed. *Understanding and Preventing Suicide*. New York: Guilford Press, 1988.

Karl Menninger. *Man Against Himself*. New York: Harcourt, Brace & World, 1938.

Israel Orbach. *Children Who Don't Want to Live: Understanding and Treating the Suicidal Child*. San Francisco: Jossey-Bass, 1988.

Seymour Perlin, ed. *A Handbook for the Study of Suicide*. New York: Oxford University Press, 1975.

David K. Reynolds and Norman L. Farberow. *Suicide: Inside and Out*. Berkeley: University of California Press, 1976.

Judith Stillion, Eugene McDowell, and Jacque May, eds. *Suicide Across the Life Span: Premature Exits*. New York: Hemisphere, 1989.

Louis Wekstein. *Handbook of Suicidology: Principles, Problems, and Practice*. New York: Brunner/Mazel, 1979.

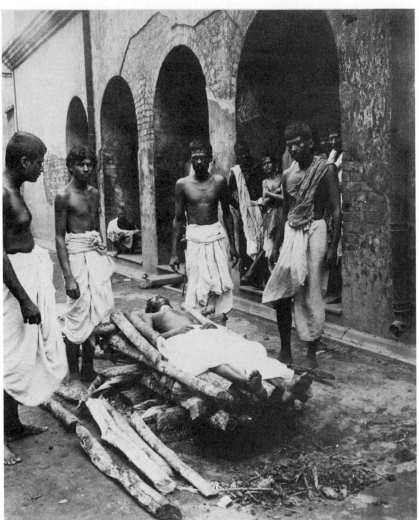

The corpse placed on the funeral pyre, these men prepare to light the cremation fire. Cremation has been a traditional practice in India, where Hindus believe that "even as the person casts off worn-out clothes and puts on others that are new, so the embodied Self casts off worn-out bodies and enters into others that are new."

CHAPTER *14*

Beyond Death/After Life

*D*eath — and then what?

Some people have a ready answer to this perennial question: "When you're dead, you're dead — that's it!" or, "You go through a transition and take birth in another body," or, "After you die you go to heaven," or, "Your body is buried until the end of time when it's resurrected and you live again." Each of these responses reflects a particular understanding of the meaning of human existence. Beliefs about life after death occupy a broad spectrum, from the notion that death spells the end, to the notion that the "soul" or "self" lives on after death in some fashion. Answering the question "What happens after I die?" has occupied the attention of human beings since the dawn of consciousness.

This concern with immortality — that is, the attribute of survival after physical death — is cut from the same cloth as questions about the meaning of life and the corollary, "How, then, should one live?" Responses to these questions reflect a person's values and beliefs about human experience and the nature of reality. Our philosophy of life influences our philosophy of death. Conversely, how we perceive death and what meaning we give it affect the way we live.

Indeed, to someone who holds a well-defined and unequivocal view about the future state of existence following this present life, death might be seen as the "meaning" of the present life. At its most extreme, such a viewpoint might postulate that some other state of existence is actually the *reason* for the present life. Stephen J. Vicchio points out, however, that such a view

527

> Every time an earth mother smiles over the birth of a child, a spirit mother weeps over the loss of a child.
>
> Ashanti saying

contains a logical fallacy because it fails to address the question of the meaning of *this* life.[1]

Many of us would agree with Socrates that "the unexamined life is not worth living." Such self-investigation includes the discovery of what one believes about death and its consequences. Ambivalence about the issue of survival after death is aptly described in an anecdote related by Bertrand Russell: A woman whose daughter had recently died was asked what she thought had become of her daughter's soul. She replied, "Oh, well, I suppose she is enjoying eternal bliss, but I wish you wouldn't talk about such unpleasant subjects."[2]

Concepts of Death and Immortality

Exploring your beliefs about immortality may not result in an easier acceptance of death — nor should it necessarily. After all, the prospect of immortality is not always looked upon favorably.[3] Even so, such an exploration can lead to a more coherent philosophy of life and death, making possible a congruence of hopes and perceptions. In this chapter we explore the meaning of mortality by investigating some of the ways that cultures ancient and modern, Eastern and Western, have answered the question, "What happens after death?" The answers voiced by ancient thinkers as well as the theories put forward by present-day researchers provide grist for the mill of our own contemplation of this ultimate human concern.

Age-Old Beliefs About Afterlife

The notion that life continues on in some form after death is one of the oldest concepts held by human beings. In some of the earliest known graves, archaeologists have uncovered skeletons that were bound by hands and feet into a fetal position, perhaps indicating beliefs about "rebirth" into other forms of existence following death. We know that in traditional societies death represents a change of status for the deceased, a transition from the land of the living to the land of the dead.

Some form of judgment is a key feature of many beliefs about what follows death. Among the various concepts of afterlife among traditional Hawaiians, for example, was the belief that a person who had offended a god or who had harmed others would suffer eternal punishment.[4] Such an unworthy soul became a wandering spirit, "forever homeless, forever hungry." The ancestor-gods had the power to punish or reward the released spirit, or even to send it back to the body. Misfortune also could result when a person had neither loving relatives to care for

William Hodges, Bishop Museum

The platform burial of a Tahitian chief is depicted in this drawing by William Hodges, made during Captain Cook's second voyage to the South Pacific in the 1770s.

In a world populated by unseen spirits who could exert their influence for good or evil upon the living, the death of a chief or other important person occasioned a spectacular display of grief, which was presided over by a chief mourner (right). Usually a priest or close relative of the deceased, the chief mourner wore an elaborate costume of pearl shells and the feathers of tropic birds. Rattling a pearl shell clapper and brandishing a long wooden weapon inset with sharks' teeth, the chief mourner was accompanied by other weapon-carrying men who could strike anyone in their way, thus helping ensure that funeral rites were carried out in a manner that would offend neither the living nor the dead.

Bishop Museum

the corpse nor the guardianship of family ancestor-gods to help souls find their way to the world of spirits. Thus, those who had lived worthily were welcomed into eternity, whereas those who had done misdeeds in life, without repenting for or correcting them, were punished. The reward for living a good life was eternity with those closest to the family-loving Hawaiian: one's own ancestors.

To understand the consciousness from which such a view of immortality arises, the notions of self that have developed in Western cultures during modern times must be put aside momentarily. Against the emphasis on individual identity and the self, imagine a mentality in which group identity is all-encompassing. The family, the clan, the people — these social groups represent the loci of communal consciousness within which the thoughts and actions of the individual are subsumed. Thus, these age-old beliefs convey less concern with individual survival than a desire for the continuation of the community and its common heritage. Having shared in the life of the group, the individual participates in its ultimate destiny, a destiny that can transcend even death.

Death and Resurrection in the Hebrew Tradition

Considered as a whole, the books of the Bible do not provide a systematic theology of death or of the afterlife. Death is not ignored, but the biblical literature about it reflects a progression of ideas over a long period of time. The biblical story describes a people whose concerns were focused on a communal destiny. Individuals were seen as actors in the unfolding drama, and its denouement was foretold in the promises made by Yahweh.

As the patriarch Abraham lay dying, his last thoughts were for the continuation of his progeny so that these promises could be realized in the unfolding of history. Abraham's vision is reiterated by the biblical writers in one circumstance after another as they affirm the destiny of the clan and of the nation of Israel. By contributing to this common destiny, the righteous person never ceased to be part of the continuing story of the people as a whole.

As the expression of Judaic thought changed over time, there were corresponding changes in the understanding of mortality and its meaning. In the story of Job's encounter with adversity and death, the human situation is described bleakly: "As a cloud fades away and disappears, so a person who goes down to the grave will not come up from it."[5] This resignation toward death is echoed in the other Wisdom books — including Proverbs, Ecclesiastes, and some of the Psalms — which present the thought of the ancient Hebrew sages on the question of human destiny. Righteous conduct is advised because it leads to harmony in the present life, not because it guarantees future rewards for the individual.

Between the time of Job and the time of the prophets there was gradual change from resignation to hopefulness in the face of death. In the apocalyptic, or visionary, writings of prophets such as Daniel and Ezekiel, we see the strands of thought that eventually are woven together in the notions that describe the resurrection of the body. Daniel envisions a future in which the "sleeping" dead will awaken, "some to everlasting life, some to everlasting disgrace."[6]

"There is always hope for a tree:
    when felled, it can start its life again;
    its shoots continue to sprout.
Its roots may be decayed in the earth,
    its stump withering in the soil,
but let it scent the water, and it buds,
    and puts out branches like a plant new set.
But man? He dies, and lifeless he remains;
    man breathes his last, and then where is he?
The waters of the sea may disappear,
    all the rivers may run dry or drain away;
but man, once in his resting place, will never rise again.
    The heavens will wear away before he wakes,
    before he rises from his sleep."

Job 14:7–12, *The Jerusalem Bible*

Hints of this change are also evident in the meanings ascribed over time to the Hebrew word *She'ol*, which in early usage is generally defined as the underworld of the dead, a shadowy realm of disembodied souls. An old story gives an account of necromancy in which King Saul requests the witch of En-dor to summon the spirit of the dead prophet Samuel. Asked by Saul to describe what she sees, the witch of En-dor replies, "I see a ghost (*elohim* = superhuman being) rising up from the earth (*She'ol*)." Later, with further refinement of these concepts, the shadowy underworld of *She'ol* is divided into two distinct realms: *Gehinom* (hell) and *Pardes* (heaven or paradise).[7]

The idea of the resurrection of the body is an important development in Hebrew thought, one that came to influence Christian theology. Stated succinctly, this view of survival after death "consists in the belief that, at the end of time, the bodies of the dead will be resurrected from the grave and reconstituted."[8]

In the main, the evolving doctrine of resurrection did not alter the essential understanding in Hebrew psychology of the human person as an undivided psychophysical entity. Although the breath or spirit was sometimes identified with a "principle of vitality" that is common to all forms of conscious life, there was no intrinsically immortal element that could be distinguished as somehow separate from the whole person. As Wheeler Robinson wrote, "The Hebrew idea of personality is an animated body, and not an incarnated soul."[9] In other words, the soul does not *take* a body, but rather the body *has* life. In this understanding of personhood, such concepts as body or soul cannot be abstracted from the essential integrity of the human person. (As we will see, this understanding is quite different from the ancient Greek ideas about the soul surviving the death of the body, ideas that have influenced all subsequent Western thought about death and immortality.)

> For the whole world is the sepulchre of famous men, and it is not the epitaph upon monuments set up in their own land that alone commemorates them, but also in lands not their own there abides in each breast an unwritten memorial of them, planted in the heart rather than graven on stone.
>
> Thucydides, *The Peloponnesian War*

The consensus expressed by the biblical writers seems to be: "Our present existence is of God; if there is life hereafter, it will also be God's gift. Thus, what need is there for anxiety about death? What matters is to live righteously and to ensure the well-being and survival of the community." The characteristic theme of Hebraic tradition concerns the importance of faith—faith in the people of Israel as a community with a common destiny, and faith in Yahweh, whose promises will be realized in the unfolding of the divine plan. The enduring concern is that one should not lose sight of the tasks at hand.

Hellenistic Concepts of Immortality

Among the ancient Greeks, or Hellenes, there were differing views about what might follow upon the death of the body. Generally, however, the afterworld was not an attractive prospect. The realm of the dead was usually pictured as a shadowy place, inhabited by bloodless phantoms. It is perhaps not surprising, therefore, that death seems to have elicited feelings of despair.

As with their contemporaries elsewhere, the ancient Greeks of the Hellenistic Age did not think about death in the same way many people do today. Rather than focusing on the status of the individual, they were preoccupied with communal concerns. In the Athenian democracy, for instance, what mattered was the survival of the *polis*, the corporate existence of the city-state. Personal immortality became important only to the extent that it affected the survival of the community. Within this context, an individual could hope to achieve social immortality by fulfilling the responsibilities of citizenship—that is, by performing actions directed toward the common good. Since heroic acts are remembered by the community, the hero achieves a renown that extends beyond a single lifetime.

For those who sought more than symbolic immortality, assurances of happiness beyond death could be had by participating in one of the mystery religions, cults whose origins are clouded in the mists of prehistory. By dedicating themselves to the rites of purification prescribed by the priests of the mystery cult, they could exchange the dire picture of the afterworld for the more promising one of an idyllic future in paradise.

Among the early Greek philosophers, speculation about the afterlife generally conformed to the popular beliefs of their culture. Most conceived of life and death as aspects of an ever-changing, eternal flux. Although they believed that the soul was the vital principle that continued in some fashion after death, they generally did not imagine that the soul would survive as a distinct entity, as the

Speak not smoothly of death, I beseech you, O famous Odysseus. Better by far to remain on earth the thrall of another . . . rather than reign sole king in the realm of bodyless phantoms.

Homer, *The Odyssey*

personality or self of a particular individual. To many early Greek thinkers, whatever it was that continued beyond death merged with the stuff of the universe.

Somewhat later, Pythagoras taught that one's conduct during life determined the destiny of the soul after death. Thus, with discipline and purification, one could influence the transmigration of the soul — successive rounds of birth and death — that led to eventual union with the Divine or Universal Absolute. These beliefs drew upon the Orphic mystery religions of earlier Greece that went back to the ancient cult of Dionysus. The notion that how a person conducted himself or herself in this life could influence the soul's existence in the afterlife contrasted with the predominant view of a rather indistinct immortality in which all participated regardless of their actions. Nevertheless, the ideas expressed by Pythagoras and his followers would eventually find a wider acceptance in somewhat altered form during the pre-Christian era, and the connection between conduct and immortality would be further refined during the early centuries of Christianity.

With Socrates, there are also indications of a belief in the possibility of personal survival after death. Precisely what Socrates believed in this regard is unclear, although he seems to have favored the notion that the individual soul would survive after the death of the body. On his deathbed, he describes his sense of anticipation at the prospect of communion with the spirits of the great in the afterworld. But, in the *Apology*, he describes death as *either* eternal bliss *or* dreamless sleep.

The concept of immortality of the soul — an idea that pervaded Orphic thought in ancient Greece and that Pythagoras and Socrates favored — was further developed in Plato's writings. In the *Phaedo*, he advances a number of

Become accustomed to the belief that death is nothing to us. For all good and evil consists in sensation, but death is deprivation of sensation. And therefore a right understanding that death is nothing to us makes the mortality of life enjoyable, not because it adds to an infinite span of time, but because it takes away the craving for immortality. For there is nothing terrible in life for the man who has truly comprehended that there is nothing terrible in not living.

Epicurus, *Letter to Menoeceus*

> ... he who has lived as a true philosopher has reason to be of good cheer when he is about to die, and that after death he may hope to receive the greatest good in the other world. ... For I deem that the true disciple of philosophy ... is ever pursuing death and dying; and if this is true, why, having had the desire of death all his life long, should he repine at the arrival of that which he has been always pursuing and desiring?
>
> Plato, *Phaedo*

"proofs" that the soul is eternal and is released from the body at death. The dualism of body and soul is emphasized, and their respective fates are distinguished from one another: Because it is mortal, the body is subject to corruption; the soul, however, is immortal and not subject to death.

Among Plato's successors, death and the prospect of immortality gained in importance. The fact of death as the common fate of all humankind could be used as a reminder of the importance of choosing wisely how to live in the present life. These thoughts are echoed by the Roman Stoic, Marcus Aurelius, who lived in the second century of the present era. "The constant recollection of death," he said, "is the test of human conduct."[10]

Christianity: Death, Resurrection, and Eternal Life

Jesus himself seems to have been little concerned with speculations about the afterlife. Rather, his message focused on the impending arrival of the Kingdom of God and the corresponding need for righteousness. Nevertheless, the ideas of resurrection that had been developing in the Judaic tradition became radically transformed in the minds of early Christians who proclaimed that death was vanquished by Christ's resurrection. Death, a universal human experience as a result of Adam's fall from grace, is no longer inevitably the enemy. The Apostle Paul wrote: "If it is certain that death reigned over everyone as the consequence of one man's fall, it is even more certain that one man, Jesus Christ, will cause everyone to reign in life who receives the free gift that he does not deserve, of being made righteous"[11]

The life, death, and resurrection of Jesus became the new model of reality for Christians. He was the prototype of the salvation from death available to all those who would share in his resurrection. The Kingdom of God described by Jesus was anticipated as a glorious event that would occur in the very near future. Eternal life was, so to speak, just around the corner.

With Jesus no longer in their midst, and as the small group of Christians began to reframe their expectations about the chronology of the Kingdom of God, their understanding of resurrection also began to change. In the writings of Paul there is an attempt to resolve some of these problems of death, afterlife, and the events foretold for the end of time. Resurrection can be understood as a special kind of bodily existence, different from historical existence. But it can also be understood as having a symbolic or spiritual meaning.

This scene from Dante's Divine Comedy *shows the guide Charon ferrying worthy souls up the River Styx toward Paradise. Unable to reach the heavenly kingdom, the unworthy, immersed in the river, struggle in despair.*

Behold, I show you a mystery; We shall not all sleep, but we shall all be changed. In a moment, in the twinkling of an eye, at the last trump: for the trumpet shall sound, and the dead shall be raised incorruptible, and we shall be changed. For this corruptible must put on incorruption, and this mortal must put on immortality. So when this corruptible shall have put on incorruption, and this mortal shall have put on immortality, then shall be brought to pass the saying that is written, Death is swallowed up in victory. O death, where is thy sting? O grave, where is thy victory?

I Corinthians, 15

The Hellenistic notion of a cosmic dualism was a persistent and pervasive influence on early Christian thought. According to this dualism, the soul was immortal, a part of the human person that existed in a disembodied state after death. During the formative period of the early Church there was constant interplay between the Hebrew traditions and the intellectual heritage of Greco-Roman culture. Milton Gatch says about this period:

> The notion of resurrection and of the restoration of an elect people continued to be prominent. But the idea of a disembodied afterlife for the soul was also current and led to the conception of some sort of afterlife between the separation and the reunion of soul and body. From a picture of death as the inauguration of a sleep which would last until the divinely instituted resurrection, there emerged a picture of death as the beginning of quiescence for the body and of a continued life for the soul, the nature of which remained more or less undefined.[12]

And so, gradually, there developed a greater emphasis on the destiny of the individual soul. Correspondingly, there was increasingly greater concern about the consequences of an individual's conduct during life. By the third or fourth century, Church doctrine more or less willingly accommodated the notion that punishment for misconduct could take place during an intermediate period between death and resurrection.[13]

By the thirteenth century, in the writings of Dante and Thomas Aquinas, the original biblical concept is almost completely subordinated to the Greek notion of dualism and its attendant concept of the soul's immortality. The interplay between these contrasting concepts is illustrated by an observation made by Stephen Vicchio of two tombstone inscriptions, dating from the colonial period, found in New Haven, Connecticut.[14]

On the first tombstone, the inscription reads, "Sleeping, but will someday meet her maker." The second is inscribed, "Gone to his eternal reward." The first inscription reflects an understanding that postulates the resurrection of the body, an event that will occur at some time in the future. The second is based on the concept of the immortality of the soul, which continues to exist even though the body dies. As Vicchio points out, the difference between these two tombstone inscriptions is particularly incongruous when you consider that these two indi-

---

Go Down, Death — A Funeral Sermon

Weep not, weep not,
She is not dead;
She's resting in the bosom of Jesus.
Heart-broken husband — weep no more;
Grief-stricken son — weep no more;
Left-lonesome daughter — weep no more;
She's only just gone home.

James Weldon Johnson

---

viduals were married to each other and are buried side by side in this New England cemetery. Yet, one of them is "sleeping," while the other is "gone."

In these inscriptions we see a curious example of how these essentially disparate ideas can coexist in time. Today, each of these notions — resurrection and immortality — has its adherents. For some, the distinction is vital. Others give little thought to either the distinction or the necessary logic that follows from each of these conceptual understandings.

Until fairly recent times, most people living in the Western world could find adequate answers to the enigma of death by relying upon the teachings of the Christian creeds. In the modern world, our understanding of death has been altered radically. The religious consciousness of the Apostle Paul — for whom the subjugation of death was a reality demonstrated by Christ's resurrection — now seems an anachronism to many people. Renee Haynes observed that persons brought up in the oldest traditional form of Christianity "will have learned to consider two things from which many of their contemporaries have been conditioned to turn away: the fact of mystery and the fact of death."[15]

Death in the Islamic Tradition

The third of the great religious traditions stemming from the patriarch Abraham is Islam, which has perhaps 900 million adherents worldwide. Like Judaism and Christianity, Islam shares the Semitic religious heritage of belief in monotheism, God's revelation through the prophets, ethical responsibility, and ultimate accountability for one's actions at the Day of Judgment. The word *Islam* means "submission to God" and, by extension, being in right relationship with the Divine. The person who adheres to this path is a Muslim, a "submitter."

The Islamic revelation came through the prophet Muhammad and was recorded in the Qur'an (perhaps more familiarly spelled phonetically as Koran in the West) over a period of about two decades. About four-fifths the size of the New Testament, the Qur'an, according to Muslims, "does not abrogate or nullify, but rather corrects, the version of scripture preserved by the Jewish and Christian communities."[16] For the most part, the theological concerns expressed in the Qur'an are generally the same as those of Judaism and Christianity. Frithjof

Schuon notes that the doctrine of Islam hangs on two statements: First, "There is no divinity (or reality) outside the only Divinity (or Absolute)" and, second, "Muhammad is the Envoy (the mouthpiece, intermediary, or manifestation)."[17]

As with the Bible, the Qur'an does not provide a systematic treatment of death, although the subject is not ignored. Alfred Welch points out that a basic premise of Qur'anic teaching about death is that God, in his omnipotence, determines the span of a person's life; "he creates man and also causes him to die."[18] Believers naturally owe obedience and gratitude to their creator, although, as John Esposito says, "The specter of the Last Judgment, with its eternal reward and punishment, remains a constant reminder of the ultimate consequences of each life."[19] Each individual's moral accountability will ultimately be assessed at the time of the Resurrection and Last Judgment, or Day of Reckoning. The Book of Deeds, wherein are recorded good and bad actions, will be opened and each person will be consigned either to everlasting bliss or everlasting torment. As Huston Smith wrote, "For the Muslim, life on earth is the seedbed of an eternal future."[20] The vision of the afterlife recorded in the Qur'an is both spiritual and physical. "Since the Last Day will be accompanied by bodily resurrection," says Esposito, "the pleasures of heaven and the pain of hell will be fully experienced."[21]

For the believer whose actions demonstrate commitment and faithfulness to the path of Islam, death is a release from the sorrows and troubles of life. When death nears, appropriate passages from the Qur'an may be read to the dying person to facilitate an easy release. After death, the body is laid out, with the head in the direction of prayer, and a ritual washing is begun—unless the deceased happens to be a martyr, in which case the washing is skipped "in order not to remove traces of blood which are the hallmark of his martyrdom, nor is it necessary to pray for his soul."[22] On hearing of someone's death, it is customary to say, "Allah Karim"—from God we came and to him we shall return, referring to the time of the Last Judgment, when all lives will be reviewed and everyone will answer for his or her deeds.[23]

Among some Muslims, it is believed that, when a person dies and the body is placed in the grave, "two black-faced, blue-eyed angels named Munkar and Nakir visit the grave and interrogate the deceased concerning his beliefs and deeds in life." Depending on the answers given, the deceased, while still in the grave, receives comfort or punishment at the hands of these "two interrogators." Thus, says Alford Welch, "At a Muslim funeral a mourner may approach a corpse as it is about to be laid in the tomb and whisper instructions for answering these questions."[24] Some Muslims believe that "no one should precede the corpse in the funeral procession because the angels of death go before it."[25] According to orthodox tradition, the funeral is to be conducted without elaborate ceremony, and the body is to be laid in a simple, unmarked grave. Some believe the grave should be deep enough for the dead person to sit up without his or her head appearing above ground when it comes time to answer questions at the Last Judgment.

The Egyptian papyrus of Hunefer depicts the Hall of Judgment and the Great Balance where the deceased's soul is weighed against the feather of truth. Beneath the scales the Devourer of Souls awaits the unjust while Horus is ready to lead the just to Osiris, the lord of the underworld, and to a pleasurable afterlife.

During the last few decades, a resurgence or revivalism of Islam has become increasingly prominent throughout much of the Muslim world. This movement, often termed Islamic fundamentalism, advocates a more pronounced emphasis on religious identity and practice in both individual and community life. Reacting to modern, and especially Western, tendencies to separate religion and politics and to offer secular alternatives as the only contemporary option, Islamic revivalism embodies the notion that politics, law, education, social life, and economics are not to be viewed as "secular institutions or areas of life" but as integral to the total and comprehensive way of life that is Islam. As John Esposito reports, from this viewpoint, "The failure of Muslim societies is due to their departure from the straight path of Islam and their following a Western secular path with materialistic ideologies and values."[26]

Concerns about the steadily increasing influence of secular and materialistic values are not limited to Muslims. Many of their "Abrahamic cousins"—Jews and Christians—are also concerned about what Esposito terms "the secular drift

> The happiness of the drop is to
> die in the river.
>
> Ghazal of Ghalib

and outlook of their societies and its impact on faith and values."[27] We will look at the impact of secularism on our relationship with dying and death in the next section.

Secular Concepts of Immortality

In modern technology-oriented and economics-driven societies — both East and West — traditional beliefs about the purpose of life or the nature of death no longer enjoy the virtually universal acceptance they did when societies and communities were more cohesive, less influenced by ideas and events outside their own domains. Granted, much of the modern world view is indeed shared to a large degree. Nevertheless, when we turn to the experience of death and speculation about what the end of life may portend, we discover a much less monochromatic situation, one that reflects the pluralistic nature of our era.

For many people, death has been divorced from its mythic and religious connotations. This secularization of death has not done away with natural human concerns about what happens afterward. But the underpinnings for the traditional beliefs no longer carry the same weight in a culture that emphasizes empirical verification and the scientific method. Theological or philosophical discussions about the afterlife may seem to resemble the famous debate about the number of dancing angels that will fit on the head of a pin. Yet vestiges of traditional concepts about death and the afterlife remain lodged in the modern consciousness.

The Abrahamic religious traditions — Judaism, Christianity, and Islam — present a linear picture of human history. These traditions describe a progression of events that begins with creation and eventuates in the resolution of the cosmic story at the end of time. Such an orientation to human experience naturally leads to an interest in eschatologies — pictures of the ultimate state, doctrines of the last things. From the wellsprings of the Judeo-Christian tradition and Hellenistic ideals of progress, the Western world has predominantly framed its beliefs about what happens after death in a historical context that is oriented toward the future. For most of its past, the Western view has been that human beings live a single life; that the soul survives death, perhaps in a disembodied state; that at some future time each soul will be judged; and that, depending upon one's conduct during earthly existence, the aftermath will be either hellish torment or heavenly bliss.

Among the most widespread of the secular alternatives to religion are positivism and humanitarianism. *Positivism*, a doctrine associated with faith in science, reflects the belief that religious or metaphysical modes of knowing are imperfect and inadequate, and that "positive knowledge" must be based on what can be observed in nature and verified by the empirical sciences. *Humanitarianism* is a doctrine or way of life that rejects the supernaturalism of religion and instead centers on human values and interests, stressing self-realization through the use of reason. In the real world, it is not unusual for a person to hold several of these competing world views at the same time, perhaps combining a vague religious faith carried over from childhood with faith in scientific modes of knowing and humanitarian ideals of conduct.

In his study of the origins of unbelief, *Without God, Without Creed*, James Turner notes that, although science and social transformation both played key roles in giving rise to the secular option of not believing in God or at least retiring him "to a private or at best subcultural role," it is in fact religion itself that bears responsibility for this major cultural upheaval.[28] As Turner points out, during medieval times, and, with slight variation, even up until about the middle of the nineteenth century,

> religious observance in some form or another remained integral to the social fabric. For the individual, swathed in communal ritual, birth meant baptism; adulthood brought marriage by the priest; and life's journey ended in the courtyard but in a sense continued amid the chanting of masses for the dead.

The change that made unbelief an option was influenced, of course, by the ideal of social and scientific progress and by the humanitarian aim of eradicating human suffering. Compassion gained prominence among the "duties of humanity" and was joined with the idea of progress to forge a new moral principle oriented largely toward earthly concerns. Instruction in "life and manners" became the principal purpose of religion, to the detriment of the transcendent concerns that had figured so prominently in the great theological traditions. In short, says Turner, religious leaders "divorced morality from spirituality." The result was to downplay the spiritual aspects of religion while making religion almost solely a moral guide.

The social reality of the average person was rapidly changing. New conceptions of knowledge, fostered by the advance of science, focused attention on the problem of verifying religious belief. Capitalist economic development influenced the ways people thought as well as how they worked. Increasingly, people were becoming "thoroughly enmeshed in the commercial networks of a market economy." Work moved indoors, distancing people from nature's cycles. The effects of this trend were amplified by the widespread adoption of electric lighting and the regulation of one's activities by the clock. In all, as impersonal business methods became commonplace, there was a lessening of self-sufficiency accompanied by rapid urbanization. Turner says, "Objects of human manufacture enveloped people, separating them from the nature attributed to God's hand," and "even God's time gave way to manmade time." This insulation from nature, as well as the growing sense of control over nature, encroached on the sense of divine activity in nature and helped to push "God's direct presence farther from everyday experience into an intangible spiritual realm."

As findings from anthropology were taken to indicate that religious beliefs were simply a "human attempt to cope with the mysteries of nature," and as brain physiology seemed to reduce the human mind to nothing more mystical than a "grid of electrical nerve impulses," it became more and more difficult to maintain traditional notions about the soul, immortality, and God. As Turner points out, the "psychic gratifications" that used to be sought in God could now be provided by a "religion of humanity" that embraced science, art, and the worship of nature. Religious leaders tried to make peace with modernity "by conceiving God and His purposes in terms as nearly compatible as possible with secular understandings and aims."

Today, despite the option of unbelief, most people still readily affirm their belief in God. A survey completed in 1991 and characterized as "perhaps the most detailed religious profile of twentieth-century Americans, found that "religion remains a constant point of identification and commonality."[29] According to a 1990 survey of Americans' beliefs about the afterlife, 78 percent reported believing in heaven and 60 percent believing in hell, with the highest percentages of belief in both realms being reported among young adults.[30] Religious ideas and messages continue to play an important role in both individual and social thought. What is different, however, is the lack of a common intellectual life founded in a shared understanding that unifies an entire culture, "a common heritage that underlies our diverse world views."

Assurances about what to expect after death, assurances that were historically part of a community's heritage of shared belief, are now less convincing. For many, perhaps most, people, the idea that immortality signifies an everlasting state of paradisiacal bliss has given way to more modest hopes. As Norman Cousins wrote in his dialogue on immortality, *The Celebration of Life*, one's expectation of the hereafter may be limited merely to "peace of mind" or, even more basically, "to be saved from an eternity in death."[31] Beyond the fact that death, absolute extinction, is unacceptable, the average person may have little concrete notion of what he or she expects of an afterlife state. "Shouldn't your quest for immortality," the docent asks in Cousin's dialogue, "involve more than the mere desire to avoid a shattering blow to your conceit?" Is it really enough, in other words, to wish merely to survive? Isn't non-death, of itself, a rather limited idea?

Within the realm of secular, or nonreligious, answers to the question of immortality, there are various possible responses. The idea of the brotherhood of man, or the essential unity of humankind, may appeal to some as a plausible avenue of immortality. "You live in others; others live in you." The exchange of love and compassion between members of the human community itself assumes a kind of immortality for the person who shares his or her life with others.

Likewise, children represent a form of biological continuity that can be seen as a form of personal immortality. Other "children" that may be construed as conveying immortality on the creator include works of art or contributions to some field of knowledge or technology, as well as heroic or helpful deeds. Notwithstanding the sense of personal continuity that these forms of immortality may bring to the individual, as Robert Lifton and others have pointed out, the modern situation is one in which even the continuity (or, if you like, the immortality) of the human species as a whole cannot be assumed absolutely. The threat of catastrophic evil, in the form of nuclear annihilation or global environmental disaster, hangs over all our heads.

Perhaps, then, our approach to immortality is best made by focusing on the present. Righteous conduct, the Hebrew sages advised, is worthy of pursuit because it contributes to harmony now. Among the Greeks, death served to foster mindfulness of the importance of choosing wisely in one's present life. Although the hope of resurrection and eternal life is surely a central feature of Christianity, it is also worth noting that Jesus' message emphasized righteousness, not rewards. In the Islamic tradition, too, the ultimate consequences of one's actions are determined in the present. In light of our religious heritage as well as the more recent changes wrought under the name of secularism, placing the approach to immortality squarely in the present may serve both those who anticipate a future heavenly state and those who scoff at any such notion of an existence beyond death.

The Place of Death and Immortality in Eastern Thought

The Western approach to experience tends to be dualistic. Experiences are analyzed as being *either* this *or* that. The Western thinker typically makes distinctions, points up contrasts, establishes differences. Within this context, life is opposed to death, death is the enemy of life; life represents affirmation, death negation. Death is "evil," life "good."

In the cultures of the East, on the other hand, the characteristic mode of thought emphasizes the integrity of the whole rather than the differences between constituent parts. It seeks to discover the unity that underlies apparently contradictory phenomena. Whereas Western thought distinguishes between "either/or," Eastern thought subsumes such distinctions within a holistic "both/and" approach. In place of the dualistic view of reality typical of Western thought, the corresponding Eastern mode of thought characteristically reflects the position that such apparent dualisms are merely illusory aspects of an essentially undivided reality.

This unitary view of reality is reflected in many of the sacred texts of the East. The *I Ching*, or *Book of Changes*, for instance, postulates a world of experience that is constantly being transformed. Life and death are manifestations of a constantly changing reality. Like the symbol of the *Tao*, these contrasting aspects of reality interpenetrate one another. Death and life are not seen as mutually exclusive opposites, but rather as complementary facets of an underlying process. We see this process in the inexorable cycles of birth, decay, and death. Like a pendulum moving through its arc, the completion of one cycle heralds the beginning of another.

Everything in the phenomenal world exhibits this pattern of constant arising and passing away. Through their observations of this process, the sages of the East developed the concept of reincarnation or transmigration. For some, reincarnation is understood as a physical reality: "I will take birth in another body

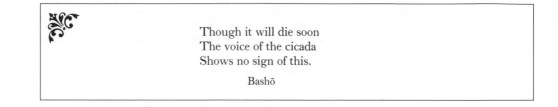

> Though it will die soon
> The voice of the cicada
> Shows no sign of this.
>
> Bashō

following the death of my present body." Others deny such a physical, materialist understanding of reincarnation, saying that there is, in fact, no "I" to be reborn. According to this view, what we identify as "I" or "self" is insubstantial, *ever-changing* process. In the constant arising and passing away of experience, something is carried over from one state to the next, but this "something" is impersonal and is essentially formless and ineffable.

Hindu Theologies of Death and Rebirth

One of the distinguishing features of Hinduism is the belief in the transmigration of souls — that is, the passing at death of the soul from one body or being to another. This process is termed *samsara*, which refers to "passing through" a series of incarnational experiences. What links these experiences together is *karma*, which can be roughly defined as the moral law of cause and effect. The thoughts and actions of the past determine the present state of being; and, in turn, present choices influence future states. This karmic process can be interpreted as pertaining to the ever-changing flow of moment-to-moment experience, as well as to the successive rounds of death and rebirth. As each moment conditions the next, *karma* sustains this reincarnational flow of being. In the *Bhagavad-Gita* Krishna tells Arjuna:

> For death is a certainty for him who has been born, and birth is a certainty for him who has died. Therefore, for what is unavoidable thou shouldst not grieve.

In his commentary on this passage, Swami Nikhilananda adds, "It is not proper to grieve for beings which are mere combinations of cause and effect."[32]

According to Hinduism, the workings of *karma* provide only a partial description of reality. Underlying the apparent separateness of individual beings is a unitary reality. Just as the ocean can be imagined as composed of innumerable drops of water, undifferentiated being is manifest in human experience in the form of an apparently separate self. Huston Smith expresses the Hindu perception this way: "Underlying man's personality and animating it is a reservoir of being that never dies, is never exhausted, and is without limit in awareness and bliss. This infinite center of life, this hidden self or *Atman*, is no less than *Brahman*, the Godhead."[33]

Difficulty and suffering arise in human experience, Hinduism says, because of not recognizing the true nature of existence; namely, that the relationship between *Atman* and *Brahman* is essentially one absolute identity. Instead, we see ourselves as separate from this essential unity. We hold to our cherished self-

The cosmic dance of the Hindu deity Shiva, an ever changing flow of creation and dissolution, embodies the fundamental equilibrium between life and death, the underlying reality behind appearances.

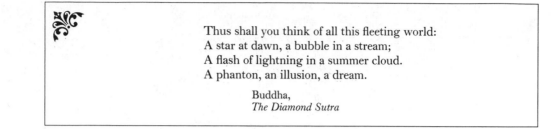

Thus shall you think of all this fleeting world:
A star at dawn, a bubble in a stream;
A flash of lightning in a summer cloud.
A phanton, an illusion, a dream.

Buddha,
The Diamond Sutra

concepts — "my" life, "my" self — ignoring the reality in which all such notions are illusory and substanceless. Our attachments to these concepts of "self" as separate and distinct cause us suffering in the present life and perpetuate the endless wheel of births and deaths, the wheel of *karma*.

To escape this fate, Hinduism teaches that we need to become free of the illusion of separate selfhood, with its attendant pain. A liberated being is one who recognizes that life and death transcend such mistaken notions of self-identity, and thereby becomes free of the conditioning effects of *karma*. The *Bhagavad-Gita* says:

> Worn-out garments are shed by the body: Worn-out bodies are shed by the dweller.

Nikhilananda explains this process: "In the act of giving up the old body or entering into the new body, the real Self does not undergo any change whatsoever. . . . Brahman, through Its inscrutable maya, creates a body, identifies Itself with it, and regards Itself as an individual, or embodied, soul."[34]

To be free of death means letting go of attachments to the phenomenal world, releasing the grasp on the false distinctions of a separate self and its unceasing desires. Death is inescapable, a natural corollary of conditioned existence. What is born passes away. Yet for the person "whose consciousness has become stabilized by the insight that it is the very nature of things to come-to-be and pass-away," there is no "occasion either for rejoicing over birth or grieving over death."[35]

To loosen the bonds of attachment, Hinduism offers various aids in the form of rites and practices that can assist in the awakening to truth. Some of these methods emphasize paying close attention to the processes that surround death. For example, one practice involves attending to the transitory and ever-changing nature of one's own body, observing its inexorable progress toward decay and dissolution, its constant transformation, moment to moment. Another practice involves imagining one's death and the ultimate fate of the body, its return to elemental matter in the grave or on the funeral pyre. Some of these meditation practices occur in the presence of a dead body or at burial or cremation grounds. Death becomes a clear reminder of the ever-changing flow of *karma*, a reminder that there is nothing to hold to, no permanence, no solid self. By confronting one's own mortality, one becomes reoriented toward the transcendent dimensions of reality. The death of the separate self is the letting go of conditioned existence, "the death that conquers death."[36]

Before we were born we had no feeling; we were one with the universe. This is called "mind-only," or "essence of mind," or "big mind." After we are separated by birth from this oneness, as the water falling from the waterfall is separated by the wind and rocks, then we have feeling. You have difficulty because you have feeling. You attach to the feeling you have without knowing just how this kind of feeling is created. When you do not realize that you are one with the river, or one with the universe, you have fear. Whether it is separated into drops or not, water is water. Our life and death are the same thing. When we realize this fact we have no fear of death anymore, and we have no actual difficulty in our life.

Shunryu Suzuki, *Zen Mind, Beginner's Mind*

The Buddhist Understanding of Death

Zen master Dōgen, founder of the Sōtō Zen sect in Japan, said, "The thorough clarification of the meaning of birth and death — this is the most important problem of all for Buddhists."[37] Although there is considerable variety in Buddhist practices and beliefs — as there is in the Hinduism that served as the background of Siddhartha Gautama's experience of awakening to become the Buddha — death holds a central place in the teachings of Buddhism. And although its meaning may be variously interpreted by different sects and schools, the ultimate aim for Buddhists is *nirvana*, which literally means "extinction" — as when a flame goes out if deprived of fuel. It is, says Philip Kapleau, the "unconditioned state beyond birth and death that is reached after all ignorance and craving have been extinguished and all karma, which is the cause of rebirth, has been dissolved."[38]

Buddhism denies the existence of a permanent, unchanging self or substantial soul that transmigrates intact from one life to the next. What we call "self" is really nothing more than a process of continuous change with no permanence. Everything is transitory and impermanent *(anicca)*, in continual unease and unrest *(dukkha)*, and substanceless *(anatta)*. *Karma* can be understood as the universal principle of causality underlying the constant stream of psychophysical events. Dōgen says, "Life constantly changes, moment by moment, in each of its stages, whether we want it to or not. Without even a moment's pause our karma causes us to transmigrate continuously."[39]

From the Buddhist perspective there are two kinds of death: continuous and regular. Continuous death is the "passing show" of phenomenal experience, constantly arising and passing away, moment by moment. Regular, or corporeal, death pertains to the physical cessation of vital body functions at the end of a lifetime.

There is no "self" to survive after death or to be reborn, yet *karma* transmigrates to the next moment of arising into being. This transmigration can be likened to impressing a seal onto wax or mud, or to the transfer of energy in a game of billiards when the cue ball strikes the cluster of balls, creating new energy events. Philip Kapleau says: "Rebirth does not involve the transfer of a substance, but the continuation of a process."

© Albert Lee Strickland

In the Japanese section of this cemetery on the island of Oahu, graves holding the
ashes of deceased members of the community are ornamented with Buddhist symbols
of the Wheel of Dharma and the Lotus.

Like Hinduism, Buddhism teaches that it is necessary to renounce the desires and cravings that maintain the delusion of a separate self. When all attachments are dropped, the wheel of *karma*, the incessant round of birth-decay-death,
is given no further fuel. How does one awaken to this reality, to *nirvana*? Dōgen
says, "Simply understand that birth and death are in themselves nirvana, there
being no birth-death to be hated or nirvana to be desired. Then, for the first time
you will be freed from birth and death."[40]

The paradox of Dōgen's statement about birth-death and the importance of
using death as a means of awakening to truth is echoed in the words of the Zen
master Hakuin, who is known as the reviver of the Rinzai sect, the other great
Buddhist lineage in Japan.[41] For those who wish to investigate their true nature,
Hakuin advised meditation on the word *shi*, the character for death. To do this,
he suggested a koan (a riddle or paradox to be meditated upon): "After you are
dead and cremated, where has the main character [the chief actor or one's "original face"] gone?" Hakuin wrote:

> Among all the teaching and instructions, the word *death* has the most unpleasant and
> disgusting connotations. Yet if you once suddenly penetrate this "death" koan, you
> will find that there is no more felicitous teaching than this instruction that serves as

the key to the realm in which birth and death are transcended, where the place in which you stand is the Diamond indestructible, and where you have become a divine immortal, unaging and undying. The word *death* is the vital essential that the warrior must first determine for himself.

Guides to After-Death States

A person who by religious persuasion perceives death as an opportunity for awakening to truth is naturally interested in influencing the character of the after-death state and the next incarnation. According to W.Y. Evans-Wentz, "Buddhists and Hindus alike believe that the last thought at the moment of death determines the character of the next incarnation."[42] On this point, Philip Kapleau says: "Rebirth arises from two causes: the last thought of the previous life as its governing principle and the actions of the previous life as its basis. The stopping of the last thought is known as decease; the appearance of the first thought as rebirth." Writings like the *Bardo Thödol*, or *The Tibetan Book of the Dead*, as it is better known in the West, are intended to direct the thought processes of the dying person during the transitional period of life-death-rebirth.

The passing from one stage of the after-death experience to another can be likened to the process of birth. The term *bardo* can be translated as "gap" or "interval of suspension" and is usually taken to mean an intermediate or transitional state between birth and death. Chögyam Trungpa suggests that *bardo* refers not only to the interval after death, but also to "suspension within the living situation."[43]

The *Bardo Thödol* offers counsel on how to use these experiences—some terrifying, some benign—to awaken to a more enlightened incarnation. Although acknowledging that these experiences are likely to appear quite real to the *bardo* traveler, the text emphasizes that the deities or demons encountered are simply apparitions, the experiencer's own projections.

Although the *Bardo Thödol* and similar texts are commonly thought to be designed to be read as a person experiences the process of dying, they have a broader application as well. Indeed, such texts can serve as a guide for the living as well as the dying. As Chögyam Trungpa says, the *Bardo Thödol* deals with "the principle of birth and death recurring constantly in this life"; thus, these writings refer not only to the interval after death, but also to the situation encountered by the living, for "the bardo experience is part of our basic psychological make-up."

Your essence was not born and will not die. It is neither being nor nonbeing. It is not a void nor does it have form. It experiences neither pleasure nor pain. If you ponder what it is in you that feels the pain of this sickness, and beyond that you do not think or desire or ask anything, and if your mind dissolves like vapour in the sky, then the path to rebirth is blocked and the moment of instant release has come.

Bassui, Zen Buddhist, comforting a dying person

As to the states described in the *Tibetan Book of the Dead*, they are intermediate states of consciousness. They do not represent ultimate or transcendent perfection but rather steps along the way. Nevertheless, the period immediately following death is considered to be an especially opportune time for gaining insight. The priest at a Buddhist funeral, for example, speaks directly to the deceased, expounding on the teachings that can awaken the intermediate being to the true nature of existence. Philip Kapleau says, "The funeral and subsequent services thus represent literally a 'once in a lifetime' opportunity to awaken the deceased and thereby liberate him from the binding chain of birth-and-death."[44]

Near-Death Experiences: At the Threshold of Death

Stories of travel to another world can be found in virtually all cultures. The traveler may be a hero, shaman, prophet, king, or even an ordinary mortal who, as Carol Zaleski says, "passes through the gates of death and returns with a message for the living."[45] Such journeys include the heavenly ascent of the prophet Muhammad and the heavenly visions of Enoch and the Apostle Paul, as well as Gilgamesh's epic adventures to the underworld and the descent of the goddess Inanna. Zaleski identifies three forms of the otherworld journey: (1) the journey to the underworld, (2) the ascent to higher worlds, and (3) the fantastic voyage. The common thread of all such journeys, says Zaleski, is the "story," which is shaped not only by universal laws of symbolic experience, but also by the transitory experiences of a given, local culture.

The publication in 1975 of Raymond Moody's *Life After Life* sparked a renewed interest in otherworld journeys and, specifically, in near-death experiences. These stories of persons who have come back from the edge of death describe fascinating glimpses of a paranormal, or scientifically unexplainable, order of existence. Some interpret these near-death experiences (NDEs) as indicating that the human personality survives death; others believe that the phenomena experienced by such near-death survivors actually represent nothing more mysterious than a psychological or neurophysiological response to the stress of facing a life-threatening danger. Despite questions about how NDEs are to be interpreted, health care professionals and others who are exposed to persons reporting near-death experiences need to be sensitive and nonjudgmental in assessing the accounts of near-death survivors.[46]

NDEs: A Composite Picture

Significantly, although researchers differ in their interpretations of near-death experiences, their studies reveal a strikingly similar picture of such phenomena. Let us imagine what might be experienced during an overwhelming encounter with death, resulting perhaps from an accident or from a life-threatening illness or acute medical crisis. Perhaps, almost beyond awareness, you hear a voice saying that you're not going to make it, you're going to die.

In Hieronymous Bosch's portrayal of the Ascent into the Empyrean—the highest heaven in medieval cosmology—the soul, purged of its impurities, approaches the end of its long journey and union with the Divine.

It's like a dream, but somehow the experience seems more real than ordinary waking consciousness. Vision and hearing are extremely acute; sensory perceptions are heightened. You experience your thought processes as clear, rational. Yet you no longer seem tied to a body. As you become aware of this feeling of disconnectedness, you notice yourself separate from the body, floating free. From a corner of the room, you look down at the body below and recognize it as your own.

Perhaps you feel a little lonely, drifting in space, yet there is a sense of calm, a serenity that was rarely if ever experienced in the body. All the usual constructs of time and space seem irrelevant, unreal. As you feel yourself moving farther away from the once-familiar world of your now-dead body, you enter a darkness, a tunnel, some transitional stage in your journey.

At this point you notice a light, more brilliant than any imagined during your earthly existence, beckoning, drawing you onward, its golden hues heralding your approach to the other side.

Perhaps now you experience the whole of your previous life in the body, a nearly instantaneous matrix of flashbacks, impressions of your former life, events, places, people: your life reviewed and projected on the transparent screen of consciousness.

You enter the light, glimpsing a world of unimaginable and unspeakable brilliance. A loved one greets you, or perhaps you become aware of Jesus or Moses or another being of ineffable grace. Only now you realize that you cannot enter fully into this light, not yet, not this time.

Dimensions of Near-Death Experiences

For most people who have experienced such phenomena as those encountered in your imaginary journey, the return to the body is a blank. Others report feeling a jolt or becoming aware of pain upon their return to consciousness in the body. Many emerge from their experience with a greater appreciation of life, a determination to make better use of the opportunities presented to them. Typically, they feel more self-confident, more able to cope with the vicissitudes of life. Loving relationships become more important and material comforts less important. Researcher Kenneth Ring says that the typical near-death experiencer "has achieved a sense of what is important in life and strives to live in accordance with his understanding of what matters."[47] In some respects, near-death experiences share many features with the "conversion" stories associated with life-changing religious experiences.

Our imaginary, composite picture of a near-death experience incorporates a number of elements that are in fact only rarely experienced. Whereas 60 percent of the respondents in Ring's sample experienced feelings of peace and well-being, 37 percent experienced themselves as separate from their bodies, 23 percent experienced the entry into a dark tunnel or transitional stage, 16 percent experienced seeing a bright light, and 10 percent experienced themselves actually entering the light, though only for a "peek" into their unearthly surroundings. Ring found that NDEs resulting from illness were more likely to be complete — to have all of these characteristic core elements — than were NDEs resulting from accidents. On the other hand, over half the accident victims experienced panoramic memory, or life review, compared to only 16 percent of the respondents whose experiences were related to illness or attempted suicide.

The *panoramic life review*, in itself an interesting feature of near-death experiences, may consist of vivid, almost instantaneous visions of the person's whole life or "selected highlights" of it.[48] The life review may appear in an orderly sequence, or it may seem to come "all at once." In any case, it apparently occurs without any conscious control or effort by the experiencer. Less frequently, the life review incorporates visions about the future, with experiencers visualizing their death, the reactions of friends and relatives, and events at the funeral.

The encounter with a presence — a feature of NDEs that is commonly related to the "tunnel" experience — usually involves seeing deceased relatives or friends, or sensing some religious presence. Although the presence thus encountered usually appears to involve some representation of the "higher self," in some instances the presence is an entity that seems otherwise.[49] William Serdahely reports the case of an eight-year-old boy who was "comforted by two of his family's pets who had died prior to the incident."[50] The encounter with a presence during a near-death experience is sometimes linked to the decision to return, to terminate the experience. Some near-death experiencers believe that the decision to return to the present earthly life is made for them, others that they arrived at this decision themselves. Usually, the decision to return is related in some way to unfinished business or responsibilities that the person believes must be attended to before his or her death.

In broad outline, the description provided in our imaginary near-death experience is typical of reports in the literature. Thus, it is possible to identify four core elements that appear to be characteristic of NDEs: The person (1) hears the news of his or her death, 2) departs from the body, (3) encounters significant others, and (4) returns to the body.

What are we to make of these experiences? How should the data regarding NDEs be interpreted?

Interpreting Near-Death Experiences

Near-death experiences are clearly a fascinating field of inquiry. To some they suggest (or confirm) hoped-for possibilities. Others view NDEs as a fertile field for research into the nature of human consciousness. To still others, NDEs illustrate the remarkable psychodynamic processes that surface when annihilation of the self is threatened. An important precipitator of the near-death experience is the belief that one is dying — whether or not one is in fact close to death.[51] Although the general features of NDEs tend not to be matters of dispute, such experiences elicit widely divergent interpretations.[52] Some of the major theories devised to explain near-death experiences are listed in Table 14-1.

TABLE 14-1   *Theories of the Near-Death Experience*

1. Neuropsychological theories:
    A. *Temporal lobe paroxysm*, or limbic lobe syndrome: Seizurelike neural discharges in the temporal lobe or, more generally, in the limbic system.
    B. *Cerebral anoxia*, or oxygen deprivation: Shortage of oxygen in the brain.
    C. *Endorphin release:* Release of certain neurotransmitters associated with analgesic (pain-killing) effects and a sense of psychological well-being.
    D. *Massive cortical disinhibition:* Loss of control over the random activity of the central nervous system.
    E. *False sight:* Hallucinatory imagery arising from structures in the brain and nervous system.
    F. *Drugs:* Side-effects.
    G. *Sensory deprivation.*
2. Psychological theories:
    A. *Depersonalization:* Psychological detachment from one's body; in this case, a defensive reaction to the perceived threat of death. May be accompanied by hyperalertness.
    B. *Motivated fantasy:* A type of "defensive" fantasy that basically proposes that experiencers have an impression of surviving death because they desire to survive death.
    C. *Archetypes:* Images associated with various elements of the near-death experience are "wired" into the brain as mythological archetypes of our common humanity.
3. Metaphysical theories:
    A. *Soul travel:* Transitional journey of the soul or spirit to another mode of existence or realm of reality (e.g., "heaven"); proof of life after death.
    B. *Psychic vision:* Glimpses into another mode of reality, though not necessarily providing proof of soul-survival after death.

For early Hawaiians, their observations of *apparent* death, or persons who had "left the body prematurely," were interpreted in accordance with beliefs about the ancestor-gods.[53] On each island, there was a special promontory overlooking the sea; this was the *leina*, or leaping place, of the soul or spirit on its journey to the realm of the ancestors. If, on its way to the *leina*, a soul was met by an ancestor-god and sent back, the body would revive. Otherwise the ancestor-god would lead it safely to and over the *leina*; once beyond that hurdle, the soul was safe with the ancestors. Notice that a specific place was designated as the point of transition between life and death.

For various reasons (often, though not always, having to do with a person's behavior), an ancestor-god might delay a soul's acceptance into eternity. For instance, if a person died before his or her earthly work was done, the ancestor-god conducted the soul back to the body. "Sometimes when it is not yet time to die," reports Mary Pukui, "the relatives [ancestors] stand in the road and make you go back. Then the breath returns to the body with a crowing sound, *o'o-a-moa*." After such a person was fully restored to life, he or she took a purifying bath and was welcomed back into the family.

Albert Heim, a Swiss geologist and mountain climber, is considered to have been the first investigator to systematically gather data on near-death experiences.[54] Working at the turn of the century, Heim interviewed some thirty skiers and climbers who had been involved in accidents resulting in paranormal experiences. Heim's subjects experienced such phenomena as detachment from their bodies and panoramic memory, or life review.

The data compiled by Heim were subsequently interpreted by psychoanalytic pioneer Oskar Pfister, who explained these experiences as being caused by shock and depersonalization in the face of impending death. In other words, when a person's life is threatened, psychological defense mechanisms may come into play, giving rise to the phenomena associated with NDEs. The psychological approach initiated by Pfister continues to be elaborated by a number of present-day researchers who believe that NDEs can be explained satisfactorily without hypothesizing life after death. Such explanations include suggestions of a possible connection between NDEs and dream states, hallucinations, side effects of pharmacological agents, and various neurophysiological causes.

The psychological model described by Russell Noyes and Roy Kletti posits that defensive reactions lead to depersonalization in the face of mortal danger.[55] Their model is perhaps the most comprehensive explanation of this type offered thus far. According to this model, NDEs can be broken down into three stages: resistance, life review, and transcendence. The first stage, *resistance*, involves recognition of the danger, fear of it and struggle against it, and finally acceptance of death as imminent. This acceptance, or surrender, marks the beginning of the second stage, *life review*. As the self is detached from its bodily representation, panoramic memories occur, often in almost simultaneous succession, appearing to encompass a person's entire life. This experience of life review is often related to a sense of affirmation of the meaning of one's existence and its integration into the universal order of things. The third stage, *transcendence*, evolves from the increased detachment from one's individual existence and is marked by an increasingly cosmic or transcendental consciousness replacing the more limited ego- or self-identity.

Experiences such as calm detachment, heightened sensory awareness, panoramic memory or life review, and mystical consciousness represent the ego's protective response when confronted by its own demise. In other words, the threat of death can set into motion various psychological processes that provide an escape for the ego, the experiencing self. Because these processes dissociate the experiencing self from the body, the threat of death is perceived as being a threat only to the *body*, not to the "self" that is doing the perceiving. Although the psychological interpretation of NDEs does not necessarily invalidate their possible spiritual significance, these findings have been used by some to support a reductionist approach that leaves no room for metaphysical interpretation.

> It is wonderful that five thousand years have now elapsed since the creation of the world, and still it is undecided whether or not there has ever been an instance of the spirit of any person appearing after death. All argument is against it; but all belief is for it.
>
> James Boswell, *Life of Johnson*

In contrast to researchers such as those just discussed, others have followed the lines of inquiry established in the late nineteenth century by parapsychologists. These investigators believe that to adequately understand NDEs one must be willing to go beyond the usual boundaries of scientific inquiry. In short, the researchers must be prepared to accept the possibility, which is not scientifically verifiable, that NDEs are what they seem to be — that is, experiences of states of consciousness that transcend the death of the body. Thus, such researchers tend to accept anecdotal reports of NDEs at face value and try to construct a model of reality that will account for such experiences.

Near-death experiences, they say, teach us that the *appearance* of death is not at all like the *experience* of death. A Gallup poll conducted during the 1980s showed that about two-thirds of all adult Americans answered yes to the question, "Do you believe in life after death?[56] Only one-fifth, however, thought that life after death would be proven scientifically. (About eight million people reported near-death experiences.) Of course, those approaching the question of survival after death with their minds already made up in the affirmative have no difficulty finding corroborative evidence. One book on the subject begins with the assertion that "human beings survive physical death," which is supported by accounts of apparitions, hauntings, out-of-body experiences, deathbed visions, resuscitations, possession experiences, reincarnation claims, and mediumistic communications or "accounts from the realm beyond death." It is unlikely that such works accomplish much more than to confirm the preconceptions of the already decided.

A more objective approach is reflected in the work of Karlis Osis and Erlendur Haraldsson, whose cross-cultural studies led them to conclude that the evidence from NDEs strongly suggests life after death.[57] In their view, "Neither medical, nor psychological, nor cultural conditioning can explain away deathbed visions." One of the points put forward in support of this conclusion is the observation that in some deathbed visions there are apparitions that are contrary to the experiencer's expectations. Osis and Haraldsson mention "apparitions of persons the person thought were still living, but who in fact were dead," as well as apparitions that do not conform to cultural stereotypes, as with dying children who are "surprised to see 'angels' without wings."

Drawing by Henry Martin, from TV Guide®, © 1978 Triangle Publications

'While on the operating table my heart stopped beating and I died.
At that moment, Merv, I learned there was a life after life and a chance
for a best selling book based on this discovery, and a hit movie
based on the book, and TV guest shots to plug the movie, and commercials
generated by TV appearances and...'

Arguments and counterarguments have been put forth in favor of each of the basic approaches to understanding the phenomena of NDEs. Casting a critical eye on this ongoing debate, Stephen Vicchio observes that "much of the literature is philosophically unsophisticated, relying too heavily on metaphysical explanations, while ignoring or disregarding alternative explanations." Indeed, the issues could be much clarified by an understanding of the theological and philosophical antecedents of the present theories formulated to explain such experiences. Near-death experiences are real, for some persons do have them. The question is how they should be interpreted.

The first explanation postulates that death is the destruction of the personality. Near-death experiences are explained as resulting from some dysfunction of the brain or nervous system, or as resulting from the ego's defensive reaction to a life-threatening situation. Thus, what are perceived as visions of an after-death existence actually arise from memories stored in the brain that express the desires, expectations, and fears of the individual, as well as the beliefs characteristic of his or her culture.

The second explanation postulates that near-death experiences indicate survival after death. Death is seen as the transition to another mode of existence. According to this hypothesis, the experiences of incorporeal entities and the glimpses of postmortem states of being result from extrasensory perception of objective phenomena. In other words, NDEs are what they seem to be: experiences of life after death.

Each explanation offers a model, or representation, of "how the world works." One's own model of reality is likely to cause more favorable treatment of one or the other of these interpretations. Louis Appleby, writing in the *British Medical Journal*, says that all of the explanations put forward to explain NDEs share one attribute: Each requires a form of faith.[58] The explanation that best suits your own perception of how things work is likely to be accepted most readily. There remains, however, another approach to understanding the significance of near-death experiences — namely, the possibility that both propositions are valid: There is life after death; and there is also a psychological phenomenon involving various defense mechanisms whereby the personality is radically altered as the transition from one state to the next is negotiated. Carol Zaleski points to the possibility that the various explanations of NDEs, taken together, might result in a comprehensive theory. "We need to find a middle path," she says, "between the extremes of dismissing near-death experience as 'nothing but' and embracing it as 'proof.'" In a similar vein, Herman Feifel says:

> What is somewhat disquieting is the claim by some that near-death experiences are evidence for and proof of the existence of an after-life. There may well be life after death, but jumping to that conclusion from reported near-death experiences reflects more a leap of faith than judicious scientific assessment. This in no way minimizes the reality of these occurrences for the people who declare them. I just think that in weighing the evidence in this area we have less far-fetched and more parsimonious interpretations within the canons of science that can explain these phenomena. What strikes me about many of these out-of-body reports is the hunger for meaning and purpose they suggest in this age of faltering faith.[59]

As mentioned earlier, modern society is characterized in part by a fragmented religious situation. Perhaps, as Zaleski suggests, the near-death experience can serve to "remind us of the need for orientation, the need to have a consecrated cosmos as the setting for a spiritual journey." But, she adds, "it cannot provide the means or material to accomplish this." Thus, however one decides to interpret near-death experiences, gleaning whatever spiritual meaning they

> Our normal waking consciousness, rational consciousness as we call it, is but one special type of consciousness, whilst all about it, parted from it by the filmiest of screens, there lie potential forms of consciousness entirely different. We may go through life without suspecting their existence; but apply the requisite stimulus, and at a touch they are there in all their completeness, definite types of mentality which probably somewhere have their field of application and adaptation. No account of the universe in its totality can be final which leaves these other forms of consciousness quite disregarded. How to regard them is the question—for they are so discontinuous with ordinary consciousness. Yet they may determine attitudes though they cannot furnish formulas, and open a region though they fail to give a map. At any rate, they forbid a premature closing of our accounts with reality.
>
> William James,
> *The Varieties of Religious Experience:*
> *A Study in Human Nature*

might have to convey ultimately throws us "back on our devices, our own partial and provisional solutions."

In considering how to interpret reports of near-death experiences, one should remember that, indeed, these are *near-death* experiences, not, strictly speaking, experiences after death. The reality that such experiences open to investigation may turn out to be much vaster than, and quite different from, what we suppose if we consider them only as glimpses of "another world." Indeed, the matrices for such experiences may lie within the depths of human consciousness. As Charles Garfield states: "If the various Eastern and Western religious traditions and parapsychological disciplines are correct, the period just before physical death is one of maximum receptivity to altered state realities."[60] It should also be noted that many people experience clinical death and after being resuscitated simply have nothing to report.

Robert Kastenbaum cautions that one needs to be careful of a too-ready acceptance of the "fantastic voyage" implied by most life-after-death accounts.[61] He says:

> The happily-ever-after theme threatens to draw attention away from the actual situations of the dying persons, their loved ones, and their care givers over the days, weeks, and months preceding death. What happens up to the point of the fabulous transition from life to death recedes into the background. This could not be more unfortunate. The background, after all, is where these people are actually living until death comes.

Finally, three points expressed by Charles Garfield, after extensive work with dying persons, should be considered:

1. Not everyone dies a blissful, accepting death.
2. Context is a powerful variable in such altered-state experiences as those involving hypnosis, meditation, psychedelics, and schizophrenia. It may be that a supportive environment for the dying person is an important factor in determining whether the outcome is a positive altered-state experience for the dying.
3. The "happily ever after" stance toward death may represent a form of denial when what is really needed by the dying is a demonstration of real concern and real caring in their present experience.

Whatever the beliefs one may hold about life after death, as Garfield says, "Let us have the courage to realize that death often will be a bitter pill to swallow."

Death in the Psychedelic Experience

The death-related experiences resulting from the use of LSD (lysergic acid diethylamide) and other psychedelic — that is, mind-manifesting or mind-opening — substances may shed light on our inquiry into the question of personality survival after death. From its earliest clinical applications, LSD was seen to have far-reaching implications for our understanding of death and human consciousness.

In the early 1960s, Eric Kast of the Chicago Medical School began pioneering studies of the analgesic effects of LSD on patients suffering intense pain.[62] Besides relieving the symptoms of physical pain and discomfort, LSD therapy also diminished emotional symptoms, such as depression, anxiety, tension, insomnia, and psychological withdrawal. LSD seemed to accomplish these impressive results by altering the patient's learned response to pain — that is, the patient's anticipation of pain based on past experiences. By becoming free of this conditioning, the patient was oriented to the present and thus able to respond to the sensations actually experienced rather than to an image of pain that had grown more and more discomforting over time. Noting that pain is a composite phenomenon that has a neurophysiological component (the pain sensation) and a psychological component (the pain affect), Stanislav Grof and Joan Halifax report that psychedelic therapy seemed to influence pain "primarily by modifying the psychological component."[63]

Perhaps even more significant than the diminution of pain was the change of attitude toward death and dying. Following the psychedelic experience, patients often showed a diminished fear of death and less anxiety about the life-threatening implications of their illness. According to Grof and Halifax: "Dying persons who had transcendental experiences developed a deep belief in the ultimate unity of all creation; they often experienced themselves as integral parts of it, including their disease and the often painful situations they were facing."

Many patients exhibited a greater responsiveness to their families and their environment. Their self-respect and morale were enhanced, and they showed a

> Death and life, usually considered to be irreconcilable opposites, appear to actually be dialectically interrelated. Living fully and with maximum awareness every moment of one's life leads to an accepting and reconciled attitude toward death. Conversely, such an approach to human existence requires that we come to terms with our mortality and the impermanence of existence.
>
> Stanislav Grof and Joan Halifax,
> *The Human Encounter with Death*

greater appreciation of the subtleties of everyday life. That LSD induced such transcendental experiences in randomly selected subjects was considered strong evidence that "matrices for such experiences exist in the unconscious as a normal constituent of the human personality."[64]

Although LSD was first synthesized in 1938 by the Swiss chemist Albert Hoffman, its chemical action on the brain is still not completely understood.[65] However, its amplifying and catalyzing effects on the mind are well documented. From the earliest studies, researchers noticed that LSD appeared to activate "unconscious material from various deep levels of the personality."[66] Of particular importance is what has been described as the "shattering encounter" with certain critical aspects of human existence: birth, decay, and death.

This encounter initiates a profound emotional and philosophical crisis that forces the individual to seriously question the meaning of existence and his or her values in life. It also opens areas of religious and spiritual experience that seem to be intrinsic to the human personality and independent of the individual's cultural or religious background.

As with the phenomena discussed in connection with near-death experiences, the psychedelic experience typically contains elements that are not scientifically explainable. Persons "unsophisticated in anthropology and mythology experience images, episodes, and even entire thematic sequences that bear a striking resemblance to the descriptions of the posthumous journey of the soul and the death-rebirth mysteries of various cultures."[67] As with NDEs, the result is often a significantly altered outlook on the meaning of life and death. The evidence gathered from accounts of near-death experiences as well as reports about psychedelic experiences have led some to call for a broader perspective on the nature of human consciousness.[68] As Stanislav Grof says, "Reality is always larger and more complex than the most elaborate and encompassing theory."[69]

Beliefs About Death: A Wall or a Door?

In the final analysis, then, what do afterlife experiences or NDEs, and other paranormal experiences, reveal concerning the perennial question of human

The absolute certainty that death is a complete and definitive and irrevocable annihilation of personal consciousness, a certainty of the same order as our certainty that the three angles of a triangle are equal to two right angles, or contrariwise, the absolute certainty that our personal consciousness continues beyond death in whatever condition (including in such a concept the strange and adventitious additional notion of eternal reward or punishment)—either of these certainties would make our life equally impossible. In the most secret recess of the spirit of the man who believes that death will put an end to his personal consciousness and even to his memory forever, in that inner recess, even without his knowing it perhaps, a shadow hovers, a vague shadow lurks, a shadow of the shadow of uncertainty, and, while he tells himself: 'There's nothing for it but to live this passing life, for there is no other!' at the same time he hears, in this most secret recess, his own doubt murmur: 'Who knows? . . .' He is not sure he hears aright, but he hears. Likewise, in some recess of the soul of the true believer who has faith in a future life, a muffled voice, the voice of uncertainty, murmurs in his spirit's ear: 'Who knows? . . .' Perhaps these voices are no louder than the buzzing of mosquitoes when the wind roars through the trees in the woods; we scarcely make out the humming, and yet, mingled in the uproar of the storm, it can be heard. How, without this uncertainty, could we ever live?

Miguel de Unamuno, *The Tragic Sense of Life*

personality survival after death? Is death the joyful and ultimately fulfilling experience it seems to be from survivors' reports of near-death experiences? Or are such experiences only psychological projections, wish-fulfilling fantasies that serve to mask the terror of confronting one's own demise? What shall we believe about survival after death?

Clyde Nabe has characterized the two basic philosophical perspectives regarding death as follows: Death is either a *wall* or it is a *door*.[70] As we have seen, in the first view, death is the "disorganization of the functional structure of the matter which is a particular human body," and thus is the "cessation of all possibility for the person who dies." In short, death is a *wall*, not a door. In the second perspective, the possibility arises that "what is real need not necessarily be equated with what is material," thus the dissolution of the body need not be viewed as necessarily resulting in the dissolution of the human person. In other words, death is a *door*, not a wall.

We can imagine many variations on these two basic positions regarding what happens at death. Indeed, the doctrines of various religions and the explanations offered for paranormal experiences of death are just such variations. For example, stating the Christian perspective, we could say that death appears to be a wall, but at some time in the future—at the Resurrection—it turns out to have been a door. The Hindu concept of reincarnation would suggest that death is a door, not

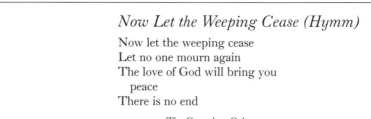

Now Let the Weeping Cease (Hymm)

Now let the weeping cease
Let no one mourn again
The love of God will bring you
    peace
There is no end

The Gospel at Colonus

a wall. Buddhists might respond that death is both a door and a wall, and is neither. The conventional psychological explanation of NDEs might seem an argument in favor of the position that death is a wall that is experienced as a door. The transpersonal and parapsychologies, on the other hand, might suggest that the door and the wall are simply alternative ways of experiencing the same reality.

In promulgating its findings on the "Assumptions and Principles of Spiritual Care," the Spiritual Care Work Group of the International Work Group on Death, Dying and Bereavement emphasized that "dying is more than a biological occurrence. It is a human, social, and spiritual event."[71] However, "too often the spiritual dimension of patients is neglected." A close relationship between religion and health has existed since ancient times. Only in the comparatively recent past has the spiritual dimension of health care been largely shunted aside in favor of a more mechanistic or scientific model. A number of practitioners, however, are now calling for a revitalized concern with their patients' spiritual health. Clifford Kuhn, for example, posits a comprehensive health model involving body, mind, society/community, and spirituality.[72] It is being increasingly recognized that caregivers need to acknowledge the spiritual component of patient care and provide appropriate resources for those who wish them. In carrying out such aims, it goes without saying that each person's spiritual beliefs and preferences must be respected.

What we believe about death and the afterlife can influence the actions taken when we or others near death. For example, if we adhere to the materialist view, seeing death as a wall, we may insist that life-sustaining efforts be carried out to the end. On the other hand, if we conceive of continued consciousness after death, we might prefer that the final hours of life on earth be spent preparing for a transition into another mode of existence. As Nabe says, "How we respond to the death of someone else, and to our own death, is thus dependent on much broader philosophical questions."

Similarly, beliefs about what happens after death may be a source of comfort and solace to the bereaved. The person who views death as the end may feel reassured that the suffering experienced during this life ends at death. Someone else may find comfort in the belief that the personality survives physical death. By understanding our own beliefs about death, says Nabe, we are able to "care more adequately for each other when death — wall or door — comes to those we love." As Thomas Attig points out, coming to terms with our own personal finiteness and mortality can be understood as a grieving process.[73] This self-mourning is a potentially lifelong process of coming to terms with impermanence, uncertainty, and vulnerability — qualities that are inherent in being mortal.

Further Readings

Paul Badham and Linda Badham, eds. *Death and Immortality in the Religions of the World*. New York: Paragon House, 1986.

Paul Barber. *Vampires, Burial, and Death: Folklore and Reality*. New Haven, Ct.: Yale University Press, 1988.

Arthur Berger, et al., eds. *Perspectives on Death and Dying: Cross-Cultural and Multi-Disciplinary Views*. Philadelphia: Charles Press, 1989.

S.G.F. Brandon. *The Judgment of the Dead: The Idea of Life After Death in the Major Religions*. New York: Charles Scribner's Sons, 1967.

James P. Carse. *Death and Existence: A Conceptual History of Human Mortality*. New York: John Wiley & Sons, 1980.

Jacques Choron. *Death and Western Thought*. New York: Macmillan, 1963.

R.C. Finucane. *Appearances of the Dead: A Cultural History of Ghosts*. Buffalo, N.Y.: Prometheus Books, 1984.

Stanislav Grof and Christina Grof. *Beyond Death: The Gates of Consciousness*. New York: Thames and Hudson, 1980.

Murray J. Harris. *Raised Immortal: Resurrection and Immortality in the New Testament*. Grand Rapids, Mich.: Eerdmans, 1985.

Frederick H. Holck, ed. *Death and Eastern Thought: Understanding Death in Eastern Religions and Philosophies*. Nashville: Abingdon, 1974.

Philip Kapleau. *The Wheel of Life and Death: A Practical and Spiritual Guide*. New York: Doubleday, 1989.

Morton T. Kelsey. *Afterlife: The Other Side of Dying*. New York: Paulist Press, 1979.

Hans Kung. *Eternal Life? Life After Death as a Medical, Philosophical, and Theological Problem*. Garden City, N.Y.: Doubleday, 1984.

Maurice Lamm. *The Jewish Way in Death and Mourning*. New York: Jonathan David, 1969.

Jung Young Lee. *Death and Beyond in the Eastern Perspective: A Study Based on the Bardo Thödol and the I Ching*. New York: Gordon and Breach, 1974.

Stephen Levine. *Who Dies? An Investigation of Conscious Living and Conscious Dying*. Garden City, N.Y.: Anchor Press/Doubleday, 1982.

Raymond Moody. *Elvis after Life: Unusual Psychic Experiences Surrounding the Death of a Superstar*. Atlanta: Peachtree, 1987.

Fazlur Rahman. *Health and Medicine in the Islamic Tradition: Change and Identity*. New York: Crossroad, 1987.

Frank E. Reynolds and Earle H. Waugh, eds. *Religious Encounters with Death: Insights from the History and Anthropology of Religions*. University Park, Pa.: Pennsylvania State University Press, 1977.

Jack Riemer, ed. *Jewish Reflections on Death*. New York: Schocken Books, 1974.

Arnold Toynbee, et al. *Man's Concern with Death*. New York: McGraw-Hill, 1968.

Emily Vermeule. *Aspects of Death in Early Greek Art and Poetry*. Berkeley: University of California Press, 1979.

Abner Weiss. *Death and Bereavement: A Halakhic Guide.* Hoboken, N.J.: KTAV, 1991.

Carol G. Zaleski. *Otherworld Journeys: Accounts of Near-Death Experiences in Medieval and Modern Times*. New York: Oxford University Press, 1988.

Photojournalist W. Eugene Smith's children appear in his 1946 photograph, "The Walk to Paradise Garden," the first taken by Smith after two years of inactivity and numerous operations to make him sound again after multiple wounds received in the Pacific during World War II. Smith said he was determined that his first frame successfully "speak of a gentle moment of spirited purity in contrast to the depraved savagery I had raged against with my war photographs."

C H A P T E R 15

The Path Ahead:
Personal and Social Choices

*D*eath may be devalued, even denied for a time, but it cannot be eluded. In our relationship with death, we are both survivors and experiencers. In previous chapters we have seen that there can be many different attitudes toward death and dying. Death may be seen as an ever-present threat, or as a benign catalyst, provoking us to greater awareness and creativity in life. Death may seem the ignominious end to even the best of human accomplishment, or it may be seen as a welcome respite from life's sufferings. Death holds many meanings.

One student in a death and dying class said, "Confronting death has put me in touch with life." Acknowledging the impact of death in our lives can awaken us to the preciousness of life. This insight can lead to a greater appreciation of the relationships in one's life. Learning about death can also bring insights concerning the death of old notions of self, as one grows beyond limited concepts of "who I am."

Death is inseparable from the whole of human experience. The study of death and dying touches on the past, the present, and the future. It takes account of individual acts as well as customs of entire societies. The study of death and dying leads naturally to the arena of political decision, and it ultimately brings us to choices of an emphatically personal nature. Death education is germane to the sphere of social relationships as well as to the confrontation with mortality that comes in the most private, personal moments of solitude and introspection.

567

I say, "Why should a spirited mortal feel proud, when like a swift, fleet meteor or fast-flying cloud, man passes through life to his rest in the grave?" They've asked me, "How do I feel?" I told them that there's nothing to it; you do things the way they ought to be done. I don't see anything to be proud about. It's pretty difficult for a man to feel proud when knowing as he does the short space of time he's here and all paths, even those of our greatest glory, lead but to the grave. So it is very difficult to feel proud when Death says this. You're here today and gone sometimes today.

"A Very Long Conversation with
James Van Der Zee at the Age of Ninety-One,"
in *The Harlem Book of the Dead*

Think about your own relationship to death. What place does death have in your life? What kinds of meanings does death hold for you? Are death and dying compartmentalized in a category all their own, or are they part of a larger fabric of human experience?

In this final chapter we touch upon some of the ways in which what we learn about death impinges on individual and social experience. Rather than providing answers, our aim will be to stimulate inquiry, to raise questions, to speculate about the path ahead.

The Value of Exploring Death and Dying: New Choices

Taking a course or reading a book about death and dying offers an opportunity to take death "out of the closet" and examine it from many perspectives. Possibly you are making new choices in your life as a result of your personal exploration of death. Reflecting on the study of death and dying, one student remarked, "The thought of death had always created a lot of fear; now I find that there's something very fascinating about exploring my own feelings about death and the way that society relates to death." Often, the study of death brings insights into past experiences in one's life. One woman said, "I see now what a big part denial and mutual pretense played in my family's experience of death; the subject of death had really been taboo." Another said, "I was surprised to find how many events in my own life had carried the same kind of emotional impact as a death. Divorce, separation, illness, disappointment—all meant coping with grief, loneliness, fear, and sadness in much the same way as when dealing with a death."

As you think about the various topics covered in this book, what do you notice concerning your understanding of death? Has learning about death and dying expanded your perspective or altered your attitude toward death? Do the terms *death* and *dying* elicit the same patterns of thought and emotion as when you began your study?

I attended your Dealing with Death and Dying class May 10 and 11. You excused me at 1:00, May 11, so that I could go to a function that I needed to attend. I agreed to write notes on an article on cancer to compensate for the class time that I'd miss.

At the same time I was driving home from the class, my Mother was admitted to a Midwestern hospital for internal bleeding due to her accelerated cancerous condition. I left the Bay Area soon after and arrived in Iowa to deal with the reality of death.

Comments on the article don't seem as important to me, now, as some other comments I'd like to make. They concern the necessity of dealing with death and dying.

Had it not been for your class, I would have had more severe problems dealing with all the things death causes us to deal with. The openness of the people in class helped me work through some of the pain I was experiencing as I knew that my Mother didn't have long to live. The class helped me during the time the mortician sat with us and helped us work out the business details, and it helped me through the Midwestern Protestant wake. I was helped as I remembered to make sure that we got what we wanted and were allowed to say our good-byes in ways we wanted. I was able to help my family think clearly about the needs they had so that after Mother was removed from us, we would not say "if only."

A student in a Death and Dying class

"When I used to think about my own death," a student remarked, "I used to slam the door, thinking of all the things I still wanted to do in my lifetime. Now, I've become a bit more calm, a bit more balanced about it." Another said, "Before I got involved in studying death, 1 was really uptight about death and dying, especially my own death, even though I haven't had many personal encounters with death. Now I feel that facing my own death is not as difficult, really, as being a survivor of other people's deaths."

Studying death and dying does not necessarily resolve the question, "Why death?" We are born and we die: We face the prospect not only of our own death, but of surviving the deaths of loved ones. For some, investigation of death and dying allows a more accurate perception of what anyone can do to protect or be responsible for another. A parent said, "I've learned something about letting go where my children are concerned. No matter how much you might wish it were otherwise, you can never shield your loved ones from everything."

Responding to this awareness, one student said, "I learned how important it is to appreciate people while you've got them." Becoming aware of death can focus attention on the importance in relationships of taking care of unfinished business, saying the things that need to be said, and not being anxious about those things that do not. As one student expressed it, her study of death and dying had impressed upon her a sense of "the precariousness of life."

Recognizing that the preciousness of the human situation is revealed not only in major changes — such as those brought about by death — but also in the less noticed changes experienced in daily life, one can choose to be attentive to the things and persons that are most highly valued.

Think about the personal and social implications of death and dying. Have your previous opinions on such issues as euthanasia, funerals and body disposition, and war been confirmed? Or have they changed as a result of your studies?

As more people willingly confront issues surrounding death and dying, and examine the options for themselves, changes are occurring throughout society. Examples are the establishment of such helping mechanisms as hospices and suicide intervention programs, as well as other support groups that aid individuals and families in crisis. As death is subjected to a less fearful scrutiny, there is movement — individually and as a society — toward gaining the knowledge that can be helpful in dealing with death intelligently and compassionately.

For some, the close examination of death brings insights that help to dissipate or resolve long-held feelings of guilt or blame attached to grief about a loved one's death. The encounter with death that comes through study can open up new and creative possibilities that result in an easier, more comfortable relationship with others and with life itself. The study of death and dying can help to put previously unsettling experiences into perspective.

The notions that may be present at the beginning of a personal exploration of death and dying are expressed in the following statement:

> When I first began to recognize the seriousness of death and dying, I fled from it in fear, although I didn't realize what I was doing. Emotionally, it was harder than I had expected. But I learned that people do survive their losses, and I now know why they are called "survivors." I also learned a lot about myself, not all pleasant. A lot of my learning occurred amidst avoidance and trepidation. I thought about things that I had neglected for a long time...all my old concepts of death, shadowed in images of hells and old horror movies.

For one man who had felt frustrated, resentful, and guilty about his brother's death twenty years earlier, the study of death provided an opportunity to open up unexpressed and unresolved grief about a number of close family deaths. As the "stored tears" began to be expressed, he summed up the benefit of his exploration of death: "It feels so good to get rid of that ache."

For some, the study of death and dying brings benefits related to professional concerns. One nurse said: "When death occurs on the ward, people often think, 'Oh, well, you're a nurse; it shouldn't bother you.' But it does. . . . I really miss the patient; it's a real loss." A ward clerk in a hospital emergency room described the new and more-helpful choices she could make use of in relating to survivors:

> My desk is in the same area with the survivors of an ER [emergency room] death. I used to feel a pain right in the pit of my stomach, wondering what to say to them. I thought I should be able to comfort them in some way, that I should somehow offer them words of wisdom. But now I don't feel that way. I've learned how important it is to simply listen, to be supportive just by being there, instead of trying to find some words that will magically make it all go away.

Ukiyo-E

What explanation is given for the phosphorus light
That you, as boy, went out to catch
When summer dusk turned to night.
You caught the fireflies, put them in a jar,
Careful to let in the air,
Then you fed them dandelions, unsure
Of what such small and fleeting things
Need, and when
Their light grew dim, you
    Let them go.

There is no explanation for the fire
That burns in our bodies
Or the desire that grows, again and again,
So that we must move toward each other
In the dark.
We have no wings.
We are ordinary people, doing ordinary things.
The story can be told on rice paper.
There is a lantern, a mountain, whatever
    We can remember.

Hiroshige's landscape is so soft.
What child, woman, would not want to go out
Into that dark, and be caught,
And caught again, by you?
Let these pictures of the floating world go on
Forever, but when
This light must flicker out, catch me,
Give me whatever a child imagines
To keep me aglow, then
    Let me go.

Siv Cedering

Others find the study of death and dying academically intriguing. The avenues of exploration into other cultures or into one's own society opened up through such study can be a rapid means of gaining insight into what is essential about a society's values and concepts. Learning about the meaning of death in feudal Japan, for example, provides the student of Japanese culture an appreciation that goes beyond the usual aesthetic or historic approach to cross-cultural understanding. Concepts about what constitutes a "good" death or about immortality reveal a great deal about the tenor and form of a culture's daily life as well as its highest achievements. Death is at the core of human experience.

Culture and individual personality shape our attitudes toward death. What we understand of death and what meanings we ascribe to it become significant to the extent that we construct a meaningful relationship with the experience of death and dying in our lives. This grave marker expresses a memorialization that is consonant with the life styles of both the deceased and her survivors.

Cultural attitudes toward death are reflected in such societal applications as social programs for the aged and medical care of the dying. The willingness of a society to engage in activities that pose risks for the well-being of its citizens also demonstrates something of the consensus with regard to the value of human life. Funeral customs reflect a society's attitudes toward death and intimate relationships. Investigating a society's relationship with death makes available a wealth of information to the person with an inquiring mind and an interest in discerning the larger patterns of belief and behavior.

Societal Applications of Death Education

What kinds of cultural values may be acquired or refined by a willingness to think and talk about death, and with what effect on society as a whole? Will frank explorations of dying and death contribute to solving the current dilemmas of medical ethics? Can a greater openness toward death help to answer thorny questions about whether, or in what circumstances, the use of life-sustaining technologies prolong life or only delay death? A willingness to speak plainly about death and to face squarely the implications of public policy decisions that relate to death can assist a society in sorting out such value-laden issues. Similarly, an awareness of the needs of the dying, coupled with knowledge about the options for meeting those needs, can lead to improvements in our health care system. Arriving at responsible and just decisions about such issues requires informed participation by citizens from all walks of life.

One student said, "Sometimes I feel there's too little space in our society for a person to scream, to cry, to shout, to sing, to touch, to be human." Death evokes all these aspects of human behavior. Yet the person who is experiencing grief may find it difficult to express these natural emotions. Elisabeth Kübler-Ross is among those who have advocated the institution, in hospitals and other such settings, of a "grief" or "screaming" room: a room set aside not only for letting out the intense emotions of loss and bereavement, but also for physicians and other caregivers to engage in open discussions with patients and family members.

In the past few decades, death has come a considerable distance out of the closet into the light of public attention. It is difficult to assess to what extent this increased awareness is the result of what seems a pervasive dread concerning the future. The experiences of the Vietnam era altered the perceptions of many people with regard to what constitutes the national interest in matters of defense and foreign affairs. Experiences such as those stemming from the American involvement in Vietnam, and more recently in the Persian Gulf, can affect more general attitudes toward death by causing an examination of previously unquestioned assumptions. Although death from such catastrophes as war has indeed touched the lives of many Americans, war has usually been thought of as something that happens "over there," not "here at home." In many countries, however, the consequences of warfare have been recent and immediate in national experience. Some persons have sought greater knowledge about death and dying as a means of

> Recently my seven-year-old son hopped in my lap and we watched the evening news together. The concluding line of a report on environmental pollution was a quote from U.N. scientists predicting that in twenty years the world would be uninhabitable. As the TV switched to a Madison Avenue jingle designed to encourage us to purchase a non-greasy hair tonic, my son turned to me with a terribly small voice and asked: "Dad, how old will I be when we all die?"
>
> Robert D. Barr, *The Social Studies Professional*

resolving disturbing personal and social issues raised by such military and political conflicts.

The threat of nuclear warfare has brought death into the consciousness of many people. Increasingly, it seems that the threat of death on a massive scale now comes not only from the possibility of nuclear catastrophe (whether accidental or intentional), but also from pollution, the deadly poisoning of our environment. The accidental poisoning of livestock feed in Michigan a few years back characterizes the kind of risk to which individuals are exposed but which they feel unable to control. Many people are angry about what is perceived as the precedence of profit over people, yet they feel powerless to affect the situation. Others feel frustrated at conflicting reports about the true nature of the hazard. This frustration is often compounded by uncertainty about whether government agencies and private industry are telling the whole story.

How do our understanding about death and our attitudes toward it affect the way we think and feel about these encounters with death? And, equally relevant, how do these encounters affect the way we relate to death? If these threats are as real as they seem, what is it about our attitudes toward death that stops us from truly confronting such threats?

Confronting the meaning of death in social as well as personal contexts may alter our political consciousness. The student of death and dying is likely to have heightened awareness about the social issues that involve death. He or she will have an appreciation of the reality underlying newspaper stories that report about death either in statistical or dramatic terms. Hazards to public safety — often expressed in tedious analyses of risks versus benefits — take on an added dimension for the person who has explored the human impact of death and dying. The person who has examined the manner in which death impinges on such issues as disarmament, environmental pollution, and crime in the streets begins to consider them in a new light, with greater understanding and concern.

The issues that confront us are not amenable to easy answers. Consider, for example, the debate over a person's "right to die" and the demand prevalent in our society that life be sustained. Such questions must be dealt with in the context of a cultural milieu with characteristic attitudes toward death and dying. Appreciating all sides of the issue can lead to more balanced and practical choices.

"Frank and Ernest," drawing by Bob Thaves, © 1984 NEA Inc.

New Directions in Death Education

The curricula of death education and standards for measuring outcome are still being defined. A clear sense of continuity and common tradition has not fully developed. Although this issue is perhaps most pressing for those in academic settings, it applies as well to persons working as counselors, caregivers, and in other such capacities within communities.

The question of accountability in death education has been difficult to address, partly because such education is conducted in a variety of settings, often with differing methodologies and goals. For example, should the aim of death education be to *alleviate* discomfort and anxiety about dying and death? If acceptance of death is thought to be a superior posture to denial, then efforts must be made to assess the validity of such notions.[1] Death education is both humanitarian and scientific, thus caring must be combined with objectivity.

Research is needed to address adequately even some of the fundamental concerns of thanatology. Robert Fulton has pointed out, for example, that there seems to be a fixation on nineteenth-century hydrostatic models of grief, which postulate a certain volume of grief that must be poured out. The "work" of mourning, Fulton says, is generally conceived of in linear terms, as a step-by-step progression, rather than as a dynamic process of "unraveling the skein of grief."[2] Little is known about how physiological processes of the brain affect the experience of grief. Fulton notes that the "anniversary reaction," for example, a phenomenon commonly experienced by the bereaved, may be a manifestation of the associative nature of brain function. Also requiring further study is a possible link between mourning and creativity.

In striving to improve care of the dying and the bereaved, paternalism may replace advocacy if answers are proposed before the necessary questions have been asked. If such care is to be provided within the context of a person's free choice and beliefs about death, we should be wary of presuppositions that derive from the caregiver's personal preferences rather than unbiased and informed appraisal. A caregiver who places a high value on resolving conflicts as part of preparing for endings may unintentionally demand, expect, or wish that his or

> Death is not the ultimate tragedy of life. The ultimate tragedy is depersonalization—dying in an alien and sterile area, separated form the spiritual nourishment that comes from being able to reach out to a loving hand, separate from the desire to experience the things that make life worth living, separated from hope.
>
> Norman Cousins, *Anatomy of an Illness*

her patients do the same. Our understanding of the phenomena associated with dying and death can grow only when we take into account the interplay between theory and application in constructing an adequate knowledge base.

Others have noted that minorities appear to be underrepresented in the resource materials commonly used in death education courses. Observing that one of the larger organizations of professionals in the field "appears to reflect a middle-class white, grassroots movement," Darrell Crase asks the rhetorical question, "Black people do die, don't they?"[3]

Much of the research in thanatology has been concerned with the measurement of attitudes toward death, and, more particularly, death anxiety with its related concepts of fear, threat, and concern in the face of one's own death. Robert Neimeyer has stated that more than 760 articles on death anxiety were published in professional journals between 1955 and 1990.[4] This area of research has been characterized as "the largest area of empirical study in the field of thanatology."[5] Virtually all of this research has made use of questionnaires in gathering data on death anxiety. Since the early 1970s a number of "death anxiety" and "fear of death" scales have been proposed by various researchers, including Donald Templer, David Lester, John Hoelter, and Robert Neimeyer, to cite several noteworthy examples.[6]

Generally speaking, the findings from this research indicate that death anxiety tends to be higher among females than among males, higher among blacks than among whites, and higher among youth and middle-aged adults than among older persons. Religious belief appears to be inversely related to death anxiety; that is, people who characterize themselves as "religious" tend to report less death anxiety than those who do not characterize themselves this way. Individuals who report a greater degree of self-actualization and internal sense of control also report less death anxiety than do their counterparts. The same general finding also applies to persons whose orientation to life is one of "living in the present," rather than looking back to the past or ahead to the future.

Despite the bulk of accumulated data, however, there remain significant questions about the research into death anxiety. Robert Neimeyer has summarized these questions as follows: First, what definition of death is implied by the various testing instruments? Second, what are the strengths and limitations of the various instruments that have been used in death anxiety research? Third, based on the answer to the first two questions, what are the implications for future research? And, finally, reviewing the data gathered up to now, what do we really know?[7] As Herman Feifel pointed out in a recent article reviewing the status of research and practice in thanatology:

> Fear of death is not a unitary or monolithic variable. . . . In the face of personal death, the human mind ostensibly operates simultaneously on several levels of reality, or finite provinces of meaning, each of which can be somewhat autonomous. We, therefore, need to be circumspect in accepting at face value the degree of fear of death affirmed at the conscious level.[8]

Robert Kastenbaum recently characterized research into death anxiety as "thanatology's own assembly line."[9] He suggests that part of the appeal of death anxiety research lies in the fact that it "allows the researcher (and the readers, if they so choose) to enjoy the illusion that death has really been studied." Just how the data obtained from death anxiety research should be applied to practical issues in death education, counseling, and care is still largely a matter of uncertainty. If we could reliably state, for example, that physicians with a high degree of death anxiety do less well in relating to dying patients, then that lesson might be applied constructively in the health care setting. For the most part, however, we are not yet in a position to adequately appraise the effects of death anxiety as they impinge on real-world issues. To cite one instance of this problem, consider the fact that some studies indicate that women have higher death anxiety scores than do men. Does this gender difference mean that women are too anxious about death, or that men are not anxious enough?[10] This question is yet to be satisfactorily answered and may be taken as representative of the difficulties in the field of death anxiety research that must be addressed.

Turning our attention to practice, there are few signs that practitioners have made much use of either research or theory in their work with patients or with the bereaved. It appears, Kastenbaum says, "that many practitioners in the area of terminal care and bereavement have neither an up-to-date mastery of thanatological research nor a secure grasp of the historical and theoretical dimensions."

Completing his portrait of thanatological research, theory, and practice, Kastenbaum concludes that,

> at the worst, perhaps, we have sketched a picture of practitioners who fail to read a literature that wouldn't help them very much anyway. The academicians continue to tread their mills . . . with only each other to amuse, while the practitioners base their services on individual experiences and a grab-bag of unexamined assumptions and "facts" whose veridicality has seldom been tested, let alone established.

Echoing such thoughts, Myra Bluebond-Langner notes that, "while the quantity of research has increased, what more do we actually know? Has progress in thanatology kept pace with publication? What differences have our efforts made in the care of dying patients and their families, and in our own responses to death and impending disasters?"[11] Herman Feifel calls attention to the need to "integrate existing knowledge concerning death and grief into our communal and public institutions."[12] Individuals involved in the areas of death education, counseling, and care must become active participants in helping to formulate the public policies affecting those areas of concern. While acknowledging that the

---

❧ *Zen Questions*

Men who have seen life and death as . . . an unbroken continuum, the swingings of an eternal pendulum, have been able to move as freely into death as they walked through life.

The Zen masters were so intimately involved with the *whole* of existence that they found overinvolvement with any of its parts, death included, to be a misplaced concern, saying to people who ask about an afterlife, "Why do you want to know what will happen to you after you die? Find out who you are now!"

Philip Kapleau

---

field of thanatology (and, by extension, the so-called death awareness movement) has many tasks facing it, Feifel concludes that it already can be credited with a number of contributions to our well-being:

> The [death] movement has been a major force in broadening our grasp of the phenomenology of illness, in helping humanize medical relationships and health care, and in advancing the rights of the dying. It is highpointing values that undergird the vitality of human response to catastrophe and loss. Furthermore, it is contributing to reconstituting the integrity of our splintered wholeness. More important, perhaps, it is sensitizing us to our common humanity, which is all too eroded in the present world. It may be somewhat hyperbolic, but I believe that how we regard death and how we treat the dying and survivors are prime indications of a civilization's intention and target.

Along this line, Robert Fulton and Greg Owen note that the message of palliative care put forward by Elisabeth Kübler-Ross, Cicely Saunders, Mother Teresa of Calcutta, and others also contains a message about "essential religious and spiritual values that extend beyond the immediate goal of care for the dying."[13] The "compassionate acts of service," which the death awareness movement has encouraged and promoted during the past several decades, are founded on a recognition of the identity and worth of each human being.

As the disciplines of death education, counseling, and care continue to evolve, one of the most persistent calls has been for a global perspective. Although personal experiences related to dying and death are indeed central to thanatological study and practice, the global dimensions of death — war, violence, nuclear threat, environmental catastrophe — are increasingly of concern. Dan Leviton and William Wendt have described a conceptual framework that focuses on the reality of death to help improve the quality of civilized life.[14] Using this model, death education may serve not only to aid individuals in their personal confrontations with death, but also to ameliorate the causes of large-scale deaths that are human-caused and unnecessary.

Leviton and Wendt use the term *horrendous death* to describe these global confrontations with death, and they define it as

> Could it be . . . that one reason why the study of death has emerged as one of the dominant concerns of our time is to help us to become globally sensitized to the experience of death precisely because the notion of death on a *planetary scale* now hangs, like the sword of Damocles, over our heads? Could this be the universe's way of "inoculating" us against the fear of death?
>
> Kenneth Ring, *Life at Death*

a form of premature death which is ugly, fashioned by man, without any trace of grace, totally unnecessary, and, as they say of pornography, lacking any redeeming social value. It is that death which is caused by war, homicide, holocaust, terrorism, starvation, and poisoning of the environment.

Benumbed by these categories of horrendous death, most of us tend to deny its presence or feel a sense of hopelessness and loss of control over our own destiny and future. It is this denial, say Leviton and Wendt, that "very much *prevents* worldwide cooperative policy designed to improve the quality of life." Death education, then, can serve a public health function of prevention and intervention in response to potential catastrophe.

The comprehensive nature of the concerns that ought to be addressed within the practice of death education has been eloquently summarized in a document formulated by the International Work Group on Death, Dying, and Bereavement:

Death, dying, and bereavement are fundamental and pervasive aspects of the human experience. Individuals and societies achieve fullness of living by understanding and appreciating these realities. The absence of such understanding and appreciation may result in unnecessary suffering, loss of dignity, alienation, and diminished quality of living. Therefore, education about death, dying, and bereavement, both formal and informal, is an essential component of the educational process at all levels.[15]

As efforts toward providing education about death continue to mature, it is likely that the vision of a comprehensive role for death education, as reflected in this statement, will serve to guide the creation of diverse forms of death education in the future.

Death in the Future

As we look to the future, what questions about death and dying will increasingly demand our attention both as individuals and as a society? We will continue to see an ever-growing older population. Over the next two decades, the U.S. population of persons ages 65 and over is expected to increase from about 31.6 million to 39.4 million, with the largest share of this increase among persons over

> ### The Past Is Not Dead
>
> Cultures that view birth as a beginning and death as an end can have no sense of a living past. For Mexicans, neither birth nor death is seen to interrupt the continuity of life and neither is considered overly important. Belief in communion with the dead is widespread, not in a psychic or spiritualist sense or as a function of a Christian faith in the afterlife, but simply as an outgrowth of the knowledge that the past is not dead.
>
> Alan Riding, *Distant Neighbors*

age 75.[16] It has been estimated there will be 2.6 million deaths annually by the year 2000, an increase of about one-third over the present number. Care of the dying is likely to become big business as corporations expand their role as surrogate caregivers for the aged and dying.

Imagine what death will be like fifty or one hundred years from now. Extrapolate from present realities and current possibilities. Think back over the key issues discussed in previous chapters. What are some of your speculations about what our relationship to death will be by the middle years of the twenty-first century?

For example, imagine the kind of rituals or ceremonies surrounding the dead that will exist several decades from now. Writing about the rapid pace of social change among South Pacific societies, Ron Crocombe remarks upon the trend in these societies of reducing the time spent on each funeral, marriage, birth, and other such occasion of community celebration, as well as diverting such activities from day to night and weekday to weekend. "Most traditional social rituals took more time than can be spared today," he says, "both because there are many more things to do, and because each person is doing different things."[17]

Although our own value judgments may determine how we spend our time, such decisions are rarely made independently of social norms and practices. For instance, if a work schedule makes it difficult to attend a midweek funeral, we may be reluctant to insist on having time off. As our notions about the use of time change, thereby affecting our attitudes and behaviors relative to death, what kinds of funeral practices and services might evolve to correspond to these changes?

As for disposition of the corpse, will there be enough land to continue the practice of burials? Some have suggested that we may see the substitution of high-rise cemeteries, cities of the dead towering above the landscape of the living. This is already happening in Japan, where burial space in large cities like Tokyo is at a premium. Although it is unlikely that current funeral practices will disappear completely within the foreseeable future, changes in methods of arranging for and conducting last rites will undoubtedly occur as consumers exercise new choices. An example of this change can already be seen in some areas of the country as casket dealers set up shop to make their wares available to the public independently of conventional funeral establishments.

In coping with the death of a loved one, what types of social services will be available? Few could have foreseen the rapid rise of specialized support groups and activist organizations such as "Parents of Murdered Children" and "Mothers Against Drunk Driving," to name but two of the groups that provide a forum for the issues and a focus for the grief resulting from particular types of bereavement. What other developments in bereavement, grief, and mourning may take place in the coming years?

Besides support groups for the bereaved, the recent past also has seen an increased emphasis on counseling or therapy following bereavement. In the future, might there be "grief clinics" available on call for emergencies? Would these clinics — much like present health institutions — send out reminders for patients or clients to come in for a bereavement checkup before the anniversary date of a significant death? Bereavement counseling is already acknowledged for its value, especially when circumstances make coping with a death difficult. Such counseling, however, is not yet widely available, partly due to a persistent belief that coping with grief — regardless of circumstances — should not require outside intervention. In addition, some health insurance providers refuse to reimburse their policyholders for therapy or counseling related to bereavement. With a greater openness in talking about death and acknowledging its place in our lives, however, the time may not be too far off when professional assistance in dealing with grief is the norm.

What diseases will frighten us and endanger our survival if the currently threatening diseases, such as cancer and heart disease, become routinely prevented or cured? What change do you imagine will occur within even as short a period as the next decade? In earlier chapters, we discussed the rapid pace of medical advances in diagnosis and treatment. The prognosis for a given disease or category of patient may change from very poor to exceptionally good within the span of a few years with new discoveries and techniques. During the same period, on the other hand, life-threatening diseases that were previously unrecognized or even nonexistent may present new threats.

As a case in point: Who could have foreseen the frightening implications of AIDS? Virtually nonexistent just a few years ago, this disease quickly assumed proportions comparable to the great plagues of the Middle Ages in terms of public fear and uncertainty. Individuals, local communities, and society as a whole were caught off guard by the outbreak and unsure about how to respond. To cite one example: When Elisabeth Kübler-Ross proposed a hospice for infants and children with AIDS, the nearby community called an emergency meeting to squelch the proposal. Can we anticipate that new diseases and threats, as yet undescribed and unknown, will cause similar hysteria in the future?

It is difficult to imagine a time when *no* disease or illness will be life-threatening. Yet we have already lived through many technological advances that make

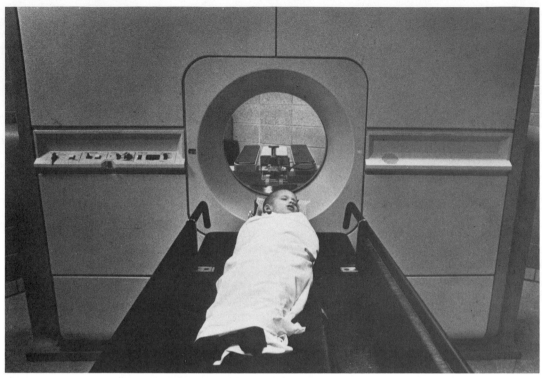

Burton Steele, Times-Picayune

Extrapolating from current medical technologies, we can foresee only faintly the questions and decisions about death and dying that the children of the future will face.

possible the sustaining of life beyond any measure conceivable by earlier generations. What technological advances will become commonplace for sustaining life in the coming decades? The future may include "off-the-shelf" replaceable body parts that will sustain life when conventional methods prove futile. In the coming years, organ transplantation may give way to organ substitution. If there is indeed a "bionic" human in our future, what values should guide the use of such innovative, life-sustaining technologies, and who will decide? In Damon Knight's science fiction story, "Masks," a man who has suffered physically devastating injuries is repaired with functional artificial body parts.[18] But his mechanically sustained life causes him to question what constitutes a living human being.

Another area of speculation is the development of techniques for accurately predicting the time of a person's death. This theme is explored in Clifford Simak's

> I was sitting by myself. The hotel had cleared. A little old lady came in, so I asked her to sit with me. And she told me her life. She had lived for twelve years in hotels. All she had was in this one little room. She had a daughter. She said her daughter wrote twice a week, but her daughter lived at a distance. She went into quite some detail, and I think, it hit me then, harder than it ever had, that some day that might be me!
>
> A student in a Death and Dying class

"Death Scene" and in Robert Heinlein's "Life-Line."[19] Both stories seem to suggest that the moment of one's death may be better left unknown. Although such explorations in speculative fiction are typically located in the future, in a setting different from our own, and often incorporate elements of fantasy, the themes investigated relate directly to present possibilities and current dilemmas of moral choice.

When members of the "baby boom" generation reach retirement age in the first decades of the twenty-first century, what will their lives be like? What changes are likely to occur in the health care system? What will be the quality of life — and of dying? In the story "Golden Acres," Kit Reed envisions a future in which the administrators of an institution for the aged make life-or-death decisions about the aged inmates in order to make room for new arrivals.[20] Golden Acres provides everything for its residents, except the possibility of living out their lives in the ways they wish. Reed's story focuses on a resident who refuses to acquiesce in society's neglect of its aged members. As the protagonist describes it, Golden Acres is "a vast boneyard." Will that description also apply to the prospects facing the aged members of our own communities?

During the decade of the 1990s, as we approach the end of one millennium and the advent of another, we can expect to encounter a variety of apocalyptic scenarios and perhaps some feelings of trepidation. Prophecies concerning "the end of the world" from ancient traditions around the globe will be dusted off and put forward for our inspection. Nostradamas, writing in the sixteenth century, prophesied that terrible events would occur in the last months before the turning of the millennium. The Bible, according to the view espoused by some readers, speaks of the cataclysmic final battle of Armageddon occurring a generation after the establishment of a Jewish nation-state. Prophecies found in the Buddhist and Hindu traditions, as well as in the Aztec and Hopi traditions, among many others, also suggest the potential for unimaginable upheaval as an accompaniment to the change of millennia.

Cullen Murphy describes a scenario apparently thought to be likely among some astronomers:

> In May of the year 2000 . . . Mercury, Mars, Jupiter, and Saturn will be aligned behind the sun, aimed directly at Earth on the other side. The pull of these planets

could, some say, be so intense as to rupture seismic faults and even to cause devastating tsunamis in the planet's underlying magma, the molten rock pulsing in powerful waves beneath the mantle. . . . The geologic disruptions could be so great that they could cause a "wobble" in Earth's rotation and possibly cause a "polar flip," with the planet falling over on its side or turning completely upside down, like an unskilled kayaker.[21]

Scientists, Murphy says, "are unanimous in the view that the result would be a real mess."

Less dramatic, but perhaps no less troublesome for life on planet Earth, are the well-known warnings we have heard concerning the greenhouse effect, acid rain, global warming, holes in the ozone layer, the decimation of the rain forests, and the deaths of species. Many observers believe that "these banner warnings of planetary trouble" bespeak clear and real dangers that "must in addressed in an unprecedented, worldwide effort before it is too late."[22] In addressing these issues, students and practitioners of thanatology have a special responsibility. They have learned from their encounters with dying and death that life is precious and precarious. The poet Gary Snyder has written:

> The extinction of a species, each one a pilgrim of four billion years of evolution, is an irreversible loss. The ending of the lines of so many creatures with whom we have traveled this far is an occasion of profound sorrow and grief. Death can be accepted and to some degree transformed. But the loss of lineages and all their future young is not something to accept. It must be rigorously and intelligently resisted.[23]

In working to improve care of the dying and provide comfort for the bereaved, we must also consider how the insights gained from a study of death can be compassionately applied to the life of the planet as a whole.

Living with Death and Dying

As you think about the various perspectives covered in your study of death and dying, take a moment to assess the areas that seem of particular value to you. What insights developed from examining how people relate to death in other cultures? How do the insights gained from study about death and children relate to your own death experiences as a child or as an adult? What about your risk-taking behaviors? What aspects of your life style involve risking death? What choices would you make regarding funeral ritual, terminal care, life-sustaining medical technologies? In sum, ask yourself: What have I learned that can be helpful to me as a survivor of others' deaths — and in confronting my own death?

In considering the personal value that is derived from thinking about and exploring the many meanings of death, you may notice that the study of death and dying engages both the cognitive faculties and the emotions. The personal exploration of death also has a rippling effect, extending outward to the social milieu and your relationships with others. What effect does your awareness of death have on the quality of your relationships with family members and friends, or perhaps

My Death

"Death is our eternal companion,"
Don Juan said with a most serious
air. "It is always to our left, at
an arm's length. . . . It has always been
watching you. It always will until
the day it taps you."

Carlos Castenada

My death
looks exactly like me.
She lives to my left,
at exactly an arm's length.
She has my face, hair, hands;
she ages
as I grow older.

Sometimes, at night,
my death awakens me

or else appears in dreams
I did not write.
Sometimes a sudden wind
blows from nowhere,
& I look left
& see my death.
Alive, I write
with my right hand only.
When I am dead,
I shall write with my left.

But later I will have to write
through others.
I may appear
to future poets
as their deaths.

Erica Jong

with the person down the street or at the neighborhood shop? Does an awareness of "the precious precariousness of life" prompt a greater sensitivity toward your own and others' needs and a greater compassion for others?

Humanizing Death and Dying

Many people are encouraged by what they see as the increasing openness about and humanizing of death in American society. There are signs that the circumstances surrounding death are being brought back into the personal control of the individuals and families who are closest to a particular death.

There is some question, however, whether this apparent openness toward death is illusory. When death is accepted as a topic of casual discussion on television talk shows, are we not minimizing or devaluing death, trying to achieve a kind of "death without regrets"? Is our discomfort with death somehow masking its reality?

As some thanatologists and persons who care for the dying emphasize, death is not necessarily what it seems to be in our rosy-colored projections and fantasies about the good death. In the urge to humanize death and dying, to accept death, might there also be a more subtle form of denial?

In one sense, of course, none of us is able to "humanize" death. Death is already an intensely human experience. We can work to balance our fears with openness, our anxieties with trust. We can begin to understand the dynamics of bereavement and grief, to make room for loss and change in our lives and in the

> It's a matter of honor, death. It's your white page, do you see? Or your shame. Either you're worthy of it or you ain't. To accept it, to face it with honor and respect and goodwill, to *earn* it, that is to be brave.
>
> N. Scott Momaday,
> *The Ancient Child*

lives of others. Death need not always be seen as something foreign, a foe to be fought valiantly to the bitter end.

But in gaining an easier familiarity with death, we should beware of becoming too casual. We may find we have confronted only our *image* of death, not death itself. There are many signs of an increased casualness toward death in modern society. One example is the increasing number of death notices, bearing the announcement, "No services are planned." Yet few people die without survivors who are affected by the loss. Is death a solitary or a communal event? Can I truly say that my death is "my own"? Or is death an event whose significance ripples outward to touch the lives not only of friends and loved ones, but also the lives of casual acquaintances and even strangers in ways little understood? What is the desired balance between the individual and the social connotations of death?

Defining the Good Death

There is no single definition of what constitutes a *good* death. In ancient Greece, to die young, in the fullness of one's creative energies, was considered to be exceptional luck. In our society, on the other hand, death at a young age is considered a misfortune; the death of a person just embarking on an independent life or of someone in the prime of life seems a great tragedy.

The good death can be defined in many ways. Take a moment to think about how you might define it. Consider the various factors — age, mode of death, surroundings, and so on — that would enter into your concept of a good death. Is your concept the same for yourself and for others?

Some may question whether there can be any such thing as a good death. "Death is never good," they might say. "It can only cause pain and sadness." A more useful concept, perhaps, is of the *appropriate* death. What makes some deaths seem more appropriate than others? Our answers are influenced by cultural values and by the social context of death. Avery Weisman has enumerated some of the conditions that define an appropriate death in most modern societies.[24]

First, an appropriate death is relatively pain-free; suffering is kept to a minimum. The social and emotional needs of the dying person are met to the fullest extent possible. There is no impoverishment of crucial human resources. Within the limits imposed by disabilities, the dying person is free to operate effectively as

The contemplation of death and its meaning will determine how we and our children think about and behave toward death in the decades ahead.

an individual and to enjoy mobility and independence. In addition, the dying person is able to recognize and resolve, as far as possible, any residual personal and social conflicts. The person is allowed to satisfy his or her wishes in ways that are consistent with the situation and with his or her self-identity and self-esteem.

As death approaches, the dying person is allowed to freely choose to relinquish control over various aspects of his or her life, turning them over to persons in whom confidence and trust have been placed. The dying person also may choose to seek out or to relinquish relationships with significant others. In other words, the person chooses a comfortable level of social interaction.

Weisman points out that to achieve an appropriate death we must first rid ourselves of the notion that death is *never* appropriate. This belief, he says, acts as a self-fulfilling prophecy: We shut ourselves off from creating the possibility of a more appropriate death.

For an appropriate death to be possible, the dying person must be protected from needless, dehumanizing, and demeaning procedures. The person's prefer-

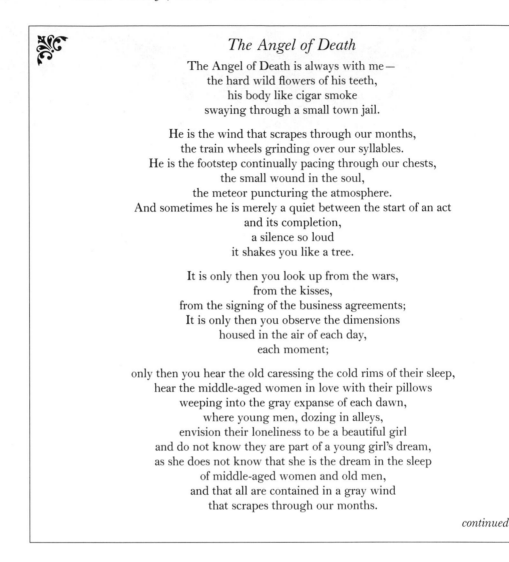

The Angel of Death

The Angel of Death is always with me —
the hard wild flowers of his teeth,
his body like cigar smoke
swaying through a small town jail.

He is the wind that scrapes through our months,
the train wheels grinding over our syllables.
He is the footstep continually pacing through our chests,
the small wound in the soul,
the meteor puncturing the atmosphere.
And sometimes he is merely a quiet between the start of an act
and its completion,
a silence so loud
it shakes you like a tree.

It is only then you look up from the wars,
from the kisses,
from the signing of the business agreements;
It is only then you observe the dimensions
housed in the air of each day,
each moment;

only then you hear the old caressing the cold rims of their sleep,
hear the middle-aged women in love with their pillows
weeping into the gray expanse of each dawn,
where young men, dozing in alleys,
envision their loneliness to be a beautiful girl
and do not know they are part of a young girl's dream,
as she does not know that she is the dream in the sleep
of middle-aged women and old men,
and that all are contained in a gray wind
that scrapes through our months.

continued

ences about pain control and consciousness, and about the extent of solitude or gregarious interaction desired, should be respected. "An appropriate death," Weisman says, "is a death that someone might choose for himself — had he a choice."

The death of Charles Lindbergh reveals many of the features of an appropriate death as defined by Weisman.[25] Lindbergh was diagnosed in 1972 as having lymphoma. Until he died two years later, he continued living an active life, traveling and promoting the cause of conservation. When chemotherapy became ineffective, Lindbergh made arrangements for his eventual burial on his beloved island of Maui, in the Hawaiian islands. As his condition worsened, Lindbergh

continued from previous page

But soon we forget that the dead sleep in buried cities,
that our hearts contain them in ripe vaults,
We forget that beautiful women dry into parchment
and ball players collapse into ash;
that geography wrinkles and smoothes like the expressions on a face,
and that not even children
can pick the white fruit from the night sky.

And how *could* we laugh while looking at the face
that falls apart like wet tobacco?
How could we wake each morning
to hear the muffled gong beating inside us,
our mouths full of shadows, our rooms filled with a black dust?

Still,
it is humiliating to be born a bottle:
to be filled with air, emptied, filled again;
to be filled with water, emptied, filled again;
and, finally, to be filled with earth.

And yet I am glad that The Angel of Death is always with me:
his footsteps quicken my own,
his silence makes me speak,
his wind freshens the weather of my day.
And it is because of him
I no longer think
that with each beat
my heart
is a planet drowning from within
but an ocean filling for the first time.

Morton Marcus

was hospitalized for several months, but the best efforts of his physicians could not alter the consequences of the disease. Lindbergh then instructed that a cabin on Maui be obtained, and he was flown "home to Maui," where, with two nurses, his physician, and his family, he spent the last eight days of his life in the environment he loved.

During this time, he gave instructions for the construction of his grave and for the conduct of his funeral, requesting that people attend in their work clothes. As Dr. Milton Howell, one of Lindbergh's physicians, describes it, "There was time for reminiscing, time for discussion, and time for laughter."

Jerry Soloway, UPI/Bettmann Newsphotos

Death can be viewed as a burden or as a blessing. Its meaning changes as circumstances change and as our understanding evolves toward new recognitions of its place in our lives.

Finally, Lindbergh lapsed into a coma and, twelve hours later, died. In accordance with his wishes, there had been no medical heroics. Dr. Howell says, "Death was another event in his life, as natural as his birth had been in Minnesota more than seventy-two years before."

Postscript and Farewell

Learning about death may have immediate, practical consequences. At the conclusion of a course on death and dying, one student said, "It has helped me and my family in dealing with my mother's serious illness." For others, the practi-

"Calvin and Hobbes," drawing by Bill Watterson, © 1991 Universal Press Syndicate

cal implications may seem less immediate. Yet, as another student expressed it, "I've gained a lot of useful information which may not be applicable to my life right now, but I know now that information and help is available and I didn't know that before."

Many people find that their explorations have consequences for their life that go beyond their previous notions about death and dying. One student said, "To me, this study has focused on more than just death and dying; it has dealt with ideas and with living, like a class on philosophy." Another student expressed the value of her death explorations as having, "expanded my faith in the resilience of the human spirit."

Death education does pertain to the practical and obvious aspects associated with the individual and social encounter with death. But an awareness of death and dying can also bring an added dimension to the experience of living, moment to moment. The remembrance of death can bring us more into the present. It can serve as a reminder of the precious precariousness of life and the value of compassion in the ordinary as well as extraordinary circumstances of human experience.

Further Readings

James Agee. *A Death in the Family*. New York: Bantam Books, 1969.

Simone de Beauvoir. *A Very Easy Death*. New York: Warner, 1973.

Ernest Becker. *The Denial of Death*. New York: The Free Press, 1973.

Norman O. Brown. *Life Against Death: The Psychoanalytical Meaning of History*. 2d ed. Middletown, Conn.: Wesleyan University Press, 1985.

Ken Dychtwald and Joe Flower. *Age Wave: The Challenges and Opportunities of an Aging America*. Los Angeles: Jeremy P. Tarcher, 1988.

David Feinstein and Peg Elliott Mayo. *Rituals for Living and Dying: From Life's Wounds to Spiritual Awakening*. San Francisco: Harper-Collins, 1990.

Rosemary Gordon. *Dying and Creating: A Search for Meaning*. London: The Society for Analytical Psychology, 1978.

Robert Kastenbaum and Beatrice Kastenbaum, eds. *Encyclopedia of Death*. Phoenix: Oryx Press, 1989.

Elisabeth Kübler-Ross. *To Live Until We Say Good-bye*. Englewood Cliffs, N.J.: Prentice-Hall, 1978.

David K. Reynolds. *Constructive Living*. Honolulu: University of Hawaii Press, 1984.

Leo Tolstoy. *The Death of Ivan Ilych and Other Stories*. New York: New American Library/Signet, 1960.

Alan Watts. *Death*. Millbrae, Calif.: Celestial Arts, 1975.

Jonathan Weiner. *The Next One Hundred Years: Shaping the Fate of Our Living Earth*. New York: Bantam Books, 1990.

Avery Weisman. *The Coping Capacity: On the Nature of Being Mortal*. New York: Human Sciences, 1984.

E P I L O G U E

It's late. I wonder what Death will look like? A drooling ogre? Perhaps an unblinking skull, the Grim Reaper? A veiled mistress with beckoning arms? The standard forms. Or maybe Death will be a polished young man in a three-piece suit, all smiles and sincerity and confidence. What a disappointment that would be. No, I prefer the scythe—no ambiguity, no surrender . . . no dickering. What's that? . . . I hear him. He's here.

"May I come in?"

I nod. It's the young man who left me two days ago to knock on the doors of his neighbors' homes. "Well . . . ?" My breath is shorter than I thought.

He smiles, looks down at his hands, then at me. "Well I did as you said. It didn't take long before I realized that I wasn't going to find a household that hadn't been touched by death."

"How many did you go to?"

He covers his mouth with his hand a moment, trying to hide his pride, I guess. "All of them."

"All?"

"Every house . . . I'm very stubborn."

We both smile. My wheezing is worse, and he notices. He shows his concern, and I can see that he understands what is happening.

"You're dying, aren't you, old man?"

I close my eyes in answer. When I open them again, he is at my side.

"Is there someone I should get for you? Your family?"

"Gone."

"Some friend?"

"Gone. All gone . . . except for you." The young man nods, then pulls his chair over next to my own. He takes my hand. I rest a moment. "There is something you

593

must do for me," I wheeze. "When I'm dead, burn this house and everything in it, including me."

"Leave nothing behind?"

"This is only a filthy old shack. I'm leaving behind the only thing that anyone really can *leave behind . . . the difference I've made in the lives of the people I've met." I squeeze his hand as best I can. He squeezes back. "Oh . . . and this." I try to lift the book in my lap—my book. He sees me struggling, and picks it up for me. "You take this. It's yours." His eyes widen.*

"But I don't deserve—"

"There isn't time for that now!" He nods, and lays the book on his lap. Good, that's done. Moments pass. It gets quieter . . . still. I must close my eyes. I witness again the glory of ten thousand mornings, ten thousand afternoons, ten thousand nights . . . then they, too, fade. All that's left is the sound of our breathing, and the wind. Time slows. Time changes. Where is the scythe? The young man's hand leaves mine and I hear his footsteps recede . . . stop . . . return. He sits down and I feel his hand on mine. He opens my fingers and lays something cool and light in my palm, all lace and limbs . . . the ballerina.

Now I can go.

David Gordon

Notes

CHAPTER 1

1. Robert G. Stevenson, "The Eye of the Beholder: The Media Look at Death Education," *Death Studies* 14 (1990): 161–170.

2. David E. Stannard, *The Puritan Way of Death: A Study in Religion, Culture, and Social Change* (New York: Oxford University Press, 1977).

3. Octavio Paz, *The Labyrinth of Solitude: Life and Thought in Mexico* (New York: Grove Press, 1961), p. 60.

4. Herman Feifel, "Psychology and Death: Meaningful Rediscovery," *American Psychologist* (April 1990): 537–543.

5. Steven Starker, "Psychologists and Self-Help Books: Attitudes and Prescriptive Practices of Clinicians," *American Journal of Psychotherapy* 63:3 (July 1988): 448–455.

6. Adapted from Kenneth J. Doka, "The Rediscovery of Death: An Analysis of the Emergence of the Death Studies Movement," paper presented at the Annual Meeting of the Forum for Death Education and Counseling, San Diego, September 1982.

7. Robert Fulton, *Death, Grief and Bereavement: A Bibliography, 1845–1975* (New York: Arno Press, 1976).

8. Hannelore Wass, M. David Miller, and Gordon Thornton, "Death Education and Grief/Suicide Intervention in the Public Schools," *Death Studies* 14 (1990): 253–268.

9. Vanderlyn R. Pine, "A Socio-Historical Portrait of Death Education," *Death Education* 1:1 (1977): 57–84. See also, by Pine, "The Age of Maturity for Death Education: A Socio-Historical Portrait of the Era 1976–1985," *Death Studies* 10:3 (1986): 209–231.

10. Feifel, "Psychology and Death," p. 539.

11. Dan Leviton, "The Scope of Death Education," *Death Education* 1:1 (1977): 41–56.

12. Darrell Crase, "Death Education: Its Diversity and Multidisciplinary Focus," *Death Studies* 13:1 (1989): 25–29.

13. Mary Ann Morgan, "Learner-centered Learning in an Undergraduate Interdisciplinary Course About Death," *Death Studies* 11:3 (1987): 183–192.

14. Leslie F. Degner and Christina M. Gow, "Evaluations of Death Education in Nursing," *Cancer Nursing* 11:3 (1988): 151–159.

15. The study referred to, *The Nurse and the Dying Patient* (New York: Macmillan), by Jeanne Quint, was published in 1967.

16. See, for example, Duane Weeks, "Death Education for Aspiring Physicians, Teachers, and Funeral Directors," *Death Studies* 13 (1989): 17–24.

17. Stephen P. Grant, "Death Education for Police Officers," unpublished paper, March 1985.

18. For material on the history and current activities of the Association (previously the Forum) for Death Education and Counseling, see: Darrell Crase and Dan Leviton, "Forum for Death Education and Counseling: Its History, Impact, and Future," *Death Studies* 11:5 (1987): 345–359; and Judith M. Stillion, "Association for Death Education and Counseling: An Organization for Our Times and for Our Future," *Death Studies* 13:2 (1989): 191–201.

19. "Expectation of Life at Birth," in *Statistical Abstract of the United States 1990*, 110th ed. (Washington: Government Printing Office, 1990), p. 72.

20. "Deaths, by Selected Cause and Selected Characteristics," in *Statistical Abstract of the United States 1990*, p. 80.

21. "Deaths and Death Rates," in *Statistical Abstract of the United States 1990*, p. 75. Statisticians consider the current death rate to be uncommonly low and something of an aberration because it reflects the significant shift in the age grouping of the American population. The death rate is expected to stabilize at about 10.0 per 1000 by the year 2000.

22. Robert Fulton, "Death, Grief, and Social Recuperation," *Omega: Journal of Death and Dying* 1 (1970): 25.

23. S. Jay Olshansky and A. Brian Ault, "The Fourth Stage of the Epidemiologic Transition: The Age of Delayed Degenerative Diseases," *The Millbank Quarterly* 64:3 (1986): 355–391.

24. "Resident Population by Age" and "Deaths, by Selected Cause and Selected Characteristics," in *Statistical Abstract of the United States 1990*, pp. 23, 80.

25. Robert Fulton, "The Many Faces of Grief," *Death Studies* 11:4 (1987): 243–256.

26. "Mobility Status of the Population," in *Statistical Abstract of the United States 1990*, p. 19.

27. Marsha McGee, "Faith, Fantasy, and Flowers: A Content Analysis of the American Sympathy Card," *Omega* 11 (1980–81): 27, 29.

28. Alynn Day Harvey, "Evidence of a Tense Shift in Personal Experience Narratives," *Empirical Studies of the Arts* 4:2 (1986): 151–162.

29. Barry Alan Morris, "The Communal Constraints on Parody: The Symbolic Death of Joe Bob Briggs," *Quarterly Journal of Speech* 73 (1987): 460–473.

30. Mary N. Hall, "Laughing As We Go," paper presented at the Annual Meeting of the Forum for Death Education and Counseling, Philadelphia, April 1985.

31. Ben H. Bagdikian, *The Information Machines: Their Impact on Men and the Media* (New York: Harper and Row, 1971). The public's reaction to the loss of significant public figures by assassination is discussed in Harold Cox, "Mourning Population: Some Considerations of Historically Comparable Assassinations," in *Death Education* 4:2 (1980): 125–138.

32. Robert Kastenbaum, *Death, Society, and Human Experience* (St. Louis: C. V. Mosby, 1977), p. 93.

33. Quoted in *Newsletter of the International Communication Association* 13:3 (Summer 1985): 8.

34. Staff article, "Why Do They React? Readers Assail Publication of Funeral, Accident Photos," *News Photographer* 36:3 (March 1981): 21–23.

35. John L. Huffman, "Putting Grief in Perspective," *News Photographer* 36:3 (March 1981): 21–22.

36. Sydney H. Schanberg, "Press Can Do Better Covering Personal Tragedy," *Newsday* (February 17, 1989): 85.

37. Barbara Hastings, "Interviews Unwelcome by Some in Accident," *Honolulu Star-Bulletin & Advertiser*, April 23, 1989.

38. Michael Arlen, "The Cold, Bright Charms of Immortality," from *The View from Highway 1* (New York: Farrar, Straus & Giroux, 1976), pp. 34–68.

39. Robert Fulton and Greg Owen, "Death and Society in Twentieth Century America," *Omega* 18 (1987–1988): 383.

40. "Utilization of Selected Media," in *Statistical Abstract of the United States 1989*, 109th ed. (Washington: Government Printing Office, 1989), p. 544.

41. Robert Abelman and Kimberly Neuendort, "Themes and Topics in Religious Television Programming," *Review of Religious Research* 29:2 (December 1987): 152–174.

42. Hannelore Wass, Jana L. Raup, and Harry H. Sisler, "Adolescents and Death on Television: A Follow-up Study," *Death Studies* 13:2 (1989): 161–173.

43. George Gerbner, "Death in Prime Time: Notes on the Symbolic Functions of Dying in the Mass Media," *Annals of the American Academy of Political and Social Science* 447 (January 1980): 64–70; see also, Fulton and Owen, "Death and Society in Twentieth Century America," pp. 381–382.

44. George Gerbner, Larry Gross, Nancy Signorielli, and Michael Morgan, "Television's Mean World: Violence Profile No. 14–15," Annenberg School of Communications, University of Pennsylvania (September 1986).

45. Roger Ebert, film critic of the Chicago *Sun-Times*, "At the Movies," NBC-TV, September 8, 1985.

46. Frederic B. Tate, "Impoverishment of Death Symbolism: The Negative Consequences," *Death Studies* 13:3 (1989): 305–317.

47. Delese Wear and Lois LaCivita Nixon, "'Is There a Text in This Class?': Reader-Response Theory in Literature and Medicine," *Journal of Medical Humanities* 11:1 (Spring 1990): 45–53.

48. For a survey of the genre, see: John Hellman, *American Myth and the Legacy of Vietnam* (New York: Columbia University Press, 1986).

49. Alvin H. Rosenfeld, *A Double Dying: Reflections on Holocaust Literature* (Bloomington: Indiana University Press, 1980), p. 12. See also Lawrence L. Langer, *Versions of Survival: The Holocaust and the Human Spirit* (Albany: State University of New York Press, 1982), and Terrence Des Pres, *The Survivor: An Anatomy of Life in the Death Camps* (New York: Oxford University Press, 1976).

50. Frederick J. Hoffman, *The Mortal No: Death and the Modern Imagination* (Princeton, N.J.: Princeton University Press, 1964).

51. Lawrence Langer explores this theme in *The Age of Atrocity: Death in Modern Literature* (Boston: Beacon Press, 1978).

52. William Ruehlmann, *Saint with a Gun: The Unlawful American Private Eye* (New York: New York University Press, 1984), p. 9.

53. Hoffman, *Mortal No*, p. 312.

54. Richard A. Pacholski, "Death Themes in the Visual Arts: Resources and Research Opportunities for Death Educators," *Death Studies* 10:1 (1986): 59–74.

55. Aron Weller, Victor Florian, and Rivka Tenenbaum, "The Concept of Death: 'Masculine' and 'Feminine' Attributes," *Omega* 19 (1988–1989): 253–263.

56. Fritz Eichenberg, *Dance of Death: A Graphic Commentary on the Danse Macabre through the Centuries* (New York: Abbeville, 1983).

57. Anita Schorsch, *Mourning Becomes America: Mourning Art in the New Nation* (Philadelphia: Main Street Press, 1976), p. 1.

58. Cindy Ruskin, *The Quilt: Stories from the Names Project* (New York: Pocket Books, 1988).

59. Miriam Horn, "The Artists' Diagnosis," *U.S. News & World Report* (March 27, 1989): 62–70.

60. Carla Gottlieb, "Modern Art and Death," in *The Meaning of Death*, edited by Herman Feifel (New York: McGraw-Hill, 1959).

61. See Richard A. Pacholski, "Death Themes in Music: Resources and Research Opportunities for Death Educators," *Death Studies* 10:3 (1986): 239–263.

62. George S. Kanahele, ed., *Hawaiian Music and Musicians* (Honolulu: University Press of Hawaii, 1979), pp. 53, 56.

63. Marguerite K. Ashford, Bishop Museum, Honolulu, personal communication.

64. See, for example, Hannelore Wass, M. David Miller, and Robert G. Stevenson, "Factors Affecting Adolescents' Behavior and Attitudes Toward Destructive Rock Lyrics," *Death Studies* 13:3 (1989): 287–303; and Hannelore Wass, Jana L. Raup, Karen Cerullo, Linda G. Martel, et al., "Adolescents' Interest in and Views of Destructive Themes in Rock Music," *Omega* 19 (1988–1989): 177–186.

65. Fulton and Owen, "Death and Society in Twentieth Century America," 379–395.

66. Kathleen B. Bryer, "The Amish Way of Death: A Study of Family Support Systems," *American Psychologist* 34:3 (March 1979): 255–261.

CHAPTER 2

1. The use of blood-red oxide to decorate corpses is generally thought to be the earliest widespread funeral custom. Ore deposits of hematite in the Bomvu (Red) Ridge in Africa are thought to be the oldest mineworks anywhere in the world. Red ochre was mined in Africa by the earliest *Homo sapiens sapiens*. It appeared in Europe in connection with Neanderthal funeral practices and was used in burials throughout Europe, Africa, Asia, Australia, and the Americas.

If we imagine the earth as a living organism, hematite is analogous to the blood of Mother Earth. Its symbolic properties, therefore, are obvious. The Christian Eucharist involves a similar symbology: the red wine that represents the blood of Christ.

2. Joseph Campbell, "Mythological Themes in Creative Literature and Art," in *Myths, Dreams, and Religion*, edited by Joseph Campbell (Dallas, Tex.: Spring Publications, 1970, 1988), pp. 138–175.

3. See, for example, Neville Drury, *The Elements of Shamanism* (Dorset: Element Books, 1989).

4. Mary Kawena Pukui, E. W. Haertig, and Catherine A. Lee, *Nana I Ke Kumu (Look to the Source)*, 2 vols. (Honolulu: Hui Hanai; Queen Lili'uokalani Children's Center,

1972). A study conducted in the 1930s found families still tracing their lineage from ancestors who were viewed as spiritual guardians of their descendants, often interceding in very practical ways. See E. S. Craighill Handy and Mary Kawena Pukui, *The Polynesian Family System in Ka-'u, Hawai'i* (Rutland, Vt.: Charles E. Tuttle, 1972).

5. Ninian Smart, *The Long Search* (Boston: Little, Brown, 1977), p. 231.

6. The persistence of such beliefs and customs in modern Japan is discussed by Robert J. Smith, *Ancestor Worship in Contemporary Japan* (Stanford, Calif.: Stanford University Press, 1974); and Yamaori Tetsuo, "The Metaphorphosis of Ancestors," *Japan Quarterly* 33:1 (January–March 1986): 50–53.

7. T. H. Gaster, in James Frazer, *The New Golden Bough* (New York: New American Library, 1964), p. 241.

8. Handy and Pukui, *Polynesian Family System in Ka-'u, Hawai'i*, pp. 98–101. About modern practices, Handy and Pukui add: "Today it is just a matter of different relatives 'giving' a name informally; such a name 'given' constitutes a bond, a token of *aloha*, an expression of gratification and mark of pride and esteem."

9. Anita J. Glaze, *Art and Death in a Senufo Village* (Bloomington: Indiana University Press, 1981), pp. 150–151.

10. Ndolamb Ngokwey, "Pluralistic Etiological Systems in Their Social Context: A Brazilian Case Study," *Social Science and Medicine* 26:8 (1988): 793–802.

11. Paul Katz and Faris R. Kirkland, "Traditional Thought and Modern Western Surgery," *Social Science and Medicine* 26:12 (1988): 1175–1181.

12. E. Clyde Smoot III, John O. Kucan, Jo Schlenker Cope, and Jon M. Aase, "The Craniofacial Team and the Navajo Patient," *Cleft Palate Journal* 25:4 (1988): 395–402.

13. For further study, see: Hans Abrahamson, *The Origin of Death: Studies in African Mythology* (New York: Arno Press, 1977); Joseph Campbell, *The Masks of God: Primitive Mythology* (New York: Viking Press, 1959); and Jacques Choron, *Death and Western Thought* (New York: Macmillan, 1963).

14. For a review of the literature on the anthropology of death, see Phyllis Palgi and Henry Abramovitch. "Death: A Cross-Cultural Perspective," *Annual Review of Anthropology* 13 (1984): 385–417.

15. Louise B. Halfe, "The Circle: Death and Dying from a Native Perspective," *Journal of Palliative Care* 5:1 (1989): 37–41.

16. Jamake Highwater, *The Primal Mind: Vision and Reality in Indian America* (New York: Harper and Row, 1981), p. 165.

17. Joseph E. Trimble and Candace M. Fleming, "Providing Counseling Services for Native American Indians: Client, Counselor, and Community Characteristics," in *Counseling Across Cultures*, 3d ed., edited by Paul B. Pedersen, Juris G. Dragus, Walter J. Lonner, and Joseph E. Trimble (Honolulu: University of Hawaii Press, 1989): 177–204.

18. See, for example, C. E. Schorer, "Two Centuries of Miami Indian Death Customs," *Omega: Journal of Death and Dying* 20 (1989–1990): 75–79; and Carl Waldman, *Atlas of the North American Indian* (New York: Facts on File, 1985).

19. Åke Hultkrantz, *Native Religions of North America: The Power of Visions and Fertility* (New York: Harper and Row, 1987), pp. 21, 33, 59. See also, by Hultkrantz, *The Religions of the American Indians* (Berkeley: University of California Press, 1979), and *The Study of American Indian Religions* (New York: Crossroad, 1983); and Sam D. Gill, *Native American Religions: An Introduction* (Belmont, Calif.: Wadsworth, 1982).

20. Malcolm Margolin, *The Ohlone Way: Indian Life in the San Francisco-Monterey Bay Area* (Berkeley, Calif.: Heyday Books, 1978), pp. 145–149.

21. Quoted in Vine Deloria, Jr., *God Is Red* (New York: Dell, 1973), pp. 176–177.

22. Concern for the proper disposition of human remains is not limited to the native peoples of North America but is an issue for many indigenous peoples around the world. For a recent discussion on this subject, see "Human Remains: Contemporary Issues," in *Death Studies* 14 (1990), a special issue edited by Glen W. Davidson and Larry W. Zimmerman.

23. David G. Mandelbaum, "Social Uses of Funeral Rites," in *The Meaning of Death*, edited by Herman Feifel (New York: McGraw-Hill, 1959), pp. 189–217.

24. Noel Q. King, *Religions of Africa: A Pilgrimage into Traditional Religions* (New York: Harper and Row, 1970), pp. 13–14. Also see, by the same author, *Christian and Muslim in Africa* (New York: Harper and Row, 1971), p. 95.

25. King, *Religions of Africa*, p. 68.

26. Kofi Asare Opoku, "African Perspectives on Death and Dying," in *Perspectives on Death and Dying: Cross-Cultural and Multidisciplinary Views*, edited by Arthur Berger, et al. (Philadelphia: The Charles Press, 1989), pp. 14–23.

27. Kwasi Wiredu, "Death and the Afterlife in African Culture," in *Perspectives on Death and Dying: Cross-Cultural and Multidisciplinary Views*, edited by Arthur Berger, et al. (Philadelphia: The Charles Press, 1989), pp. 24–37.

28. From a story by Robert Dvorchak, *Los Angeles Times*, July 8, 1990.

29. Jack Goody, *Death, Property, and the Ancestors: A Study of the Mortuary Customs of the LoDagaa of West Africa* (Stanford, Calif.: Stanford University Press, 1962).

30. Gillian Feeley-Harnik, "The Political Economy of Death: Communication and Change in Malagasy Colonial History," *American Ethnologist* 11:1 (1984): 1–19.

31. Olatunde Bayo Lawuyi, "Obituary and Ancestral Worship: Analysis of a Contemporary Cultural Form in Nigeria," *Sociological Analysis* 48:4 (1988): 372–379.

32. Octavio Paz, *The Labyrinth of Solitude: Life and Thought in Mexico* (New York: Grove Press, 1961).

33. For further information, see: Ignacio Aguilar and Virginia N. Wood, "Therapy Through a Death Ritual," in *Death and Dying: Theory, Research, and Practice*, edited by Larry Bugen (Dubuque, Iowa: William C. Brown, 1979), pp. 131–141; Barbara Brodman, *The Mexican Cult of Death in Myth and Literature* (Gainesville: University of Florida Press, 1976); Patricia Fernández Kelly, "Death in Mexican Folk Culture," *American Quarterly* 26:5 (December 1974): 516–535; Oscar Lewis, *A Death in the Sanchez Family* (New York: Vintage Books, 1970); and Joan Moore, "The Death Culture of Mexico and Mexican Americans," in *Death and Dying: Views from Many Cultures*, edited by Richard A. Kalish (New York: Baywood, 1980), pp. 72–91.

34. Jose Antonio Burciaga, "A Day to Laugh at Death," San Jose *Mercury-News*, November 1, 1985.

35. Judith Strupp Green, "The Days of the Dead in Oaxaca, Mexico: An Historical Inquiry," in *Death and Dying: Views from Many Cultures*, edited by Richard A. Kalish (New York: Baywood, 1980), pp. 56–71.

36. Glenn Whitney, "Mexico's Day of the Dead Is Actually Very Lively," UPI story, in the Honolulu *Star-Bulletin & Advertiser*, November 1, 1987. The quotations by Marie Nunez are from this article.

37. Joan Moore, "The Death Culture of Mexico and Mexican Americans," in *Death and Dying: Views from Many Cultures*, edited by Richard A. Kalish (New York: Baywood, 1980): pp. 72–91.

38. Philippe Ariès, *Western Attitudes Toward Death: From the Middle Ages to the Present* (Baltimore: Johns Hopkins University Press, 1974), and, also by Ariès, *The Hour*

of Our Death (New York: Alfred A. Knopf, 1981), and *Images of Man and Death* (Cambridge, Mass.: Harvard University Press, 1985). Except where otherwise noted, material appearing within quotation marks is drawn from Ariès' works. See also: T. S. R. Boase, *Death in the Middle Ages: Mortality, Judgment and Remembrance* (New York: McGraw-Hill, 1972); Jacques Choron, *Death and Western Thought* (New York: Macmillan, 1963); Donna C. Kurtz and John Boardman, *Greek Burial Customs* (Ithaca, N.Y.: Cornell University Press, 1971).

39. Ian Gentles, "Funeral Customs in Historical Context," *Journal of Palliative Care* 4:3 (1988): 16–20.

40. Alain Erlande-Brandenburg, Jules Mazé, and Brooks Walker, "Royal Dreams: The Final Cortège," *FMR*, number 43 (April 1990): 65–96.

41. Rob Kay, *Santa Cruz Sentinel*, March 20, 1983.

42. F. Gonzalez-Crussi, "Anatomy and Old Lace: An Eighteenth-Century Attitude Toward Death," *The Sciences* (January–February 1988): 48–49.

43. These paintings, originally in the Cemetery of the Innocents in Paris, were destroyed in the late seventeenth century, but reproductions or copies can be seen in the woodcuts of the Paris printer Guy Marchant. The Flemish artist Hans Holbein the Younger executed a series of drawings on the theme in 1523–1526, depicting the skeletal figure of Death surprising victims in the midst of their daily life. In music, the Dance of Death theme survives in the German *Totentanz*, which dates from the sixteenth century.

44. Robert S. Gottfried, "Of Rats and Men," *The Sciences* (November–December 1985): 59–61; and Johan Goudsblom, "Public Health and the Civilizing Process," *The Millbank Quarterly* 64:2 (1986): 161–188. See also: Lawrence Biemiller, "Plagues: How People Responded to Them in the Past Is Studied by Scholars as a Guide in AIDS Crisis," *Chronicle of Higher Education* 34 (January 27, 1988): A6–A8.

45. See Georges Bataille, *Death and Sensuality: A Study of Eroticism and the Taboo* (New York: Walker and Company, 1962).

46. Gentles, "Funeral Customs in Historical Context."

47. For more on these historical developments, see the following authors: Diana Williams Combs, *Early Gravestone Art in Georgia and South Carolina* (Athens: University of Georgia Press, 1986); James J. Farrell, *Inventing the American Way of Death, 1830–1920* (Philadelphia: Temple University Press, 1980), and "The Dying of Death: Historical Perspectives," *Death Education* 6 (1982): 105–123; Gordon E. Geddes, *Welcome Joy: Death in Puritan New England* (Ann Arbor: UMI Research Press, 1981); David E. Stannard, *The Puritan Way of Death: A Study in Religion, Culture, and Social Change* (New York: Oxford University Press, 1977), "Calm Dwellings: The Brief, Sentimental Age of the Rural Cemetery," *American Heritage* 30:5 (August/September 1979): 42–55, and, edited by Stannard, *Death in America* (Philadelphia: University of Pennsylvania Press, 1975); Michael Vovelle, "A Century and One-Half of American Epitaphs (1660–1813): Toward the Study of Collective Attitudes About Death," *Comparative Studies in Society and History* 22:4 (October 1980): 534–547.

48. Herman Feifel, "The Meaning of Death in American Society," in *Death Education: Preparation for Living*, edited by Betty R. Green and Donald P. Irish (Cambridge, Mass.: Schenkman, 1971).

49. Norbert Elias, *The Loneliness of the Dying* (New York: Basil Blackwell, 1985).

50. Gentles, "Funeral Customs in Historical Context."

51. Charles O. Jackson, "Death Shall Have No Dominion: The Passing of the World of the Dead in America," in *Death and Dying: Views from Many Cultures*, edited by Richard A. Kalish (New York: Baywood, 1980), pp. 47–55.

CHAPTER 3

1. Adah Maurer, "Maturation of Concepts of Death," *British Journal of Medicine and Psychology* 39 (1966): 35–41.

2. Information about death anxiety can be found in the following sources: James B. McCarthy, *Death Anxiety: The Loss of the Self* (New York: Gardner Press, 1980); C. W. Wahl, "The Fear of Death," in *The Meaning of Death* (New York: McGraw-Hill, 1959), edited by H. Feifel, pp. 16–29; and Martin P. Seligman, *Helplessness: On Depression, Development, and Death* (San Francisco: W. H. Freeman, 1975). Also see John Bowlby's classic works on attachment and loss: vol. 1, *Attachment* (1969); vol. 2, *Separation: Anxiety and Anger* (1973); vol. 3, *Loss: Sadness and Depression* (1982) (New York: Basic Books).

3. Mark W. Speece, "Very Young Children's Experiences with and Reactions to Death" (Master's thesis, Wayne State University, 1983).

4. Sandor B. Brent, "Puns, Metaphors, and Misunderstandings in a Two-Year-Old's Conception of Death," *Omega: Journal of Death and Dying* 8 (1977–1978): 285–293. In a subsequent conversation, the father, Dr. Sandor Brent, reported that his son — now a teenager — has no recollection of this death-related experience. Dr. Brent believes that the lack of memory regarding this experience indicates a successfully managed event. (Personal communication.)

5. For a review of the literature, see Mark W. Speece and Sandor W. Brent, "Children's Understanding of Death: A Review of Three Components of a Death Concept," *Child Development* 55:5 (October 1984): 1671–1686. Sources of information on early research in death and children include: Irving E. Alexander and Arthur M. Adlerstein, "Affective Responses to the Concept of Death in a Population of Children and Early Adolescents," *Journal of Genetic Psychology* 93 (1958): 167–177; Sylvia Anthony, *The Discovery of Death in Childhood and After* (New York: Basic Books, 1972); Robert Kastenbaum, "Childhood: The Kingdom Where Creatures Die," *Journal of Clinical Child Psychology* 3 (Summer 1974): 11–13; Maria H. Nagy, "The Child's View of Death," *Journal of Genetic Psychology* 73 (1948): 3–27; Paul Schilder and David Wechsler, "The Attitudes of Children Toward Death," *Journal of Genetic Psychology* 45 (1934): 406–451.

6. See, for example, Sigal Ironi Hoffman and Sidney Strauss, "The Development of Children's Concepts of Death," *Death Studies* 9 (1985): 469–482; and William Lee, Jr., "Children's Conceptions of Death: A Study on Age and Gender as Factors in Concept Development" (Doctoral dissertation, Harvard University, 1987).

7. Erik Erikson, *Childhood and Society* (New York: W. W. Norton, 1950).

8. Jean Piaget, *The Child and Reality: Problems of Genetic Psychology*, translated by Arnold Rosin (New York: Grossman Publishers, 1973), and *The Child's Conception of the World* (London: Routledge and Kegan Paul, 1929). Also see: Mary Ann Spencer Pulaski, *Understanding Piaget: An Introduction to Children's Cognitive Development* (New York: Harper and Row, 1980); Howard E. Gruber and J. Jacques Vonèche, eds., *The Essential Piaget* (New York: Basic Books, 1977); and Hugh Rosen, *Pathway to Piaget: A Guide for Clinicians, Educators, and Developmentalists* (Cherry Hill, N.J.: Postgraduate International, 1977).

9. From a conversation with Jean Piaget in Richard I. Evans, *The Making of Psychology: Discussions with Creative Contributors* (New York: Alfred A. Knopf, 1976), p. 46.

10. Gerald P. Koocher, "Childhood, Death, and Cognitive Development," *Developmental Psychology* 9:3 (1973): 369–375; "Talking with Children About Death," *American Journal of Orthopsychiatry* 44:3 (April 1974): 404–411; and "Conversations with Children About Death," *Journal of Clinical Child Psychology* (Summer 1974): 19–21. Of

the children in Koocher's study group, the mean age of those classified as preoperational was 7.4 years; of those who used concrete operations, 10.4 years; and of those who used formal operations, 13.3 years.

11. Helen L. Swain, "Childhood Views of Death," *Death Education* 2:4 (1979): 341–358.

12. See Gregory Rochlin, "How Younger Children View Death and Themselves," in *Explaining Death to Children*, edited by Earl A. Grollman (Boston: Beacon Press, 1967), pp. 51–85.

13. Hedda Sharapan, "'Mister Rogers' Neighborhood': Dealing with Death on a Children's Television Series," *Death Education* 1:1 (1977): 131–136.

14. Martha Wolfenstein and Gilbert Kliman, eds., *Children and the Death of a President: Multi-Disciplinary Studies* (Garden City, N.Y.: Anchor Press/Doubleday, 1965), especially pp. 217–239.

15. From an Associated Press wire story, "First Graders Paint a Happy Ending" (January 31, 1986) and other newspaper sources.

16. Reported by Richard Lonetto, *Children's Conceptions of Death* (New York: Springer, 1980), p. 9.

17. Kalle Achte, Ritva Fagerstrom, Juha Pentikainen, and Norman L. Farberow, "Themes of Death and Violence in Lullabies of Different Countries," *Omega* 20 (1989–1990): 193–204.

18. Gloria Goldreich, "What Is Death? The Answers in Children's Books—From Fairy Tales to Harsh Reality," *The Hastings Center Report* 7:3 (June 1977): 18–20.

19. A. Cordell Perkes and Roberta Schildt, "Death-Related Attitudes of Adolescent Males and Females," *Death Education* 2 (1979): 359–368. For coverage of gender differences in adults as well as children, see Judith M. Stillion, *Death and the Sexes: An Examination of Differential Longevity, Attitudes, Behaviors, and Coping Skills* (Washington, D.C.: Hemisphere, 1985).

20. Ernest Becker, *The Denial of Death* (New York: The Free Press, 1973). On the pathological fear of death, see, for example, Vladan Starcevic, "Pathological Fear of Death, Panic Attacks, and Hypochondriasis," *American Journal of Psychoanalysis* 49 (1989): 347–361.

21. Barbara Kane, "Children's Concepts of Death," *Journal of Genetic Psychology* 134 (1979): 141–153.

22. *Newsweek*, May 5, 1980. See also Roger Rosenblatt, *Children of War* (New York: Anchor/Doubleday, 1983); Claudine Vegh, *I Didn't Say Goodbye: Interviews with the Children of the Holocaust* (New York: E. P. Dutton, 1985); and Robert Westall, *Children of the Blitz: Memories of Wartime Childhood* (New York: Viking, 1986).

23. See, for example, David J. Schonfeld and Sara Smilansky, "A Cross-Cultural Comparison of Israeli and American Children's Death Concepts," *Death Studies* 13 (1989): 593–604.

C H A P T E R 4

1. "National Health Expenditures," in *Statistical Abstract of the United States, 1990*, 110th edition (Washington: Government Printing Office, 1990), p. 92.

2. Charles E. Rosenberg, "Institutionalized Ambiguity: Conflict and Continuity in the American Hospital," *Second Opinion* 12 (November 1989): 63–73.

3. See, for example, "Confronting the Crisis in Health Care: An Interview with Arnold Relman," *Bulletin of the Park Ridge Center* (September 1989): 35–42.

4. Rosemary Stevens, *In Sickness and in Wealth: American Hospitals in the Twentieth Century* (New York: Basic Books, 1989), p. 343; see also: Gordon K. Douglas, "Ethical Implications of the Revolution in Health Care Finance," in *Health Care and Its Costs*, edited by Walter E. Wiest (Lanham, Md.: University Press of America, 1988); and Victor R. Fuchs, "Has Cost Containment Gone Too Far?," *Millbank Quarterly* 64:3 (1986): 479–488.

5. Peter E. Dans, "The Health Care Revolution: A Preliminary Report from the Front," *Journal of the American Medical Association* 259 (June 17, 1988): 3452–3453.

6. Diana B. Dutton, Thomas A. Preston, and Nancy E. Pfund, *Worse Than the Disease: Pitfalls of Medical Progress* (New York: Cambridge University Press, 1988), p. 4.

7. Edward R. Pinckney and Cathey Pinckney, "Unnecessary Measures: Physicians Are Relying Too Heavily on Medical Tests," *The Sciences* 29:1 (January/February 1989): 21–27.

8. Quoted in Paul E. Kalb and David H. Miller, "Utilization Strategies for Intensive Care Units," *Journal of the American Medical Association* 261:16 (1989): 2389–2395.

9. Graham Loomes and Lynda McKenzie, "The Use of QALYs in Health Care Decision Making," *Social Science and Medicine* 28 (1989): 299–308.

10. Daniel Callahan, "The Limits of Medical Progress: A Principle of Symmetry," *The Center Report* 2, The Center for Public Policy and Contemporary Issues, University of Denver (Winter/Spring 1990): 2. See also, by Callahan, "Modernizing Mortality: Medical Progress and the Good Society," *Hastings Center Report* (January/February 1990): 28–32.

11. Leonard Stein, David Watts, and Timothy Howell, "The Doctor-Nurse Game Revisited," *New England Journal of Medicine* 322 (February 22, 1990): 546–549.

12. Robert Blauner, "Death and Social Structure," *Psychiatry* 29:4 (November 1966): 378–394. See also Diana Crane, *The Sanctity of Social Life: Physicians' Treatment of Critically Ill Patients* (New York: Russell Sage Foundation, 1975).

13. Elisabeth Kübler-Ross, *On Death and Dying* (New York: Macmillan, 1969), p. 249.

14. Eric J. Cassell, "Dying in a Technological Society," in *Death Inside Out: The Hastings Center Report*, edited by Peter Steinfels and Robert M. Veatch (New York: Harper and Row, 1974), pp. 43–48. See also Orville G. Brim, Jr., Howard E. Freeman, Sol Levine, and Norman A. Scotch, eds., *The Dying Patient* (New York: Russell Sage Foundation, 1970); David Sudnow, *Passing On: The Social Organization of Dying* (Englewood Cliffs, N.J.: Prentice-Hall, 1967); and the seminal work by Barney G. Glaser and Anselm L. Strauss, *Awareness of Dying* (Chicago: Aldine, 1965).

15. E. Alison Holman, "Death and the Health Professional: Organization and Defense in Health Care," *Death Studies* 14 (1990): 13–24.

16. See Margaretta K. Bowers, et al., *Counseling the Dying* (New York: Thomas Nelson & Sons, 1964).

17. Robert Kastenbaum and Ruth Aisenberg, *The Psychology of Death, Concise Edition* (New York: Springer, 1976), p. 179. See also: Richard Schulz and David Alderman, "How the Medical Staff Copes with Dying Patients: A Critical Review," *Omega: Journal of Death and Dying* 7 (1976): 11–21.

18. William M. Buchholz, "Medical Eschatology: Combined Role for Caregiver and Scientist," *American Journal of Hospice Care*, (January–February 1985): 22–24.

19. "Deaths, by Selected Cause and Selected Characteristics" and "Deaths and Death Rates from Accidents," in *Statistical Abstract of the United States 1990*, pp. 80, 85;

and National Center for Health Statistics, *Health, United States, 1989* (Hyattsville, Md.: Public Health Service, 1990), p. 123.

20. Seth B. Golbey, "Critical Cares: Life-Saving Aeromedical Helicopter Services," *AOPA Pilot* 30:4 (April 1987): 39–46, and "Dust Off," pp. 46–48.

21. John Grossman, "Emergency! Emergency!" *Health* 21:7 (July 1989): 76–94.

22. Ralph Hingson, Norman A. Scotch, James Sorenson, and Judith P. Swazey, *In Sickness and in Health: Social Dimensions of Medical Care* (St. Louis: C. V. Mosby, 1981), pp. 120, 139–140, 257–265.

23. C. D. Bessinger, "Doctoring: The Philosophic Milieu," *Southern Medical Journal* 81:12 (1988): 1558–1562. See also Edmund D. Pellegrino and David C. Thomasma, *A Philosophical Basis for Medical Practice: Toward a Philosophy and Ethic of the Healing Professions* (New York: Oxford University Press, 1981).

24. Clyde Nabe, "Health Care and the Transcendent," *Death Studies* 13 (1989): 557–565.

25. Cited in Bessinger, "Doctoring."

26. Richard B. Gunderman, "Medicine and the Question of Suffering," *Second Opinion* 14 (July 1990): 15–25.

27. Candace West, *Routine Complications: Troubles with Talk Between Doctors and Patients* (Bloomington: Indiana University Press, 1984).

28. Sandra L. Bertman, Michael D. Wertheimer, and H. Brownell Wheeler, "Humanities in Surgery, a Life-Threatening Situation: Communicating the Diagnosis," *Death Studies* 10 (1986): 431–439. On the reliance of physicians on medical tests, see Edward R. Pinckney and Cathey Pinckney, "Unnecessary Measures," *The Sciences* 29 (January/February 1989): 21–27.

29. Ernest Rosenbaum, "Oncology/Hematology and Psychosocial Support of the Cancer Patient," in *Psychosocial Care of the Dying Patient*, edited by Charles A. Garfield (New York: McGraw-Hill, 1978), pp. 169–184. See also David Barton, ed. *Death and Dying: A Clinical Guide for Caregivers* (Baltimore: Williams and Wilkins, 1977).

30. "Tapping Human Potential: An Interview with Norman Cousins," *Second Opinion* 14 (July 1990): 57–71.

31. See, for example, *Foundations of Psychoneuroimmunology*, edited by Steven Locke, et al. (New York: Aldine, 1985); and *Psychoneuroimmunology*, edited by Robert Ader, David L. Felten, and Nicholas Cohen (San Diego: Academic Press, 1990).

32. See, for example, David A. Alexander, "'Stressors' and Difficulties in Dealing with the Terminal Patient," *Journal of Palliative Care* 6:3 (1990): 28–33.

33. Jeanne Quint Benoliel, "Health Care Providers and Dying Patients: Critical Issues in Terminal Care," *Omega* 18 (1987–1988): 341–363.

34. C. A. J. McLauchlan, "Handling Distressed Relatives and Breaking Bad News," *British Medical Journal* 301 (November 17, 1990): 1145–1149.

35. See, for example, Egilde P. Seravalli, "The Dying Patient, the Physician, and the Fear of Death," *New England Journal of Medicine* 319 (December 29, 1988): 1728–1730.

36. See Marilee Ivars Donovan and Sandra Girton Pierce, *Cancer Care Nursing* (New York: Appleton-Century-Crofts, 1976).

37. Jeanne Brimigion, "Living with Dying," in Nursing Skillbook, *Dealing with Death and Dying*, 2d ed. (Horsham, Pa.: Intermed Communications, 1980), pp. 91–96.

38. M. L. S. Vachon, W. A. L. Layall, and S. J. J. Freeman, "Measurement and Management of Stress in Health Professionals Working with Advanced Cancer Patients," *Death Education* 1 (1978): 365–369.

39. Quoted in Donovan and Pierce, *Cancer Care Nursing*, p. 32.

40. Eileen Renear, "Confronting Expected Death," in Nursing Skillbook, *Dealing with Death and Dying*, pp. 63–72.

41. The early history of AIDS is derived in part from reports published in *Science* and from a report by the U. S. Congress's Office of Technology Assessment, *Review of the Public Health Services' Response to AIDS* (Washington: Government Printing Office, 1985).

42. Initially Gallo used the term HTLV-III (for human lymphotropic virus); other terms, such as LAV (lymphadenopathy-associated virus) were also used by researchers. HIV is now the official designation.

43. A measure of premature mortality, "years of potential life lost" (YPLL), points up the effect of the high fatality rate and relative youth of persons afflicted with AIDS.

44. Statistics from "AIDS Cases Reported" and "AIDS Cases, Expenditures, and Appropriations," in *Statistical Abstract of the United States 1990*, p. 117, and other sources.

45. Nicholas A. Christakis, "Responding to a Pandemic: International Interests in AIDS Control," *Daedalus* 118:2 (Spring 1989): 113–134.

46. Paul Wallich, "AIDS Counts: Planning for an Epidemic Whose Size Is Still Unknown," *Scientific American* 260:4 (April 1989): 17–18.

47. Larry O. Gostin, "Public Health Strategies for Confronting AIDS: Legislative and Regulatory Policy in the United States," *Journal of the American Medical Association* 261: 11 (March 17, 1989): 1621–1630.

48. On the political and social response to AIDS, see: Dennis Altman, *AIDS in the Mind of America* (New York: Anchor Press/Doubleday, 1986); Mary Catherine Bateson and Richard Goldsby, *Thinking AIDS: The Social Response to the Biological Threat* (Reading, Mass.: Addison-Wesley, 1988); Inge B. Corliss and Mary Pittman-Lindeman, eds., *AIDS: Principles, Practices, and Politics* (New York: Hemisphere, 1989); Douglas Crimp, ed., *AIDS: Cultural Analysis, Cultural Activism* (Cambridge, Mass.: MIT Press, 1988); Institute of Medicine/National Academy of Sciences, *Confronting AIDS: Update 1988* (Washington: National Academy Press, 1988); Eve K. Nichols, *Mobilizing Against AIDS*, rev. ed. (Cambridge, Mass.: Harvard University Press, 1989); Randy Shilts, *And the Band Played On: Politics, People, and the AIDS Epidemic* (New York: Viking Penguin, 1988).

49. "Hospital Utilization Rates," in *Statistical Abstract of the United States 1990*, p. 108.

50. Inge B. Corliss, "Settings for Terminal Care," *Omega* 18 (1987–1988): 319–340.

51. Corliss, "Settings for Terminal Care," p. 331; see also, Josefina B. Magno, "The Hospice Concept of Care: Facing the 1990s," *Death Studies* 14 (1990): 109–119.

52. Bart Collopy, Nancy Dubler, and Connie Zuckerman, "The Ethics of Home Care: Autonomy and Accommodation," *Hastings Center Report* (March/April 1990): Supplement.

53. David S. Greer, Vincent Mor, and Robert Kastenbaum, "Concepts, Questions, and Research Priorities," in *The Hospice Experiment*, edited by Mor, Greer, and Kastenbaum (Baltimore: Johns Hopkins University Press, 1988), p. 249.

54. James Luther Adams, "Palliative Care in the Light of Early Christian Concepts," *Journal of Palliative Care* 5:3 (1989): 5–8.

55. Sandol Stoddard, "Hospice in the United States: An Overview," *Journal of Palliative Care* 5:3 (1989): 10–19.

56. The description of St. Christopher's is derived mainly from "St. Christopher's Hospice" by Thelma Ingles, in Michael P. Hamilton and Helen F. Reid, *A Hospice Hand-*

book: A New Way to Care for the Dying (Grand Rapids, Mich.: Wm. B. Eerdmans, 1980); pp. 45–56.

57. William E. Phipps, "The Origin of Hospices/Hospitals," *Death Studies* 12:2 (1988): 91–99.

58. Quoted in Constance Holden, "Hospices for the Dying, Relief from Pain and Fear," in Hamilton and Reid, *Hospice Handbook*, p. 61.

59. Robert W. Buckingham, *The Complete Hospice Guide* (New York: Harper and Row, 1983), pp. 13–15.

60. See Charles A. Corr and Donna M. Corr, eds., *Hospice Approaches to Pediatric Care* (New York: Springer, 1985).

61. Pam Brown, Betty Davies, and Nola Martens, "Families in Supportive Care — Part II: Palliative Care at Home: A Viable Care Setting," *Journal of Palliative Care* 6:3 (1990): 21–27.

62. Brown, et al., "Palliative Care at Home," p. 24.

63. Barbara McCann, "Hospice Care in the United States: The Struggle for Definition and Survival," *Journal of Palliative Care* 4:1–2 (1988): 16–18.

64. Clive F. Seale, "What Happens in Hospices: A Review of Research Evidence," *Social Science and Medicine* 28:6 (1989): 551–559.

65. The importance of volunteers in hospice programs is discussed by Michael A. Patchner and Mark B. Finn, "Volunteers: The Life-Line of Hospice," *Omega* 18 (1987–1988): 135–144.

66. See "The Shanti Project: A Community Model of Psychosocial Support for Patients and Families Facing Life-Threatening Illness," in *Psychosocial Care of the Dying Patient*, edited by Charles A. Garfield (New York: McGraw-Hill, 1978), pp. 355–364.

67. Mary-Ellen Siegel, "I Can Cope with Cancer," *Cancer News* 38:2 (Spring/Summer 1984): 10–12.

68. For further information, contact The Elisabeth Kübler-Ross Center, South Route 616, Head Waters, VA 24442.

69. Talcott Parsons, *The Social System* (New York: Free Press, 1951). See also: Russell Noyes, Jr., and John Clancy, "The Dying Role: Its Relevance to Improved Patient Care," in *Psychiatry* 40 (February 1977): 41–47.

70. Ross E. Gray and Brian D. Doan, "Empowerment and Persons with Cancer: Politics in Cancer Medicine," *Journal of Palliative Care* 6:2 (1990): 33–45.

71. See, for example, Robert J. Baugher, Candice Burger, Roberta Smith, and Kenneth A. Wallston, "A Comparison of Terminally Ill Persons at Various Time Periods to Death," *Omega* 20 (1989–1990): 103–155.

72. Allan Kellehear and Terry Lewin, "Farewells by the Dying: A Sociological Study," *Omega* 19 (1988–1989): 275–292.

CHAPTER 5

1. A. D. Lopez, "Competing Causes of Death: A Review of Recent Trends in Mortality in Industrialized Countries with Special Reference to Cancer," *Annals of the New York Academy of Science* 609 (1990): 58–74.

2. G. P. Sholevar and R. Perkel, "Family Systems Intervention and Physical Illness," *General Hospital Psychiatry* 12 (1990): 363–372.

3. M. E. Koster and J. Bergsma, "Problems and Coping Behavior of Facial Cancer Patients," *Social Science and Medicine* 30 (1990): 569–578.

4. See, for example, D. Welch-McCaffrey, B. Hoffman, S. A. Leigh, L. J. Loescher,

and F. L. Meyskens, Jr., "Surviving Adult Cancers: Part 2, Psychosocial Implications," *Annals of Internal Medicine* (1989): 517–524.

5. Elisabeth Kübler-Ross, *On Death and Dying* (New York: Macmillan, 1969). See also: Edwin S. Shneidman, "Death Work and the Stages of Dying," in Robert Fulton, et al., *Death and Dying: Challenge and Change* (Reading, Mass.: Addison-Wesley, 1978), pp. 181–182.

6. Herman Feifel, "Psychology and Death: Meaningful Rediscovery," *American Psychologist* 45 (1990): 537–543.

7. Avery D. Weisman, *On Dying and Denying: A Psychiatric Study of Terminality* (New York: Behavioral Publications, 1972). See also: Avery D. Weisman, *Coping with Cancer* (New York: McGraw-Hill, 1979).

8. Robert Kastenbaum and Claude Normand, "Deathbed Scenes as Imagined by the Young and Experienced by the Old," *Death Studies* 14 (1990): 201–217.

9. Mickey S. Eisenberg, Lawrence Bergner, Alfred P. Hallstrom, and Richard O. Cummins, "Sudden Cardiac Death," *Scientific American* 254:5 (May 1986): 37–43.

10. Gideon Gil, "The Artificial Heart Juggernaut," *Hastings Center Report* 14:2 (March–April 1989): 24–31.

11. *Carcinomas* — that is, cancers of the skin, mucous membranes, and glandular tissues — are more likely to exhibit metastasis than are *sarcomas* — cancers of the connective tissues such as cartilage, muscle, and bone. Examples of carcinomas include cancers of the skin and breast, as well as cancers of the liver, pancreas, intestines, prostate, and thyroid.

12. Anson Shupe and Jeffrey K. Hadden, "Symbolic Healing," *Second Opinion* 12 (November 1989): 74–97.

13. Shupe and Hadden, "Symbolic Healing," p. 80. See also Robert Ornstein and David Sobel, *The Healing Brain: Breakthrough Discoveries About How the Brain Keeps Us Healthy* (New York: Simon and Schuster, 1987).

14. "Tapping Human Potential: An Interview with Norman Cousins," *Second Opinion* 14 (July 1990): 57–71.

15. Ross E. Gray and Brian D. Doan, "Heroic Self-healing and Cancer: Clinical Issues for the Health Professions," *Journal of Palliative Care* 6:1 (1990): 32–41.

16. Michael H. Levy, "Pain Control Research in the Terminally Ill," *Omega* 18 (1987–1988): 265–279.

17. Linda C. Garro, "Culture, Pain and Cancer," *Journal of Palliative Care* 6:3 (1990): 34–44.

18. See, for example, Pam Brown, Betty Davies, and Nola Martens, "Families in Supportive Care — Part II: Palliative Care at Home: A Viable Care Setting," *Journal of Palliative Care* 6:3 (1990): 21–27.

19. Levy, "Pain Control Research," p. 266.

20. See Arnold A. Hutschnecker, *The Will to Live* (New York: Doubleday, 1954); Meyer Friedman and Ray H. Rosenman, *Type A Behavior and Your Heart* (New York: Alfred A. Knopf, 1974); Lawrence LeShan, *You Can Fight for Your Life* (New York: M. Evans, 1977); O. Carl Simonton, Stephanie Matthews Simonton, and James Crieghton, *Getting Well Again: A Step-by-Step Guide to Overcoming Cancer for Patients and Their Families* (Los Angeles: J. P. Tarcher, 1978).

21. Stephanie Matthews Simonton, *The Healing Family: The Simonton Approach for Families Facing Illness* (New York: Bantam, 1984). See also O. Carl Simonton and Stephanie Matthews Simonton, "Belief Systems and Management of the Emotional Aspects of Malignancy," *Journal of Transpersonal Psychology* 7 (1975): 29–47; and Dennis T. Jaffe

and David E. Bresler, "The Use of Guided Imagery as an Adjunct to Medical Diagnosis and Treatment," *Journal of Humanistic Psychology* 20:4 (Fall 1980): 45–59.

22. David K. Reynolds, *A Thousand Waves: A Sensible Life Style for Sensitive People* (New York: Quill/Morrow, 1990).

23. Orville Kelly, "Making Today Count," in *Death and Dying: Theory/Research/ Practice*, edited by Larry A. Bugen (Dubuque, Iowa: William C. Brown, 1979), pp. 277– 283. See also: Orville E. Kelly, *Until Tomorrow Comes* (New York: Everest House, 1979).

24. Jeanette Pickrel, "'Tell Me Your Story': Using Life Review in Counseling the Terminally Ill," *Death Studies* 13 (1989): 127–135.

25. Betty Davies, Joanne Chekryn Reimer, and Nola Martens, "Families in Supportive Care — Part I: The Transition of Fading Away: The Nature of the Transition," *Journal of Palliative Care* 6:3 (1990): 12–20.

CHAPTER 6

1. This account draws upon material from the following sources: "Coffins and Sarcophagi," exhibition notes provided by the Metropolitan Museum of Art, New York; Henri Frankfort, *Ancient Egyptian Religion: An Interpretation* (New York: Harper and Row, 1948, 1961); Manfred Lurker, *The Gods and Symbols of Ancient Egypt* (New York: Thames & Hudson, 1980); and Barbara Watterson, *The Gods of Ancient Egypt* (New York: Facts on File, 1984). See also: Morris Bierbrier, *The Tomb-Builders of the Ancient Pharaohs* (New York: Charles Scribner's Sons, 1982); John Romer, *Ancient Lives: Daily Life in Egypt of the Pharaohs* (New York: Holt, Rinehart and Winston, 1984); and A. J. Spencer, *Death in Ancient Egypt* (New York: Penguin, 1982).

2. David Sudnow, "Notes on a Sociology of Mourning," in *Passing On: The Social Organization of Dying* (Englewood Cliffs, N.J.: Prentice-Hall, 1967), pp. 153–168.

3. Ben H. Bagdikian, *The Information Machines: Their Impact on Men and the Media* (New York: Harper and Row, 1971), pp. 39, 59. Also see Bradley Greenberg, "Diffusion of News of the Kennedy Assassination," *Public Opinion Quarterly* 28: 225–232.

4. J. Z. Young, *Programs of the Brain* (New York: Oxford University Press, 1978), p. 255.

5. John R. Elliott, "Funerary Artifacts in Contemporary America," *Death Studies* 14 (1990): 601–612.

6. See Robert Fulton, "The Sacred and the Secular: Attitudes of the American Public Toward Death, Funerals, and Funeral Directors," in *Death and Identity*, rev. ed., edited by Robert Fulton and Robert Bendiksen (Bowie, Md.: Charles Press, 1978), pp. 158–172; Robert Fulton, "Death and the Funeral in Contemporary Society," in *Dying: Facing the Facts*, edited by Hannelore Wass (Washington: Hemisphere, 1979), pp. 236– 255; Richard A. Kalish and Helene Goldberg, "Clergy Attitudes Toward Funeral Directors," *Death Education* 2:3(1978): 247–260; Richard A. Kalish and Helene Goldberg, "Community Attitudes Toward Funeral Directors," *Omega: Journal of Death and Dying* 10:4 (1979–1980): 335–346; and Amy Seidel Marks and Bobby J. Calder, *Attitudes Toward Death and Funerals* (Evanston, Ill.: Center for Marketing Sciences, Northwestern University, 1982), pp. 79–82.

7. Leroy Bowman, *The American Funeral: A Study in Guilt, Extravagance, and Sublimity* (Washington: Public Affairs Press, 1959).

8. Jessica Mitford, *The American Way of Death* (New York: Simon & Schuster, 1963), pp. 16–19.

9. Robert Fulton, "The Funeral and the Funeral Director: A Contemporary Analysis," in *Successful Funeral Service Practice*, edited by Howard C. Raether (Englewood Cliffs, N.J.: Prentice-Hall, 1971), p. 229.

10. Frank Minton, "Clergy Views of Funeral Practice (Part One)," *National Reporter* 4:4 (April 1981): 4.

11. Richard A. Kalish and Helene Goldberg, "Community Attitudes Toward Funeral Directors," *Omega* 10:4 (1979–1980): 335–346.

12. Federal Trade Commission, *Compliance Guidelines: Trade Regulation Rule on Funeral Industry Practices* (Washington, D.C.: Government Printing Office, 1984).

13. Vanderlyn Pine, "The Care of the Dead: A Historical Portrait," in *Death and Dying: Challenge and Change*, edited by Robert Fulton, et al. (Reading, Mass.: Addison-Wesley, 1978), p. 274.

14. See, for example: Steven D. Rosenbaum and John A. Ballard, "Educating Air Force Mortuary Officers," *Death Studies* 14 (1990): 135–145.

15. Vanderlyn R. Pine, *A Statistical Abstract of Funeral Service Facts and Figures of the United States, 1984 Edition* (Milwaukee: National Funeral Directors Association, 1984), pp. 7, 62. This includes charges for professional services, use of facilities and equipment, and the casket as selected by the customer. It does not include the cost of an interment receptacle, cemetery or crematory expenses, monument or marker, or miscellaneous items such as clergy honorarium, flowers, additional transportation, burial clothing, or newspaper notices. Since funeral costs vary among regions of the country as well as between rural and metropolitan areas, average costs can be a useful statistical measure, but cannot be used as a guide for what one may expect to pay in his or her own locale.

16. "Service Industries — Annual Receipts," in *Statistical Abstract of the United States 1990*, 110th ed. (Washington: Government Printing Office, 1990), p. 785.

17. Figures compiled in 1983 by Vanderlyn Pine (*Funeral Service Facts and Figures*) showed an average investment in facilities, land, and equipment of $201,121. This figure ranged from $114,821 for firms performing fewer than 100 funerals per year, to $1,199,303 for firms performing 500 or more. These figures do not include compensation for employees, other operating expenses, or the investment in merchandise inventory.

18. Ronny E. Turner and Charles Edgley, "Death as Theatre: A Dramaturgical Analysis of the American Funeral," *Sociology and Social Research* 60:4 (1976): 377–392, reprinted in *Death and Dying: Theory, Research, and Practice*, edited by Larry A. Bugen (Dubuque, Iowa: William C. Brown, 1979), pp. 191–202.

19. Briefly summarized, exceptions to this requirement occur when: (1) state or local law requires embalming; or (2) there are "exigent circumstances," such as: (a) when a family member or other authorized person cannot be contacted despite diligent efforts, and (b) there is no reason to believe the family does not want embalming, and, (c) after the body has been embalmed, the family is notified that no fee will be charged if they choose a funeral that does not require embalming.

20. Casket Manufacturers Association of America, "Nationwide Summary — Estimate of Sales to Funeral Directors, Unit Volume (July–September 1985)." These sales represent more than 1,800,000 casketed deaths out of slightly more than 2 million total deaths occurring in the United States during this period.

21. From a story by Sylvia Wieland Nogaki, *Honolulu Star-Bulletin & Advertiser* (November 26, 1989).

22. Vivian Spiegelman and Robert Kastenbaum, "Pet Rest Memorial: Is Eternity Running Out of Time?" *Omega* 21 (1990): 1–13.

23. Honolulu *Star-Bulletin and Advertiser* (June 3, 1984).

24. James M. Weir, "Cremation: Statistics to Year 2000, A Presentation to the Cremation Association of North America," Keystone, Colorado (August 1985), Table 1.

25. William Lamers, quoted in *Concerning Death: A Practical Guide for the Living*, edited by Earl Grollman (Boston: Beacon Press, 1974), and in Raether, *Successful Funeral Service Practice*.

26. Robert Fulton and Greg Owen, "Death and Society in Twentieth Century America," *Omega* 18 (1987–1988): 389.

27. Personal communication.

28. Robert Fulton, in *Dying: Facing the Facts*, edited by H. Wass.

29. E. S. Craighill Handy and Mary Kawena Pukui, *The Polynesian Family System in Ka-'u, Hawai'i* (Rutland, Vt.: Charles E. Tuttle, 1972), p. 157; and Mary Kawena Pukui, E. W. Haertig, and Catherine A. Lee, *Nana I Ke Kumu (Look to the Source)*, Vol. 1 (Honolulu: Hui Hanai; Queen Lili'uokalani Children's Center, 1972), p. 139.

CHAPTER 7

1. Philippe Ariès, "The Reversal of Death: Changes in Attitudes Toward Death in Western Societies," in *Death in America*, edited by David E. Stannard (Philadelphia: University of Pennsylvania Press, 1975), pp. 134–158.

2. Mary Caroline Crawford, *Social Life in Old New England* (Boston: Little, Brown, 1914), p. 461.

3. Sidney Zisook and Lucy Lyons, "Bereavement and Unresolved Grief in Psychiatric Outpatients," *Omega: Journal of Death and Dying* 20 (1989–1990): 307–322.

4. Sylvia Sherwood, Robert Kastenbaum, John N. Morris, and Susan M. Wright, "The First Months of Bereavement," in *The Hospice Experiment*, edited by Vincent Mor, David S. Greer, and Robert Kastenbaum (Baltimore: Johns Hopkins University Press, 1988), pp. 149–150.

5. Sarah Brabant, "Old Pain or New Pain: A Social Psychological Approach to Recurrent Grief," *Omega* 20 (1989–1990): 273–279.

6. Ira O. Glick, Robert S. Weiss, and C. Murray Parkes, *The First Year of Bereavement* (New York: John Wiley & Sons, 1974), p. viii.

7. Erich Lindemann, "Symptomatology and Management of Acute Grief," *American Journal of Psychiatry* 101 (1944): 141–148.

8. Sigmund Freud, "Mourning and Melancholia," *Collected Papers*, vol. 4 (New York: Basic Books, 1959), pp. 152–170. Originally published in 1917.

9. In addition to the classic work by Freud, see John Bowlby's three-volume work, *Attachment and Loss* (New York: Basic Books): vol. 1, *Attachment* (1969); vol. 2, *Separation: Anxiety and Anger* (1973); and vol. 3, *Loss: Sadness and Depression* (1982). A summary of Bowlby's stages of mourning can be found in Dale Vincent Hardt's "An Investigation of the Stages of Bereavement," *Omega* 9 (1978–1979): 279–285. On inadequacies found in Bowlby's model, see Dennis Klass, "John Bowlby's Model of Grief and the Problem of Identification," *Omega* 18 (1987–1988): 13–32.

10. Some believe that the attachments developed by animals for others of their kind, or by domestic pets for their human owners, can result in at least elemental forms of grief (as exhibited through such behaviors as "pining" for a lost home or caretaker) when events occur that threaten or break these bonds of attachment. See, for example: Ute Carson, "Do Animals Grieve?," *Death Studies* 13 (1989): 49–62.

11. C. M. Parkes, "Research: Bereavement," *Omega* 18 (1987–1988): 365–377.

12. Selby C. Jacobs, Thomas R. Kosten, Stanislav V. Kasl, Adrian M. Ostfeld, Lisa

Berkman, and Peter Charpentier, "Attachment Theory and Multiple Dimensions of Grief," *Omega* 18 (1987–1988): 41–52.

13. Klass, "John Bowlby's Model of Grief," p. 31.

14. This discussion of the phases of grief draws particularly on the following works: Geoffrey Gorer, *Death, Grief, and Mourning in Contemporary Britain* (London: Cresset Press, 1965); Robert E. Kavanaugh, *Facing Death* (Los Angeles: Nash Publishing, 1972), pp. 107–124; Beverly Raphael, *The Anatomy of Bereavement* (New York: Basic Books, 1983), pp. 33–51; and Savine Gross Weizman and Phyllis Kamm, *About Mourning: Support and Guidance for the Bereaved* (New York: Human Sciences Press, 1985), pp. 42–63.

15. J. William Worden, *Grief Counseling and Grief Therapy: A Handbook for the Mental Health Practitioner* (New York: Springer, 1982), pp. 11–16.

16. W. D. Rees and S. G. Lutkins, "The Mortality of Bereavement," *British Medical Journal* 4 (1967): 13–16.

17. Arthur C. Carr and Bernard Schoenberg, "Object-Loss and Somatic Symptom Formation," in *Loss and Grief: Psychological Management in Medical Practice*, edited by Bernard Schoenberg, et al. (New York: Columbia University Press, 1970), pp. 36–47.

18. See Nicholas R. Hall and Allan L. Goldstein, "Thinking Well: The Chemical Links Between Emotions and Health," *The Sciences* 26:2 (March/April 1986): 34–40. See also Jerome F. Fredrick, "Grief as a Disease Process," *Omega* 7 (1976–1977): 297–305; and Edgar N. Jackson, "The Physiology of Crisis," in his *Coping with the Crises of Your Life* (New York: Hawthorne Books, 1974), pp. 48–55.

19. For a brief review of these studies, see Parkes, "Research: Bereavement," p. 367.

20. Hans Selye, *The Stress of Life*, rev. ed. (New York: McGraw-Hill, 1976), pp. 36ff.

21. George L. Engel, "Sudden and Rapid Death During Psychological Stress," *Annals of Internal Medicine* 74 (1971). See also, by Engel, "Emotional Stress and Sudden Death," *Psychology Today*, November 1977.

22. Colin Murray Parkes, "The Broken Heart," in his *Bereavement: Studies of Grief in Adult Life*, 2d ed. (Madison, Conn.: International Universities Press, 1987) p. 37. See also Gerald Epstein, Lawrence Weitz, Howard Roback, and Embry McKee, "Research on Bereavement: A Selective and Critical Review," *Comprehensive Psychiatry* 16 (1975): 537–546.

23. Itzhak Levav, "Second Thoughts on the Lethal Aftermath of a Loss," *Omega* 20 (1989–1990): 81–90.

24. Robert L. Fulton, "Death, Grief, and Social Recuperation," *Omega* 1 (1978): 23–28.

25. Kenneth J. Doka, "Disenfranchised Grief" (Paper presented at the Annual Meeting of the Association for Death Education and Counseling, Atlanta, Spring 1986).

26. Darlene A. Kloeppel and Sheila Hollins, "Double Handicap: Mental Retardation and Death in the Family," *Death Studies* 13 (1989): 31–38.

27. Edgar N. Jackson, *Understanding Grief: Its Roots, Dynamics, and Treatment* (Nashville: Abingdon Press, 1957), p.27. In an unpublished interview with the authors, Jackson described how the death of his young son became the impetus for his studies of grief. In effect, his studies of grief were in part a mechanism for coping with, understanding, and coming to terms with the loss. This is an example of how an individual survivor's value system shapes the means of coping with a loss.

28. Karen S. Pfost, Michael J. Stevens, and Anne B. Wessels, "Relationship of Purpose in Life to Grief Experiences in Response to the Death of a Significant Other," *Death Studies* 13 (1989): 371–378.

29. Richard A. Kalish and David K. Reynolds, *Death and Ethnicity: A Psychocultural Study* (Los Angeles: Ethel Percy Andrus Gerontology Center, University of Southern California, 1976), p.30.

30. Robert J. Smith, John H. Lingle, Timothy C. Brock, "Reactions to Death as a Function of Perceived Similarity to the Deceased," *Omega* 9 (1978–1979): 125–138.

31. Glenn M. Vernon, *Sociology of Death: An Analysis of Death-Related Behavior* (New York: Ronald Press, 1970).

32. Richard M. Leliaert, "Spiritual Side of 'Good Grief': What Happened to Holy Saturday?" *Death Studies* 13 (1989): 103–117.

33. Arlene Sheskin and Samuel E. Wallace, "Differing Bereavements: Suicide, Natural, and Accidental Death," *Omega* 7 (1976): 229–242.

34. Yvonne K. Ameche, "A Story of Loss and Survivorship," *Death Studies* 14 (1990): 185–198.

35. Bernard Schoenberg, Arthur C. Carr, Austin H. Kutscher, David Peretz, and Ivan K. Goldberg, eds., *Anticipatory Grief* (New York: Columbia University Press, 1974), p. 4. Also see Lindemann, "Acute Grief," p. 141, and Therese A. Rando, *Loss and Anticipatory Grief* (Lexington, Mass.: Lexington Books, 1985).

36. Sherwood, Kastenbaum, Morris, and Wright, "The First Months of Bereavement," p. 150.

37. Lea Barinbaum, "Death of Young Sons and Husbands," *Omega* 7 (1976): 171–175.

38. Francoise M. Reynolds and Peter Cimbolic, "Attitudes Toward Suicide Survivors as a Function of Survivors' Relationship to the Victim," *Omega* 19 (1988–1989): 125–133.

39. Gordon Thornton, Katherine D. Whittemore, and Donald U. Robertson, "Evaluation of People Bereaved by Suicide," *Death Studies* 13 (1989): 119–126.

40. Robert G. Dunn and Donna Morrish-Vidners, "The Psychological and Social Experience of Suicide Survivors," *Omega* 18 (1987–1988): 175–215; David E. Ness and Cynthia R. Pfeffer, "Sequelae of Bereavement Resulting from Suicide," *American Journal of Psychiatry* 147 (1990): 279–285; Lillian M. Range and Nathan M. Niss, "Long-Term Bereavement from Suicide, Homicide, Accidents, and Natural Deaths," *Death Studies* 14 (1990): 423–433; and Jan Van der Wal, "The Aftermath of Suicide: A Review of Empirical Evidence," *Omega* 20 (1989–1990): 149–171.

41. See, for example, June S. Church, "The Buffalo Creek Disaster: Extent and Range of Emotional and Behavioral Problems," *Omega* 5 (1974): 61–63.

42. Terrence Des Pres, *The Survivor* (New York: Oxford University Press, 1976; Pocket Books, 1977). This is an intense exploration of the survivors of the Holocaust.

43. Lula M. Redmond, *Surviving When Someone You Love was Murdered: A Professional's Guide to Group Therapy for Families and Friends of Murder Victims* (Clearwater, Fla.: Psychological Consultation and Education Services, 1989), pp. 38–39, 46–49, 52–53.

44. Fred Sklar and Shirley F. Hartley, "Close Friends as Survivors: Bereavement Patterns in a 'Hidden' Population," *Omega* 21 (1990): 103–112.

45. Larry A. Bugen, "Human Grief: A Model for Prediction and Intervention," *American Journal of Orthopsychiatry* 47:2 (1977): 196–206.

46. Vernon, *Sociology of Death*, p. 159.

47. Mary Kawena Pukui, E. W. Haertig, and Catherine A. Lee, *Nana I Ke Kumu* (Look to the Source), vol. 1 (Honolulu: Hui Hanai; Queen Lili'uokalani Children's Center, 1972), pp. 135–136, 141.

48. See Kalish and Reynolds, *Death and Ethnicity: A Psychocultural Study*; and Jean

Masamba and Richard A. Kalish, "Death and Bereavement: The Role of the Black Church," *Omega* 7 (1976): 23–34.

49. Nissan Rubin, "Social Networks and Mourning: A Comparative Approach," *Omega* 21 (1990): 113–127.

50. Onno van der Hart, *Coping with Loss: The Therapeutic Use of Leave-Taking Ritual* (New York: Irvington, 1988); and "An Imaginary Leave-Taking Ritual in Mourning Therapy: A Brief Communication," *The International Journal of Clinical and Experimental Hypnosis* 36:2 (1988): 63–69.

51. Nancy C. Reeves and Frederic J. Boersma, "The Therapeutic Use of Ritual in Maladaptive Grieving," *Omega* 20 (1989–1990): 281–291.

52. Vamik Volkan and C. R. Showalter, "Known Object Loss, Disturbance in Reality Testing, and 'Re-grief' Work as a Method of Brief Psychotherapy," *Psychiatric Quarterly* 42 (1968): 358–374; and, Vamik Volkan, "A Study of a Patient's 'Re-grief' Work," *Psychiatric Quarterly* 45 (1971): 255–273.

53. Giorgio Di Mola, Marcello Tamburini, and Claude Fusco, "The Role of Volunteers in Alleviating Grief," *Journal of Palliative Care* 6:1 (1990): 6–10.

54. Parkes, "Bereavement: Research," p. 373.

55. John Schneider, *Stress, Loss, and Grief: Understanding Their Origins and Growth Potential* (Baltimore: University Park Press, 1984), pp. 66–76.

56. Lawrence G. Calhoun and Richard G. Tedeschi, "Positive Aspects of Critical Life Problems: Recollections of Grief," *Omega* 29 (1989–1990): 265–272.

57. Julie Fritsch with Sherokee Ilse, *The Anguish of Loss* (Maple Plain, Minn.: Wintergreen Press, 1988).

CHAPTER 8

1. Committee on Trauma Research, National Research Council, *Injury in America: A Continuing Public Health Problem* (Washington: National Academy Press, 1985).

2. Myra Bluebond-Langner, *The Private Worlds of Dying Children* (Princeton, N.J.: Princeton University Press, 1978), and "Worlds of Dying Children and Their Well Siblings," *Death Studies* 13 (1989): 1–16.

3. Sara Dubik-Unruh, "Children of Chaos: Planning for the Emotional Survival of Dying Children of Dying Families," *Journal of Palliative Care* 5:2 (1989): 10–15.

4. Thesi Bergmann and Anna Freud, *Children in the Hospital* (New York: International Universities Press, 1965), pp. 27–28.

5. Donna Juenker, "Child's Perception of His Illness," in *Nursing Care of the Child with Long-Term Illness*, 2d ed., edited by Shirley Steele (New York: Appleton-Century-Crofts, 1977), p. 177.

6. See, for example: Maurice Levy, Ciaran M. Duffy, Pamela Pollock, Elizabeth Budd, Lisa Caulfield, and Gideon Koren, "Home-Based Palliative Care for Children—Part 1: The Institution of a Program," *Journal of Palliative Care* 6:1 (1990): 11–15; Ciaran M. Duffy, Pamela Pollock, Maurice Levy, Elizabeth Budd, Lisa Caulfield and Gideon Koren, "Home-Based Palliative Care for Children—Part 2: The Benefits of an Established Program," *Journal of Palliative Care* 6:2 (1990): 8–14; D. F. Dufour, "Home or Hospital Care for the Child with End-Stage Cancer: Effects on the Family," *Issues in Comprehensive Pediatric Nursing* 12 (1989): 371–383; Ida M. Martinson, ed., *Home Care for the Dying Child: Professional and Family Perspectives* (Norwalk, Conn.: Appleton-Century-Crofts, 1976); Ida M. Martinson, et al., "Home Care for Children Dying of Cancer," *Pediatrics* 62 (1978): 106–113; and D. Gay Moldow, Ida M. Martinson, and Arthur

Kohrman, *Home Care for Seriously Ill Children: A Manual for Parents* (Alexandria, Va.: Children's Hospice of Virginia, 1984).

7. A. E. While, "The Needs of Dying Children and Their Families," *Health Visitor* 62:6 (1989): 176–178.

8. Jo-Eileen Gyulay, "What Suicide Leaves Behind," *Issues in Comprehensive Pediatric Nursing* 12 (1989): 103–118.

9. Richard Lonetto, *Children's Conceptions of Death* (New York: Springer, 1980), p. 186. This phenomenon is also dealt with in Sylvia Anthony's classic work, *The Discovery of Death in Childhood and After* (New York: Basic Books, 1972).

10. Ute Carson, "A Child Loses a Pet," *Death Education* 3 (1980): 399–404.

11. Jane Brody, "When Your Pet Dies," Honolulu *Star-Bulletin & Advertiser*, December 8, 1985.

12. Randolph Picht, "Fido's Final Resting Place," Associated Press story (January 5, 1986).

13. In February 1989, a group of veterinary faculty and students associated with the Human-Animal Program at the University of California at Davis inaugurated a Pet Loss Support Hotline. The phone number is (916) 752-4200. Hours are from 6:30 P.M. to 9:30 P.M., Monday through Friday.

14. Sons and Daughters in Touch can be contacted in care of Friends of the Vietnam Veterans Memorial, 1350 Connecticut Avenue, N.W., Suite 300, Washington, DC 20036.

15. From an article by Al Santoli, "We Never Knew Our Fathers," *Parade* (May 27, 1990), pp. 21–22.

16. For further information on the use of spontaneous drawings, see Robert C. Burns and S. Harvard Kaufman, *Kinetic Family Drawings: An Introduction to Understanding Children Through Kinetic Drawings* (New York: Brunner/Mazel, 1970), and *Actions, Styles and Symbols in Kinetic Family Drawings* (New York: Brunner/Mazel, 1972); Joseph H. DiLeo, *Young Children and Their Drawings* (New York: Brunner/Mazel, 1970), and *Children's Drawings as Diagnostic Aids* (New York: Brunner/Mazel, 1973); and Gregg M. Furth, *The Secret World of Drawings: Healing Through Art* (Boston: Sigo Press, 1988).

17. Barbara Betker McIntyre, "Art Therapy with Bereaved Youth," *Journal of Palliative Care* 6:1 (1990): 16–23.

18. David E. Balk, "Sibling Death, Adolescent Bereavement, and Religion," *Death Studies* 15 (1991): 1–20.

19. This and the following anecdote from Jo-Eileen Gyulay, *The Dying Child* (New York: McGraw-Hill, 1978), pp. 17–18.

20. John Graham-Pole, Hannelore Wass, Sheila Eyberg, and Luis Chu, "Communicating with Dying Children and Their Siblings: A Retrospective Analysis," *Death Studies* 13 (1989): 465–483; see also S.J. Bendor, "Preventing Psychosocial Impairment in Siblings of Terminally Ill Children," *Hospice Journal* 5 (1989): 151–163; and Linda K. Birenbaum, Michaelle A. Robinson, David S. Phillips, Barbara J. Stewart, et al., "The Response of Children to the Dying and Death of a Sibling," *Omega: Journal of Death and Dying* 20 (1989–1990): 213–228.

21. Myra Bluebond-Langner, "Worlds of Dying Children and Their Well Siblings," *Death Studies* 13 (1989): 9.

22. For more information about these groups, contact: Brass Ring Society, 7020 South Yale Avenue, Suite 103, Tulsa, OK 74136; Starlight Foundation, 9021 Melrose Avenue, Suite 204, Los Angeles, CA 90069; Sunshine Foundation, 2842 Normandy Drive, Philadelphia, PA 19154.

CHAPTER 9

1. Charles W. Brice, "Mourning Throughout the Life Cycle," *American Journal of Psychoanalysis* 42:4 (1982): 320–321.

2. Louis E. LaGrand, "Loss Reactions of College Students: A Descriptive Analysis," *Death Education* 5 (1981): 235–248.

3. Erik H. Erikson, *The Life Cycle Completed: A Review* (New York: W. W. Norton, 1982), p. 67. Neil Salkind says the final psychosocial stage described by Erikson contains mystical elements and has much in common with the state of self-actualization discussed by Abraham Maslow; see Salkind, *Theories of Human Development*, 2d ed. (New York: Wiley, 1985), p. 117.

4. Example from Robert Kastenbaum, *Death, Society, and Human Experience*, 3d ed. (Columbus, Ohio: Charles E. Merrill, 1986), pp. 223ff.

5. Gina Gesser, Paul T. P. Wong, and Gary T. Reker, "Death Attitudes Across the Life-Span: The Development and Validation of the Death Attitude Profile (DAP)," *Omega: Journal of Death and Dying* 18 (1987–1988): 113–128.

6. Russell A. Ward, "Age and Acceptance of Euthanasia," *Journal of Gerontology* 35:3 (May 1980): 428–429.

7. Exhibition note, "Native Peoples," Glenbow Museum, Calgary, Alberta, Canada.

8. Dennis Klass and Samuel J. Marwit, "Toward a Model of Parental Grief," *Omega* 19 (1988–1989): 31–50.

9. Elliott J. Rosen, "Family Therapy in Cases of Interminable Grief for the Loss of a Child," *Omega* 19 (1988–1989): 187–202.

10. Kathleen R. Gilbert, "Interactive Grief and Coping in the Marital Dyad," *Death Studies* 13 (1989): 605–626.

11. Cynthia Bach-Hughes and Judith Page-Lieberman, "Fathers Experiencing a Perinatal Loss," *Death Studies* 13 (1989): 537–556.

12. Judy Rollins Bohannon, "Grief Responses of Spouses Following the Death of a Child: A Longitudinal Study," *Omega* 22 (1990–1991): 109–121. See also Nancy Feeley and Laurie N. Gottlieb, "Parents' Coping and Communication Following Their Infant's Death," *Omega* 19 (1988–1989): 51–67; and Reiko Schwab, "Paternal and Maternal Coping with the Death of a Child," *Death Studies* 14 (1990): 407–422.

13. Gilbert, "Interactive Grief and Coping in the Marital Dyad."

14. "Fetal and Infant Deaths," in *Statistical Abstract of the United States 1990*, 110th ed. (Washington: Government Printing Office, 1990), p. 77.

15. *Dorland's Illustrated Medical Dictionary*, 26th ed. (Philadelphia: W. B. Saunders, 1985), p. 828.

16. Ellen Fish Lietar, "Miscarriage," in *Parental Loss of a Child*, edited by Therese A. Rando (Champaign, Ill.: Research Press, 1986), p. 122.

17. *Dorland's Illustrated Medical Dictionary*, 26th ed., pp. 664, 1251.

18. Peter Wingate, *The Penguin Medical Encyclopedia*, 2d ed. (New York: Penguin, 1976), p. 177.

19. Judith A. Savage, *Mourning Unlived Lives: A Psychological Study of Childbearing Loss* (Wilmette, Ill.: Chiron Publications, 1989).

20. Savage, *Mourning Unlived Lives*, p. xiii.

21. Savage, *Mourning Unlived Lives*, p. 108.

22. J. A. Menke and R. E. McClead, "Perinatal Grief and Mourning," *Advances in Pediatrics* 37 (1990): 261–283.

23. Anne C. Smith and Sherry B. Borgers, "Parental Grief: Response to Perinatal Death," *Omega* 19 (1988–1989): 203–214.

24. Irwin J. Weinfeld, "An Expanded Perinatal Bereavement Support Committee: A Community-Wide Resource," *Death Studies* 14 (1990): 241–252.

25. Glen W. Davidson, "Death of the Wished-for Child: A Case Study," *Death Education* 1 (1977): 265–275.

26. "Legal Abortions — Estimated Number, Rate, and Ratio" and "Legal Abortions by Selected Characteristics," in *Statistical Abstract of the United States 1989*, p. 70.

27. Larry G. Peppers, "Grief and Elective Abortion: Breaking the Emotional Bond?," *Omega* 18 (1987–1988): 1–12.

28. Marie Okabe, UPI writer, "Japan Shrine Honors Infants Never Born," *Los Angeles Times* (November 13, 1982); and Tom Ashbrook of the Boston Globe, "Japanese Temples Exploit Superstitions of Abortion," *Honolulu Star-Bulletin & Advertiser* (October 13, 1985).

29. Kenneth J. Doka, "Disenfranchised Grief" (Paper presented at the Annual Meeting of the Association for Death Education and Counseling, Atlanta, Spring 1986); see also *Disenfranchised Grief: Recognizing Hidden Sorrow*, edited by Ken Doka (Lexington, Mass.: Lexington Books, 1989).

30. John De Frain, Leona Martens, Jan Stork, and Warren Stork, "The Psychological Effects of a Stillbirth on Surviving Family Members," *Omega* 22 (1990–1991): 81–108.

31. Jay Ruby, "Portraying the Dead," *Omega* 19 (1988–1989): 1–20; and Joy Johnson and S. Marvin Johnson, with James H. Cunningham and Irwin J. Weinfeld, *A Most Important Picture: A Very Tender Manual for Taking Pictures of Stillborn Babies and Infants Who Die* (Omaha: Centering Corp., 1985).

32. De Frain, et al., "Psychological Effects of a Stillbirth," p. 87.

33. Beverly Raphael, *The Anatomy of Bereavement* (New York: Basic Books, 1983), p. 229.

34. Barney G. Glaser and Anselm L. Strauss, *Awareness of Dying* (Chicago: Aldine, 1965).

35. Shirley Steele, ed., *Nursing Care of the Child with Long-Term Illness*, 2d ed. (New York: Appleton-Century-Crofts, 1977), p. 531.

36. Jerome L. Schulman, *Coping with Tragedy: Successfully Facing the Problem of a Seriously Ill Child* (Chicago: Follett, 1976), p. 335.

37. Raphael, *The Anatomy of Bereavement*, p. 280.

38. Victor Florian, "Meaning and Purpose in Life of Bereaved Parents Whose Son Fell During Active Military Service," *Omega* 20 (1989–1990): 91–102.

39. See, for example, De Frain, et al., "Psychological Effects of a Stillbirth," pp. 95–97, 107.

40. Savine Gross Weizman and Phyllis Kamm, *About Mourning: Support and Guidance for the Bereaved* (New York: Human Sciences, 1985), p. 130.

41. Notable studies include Colin Murray Parkes, "The Effects of Bereavement on Physical and Mental Health: A Study of Medical Records of Widows," *British Medical Journal* 1 (1964): 272–279, and "Recent Bereavement as a Cause of Mental Illness," *British Journal of Psychiatry* 110 (1964): 198–204, as well as *Bereavement: Studies of Grief in Adult Life* (New York: International Universities Press, 1972); Ira O. Glick, Robert S. Weiss, and Colin Murray Parkes, *The First Year of Bereavement* (New York: John Wiley, 1974), and its follow-up by Colin Murray Parkes and Robert S. Weiss, *Recovery from Bereavement* (New York: Basic Books, 1983); Helena Z. Lopata, *Widowhood in*

an American City (Cambridge, Mass.: Schenkman, 1973) and *Women as Widows: Support Systems* (New York: Elsevier, 1979); Paula J. Clayton, "Mortality and Morbidity in the First Year of Widowhood," *Archives of General Psychiatry* 125 (1974): 747–750, and "The Sequelae and Non-Sequelae of Conjugal Bereavement," *American Journal of Psychiatry* 136 (1979): 1530–1543; Herbert H. Hyman, *Of Time and Widowhood: Nationwide Studies of Enduring Effects* (Durham, N.C.: Duke University Press, 1983).

42. The question of possible sampling bias in bereavement research is discussed by Margaret S. Stroebe and Wolfgang Stroebe in "Who Participates in Bereavement Research? A Review and Empirical Study," *Omega* 20 (1989–1990): 1–29.

43. Brice, "Mourning Throughout the Life Cycle," pp. 320–321.

44. Justine F. Ball, "Widows' Grief: The Impact of Age and Mode of Death," *Omega* 7 (1976–1977): 307–333.

45. Paul J. Hershberger and W. Bruce Walsh, "Multiple Role Involvements and the Adjustment to Conjugal Bereavement: An Exploratory Study," *Omega* 21 (1990): 91–102.

46. Linda J. Solie and Lois J. Fielder, "The Relationship Between Sex Role Identity and a Widow's Adjustment to the Loss of a Spouse," *Omega* 18 (1987–1988): 33–40.

47. Judith M. Stillion, *Death and the Sexes: An Examination of Differential Longevity, Attitudes, Behaviors, and Coping Skills* (Washington: Hemisphere, 1985).

48. Ann Bowling, "Who Dies After Widow(er)hood? A Discriminate Analysis," *Omega* 19 (1988–1989): 135–153.

49. "Marital Status of the Population," in *Statistical Abstract of the United States 1990*, 110th ed. (Washington: Government Printing Office, 1990), p. 43.

50. Dale A. Lund, Michael S. Caserta, Jan Van Pelt, and Kathleen A. Gass, "Stability of Social Support Networks After Later-Life Spousal Bereavement," *Death Studies* 14 (1990): 53–73.

51. David M. Bass, Linda S. Noelker, Aloen L. Townsend, Gary T. Deimling, "Losing an Aged Relative: Perceptual Differences Between Spouses and Adult Children," *Omega* 21 (1990): 21–40.

52. Molly Hill Folken, "Moderating Grief of Widowed People in Talk Groups," *Death Studies* 14 (1990): 171–176. On Silverman's work, see Phyllis R. Silverman and Adele Cooperband, "On Widowhood: Mutual Help and the Elderly Widow," *Journal of Geriatric Psychiatry* 8: (1975): 9–27; and, by Silverman, "The Widow-to-Widow Program: An Experiment in Preventive Intervention," *Mental Hygiene* 53:3 (1969), which describes the work at Harvard Medical School's Laboratory of Community Psychiatry. See also Mary Vachon, et al., "A Controlled Study of Self-Help Intervention for Widows," *American Journal of Psychiatry* 137:1 1 (1980): 1380–1384.

53. Folken, "Moderating Grief," p. 175.

54. Joan Delahanty Douglas, "Patterns of Change Following Parent Death in Midlife Adults," *Omega* 22 (1990–1991): 123–137.

55. Marion Osterweis, Fredric Solomon, and Morris Green, eds. *Bereavement: Reactions, Consequences, and Care* (Washington: National Academy Press, 1984), p. 85.

56. Bernice L. Neugarten, "Growing as Long as We Live," *Second Opinion* 15 (November 1990): 42–51.

57. Robert M. Sapolsky and Caleb E. Finch, "On Growing Old," *The Sciences* 31 (March/April 1991): 30–38.

58. Sandra L. Bertman, "Aging Grace: Treatment of the Aged in the Arts," *Death Studies* 13 (1989): 517–535. See also Pamela T. Amoss and Steven Harrell, eds., *Other Ways of Growing Old: Anthropological Perspectives* (Palo Alto, Calif.: Stanford University Press, 1981).

59. M. Powell Lawton, Miriam Moss, and Allen Glicksman, "The Quality of the Last Year of Life of Older Persons," *Millbank Quarterly* 68 (1990): 1–28.

60. Daniel Callahan, "Can Old Age Be Given a Public Meaning," *Second Opinion* 15 (November 1990): 12–23.

61. Melvin A. Kimble, "Religion: Friend or Foe of the Aging?," *Second Opinion* 15 (November 1990): 70–81.

62. Robert N. Butler, *Why Survive? Being Old in America* (New York: Harper and Row, 1975).

63. Hannelore Wass, "Aging and Death Education for Elderly Persons," *Educational Gerontology: An International Quarterly* 5 (1980): 79–90.

64. James F. Fries, Lawrence W. Green, and Sol Levine, "Health Promotion and the Compression of Morbidity," *Lancet* (March 4, 1989): 481–483; see also Fries, "The Compression of Morbidity," *Millbank Memorial Fund Quarterly* 61 (1983): 397–419.

65. William J. Bicknell and Cindy Lou Parks, "As Children Survive: Dilemmas of Aging in the Developing World," *Social Science and Medicine* 28 (1989): 59–67.

66. Saga Johansson, "Longevity in Women," *Cardiovascular Clinics* 19:3 (1989): 3–16.

67. Jon Hendricks and C. Davis Hendricks, *Aging in Mass Society: Myths and Realities* (Cambridge, Mass.: Winthrop, 1977), pp. 284–285.

68. Ibid., p. 282. See also Colleen L. Johnson and Leslie A. Grant, *The Nursing Home in American Society* (Baltimore: Johns Hopkins University Press, 1985).

CHAPTER 10

1. Cited in "Transplants: Are They Worth It?" *Second Opinion* 12 (November 1989): 11. See also "Organ Transplants and Grafts," in *Statistical Abstract of the United States 1990,* 110th ed. (Washington: Government Printing Office, 1990), p. 110.

2. The Hippocratic Oath, named for the ancient Greek physician Hippocrates, has been an enduring guide for the conduct of physicians since the fourth century B.C.E. (before the common era). Modified during the twentieth century—most notably by the World Medical Association in its "Declaration of Geneva" (1949)—Hippocratic principles continue to exert a strong moral force in medical practice.

3. Charles L. Sprung, "Changing Attitudes and Practices in Forgoing Life-Sustaining Treatments," *Journal of the American Medical Association* 263 (April 25, 1990): 2211–2215.

4. Edmund D. Pellegrino, "Character, Virtue, and Self-Interest in the Ethics of the Professions," *Journal of Contemporary Health Policy and Law* 5 (Spring 1989): 53–73.

5. Alexander Morgan Capron, "The Burden of Decision," *Hastings Center Report* (May–June 1990): 36–41.

6. Leon R. Kass, "Practicing Ethics: Where's the Action?" *Hastings Center Report* (January–February 1990): 5–12.

7. The issue of patient autonomy versus medical/social paternalism is highlighted in the experience of Don (Dax) Cowart, whose case has become a classic in the literature of medical ethics. See *Dax's Case: Essays in Medical Ethics and Human Meaning*, edited by Lonnie D. Kliever (Dallas: Southern Methodist University, 1989); and "Symposium on Dax's Case," *Bulletin of the Park Ridge Center* (May 1990): 16–33.

8. James F. Childress, "The Place of Autonomy in Bioethics," *Hastings Center Report* (January–February 1990): 12–17.

9. Marshall B. Kapp, "Medical Empowerment of the Elderly," *Hastings Center Report* (July–August 1989): 5–7.

10. John Hardwig, "What About the Family?" *Hastings Center Report* (March–April 1990): 5–10.

11. Nancy S. Jecker, "The Role of Intimate Others in Medical Decision Making," *Gerontologist* (February 1990): 65–71.

12. Donald Oken, "What to Tell Cancer Patients: A Study of Medical Attitudes," in *Journal of the American Medical Association* 175 (1961): 1120–1128.

13. D. H. Novack, et al., "Changes in Physician's Attitudes Toward Telling the Cancer Patient," *Journal of the American Medical Association* 241 (March 2, 1979): 897–900.

14. D. H. Novack, et al., "Physicians' Attitudes Toward Using Deception to Resolve Difficult Ethical Problems," *Journal of the American Medical Association* 261 (May 26, 1989): 2980–2985.

15. The President's Commission for the Study of Ethical Problems in Medicine and Biomedical and Behavioral Research, *Making Health Care Decisions: The Ethical and Legal Implications of Informed Consent in the Patient-Practitioner Relationship*; vol. 1, *Report*; and vol. 3, *Studies on the Foundations of Informed Consent* (Washington: Government Printing Office, 1982).

16. E. A. Green, "Placebo," *Academic American Encyclopedia* (March 1991), in press.

17. David W. Towle, "Medical Ethics," *Academic American Encyclopedia* (March 1991), in press; see also Alan Leslie, "Ethics and Practice of Placebo Therapy," *American Journal of Medicine* 16 (1954): 854–862.

18. Howard Brody, "Transparency: Informed Consent in Medical Practice," *Hastings Center Report* (September–October 1989): 5–9.

19. Marshall B. Kapp, "Enforcing Patient Preferences: Linking Payment for Medical Care to Informed Consent," *Journal of the American Medical Association* 261 (April 7, 1989): 1935–1938.

20. *In the Matter of Karen Quinlan: The Complete Legal Briefs, Court Proceedings and Decisions in the Superior Court of New Jersey* (1975) and *In the Matter of Karen Quinlan, Volume 2: the Complete Briefs, Oral Arguments, and Opinion in the New Jersey Supreme Court* (1976; Arlington, Va.: University Publications of America).

21. Joseph Fletcher, "The Patient's Right to Die," in *Euthanasia and the Right to Die: The Case for Voluntary Euthanasia*, edited by A. B. Downing (London: Peter Owen Ltd., 1969), p. 30.

22. On the potential value of talking to comatose patients, despite their unresponsiveness and inability to talk back, see John LaPuma, David L. Schiedermayer, Ann E. Gulyas, and Mark Siegler, "Talking to Comatose Patients," *Archives of Neurology* 45 (January 1988): 20–22.

23. Richard M. Gula, "Moral Principles Shaping Public Policy on Euthanasia," *Second Opinion* 14 (July 1990): 73–83.

24. A brief discussion of how the term *euthanasia* is used by various ethicists can be found in John J. Cole, "Moral Dilemma: To Kill or Allow to Die?," *Death Studies* 13 (1989): 393–406, esp. pp. 397–398; see also Richard M. Gula, "Moral Principles," *Second Opinion* 14 (July 1990): 73–83.

25. On institutional guidelines for terminating treatment, see U.S. Congress, Office of Technology Assessment, *Institutional Protocols for Decisions about Life-Sustaining Treatments — Special Report* (Washington, D.C.: Government Printing Office, 1988); and Hastings Center, *Guidelines on the Termination of Life-Sustaining Treatment and the Care of the Dying* (Bloomington: Indiana University Press, 1988).

26. President's Commission for the Study of Ethical Problems in Medicine and Bio-

medical and Behavioral Research, *Summing Up: Final Report on Studies of the Ethical and Legal Problems in Medicine and Biomedical and Behavioral Research* (Washington Government Printing Office, March 1983), p. 31. See also the companion volume, *Deciding to Forego Life-Sustaining Treatment: A Report on the Ethical, Medical, and Legal Issues in Treatment Decisions* (Washington: Government Printing Office, March 1983).

27. See, for example, Tom Tomlinson and Howard Brody, "Futility and the Ethics of Resuscitation," *Journal of the American Medical Association* 264 (September 12, 1990): 1276–1280; and J. Chris Hackler and F. Charles Hiller, "Family Consent Orders Not to Resuscitate," *Journal of the American Medical Association* 264 (September 12, 1990): 1281–1283.

28. M. A. M. de Wachter, "Active Euthanasia in the Netherlands," *Journal of the American Medical Association* 262 (December 15, 1989): 3316–3319. See also Sidney H. Wanzer, et al., "The Physician's Responsibility Toward Hopelessly Ill Patients," in *Euthanasia: The Moral Issues*, edited by Robert M. Baird and Stuart E. Rosenbaum (New York: Prometheus, 1989), pp. 163–177, and, in the same source, Pieter Admiraal, "Justifiable Active Euthanasia in the Netherlands," pp. 125–128.

29. Neil Macdonald and Balfour Mount, "Controversies in Palliative Care," *Journal of Palliative Care* 4:1–2 (1988): 6–8.

30. Richard M. Gula, "The Virtuous Response to Euthanasia," *Health Progress* 70 (December 1989): 24–27.

31. See Gretchen L. Johnson, *Voluntary Euthanasia: A Comprehensive Bibliography* (Eugene, Ore.: Hemlock Society, 1987).

32. Joseph Fletcher, "The Right to Choose When to Die," *Hemlock Quarterly* 34 (January 1989): 3. A similar position is espoused by James Rachels, *The End of Life: Euthanasia and Morality* (New York: Oxford University Press, 1986).

33. Sprung, "Changing Attitudes and Practices," p. 2214.

34. "It's Over, Debbie," *Journal of the American Medical Association* 259 (1989): 272.

35. Robert W. Carton, "The Road to Euthanasia," *Journal of the American Medical Association* 263 (April 25, 1990): 2221.

36. David J. Roy, "Euthanasia—Taking a Stand," *Journal of Palliative Care* 6:1 (1990): 3–5.

37. "Florida District Court of Appeals Decides Landmark Case Concerning Life-Sustaining Measures," PR Newswire, April 22, 1986.

38. N. L. Cantor, "The Permanently Unconscious Patient, Non-Feeding, and Euthanasia," *American Journal of Law and Medicine* 15 (1989): 381–437.

39. R. J. Connelly, "The Sentiment Argument for Artificial Feeding of the Dying," *Omega: Journal of Death and Dying* 20 (1989–1990): 229–237; see also: Steven H. Miles, "Nourishment and the Ethics of Lament," *Linacre Quarterly* 56 (August 1989): 64–69.

For opposing views on the "bond of human communion" that is maintained by artificially nourishing patients in a persistent vegetative state, see Germain Grisez and Kevin O'Rourke, "Should Nutrition and Hydration Be Provided to Permanently Unconscious and Other Mentally Disabled Persons?" *Issues in Law and Medicine* 5 (1989): 165–196.

40. James J. McCartney and Jane Mary Trau, "Cessation of the Artificial Delivery of Food and Fluids: Defining Terminal Illness and Care," *Death Studies* 14 (1990): 435–444.

41. Dena S. Davis, "Old and Thin," *Second Opinion* 15 (November 1990): 26–32; see also, in the same issue, Ronald M. Green, "Old and Thin: A Response," pp. 34–39.

42. Quoted from an article by Joseph F. Sullivan, *New York Times* (June 25, 1987).

43. Background to the Cruzan case and arguments on both sides of the issue can be found in *Hastings Center Report* (January–February 1990): 38–50.

44. Ron Hamel, "The Supreme Court's Decision in the *Cruzan* Case: A Synopsis," *Bulletin of the Park Ridge Center* (September 1990): 18, 20.

45. Ellen Goodman, "Death in the Technological Age," *Los Angeles Times* (December 28, 1990).

46. The Patient Self-Determination Act is discussed in Chapter 11.

47. Callahan and Caplan quoted in "Cruzan Case Leaves Unresolved Issues," *Washington Post* (December 15, 1990). Other newspaper sources consulted for this account of the Cruzan case include Don Colburn, "When to Let Death Come," *Washington Post* (January 1, 1991); Malcolm Gladwell, "Woman in Right-to-Die Case Succumbs," *Washington Post* (December 27, 1990); Don Colburn, "Missouri Seeks to Withdraw from Legal Case It Has Long Pursued," *Washington Post* (October 16, 1990); and Jerry Nachtigal, "Comatose Woman in Right-to-Die Case Likely to Live Under Two Weeks," *Honolulu Star-Bulletin & Advertiser* (December 16, 1990).

48. Case reported in the *Bulletin of the Park Ridge Center* (May 1989): 24–25.

49. For discussion of the legal concept of "personhood" as applied in the Bouvia case, as well as the cases of Hilda Peter (discussed earlier in this section), Claire Conroy, and Paul Brophy, see Edward J. Larson, "Personhood: Current Legal Views," *Second Opinion* 14 (July 1990): 41–53.

50. President's Commission, *Summing Up*, p. 34.

51. Hastings Center, "Imperiled Newborns," *Hastings Center Report* 17 (December 1987): 5–32.

52. Marie C. McCormick, "Long-Term Follow-Up of Infants Discharged from Neonatal Intensive Care Units," *Journal of the American Medical Association* 261 (March 24/31, 1989): 1767–1772.

53. Robert McCormick, in *Ethical Issues in Death and Dying*, edited by Robert F. Weir (New York: Columbia University Press, 1977), p. 133.

54. James M. Gustafson, "Mongolism, Parental Desires, and the Right to Live," ibid., pp. 145–172.

55. D. Alan Shewmon, "Anencephaly: Selected Medical Aspects," *Hastings Center Report* (October/November 1988): 11–19.

56. Arthur L. Caplan, "Should Foetuses or Infants Be Used as Organ Donors?" *Bioethics* 1 (1987); see also Michael R. Harrison, "Organ Procurement in Children: The Anencephalic Fetus as Donor," *The Lancet* (December 13, 1986); and Task Force for the Determination of Brain Death in Children, "Guidelines for the Determination of Brain Death in Children," *Pediatrics* 80 (1987): 298–300.

57. D. Alan Shewmon, "Commentary on Guidelines for the Determination of Brain Death in Children," *Annals of Neurology* 24 (1988): 780–791; see also D. Alan Shewmon, Alexander M. Capron, Warwick J. Peacock, and Barbara L. Schulman, "The Use of Anencephalic Infants as Organ Sources: A Critique," *Journal of the American Medical Association* 261 (March 24/31, 1989): 1773–1781.

58. President's Commission, *Deciding to Forego Life-Sustaining Treatment*, p. 7.

59. Hastings Center, "Imperiled Newborns," pp. 5–32.

60. Leonard L. Bailey, "Organ Transplantation: A Paradigm of Medical Progress," *Hastings Center Report* (January–February 1990): 24–28.

61. "Organ Transplants and Grafts," in *Statistical Abstract of the United States 1990*, p. 110.

62. A description of the psychological issues relative to transplants from a recipient's viewpoint can be found in Robert G. Clouse, "A New Heart in the Face of Old Ethical Problems," *Second Opinion* 12 (November 1989): 13–26. Responses to Clouse's article in the same journal issue are provided by Patricia M. Park, a transplant research nurse, "The Transplant Odyssey," pp. 27–32; George J. Annas, a medical ethicist, "Feeling Good about Recycled Hearts," pp. 33–39; and a transplant-program chaplain, Leslie G. Reimer, "The Power of the Individual's Story," pp. 40–45.

63. See Renee C. Fox and Judith P. Swazey, *The Courage to Fail: A Social View of Organ Transplants and Dialysis* (Chicago: University of Chicago Press, 1974).

64. Douglas N. Walton, *On Defining Death: An Analytic Study of the Concept of Death in Philosophy and Medical Ethics* (Montreal: McGill-Queen's University Press, 1979), pp. 20ff. Also see Eric Cassell, Leon Kass, et al., "Refinements in Criteria for the Determination of Death: An Appraisal," in *Journal of the American Medical Association* 221 (1972): 48–53.

65. When patients continue in a comatose state for longer than a month or so, the condition is described as a "persistent vegetative state" and is usually considered irreversible.

66. Editorial, "Brain Damage and Brain Death," *Lancet* (1974): 342.

67. Clyde M. Nabe, "Presenting Biological Data in a Course on Death and Dying," *Death Education* 5:1 (Spring 1981): 56.

68. Aaron D. Freedman, "Death and Dying," *Academic American Encyclopedia* (March 1991), in press.

69. Nabe, "Presenting Biological Data," p.53.

70. Robert M. Veatch, *Death, Dying, and the Biological Revolution: Our Last Quest for Responsibility*, rev. ed. (New Haven: Yale University Press, 1989).

71. Duncan MacDougall, "Hypothesis Concerning Soul Substance Together with Experimental Evidence of the Existence of Such Substance," *Journal of the American Society for Psychical Research* 1:5 (May 1907): 237–244.

72. Karen G. Gervais, "Advancing the Definition of Death: A Philosophical Essay," *Medical Humanities Review* 3 (July 1989): 7–19.

73. President's Commission for the Study of Ethical Problems in Medicine and Biomedical and Behavioral Research, *Defining Death: A Report on the Medical, Legal and Ethical Issues in the Determination of Death* (Washington: Government Printing Office, July 1981), p. 45.

74. Alexander M. Capron and Leon R. Kass, "A Statutory Definition of the Standards for Determining Human Death: An Appraisal and a Proposal," *University of Pennsylvania Law Review* 121 (1972): 87–118.

75. President's Commission, *Defining Death*.

C H A P T E R 11

1. Annalisa Pizzarello, "Policy and Attitudes on Advance Directives," *Bulletin of the Park Ridge Center* (May 1990): 42. Current information about legislation related to living wills in the various states may be obtained from Concern for Dying, 250 West 57th Street, New York, NY 10107.

2. George P. Smith, III, "Recognizing Personhood and the Right to Die with Dignity," *Journal of Palliative Care* 6:2 (1990): 24–32.

3. Steven H. Miles and Allison August, "Courts, Gender and the 'Right to Die,'" *Law, Medicine and Health Care* 18 (Spring–Summer 1990): 85–95.

4. Smith, "Recognizing Personhood," p. 28.

5. See Kent W. Davidson, et al., "Physicians' Attitudes on Advance Directives," *Journal of the American Medical Association* 262 (November 3, 1989): 2415–2419.

6. S. Van McCrary and Jeffrey R. Botkin, "Hospital Policy on Advance Directives," *Journal of the American Medical Association* 262 (November 3, 1989): 2411–2414.

7. See, for example, Steven H. Miles, "The Case: A Story Found and Lost," *Second Opinion* 15 (November 1990): 55–59, with commentary by Kathryn Montgomery Hunter, pp. 60–67; and Kenneth V. Iverson, "Prehospital DNR Orders," *Hastings Center Report* (November/December 1989): 17–19, with commentary by Fenella Rouse, p. 19.

8. Section 4206 of Public Law 101–508, 101st Congress. We thank Senator John C. Danforth of Missouri, a sponsor of this measure, for providing information about its provisions.

9. Leonard Sloane, "'91 Law Says Failing Patients Must Be Told of Their Options," *New York Times* (December 8, 1990), p. 50.

10. Larry R. Churchill, "Trust, Autonomy, and Advance Directives," *Journal of Religion and Health* 28 (Fall 1989): 175–183.

11. Rosemary A. Robbins, "Signing an Organ Donor Card: Psychological Factors," *Death Studies* 14 (1990): 219–229.

12. "Organ Transplantation — Questions and Answers" (Rockville, Md.: Division of Organ Transplantation, U.S. Department of Health and Human Services, October 1988).

13. See, for example, Sheila Howard, "How Do I Ask? Requesting Tissue or Organ Donations from Bereaved Families," *Nursing* 89 (January 1989): 70–73.

14. David A. Peters, "An Individualistic Approach to Routine Cadaver Organ Removal," *Health Progress* (September 1988): 25–28.

15. David C. Thomasma, "The Quest for Organ Donors: A Theological Response," *Health Progress* (September 1988): 22–24.

16. Robert Fulton and Greg Owen, "Death and Society in Twentieth Century America," *Omega: Journal of Death and Dying* 18 (1987–1988): 388.

17. See, for example, Council on Scientific Affairs and Council on Ethical and Judicial Affairs, "Medical Applications of Fetal Tissue Transplantation," *Journal of the American Medical Association* 263 (January 26, 1990): 565–570; and Richard B. Miller, "On Transplanting Human Fetal Tissue: Presumptive Duties and the Task of Casuistry," *Journal of Medicine and Philosophy* 14 (1989): 617–640.

18. It was announced in 1989 that a new form of the death certificate has been designed by the National Center for Health Statistics and is expected to be adopted by all fifty states. The new death certificates will provide more information about long-term causes of death rather than just the immediate physiological malfunction that proved fatal. For example, doctors will be asked to check a box indicating whether tobacco use contributed to the death.

19. Edwin S. Shneidman, "The Death Certificate," *Deaths of Man* (New York: Quadrangle/The New York Times Book Company, 1973), pp. 121–130.

20. Peter L. Petrakis, "Autopsy," *Academic American Encyclopedia* (March 1991), in press. See also James Adams and Robert D. Mader, *Autopsy* (Ann Arbor, Mich.: UMI Research Press, 1990); and Ludwig Jurgen, *Current Methods of Autopsy Practice*, 2d ed. (Philadelphia: Saunders, 1979).

21. Clyde Collins Snow, Eric Stover, and Kari Hannibal, "Scientists as Detectives: Investigating Human Rights," *Technology Review* (February/March 1989): 42–51.

22. See Bruce A. Iverson, "Bodies for Science," *Death Studies* 14 (1990): 577–587; Robert D. Reece and Jesse H. Ziegler, "How a Medical School (Wright State University)

Takes Leave of Human Remains," *Death Studies* 14 (1990): 589–600; and Kathleen A. Schotzinger and Elizabeth Kirkley Best, "Closure and the Cadaver Experience: A Memorial Service for Deeded Bodies," *Omega* 18 (1987–1988): 217–227.

23. Barton E. Bernstein: "Lawyer and Counselor as an Interdisciplinary Team: Interfacing for the Terminally Ill," *Death Education* 1:3 (Fall 1977): 277–291; and "Lawyer and Therapist as an Interdisciplinary Team Serving the Terminally Ill," *Death Education* 3:1 (Spring 1979): 11–19.

24. Barton E. Bernstein, "Lawyer and Therapist as an Interdisciplinary Team: Serving the Survivors," *Death Education* 4:2 (Summer 1980): 179–188.

25. Everyone should maintain a record of important family information and pertinent documents. Such records include the vital statistics for each family member; military service records and VA (Veterans Administration) number; marriage, divorce, and adoption papers; names, addresses, and phone numbers of relatives and close friends who should be notified if a death occurs; professional and social organizations that should receive notification; location of wills and other important documents, including insurance policies, property deeds, and tax returns; names and addresses of persons to be contacted upon the death of a family member, including executors, attorneys, bank officials, accountants, funeral or cemetery directors, brokers, and mortgage companies; information about notes receivable and accounts outstanding; information regarding funeral plans and wishes for the disposition of the body.

26. Paul Ashley, *You and Your Will: The Planning and Management of Your Estate* (New York: New American Library, 1977), p. 14.

27. The authors thank Richard G. Polse, attorney-at-law, for providing information used in drafting this section.

28. Ashley, *You and Your Will*, pp. 76–77.

29. "Life Insurance Companies," *Statistical Abstract of the United States 1990*, 110th ed. (Washington: Government Printing Office, 1990), p. 514.

30. "Life Insurance Ownership by Households and Adults," *Statistical Abstract of the United States 1989*, 109th ed. (Washington: Government Printing Office, 1989) p. 509.

CHAPTER 12

1. From Letters of E. B. White, collected and edited by Dorothy Lobrano Guth (New York: Harper and Row, 1976), p. 558.

2. Cited in Daniel M. Berman, *Death on the Job: Occupational Health and Safety Struggles in the United States* (New York: Monthly Review Press, 1978), pp. 179–180.

3. James A. Thorson and F. C. Powell, "To Laugh in the Face of Death: The Games That Lethal People Play," *Omega: Journal of Death and Dying* 21 (1990): 225–239.

4. Kenneth J. Doka, Eric C. Schwarz, and Catherine Schwarz, "Risky Business: Reactions to Death in Hazardous Sports" (Paper presented at the Annual Meeting of the Association for Death Education and Counseling, Atlanta, 1986); see also, by the same authors, "Risky Business: Observations on the Nature of Death in Hazardous Sports," *Omega* 21 (1990): 215–223.

5. "Deaths by Selected Cause and Selected Characteristics," in *Statistical Abstract of the United States 1990*, 110th ed. (Washington: Government Printing Office, 1990), p. 80; and National Center for Health Statistics, *Health, United States, 1989* (Hyattsville, Md.: Public Health Service, 1990), p. 123.

6. "Licensed Drivers, Fatal Motor-Vehicle Accidents, and Alcohol Involvement, by Age of Driver," in *Statistical Abstract of the United States, 1990*, p. 608. See also National Center for Health Statistics, *Health, United States, 1989*, pp. 70–71.

7. Robert Kastenbaum and Ruth Aisenberg, *The Psychology of Death: Concise Edition* (New York: Springer, 1976), p. 319.

8. K. David Pijawka, Beverly A. Cuthbertson, and Richard S. Olson, "Coping with Extreme Hazard Events: Emerging Themes in Natural and Technological Disaster Research," *Omega* 18 (1987–1988): 281–297.

9. For an account of the personal response of nearby residents to one such disaster, see Robert Leppzer, *Voices from Three Mile Island: The People Speak Out* (Trumansburg, N.Y.: Crossing Press, 1980).

10. Robert Kastenbaum, *Death, Society, and Human Experience* (St. Louis: C. V. Mosby, 1977), p. 98.

11. Ibid., p. 103.

12. Robert I. Tilling, U.S. Geological Survey, *Eruptions of Mount St. Helens: Past, Present, and Future* (Washington: Government Printing Office, n.d.); see also Robert D. Brown, Jr., and William J. Kockelman, "Geology for Decisionmakers: Protecting Life, Property, and Resources," *Public Affairs Report* 26: 1.

13. Pijawka, Cuthbertson, and Olson, "Coping with Extreme Hazard Events," pp. 291–293.

14. Gail Walker, "Crisis-Care in Critical Incident Debriefing," *Death Studies* 14 (1990): 121–133.

15. Beverly McLeod, "In the Wake of Disaster," *Psychology Today* (October 1984): 54–57.

16. Harvey M. Sapolsky, "The Politics of Risk," *Daedalus: Journal of the American Academy of Arts and Sciences* 119 (Fall 1990): 83–96.

17. "Murder Circumstances/Motives and Weapons Used or Cause of Death: 1980 to 1988," in *Statistical Abstract of the United States 1990*, 110th ed. (Washington: Government Printing Office, 1990), p. 173.

18. "'Vietnam Style' Triage Techniques Used to Treat Urban Assault Weapon Injuries," *Bulletin of the Park Ridge Center* (May 1989): 11–12.

19. American Medical Association, Council on Scientific Affairs, "Firearms Injuries and Deaths: A Critical Public Health Issue," *Public Health Reports* 104 (1989): 111–120.

20. Jane Caputi and Diana E. H. Russell, "'Femicide': Speaking the Unspeakable," *Ms.* (September–October 1990): 34–37; see also Susan Brownmiller, *Against Our Will: Men, Women and Rape* (New York: Simon and Schuster, 1975).

21. Walter Laqueur, *The Age of Terrorism* (Boston: Little, Brown, 1987), p. 72.

22. Henry Lundsgaarde, *Murder in Space City: A Cultural Analysis of Houston Homicide Patterns* (New York: Oxford University Press, 1977). See also *Homicide: A Bibliography*, edited by Ernest L. Abel (Westport, Ct.: Greenwood Press, 1987).

23. Quoted in Kastenbaum and Aisenberg, *Psychology of Death*, pp. 269ff (italics in original).

24. Glenn M. Vernon, *Sociology of Death: An Analysis of Death-Related Behavior* (New York: Ronald Press, 1970), p. 95.

25. Hugh A. Bedau, "Capital Punishment," *Academic American Encyclopedia* (March 1991), in press. See also *The Death Penalty in America*, 3d ed., edited by Hugo A. Bedau (New York: Oxford University Press, 1982); and *Capital Punishment in the United States*, edited by Hugo A. Bedau and Chester M. Pierce (New York: AMS Press, 1976).

26. "Movement of Prisoners Under Sentence of Death: 1975 to 1988," in *Statistical Abstract of the United States 1990*, 110th ed. (Washington: Government Printing Office, 1990), p. 191.

27. Polls conducted by the National Opinion Research Center, CBS News/New York Times, and NBC News/Wall Street Journal.

28. Kastenbaum and Aisenberg, *Psychology of Death*, pp. 95–96, 284–285.

29. Lundsgaarde, *Murder in Space City*, p. 146.

30. Kastenbaum and Aisenberg, *Psychology of Death*, pp. 296–297.

31. Ibid., pp. 281–282.

32. Lula M. Redmond, *Surviving When Someone You Love Was Murdered: A Professional's Guide to Group Grief Therapy for Families and Friends of Murder Victims* (Clearwater, Fla.: Psychological Consultation and Education Services, 1989), p. 37.

33. Arnold Toynbee, "Death in War," in *Death and Dying: Challenge and Change*, edited by Robert Fulton, et al. (Reading, Mass.: Addison-Wesley, 1978), p. 367.

34. Dalton Trumbo, *Johnny Got His Gun* (New York: Bantam Books, 1970), pp. 214, 224.

35. See Ervin Staub, *The Roots of Evil: The Origins of Genocide and Other Group Violence* (New York: Cambridge University Press, 1989).

36. World Campaign for the Protection of Victims of War, International Red Cross and Red Crescent Movement.

37. Vernon, *Sociology of Death*, p. 46.

38. Toynbee, "Death in War," p. 367.

39. Sam Keen, *Faces of the Enemy: Reflections of the Hostile Imagination* (San Francisco: Harper and Row, 1986), p. 12.

40. Vernon, *Sociology of Death*, p. 47.

41. Joel Baruch, "Combat Death," in *Death: Current Perspectives*, edited by Edwin S. Shneidman (Palo Alto, Calif.: Mayfield, 1976), pp. 92–93.

42. Personal communication.

43. On the process of readjustment of the combat veteran, see Harvey J. Schwartz, "Fear of the Dead: The Role of Social Ritual in Neutralizing Fantasies from Combat," in *Psychotherapy of the Combat Veteran*, edited by H. J. Schwartz (New York: SP Medical & Scientific Books, 1984), pp. 253–267.

44. Paul Recer, AP Science Writer, "A Different Johnny," Associated Press wire story (March 3, 1991).

45. Robert Jay Lifton and Eric Olson, *Living and Dying* (New York: Bantam Books, 1975), pp. 8, 123–124.

46. See, for example, Harold A. Widdison and Howard G. Salisbury, "The Delayed Stress Syndrome: A Pathological Delayed Grief Reaction?" *Omega* 20 (1989–1990): 293–306.

47. Cited by Maja Beckstrom, "Vietnam Vets Find Peace in Healing Ceremonies: Rituals Help End the War Within," *Utne Reader* (March/April 1991): 34–35. See also Rod Kane, *Veteran's Day: A Vietnam Memoir* (New York: Crown/Orion, 1989), and Michael Norman, *These Good Men: Friendships Forged from War* (New York: Crown, 1989).

48. Ibid.

49. Paul Recer, AP Science Writer, "A Different Johnny."

50. Quoted in Recer, "A Different Johnny."

51. From an account by Barbara Carton of the Washington Park Service, Honolulu *Star-Bulletin & Advertiser* (August 11, 1985).

52. From an Associated Press wire story, March 9, 1991.

53. Marian Faye Novak, *Lonely Girls with Burning Eyes: A Wife Recalls Her Husband's Journey Home from Vietnam* (Boston: Little, Brown, 1991), p. 3.

54. Susan Fromberg Schaeffer, back cover comment in Novak, *Lonely Girls with Burning Eyes*.

55. According to reports published shortly after war's end, 141 Americans were killed in action, and 110 deaths were attributed to noncombat accidents or natural causes (disease). Another 106 reportedly died in accidents during the buildup before the war erupted on January 17, 1991. Of the total dead, it was reported that eight were women.

56. Dana Priest, "From All Walks, to Death in War," *Washington Post* (March 10, 1991).

57. Major John I. Alger, "War," *Academic American Encyclopedia* (March 1991), in press.

58. Staub, *The Roots of Evil*, p. 62.

59. Keen, *Faces of the Enemy*, pp. 10, 11. Unless otherwise noted, material attributed to Keen in this section is from the chapter "Homo Hostilis, the Enemy Maker," pp. 10–14.

60. Staub, *The Roots of Evil*. Material attributed to Staub in this section is from Chapter 16, "The Cultural and Psychological Origins of War"; Chapter 17, "The Nature of Groups: Security, Power, Justice, and Positive Connection"; and Chapter 18, "The Creation and Evolution of Caring, Connection, and Nonaggression."

61. J. Krishnamurti, "The Way of Peace," a talk broadcast in Bombay, India, on April 3, 1948, reprinted in *Bulletin of the Krishnamurti Foundation of America* 65 (Spring/Summer 1991). Subsequent conflicts between India and Pakistan occurred in 1965 and 1971.

62. See Robert S. Meyer, *Peace Organizations Past and Present: A Survey and Directory* (Jefferson, N.C.: McFarland, 1988).

63. Keen, *Faces of the Enemy*, pp. 180–181.

64. Ibid., pp. 91–93.

65. Ibid., p. 178.

66. Ibid., p. 137.

67. Ibid., p. 138.

68. Staub, *The Roots of Evil*, p. 265.

69. Keen, *Faces of the Enemy*, p. 71.

70. Gil Elliot, "Agents of Death," in *Death: Current Perspectives*, edited by Edwin S. Shneidman, 3d ed. (Palo Alto, Calif.: Mayfield, 1984), pp. 422–440.

71. In the aftermath of the Persian Gulf War, some military analysts called attention to a "firepower revolution" exemplified by "smart" weapons (such as laser-guided bombs) that make extremely precise targeting possible, thus reducing the number of civilian deaths. Francois Heisbourg of the International Institute for Strategic Studies observed that bombing need no longer entail "the mass murder of civilian populations." John Keegan remarked that "during the [Persian Gulf] war, television brought us the extraordinary spectacle of the population of Baghdad going about its business while the necessities of everyday life — electrical power supply, water, filtration, telecommunications — were destroyed about its ears." See John Keegan, "The Lessons of the Gulf War," *Los Angeles Times Magazine* (April 7, 1991), pp. 21, 62.

72. John E. Mack, "Psychosocial Effects of the Nuclear Arms Race," in the *Bulletin of the Atomic Scientists* 37:4 (April 1981): 19–20. See also Edwin S. Shneidman, "Megadeath: Children of the Nuclear Family," in *Death and Dying: Challenge and Change*, edited by R. Fulton, et al., pp. 372–376; and Judith M. Stillion, "Examining the Shadow: Gifted Children Respond to the Nuclear Threat," *Death Studies* 10: 1 (1986): 27–41.

73. Jerald Bachman, "High School Seniors View the Military, 1976–1982," *Armed Forces and Society* 10 (1983): 86–94.

74. Judith M. Stillion, Eugene E. McDowell, and Jacque H. May, *Suicide Across the Life Span—Premature Exits* (New York: Hemisphere, 1989), p. 98.

75. Cited by Robert Fulton and Greg Owen, "Death and Society in Twentieth Century America," *Omega* 18 (1987–1988): 391.

76. Ibid., pp. 390–391.

77. Sam Keen, *Fire in the Belly: On Being a Man* (New York: Bantam, 1991), p. 46.

78. On the development of the bomb, see Richard Rhodes, *The Making of the Atomic Bomb* (New York: Simon and Schuster, 1987).

79. Joanne Silberner, "Hiroshima and Nagasaki: Thirty-Six Years Later, the Struggle Continues," in *Science News* 120:18 (October 31, 1981): 284–287.

80. Robert Jay Lifton, "Psychological Effects of the Atomic Bomb in Hiroshima: The Theme of Death," in *The Threat of Impending Disaster: Contributions to the Psychology of Stress*, edited by George H. Grosser, Henry Wechsler, and Milton Greenblatt (Cambridge, Mass.: MIT Press, 1964), pp. 152–193.

81. Lawrence Badash, "Atomic Bomb" and "Hydrogen Bomb," *Academic American Encyclopedia* (March 1991), in press.

82. See, for example, Anatolii Andreevich Gromyko and Martin E. Hellman, *Breakthrough / Emerging New Thinking: Soviet and Western Scholars Issue a Challenge to Build a World Beyond War* (New York: Walker, 1988).

83. Ruth Sivard, *World Military and Social Expenditures—1989*, 13th ed. (Washington: World Priorities, 1989). See also Christine K. Cassel and Victor W. Sidel, "Prescribing Global Health," *Second Opinion* 10 (March 1989): 126–133.

84. Scott B. Hamilton, William G. Keilin, and Thomas A. Knox, "Thinking About the Unthinkable: The Relationship Between Death Anxiety and Cognitive/Emotional Responses to the Threat of Nuclear War," *Omega* 18 (1987–1988): 53–61.

85. Lester Grinspoon, "Fallout Shelters and the Unacceptability of Disquieting Facts," in *The Threat of Impending Disaster*, edited by G. H. Grosser, et al. (Cambridge, Mass.: MIT Press, 1964), pp. 117–130. See also Jerome D. Frank, *Sanity and Survival: Psychological Aspects of War and Peace* (New York: Random House, 1967).

86. M. Scott Peck, *The Different Drum: Community-Making and Peace* (New York: Simon and Schuster, 1987), p. 19.

87. Lifton and Olson, *Living and Dying*, p. 104.

88. Kawahito Hiroshi, "Death and the Corporate Warrior," *Japan Quarterly* 38 (April–June 1991): 149–157.

89. Thomas H. Holmes and Richard H. Rahe, "The Social Readjustment Rating Scale," *Journal of Psychosomatic Research* 11 (1967): 213–218; see also Richard H. Rahe, "Social Stress and Illness Onset," *Journal of Psychosomatic Research* 8 (1964): 35–43. On stress related to general environmental conditions, see Manfred F. R. Kets de Vries, "Ecological Stress: A Deadly Reminder," *The Psychoanalytic Review* 67:3 (Fall 1980): 389–408.

90. Paul J. Rosch, "Stress and Cancer: A Disease of Maladaptation?" in *Cancer, Stress, and Death*, edited by Jean Tache, et al. (New York: Plenum, 1979), pp. 211–212.

91. Jean Tache, "Stress as a Cause of Disease," in *Cancer, Stress, and Death*, p. 8.

92. Hans Selye, "Stress Without Distress," in *Stress and Survival: The Emotional Realities of Life-Threatening Illness*, edited by Charles A. Garfield (St. Louis, Mo.: C.V. Mosby, 1979), p. 15. See also, by Selye, *The Stress of Life* (New York: McGraw-Hill,

1976); and "Stress, Cancer, and the Mind," in *Cancer, Stress, and Death*, edited by Jean Tache, et al. (New York: Plenum, 1979), pp. 11–19. The positive uses of stress are discussed in an interview with Hans Selye by Laurence Cherry, "On the Real Benefits of Distress," *Psychology Today* 11:10 (March 1978), 60–70.

C H A P T E R   13

1. Judith M. Stillion, Eugene E. McDowell, and Jacque H. May, *Suicide Across the Life Span: Premature Exits* (New York: Hemisphere, 1989), p. 1.

2. P. L. McCall, "Adolescent and Elderly White Male Suicide Trends," *Journal of Gerontology* 46 (1991): 43–51.

3. Judith M. Stillion, Hedy White, Pamela J. Edwards, and Eugene E. McDowell, "Ageism and Sexism in Suicide Attitudes," *Death Studies* 13 (1989): 247–261.

4. John L. McIntosh, "Trends in Racial Difference in U.S. Suicide Statistics," *Death Studies* 13 (1989): 275–286.

5. Committee on Cultural Psychiatry, "Suicide and Ethnicity in the United States," *Report: Group for the Advancement of Psychiatry* 128 (1989): 1–131. See also Philip A. May, "A Bibliography on Suicide and Suicide Attempts Among American Indians and Alaska Natives," *Omega: Journal of Death and Dying* 21 (1990): 199–214.

6. Jon B. Ellis and Lillian M. Range, "Characteristics of Suicidal Individuals: A Review," *Death Studies* 13 (1989): 485–500.

7. See, for example, P. W. O'Carroll, "A Consideration of the Validity and Reliability of Suicide Mortality Data," *Suicide and Life Threatening Behavior* 19 (1989): 1–16.

8. *The Encyclopedia of Suicide*, edited by Glen Evans and Norman L. Farberow (New York: Facts on File, 1988), p. 70.

9. Evans and Farberow, *Encyclopedia of Suicide*, p. 26.

10. Ezra H. E. Griffith and Carl C. Bell, "Recent Trends in Suicide and Homicide Among Blacks," *Journal of the American Medical Association* 262 (1989): 2265–2269; also see F. M. Baker, "Black Youth Suicide: Literature Review with a Focus on Prevention," *Journal of the National Medical Association* 82 (1990): 495–507.

11. Evans and Farberow, *Encyclopedia of Suicide*, p. 268.

12. Edwin S. Shneidman, "Suicide," in *Death: Current Perspectives*, 2d ed., edited by E. S. Shneidman (Palo Alto, Calif.: Mayfield, 1980), p. 432.

13. Evans and Farberow, *Encyclopedia of Suicide*, pp. 26, 230–231. See also Norman L. Farberow, "The History of Suicide," in *The Encyclopedia of Suicide*, edited by Evans and Farberow, p. xxv; and *The Cry for Help*, edited by Norman L. Farberow and Edwin S. Shneidman (New York: McGraw-Hill, 1961).

Other resources on the psychological autopsy include: Edwin S. Shneidman, *Clues to Suicide* (New York: McGraw-Hill, 1957); and, by Avery D. Weisman, *The Psychological Autopsy* (New York: Human Sciences Press, 1968) and *The Realization of Death: A Guide for the Psychological Autopsy* (Northvale, N.J.: Aronson, 1974).

A forerunner of the psychological autopsy was initiated by S. Serin in France during the 1920s. See S. Serin, *Les cases du suicide d'après une enquête médico-sociale dans la Ville de Paris* (Presse médic, 1926), and "Une enquête médico-sociale sur le suicide á Paris," *Annales Medico-Psychologie* 84 (1926): 356.

14. Evans and Farberow, *Encyclopedia of Suicide*, pp. 230–231.

15. David A. Brent, "The Psychological Autopsy: Methodological Considerations for the Study of Adolescent Suicide," *Suicide and Life Threatening Behavior* 19 (Spring 1989): 43–57.

16. Ibid. See also David Shaffer, "The Epidemiology of Teen Suicide: An Examination of Risk Factors," *Journal of Clinical Psychiatry* 49 (September 1988): Supplement, 36–41; and Mohammad Shafi, Shahin Carrigan, J. Russell Whittinghill, and Ann Derrick, "Psychological Autopsy of Completed Suicide in Children and Adolescents," *The American Journal of Psychiatry* 142 (1985): 1061–1064.

17. Edwin S. Shneidman, "Perturbation and Lethality as Precursors of Suicide in a Gifted Group," *Suicide and Life-Threatening Behavior* 1 (Spring 1971): 23–45.

18. Emile Durkheim, *Suicide: A Study in Sociology* (New York: Free Press, 1951). Additional material from Evans and Farberow, *The Encyclopedia of Suicide*, pp. xxiii, 11, 14, 102.

19. E. Hunter, "Using a Socio-Historical Frame to Analyse Aboriginal Self-Destructive Behavior," *Australian and New Zealand Journal of Psychiatry* 24 (1990): 191–198.

20. Durkheim, *Suicide*, p. 209.

21. Ronald Maris, "Sociology," in *A Handbook for the Study of Suicide*, edited by Seymour Perlin (New York: Oxford University Press, 1975), pp. 95–96.

22. Norman L. Farberow, "The History of Suicide," in *The Encyclopedia of Suicide*, edited by Glen Evans and Norman L. Farberow (New York: Facts on File, 1988), p. xxiii.

23. For more on this topic, see: Robert Jay Lifton, Shuichi Kato, and Michael R. Reich, *Six Lives, Six Deaths: Portraits from Modern Japan* (New Haven, Conn.: Yale University Press, 1979); Bernard Millot, *Divine Thunder: The Life and Death of the Kamikazes*, translated by Lowell Bair (New York: McCall, 1971); Jack Seward, *Hara-Kiri: Japanese Ritual Suicide* (Rutland, Vt., and Tokyo: Charles E. Tuttle, 1968). In addition, the following historical accounts include descriptions of how *seppuku* was practiced in the context of feudal Japanese culture: Helen Craig McCullough, *The Taiheiki: A Chronicle of Medieval Japan* (Rutland, Vt., and Tokyo: Charles E. Tuttle, 1959, 1979); A. L. Sadler, *The Maker of Modern Japan: The Life of Shogun Tokugawa Ieyasu* (Rutland, Vt., and Tokyo: Charles E. Tuttle, 1937, 1978). Current patterns of suicide in Japan are surveyed in "Japanese Suicide," *The East* 21:5 (October 1985): 46–52.

24. Norman L. Farberow, "The History of Suicide," in *Encyclopedia of Suicide*, p. viii.

25. The following sources provide differing perspectives on the mass suicide of members of the People's Temple in Jonestown, Guyana: David Chidester, *Salvation and Suicide: An Interpretation of Jim Jones, the People's Temple, and Jonestown* (Bloomington: Indiana University Press, 1988); Marshall Kilduff and Ron Javers, *The Suicide Cult: The Inside Story of the People's Temple Sect and the Massacre in Guyana* (New York: Bantam Books, 1978); Jose I. Lasaga, "Death in Jonestown: Techniques of Political Control by a Paranoid Leader," *Suicide and Life-Threatening Behavior* 10:4 (Winter 1980): 210–213; Shiva Naipaul, *Journey to Nowhere: a New World Tragedy* (New York: Simon & Schuster, 1979); James Reston, Jr., *Our Father Who Art in Hell* (New York: Times Books, 1978); and Richard H. Seiden, "Reverend Jones on Suicide," *Suicide and Life-Threatening Behavior* 9:2 (Summer 1979): 116–119.

26. Charles Brenner, *An Elementary Textbook of Psychoanalysis*, rev. ed. (Garden City, N.Y.: Anchor Press/Doubleday, 1975), pp. 100–101.

27. Erwin Stengel, "A Matter of Communication," in *On the Nature of Suicide*, edited by Edwin S. Shneidman (San Francisco: Jossey-Bass, 1969), pp. 78–79.

28. A. L. Evans, "Dreams and Suicidal Behavior," *Crisis* (May 1990): 12–19.

29. Unattributed article, "View of Suicide as a Right Disturbs Philosophers," *Bulletin of the Park Ridge Center* (September 1990): 6–7.

30. Lillian M. Range and Stephen K. Martin, "How Knowledge of Extenuating Circumstances Influences Community Reactions Toward Suicide Victims and Their Bereaved Families," *Omega* 21 (1990): 191–198.

31. Evans and Farberow, *Encyclopedia of Suicide*, p. 250.

32. Richard H. Seiden and Molly Gleiser, "Sex Differences in Suicide Among Chemists," *Omega* 21 (1990): 177–189.

33. Roy F. Baumeister, "Suicide as Escape from Self," *Psychological Review* 97 (1990): 90–113.

34. Evans and Farberow, *Encyclopedia of Suicide*, p. 231.

35. See, for example, Joaquim Puig-Antich, et al., "A Controlled Family History Study of Prepubertal Major Depressive Disorder," *Archives of General Psychiatry* 46 (1989): 406–418.

36. G. D. Tollefson, "Recognition and Treatment of Major Depression," *American Family Physician* 41 (1990): Supplement, 59–66; and A. T. Davis and C. Schrueder, "The Prediction of Suicide," *Medical Journal of Australia* 153 (1990): 552–554.

37. See, for example, Gabor I. Keitner and Ivan W. Miller, "Family Functioning and Major Depression: An Overview," *American Journal of Psychiatry* 147 (1990): 1128–1137.

38. George Beaumont, "Suicide and Antidepressant Overdosage in General Practice," *British Journal of Psychiatry* (October 1989): Supplement, 27–31.

39. Edwin S. Shneidman, *Deaths of Man* (New York: Quadrangle Books, 1973), pp. 81–90.

40. See, for example, M. A. Fine and R. A. Sansone, "Dilemmas in the Management of Suicidal Behavior in Individuals with Borderline Personality Disorder," *American Journal of Psychotherapy* 44 (1990): 160–171.

41. Evans and Farberow, *Encyclopedia of Suicide*, p. 21.

42. See, for example, Ronald W. Maris, *Pathways to Suicide: A Survey of Self-Destructive Behaviors* (Baltimore: Johns Hopkins University Press, 1981).

43. David Lester, "The Study of Suicide from a Feminist Perspective," *Crisis* 11 (May 1990): 38–43.

44. See Stillion, et al., *Suicide Across the Life Span*, p. 69; and James Overholser, Steven Evans, and Anthony Spirito, "Sex Differences and Their Relevance to Primary Prevention of Adolescent Suicide," *Death Studies* 14 (1990): 391–402.

45. Stillion, et al., *Suicide Across the Life Span*, pp. 103–104.

46. Stillion, et al., *Suicide Across the Life Span*, p. 102.

47. Richard H. Seiden and Raymond P. Freitas, "Shifting Patterns of Deadly Violence," *Suicide and Life-Threatening Behavior* 10:4 (Winter 1980): 209.

48. Brian Barry, "Suicide: The Ultimate Escape," *Death Studies* 13 (1989): 185–190.

49. Jack D. Douglas, "Suicide," *Academic American Encyclopedia* (March 1991), in press.

50. Evans and Farberow, *Encyclopedia of Suicide*, p. 240; see also Alfred Alvarez, *The Savage God: A Study of Suicide* (New York: Random House, 1971).

51. On Plath's suicide, see David Lester, "Application of Piotrowski's Dark Shading Hypothesis to Sylvia Plath's Poems Written Before Her Suicide," *Perceptual and Motor Skills* 68 (1989): 122.

52. J. Michael Olivero and James B. Roberts, "Jail Suicide and Legal Redress," *Suicide and Life-Threatening Behavior* 20 (1990): 138–147.

53. John M. Memory, "Juvenile Suicides in Secure Detention Facilities: Correction of Published Rates," *Death Studies* 13 (1989): 455–463.

54. D. E. Ness and C. R. Pfeffer, "Sequelae of Bereavement Resulting from Suicide," *American Journal of Psychiatry* 147 (March 1990): 279–285.

55. See, for example, S. Vomvouras, "Psychiatric Manifestations of AIDS Spectrum Disorders," *Southern Medical Journal* 82 (1989): 352–357.

56. Donald H. Rubenstein, "Epidemic Suicide Among Micronesian Adolescents," *Social Science and Medicine* 17 (1983): 657–665; and "Suicide in Micronesia," in *Culture, Youth and Suicide in the Pacific: Papers from an East-West Center Conference*, edited by Francis X. Hezel, Donald H. Rubinstein, and Geoffrey M. White (Honolulu: Pacific Islands Study Program, University of Hawaii, 1985), pp. 88–111.

57. Representative studies include: K. Y. Little and D. L. Sparks, "Brain Markers and Suicide: Can a Relationship Be Found?" *Journal of Forensic Science* 35 (1990): 1393–1403; J. J. Mann, V. Arango, and M. D. Underwood, "Serotonin and Suicidal Behavior," *Annals of the New York Academy of Science* 600 (1990): 476–484; Lorna Cameron Ricci and Mary M. Wellman, "Monoamines: Biochemical Markers of Suicide?" *Journal of Clinical Psychology* 46 (1990): 106–116; and Michael Stanley and Barbara Stanley, "Postmortem Evidence for Serotonin's Role in Suicide," *Journal of Clinical Psychiatry* 51 (April 1990): Supplement, 22–28.

58. See, for example, Stillion, et al., *Suicide Across the Life Span*, p. 67.

59. Evans and Farberow, *Encyclopedia of Suicide*, p. 253.

60. Cynthia R. Pfeffer, "Preoccupations with Death in 'Normal' Children: The Relationship to Suicidal Behavior," *Omega* 20 (1989–1990): 205–212.

61. "Suicide Rates by Sex, Race, and Age Group: 1970 to 1986," in *Statistical Abstract of the United States 1989*, 109th ed. (Washington: Government Printing Office, 1989), p. 84.

62. L. Bender and P. Schilder, "Suicidal Preoccupations and Attempts in Children," *American Journal of Orthopsychiatry* 7 (1937): 225–234.

63. René F. W. Diekstra, "Suicidal Behavior and Depressive Disorders in Adolescents and Young Adults," *Neuropsychobiology* 22 (1989): 194–207.

64. Cynthia R. Pfeffer, "Self-Destructive Behavior in Children and Adolescents," *Psychiatric Clinics of North America* 8:2 (June 1985): 215–226; see also, by Pfeffer, "Assessment of Suicidal Children and Adolescents," *Psychiatric Clinics of North America* 12 (1989): 861–872, and "Studies of Suicidal Preadolescent and Adolescent Inpatients: A Critique of Research Methods, *Suicide and Life-Threatening Behavior* 19 (Spring 1989): 58–77.

65. S. J. Blumenthal, "Youth Suicide: Risk Factors, Assessment, and Treatment of Adolescent and Young Adult Suicidal Patients," *Psychiatric Clinics of North America* 13 (1990): 511–556.

66. P. D. Trautman and D. Shaffer, "Pediatric Management of Suicidal Behavior," *Pediatric Annals* 18 (1989): 134ff.

67. Michael Peck, "Youth Suicide," *Death Education* 6 (1982): 29–47.

68. Evans and Farberow, *Encyclopedia of Suicide*, p. 262.

69. Evans and Farberow, *Encyclopedia of Suicide*, pp. 161–162. See also M. S. Gould, S. Wallenstein, and L. Davidson, "Suicide Clusters: A Critical Review," *Suicide and Life-Threatening Behavior* 19 (Spring 1989): 17–29.

70. Examples cited by Evans and Farberow, *Encyclopedia of Suicide*, pp. 26–27, 72,

254. See also R. Milin and A. Turgay, "Adolescent Couple Suicide: Literature Review," *Canadian Journal of Psychiatry* 35 (March 1990): 183–186.

71. Evans and Farberow, *Encyclopedia of Suicide*, pp. 83–84.

72. R. D. Goldney, "Suicide: The Role of the Media," *Australian and New Zealand Journal of Psychiatry* 2 (March 1989): 30–34.

73. Evans and Farberow, *Encyclopedia of Suicide*, p. 2.

74. Evans and Farberow, *Encyclopedia of Suicide*, p. 97.

75. Frank E. Crumley, "Substance Abuse and Adolescent Suicidal Behavior," *Journal of the American Medical Association* 263 (1990): 3051–3056.

76. Stillion, et al., *Suicide Across the Life Span*, pp. 111–116.

77. B. P. Low and S. F. Andrews, "Adolescent Suicide," *Medical Clinics of North America* 74 (1990): 1251–1264.

78. Stillion, et al., *Suicide Across the Life Span*, p. 126.

79. Stillion, et al., *Suicide Across the Life Span*, p. 134.

80. "Death Rates by Selected Causes and Selected Characteristics: 1970 to 1988," in *Statistical Abstract of the United States 1990*, 110th ed. (Washington: Government Printing Office, 1990), p. 81. See also John L. McIntosh, "Middle Age Suicide: A Literature Review and Epidemiological Study," *Death Studies* 15 (1991): 21–37.

81. Dennis L. Peck, "Evaluation of a Suicide Diary: A Content and Situational Analysis," *Omega* 19 (1988–1989): 293–309.

82. Stillion, et al., *Suicide Across the Life Span*, p. 159.

83. Sidney R. Saul and Shura Saul, "Old People Talk About Suicide: A Discussion About Suicide in a Long-Term Care Facility for Frail and Elderly People," *Omega* 19 (1988–1989): 237–251. See also Nancy J. Osgood, Barbara A. Brant, and Aaron A. Lipman, "Patterns of Suicidal Behavior in Long-Term Care Facilities: A Preliminary Report," *Omega* 19 (1988–1989): 69–78.

84. Stillion, et al., *Suicide Across the Life Span*, p. 163.

85. Stillion, et al., *Suicide Across the Life Span*, p. 169.

86. Stillion, et al., *Suicide Across the Life Span*, p. 154.

87. Stillion, et al., *Suicide Across the Life Span*, p. 165.

88. Stillion, et al., *Suicide Across the Life Span*, pp. 180–181.

89. Antoon A. Leenaars and David Lester, "The Significance of the Method Chosen for Suicide in Understanding the Psychodynamics of the Suicidal Individual," *Omega* 19 (1988–1989): 311–314.

90. American Medical Association Counsel on Scientific Affairs, "Firearms Injuries and Deaths: A Critical Public Health Issue," *Public Health Reports* 104 (March–April 1989): 111–120.

91. Josefina Jayme Card, "Lethality of Suicidal Methods and Suicide Risk: Two Distinct Concepts," *Omega* 5:1 (1974): 37–45.

92. Edwin S. Shneidman, "Self-Destruction: Suicide Notes and Tragic Lives," in *Death: Current Perspectives*, 2d ed., p. 467. See also, by Shneidman, "A Bibliography of Suicide Notes: 1856–1979," in *Suicide and Life-Threatening Behavior* 9:1 (Spring 1979): 57–59.

93. Antoon A. Leenaars and David Lester, "What Characteristics of Suicide Notes Are Salient for People to Allow Perception of a Suicide Note as Genuine?" *Death Studies* 14 (1990): 25–30, and "Myths About Suicide Notes," *Death Studies* 15 (1991): 303–308.

94. Evans and Farberow, *Encyclopedia of Suicide*, p. 187.

95. Stillion, et al., *Suicide Across the Life Span*, p. 13.

96. Ralph Beer, "Holding to the Land: A Rancher's Sorrow," *Harper's* (September 1985), p. 62.

97. Stillion, et al., *Suicide Across the Life Span*, p. 194.

98. Stillion, et al., *Suicide Across the Life Span*, p. 194.

99. See, for example, Cathie Stivers, "Promotion of Self-Esteem in the Prevention of Suicide," *Death Studies* 14 (1990): 303–327.

100. See Linda Sattem, "Suicide Prevention in Elementary Schools," *Death Studies* 14 (1990): 329–346; Roger Tierney, Richard Ramsey, Bryan Tanney, and William Lang, "Comprehensive School Suicide Prevention Programs," *Death Studies* 14 (1990): 347–370; and Diane Ryerson, "Suicide Awareness Education in Schools: The Development of a Core Program and Subsequent Modifications for Special Populations or Institutions," *Death Studies* 14 (1990): 371–390.

101. See, for example, Jane Mersky Leder, *Dead Serious: A Book for Teenagers About Teenage Suicide* (New York: Atheneum, 1987). Other titles can be found through a search of *Books in Print*.

102. James Overholser, Steven Evans, and Anthony Spirito, "Sex Differences and Their Relevance to Primary Prevention of Suicide," *Death Studies* 14 (1990): 391–402.

103. Stanley Beardy and Margaret Beardy, "Healing Native Communities Through 'Helping Hands'" (Paper presented at the annual meeting of the Association for Death Education and Counseling, Duluth, Minnesota, April 1991).

104. Evans and Farberow, *Encyclopedia of Suicide*, pp. 171–173.

105. Stillion, et al., *Suicide Across the Life Span*, pp. 200–202.

106. K. D. Atala and R. F. Baxter, "Suicidal Adolescents: How to Help Them Before It's Too Late," *Postgraduate Medicine* 86 (1989): 229–230.

107. Evans and Farberow, *Encyclopedia of Suicide*, p. 225. See also Edwin S. Shneidman, "Postvention and the Survivor Victim," in *Death: Current Perspectives*, 3d ed., edited by E. S. Shneidman (Mountain View, Calif.: Mayfield, 1984), p. 413.

108. Evans and Farberow, *Encyclopedia of Suicide*, pp. 58–59, 63.

109. Charles Neuringer, "The Meaning Behind Popular Myths About Suicide," *Omega* 18 (1987–1988): 155–162. See also George Domino, "Popular Misconceptions About Suicide: How Popular Are They?" *Omega* 21 (1990): 167–175.

110. This tendency to devalue talk about suicide is discussed by Jack D. Douglas in *The Social Meanings of Suicide* (Princeton, N.J.: Princeton University Press, 1967), pp. 324ff.

111. Stillion, et al., *Suicide Across the Life Span*, p. 24.

C H A P T E R 14

1. Personal communication.

2. Bertrand Russell, *Unpopular Essays* (New York: Simon & Schuster, 1950), p. 141.

3. See, for example, "The Problem of Immortality," in Jacques Choron, *Death and Modern Man* (New York: Collier Books, 1964).

4. Mary Kawena Pukui, E. W. Haertig, and Catherine A. Lee, *Nana I Ke Kumu (Look to the Source)*, vols. 1 and 2 (Honolulu: Hui Hanai; Queen Lili'uokalani Children's Center, 1972). See also E. S. Craighill Handy and Mary Kawena Pukui, *The Polynesian Family System in Ka-'u, Hawai'i* (Rutland, Vt.: Charles E. Tuttle, 1972).

5. Job 7:9, *The Jerusalem Bible*. See also Job 14:7–12.

6. Daniel 12:2, *The Jerusalem Bible*.

7. See Lou H. Silberman in "Death in the Hebrew Bible and Apocalyptic Literature," in *Perspectives on Death*, edited by L. O. Mills (Nashville: Abingdon Press, 1969), pp. 13–32. The "Samuel" story is told in the first book of Samuel (28:3–25).

8. Stephen J. Vicchio, "Against Raising Hope of Raising the Dead: Contra Moody and Kübler-Ross," in *Essence: Issues in the Study of Ageing, Dying and Death* 3:2 (1979): 63.

9. H. Wheeler Robinson, "Hebrew Psychology," in *The People and the Book*, edited by Arthur S. Peake (London: Oxford University Press, 1925), pp. 353–382.

10. *The Meditations of Marcus Aurelius*, translated by George Long, *The Harvard Classics*, vol. 2, edited by Charles W. Elliot, pp. 193–301; see especially section II, 5 and 11, pp. 201–202.

11. Romans 5:17, *The Jerusalem Bible*. See also Genesis 3:6 and Romans 5:12–15.

12. Milton McC. Gatch, *Death: Meaning and Mortality in Christian Thought and Contemporary Culture* (New York: Seabury Press, 1969), p. 78.

13. For more on these developments, see Jacques Le Goff, *The Birth of Purgatory* (Chicago: University of Chicago Press, 1984).

14. Vicchio, "Against Raising Hope of Raising the Dead," p. 62. Historian David Stannard's research into the origins and effects of such changing views in early American history reveals the extent to which such conceptual developments can alter people's lives. See, for example, David E. Stannard, *The Puritan Way of Death: A Study of Religion, Culture, and Social Change* (New York: Oxford University Press, 1977); "Calm Dwellings: The Brief, Sentimental Age of the Rural Cemetery," in *American Heritage* 30 (August–September 1979): 42–56; and, edited by Stannard, *Death in America* (Philadelphia: University of Pennsylvania Press, 1975). See also Gordon E. Geddes, *Welcome Joy: Death in Puritan New England* (Ann Arbor, Mich.: UMI Research Press, 1981).

15. Renee Haynes, "Some Christian Imagery," in *Life After Death*, edited by Arnold Toynbee, et al. (New York: McGraw-Hill, 1976), pp. 132ff.

16. John L. Esposito, *Islam: The Straight Path* (New York: Oxford University Press, 1988), p. 22.

17. Frithjof Schuon, *Understanding Islam* (Baltimore: Penguin, 1972), p. 16.

18. Alfred T. Welch, "Death and Dying in the Qur'an," in *Religious Encounters with Death: Insights from the History and Anthropology of Religions*, edited by Frank E. Reynolds and Earle H. Waugh (University Park: Pennsylvania State University Press, 1977), p. 184.

19. Esposito, *Islam: The Straight Path*, p. 34.

20. Huston Smith, *The Religions of Man* (New York: New American Library, 1958), p. 215.

21. Esposito, *Islam: The Straight Path*, p. 35.

22. D. S. Roberts, *Islam: A Concise Introduction* (San Francisco: Harper and Row, 1981), p. 128.

23. Abdul Latif Al Hoa, *Islam* (New York: Bookwright Press, 1987), p. 20.

24. Welch, "Death and Dying in the Qur'an," p. 193.

25. Roberts, *Islam: A Concise Introduction*, p. 128.

26. Esposito, *Islam: The Straight Path*, pp. 162–170.

27. Ibid., p. 202.

28. James Turner, *Without God, Without Creed: The Origins of Unbelief in America* (Baltimore: Johns Hopkins University Press, 1985).

29. David E. Anderson, "Survey Shows Americans a Religious People," United Press International (April 3, 1991).

30. Jeffery L. Sheler, "Hell's Sober Comeback," *U.S. News & World Report* (March 25, 1991): 56–57. See also Daniel J. Klenow and Robert C. Bolin, "Belief in an Afterlife: A National Survey," *Omega: Journal of Death and Dying* 20 (1989–1990): 63–74.

31. Norman Cousins, *The Celebration of Life: A Dialogue on Immortality and Infinity* (New York: Harper and Row, 1974).

32. *Bhagavad-Gita* II.27, translated by Swami Nikhilananda (New York: Ramakrishna-Vivekananda Center, 1952), p. 79.

33. Smith, *The Religions of Man*, p. 34.

34. *Bhagavad-Gita* II.22, trans. Nikhilananda, p. 77.

35. J. Bruce Long, "Death as a Necessity and a Gift in Hindu Mythology," in *Religious Encounters with Death*, ed. Reynolds and Waugh, p. 92; see also pp. 73–96.

36. This theme is explored by David R. Kinsley in "The 'Death That Conquers Death': Dying to the World in Medieval Hinduism," in *Religious Encounters with Death*, ed. Reynolds and Waugh, pp. 97–108.

37. Dōgen, "The Meaning of Practice-Enlightenment (Shushō-gi)," in Yūhō Yokoi, *Zen Master Dōgen: An Introduction with Selected Writings* (New York/Tokyo: Weatherhill, 1976), p. 58.

38. Philip Kapleau, *Zen: Dawn in the West* (Garden City, N.Y.: Anchor Press/Doubleday, 1979). See also, edited by Kapleau, *The Wheel of Death: A Collection of Writings from Zen Buddhist and Other Sources on Death-Rebirth-Dying* (New York: Harper and Row, 1971).

39. Dōgen, "Awakening to the Bodhi-Mind (Hotsu Bodai-shin)," from the Shōbō-Genzō, in Yokoi, *Zen Master Dōgen: An Introduction with Selected Writings*, p. 109.

40. Dōgen, "The Meaning of Practice-Enlightenment (Shushō-gi)," in Yokoi, *Zen Master Dōgen: An Introduction with Selected Writings*, p. 58.

41. *The Zen Master Hakuin: Selected Writings*, translated by Philip B. Yampolsky (New York: Columbia University Press, 1971).

42. W. Y. Evans-Wentz, *The Tibetan Book of the Dead: or, the After-Death Experiences on the Bardo Plane, According to Lama Kazi Dawa-Samdup's English Rendering* (New York: Oxford University Press, 1960).

43. Francesca Fremantle and Chögyam Trungpa, eds., *The Tibetan Book of the Dead: The Great Liberation Through Hearing in the Bardo, by Guru Rinpoche According to Karma Lingpa* (Boulder, Colo.: Shambhala, 1975).

44. Kapleau, *Zen: Dawn in the West*, p. 69. The crucial period is the first forty-nine days following death. Services may be held every day for the first seven days, then once a week thereafter for the remainder of the seven-week period. After that, similar rites are extended into the third year, the seventh year, the thirteenth, and so on, up to fifty years.

45. Carol Zaleski, *Otherworld Journeys: Accounts of Near-Death Experience in Medieval and Modern Times* (New York: Oxford University Press, 1987).

46. Barbara A. Walker, "Health Care Professionals and the Near-Death Experience," *Death Studies* 13 (1989): 63–71. See also Evelyn R. Hayes and Linda D. Waters, "Interdisciplinary Perceptions of the Near-Death Experience: Implications for Professional Education and Practice," *Death Studies* 13 (1989): 443–453.

47. Kenneth Ring, *Life at Death: A Scientific Investigation of the Near-Death Experience* (New York: Coward, McCann, and Geoghegan, 1980; and *Heading Toward Omega:*

In Search of the Meaning of the Near-Death Experience (New York: William Morrow, 1984). See also Raymond A. Moody, Jr., *Life After Life*, and its sequel, *Reflections on Life After Life* (various editions); and Elisabeth Kübler-Ross, "Death Does Not Exist," *CoEvolution Quarterly* 14 (Summer 1977): 100–107.

48. H. J. Irwin, *An Introduction to Parapsychology* (Jefferson, N.C.: McFarland, 1989), pp. 188–190.

49. William J. Serdahely, "The Near-Death Experience: Is the Presence Always the Higher Self?" *Omega* 18 (1987–1988): 129–134.

50. William J. Serdahely, "A Pediatric Near-Death Experience: Tunnel Variants," *Omega* 20 (1989–1990): 55–62. See also William J. Serdahely and Barbara A. Walker, "A Near-Death Experience at Birth," *Death Studies* (1990): 177–183.

51. Ian Stevenson, Emily W. Cook, Nicholas McClean-Rice, "Are Persons Reporting 'Near-Death Experiences' Really Near Death? A Study of Medical Records," *Omega* 20 (1989–1990): 45–54.

52. An excellent introduction to the main points of view can be found in Stephen J. Vicchio's review article, "Near-Death Experiences: A Critical Review of the Literature and Some Questions for Further Study," in *Essence: Issues in the Study of Ageing, Dying and Death* 5:1 (1981): 77–89. Also see James E. Alcock, "Psychology and Near-Death Experiences," in *The Skeptical Inquirer* 3:3 (Spring 1979): 25–41; Michael B. Sabom, *Recollections of Death: A Medical Investigation* (New York: Harper and Row, 1981); and Stephen J. Vicchio, "Near-Death Experiences: Some Logical Problems and Questions for Further Study," in *Anabiosis: The Journal of the International Association for Near-Death Studies* (1981): 66–87. The history of research into near-death experiences is also traced in Chapter 7, "Consciousness and the Threshold of Death," in Stanislav Grof and Joan Halifax, *The Human Encounter with Death* (New York: E. P. Dutton, 1978), pp. 131–157.

53. See Handy and Pukui, *The Polynesian Family System in Ka-'u, Hawai'i*; Donald D. Kilolani Mitchell, *Resource Units in Hawaiian Culture* (Honolulu: Kamehameha Schools Press, 1982); and Pukui, et al., *Nana I Ke Kumu (Look to the Source)*, vols. 1 and 2.

54. See Roy Kletti and Russell Noyes, Jr., "Mental States in Mortal Danger," which includes a translation of Oskar Pfister's 1930 paper commenting on Heim's observations, in *Essence: Issues in the Study of Ageing, Dying and Death* 5:1 (1981): 5–20.

55. See Russell Noyes, Jr., "Dying and Mystical Consciousness," *Journal of Thanatology I (1971)*: 25–41; Russell Noyes, Jr., and Roy Kletti, "Depersonalization in the Face of Life-Threatening Danger: An Interpretation," *Omega* 7 (1976): 103–114; Russell Noyes, Jr., and Roy Kletti, "Panoramic Memory: A Response to the Threat of Death," *Omega* 8 (1977): 181–194; Russell Noyes, Jr., "Near-Death Experiences: Their Interpretation and Significance," in *Between Life and Death*, edited by Robert Kastenbaum (New York: Springer, 1979), pp. 73–78; and Russell Noyes, Jr., "The Encounter with Life-Threatening Danger: Its Nature and Impact," *Essence: Issues in the Study of Aging, Dying and Death* 5:1 (1981): 21–32.

56 George Gallup, Jr., *Adventures in Immortality* (New York: McGraw-Hill, 1982).

57. Karlis Osis and Erlendur Haraldsson, "Deathbed Observations of Physicians and Nurses: A Cross-Cultural Survey," in *The Signet Handbook of Parapsychology*, edited by Martin Ebon (New York: Signet/NAL, 1978); and, by Osis and Haraldsson, *At the Hour of Death* (New York: Avon Books, 1977). See also, by Haraldsson, "Survey of Claimed Encounters with the Dead," *Omega* 19 (1988–1989): 103–113.

58. Louis Appleby, *British Medical Journal* 298 (April 15, 1989): 976–977.

59. From a conversation between Herman Feifel and John Morgan, "Humanity Has to Be the Model," *Death Studies* 10 (1986): 1–9.

60. Charles A. Garfield, "The Dying Patient's Concern with 'Life After Death,'" in *Between Life and Death*, edited by Robert Kastenbaum (New York: Springer, 1979), pp. 52–57.

61. Robert Kastenbaum, "Happily Ever After," in *Between Life and Death*, ed. Kastenbaum, pp. 17, 19.

62. Early studies of LSD are reviewed by Stanislav Grof, *LSD Psychotherapy* (Pomona, Calif.: Hunter House, 1980), pp. 252ff; Stanislav Grof and Joan Halifax, *The Human Encounter with Death* (New York: E. P. Dutton, 1978), pp.16ff; and Peter Stafford, *Psychedelics Encyclopedia* (Berkeley, Calif.: And/Or Press, 1977), pp. 23–39.

63. Grof and Halifax, *Human Encounter with Death*, pp. 120–121.

64. Stanislav Grof and Christina Grof, *Beyond Death: The Gates of Consciousness* (New York: Thames and Hudson, 1980), p. 24.

65. Some evidence suggests that LSD may function by interfering with the transfer of oxygen on the enzymatic level. Anoxia, or diminished levels of oxygen in the bodily tissues, is also frequently found in dying patients as well as in conjunction with certain yogic techniques involving breath control. The chemical changes caused by anoxia in all these instances may somehow activate certain transpersonal matrices in the unconscious, giving rise to the experiences associated with NDEs, certain yogic states, and LSD sessions. For a discussion of this, see Grof and Halifax, *Human Encounter with Death*, pp. 183ff.

66. Stanislav Grof, *Realms of the Human Unconscious: Observations from LSD Research* (New York: E. P. Dutton, 1976).

67. Stanislav Grof and Joan Halifax, "Psychedelics and the Experience of Dying," in *Life After Death*, ed. Toynbee, et al., pp. 192–193.

68. See, for example: Seymour Boorstein, ed., *Transpersonal Psychology* (Palo Alto, Calif.: Science and Behavior Books, 1980); Abraham H. Maslow, *The Farther Reaches of Human Nature* (New York: Viking Penguin, 1971); Robert E. Ornstein, ed., *The Nature of Human Consciousness: A Book of Readings* (San Francisco: W. H. Freeman, 1973); Kenneth R. Pelletier and Charles A. Garfield, *Consciousness: East and West* (New York: Harper and Row, 1976); Charles T. Tart, ed., *Transpersonal Psychologies* (New York: Harper and Row, 1975); Roger N. Walsh and Frances Vaughan, eds., *Beyond Ego: Transpersonal Dimensions in Psychology* (Los Angeles: J. P. Tarcher, 1980).

69. Grof, *LSD Psychotherapy*, p. 294.

70. Clyde M. Nabe, "'Seeing As': Death as Door or Wall," in *Priorities in Death Education and Counseling*, edited by Richard A. Pacholski and Charles A. Corr (Arlington, Va.: Forum for Death Education and Counseling, 1982), pp. 161–169. The metaphorical presentation of death as door or wall has been credited by Nabe and others to Herman Feifel, *The Meaning of Death* (New York: McGraw-Hill, 1959), p. xii.

71. Spiritual Care Work Group, International Work Group on Death, Dying and Bereavement, "Assumptions and Principles of Spiritual Care," *Death Studies* 14 (1990): 75–81.

72. Clifford C. Kuhn, "A Spiritual Inventory of the Medically Ill Patient," *Psychiatric Medicine* 6 (1988): 87–100.

73. Thomas Attig, "Coping with Mortality: An Essay on Self-Mourning," *Death Studies* 13 (1989): 361–370.

CHAPTER 15

1. J. Eugene Knott and Richard W. Prull, "Death Education: Accountable to Whom? For What?" *Omega: Journal of Death and Dying* 7 (1976): 178.

2. Robert Fulton, "Unanticipated Grief" (Paper presented at the Annual Meeting of the Forum for Death Education and Counseling, Philadelphia, April 12, 1985).

3. Darrell Crase, "Black People Do Die, Don't They?" *Death Studies* 11:3 (1987): 221–228.

4. Robert A. Neimeyer, "Death Anxiety Research: The State of the Art" (Paper presented at the annual meeting of the Association for Death Education and Counseling, Duluth, Minnesota, April 1991).

5. Robert A. Neimeyer and Marlin K. Moore, "Assessing Personal Meanings of Death: Empirical Refinements in the Threat Index," *Death Studies* 13 (1989): 227–245.

6. For an introduction to the literature, see Robert A. Neimeyer, "Death Anxiety," in *Dying: Facing the Facts*, 2d ed., edited by Hannelore Wass, Felix Berardo, and Robert A. Neimeyer (New York: Hemisphere, 1988), pp. 97–135.

7. Neimeyer, "Death Anxiety Research," ADEC, April 1991.

8. Herman Feifel, "Psychology and Death: Meaningful Rediscovery," *American Psychologist* (April 1990): 539.

9. Robert Kastenbaum, "Theory, Research, and Application: Some Critical Issues for Thanatology," *Omega* 18:4 (1987–1988): 397–410.

10. Example cited by Kastenbaum, "Theory, Research, and Application," p. 401.

11. Myra Bluebond-Langner, "Wither Thou Goest?" *Omega* 18:4 (1987–1988): 257–263.

12. Feifel, "Psychology and Death," p. 542.

13. Robert Fulton and Greg Owen, "Death and Society in Twentieth Century America," *Omega* 18 (1987–1988): 390.

14. Dan Leviton and William Wendt, "Death Education: Toward Individual and Global Well-Being," *Death Education* 7 (1983): 369–384. See also Richard A. Pacholski, "Teaching Nuclear Holocaust, the Basic Thanatological Topic," *Death Studies* 13 (1989): 175–183.

15. Education Work Group, International Work Group on Death, Dying, and Bereavement, "A Statement of Assumptions and Principles Concerning Education about Death, Dying, and Bereavement." The three documents on death education prepared by this group are scheduled for publication in the following journals: *Death Studies* (on education in general), *Omega: Journal of Death and Dying* (on education for professionals in health care and human services), and *The American Journal of Hospice and Palliative Care* (on education for volunteers and nonprofessionals).

16. "Projections of the Total Population by Age," in *Statistical Abstract of the United States, 1989*, 109th edition (Washington: Government Printing Office, 1989), p. 15.

17. Ron Crocombe, *The South Pacific: An Introduction* (Auckland, New Zealand: Longman Paul, 1983), p. 73.

18. Damon Knight, "Masks," in *A Pocketful of Stars*, edited by Damon Knight (New York: Doubleday, 1971).

19. Clifford Simak, "Death Scene," in *The Worlds of Clifford Simak* (New York: Simon & Schuster, 1960); Robert A. Heinlein, "Life-Line," in *The Man Who Sold the Moon; Harriman and the Escape from the Earth to the Moon!* edited by Robert A. Heinlein (New York: Shasta Publications, 1950).

20. Kit Reed, "Golden Acres," in *Social Problems Through Science Fiction*, edited by John W. Miestead, et al. (New York: St. Martin's, 1975).

21. Cullen Murphy, "The Way the World Ends," *The Wilson Quarterly* (Winter 1990): 50–55.

22. See, for example, Jonathan Weiner, *The Next One Hundred Years: Shaping the Fate of Our Living Earth* (New York: Bantam, 1990).

23. Gary Snyder, *The Practice of the Wild: Essays* (San Francisco: North Point Press, 1990), p. 176.

24. Avery Weisman, *On Dying and Denying: A Psychiatric Study of Terminality* (New York: Behavioral Publications, 1972), pp. 39–40.

25. This account of Lindbergh's death draws from various sources, including a description by Dr. Milton H. Howell, one of Lindbergh's physicians, reported by Ernest H. Rosenbaum, "The Doctor and the Cancer Patient," in *A Hospice Handbook*, edited by Michael P. Hamilton and Helen F. Reid (Grand Rapids, Mich.: Wm. B. Eerdmans, 1980), pp. 19–43.

Credits and Sources

Prologue and Epilogue: Copyright © 1982 by David Gordon. Used by permission.

Page 7: Excerpt from "Death in the Open" from *The Lives of a Cell: Notes of a Biology Watcher* by Lewis Thomas. Originally published in *The New England Journal of Medicine*. Copyright © 1973 by Massachusetts Medical Society. Reprinted by permission of Viking Penguin Inc. and Penguin Books Ltd.

Page 16: From *Small Town America: A Narrative History, 1620–Present*, by Richard R. Lingeman, G. P. Putnam's Sons, 1980.

Page 20: "Grandmother, When Your Child Died," first published by the California State Poetry Society. Used by permission of Joan Neet George.

Page 26: Reprinted by permission of G. P. Putnam's Sons from *Cruel Shoes* by Steve Martin. Copyright © 1977, 1979 by Steve Martin.

Page 34: From an interview first published in *The Paris Review* and reprinted in *The Writer's Chapbook*, edited by George Plimpton; Viking Penguin, 1989.

Page 36: "Buffalo Bill's" is reprinted from *Tulips & Chimneys* by E. E. Cummings, edited by George James Firmage, by permission of Liveright Publishing Corporation. Copyright 1923, 1925 and renewed 1951, 1953 by E. E. Cummings. Copyright © 1973, 1976 by the Trustees for the E. E. Cummings Trust. Copyright © 1973, 1976 by George James Firmage. From *Complete Poems 1913–1962*, by permission of Grafton Books.

Page 41: "One Tree Hill," music by U2, words by Bono. Copyright © 1987 by U2. All rights administered by Chappell & Co., Inc. All rights reserved.

Pp. 43, 84, 208, & 373: Courtesy of Edward C. and Gail R. Johnson.

Page 44: "Luke Stanos" copyright © Morton Marcus. Used by permission of the author.

Page 51: Illustration copyright © 1982 by Eric Mathes. Courtesy of Eric Mathes.

Page 52: From *The Four Seasons: Japanese Haiku Second Series*, translated by Peter Beilenson. Copyright © 1958 by The Peter Pauper Press.

Page 55: From *Death Customs* by E. Bendann; Knopf, 1930.

Page 56: "When Hare Heard of Death," an excerpt from pp 23–24 of *The Road of Life and Death: A Ritual Drama of the American Indians* by Paul Radin, Bollingen Series V. Copyright © 1945, renewed 1973, by Princeton University Press. Reprinted by permission of Princeton University Press and Doris Woodward Radin.

Page 57: Aesop's "Eros and Death" reworked by Steve Sanfield, from *Death: An Anthology of Ancient Texts, Songs, Prayers, and Stories*, edited by David Meltzer; North Point Press, 1984.

Page 59: Papago song by Juana Manwell. By permission of Smithsonian Institution Press from *Papago Music* by Frances Densmore. Bureau of American Ethnology Bulletin 90. Smithsonian Institution, Washington, D.C. 1929.

Page 59: Dakota song from *The Primal Mind: Vision and Reality in Indian America* by Jamake Highwater; Harper & Row, 1981.

Page 60: "Burial Oration" (Wintu Indian) from "Wintu Ethnography" by Cora Du Bois, in *University of Cal-*

ifornia Publications in American Archaeology and Ethnology 36 (1935). Reprinted by permission of the University of California Press.

Page 61: "Warrior song" (Omaha) from The Omaha Tribe by Alice Fletcher and Francis LaFlesche. Bureau of American Ethnology, 27th Report, 1911.

Page 63: From Religions of Africa: A Pilgrimage into Traditional Religions by Noel Q. King; Harper & Row, 1970.

Page 70: From "The Next in Line" in The October Country by Ray Bradbury; Ballantine, 1955.

Page 74: From Strange Facts About Death by Webb Garrison. Copyright © 1978 by Webb Garrison. Used by permission of the publisher, Abingdon Press.

Page 75: From Writings from the Philokalia on Prayer of the Heart, translated by E. Kadloubovsky and G. E. H. Palmer; Faber and Faber, 1951.

Page 83: From CoEvolution Quarterly 17 (Spring 1978): 135, "Little Prigs & Sages." Used by permission of CoEvolution Quarterly.

Page 90: "Death Education for Children and Youth" by Dan Leviton and Eileen C. Forman in Journal of Clinical Child Psychology (Summer 1974).

Page 92: From The Interpretation of Dreams by Sigmund Freud, translated and edited by James Strachey; Basic Books, 1953.

Page 99: Adapted from Behavior and Life: An Introduction to Psychology by Frank J. Bruno. Copyright © 1980 by John Wiley and Sons, Inc. Reproduced by permission of John Wiley and Sons, Inc.

Page 102: From The Words by Jean Paul Sartre; George Braziller, 1964.

Pp. 103, 230, & 284: Used with permission of Joe Allen, Brooks Allen, and Janice Laurent.

Page 112: "The Shroud" from Grimms' Tales for Young and Old, translated by Ralph Manheim. Reprinted by permission of Doubleday & Company, Inc.

Pp. 114 & 115: From Journeys Through Bookland, Volume One, edited by Charles H. Sylvester; published by Bellows-Reeve Company, Publishers, Chicago, 1922.

Page 116: From Trinity by Leon Uris; Doubleday & Company, Inc., 1976.

Page 119: From My Grandson Lew by Charlotte Zolotow; Harper & Row, 1974.

Page 131: From Dying and Death: A Clinical Guide for Caregivers, edited by David Barton. Copyright © 1977 by The Williams and Wilkins Company. Used with permission of The Williams and Wilkins Company and by courtesy of David Barton, M.D.

Pp. 134 & 235: From Passing On: The Social Organization of Dying by David Sudnow; Prentice-Hall, 1967.

Page 136: From the Honolulu Star-Bulletin, October 20, 1985.

Page 137: From "Medicine and the Question of Suffering," by Richard B. Gunderman, in Second Opinion: Health, Faith, and Ethics 14 (July 1990).

Page 142: Excerpt from A Gradual Awakening by Stephen Levine. Copyright © 1979 by Stephen Levine. Reprinted by permission of Doubleday & Company, Inc.

Page 149: From Cancer Care Nursing by Marilee Ivars Donovan and Sandra Girton Pierce. Used by permission of Appleton-Century-Crofts.

Pp. 155 & 576: From Anatomy of an Illness by Norman Cousins. Copyright © 1979 by W. W. Norton & Company, Inc. Used by permission of W. W. Norton & Company, Inc. United Kingdom rights by permission of Transworld Publishers Ltd.

Page 164: "Of Dragons and Garden Peas: A Cancer Patient Talks to Doctors," by Alice Stewart Trillin in The New England Journal of Medicine, March 19, 1981.

Page 166: "Scream of Consciousness," by Ruth Kramer Ziony, in Neworld, 1977.

Page 170: From Experiment Perilous by Renee Fox, published by University of Pennsylvania Press, 1974.

Pp. 172 & 365: Used by permission of Elizabeth Bradbury.

Page 173: Used by permission of Joan J. Conn.

Page 179: Adapted from Living with Cancer by Ernest H. Rosenbaum; The Mosby Medical Library series, The C. V. Mosby Company, St. Louis, 1982. Used with permission of the C. V. Mosby Company.

Page 188: From There is a Rainbow Behind Every Dark Cloud, compiled by the Center for Attitudinal Healing; published by Celestial Arts, 1978. Used with permission of the Center for Attitudinal Healing.

Pp. 189 & 258: Used by permission of The Centre for Living with Dying.

Page 191: "But You Look So Good," from No Pain, No Gain; reprinted by permission of Judith L. Ellsworth.

Pp. 193 & 588: From Big Winds, Glass Mornings, Shadows Cast by Stars: Poems 1972–80 by Morton Marcus (Jazz Press, 1981, Los Angeles). Copyright © by Morton Marcus. Used by permission of Morton Marcus.

Page 202: From "Clergy Views of Funeral Practice (Part One)," by Frank Minton, in National Reporter 4 (April 1981).

Page 206: Used by permission of Edgar N. Jackson.

Page 207: From "Death and Social Values," by Robert Fulton and Gilbert Geis in Death and Identity, edited by Robert Fulton; John Wiley and Sons, 1965.

Page 209: Athenaeum of Philadelphia Collection.

Page 210: From The Loved One by Evelyn Waugh; Little, Brown & Co., 1948.

Page 221: From *The History of American Funeral Directing* by Robert W. Habenstein and William M. Lamers; Bulfin Printers, 1962.

Page 223: From *Working: People Talk About What They Do All Day and How They Feel About What They Do* by Studs Terkel. Copyright © 1972, 1974 by Studs Terkel. Reprinted by permission of Pantheon Books, a Division of Random House, Inc., and Wildwood House Ltd., London.

Page 234: From *Living Your Dying* by Stanley Keleman; Random House, Inc., 1974.

Page 238: From *A Death in the Sanchez Family* by Oscar Lewis; Random House, Inc., 1969.

Page 239: From *Nana I Ke Kumu (Look to the Source)* by Mary Kawena Pukui et al., published by Hui Hanai, 1972. Courtesy of Queen Lili'uokalani Children's Center, Lili'uokalani Trust.

Page 242: From "Notes on Grief in Literature," by Morris Freedman, in *Loss and Grief: Psychological Management in Medical Practice*, edited by Bernard Schoenberg et al.; Columbia University Press, 1970.

Page 245: From *A Harvest Yet to Reap: A History of Prairie Women* by Linda Rasmussen et al.; Women's Press, Toronto, Ontario, 1976.

Page 253: Excerpt from *Who Dies?* by Stephen Levine. Reprinted by permission of Doubleday & Company, Inc.

Page 260: From *Class: A View from Middle England* by Jilly Cooper; Methuen, 1979.

Page 264: "Anguish of Loss," "Sharing the Grief," and "Collapsing" from the book *The Anguish of Loss*, Copyright © 1988 by Julie Fritsch with Sherokee Ilse. Photographs by Paul Schraub. Reprinted with permission from Wintergreen Press.

Page 275: From *The Accident* by Carol and Donald Carrick; Seabury, 1976.

Page 278: Caption to cartoon by E. H. Shepard, © Punch, reprinted by permission of Rothco Cartoons, Inc.

Page 279: From *Winesburg, Ohio* by Sherwood Anderson; Viking Press, 1958.

Page 280: Used with permission of Christine and Donovan Longaker.

Page 285: From *A Tropical Childhood and Other Poems* by Edward Lucie-Smith; Copyright © Oxford University Press, 1961. Reprinted by permission of Oxford University Press.

Page 287: From *Collected Poems*; Harper & Row. Copyright 1921, 1948 by Edna St. Vincent Millay.

Page 300: From *The Oxford Book of Death*, edited by D. J. Enright; Oxford University Press, 1983.

Page 301: From *Love and Profit: The Art of Caring Leadership* by James A. Autry; William Morrow, 1991.

Page 310: From *Surviving Pregnancy Loss* by Rochelle Friedman and Bonnie Gradstein; Little, Brown, 1982.

Pp. 313 & 522: Used by permission of Maude Meehan.

Page 318: From "Psychological Aspects of Sudden Unexpected Death in Infants and Children," by Abraham B. Bergman in *Pediatric Clinics of North America 21* (February 1974).

Page 323: From *Alone: Surviving as a Widow* by Elizabeth C. Mooney; G. P. Putnam's Sons, 1981.

Page 329: From *Widow* by Lynn Caine. Copyright © 1974 by Lynn Caine. Used by permission of William Morrow & Company and Macdonald & Company (Publishers) Ltd.

Page 333: From *Chipping Bone: Collected Poems* by Maude Meehan; Embers Press, 1985. Courtesy of Maude Meehan.

Page 335: From *Living with Huntington's Disease: A Book for Patients and Families* by Dennis H. Phillips; University of Wisconsin Press, 1982.

Page 340: From *Aging in Mass Society: Myths and Realities* by Jon Hendricks and C. Davis Hendricks; Winthrop, 1977.

Page 348: From "Tapping Human Potential," by Norman Cousins, in *Second Opinion: Health, Faith, and Ethics 14* (July 1990).

Page 353: From *Making Health Care Decisions: A Report on the Ethical and Legal Implications of the Patient-Practitioner Relationship*; Government Printing Office, 1982.

Page 356: From *Care of the Dying* by Richard Lamerton; Technomic Publishing, 1976.

Page 359: From *The Pursuit of Virtue & Other Tory Notions* by George F. Will; Simon & Schuster, 1982.

Page 378: From *Mystics, Magicians, and Medicine People: Tales of a Wanderer* by Doug Boyd. © 1989 by Doug Boyd. By permission of Paragon House.

Page 380: From "Law Versus Medicine," an editorial that appeared November 8, 1981, in *The Boston Globe*. Reprinted courtesy of The Boston Globe.

Page 399: From "The Coroner and Death," by Cyril H. Wecht, in *Concerning Death: A Practical Guide for the Living*, edited by Earl A. Grollman; Beacon Press, 1974.

Page 405: From *The Warming of Winter* by Maxine Dowd Jensen; Abingdon Press.

Page 406: Will of Tomas Antonio Yorba, translated by H. Noya [HM26653], reproduced by permission of The Huntington Library, San Marino, California.

Page 408: From *You and Your Will* by Paul P. Ashley; New American Library, 1977.

Page 409: From *To A God Unknown* by John Steinbeck; R. O. Ballou, 1933.

Page 415: From *News from Native California 4* (August-October 1990).

Page 420: From the Honolulu *Star-Bulletin & Advertiser*, August 26, 1990.

Page 424: From "Groundfall," by William G. Higgins, in *Sierra* (November-December 1979).

Page 429: Reprinted with the permission of Pacific Gas & Electric Company.

Page 433: Courtesy of the Unocal Corporation.

Page 436: From *Custer Died for Your Sins: An Indian Manifesto* by Vine Deloria, Jr.; Macmillan, 1969.

Page 437: From *American Blood* by John Nichols; Henry Holt, 1987.

Pp. 440 & 441: From *Murder in Space City: A Cultural Analysis of Houston Homicide Patterns* by Henry P. Lundsgaarde. Copyright © 1977 by Oxford University Press, Inc. Reprinted by permission.

Page 450: From *A Rumor of War* by Philip Caputo. Copyright © 1977 by Philip Caputo. Reprinted by permission of Holt, Rinehart and Winston, Publishers. Used by permission of Macmillan Press, Ltd., London and Basingstoke.

Page 453: Copyright © 1981 New York Times Company. Reprinted by permission. Courtesy of Harvey J. Schwartz, M.D.

Page 457: Reprinted from *War* by Gwynne Dyer. Copyright © 1985 by Media Resources. Used by permission of Crown Publishers, Inc.

Page 465: From *Publishers Weekly*, October 25, 1985. Copyright © by Bowker Magazine Group, Reed Publishing USA. Used by permission.

Page 471: Reprinted with permission from *Journal of Psychosomatic Research 11* (2): 213–218, T. H. Holmes and R. H. Rahe, "The Social Readjustment Rating Scale." Copyright © 1967, Pergamon Press, Ltd., and Thomas H. Holmes, M.D.

Page 480: Edwin Arlington Robinson, "Richard Cory," in *The Children of the Night*. Copyright under the Berne Convention (New York: Charles Scribner's Sons, 1897). Reprinted with the permission of Charles Scribner's Sons.

Page 482: Courtesy of Magaret Macro.

Pp. 485, 489, 506, 507, 509, & 514: Suicide notes courtesy of Edwin S. Shneidman.

Page 487: From *The Goodbye Book* by Robert Ramsey and Randall Toye. Copyright © 1979 by Robert Ramsey. Reprinted by permission of Van Nostrand Reinhold Company.

Page 491: Adapted from *Death, Society, and Human Experience*, 2nd Edition, by Robert J. Kastenbaum (St. Louis: The C. V. Mosby Company, 1981). Used with permission of The C. V. Mosby Company and Robert J. Kastenbaum.

Page 494: From *Deaths of Man* by Edwin S. Shneidman; Quadrangle Books, 1973. Courtesy of Edwin S. Shneidman.

Page 499: From *The Savage God: A Study of Suicide* by A. Alvarez; Random House, 1972.

Page 512: "Resume," by Dorothy Parker, from *The Portable Dorothy Parker*, revised and enlarged Edition, edited by Brendan Gill. Copyright 1926 by Dorothy Parker. Reprinted by permission of Viking Penguin, Inc.

Page 518: From *A Hole in the World: An American Boyhood* by Richard Rhodes; Simon & Schuster, 1990.

Page 537: Excerpt from "Go Down Death — a Funeral Sermon," from *God's Trombones* by James Weldon Johnson. Copyright 1927 by Viking Press, Inc. Copyright renewed 1955 by Grace Nail Johnson. Reprinted by Permission of Viking Penguin Inc.

Page 540: From *Religious Encounters with Death: Insights from the History and Anthropology of Religions*, edited by Frank E. Reynolds and Earle H. Waugh; Pennsylvania State University Press, 1977.

Page 547: From *Zen Mind, Beginner's Mind* by Shunryu Suzuki. Reprinted by permission of John Weatherhill, Inc., 1970.

Page 559: From *The Varieties of Religious Experience: A Study in Human Nature* by William James; New American Library, 1958.

Page 561: From *The Human Encounter with Death* by Stanislav Grof and Joan Halifax; E. P. Dutton, 1977.

Page 562: From *Selected Works of Miguel de Unamuno*, Bollingen Series LXXXV, Vol. 4: *The Tragic Sense of Life in Men and Nations*, translated by Anthony Kerrigan. Copyright © 1972 by Princeton University Press.

Page 563: From *The Gospel at Colonus*. Music by Bob Telson, lyrics by Lee Breuer.

Page 568: From *Harlem Book of the Dead* by James Van Der Zee; Morgan and Morgan, 1978.

Page 571: Used by permission of Siv Cedering. Copyright © 1981 by Siv Cedering. First published in *Harper's Magazine*, 1981.

Page 578: From *The Wheel of Death: A Collection of Writings from Zen Buddhist and Other Sources on Death, Rebirth, Dying* by Philip Kapleau; Harper & Row, 1971.

Page 579: From *Life at Death* by Kenneth Ring; Coward, McCann & Geoghegan, Inc., 1980.

Page 580: From *Distant Neighbors* by Alan Riding; Vintage, 1986.

Page 585: From *At the Edge of the Body* by Erica Jong. Copyright © 1979 by Erica Mann Jong. Reprinted by permission of Henry Holt and Company and the Sterling Lord Agency. Copyright © 1979 by Erica Jong.

Page 586: From *The Ancient Child* by N. Scott Momaday; Doubleday, 1989.

Subject Index